# REGENCY DESIGN

# 1790–1840

. . . the English were a very good nation, but they
positively know not how to make anything but a kitchen
poker. *King George IV*

GARDENS                    BUILDINGS

# John Morley

# REGENCY DESIGN

## 1790–1840

Zwemmer

INTERIORS            FURNITURE

For my wife Jacqueline

© 1993 John Morley

First published 1993 by A. Zwemmer Ltd,
26 Litchfield Street, London
WC2H 9NJ

ISBN 0 302 00615 X

Designed by Andrew Shoolbred
Typeset by Tradeset Photosetting Ltd,
Welwyn Garden City
Colour origination by Columbia Offset Ltd,
Singapore
Printed and bound in Italy by New Interlitho,
Milan

# Contents

---

**PART I**

**PARKS AND GARDENS**

---

---

**PART II**

**EXTERIOR ARCHITECTURE**

---

# PART III
# INTERIOR DECORATION

```
┌─────────────────────────────────┐
│  ┌───────────────────────────┐  │
│  │                           │  │
│  │        PART IV            │  │
│  │                           │  │
│  │      FURNITURE            │  │
│  │                           │  │
│  └───────────────────────────┘  │
└─────────────────────────────────┘
```

# List of Colour Plates

# Foreword and Acknowledgements

This book discusses gardens, buildings, interiors and furniture in four separate parts, but the parts are interdependent and the book is meant to be read as a whole. The author has, where it has seemed appropriate, mentioned furniture in the context of interior decoration. The scope of the book would have made a bibliography of impracticable length, but the footnotes give an idea of the principal sources. All quotations are given in the original, save that the wayward accents in the editions of Laugier used by the author have been corrected. Most persons mentioned in the text are given their dates of birth and death, and principal occupations, in the index.

The author thanks Her Majesty the Queen for permission to reproduce designs and other material from the Royal Library; many of the other illustrations are drawn from the collections of the British Library, the Royal Institute of British Architects, the Soane Museum, and the Victoria and Albert Museum, the custodians and curators of which have been unfailingly helpful. In the face of the effective transformation of the local reference library into a citizens' advice bureau and the scattering of the superb Regency collection built up by Clifford Musgrave and his predecessors, the national libraries and their anonymous but (usually) angelic assistants have become ever more essential; thanks must be given to the British Library, where the bulk of the research has been done, and to Mr. Peter Thornton, who allowed access to the Regency library of the Soane Museum; the London Library has, as always, been an invaluable resource, and is to be thanked for continuing the noble tradition of allowing free reproduction from books in its collection.

Miss Claudia Kinmouth insisted, after the author had twice written out the text by hand, that he should use a word processor: Mount Sinai was less of a revelation. The author's wife has given invaluable help; she assisted in research, discussed knotty points, and cast a steely eye over grammar and vocabulary.

The following have also helped in various ways: Miss Norma Armstrong, Dr. Neil Bingham, Miss Gaye Blake, Miss Stella Beddoe, Lady Brigstocke, Mr. Peter Day, Mr. William Drummond, Mrs. Sara Elliott, Mr. Richard Edgcumbe, Mr. Nigel Foxell, Mr. James Grasby, Mrs. Sidney Harpley, Mr. John Harris, Mr. Hugh Honour, Miss Claire Johnson, Mr. Michael Jones, Mr. Timothy Knox, Mr. Lionel Lambourne, Miss Santina Levey, Mr. Ronald Lightbown, Mr. John Mallet, Mr. Charles McCorquodale, Mr. Peter Miall, Mrs. Barbara Morris, Mr. Piers Oakey, Miss Susan Palmer, Dr. Nicholas Penny, Mrs. Margaret Richardson, Miss Susannah Robson, Miss Jane Rick, the Hon. Mrs. Hugh Roberts, Mr. Julian Roberts, Miss Christina Scull, Mr. Derek Shrub, Mrs. Sheena Stoddard, Mrs. Janet Storrie, Mr. Peter Thornton, Mr. David Vaisey, Mr. Philip Vanker, Miss Marion Waller, Mr. Rowan Watson, Miss Mary Webster, Miss Caroline Whitehead, Mr. and Mrs. Christopher Wightwick, Miss Hilary Williams, Mr. Christopher Wood.

*Brighton 1990*

# Introduction

This book is concerned with design as expressed in gardens, buildings, interior decoration and furniture between the years 1790 to 1840, employing the term 'Regency' as an umbrella for the whole. The political Regency of George Prince of Wales lasted only from 1811 to 1820, but the extended application of the term has become generally accepted and understood. Fifty years is a long time, but those particular fifty years contained the discernible growth, maturity, and decadence of a distinct style; as Clifford Musgrave wrote, 'the age of Regency furniture may be said to have begun when the Prince of Wales appointed Henry Holland to rebuild and refurbish Carlton House . . . in August 1783';[1] 'Regency' was still the prevailing style in 1833, when Loudon published his *Encyclopaedia*, and traces of it lingered into the 1840s and even beyond.

The scope of the book makes for diffuseness, and there is no attempt to be encyclopaedic. Its broad theme is justified by the fact that taste exhibits, in any given period, an essential unity; consideration of the whole rather than the parts can shed a light of its own. This unity was recognised by some of the most prescient and influential theorists of the Regency itself. Uvedale Price wrote that it 'might be somewhat strained to suppose, that the most fashionable style of writing in any age should at all influence the character of other arts: yet something of the same general taste is apt to prevail in them all during the same period, and a distaste for whatever is opposed to it . . .';[2] he thought it no coincidence that 'fugues and imitations in music began to grow out of fashion, about the time that terraces and avenues were demolished'.[3] His friend and antagonist Payne Knight saw an accord between dress and other stylistic manifestations: 'The corruptions of art and the extravagancies of dress have . . . universally accompanied each other . . . perhaps one great cause of the permanency of style, and continued identity of taste, in ancient art, was the permanency and unvaried simplicity of dress'.[4]

Both these writers speak of style as the visible expression of 'taste'. The concept of 'taste' implies some freedom to choose, and the choice will vary with the predilections of the client and the possibilities to hand. The Regency period offered a bewildering array of choices, as the following pages will attempt to make clear. But unless the client were unusually independent (or unaware), the decision was affected by that collective opinion known as fashion. Fashion was increasingly manipulated during the Regency period; the docility and growing ignorance of its adherents eventually affected — and degraded — the nature of taste itself. It is difficult for us to appreciate the subtle distinctions of dead fashions, for succeeding generations lose acute awareness of the nuances, just as they lose awareness of superseded social niceties: the two are closely connected.

The pace of fashion is associated with social and economic change, and all accelerated during the course of the eighteenth century. The word 'taste' was itself increasingly used; popularised at the beginning of the century by a theoretician of aesthetics, the third Earl of Shaftesbury, it had, by the 1730s, become well established, and 'we have scarce a grave Matron at Covent Garden, or a jolly Dame at Stocks-Market, but what is elegant enough to have a Taste for things . . .'.[5] The growing influence of women in matters of taste (to be later so deplored by the ancient Sir John Soane (see p.305)) was increasingly noticed.[6]

It had become clear to perceptive observers by the beginning of the nineteenth century that fashion had, in many quarters, subjugated taste. The situation is encapsulated in the banter of Mrs. Pinmoney: 'Tastes, — they depend on the fashion. There is always a fashionable taste . . . but no gentlemen would be so rash as to have a taste of his own, or his last winter's taste, or any taste, my love, but the fashionable taste. Poor dear Mr. Pinmoney was reckoned a man of exquisite taste among all his acquaintants; for the new taste, let it be what it would, always fitted him as well as his new coat, and he was the very pink and mirror of fashion, as much in the one as in the other — So much for tastes, my dear.'[7]

Mr. Pinmoney's social position was not over-secure, a disadvantage he shared with many of his fellows; his servility to fashion was part of his struggle for status. Lord Chesterfield had advised his son to cultivate the Graces. Mr. Pinmoney was not Lord Chesterfield; he lacked position and confidence, he needed to be told who the Graces were. The change had been rapid. In 1790, people were still sure of their ground: 'No man, in general, is sensible to beauty, in those subjects with regard to which he had not previous ideas. . . . The beauty of a theory, or of a relic of antiquity, is unintelligible to a peasant. . . . It is only in the higher stations . . . or in the liberal professions of life, that we expect to find men either of a delicate or comprehensive taste.'[8] Such an opinion emphasises the importance of 'previous ideas' — knowledge — in forming aesthetic judgments; in effect, taste is denied to the peasant and to the merchant because they lack knowledge. Power, however, has a louder voice than knowledge, and power was about to pass to a class, the commercial class, that as a whole (although there are shining examples of knowledge and connoisseurship amongst merchants)[9] was not of a 'delicate or comprehensive taste'.

The arts of design during the Regency were progressively affected by the adjustment of fashionable taste to the growth and demands of the new ruling commercial classes; whether or not 'commerce' contributed to their debasement — and contemporary witness emphatically asserts that it did — it certainly accompanied it.[10] The complaint that 'our national habit of seeking wealth through commerce has become too general not to have impeded our advances in matters of taste',[11] made in 1827 by an old connoisseur who had seen the changes of the preceding thirty years, had been voiced in recent decades in wearisome repetition. A particular charge, which echoed complaints made in imperial Rome well known to the educated person, was that of tasteless flamboyance, the concern that expense should be made obvious: 'The reverse of true taste is shown in magnificence, parade, and luxury; and in whatever is horribly glaring, extravagant, and unnatural in the least degree. Gold, showy colours, gaudy tapestry . . . will ever pass with the vulgar for elegance and greatness. So persons of a bad taste will prefer the forced, unnatural, and exaggerated . . . to the truly simple, noble, and beautiful.'[12]

A greater evil than the corruption of taste by fashion and ignorance was to come. It is presaged in words, comic and sinister, spoken in December 1822 at a public meeting held to inaugurate the foundation of the Sheffield Literary and Philosophical Society. The speaker, a Mr. J. Montgomery, had been stung by a passing but scornful personal allusion made by Byron in *English Bards and Scotch Reviewers*. The mocking term '*classic* Sheffield' had been uttered. Mr. Montgomery

declared to his audience that: 'the term "classic" operates like a spell upon our imagination: without affixing to it any definite meaning, we associate with it all that is great and splendid, beautiful and excellent, in the surviving pages of ancient authors, as well as all that is venerable, sublime, and almost super-human, in the relics of Egyptian, Greek, and Roman architecture and sculpture. . . . So far as the epithet classic is an accomodated word . . . I am bold to affirm that Sheffield is as classic as Egypt was in the days of Sesostris, as Greece was in the days of Homer, as Rome was . . . etc. etc.'

He followed this with a denunciation of the 'aristocracy of learning' that 'has been the veriest despotism that was ever exercised on earth; for it was bondage both to soul and body . . .'.[13] Mr. Montgomery's target, the 'aristocracy of learning', was the whole body of antique art and letters, the knowledge of which prevented the cognoscenti from confusing the achievements of Sheffield with those of Athens. In attacking learning, he was attacking the very basis of the arts of the Regency; the attack was to be successful, but not in his time.

It was 'the aristocracy of learning', or in another word, 'scholarship', that had made the artefacts and the literature of antiquity generally available to the educated reader. Despite the large number of pieces of antique sculpture that had entered collections in England and France, the subject of fierce competition between those rich enough to afford them, the majority remained in Italy and Greece; buildings were to a large extent (by no means altogether) immovable. Since the seventeenth century a series of publications devoted to antique artefacts of all kinds had appeared, which by 1790 constituted a formidable resource; these established the authority and supplied the rules that governed those arts that turned for inspiration and sanction to antiquity. The task of collecting classical literature had begun earlier; dissemination of the word was easier than that of the artefact. The importance of both for the designer cannot be overstressed.

The continuing significance of publications dealing with ancient architecture and artefacts is reflected in constant use and frequent reprinting. A basic source like Desgodetz's *Les Edifices Antiques de Rome*, first published in 1682, remained an authority up to the Regency period and long beyond; even the scorned Batty Langley's *Ancient Architecture Restored & Improved* of 1742, of which the subject, despite the title, was Gothic architecture, was still being reprinted after 1787. As time went on pedantry increased, and fidelity to the original was encouraged by the accessibility of artefacts in museums, both public and private. The scholars had always protested the accuracy of their publications; the Comte de Caylus, for instance, vouched on the first page of his influential survey of Egyptian and classical antiquities for the fidelity of its illustrations: 'je les ai fait dessiner avec la plus grande exactitude . . .'.[14] In 1766 d'Hancarville (who knew that the jealous exclusivity of

Ferdinand IV of Naples had forced Caylus to draw artefacts disinterred from Herculaneum from memory), spoke slightingly of the 'idées générales' and 'notions vagues' of Caylus and his encyclopaedic predecessor Montfaucon; d'Hancarville emphasised the need for exactitude in reproducing the laws, rules, and proportions of the ancients, whether the modern artist wished to copy or to invent.[15] The influential Abbé Laugier, whose insistence on architectural rules and architectural logic created a scandal, did not doubt that the rules were better known in his time than ever before, enabling the artist to work with precision; he spoke of the 'principes véritables et primordiaux' that should be followed.[16] Carried to an 'archaeological' extreme, this resulted in the cheerless Cantabrigian pedantry of William Wilkins.[17]

The textual accuracy of Greek and Latin literature was equally important, especially that of poetry, the most powerful of literary forms. Classical poetry had so deeply affected the educated eighteenth-century imagination as to have acquired a direct contemporary relevance; as Alison, one of the most important legislators of Regency aesthetics, said: 'The descriptions of ancient authors, so long admired, and so deserving of admiration, occur to [educated people] at every moment'.[18] These descriptions were available to a wider audience than might be nowadays imagined; the modern equivalent of the rumbustious, amorous, fox-hunting tearaway, Tom Jones, would, no matter how classically educated, be hardly as likely to quote eight lines of Horace under the stress of generous emotion. In the opinion of his creator, Henry Fielding, 'the ancients may be considered as a rich common, where every person who hath the smallest tenement in Parnassus hath a free right to fatten his muse . . . we moderns are to the ancients what the poor are to the rich'.[19] Classical associations were of the utmost consequence; to Thomas Hope, who could not be accused of indifference to aesthetics, the associations of an artefact were more important than its aesthetic quality (see p.138).

A correctly interpreted text was as essential as the accurate delineation of artefacts. This imperative prompted Alison's disagreement with the poet Gray on Pindar's then famous description of the plumage of the eagle; the contention was whether Pindar had described it as smooth or ruffled, a matter of import since two of Edmund Burke's aesthetic categories were in question, the beautiful (smooth) and the sublime (rough).[20] Most Regency eagle console tables are conspicuously ruffled, appropriate to the associations of the eagle with war. Another example of fidelity to the word, a minor accompaniment to the Napoleonic Wars, was the reconstruction of Achilles' shield from the descriptions of Homer. The French attempt remained theoretical;[21] the British materialised, in triumphantly grandiloquent form.[22]

Payne Knight opined that although the English language was surprisingly good for a 'corrupt dialect', the 'polished languages of modern Europe, could never rival those of the Greeks and Romans in poetical diction'.[23] Despite this generally acknowledged handicap, modern poetry played a major part in forming taste. Milton furnished Addison and eighteenth-century gardeners with the most abiding evocation of Paradise in the English language, more circumstantial than that in the Authorized Version; he evoked in 'Il Penseroso' the power of Gothic in a few lines that haunted imagination for centuries; his infernal temple of Pandemonium is the most impressive modern Doric structure conceived, beside which the images of the Eidophukison pale[24] and John Martin's inventions appear jejune. Dryden and Pope turned Homer and Virgil into splendid English; Dyer, Thomson and other poets provided the vision of Nature that helped to create the Picturesque. The less than poetic talents of Mason and Payne Knight (the latter could rarely quote Shakespeare with accuracy) did not inhibit them from using poetry as an effective vehicle of propaganda; poetry itself invaded the garden in the form of inscriptions. The persuasive force of Burke's aesthetic hypotheses which, to borrow a phrase from Gibbon, 'in the composition of a specious argument, [were] artfully confounded in one splendid and brittle mass' owed much to the allurements of style, without which it is doubtful whether, the 'brilliant, but absurd and superficial theories of the "Inquiry into the Sublime and Beautiful"'[25] would have been so widely accepted. The taste for Gothic was fostered by novels and poetry; Alison said that through the influence of the latter 'the awful forms of Gothic superstition, the wild and romantic imagery . . . arise to the imagination in every scene'.[26] The antiquarian movement was accompanied by Charles Lamb's revival of the seventeenth-century cadences of Browne and quaintnesses of Burton.

There was a cult of Italian poetry; there cannot have been many periods when an English young lady could encourage an English young gentleman, even in the pages of an unusually learned novelist, by leaving open a page describing the enchanted garden in Boiardo's *Orlando Innamorato*.[27] Italy, moreover, had furnished a concept that had leavened English social mores since Elizabethan days, that permanently marked the temperament of the English gentleman and reached perfection in the most finished of dandies, Beau Brummel;[28] Brummell was the incarnation of 'sprezzatura', best perhaps rendered as 'careless and graceful off-handedness', the quality that is the kernel of the 'Courtier' of Castiglione.[29] In its English form the concept has its darker side; it encouraged amateurism, and carried within it the seeds of philistinism and anti-intellectualism. The notion of 'sprezzatura' is, incidentally, uncannily close to the postulated original meaning of another resonant 'foreign' word, 'sharawadgi' or 'sharawaggi' — 'the quality of being impressive or surprising through careless or unorderly grace';[30] is this one reason why 'sharawaggi' was so readily adopted by English gardeners? It accorded with an attitude entrenched in English social training.

'Is not Painting the mistress of all the Arts, or at least their principal Ornament? . . . there is hardly any occupation, tho' ever so mean, but what has some relation to Painting . . .'.[31] So wrote Alberti at the dawn of the Renaissance; his words were equally valid for the late eighteenth and early nineteenth centuries, and both old and modern painting played their part. The ancient decorative painting of Herculaneum, Pompeii, and Rome contributed significantly to the arts of the Regency, which at times imitated even its technique and handling (as had happened in earlier centuries). The inventions and adaptations of architecture and artefacts by modern painters, especially the Italians and the Italianate French, often preceded three-dimensional realisations by architects, decorators, and furniture makers. Their influence on the revival of antique styles was profound, from Mantegna and Raphael (the latter the most influential of all) to Poussin and Vien and beyond. The influence of Claude, Salvator Rosa, the Poussins, and the Dutch (Pls X, XI) on the art of the Picturesque and of landscape is a commonplace; it extended to the appearance and planning of the English country villa (Pl. II). Minor painters made their contribution; the landscape of Regent's Park combines the visions of Pannini and Hubert Robert. The renewed interest in Parmigianino and Mannerism in the later eighteenth century contributed to the singular mixture of sweetness and frigidity that is seen in Regency decoration and in neo-classical imagery. The list is extensive, and should include theatrical scene-painting, closely allied as it was to fashion and to techniques of interior decoration. The conception of the generative power of painting is present in Hope's concern that the liberal arts should rescue the artisan from mechanical commercial production and bring the act of creation into industry.

One is struck, in considering the various influences that helped to mould the style of the Regency — ancient architecture, sculpture, painting, and poetry; the mediaeval cathedrals; modern painting and poetry; the labours of scholars and critics, the careful and often humble expositions of the past — by the nobility of the sources whence the style sprang. The harvest was abundant and splendid, but the arts of the Regency, despite their manifold beauties and brilliancies, never reached the heights of their august exemplars, even in the earlier and more virtuous phases of the style. It is in the nature of an Indian summer that its felicities are autumnal.

PART I

# PARKS AND GARDENS

## Chapter one

# Before 1790: The Antecedents

. . . little would be left you, I'm afraid,
If all your debts to Greece and Rome were paid.
*Alexander Pope*[1]

The English parks and gardens of the eighteenth century were made by the grandees and gentry who went on the Grand Tour, read the right poets, looked at the approved pictures, built houses in the correct style, and filled them with fashionable paintings, sculpture and furniture. Not surprisingly, their intellectual and aesthetic partialities informed their parks and gardens as much as they did their other creations, although the wayward forces of nature have frequently blurred original intentions for succeeding generations. Gardens and parks were not an activity peripheral to other cultural pursuits; their changing styles during the eighteenth century fundamentally affected architecture, encouraging the use of Gothic, late mediaeval, and primitive classical forms; they influenced the design, planning and furnishing of houses, whether in rural isolation or surrounded by other houses and streets. During the Regency period the garden, as far as could be reconciled with practicality and social habits, entered the house; the purlieus of the house were treated as an extension of its interiors. In order to understand the course taken by much Regency design, one must begin out of doors.

## The influence of antiquity: formality

Surviving gardens in England and Europe exhibited a wide range of styles. In Italy, one could see richly modelled Renaissance and baroque gardens, still amongst the most exhilarating and inventive of all; in France, the stately formality that had reached its extreme form of expression in the Versailles of Louis XIV had survived the regime that gave it birth. Contrasting with these grand architectural styles were the neat compartments of the Dutch; the movement towards nature in England had culminated in the formalised naturalism of Capability Brown and the shaggy Picturesque of Payne Knight. Profoundly

different as each type was from the others, all had found inspiration, directly or indirectly, in the classical gardens that had been depicted by ancient writers and painters, recreated by modern painters and designers, and excavated from such ancient sites as that of Hadrian's Villa at Tivoli. Antique influence was not the whole story; modern gardens could not escape the influence of modern conditions, as the strongly differentiated individual and national characters that had evolved make clear. All post-mediaeval garden styles were to contribute to the synthesis that became the Regency garden.

One of the most striking tendencies of the eighteenth century in the visual arts (once the rococo had lost its initial attractions), was a steady progression towards ever more rigidly 'archaeological' re-creations of classical antiquity; this movement reached its height in the early years of the nineteenth century. It affected virtually all artefacts and appurtenances that had any pretensions to fashion or style — buildings, interiors, dress, textiles, silver and ceramics; the appearance of such distractions as revivalist Gothic did not deflect the persistent advance towards neo-classical antiquarianism. It would be surprising if gardens alone, despite the unattainability of an academic copy of an ancient garden (given eighteenth-century standards of archaeological excavation), had escaped antique influences (it was comparatively easy to reproduce an ancient chair such as the klismos, or a whole building such as the Parthenon). The intention to design parks and gardens in what was seen as an antique style is therefore often less self-evident (apart from in such objects as classical statuary and classical garden buildings) than it is in artefacts based on antique objects still in three-dimensional existence; other difficulties are caused by the widely varying interpretations to which the ancient literature that influenced modern gardens was subject.

Horace Walpole's sparkling essay on the 'Modern Taste in

Gardening', through which wit flickers like summer lightning, was written in 1770, a period when the ingredients that were to make the Regency garden were in fermentation. He detected a striking likeness between post-mediaeval garden styles and those of the antique world, frequently referring to the description of the villa gardens in Tuscany and at Laurentinum to be found in the letters of Pliny the Younger which, written in the well regulated days of the Emperor Trajan, contain the most explicit and sustained of all literary references to ancient gardens.

The most immediately noticeable aspect of Pliny's gardens was their ordered formality; the garden in Tuscany is described at length. In front of the villa was a portico, beyond which 'is a terrace, adorned with various figures, and bounded with an edging of box. Below this is a gravel walk; on each side of which, a little upon the descent, are figures of divers animals cut in box . . . round the Acanthus is a walk bounded by a close hedge of evergreens, cut into a variety of shapes . . . and a row of dwarf trees, that are always kept sheared. . . . Almost opposite to the middle of the portico is a summer-house, which surrounds a small court shaded by four plane-trees; in the midst of which a marble fountain gently plays. . . . When you are arrived at the end of all these winding alleys, you come out into a strait walk; nay, not into one, but several; divided, in some places, by grass-plots, in others, by box-trees, cut into a thousand shapes; some of which are letters forming my name; and others the name of my gardiner. In these are mixt, alternately, small pyramids and apple-trees.'[2]

Walpole's comment was that 'the English gardens . . . in the reign of Elizabeth, are exact copies of those of Pliny'. He expressed incredulity at the coexistence of what he saw as the trivialities of Pliny's garden with the contemporary glories of Roman architecture; 'what was the principal beauty of that pleasure ground? Exactly what was the admiration of this country about threescore years ago; box trees cut with monsters, animals, letters. . . . In an age when architecture displayed all its grandeur, all its purity, and all its taste . . . a Roman consul, a polished Emperor's friend, and a man of elegant literature and taste, delighted in what the mob now scarce admire in a college-garden. All the ingredients of Pliny's corresponded exactly with those laid out by London and Wise on Dutch principles . . . there wants nothing but the embroidery of a parterre, to make a garden in the reign of Trajan serve for a description of one in that of King William.'[3]

Walpole's unrestrained contempt for the style of Pliny's gardens, despite their incontestable antiquity and excellent provenance, reflects the complete fall from fashion of their English and Dutch descendants and the modern preference for 'natural' gardens. The contempt for the formal garden was on occasions justified by the argument that it owed its original formality to the demands of husbandry. This debt was well known; for example, a text book greatly respected and used throughout

the Regency period, the *De Re Aedificatoria* of Alberti, first published in about 1452, shows the very process of husbandry producing formal design in a vineyard and its irrigation canals: 'Dig trenches running . . . in strait lines, at equal distances from each other. . . . Dig a long square trench . . . with its sides all equally high and exactly level. . . . plant Willows Elder, Poplar . . . in close rows'.[4] Walpole was aware that 'the word garden . . . meant no more than a kitchen-garden or orchard for several centuries'[5] and that formality arose from utility. The utilitarian origin of formality enabled its opponents to claim that formality in gardens was an infant taste (see p.34); it is indeed true that the 'natural' garden was a more sophisticated concept than was that of the formal garden evolved from agriculture, since the former presupposes an idea of the 'artificial' from which it consciously departs. This idea leads logically to Rousseau's concept of nature controlled by art (see p.22). Even such a formal gardener as Le Nôtre was regarded in this light; a contemporary remarked that 'Le Nôtre . . . ne cherchait qu'à aider la nature, et à réduire le vrai beau aux moins de frais qu'il pouvoit'.[6]

One beguiling and evocative garden motif originally born of formal utility was treillage. Walpole mentions with interest the symmetrical town gardens of Roman antiquity, which used treillage extensively, implicitly equating them with modern Parisian gardens: 'In the paintings at Herculaneum are a few traces of gardens [Fig. 6]. . . . They are small square enclosures formed by trellis-work, and espaliers, and regularly ornamented with vases, fountains, and careatides, elegantly symmetrical, and proper for the narrow spaces allotted to the garden of a house in a capital city. From such I would not banish those playful waters [fountains were out of fashion in 1770] . . . nor the neat trellis. . . . Those treillages in the gardens at Paris . . . have a gay and delightful effect — They form light corridores, and transpicuous arbours through which the sun-beames play and chequer the shade, set off the statues, vases and flowers, that . . . suit the galant and idle society who . . . realize the fantastic society of Watteau and Durfé.'[7] Walpole in this passage anticipated the conversion to treillage of Uvedale Price (see p.46); his evocation of the enclosures of Herculaneum preceded their re-creation in the trellised compartments of Humphry Repton (Pl. XII). Repton would surely have read Walpole's essay with close attention.

Antique sources contributed the stately classical temples that so enhanced the landscapes of eighteenth and early nineteenth century England. From the antique came the statues, vases, urns, bas-reliefs and fountains that thronged the Renaissance and post-Renaissance garden, and that were to return in the Regency period after having suffered diminution at the height of the vogue for 'nature'. Pliny the Elder had attributed some uses of garden statuary to magic purposes: 'they use to set up in gardens, ridiculous and foolish images of Satyres, Antiques and such like, as good keepers and remedies against envy and witchcraft, howsoever Plautus assigneth the custodie of gardens to the protection of the goddess Venus'.[8] The last tradition was continued in the garden at Rousham, installed from 1737 onwards, where a version of the *Venus Pudica* presided over the Vale of Venus; this garden was described by Walpole as the 'most engaging of all Kent's works. . . . The whole is as elegant and antique as if the Emperor Julian had selected the most pleasing solitude about Daphne to enjoy a philosophic retirement.'[9] The association between gardens and philosophy was of long classical standing.

Like Rousham's *Venus*, many garden statues were modern versions of celebrated classical statues that had adorned Renaissance gardens before being moved indoors to the galleries of large houses and, later, to museums; the famous statues installed in the Belvedere by Pope Julius II in the early years of the sixteenth century, and the statues displayed before the garden loggia of the Villa Medici in Rome, had all been exposed to the open air.[10] During the eighteenth century, the heathen gods and goddesses, together with such famous works as the *Dancing Faun* from the Tribune of the Uffizi, the *Discobolus*, the *Dying Gladiator*, and such ornaments as the Medici and Borghese Vases, were multiplied in bronze, lead, stone, and Coade stone; garden statues in England were usually copied from the antique, whereas many statues in French gardens were in contemporary style. This taste continued; in 1792 Flaxman's father bought the remaining moulds used for casts by John Cheere in the mid-eighteenth century.[11] The fashion reached its height in the early nineteenth century, when garden ornamentation became indiscriminate, and reproductions of the Medici and Borghese vases were not thought inappropriate in the garden of a cottage orné.

The gardens of the ancient world gave to the modern European garden formal planting and canals, fountains, topiary, treillage, pergolas, temples, aviaries, grottoes decorated with shells, practically all the impedimenta of Renaissance and post-Renaissance gardens save the balustrade (the baluster was thought during the Regency to have been invented by Raphael).

## The influence of antiquity: nature

The sentiment for nature unadorned grew strongly in England during the eighteenth century, reaching its height in the 1790s. Sanctions for this could be found in antique literature. Much classical poetry celebrates nature and the bucolic life; Theocritus, Horace, and Virgil, for instance, were as affected by Nature in their way as was Wordsworth in his. Such sentiments seem to have influenced gardening practice within the classical period itself. Walpole found a hint of 'natural' gardening in Pliny's Tuscan garden, an approach congenial to Walpole's own tastes and to contemporary developments. 'In one passage . . . Pliny seems to have conceived that natural irregularity might be a beauty: "in opere urbanissimo . . . subita velut illati ruris imitatio". Something like a rural view was contrived among so much polished composition'.[12] The passage in question was translated thus in 1751: 'in the midst of a plot, improved with all imaginable art, you meet, on a sudden, with a spot of ground, wild, and uncultivated, as if transported hither on purpose . . .'.[13]

Another passage in Pliny, this time on the Laurentinum villa, not quoted by Walpole but doubtless noted by contemporaries, gave classical sanction to the home park and the ferme ornée: 'The prospects on every side are finely diversified; sometimes your view is limited by woods; then again is opened and extended by spacious meadows. Here, you see flocks of sheep; there, studs of horses and herds of cattle.'[14] Tacitus gave Walpole an instance of a 'natural' garden created by one of the more disreputable Roman emperors, Nero. 'There had been a prince, who, amidst a wildness of extravagant expense (one of his slightest faults) had discovered real taste . . . and his ideas had anticipated the principles of modern gardening'; he 'built a house [the "Domus Aurea", perhaps the greatest single influence on Renaissance and, hence, post-Renaissance interior decoration] in which gems and gold . . . were not so much to be admired as fields and lakes, and as in deserts, here woods, there open spaces and prospects'.[15] Nero, who was a compound of sophistication and brutality, a type that may have been consciously revived in the Renaissance, had perhaps been influenced by Horace, himself greatly admired in the eighteenth century: 'What inconceivable Pleasure do I enjoy while I am in these unfrequented Paths, admiring the steep Rocks and Solitary Groves.'[16]

Alberti, whose writings often display a strong romantic associationalism, recommended wild features in gardens, suggesting that they be associated with antique ruins: 'Promontories, Rocks, broken Hills vastly high and sharp, Grottoes, Caverns, Springs and the like; near which, if you wou'd have our situation strike the beholders with surprize [and fear? anticipations of Burke's "Sublime" and Chambers' Chinese horticultural extravaganzas?] we may build to our heart's desire. Nor shou'd there be wanting in the prospect Remains of Antiquity, on which we cannot turn our eyes without considering the various revolutions of men and things . . .'.[17] Already, we have the ingredients of the extreme Picturesque, of the Sublime, and of the 'Pleasure of Ruins'.

The descriptions of nature in the work of ancient poets were recommended as a source of direct inspiration to gardeners. In the early eighteenth century the well-known gardener Stephen Switzer, emphasising that the garden designer should 'take as much pains in forming his Imagination, as a Philosopher in cultivating his Understanding' mentioned Homer, Virgil and Ovid as sources: 'From these three and from some others of our own Time, and Country; the ingenuous designer . . . may collect . . . from the first what is Great, from the second what is Beautiful, and from the last what is strange' (again, these categories approach the Sublime, the Beautiful, and the Picturesque; see p.22). From Homer, the gardener should take 'something stupendously Great: such are Huge Forests mishapen Rocks and Precipices: these a designer, if possible, ought always to draw into his View . . .'. Elsewhere, Switzer speaks of trees in terms that recall Claude's drawings (of which Payne Knight, who fervently advocated the wild Picturesque garden, had a large collection): 'the careless and loose tresses of Nature, that are easily mov'd by the least Breath of Wind [that] offer more to the imagination than the most delicate Pyramid, or . . . [the] most elaborately clipp'd Espalier. . . .'[18]

Wild and irregular features in gardens did not remain as academic recommendations; 'natural and irregular planting in Italian, English and French gardens in the late 16th and 17th centuries, forms an integral part of the whole design'.[19] An English 'Essay of a Country house' of 1700 suggested that the garden should be separated into three parts; two would be formal, and the 'Third Region or Wilderness' would be 'Natural-Artificial . . . to deceive us into the belief of a real Wilderness or Thicket, and yet to be furnished with all the Varieties of Nature.'[20] Such ideas may have come from Holland; included as part of a garden near the Prinsenhof in Cleves in the late seventeenth century was a wild garden, and the garden of Zorgvliet in Holland in the same period had a wild area of sand dunes. The classical inspiration was important; 'In classical circles particularly . . . the geometric and the informal could be simultaneously realized in a garden'.[21] When, after the hiatus of Capability Brown, the combination of geometric and informal was revived, the instrument of revival was Repton, who had spent formative years in Holland.

## Modern influences

The literary remains of antiquity were used by painters in re-creating classical landscape; the most significant practitioners of this art for the eighteenth century were the two great French seventeenth-century painters based in Rome, Claude and Poussin; of the two, Claude exerted the greater influence on landscape design. As James Dallaway said in 1827, in a judgment that could have been uttered at any time within the preceding hundred years, Claude appropriated 'all that is elegant or refined in art or nature to make his pictures partake of the poetical beauties of Virgil or Tasso'.[22]

It is not difficult to account for the overwhelming effect of Claude's numinous landscapes on eighteenth-century sensibilities; steeped in the elegiac stillness that was in Claude's particular gift, the paintings were the ideal medium for reproducing such sacred landscapes of antiquity as that of the grove of Clitumnus as described by Pliny: 'A dark and shady wood of old cypress trees stands upon a small hill; under which a spring makes a passage, and breaks out in many branches . . . it forms itself

into a large basin of water, so clear and transparent . . . here it appears a fountain, and there immediately a very noble river. . . . Adjoining it is an old and awful temple. . . . There are little temples scattered up and down . . . a bridge terminates the sacred from the profane places. . . .'[23] From the evidence of his landscapes alone, it seems inconceivable that Claude was not directly inspired by the paintings of classical antiquity; apart from anything else, the extraordinarily elongated and disjointed figures that inhabit his late paintings resemble those that occur in Roman decorative wall paintings in a way that can hardly be accidental:[24] in 1661 he drew an exact copy of the largest mural of an ancient landscape known at that time.[25] Claude's paintings were, beautifully but imperfectly, translated into reality in English eighteenth-century gardens; at Stourhead the reality most nearly approached the dream.

Stourhead and Stowe are the pre-eminent examples of the mid-eighteenth century English landscape garden; ideally composed, full of classical reminiscences, scattered with temples and monuments which may have anticipated later use of Greek motifs but which were there in the first place as antique references. Stourhead, largely created from the 1740s to the 1760s, was consciously designed after Claude and Gaspar Poussin; in this it is 'pittoresque', to use the earlier eighteenth-century word, rather than 'Picturesque', to use the later one. The programme behind its design may have been planned with Virgil's *Aeneid* as inspiration.[26]

It seems probable that the early appearance in gardens of the motifs of neo-classical architecture was paralleled by the early appearance in garden design of what one might call the neo-classical spirit; the qualities of purity and economy of means, Attic simplicity, are as apparent in the Elysian fields of Stowe as in those of Gluck's *Orpheus*. The spirit of generalisation, sometimes tending towards abstraction, that is present in so much neo-classical art, is strongly expressed in the art of Capability Brown, and is emphasised by his spare use of classical ornament. Lakes, clumps, belts of trees and bare grassy meadows have in his gardens something of the same mutual relationships as do vestigial ornament and unadorned mass in the most advanced French architectural projects of the period. The faults of formalism and sterility for which he was castigated by the Picturesque propagandists of the 1790s are the faults with which much neo-classicism has been commonly charged, and for which the Greek Revivalists were later to be condemned.

## Art, Nature, and the Picturesque

Walpole, who knew that their native literary tradition influenced the way the English perceived nature, did not allow Claude sole credit for the beauties of the new gardens, but advanced the claims of Milton (he was not the first to do so): 'The description of Eden is a warmer and more just picture of the present style than Claud Lorrain could have painted from Hagley or Stourhead'. He annotated his praise of Milton's Eden for anticipating later developments with a quotation from 'Paradise Regained':

> . . . and entered soon the shade;
> High-rooft, and walks beneath, and alleys brown,
> That opened in the midst a woody scene.
> Nature's own work it seemed (Nature taught Art)

The passage, as Walpole chose to quote it (he omitted a succeeding reference to wood nymphs),[27] sounds almost Gothic, with its echo of 'Il Penseroso's' 'high-embowed roof'; the Gothic taste had affinities with the growing interest in 'nature' for various reasons, one of which may have been the difficulties encountered in the search for the 'rules' of Gothic architecture; the mark of the Goth was freedom (see p.159).

Walpole himself saw the ambiguities of the relationship between art and nature; next to his citation of Milton's 'Nature taught Art', he quoted a canto of analogous description from Tasso which concluded 'L'Arte che tutto fa, nulla si scopre'.[28] This last notion, that of art concealed, lay at the heart of the famous imaginary garden of Julie created by Rousseau in his novel of 1759, *La nouvelle Héloise*. Albeit imaginary, it was influential. It contained all the paradisical and primitive aspirations, the feeling for nature and longing for an incorrupt spontaneity, that were felt by a society conscious of the need for reform. Rousseau described the wonderful richness of the vegetation, the grassy glades, the rivulets bordered with flowers; the trees, with climbing plants flung negligently from one to the other; the birds, not penned into aviaries but flying free in the forest. Rousseau's gardener emphasised that this Eden was not natural; nature had done all 'sous ma direction'. But the art employed had been carefully concealed, and an error avoided; 'l'erreur . . . est de vouloir de l'art partout, et de n'être jamais content que l'art ne paraisse; au lieu que c'est à le cacher que consiste le véritable goût. . . .'[29]

Tasso and Rousseau agreed that art should not obtrude; in this liking for apparent spontaneity one recognises another manifestation of '*sprezzatura*'. Equally, neither believed that uncontrolled nature could be left to make a garden; the same sense of an ultimate controlling power lay behind the enjoyment of uncultivated nature felt by such diverse spirits as Pliny, Alberti, and the Earl of Shaftesbury;[30] all thought of wilder nature merely as part of the seasoning of a civilised garden, with 'art' as the master. A different concept emerged towards the end of the eighteenth century, by virtue of which Nature took its place as one of the elemental Romantic powers; Nature

> as if with voluntary power instinct
> Upreared its head . . .
> For so it seemed, with purpose of its own. . . .[31]

In 1756 Edmund Burke made his celebrated division of the categories of beauty into the Sublime and the Beautiful.[32] The Beautiful included the more amenable beauties of landscape, as epitomised in Claude (Pl. X) and in the real landscapes formed after his model; it was characterised by smallness, smoothness, roundness, and delicacy. The Sublime was founded in terror and awe, and included roughness, largeness, darkness and gloominess (Pl. XI). Burke considered the sensation of the Beautiful to be founded on pleasure, that of the Sublime on the consciousness of danger and pain. Placed in theoretical opposition as the Sublime and the Beautiful were, it is not surprising that they attracted mutually hostile disciples.

More possibilities of aesthetic argument were introduced with the concept of the Picturesque, especially as developed in the various *Tours* published between 1782 and 1809 (the last posthumously) by the Rev. William Gilpin. His notion of the Picturesque, which was closely linked with his practice of the art of watercolour, may briefly be defined as the technique of judging a scene using the same rules as one would use in judging a picture. It may be easily seen that if one uses these criteria in composing a garden, all kinds of qualities not normally associated with gardens gain admittance. One such subversive quality, the Sublime as defined by Burke, was given further sanction by the Picturesque. The pictorial Sublime was exemplified above all in the landscapes of Salvator Rosa, especially valued for their sense of terror, terror being an element of the Sublime. Walpole's description of Salvator gives an idea of some of the qualities now sought in gardens; he spoke of the 'picturesque painters, like Salvator Rosa, [who] consider colour and chiar'oscuro as their sole aim and end; consequently objects rugged and irregular, suited to produce the most brilliant effects of light and shadow, are by them preferred and selected'.[33] Jacob Ruysdael was Picturesque in a less sinister way; his disordered vegetation was to be attractive to Payne Knight and to Loudon in his early years (Pl. XI). As early as the 1780s the undisciplined wildness of Payne Knight's garden at Downton Castle anticipated the Picturesque confusion that was to find its way twenty-five years later into the arrangement of Regency drawing rooms.

The question was, who wielded the sceptre — Art or Nature? A chance remark by Walpole revealed both his perception and its limitations. After a rhapsody on the present beauties of the English countryside, he continued: 'Enough has been done to establish such a school of landscape, as cannot be found on the rest of the globe. If we have the seeds of a Claud or a Gaspar amongst us, he must come forth. If wood, water, groves, vallies, glades, can inspire a poet or painter, this is the country, this is the age to produce them.'[34] He was a prophet; the poet and the painter did appear. They were not, however, a Milton or a Claude; they were a Wordsworth and a Constable, artists who had stepped decisively outside the antique and classical tradition. The

**1** A castle in picturesque scenery, by Robert Adam, c.1782

**2** 'Vue Générale de la Villa Pia' at Rome, pictured by Percier and Fontaine, 1809

development was presaged by Gilpin, who was not interested in the dryads and the hamadryads; his book *Forest Scenery*, for example, first published in 1791, considers trees as 'individuals' as well as viewed in compositions — although his description of the oak takes virtually all its features from Virgil.[35] Despite his use of Virgil, Gilpin's attitude was very much that of the new century.

In effect, Nature had won the day, at least in painting and poetry; her victory in gardening was partial and short-lived. The extreme Picturesque in gardening was too much to be supportable for long. In a real sense, the formal garden and the ordered park, whether designed by Le Nôtre at one extreme or Capability Brown at the other, represented the classical inheritance. The extreme Picturesque landscape represented the inheritance of the Goths and Vandals; it was the kind of 'romantic' setting for which the Regency buildings that reproduced the castles of the Middle Ages were thought especially suitable, a perception anticipated by Robert Adam (Fig. 1).

Picturesque natural landscape was associated with another quality, most obvious in the poetry of Wordsworth but powerful elsewhere. It was perceived as having a moral content, now seen as somehow irreconcilable with art, whether literary or visual. This troubled even Repton, who more than any other Regency gardener was moulded by the classical past. He recorded that when he went to see the Lake District, 'the only instance in which I have made an excursion of a hundred miles to which I was not called by my profession', the magnificent landscape disquieted him: 'It gave me a humiliating idea of the vanity of my profession: The vast Lakes and their mountainous accompaniments of Nature, had the effect of making me feel how little were the humble efforts of my art — which had so often been extolled! — and I felt regret that Nature and Art were at such an immeasurable distance!'[36]

## Modern gardens

These ideas were in restless circulation as the age of the Regency opened; more reassuring, perhaps, was the sight of existing gardens, which included examples of all the great historical styles. Better roads and the new fashion of 'tourism' laid them open for inspection on a scale hitherto impracticable; the Grand Tour took travellers to the great foreign gardens as a matter of course.

Italy, and especially Genoa and Rome, provided some of the most memorable gardens in the world, with the added attraction that they were redolent of antiquity. To authentic antique detritus was added the convincing Renaissance re-creation of antiquity; in 1780 the young Beckford wrote that the Boboli Gardens in Florence 'brought the scenery of an antique Roman garden' so vividly to mind, that he 'expected every instant to be called to the table of Lucullus . . . and to

stretch [himself] on his purple triclinias'; the garden of the Villa Negroni in Rome he imagined 'as old as the baths of Dioclesian, which peep over one of its walls.'[37] The unfashionable standing of the Italian Renaissance and baroque garden at the beginning of the 1790s did not prevent their beauty from making an ineffaceable impression on such other visitors as Uvedale Price and Thomas Hope (Fig. 2); they were to have a profound influence on the Regency garden. As did the formal French garden; if, when one thinks of gardens as a type, Versailles springs more readily to mind than any other, it is a tribute to the force with which the formal and absolutist society of Louis XIV imposed its concept on the garden, as it did on the palace and the state. The absolutist element was real, and it was impossible for anybody, least of all an Englishman of the Hanoverian settlement, to regard the French style as neutral: Dallaway wrote of Le Nôtre that his planting of avenues and 'radiations, diverging from a centre, in an open champain' had led 'many to adopt it among the nobility, for it was the subjection of a whole district of country to one grand mansion'.[38]

Saint-Simon, a courtier of Louis XIV, said of the gardens of Versailles that 'one admires and avoids them';[39] succeeding generations admitted the magnificence, but regretted the frigidity. Laugier, the powerful architectural theorist (see p.91 et seq.), remarked in the middle of the eighteenth century that the gardens of Versailles had long passed amongst French and foreigners as one of the wonders of the world, but asked whether they had anything 'de quoi fournir aux plaisirs de l'âme et à l'amusement des yeux, un agréable et riant spectacle?' Astonishment and admiration were followed by 'la tristesse et . . . l'ennuie'. Most noticeably lacking were 'de l'heureuse négligence, et de la piquante bisarrerie de la nature'.[40] Others perceived similar wants, similar boredom, and a similar rejection of happy accidents of nature in the formal gardens of England; the bourgeois and miniaturised Dutch gardens were less forbidding, and when Repton returned formality to fashion in the 1790s the Dutch influence played its part (see p.43).

The Regency period saw an acceleration of social informality, lamented by Repton and frequently noted by others; Samuel Rogers, for instance, looked back towards the end of a long life to recall with some astonishment the scene in his youth at Ranelagh, when the mixture of people from different ranks of society prescribed silence, and all 'was so orderly and still, that you could hear the whisking sound of the ladies' trains, as the immense assembly walked round and round the room'.[41] Yet Regency society was still largely formal; its return to a degree of formality in gardens, partly perhaps a reaction to the

1 *The Flower Cart in Spring*, 1822, by J. L. Agasse

II Villa designed 'as the Residence of an Artist', by J. B. Papworth, 1818

III 'French Drapery Window Curtains', from the *Repository*, 1811

Plate 27. Vol. 6

IV 'Flower Garden, Valley-Field', Fife, designed by Humphry Repton, 1800

v 'The House . . . from the Drying Grounds',
the Deepdene, Surrey

29

Peacock by P. William

30

VI 'Steps to Ampitheatre and Conservatory', the Deepdene, Surrey

VII The terrace and conservatory, Mamhead, Devon, designed 1828–38 by Anthony Salvin

VIII Brighton Pavilion, detail of the garden designed by John Nash, c.1820

Picturesque threat to return gardening to the wild, was possibly also a response to the threat of social disintegration, epitomised in the recent career of the guillotine.

There was perhaps another reason. Formal gardens were prohibitively costly, and easily fell into disrepair. A visitor to Versailles in a fiction of 1766 found the garden 'doubtless extremely well laid out, but the walks were insupportably dusty, for want of gravel. Many of the statues were mutilated, and most of the water-works were in a state of inactivity by reason of the pipes being out of repair.'[42] When money was short, it was often cheaper to redesign, and 'Capability' Brown may have owed some of his success to this fact. But by the early nineteenth century the English magnates were as rich as Croesus, and notoriously anxious to display their riches. A grand formal garden was a good way of doing this; everybody knew that such gardens needed more than scythe or sheep, sufficient for the Brownian park, to keep them up.

The spate of Brownian destruction had spared some old formal gardens in England to inspire the new; the old garden of Bramham Park in Yorkshire, for example, was described thus in 1818: 'the Gardens correspond in their style with the house, and consist of fine timber cut in strait hedges of the height of the trees, the whole kept up with the greatest precision, and are said to resemble those of St. Cloud in France; gravelled walks extend for miles through the Pleasure Grounds. . . .'[43] Chiswick provided an excellent example of the so-called 'rococo' garden, a combination of axial planning and irregularity, a mixture of 'sharawadgi' and aligned paths and groves, obelisks and sphinxes. Irregularity had been recommended in gardens for some considerable time; Walpole quoted the opinion of Sir Henry Wootton, who was writing in the early seventeenth century, that 'as fabricks should be regular, so gardens should be irregular, or at least cast into a very wide regularity'.[44] The resultant informality was as artificial as a Lancret hat, but markedly 'agréable et riant'. It is likely that Walpole,

had he used such terms, would have regarded such gardens as 'neo-classical' rather than 'rococo'; he said of Kent that 'We owe the restoration of Greece and the diffusion of architecture to his skill in landscape'.[45] Lord Burlington must have intended the garden at Chiswick to harmonise with the Palladian house. Rococo or neo-classical, some later Regency gardens are remarkably reminiscent of the Chiswick type.

The style of Capability Brown, in high fashion when Walpole was writing, was by 1790 being attacked on both sides, by the lovers of the old formal gardens and by the lovers of the extreme Picturesque. The former were ably represented by Sir William Chambers, whose opinions influenced Repton; Chambers spoke of the 'improvers'' work with bitter sarcasm: 'the havock it has made in our old plantations, must ever be remembered with indignation . . . thousands of venerable plants, whole woods of them, have been swept away, to make room for a little grass, and a few American weeds'.[46] The exponents of the extreme Picturesque found in Brown nothing save manner, con-trivance, boredom and vacuity; of these the most vocal were Knight and Price. The tourists, the 'Ejaculating and Epitheting Societies', who loved '"Ahs!" and "Ohs"'[47] and preferred nature untrammelled, equally disliked Brown; a little later Wordsworth, from the height of his moral position, described the revolution accomplished in Nature's name by the 'genteel school of landscape' as 'founded in false taste, false feeling, and its effects disgusting in the extreme'.[48]

There were thus sufficient ingredients for the most determined eclecticist to experiment with — formality and informality, Nature and Art, the classical and the Gothic — and the age was not timid. Walpole, acute as ever, pointed to a peril that was to prove destructive '. . . there is a more imminent danger that threatens the present . . . I mean the pursuit of variety. . . . The more we exact novelty, the sooner will our taste be vitiated.'[49] His predictions were to prove accurate.

IX A garden temple in primitive style with wooden Doric columns and 'rope' capitals, c.1785

## Chapter two

# The 1790s: Associationalism and the Picturesque

His Majesty has also graciously permitted me to tell you, that in the controversy between you and Mr. Price his opinion entirely coincides with yours.
*Lord Harcourt to Humphry Repton*[1]

During the 1790s three men published works of fundamental importance for Regency design. They gathered together contemporary sentiments concerning associationalism and the Picturesque and presented them as coherent theory and as recommended action; they gave the signal for a rapidly accelerating implementation of Picturesque concepts, which affected architecture as deeply as they affected parks and gardens. The three men were Archibald Alison, Uvedale Price and Richard Payne Knight.

## Associationalism: Alison

The decade opened with the publication by Alison of *Essays on the Nature and Principles of Taste*; the keystone of Regency aesthetics, it had gone into six editions by 1825. Alison was a country clergyman, whose ideas had been developed from theories propounded by an eminent episcopal fantasist, Bishop Berkeley. Berkeley had defined two types of beauty; the 'Free Beauty' of direct aesthetic reactions, and the 'Relative Beauty' of associated ideas; he distinguished between, for example, the visual beauties of Gothic architecture and the associated ideas of religion and antiquity that Gothic churches convey. Berkeley had died in 1753, three years before the publication of Burke's enquiry into the Sublime and the Beautiful, the conclusions of which Alison incorporated in his own work; Alison uses such terms as 'beauty' and 'sublimity' throughout in the technical senses given to them by Burke.

Alison surpassed Berkeley by denying absolutely the existence of objective beauty; he attributed all sensations of beauty to the stimulation of the imagination by associated ideas.[2] 'Whatever increases this exercise or employment of Imagination, increases also the Emotion of beauty or sublimity. This is very obviously the effect of all Associations.[3] As a corollary, the imaginative stimulation produced by

associations 'is produced also . . . by what are generally termed Picturesque objects'.[4] Another corollary, revolutionary in import, was Alison's view that criticism destroys the sense of beauty, since critics 'accustom us to consider every composition in relation to rules . . . '.[5] Such a view must have astounded readers of the 1790s, to whom aesthetic rules were the tools of creation.

Payne Knight largely accepted Alison's propositions, save that he considered colour and sound to have undeniable objective qualities. It is surprising that sound was not further developed as a quality of the Picturesque. Alison was conscious of its importance; he mentioned, for instance, that although the beauty of a sunset on a fine autumnal evening, the various colours of the clouds and the calm and deep repose, seem incapable of enhancement, yet 'there is no man who does not know how great an addition this fine scene is capable of receiving from the circumstance of the evening bell'.[6] As Coleridge found in reverse, when, settling himself in self-conscious melancholy at Denbigh Castle in 1794, he was disturbed by the rude music of rustic revelry.[7]

A subject on which Alison's pronouncements were of significance was that of irregularity. As early as 1728 Batty Langley had written that nothing was more 'Shocking than a stiff, Regular garden',[8] but the notion of 'irregularity' had never quite thrown off its dubious origins: 'not in conformity with rule or principle; contrary to rule; disorderly in action or conduct; anomalous; abnormal'.[9] Regularity was preordained; the bright seraphim stood 'in burning row', unlike the promiscuous mass of the damned. As far as architecture was concerned, no less an authority than Wren had said that 'straight lines are more beautiful than curved'.[10]

Alison declared that 'the Form, which . . . universally characterizes the productions of infant Taste, is Uniformity or Regularity'; this was true of gardens, 'as, even at present, when so different a style of gardening prevails, the Common People universally follow the first System';[11] this equated the ancient formal garden with the taste of the common people. Alison himself concluded that 'those nations of antiquity, who had carried the Arts of Taste to the greatest perfection which they have ever yet attained, while they had arrived at Beauty in every other species of Form, seem never to have imagined, that the principle of Variety was applicable to Gardening, or to have deviated in any respect from the Regularity or Uniformity of their Ancestors'.

The advocacy of irregularity appears to condone 'rococo' and Brownian principles of gardening. Alison had loftier ambitions, in that his purpose was to create in actuality an ideal landscape of the imagination which transcended the mundane beauties of Nature: 'What we thus attempt in imagination, it is the business of the art of Gardening to execute . . . to awaken an emotion more full, more simple, and more harmonious than any we can feel from the scenes of Nature itself'.[12] To this end Alison was ready to admit, as were Uvedale Price and Payne Knight, more than one style of gardening; traditions formerly regarded as warring and incompatible were to exist side by side, as they had already begun to do in Repton's synthesis (see pp.44–5).

Alison left the propriety of architectural formality in gardens open. He approved of the removal of 'Statues, Temples, Urns, Ruins, Colonnades etc.', where they became profuse, for the beauty of the landscape remained. However, he did not exclude ornaments, for 'Jet d'Eaus, artificial Fountains, regular cascades, Trees in the form of Animals etc., have in all countries been the principle ornaments of gardening. The violation of the usual appearances of Nature in such objects, strongly exhibited the employment of Art. They accorded perfectly, therefore, with the character which the scene was intended to have; and they increased the effect of that quality upon which this Beauty was founded, and *intended to be founded* [author's italics].'[13] This recognised that the formal garden, including the much-ridiculed topiary, had an ordered and deliberate beauty peculiar to itself.

## The Picturesque and the formal garden: Price

In 1794, Uvedale Price and Richard Payne Knight published their contributions to the debate. Price was especially influential; he proposed a Trinity in which the Picturesque took its rank as a separate aesthetic category beside the Sublime and the Beautiful. This provoked an intense argument of which the 'difference is almost invisible to the nicest theological eye' (as Gibbon said of the Nicaean disputes). Price exhibited good sense, sensitivity, practicality and tolerance — except when discussing Capability Brown.

He derided the claims to naturalism of the rococo and Brownian schools; before Kent, 'everything was in squares and parallelograms;

now everything is in segments of circles, and ellipses; the formality still remains'.[14] Taking up the complaint of Chambers against Brown — 'our gardens differ very little from common fields . . . the offspring of chance rather than design'[15] — he castigated Brown's banality and boredom; the wretch who is forced to walk with an 'improver' around his grounds will allow 'that a snake with its tail in its mouth is comparatively but a faint symbol of eternity'.[16] He put his finger on Brown's main characteristic: 'the particulars are smooth and flowing; the effect . . . of the whole hard, unvaried, and unconnected'[17] (this discordance is often seen in neo-classical art, as for instance in Flaxman's illustrations). He condemned Brown's clumps, belts, and serpentine canals. Painting was in the forefront of his mind; the worst insult he could offer Brown, and to a devotee of the Picturesque it would have been the final insult, was to say that his work had affinities with that of a 'house-painter', rather than that of a landscape painter.[18]

Price recommended Claude as inspiration (Pl. X); his 'air de fête'[19] was beguiling, and he had a 'soft and pleasing repose' that is 'the characteristic of the beautiful'.[20] Variety and intricacy (qualities that were to be constantly invoked by Repton),[21] were important sources of pleasure. Fir plantations were dreary; of 'all dismal scenes it seems to me the most likely for a man to hang himself, though . . . there is rarely a single side branch to which a rope could be fastened'[22] (this was perhaps a riposte to Gilpin, who three years earlier had strongly defended the Scotch fir against its 'many enemies').[23] Avenues gave romantic effect and were like 'a grand gothic aisle with its natural columns and vaulted roof' (Fig. 106);[24] this echoed, amongst others, Pope, for whom 'aged trees cathedral walks compose'.[25]

Price rejected two shibboleths, the first being the cult of simplicity that went with the artifice of smooth banks and shaven lawns; Mason had invoked Simplicity at the opening of his well-known poetical history of the English garden, published in 1783, but Price's comment was that 'to make simplicity the arbiter of ornament, is . . . like making mercy the arbitress of justice, or frugality of generosity'.[26] The second was the excessive cult of nature; 'in the old gardens art was meant to be apparent, and to challenge admiration on its own account, not under the disguise of nature'.[27] Adieu Rousseau, but by 1794 Rousseau had been discovered to be an edged tool; a palace set down in a field, as if by the magic of Aladdin's lamp,[28] was left dangerously open to the peasantry. Price had the unlikely belief that the Brownian 'revolution' was 'stamped with the character of all those, which either in religion or politics have been carried into execution by the lower, or less enlightened part of mankind'. We are not so far from the Prince of Wales' fear that the antique republican style of his French furniture might convict it of Jacobinism.[29]

Price thought he might be accused of 'endeavouring to bring about a counter-revolution, and to restore the ancien régime, with all its despotism of straight lines and perpetual symmetry. It is true that I have some attachment to the old monarchy. . . .' He protested he would prefer the toleration of all forms of worship, where a man who had a taste for the Dutch style (the style most scorned by the improvers) might 'enjoy his tulips, amidst box or yew hedges, labyrinths etc. . . .'.[30] He was, in effect, attempting to set up Art and Nature as equals. In tolerating eclecticism, he did not foresee the democratisation and commercialisation of taste that was to accompany it.

Price's defence of the formal garden atoned for youthful vandalism; he had destroyed his own old formal garden in deference to fashion. He was aware 'how much more difficult it is to add any of the old decorations to modern improvements, than to soften the old style by blending it with a proper portion of the new'[31] — what once destroyed, can never be supplied. He refers nostalgically to the sense of seclusion and safety given by the enclosures in old gardens.[32] Nostalgia suffuses his memories of Roman villa gardens seen on the Grand Tour: 'I remember the rich and magnificent effects of balustrades, fountains, marble basons, and statues, blocks of ancient ruins, with remains of ancient sculpture, the whole mixed with pines and cypresses' (Fig. 2).[33] One suspects that Price did not dislike the baroque, in buildings or in gardens; he expressly regretted that Vanbrugh had not attended more to gardens: 'I am convinced he would have struck out many peculiar and characteristic effects'.

Price helped to prepare opinion for the return of the parade of the formal garden. The 'insipid' Brownian fashion of lawn and gravel next to the house was to be replaced by architectural ornament (Chambers had already advocated a contrast between formal symmetry next to the house and informal nature beyond): 'However unnatural raised terraces, fountains, flights of steps, parapets, with statues, vases, balustrades, etc. may be called — however our ancestors may have been laughed at . . . for "walking up and down stairs in the open air" [a reference to Walpole's mockery in his *Essay on Modern Gardening*], the effect of all these objects is very striking; and they are not more unnatural, that not more artificial, than the homes which they are intended to accompany.'[34]

## The extreme Picturesque: Knight

Knight's didactic poem 'The Landscape' was published in the same year as Price's book (1794) and was addressed to Price; it cannot be called weighty or reasoned, but its invective reinforced Price's message. Knight trounced Brown with vigour and relish, accusing the improver's acolytes, in the famous words that echo the polished indecencies of Pope, of shaving 'the goddess, whom they came to dress . . .'.[35] He advocated the revival of the formal garden as an antidote to the eternal boredom of Brown:

Tir'd with th'extensive scene, so dull and bare.
To Heav'n devoutly I've address'd my pray'r, —
Again the moss-grown terraces to raise,
And spread the labyrinth's perplexing maze;
Replace in even lines the ductile yew,
And plant again the ancient avenue[36]

Knight included in his book two 'before and after' scenes that attracted much comment. The first showed a classical house in a trim Brownian landscape; the second an Elizabethan or Jacobean house in an untidy Picturesque landscape. Repton, not unfairly, said that rather than showing examples of bad and good taste as intended, they served 'to exemplify bad taste in the two extremes of artificial neatness and wild neglect'.[37] None the less, they startlingly illustrated that change in taste effected by the Picturesque; the Elizabethan house, an exercise in historicism (for a change of style is implied, the other house being modern) was not intended to dominate its surroundings in the accepted way, but to merge into them '. . . A mere component part of what you see'.[38]

The difficulties of blending into the landscape the modern classical house, the 'poor square edifice'[39] with its unbroken skyline and concealed offices, may easily be seen. In order to mix and blend, a broken silhouette was needed, together with an irregular and extended outline; such were to be seen everywhere in the ancient dwellings of England, in mediaeval castles, in Tudor and Jacobean manor houses — and in the grandiose creations of Vanbrugh (see p.101, Pl. XXVII). Knight perceived this, and so did others.

## Prospect and the irregular house

Payne Knight practised what he preached; between 1772 and 1778 he designed and built a new house in the castle style on his property at Downton (Fig. 116). Its predecessors had included Sanderson Miller's sham castle at Edgehill (1746–7) and Vanbrugh's Castle at Greenwich (begun in 1718). In 1805 Knight wrote: 'It is now more than thirty years since the author . . . ventured to build a house, ornamented with what are called Gothic towers and battlements without, and with Grecian ceilings, columns and entablatures within; and although his example has not been much followed [broadly true at that date] he has every reason to congratulate himself upon the success of the experiment — [which provided] the advantage of a picturesque object and of an elegant and convenient dwelling; . . . capable of receiving alterations and additions in almost any direction, without any injury to its genuine and original character'.[40]

Knight regretted that the house reflected the imperfections of his own immaturity; it is a pity that he did not have a second chance, since he might then have built in 'that mixed style, which characterizes the buildings of Claude and the Poussins'[41] (see p.102 and Pl. X) and have achieved as distinguished a synthesis as that of Thomas Hope's Deepdene. None the less Knight's castle, although as architecture less remarkable than the Deepdene, is remarkable enough: it 'would seem that Downton is the first country house of any importance erected since the Renaissance which was designed from the outset with an irregular plan';[42] its descendants include unnumerable irregular, historicist country houses, to be seen all over the world. Downton marks the point where Picturesque precepts began to affect the form, planning, and disposition of country houses, and thence the whole system of living.

One of the first to follow Knight's example was Uvedale Price. Price wrote in his *Essays* that where there were good features in the landscape, the house, 'instead of making a regular front and sides' should have 'many of the windows turned towards those points where the objects were most happily arranged . . . the architect would be forced into a number of picturesque forms and combinations, which otherwise might never have occurred to him; and would be obliged to do what so seldom has been done — accomodate his building to the scenery, not make that give way to his building'.[43] This is the 'mix and blend' recipe of Knight, but approached from the inside rather than from the outside of the building. Taken together, the two approaches, with their different emphases, provided a double justification for the irregular house.

Price built his irregular house at Aberystwyth in about 1795. The site had spectacular views, on one side lay the ocean, on another a castle, on a third were ragged cliffs. The obvious solution was adopted, and the house was designed to face the views. There was classical precedent; Pliny had built a tower 'with a banquetting room, from whence there is a view of a very wide ocean, a very extensive continent, and numberless beautiful villas'.[44] Price's house was built as a triangle; this was not particularly startling, in that there had been a tradition of triangular prospect towers, but it was unusual. According to Price, his architect had first proposed a square house, but Price 'told him . . . that I must have, not only some of the windows but some of the rooms turned to particular points. . . . I expressed to him the reasons why I built it so close to the rock . . . and . . . how the foreground was connected with the rocks in the second ground, all of which would be lost by placing it further back. He was excessively struck with these reasons, which he said he had never thought of before in the most distant degree . . . the form of it is certainly extremely varied from my having obliged him to run the rooms to different aspects'.[45] The house was a success, and Royal Worcester made a china model of it. The architect who had been instructed by this pedagogue of the Picturesque was John Nash; Sir George Beaumont had recommended 'his little friend, Nash' as being 'very docile'.[46] Docile he may have been when it

suited him; he was also quick, and an opportunist, and no better person could have been selected as a vehicle for the new style.

Its course was not altogether smooth. Most people would have agreed that a good prospect was desirable, whether they were amateurs of the Picturesque or not; this went back to Roman times. In England, Moor Park in 1685 had its best rooms ranged 'upon the breadth of the garden, the great parlours open[ing] into the middle of a terrace gravel-walk that lies even with it . . . from this walk are three descents . . . into a very large parterre'.[47] Here the prospect was of a 'princely garden'. In June 1750, Lord Chesterfield wrote: 'The shell of my gallery is finished, which, by three bow-windows, gives me three different, and the finest, prospects in the world',[48] a remark that gives a very 'Regency' impression. The novel question was whether the irregularity that had been fairly readily accepted in gardens would be accepted also in architecture, both as a means to an end — that of acquiring the best prospect, and of blending the house in the landscape — and as an end in itself, a conscious aesthetic choice.

That jump, from gardens to buildings, had been made, explicitly, by Walpole, who expressed a conscious preference for irregularity: 'The Grecian is only proper for magnificent and public buildings. . . . The variety is little, and admits no charming irregularities. I am almost as fond of the Sharawaggi, of Chinese want of symmetry, in building, as in grounds or gardens'.[49] And Sir Joshua Reynolds, speaking of additions made to houses, had asked a question that had the same import: 'As such buildings depart from regularity, they now and then acquire something of scenery . . . which I think might not unsuccessfully be adopted by an Architect. . . . Variety and intricacy is a beauty and excellence in every other of the arts which address the imagination; and why not in Architecture?'[50] The answer was that the weight of traditional opinion was on the other side. As well as preferring straight to curved lines, Wren had declared that 'Geometrical figures are naturally more beautiful than other irregular figures: in this all consent as to a law of nature'.[51] In the 1730s, Roger Morris laid down that 'The Joint Union and Concordance of the Parts, in an exact Symmetry, forms the whole, a compleat Harmony'; buildings should 'unite the Beholder to consider the taking in of the whole Scene at one view . . . without moving the Eye';[52] a 'Vista through the Middle of the Building should be always had . . . and the Doors of one Room, in a Range of Rooms should be dispos'd to answer each other in a Line, to preserve a Grandeur'.[53] This regularity applied not only to palaces; in 1747, Daniel Garret wrote that 'the Palace or Cottage require different forms . . . yet regularity is necessary in both'.[54]

Many Regency architects agreed with such precepts. In 1800, for instance, John Plaw wrote in the preface to a book of country house designs that 'the following Designs are constructed on the principles of symmetry and correspondence of parts'.[55] Busby inveighed against

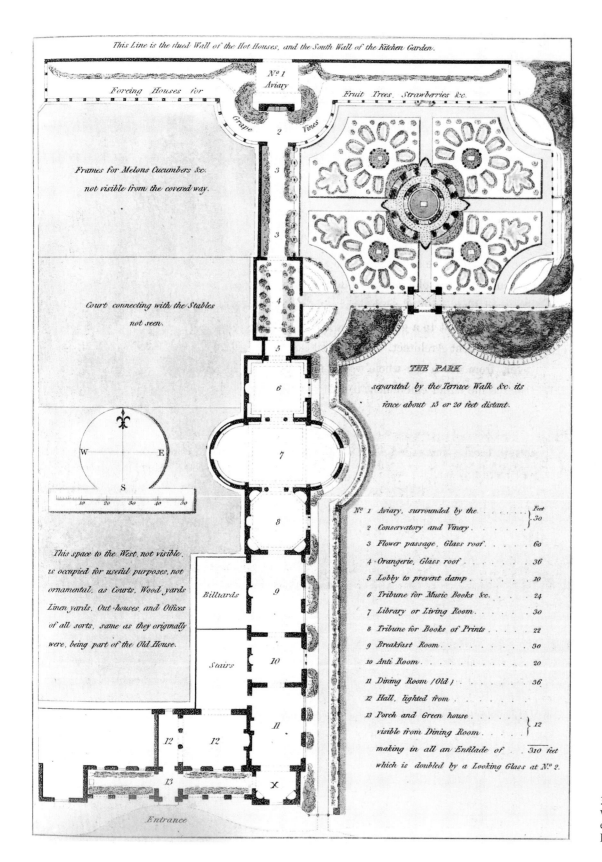

**3** 'A Ground Plan, explained to a lady, who confessed that she did not understand either a plan or map', by Humphry Repton, 1816

4 St. Dunstan's Villa, Regent's Park, from the south in 1832

irregularity. Gandy preferred irregularity, but gave the client latitude: 'Those [designs] which are regular may be changed into the picturesque, by taking away one wing; and the picturesque or irregular Designs will become regular by selecting a centre, and repeating the parts on each side, if the builder prefers such dull monotony'.[56] Knight wrote in 1805 that 'regularity, of which the moderns have been so tenacious in the plans of their country houses, was taken from the sacred, and not from the domestic architecture of the ancients . . .',[57] an attempt to explode regularity at source. It failed.

Repton seemed in 1792 to equate 'correctness' with symmetry; 'it would not be difficult for the inventive genius of my friend Mr. Wilkins to depart from all quadrangular ideas, bow windows and other hackneyed forms, and adapt a building to this situation which fronts towards only the most favourable points, excluding all that is defective: and yet be a beautiful example of correct architecture'.[58] This was a tall order, quite beyond the inventive genius of Mr. Wilkins. There were two possible solutions; either the definition of 'correct' architecture had to change to admit irregularity, or an architectural style that made a boast of irregularity had to be adopted. Both solutions were adopted, although not by all architects.

There were other difficulties. The stress laid on the view — the prospect, to use the Regency term — was not a matter merely of constructing a window that faced the desired feature. To obtain a prospect, a direct view was not deemed sufficient; it had to have obliquities also, which could be obtained only by a bow or bay window (classical or Gothic). Fenestration should not restrict the view (Gandy tried horizontal windows); the desirability of an unobstructed view encouraged the use of plate glass, whether in new houses, as in Beckford's Lansdown Tower (Pl. XXX) or in old ones; the sensitive and aesthetically inclined sixth Duke of Devonshire, whose plans for Chatsworth were 'formed on the Principle of adhering to the Character of the present building . . .',[59] did not hesitate to replace the seventeenth-century windows with plate glass, which he had admired in Russia. The need for a clear view meant that Gothic windows were normally given stained glass only in their upper reaches, and, where the owner was rich enough, stained glass and tracery were combined with plate glass in a not unpleasing but manifestly unmediaeval way (Pl. LXXXIX).

It was sometimes difficult to decide which prospect was the most desirable; great ingenuity was exercised in devising plans that satisfied contradictory needs. These could prove irreconcilable, especially where prospect conflicted with aspect, the relationship of the house with the diurnal journey of the sun (the latter not being amenable to improvement). Repton felt strongly that aspect was more important than prospect, and of all aspects, south-eastern was the best. The south-west was bad; 'no window, nor hardly any brick walls, will keep out the wet, where a front is exposed to the south west'; he noted how at Brighton, houses facing south-west had had to be covered with bricks and pendant tiles, and double sashes used in the windows. He also observed that almost all the finest classical porticos in England faced north, where their intercolumniations lacked sun to throw them into effective relief.[60]

Such considerations caused arguments in the building of Coleorton, where Dance had not only an exacting and opinionated patron in Sir George Beaumont, but contending advisers such as Uvedale Price and Wordsworth (the latter designed the winter garden). In 1804 a hot discussion took place on whether the view should be sacrificed for the aspect; in the event the house had neither a bow window nor a conservatory, much to Price's disappointment.[61]

The attached or integrated conservatory was one of the principal manifestations of the way in which the garden not only affected the plan and form of the house, but actually entered it; the conservatory not infrequently became an essential part of an enfilade, in which old-fashioned formal grandeur was united with the spontaneities of nature (Figs 3, 4; see p.77).[62] A further intermediate stage between garden and house was provided by verandahs and colonnades, intertwined with climbing plants and laden with pots of flowers (Pl. LIII); these sometimes became extraordinarily extensive, the centuries-old English pre-disposition for long galleries taking a new form (see p.105). French windows gave unimpeded access to the covered walks, terraces and lawns that extended the house into the garden and, flung open, let the garden into the house, an impression that was strengthened by the frequent use of garden motifs and plants in decoration (especially inside the cottage orné) (see pp.348, 351 and Pl. I). The offices, far from being concealed, were now used as part of the Picturesque composition, connected to the main house by colonnades and loggias.

Thus, largely owing to ideas and theories concerning gardens and the landscape, the English house had opened itself to new possibilities; it lay (Figs 3, 4, 123, Pl. III) 'all Danae' to nature, or at least to the highly organised form of nature that became the Regency ideal for the garden. The park succumbed only partly to the undiluted Picturesque; the garden assumed a new and exquisite artificiality. The paramount taste that shaped both park and garden was that of Humphry Repton.

x *Landscape with Psyche outside the Palace of Cupid (The Enchanted Castle)*,
by Claude

xi *A Waterfall by a Cottage*, by Jacob van Ruysdael

*Overleaf* **xii** 'Contrasts; Sunshine after Rain', by Humphry Repton, 1816

Chapter three

# Eclecticism

'I do not think,' said Mr Forester, as they proceeded through part of the grounds, 'that the most determined zealot of the picturesque would quarrel with me here. I found the woods around the abbey matured by time and neglect into a fine estate of wilderness and intricacy, and I think I have left enough of them to gratify their most ardent admirer.'

'Quite enough, in all conscience,' said Sir Telegraph, who was in white jean trousers, with very thin silk stockings and pumps. 'I do not generally calculate on being . . .

> Forced to scramble,
> When I ramble,
> Through a copse of furze and bramble;

which would all be very pleasant perhaps, if the fine effect of picturesque roughness were not unfortunately, as Macbeth says of his dagger, 'sensible to feeling as to sight'.

*Thomas Love Peacock*

## The rejection of the extreme Picturesque

The person who, more than any other, provided an attractive alternative to 'picturesque roughness' was Humphry Repton. Repton's ideas were disseminated by his publications, in which his talents for water-colour and flattery were given full play, and by the architects with whom he came into professional contact; indeed, it has been said that his intercourse with architects rendered his the most important single contribution to Regency style.[2] This has some truth, especially if hints of his influence on Nash are justified (see pp.177–9, 213).

The changes wrought by time to Repton's gardens have left his publications and 'Red Books' the clearest surviving exposition of his work and views. In producing the Red Books, the 'before' and 'after' views of which enabled his clients to assess the effect of his proposals, Repton acted fully in correspondence with advanced Picturesque views on how to make a garden with the aid of a painter. An instruction manual of 1790, for instance, recommended the client to have walls and avenues (of trees) removed from the garden and 'these things, then, out of the way . . . [to] take the painter with you, (and let him be an ingenious one in the art of landscape painting)' and compose the new garden; 'the ground before you is like the canvas of a picture'.[3] The author recommended such aids as mock buildings and the use of white cloth to simulate water; the water-colour talents of Repton — which may have extended to oil (see p.213) — would have made these expedients unnecessary. He had the eye of an artist of sensitivity and discrimination; whilst rejecting the hirsute extremes of the painterly Picturesque, he himself looked at Nature as does a painter, albeit with the eyes of Hubert Robert or Fragonard rather than those of Ruysdael or Hobbema. It is odd that this escaped Price and Knight, but perhaps it escaped Repton himself.[4]

Repton claimed to be the first person to use the term 'Landscape Gardening',[5] but his writings betray that the meaning he attached to the term altered; one of his virtues is that his approach was latitudinarian; he was flexible and liberal in a situation where others tended to be doctrinaire. Early influences — in 1788 he wrote that 'Mason, Gilpin, Whateley and Gerardin have been of late my Breviary, and the works of Kent, Brown, and Richmond have been the places of my worship . . .'[6] — were tempered by intercourse with Price and Knight. One early, and perhaps decisive influence, was his childhood residence in Holland; he never forgot the Dutch gardens, where 'frequently, by arches and other contrivances, the eye was led across many compartments of an extensive garden . . . all was neatness . . .'.[7]

He had enjoyed a friendship with Uvedale Price and Payne Knight; in 1789 he had sketched Knight cutting their names on a tree in Epping Forest. His common sense — he, after all, had to make a living — and liberal attitudes led him to repudiate the undiluted central doctrine of the Picturesque; he acknowledged that he had fancied 'greater affinity between Painting and Gardening, than [he] found to exist after more mature consideration and more practical experience'.[8] The recantation provoked retort; he was buffeted by the fiercer apostles of the Picturesque, whose methods in controversy were not those of the more complaisant Repton; their language alienated impartial witnesses of the contest,[9] who were inclined to agree with Repton.

Appealing as Knight's depiction of the Elizabethan house in its Picturesque grounds had looked, the scene had been presented as a picture, a form in which people were accustomed to approving wild landscapes; the actuality struck them differently, as in John Britton's account of his visit to Downton in 1798. 'The lawn and grounds, immediately adjoining the mansion, when I saw them, presented more of the wildness and ruggedness of nature than the dress and decoration of

**5** View of a 'House calculated for being decorated with Ivy and Creeper', a design by J. C. Loudon, 1806

the landscape garden; for large heaps of stones, with briers, thorns, and even thistles, were to be seen in many places'.[10] Knight's thistles became notorious; it was unreasonable, as Repton saw, to expect the kind of people who wore white silk stockings in the country to be initiated into Picturesque principles in order to appreciate the charms of briers, thorns, and thistles. As he put it in 1794, in one of the documents born of the controversy; 'Mr Knight and you [Price] are in the habit of admiring fine pictures, and both live amidst bold and picturesque scenery; this may have rendered you insensible to the beauty of the milder scenes that have charms for common observers. I will not arraign your taste . . . but your palette certainly requires a degree of "irritation" rarely to be expected in garden scenery'.[11] 'Irritation' is well chosen. He quoted a letter which referred to Payne and Knight as 'these wild improvers', and asserted that 'gravel walks and neat mown lawns, and in some situations, straight alleys, fountains, terraces, and, for aught I know, parterres and cut hedges, are in perfect good taste . . . rather than docks and thistles that look better in a picture';[12] the true criteria should be use and enjoyment.

The docks and thistles were for a time a real threat. The Picturesque in its most extreme form was eagerly taken up by the youthful Loudon, who in 1803 would have placed Scone Palace in a forest and in 1806 would have smothered all the architectural features of a house in creepers (Fig. 5);[13] this was the opposite extreme from Brown's placing a house in a field. Repton saved the Regency garden

from this fate; he led away from the thistles, from the substitution of 'negligence for ease, and slovenly dogmatic weeds for native beauty'[14] towards a compromise that admitted the charms both of natural landscape and the formal garden. And it cannot be forgotten that the revival of the latter had been advocated by both Price and Knight. At the heart of their arguments lay something of a contradiction.

## The Reptonian synthesis

Repton was the most renowned gardener of his age. By 1794 he had 'improved' over fifty places, by 1803 nearly two hundred, and by 1816 more than four hundred. His sensibility alone would not have ensured success; the other two essential ingredients were a shrewd sense of what his clients wanted and, above all, practicality. His practicality is revealed in the list, given in his *Sketches and Hints on Landscape Gardening* of 1795, of the qualities that give pleasure in gardens; it is a peculiar assemblage, containing categories culled from various works of criticism but lacking the consistency of armchair theorising. It comprises Picturesque Effect, Intricacy, Simplicity, Variety, Novelty, Contrast, Association, Grandeur, Appropriation (the extent, or apparent extent, of property), Animation, and the Seasons.[15] His other dicta convey the same impression of empiricism; for example, 'All rational improvement of grounds is . . . founded on a due attention to the CHARACTER and SITUATION of the place to be improved . . .';[16] a strict symmetry in two sides of the landscape is not required, but 'a certain balance of composition' is needed to satisfy the eye.[17] And, most important, 'utility must often take the lead of beauty, and convenience be preferred to picturesque effect'.[18]

He listed four requisites: the gardener must display natural beauties and hide natural defects; he must disguise boundaries; he must disguise art; unornamental objects must be removed or concealed.[19] The second and third of these were in many later cases dropped, as Repton developed his penchant for the formal enclosed garden.

Repton's attitude to the old English formal garden was intimately linked with his sense of the immutability, or the desired immutability, of the English social order, founded as that order was on Locke's and Burke's ideas of property, not on commerce. His hierarchical ideas were parodied by Peacock in the person of Mr. Milestone;[20] Repton had proposed that a 'mere stone' — not a milestone — should be marked with the arms of the local family, because 'the proportion of interest belonging to [it] should impress the mind with a sense of its influence'.[21] Knight made savage fun of this, in a way that was slightly unfair but that recognised the importance to Repton of romantic snobbery. Repton wrote in his autobiography: 'I remember the time when state and dignity were more externally mark'd. When every man who had a right to wear a Star, was sure to wear it and when if the head

6 A Roman garden, from a Pompeian wall-painting, published in 1760

had little in it, there was always something on it to distinguish the importance of the wearer'.[22] A similar sentiment informed his attitude to formal gardening; he desired to retain the Terraces at Burley because 'there is a certain dignity of style in BURLEY, which, like the cumbrous robes of our nobility, neither can nor ought to be sacrificed to the innovation of fashion or the affectation of ease and simplicity'.[23]

His advocacy of formal gardening developed quickly. At first, under the influence of the Picturesque, he rejected all symmetrical gardens, but as early as 1790 he recommended that the terrace at The Hassells, a 'remnant of the geometric gardening of the last century', should not be disturbed. His reason — that the terrace in summer may sometimes answer the purpose of an additional room or gallery[24] — became a Regency commonplace. By 1794, he was prepared to state in print that, following the precepts of Montesquieu, he had frequently advised 'the most perfect symmetry' in the flower-gardens, which he often placed adjacent to an orangery; in such small enclosures, 'irregularity would appear like affectation'. Symmetry was also necessary next to the façade of a symmetrical building, or 'the house itself will appear twisted and awry'.[25] He thought that there was in the human mind an inborn love of order and symmetry.[26]

Fashion changed quickly; referring in 1803 to the retention of the terrace at The Hassells, Repton confessed that twelve years before he had been cautious in advancing such opinions, but that now 'the good sense of the country admits their propriety'. He felt free to state his considered position, his frank advocacy of a synthesis that excluded the wilder excesses of the Picturesque; he wished to follow neither Le Nôtre nor Brown, but to select beauties from each, to adopt as much of the grandeur of Le Nôtre as may accord with a palace, and as much of the grace of Brown as 'may call forth the charms of natural landscape. Each has its proper situation; and good taste will make fashion subservient to good sense'.[27] That last observation could never have been made by a fully-fledged Romantic; Repton's feet, like those of Jane Austen, were firmly in the eighteenth century.

The revolution, or rather the counter-revolution, which Repton forwarded is illustrated by the scheme for Valleyfield, Fife, designed just at the turn of the century (Pl. IV); it is a domesticated Versailles, with an emphasis on the flowers that Le Nôtre had admitted only for the nursery maids. Repton wrote: 'I should condemn a long straight line of water in an open park, where everything else is natural; I should equally object to a meandering canal or walk, by the side of a long straight wall, where everything else is artificial . . . the banks of this canal, or fish pond, may be enriched with borders of curious flowers . . .'.[28] At the far end is a covered seat, between two aviaries. Aviaries were soon to become extremely popular; Rousseau's rejection of all aviaries save those provided by trees had been forgotten.

The design of Valleyfield is dominated by trellis. Of all the Reptonian contrivances, treillage is the most immediately conspicuous. Repton especially depended upon it in devising the compartmentalism that provided the 'intricacy' he thought crucial as a means of retaining interest; his references to 'intricacy' are innumerable, and he considered it essential in interiors (see p.281). In this he followed Burke.

Treillage was identified with France and antiquity (see pp.19, 20); it shared unimpeachable classical origins with compartmentalism and fountains (Fig. 6), as was recognised during the Regency period. Baskets of flowers, uncannily Reptonian, appear in many classical sources.[29] There is, incidentally, a curious resemblance between the lozenges and circles of trellis decoration and some of the border motifs of the 'Etruscan' style (in fashion during the 'Regency' period; see pp.236, 239); a fact that would become more explicable were certain of the non-architectural motifs on Greek vases to prove to have

**7** 'Fence near the House', by Humphry Repton, 1816

antecedents in wicker or basket work. The use in gardens of such motifs as treillage and baskets (Pl. XII) is significantly of a piece with the general interest in 'archaeological' authenticity so noticeable in buildings, interiors, furniture, and objets d'art. It was during the 1790s that, as Alison records, the passion for antiquity reached its height, a period when Repton was girding himself openly to advocate the revival of formal gardening. And those seeking the ancient world in Rome would have seen treillage and other devices in Italian gardens around which the scents of antiquity so heavily hung; the villa of Cardinal Albani, for example, with its famous collections of art and antiquities, had elaborate and lofty constructions of trellis.[30]

Price had explicitly commended the use of trellis: 'Trellises, with the different plants twining around them, and even the small basket-work or parterres have a mixture of natural and of artificial . . . of firmness and playfulness . . . I therefore regret that fashion has so much banished them from gardens . . .'.[31] Repton, who claimed to have been the agent of their reintroduction,[32] insisted that trellis should be used only where climbing plants were to be fastened to it; when added to 'architectural houses, and made the supporters of a heavy roof, or even a canvas awning, it looks as if the taste of the country were verging to its decline'.[33] Loudon obtusely distorted this statement to 'trelliswork in gardens is to be considered more with reference to floriculture and horticulture than to landscape Gardening or Architecture'.[34] So much for Versailles and the Italian villa garden!

Repton's trellises were usually in wood, although he also used the cast iron that was about to invade the garden in large quantities; its

nature stamps it with an unmistakable nineteenth-century character. The revival of the popularity of trellis work in interior decoration (see p.258) emphasised the connection between the garden and the interior; it has, perhaps unfairly, affected perceptions of Repton — 'when painting at last takes nature close to her heart Repton converts gardening into a department of furnishing'.[35]

The 'Ground Plan explained to a lady' (Fig. 3) gives the full range of Reptonian devices for enlivening the garden near the house, including an aviary, conservatory, 'flower passage', green-house, and constructions in trelliswork; there is a formal fountain and at least one statue. One essential feature is the terrace. Elsewhere, Repton remarks that he has often had to remove an entrance hall from the centre of a façade that enjoys a south-western aspect, in order to provide a sequence of rooms; he has then made 'a broad terrace dressed with flowers . . . if the house be Grecian, there is no fence so beautiful and proper as an open balustrade . . .' (Fig. 7).[36] Such terraces were to become ubiquitous, their balustrades constructed in every style (Figs 65, 125, Pls. VI, VII, XV).

The variety of decorative expedients used by Repton in the small enclosures in which he came to delight is seen in the 'gaudy sketch' called 'Contrasts; Sunshine after Rain' (Pl. XII); in this charmed enclosure the enchanted gardens of Pompeii and Herculaneum (Fig. 6) appear to be resurrected. The picture illustrates the delights of contrast, between colour, texture, and size of plants, between those that aspire and those that droop, between light and shade. Full as is the scene of Reptonian artifice, he quotes Rousseau on the significance of the small: 'Si la Nature est grande dans les grandes choses, Elle est très grandes dans les petites'.[37] Here we see trellis, pergolas, baskets, formal beds edged with wire, goldfish bowls, vases, and a fountain, approached by a straight path. One Reptonian conceit missing is that of the bed of flowers enclosed by a wire basket, as used in the designs for the Pavilion at Brighton and elsewhere. The self-conscious prettiness of the scene is redolent of the age; it is curious how the same ingredients, used in the seventeenth century, had produced such a different effect.

The proposals put forward in 1814 for the sixth Duke of Bedford's cottage orné at Endsleigh (see p.217) are quintessential Repton; all appear to have been executed; they included a Pheasantry and a Children's Cottage and Garden, which had formal beds radiating from a fountain. The Terrace Walk (Pl. XV) had a conservatory, rock plants and fruit walls; the 'long sketch is supposed to be taken from the window of the Dining-room; the terraces, grass, and gravel, seem to justify the boldest interference of Art in the accompaniments of the Garden Scene. The style of Conservatory, the Alcove in the Children's Garden, and the fountain and artificial Trimness of the Parterre, must all be considered with reference to the Noble Occupier rather than to the humble character of a Cottage'.[38] Repton's painting perfectly illustrates his ideal; the Terrace and its appurtenances are the pink of artificial neatness and order; beyond is the countryside, picturesque but not unrestrainedly so; the inhabitants of this Arcadia never lacked their bibs and tuckers, and there was never a skull in sight.

Repton's effect on the park was less radical than on the garden; his definition of it was a practical one: 'I always distinguish by the name of Park that portion of wood and lawn which is seen from the windows of a mansion . . . it must appear to have no boundary';[39] to Repton, Knight confounded the two separate ideas of park and forest.[40] Repton never entirely repudiated the heritage of Capability Brown; curiously enough, he brought formality back into the garden but relaxed the smooth formalities of the Brownian park.

He compromised on the avenue, the clump, and the belt, the three most vilified aspects of Brown. The first was to be neither entirely removed nor retained, but certain trees were to be removed to allow interesting views through the 'curtain' of the avenue; 'its venerable appearance from the windows of the saloon will not be injured, because the trees removed from the rows will hardly be missed in the general perspective from the house'.[41] He defended the hated clump as an intermediate expedient; he defended the belt (a device that he said he himself had never used) when not over long and narrow; Brown had 'had equal difficulties to surmount from the profusion and the parsimony of his employers, or he would never have consented to those meagre girdles of plantation'.[42]

A late (1813–14) and unexecuted design, for Beaudesert in Staffordshire, shows Repton attempting a grand manner unusual in his work (Fig. 8). His scheme was prompted by the 'character' of the site; 'the venerable dignity of this place is not to be measured by the scale of

**8** 'View to the South after Improvement', Beaudesert, Staffs., a design by Humphry Repton, 1814

a villa, or the spruce modern seat of sudden affluence . . . No — rather let us go back to former times . . .', although 'to this may be added, the modern luxury of hot-houses and conservatories, with all the agremens'.[43] The plan involved removing tall trees to reveal two streams, and the conversion of a meadow into a lake. Beaudesert's synthesis of disciplined formality (the house, the terraces) and the Picturesque (the trees, the cascade, more in Payne Knight's idiom than was the Endsleigh landscape), is complete. Repton congratulated himself on his discovery 'from old labourers on the premises, that in the line of the terrace, and other parts of this artificial and architectural Garden, we are restoring the place to what they remember it in the beginning of the last century.'[44] They must have been very old labourers.

The architectural manner of the terraces and 'bridge' in this design is uncompromising; even the line of the wall that slopes down beside the terraces is straight, and not stepped, as one might have expected. Is it possible that this rigidity results from a Reptonian essay in the sublime? Repton recorded that many years before he had been present 'when Mrs. Siddons objected to the straight braids represented in the celebrated picture in the character of the Tragic Muse, and requested Sir Joshua Reynolds to let the hair flow in more graceful ringlets; but that great master observed, that without straight lines there might be grace or beauty, but there could be no greatness or sublimity; and this same rule applies to gardening . . .'.[45]

Throughout his career Repton had been aware that it was necessary for the landscape gardener to have a competent knowledge of architecture, since 'art declares herself openly' with buildings.[46] For several years he worked with William Wilkins the elder; he was then introduced to John Nash by a mutual friend with the words, 'If you two, whom I consider the cleverest men in England, could agree to *act together*, you "might carry the whole world before you"'. As a result, 'We jointly design'd and built houses at places where I or he had previously been concerned . . .'.[47] The introduction brought together two talents of a high order that, impressive apart, in concert were incomparably more significant, both for their contemporaries and for the future; they popularised the irregular house, and it is hardly too much to say that they invented the idea of the garden city.

## Early nineteenth-century eclecticism

It is ironic, given Repton's aristocratic prejudices, that the victory of his garden style was assisted by those social changes the effects of which he deplored; in taking his style to its heart the public corrupted it. It has to be admitted that it carried the seeds of that corruption. His skilful and tasteful synthesis was succeeded by a babel of styles, sometimes an eclectic hugger-mugger and sometimes an attempt at a correct historical revival.

The propagandist of these developments, in what seems to be an inexhaustible flood of prose, was J. C. Loudon. In many ways he was paradigmatical of the new clientele that he served, except that he must have been nicer than most of them. Virtuous, industrious, brave, benevolent in intention, speculative, broad-minded, intelligent and socially responsible — a thoroughly likeable man — he had a flaw that tainted most of what he did; his taste was naturally and enthusiastically bad. The tendencies of the times fostered vulgarisation; he prosecuted it with vigour and success. And with Price's opinions on the unity of taste in mind, one notes that he did so in a language that is callow, cliché-ridden, and full of jargon.

## New plants

One of the most striking features of the Regency garden and park was the vast increase in the variety of plants they contained. New importations of exotic species had begun to grow during the 1770s; by 1789 there were 5,500 species at Kew; by 1813 there were over 11,000. The foundation in 1804 of the Royal Horticultural Society was a response to this development; in that same year the naval excursions that accompanied the resumption of the Napoleonic Wars brought plants into Europe from every corner of the earth. The new varieties included wistaria, paeonies, roses and chrysanthemums from China; dahlias from Mexico; fuschia from Central America; clarkias, galliardas, lupins, penstemons and many others. New trees, especially conifers, came from North America.[48]

One result was that the pleasure garden moved closer towards the botanical garden; another was that the quantity of new plants provided a bane rather than a blessing (see p.57). Loudon 'put his finger on the essential change of outlook between the eighteenth and the nineteenth centuries. He pointed out that the stream of books on the aesthetics of gardens had narrowed to a trickle, dried up, and been replaced by a flood of gardening literature almost solely concerned to introduce new varieties of plants to its readers and to instruct them how they should be grown'.[49] The new method of 'bedding out', first suggested by Chambers to allow the use of exotic plants that would not survive the English winter, was widely adopted.

In 1840 Loudon listed five styles of gardening in his introduction to the collected and republished works of Repton; he declared his intention of devoting an individual volume to each before producing one volume to include all. The total acceptability of all styles by that date is clear; the last volume's intent was that 'the idea that any one of them is better than another will be neutralised, and the true art of laying out grounds shown to consist in the choice and application of a school, or of parts of different schools, adapted to the particular case under consideration'.[50] The five styles were: French and Italian gardens, or the 'Geometric' school; the Modern or Landscape, or Kent's School; the Picturesque School; Repton's School (which had succeeded Kent's School); and the Gardenesque, a term used first by Loudon in 1832.[51] Although Loudon did not say so, the Gardenesque had succeeded Repton's School as Repton's had succeeded Kent's, and one of its characteristics was a coarsened use of Reptonian mannerisms; it survives today in its ideal form in unnumerable depictions on early nineteenth-century blue and white Staffordshire ware.

## The 'Geometric' school

French and Italian 'geometric' gardens were regarded as different in their kind. The French had an absolutist taint from which the Italian was free. Mention has already been made of Price's nostalgic recollections of Italian gardens; those in Genoa and Rome glowed in the memory of Hope. In 1808 Hope wrote in an influential essay of 'the suspended gardens within Genoa, and of the splendid villas about Rome . . . those mixtures of statues, and vases, and balustrades, with cypresses, and pilasters, and bays . . . those ranges of aloes and of cactuses growing out of vases of granite and of porphyry scarce more symmetric by art than these plants are by nature' (that is, nature also could deal in symmetry). In this ideal world of order and beauty the gardens were unified with their villas in a Picturesque manner; the 'cluster of highly adorned and sheltered apartments that form the mansion in the first instance shoot out, as it were, into certain more or less extended ramifications of arcades, porticoes, terraces, parterres, treillages, avenues . . . calculated by their architectural and measured forms, at once to afford a striking contrast with, and a dignified and comfortable transition to . . . more undulating and rural features'.[52] In 1809 Percier and Fontaine, whose early years in Italy were also never forgotten, published their *Maisons de Plaisance de Rome et ses environs*, picturing some of the most wonderful of the Italian formal gardens (Fig. 2).[53]

At the Deepdene, Hope created a garden that, of all Regency gardens, best illustrated Regency innovations and idiosyncrasies, and presented them in their most alluring forms. Loudon, with unusual perception, called it 'the finest example in England of an Italian Villa, united with the grounds by architectural appendages . . . one of the most extraordinary combinations of garden building with garden scenery, any where existing in Europe'.[54] Hope had absorbed the rich atmosphere of the palace gardens of Genoa and Rome, and had set his own sanctuary in the valley of Dorking, 'so beautiful that even Rasselas would not have desired to escape from that happy valley'.[55] The formal and semi-formal gardens, attached to a house that was as fully integrated with them as the English climate allows, were furnished with

terraces, vases, formally shaped beds, with triangular railings echoing the triangular windows of the façade of the 'Ampitheatre' (Pl. VI), Chinese seats, sculpture, peacocks, aloes — all the accoutrements of a Regency Elysium. The whole arose from a wonderfully Picturesque landscape, where, 'Forest on forest hung about [one's] head, Like cloud on cloud'.[56] One of the delightful paintings made for a book on the house by John Britton that, sadly, never attained publication, shows a Boucheresque scene from the Drying Grounds (Pl. V) with the house rising beyond the trees like a vision, touched with memories of the antique and of Italy but completely of its own period. In the Deepdene, the Regency concept of united garden and house attained its apotheosis.

Italy supplied patterns for the garden decorations that returned to fashion in the first years of the nineteenth century. Many were made by the modellers at the Coade stone manufactory, who at the beginning of the nineteenth century were two Italians, Rossi and Panzetta. Famous antiques that were imitated included the Borghese and Medici Vases, the Egyptian Lion from the Campidoglio (Hope owned a copy of one of these), Romano-Egyptian figures after the Hadrianic Antinous, and a sundial adapted from the stool with three monopodia from the House of the Cervi at Herculaneum.[57] A later advocate of the Italian garden, Gilbert Laing Meason, stressed a fact of which Price, Hope, and Percier and Fontaine would have been aware, that 'the architecture, sculpture and gardens of these villas were often designed by the same hand . . .';[58] they would have known also that the earliest post-antique villa in which garden and house interpenetrated, the Villa Madama, had been designed by that prince of universal geniuses, Raphael.[59] In the early 1830s a house of almost symbolic significance, Wilton, had its vanished early seventeenth-century formal gardens (designed by de Caux) 'restored' in the Italian manner by Richard Westmacott, using the remnants of the old ornaments. The fact that one who was primarily a sculptor was brought in to restore a garden makes clear the nature of the counter-revolution.

Hope's comments on Italian gardens were attended to by, amongst others, Loudon. The latter follows a quotation from Hope with a statement by 'an eloquent writer' that clearly displays the synthesising tendencies of the period. The subject is the incongruities that often existed between villa and garden; the writer reviews the various styles in country houses, from the 'baronial' or 'monastic' to the Elizabethan and Palladian, concluding that every 'style of building would give us permission, as it were, to ornament, to furnish highly our gardens, to decorate them with masonry; to place statues, and vases, and balustrades, and steps about them; and to enrich them with that most charming of all garden ornaments, the terrace; all of which rich accompaniments, by carrying the eye from the interior ornaments of the chambers to the garden, would . . . connect our gardens with our

**9** Drumlanrig Castle, Dumfries, a design for the garden, 1840, by Sir Charles Barry

houses . . . '.[60] This assimilated the geometric garden with not only Palladianism, but with the different varieties of historicism and romantic antiquarianism; such houses as Salvin's Mamhead (Pl. VII), Shaw's restoration of Newstead Abbey (Fig. 126), and Shaw's Ilam (Fig. 125), were thought 'correct' in being equipped with terraces, garden ornaments, and balustrades; a concession to historicism was frequently made in that the balustrades for such houses were decorated with strapwork in place of the classical baluster.

In 1828 Sir Walter Scott supported Loudon's 'eloquent writer' with his own eloquence; he made the point that the old formal garden was 'indeed, in the highest degree artificial, but it was a sight beautiful in itself — a triumph of human art over the elements, and, connected as these ornamental gardens were with splendid mansions, in the same character, there was a symmetry and harmony betwixt the baronial palace itself, and these its natural appendages, which recommended them to the judgment as well as to the eye.'[61] The essay hints at an interest in topiary, out of favour since the days of Pope's ridicule but for some time showing signs of revival; the reason given was antiquarian rather than aesthetic: 'these ridiculous anomalies have fallen into disuse. . . . Their rarity now entitles them to some care as a species of antiques . . .'.[62] The long animus against topiary is an

indication of how deep-seated the reaction against formality had been.

It is probable that the courtier in Sir Walter was aware that coincident with his essay King George IV was constructing a 'geometric' garden at Windsor Castle. George IV's gardens were as diverse as his buildings. At Brighton he had rejected the intensely wrought designs suggested by Repton (despite his commendation of the fact that Repton had 'dared to make a perfectly straight gravel walk')[63] in favour of a restrained Picturesque (almost 'Gardenesque') plan by Nash, with not a single straight path in the grounds (Pls VIII, XLIX); at Windsor the Cottage had not lacked formal elements in the garden, including Coade versions of the Borghese and Medici Vases, ordered by Nash in 1825.[64]

It was doubtless the King's francophile tendencies and self-identification with Louis XIV that led him to conceive the East Terrace garden at Windsor as French, a less common choice, rather than Italian; it made a consistent whole with the rococo and 'Louis Quatorze' interiors of the Castle that overlooked it (see p.307). Windsor Castle's French garden was installed by Wyatville at the time that he was assembling the ruins at nearby Virginia Water (Fig. 12); the King had a hand in both designs. The East Terrace garden evoked varying responses. In August 1830 the *Windsor and Eton Express*

XIII The Dairy, Hamels, Herts., designed by Sir John Soane, 1783

XIV The Gardens at Battlesden House, Beds., designed by Humphry Repton, 1808

**XV** 'View from the South and East Fronts of the Cottage at Endsleigh, Devonshire', designed by Humphry Repton, 1814

XVI 'South Front of Mansion House & Conservatory', Sezincote House, Gloucs., c.1805, designed by S. P. Cockerell

XVII 'The Fountain surrounding a marble statue at the Colosseum, Regent's Park', designed 1823 by Decimus Burton

reported that 'the coup d'oeil was truly magical. A considerable space of ground from the park has been taken in and laid out in flower beds interspersed with vases and statues after the manner of The Tuileries gardens at Paris'.[65] Earlier, Princess Augusta had reported; 'All the Castle is Magnificent, but the new Garden and Bastion near to the East Front is frightfull to the greatest degree. Wyattville says it's Classical'.[66] Included amongst the ornaments to the garden were '34 fine orange-trees', presented by the King of France.'[67] The King of England rifled the buildings and garden of his predecessors at Hampton Court; in September·1829 '4 Marble Vases 4 Bronze Statues 5 Marble Statues. 2 Colossal Lead Ditto. 14 Leaden Vases' were transported to Windsor,[68] and in the same month 'His Majesty inspected a collection of bronze figures and vases . . . and gave directions for their erection . . .'. By October 13th they were in position.[69]

Another 'baronial palace', that of Drumlanrig in Scotland, may also have been in Scott's mind, as the seat of a family that, although not royal, was in Scotland the next best thing. The Buccleuchs had had its terraces and flower gardens restored 'with the happiest effect', in the opinion of Gilbert Laing Meason;[70] it did not content them, since in 1840 they commissioned Barry to redesign the gardens. His stately project shows the formal garden completely re-established (Fig. 9). Barry would have probably taken the lead in designing the architectural parts of the garden; his colleague, Nesfield, would have concentrated on the Picturesque elements, and one notices that the design establishes the Picturesque on the confines of the geometric areas.

## The Picturesque school

It has been mentioned above that Loudon was one of the few who took his third category of garden styles, the Picturesque, to the wild extreme as defined by Price and Knight, and that his designs of 1803 for Scone Palace show him clasping it thistles and all to his bosom. His description of the Scone scheme uses jargon with discordant relish; all was to be disposed according to the dictates of Nature, Taste, and Utility; in the scheme, the Romantic would prevail, but the Picturesque, the Beautiful, the Pastoral and the Sublime would co-exist within the romantic.[71] The verbiage does not conceal the wild Picturesqueness of the Scone proposals, nor that Loudon had imbibed the message that 'roughness, . . . sudden variation, joined to ir-regularity, are the most efficient causes of the Picturesque' and that picturesque quality is always reduced by 'high polish and refinement . . . the same analogy prevails in language, in manners'.[72]

Unfortunately for Loudon, taste seems to have been travelling in the opposite direction; a vignette from Jane Austen gives the picture — a seaside village that 'contained little more than cottages, but the *spirit of the day* [author's italics] had been caught . . . and . . . in the little

green court of an old farm house, two females in elegant white were actually to be seen with their books and camp stools; and in turning the corner of the baker's shop, the sound of a harp might be heard through the upper casement'.[73] One has only to imagine the sound of a harp coming through the shaggy windows of Loudon's unbridled 'picturesque or perhaps romantic' house of 1806 (Fig. 5) (supposed to 'combine Architectural Fitness with Picturesque Effect'), to realise how very singular the combination would have been. This last proposal well illustrates the caveman element in Loudon; 'Where Loudon was a troglodyte, Repton was a camper. One's house tended to be a glorified version of a cave, the other's an elaboration of the tent'.[74] Loudon's conversion from the extreme Picturesque to the 'Gardenesque' took him from one extreme of anarchic naturalism to the other of tightly ordered artificiality.

Undiluted, the Picturesque was impossible; diluted, it became an inseparable part of the way in which nature, cultivated or uncultivated, was regarded. Handled with taste and restraint, it was capable of great achievements. Its presence, however disciplined by Italianate formality, was inescapable at Hope's Deepdene; it produced scenes of great beauty at Beckford's houses of Fonthill and Lansdown Crescent. The former employed a great avenue in eighteenth-century style together with richly Picturesque plantings; there was 'much diversified, picturesque, beautiful, and romantic scenery — an alternation of hill and dale, of terrace and valley, of wood and lawn, or rugged wildness and dressed parterres, with a sort of mountain lake . . .'.[75] At Lansdown Crescent, Beckford took full advantage of the hilly site to create a wonderfully intricate scene that had as its *coup d'oeil* the symmetrical terraces and crescents of the town of Bath, then at the height of its splendour.

## The Gardenesque

The characteristic feature of the Gardenesque, Loudon's fifth category, was defined by him as 'the display of the beauty of trees, and other plants, individually . . . all the trees and shrubs planted are arranged in regard to their kinds and dimensions . . . the aim of the Gardenesque is to add, to the acknowledged charms of the Repton School, all those which the sciences of gardening and botany, in their present advanced state, are capable of producing.' He added that the Gardenesque may be seen in its 'most decided' form in arboretums, or in flower beds without trees or shrubs; with a fine social impartiality, he declared that it was first applied in a country house by the Marquess of Blandford at White-Knights, and was 'nowhere better exemplified than in the villa of W. Harrison Esq. at Cheshunt'.[76] The former was sufficiently proud of his creation to commission, as Duke of Marlborough, an account of the mansion and gardens from Mrs. Hofland, printed in 1816; the circumstantial description pictures a garden that is an extreme example of a typical Regency synthesis. It seems likely that J. B. Papworth had a hand in it, although the Marquess was given the credit.[77]

White-Knights was not short of incident. It possessed a Botanic Garden, with a lawn of Reptonian baskets containing begonia and scarlet sage grown separately — already the palette becomes apparent; a Hexagon Seat, a Rustic Bower, a Gothic Bower, an Orange Grove with trees in tubs (obviously brought out in spring in seventeenth and eighteenth-century manner), a Temple of Pomona (a greenhouse), a Terrace Garden, a Greenhouse Aquarium, a Hothouse Aquarium, an Orangery; a Magnolia Walk 20 feet high by 140 feet long (no doubt classed by Chambers as a 'few American weeds') in which the plants were attached to a wall and trellis; a Japan Garden, with Japanese and American plants, from which an avenue lined with trellis, 198 feet long, led to a conservatory. A Dolphin Fountain, designed by Lady Diana Beauclerk, displayed dolphins supported by six rock columns with specimens of sea weed, petrified fungi, brainstone, white and purple fluorspar, Blue John, and various shells; it was surrounded by Repton's 'rouged beauties', China Roses. This kind of baroque marine symbolism had been long available;[78] later Regency taste is present fully fledged in the 'Romantic Arches, with Cascades', published by William Wrighte in 1767 and last reissued in 1815 (Fig. 10).

Lady Diana's fountain was supplied with a British Aquarium, containing two bronze vases from Malmaison; after this came The Woods, containing a Catalpa Walk, an Antique Vase, Acacia and Laburnum Bowers, a Rustic Orchestra, and a Seat (Fig. 16), the supporting pillars of which were of hazel, braced together 'in the manner of the ornamental Gothic pillars'. The 'Seat' was of natural brick and hazel in panels, the centre panel made of yew; 'the pediment is also ornamented in the same way'. (Papworth gives a very similar design, which he says is to be constructed chiefly of unbarked wood.)[79]

10 'Romantic Arches, with Cascades', a design by William Wrighte, 1767, reissued in 1815

Also to be found were the Chantilly Gardens in the French manner, a Vineyard, a Swiss Cottage, a Rustic Bridge, a Grotto, a Sheep Walk, and a 'Pavilion'.[80]

White-Knights may have appeared 'Gardenesque' to Loudon, but its fanciful and light-hearted agglomerations remind one that these were the years in which the rococo was returning to favour. The garden's more nineteenth-century aspect appears in its Linnaean garden, called a 'scientific museum' (which contained a hexagon Chinese Temple adorned with clematis).

Loudon's ideal of the Gardenesque, Mr. Harrison's villa at Cheshunt — 'a cottage or rather a villa assuming a cottage character'[81] — sounds much like a down-market version of White-Knights, lacking the taste that Papworth brought to all he did. Mr. Harrison began, in about 1809, by purchasing at a sale dauntingly large lots of evergreens; the gloom of the Victorian shrubbery needed only time to develop. Botanical apartheid appears to have been carried further than at White-Knights, including a garden of 'florists' flowers', and 'two semicircles for dahlias'. The trees and shrubs on the lawn were 'disposed in the gardenesque manner: that is, so that each individual plant may assume its natural shape and habit of growth . . . at the same time, in order to produce as much variety as possible, the picturesque style of planting, in which trees and shrubs are so closely grouped together as partially to injure each other's growth, occasionally occurs, for the sake of producing variety' (the slipshod repetition is typical of Loudon's publications). A particular feature was the use of slate: 'In no garden structures have we seen a more judicious use of the Penryhn slate: paths, edgings, shelves, cisterns, boxes for plants, copings, kerbs, partitions, and substitutes for dwarf walls, being all made of it'. It sounds as if Mr. Harrison bought his slate as he bought his evergreens, by lot.

The garden contained the usual agglomeration of architectural incident, including a Chinese temple; a thatched rustic alcove, containing a white marble statue of the Indian god 'Guadama' and 'three Elizabethan benches'; a grotto — 'formerly an ice-house, but it failed as such'; and a 'hermit's seat'. One uncommon feature was the 'Ship-Room'; it contained models of ships of various sorts, which in summer 'continue[d] constantly traversing the pond when there is any wind'. Perhaps Mr. Harrison had read Repton: 'a large lake, without boats, is a dreary waste of water',[82] and conjectured that a Lilliputian pond needed Lilliputian boats; before assuming a natural affiliation between suburban villas and model boats, one should recollect that Lord Shrewsbury used stucco sheep at Alton Towers.[83]

## Vulgarity and philistinism

The rapid increase in availability of novel and exotic plants aggravated existing tendencies towards flamboyance and allowed the gaudy colour that had become fashionable within to be expressed out of doors; the liking for the garish and meretricious, singled out by the cognoscenti as typical of the taste of the new commercial classes, was as fully expressed in gardening as in interior decoration. Gardeners in the late eighteenth and early nineteenth centuries were, like painters presented with an extended palette of brilliant colours.

The temptation to use the new plants was irresistible, even for Repton, whose sensitive eye discerned their shortcomings: 'I must confess I have of late viewed with a jealous eye the irruption recently made by the new China Rose, which however valuable in winter from its dark glossy foliage and hardy flower is but like a rouged beauty — and must not attempt to vie with the genuine English scented rose'.[84] Loudon was untroubled by such hesitancies; 'he had observed that flower-gardens looked best when the flowers were so arranged as to have a compound colour next the simple one . . . he advises that purple flowers should have yellow next them: that orange flowers . . . should be contrasted with blue: and that green flowers . . . should be relieved by red'.[85] A Bavarian horticulturalist observed: 'Considered with respect to real landscape beauties . . . the English garden style is . . . markedly retrograde. When I was in England, in 1817, I found the gardens in the new English style . . . oppressed with the burthen of their own ornaments. . . . The immense multitude of landscape-gardener with an inexhaustible grounds. . . . Thus I found the English unconnected beauties.'[86] The interest in the flowers affected interior decoration, in which they became ever more over-blown (Pl. LXI); they found their way, in highly realistic depictions, on to china, wallpaper, and textiles; Mrs. Hofland recounts how each chair seat at White-Knights was 'enwreathed with flowers'.[87]

The variety of available garden plants was matched by that of garden styles; the speed with which the new freedom degenerated into vulgarity is seen in a publication of 1812, *Hints on the Formation of Gardens and Pleasure Grounds*, by John Harding. It was directed towards people of middling income; the plans include some suitable for 'small plots of ground, from a perch to an acre'. Everything seems acceptable. The 'ancient geometrical style' is revived; the treatise comments that the old books by Switzer and Le Blond (on parterres and kitchen gardens), and by Batty Langley and Le Meagre (on town gardens) have never been superseded. The book is sufficiently broadminded to include a scheme in the manner of Brown. Also present are gardens in the 'old French style'[88] and 'a design in the French style, intermingled with what may be called the picturesque manner'; this shows a lawn

11 'Modern English Parterre' (lower right),
a design by John Harding, 1812

covered with picturesque patches of strawberries, camomile, creeping thyme, and daisy, with shell work and borders of 'dug work' on the turf; the borders are intended to prevent spectators from stepping on to the lawn and realising how small the 'lake' is.

Other motifs include a 'curiously clipt holly hedge', an 'old English parterre' in the 'German and Scotch style', and wicker or lattice baskets in cast iron or wood — the Reptonian influence. One design, in 'the flowery style of the French', includes a 'hedge of yew tree, cut into niches or colonnades, and surmounted with equestrian statues of yew', a clear reference to a revival of topiary. Yet another (Fig. 11) shows a 'Modern English Parterre'; this squirmy confection, which looks as if it might be an attempt to translate Decorated Gothic tracery into a garden idiom, is described as 'in the modern English style, with additions in the French manner; it includes a covered trellis walk, compartments of basket work, cones, columns, wire statues to take creepers, trellises for roses, a conservatory and aviary'. This distressing book is dignified with long quotations from Chambers and Price. By comparison, Loudon seems refined.

Repton would have been quite clear where to lay the blame for all this. Wealth was no substitute for aristocracy; 'Good taste can only be acquired by leisure and observation; it is not, therefore, to be expected in men, whose taste is fully employed in the more important acquirement of wealth or fame. . . .'[89] This opinion was not Repton's alone; there was a remarkable unanimity concerning the causes of the decline in taste apparent in so many activities; connoisseurs in general considered that commerce had corrupted taste. The decline in taste had begun to affect the English artefact that had most attracted the eulogies of foreigners, and that had called forth one of the few passages in which Horace Walpole disclosed heartfelt emotion — the English countryside. Towards the end of his life, Repton revealed his hitherto concealed opinion that the increased wealth of the country had impaired its beauty; 'I may now speak the truth, without fear of offending, since time has brought about those changes which I long ago expected. . . . Too few now think of the beauty of scenery — What will it cost? or what will it yield? not, how will it look? seems the general object of inquiry in all improvements . . . the riches of individuals have changed the face of the country.' The eager pursuit of profit had extended from the new proprietor to the ancient hereditary gentleman, who 'gives up beauty for gain'.[90] Repton was a prophet who did not stop at concern for destroyed beauty; 'the monopolist only can contemplate with delight his hundred acres of wheat in a single enclosure; such expanded avarice may enrich the man, but will impoverish and distress, and (I had almost added) will ultimately starve mankind'.[91] One dare not think what Repton would have thought of the present state of the English landscape. Of the two 'before' and 'after' illustrations that he supplies, the latter has a familiar arid and blighted look.

## Chapter four

# Garden Buildings and Furnishings

The desire to ornament garden and park has its roots deep in antiquity; one's temple embellished the prospect, as the Temple of Vesta embellished that of Hadrian's Villa at Tivoli. In 1681 Charles Cotton made his list: 'Let every site have its proper parerga, adjuncts or additional graces, as the Farm-house, Wind-mill, Water-mill, Woods, Flocks of Sheep, Herds of cattle, Pilgrims, Ruines of temples, Castles, and Monuments'.[1]

The eighteenth century showed itself generous in bestowing 'additional graces' upon the landscape, often planting them in secluded and inaccessible spots. It was adventurous in the form that it gave garden buildings, not minding if a cheap and perhaps temporary structure took a shape that would have seemed outré and foolish applied to the more permanent and costly dwelling. Restraint in such a situation has no attractions: 'In Garden Delights it is not easy to hold a Mediocrity; that insinuating Pleasure is seldom without some Extremity'.[2] At the worst, mistakes could be easily retrieved.

The stylistic extremes practised in garden structures not infrequently rehearsed their later employment in the big house; the 'fullest freedom of visualization of the artistic goals of a period belongs only to designs emanating from the unrestricted fantasy of the architect'.[3] Stowe, so despised by Rousseau, provided the Temple of Concord of 1748, which 'probably ranks as the first neo-classical building in Europe'.[4] The Pantheon at Stourhead has the dome, copied from its Roman original, that was to be used so extensively by French and English neo-classical architects. 'Athenian' Stuart built a Doric Temple at Hagley in 1758; Shugborough was given a copy of the Tower of the Winds (Fig. 86) and of the Choragic Monument of Lysicrates.[5] All displayed motifs which were to be extensively used in 'serious' buildings during the Regency period; in these parks, however, the prime function of the then outlandish architecture was associational.

Towards the end of the Regency period Loudon wrote that 'sepulchral cenotaphs are frequently erected on the grounds of villas', and gave a few designs; he regarded these as monuments, not tombs, and said they 'may often find a place among the architectural decorations of pleasure grounds'.[6] Indeed, in a period when ancient sepulchral monuments provided many of the motifs of architecture and interior decoration, a practice carried to a point where it aroused disquiet (see p.292), it would have been surprising had not tombs themselves been treated as architectural monuments. An unrealised cemetery project of 1830 (Pl. XXXV) was intended to create a Picturesque architectural garden of the utmost beauty and magnificence, in which piety and ostentation would join hands with instruction: 'public taste and private affection will be afforded ample scope for encouragement of the architectural and sculptural skill of the British School of art; and the scene thus created will call forth all those endearing sentiments, which are so universally excited in visiting the monumental region of the consecrated cemetery of Père la Chaise'.[7] The utilitarian content is characteristic of the new age. The area, a hundred and twenty-two acres in all, was to have been laid out 'in the modern style of ornamental gardening'. The temples and other buildings depicted include some of the most illustrious of Greek and Roman piles, a pagan paradise conjured up in the twilight of classicism itself.

Gothic garden buildings performed the same service for the Gothic style as did antique buildings for the classical. In addition to its Grecian temples, Stowe prominently displayed James Gibbs' Gothic Temple of 1741. Cirencester Park had Alfred's Hall, the first castellated 'Folly' (it is in fact habitable); created by Pope and Lord Bathurst in 1721 and enlarged in 1732,[8] it was placed originally in a formal setting that terminated in a *patte d'oie*.[9] Antiquity, associationalism, and aesthetic adventure united to fill parks with temples and fanes, obelisks, ruins, grottoes, castles, bridges, together with a host of smaller structures: they took every singular form — classical, Gothic, Chinese, primitive — that fancy could devise.

## Ruins and temples

The pleasure of ruins had been long implanted in romantic consciousness, at least since the Anglo-Saxon poet had indulged in pleasing melancholy before the ruins of Roman Bath; Alberti (see p.20) had recommended them as an ingredient in the garden. Alberti came from a country that possessed classical ruins of an unparalleled size and splendour; they were not so easily to be got in a place that had been a barbaric outpost of Roman civilisation. And although the English acquired a taste for their native Gothic ruins, it was the classical ruin that appealed most, aesthetically and associationally. Ruined and entire classical buildings were early 'in the picture', literally so in Claude (Pl. X), in whose paintings they became part of the elegiac romanticism that proved so irresistible during the eighteenth century and beyond: 'Oh! matchless scenes, oh! orient skies, bright with purple and gold: ye opening glades and distant sunny vales, glittering with fleecy flocks, pour all your enchantment into my soul'.[10]

**12** The Ruins at Virginia Water, Windsor, erected 1826–9

The rational century undertook the fantastic activity of manufacturing ruins. They multiplied all over England, indeed all over Europe. They could be Gothic, or classical, or mixed in style; the last was chosen for what is perhaps the earliest purpose-built ruin in Europe, the Magdalenaklause at Schloss Nymphenburg in Munich; built in an extraordinarily hybrid style, with deliberately cracked and eroded walls, it employed the primitivistic triangular arches later used by Hope at the Deepdene (see p.116); the purpose of the building was to induce meditation.[11] This was an important ruin function; for the eighteenth century, new ruins were not a contradiction in terms; there was no reason why they should not work as illusionistically as did theatrical scenery or a play. It was the utilitarian spirit and the pedantry of archaeology that deprived purpose-built ruins of emotional power. The new fundamentalism in Nature-worship may have played a part in destroying their illusionistic authority; the vision of Claude changed imperceptibly into that of Samuel Palmer, to a point where artificial ruins became embarrassing.

An objection increasingly raised against classical ruins in England was that they were historically incorrect. Lord Kames, a respected authority on aesthetics throughout the Regency, took a slightly different stance; he preferred the Gothic ruin 'because it exhibits the triumph of time over strength; a melancholy but not unpleasing thought; a Grecian ruin suggests rather the triumph of barbarity over taste; a gloomy and discouraging thought'.[12] This is a pleasant example of eighteenth-century rationalism and aspiration, held within a framework of a willing suspension of disbelief. Payne Knight thought classical ruins stood 'wholly unconnected with all that surrounds them. . . . Even if the landscape scenery should be rendered beautiful by such ornaments its beauty will be thought of as a vain and affected coquette which offends the understanding . . .'.[13] Soane agreed: 'Ruins representing the remains of Grecian or Roman buildings, however beautiful and picturesque, can never be introduced into the Decorative Gardening of this Country';[14] the emphasis on 'Decorative' may be deliberate, since Soane himself constructed artificial ruins next to his house at Ealing, ostensibly in order to educate his son. They have an echo of Vanbrugh. Soane was self-contradictory, as so often; artificial ruins 'if so cunningly contrived, so well conceived, as to excite such reflections and convey such useful, though melancholy lessons, then too much cannot be said in favour of their introduction on every occasion'.[15] King George IV ignored such scruples, and relieved Sir Charles Long and the British Museum of the embarrassment of a cargo of huge columns from Palmyra by re-erecting them as a ruin at Windsor (Fig. 12).

The English liked Gothic ruins, new or old; their appeal was reinforced by their use in poetry and novels. When the ruins were genuine, a feeling grew that associationalism had to be consistent;

objections were made to the landscaping of ancient ruins. Gilpin disliked Brown's treatment of Roche Abbey (1776): 'the ruin stands now on a neat bowling-green like a house just built, and without any kind of connection with the ground it stands on'.[16] This objection was voiced most frequently against the treatment of Fountains Abbey, the grandest ruin and most compelling eye-catcher in the land: 'amid the natural awe that hangs around one in this noble part of the Abbey, we suddenly enter a modern plot, dispersed with neat walks, and elegant parterres of flowers, weeded with a scrupulous attention!!'.[17] Neatness was incompatible with ruins, with Gothic associations, with melancholy.

From the Romantic literary point of view, the ideal house was a ruin.[18] The first intention at Fonthill had been to build an inhabited ruin (see p.180). Byron was born to one (Fig. 126); in letters and poetry alike, he emphasised the ruinous state of the ancestral mansion, the gaping façade of which supported his romantic image — an ancient title (or what passes for ancient in England), beauty, danger, and poetry together, a heady mixture. This was a period when people proposed to stall their cattle (Fig. 13) and to install their peasantry in Gothic ruins; Robert Lugar's ready-made design provided 'an ornamented Cottage with ruins; contains rooms sufficient for a numerous and respectable family, partly formed in ruins, together with a chaise-house and stable, connected with a gateway; this design was made at the express desire of a gentleman in the neighbourhood of town. The ruins were intended to be an object for his grounds. The idea to be conveyed

**13** 'Cattle Shed & Ruins', a design by Thomas Elison, c.1800–10

**14** 'An Ornamental Cottage with Ruins', a design by Robert Lugar, 1805

was an abbey mutilated, and to show the Cottage as if dressed out of the remains' (Fig. 14).[19]

When the use of the Gothic style spread from garden follies to the main house, the whole garden occasionally became Gothic, as it did at the spikily Gothic Eaton Hall in Cheshire (see p.317). The fifty acre lawn, which had no fewer than three gravelled terraces parallel with the house, was interspersed with 'clumps or knots of shrubs and flowers, mostly describing some appropriate Gothic figure . . .'.[20] This garden was a failure; in 1831 Loudon said that 'a highly enriched geometrical style, corresponding to the house' would have been better;[21] did he mean Gothic geometry, like some Early English window tracery? Prince Pückler-Muskau found the park and gardens of Eaton 'the most unmeaning of any of their class I had seen, although of vast extent'.[22] Soon afterwards the gardens were completely altered.

## The rustic and the primitive

The rustic, and the primitive with which it was associated, early became popular; a Hermit's Cell or Root House existed at Badminton by 1750, before the publication of the theories of Laugier that made primitivism

**15** Merlin's Cave, Richmond, designed by William Kent, 1735

**16** 'A Seat' at White-Knights, 1819, probably designed by J. B. Papworth

**XVIII** 'The Pheasantry', a design by Humphry Repton for Brighton Pavilion, 1805

Plate 13

**17** 'Lady seated with her umbrella, footstool, & pyxis, or jewel box from a greek vase', published by Thomas Hope, 1809

**XIX** Garden seats, designs by J. B. Papworth, c.1818

so popular (see p.108). By 1735, Kent had associated thatch with Gothic in 'Merlin's Cave' at Richmond (Fig. 15), which preceded the fashion for thatched garden buildings and the thatched cottage orné; the idiosyncratic 'beehive' shapes of the roof remind one of J. B. Papworth, who occasionally used the same combination of beehive and triangle.

Robert Adam was a pioneer of decorative cottages in the park, as at Kedleston in the 1770s (Fig. 18; see p.212). Soane's dairy of 1783 at Hamels in Hertfordshire (Pl. XIII; see p.108), built in 1783 for Lady Elizabeth Yorke, brought together Laugierian primitivism (Fig. 44) and thatch in a style that might have extended to his houses had his patrons found it acceptable (Fig. 49); the dairy had marble counters and stained glass, the latter probably old and a precursor of his use of it in his house at Lincoln's Inn Fields. The primitive theme was employed in a dairy designed by Elison in about 1800–10 (Fig. 19), and in the columns of a rustic bridge in the same publication; it had become a commonplace by 1813, when Joseph Gwilt used primitive Doric timber columns in the design of a 'rustic apiary' (Fig. 20).

The rustic, as opposed to the primitive, was subject to the scorn of Payne Knight: 'Rustic lodges to parks, dress cottages, pastoral seats, gates, and gateways, made of unhewn branches and stems of trees', were, he thought, all affected; the rusticity of the first being that of 'a clown in a pantomime, and the simplicity of the others, that of a shepherdess in a French opera'.[23] He did not make known his feelings about the wilder shores of twigginess. Henry Roberts, who had travelled with Cook on his second voyage, bedecked the grounds of his house, Mareham Manor in Lincolnshire, with versions of the huts of the brutish Indians of the Terra del Fuego;[24] even they had been dignified by Rousseau's vision of the Noble Savage (eventually to be succeeded by the equally unrealistic stereotype of the Ignoble Savage, as invented by the Missionary Society after 1818.[25] The noble grace of the Tahitians led to comparisons with the ancient Greeks; 'civilisation had advanced to that state, in which the manners of men are polished, but yet natural'.[26] The fashion for Tahitian huts in gardens became common; their similarities with primitive Greek timber architecture are clear (Fig. 21). Some rational spirits found this romantic idealism funny: in 1817 or 1818 Peacock wrote a fragment of his projected 'Sir Calidore', alas never completed, in which King Arthur and his Court settle down on a South Sea island with the exiled gods and goddesses of Greece; Offenbach seems not far away.

Stonehenge attracted some attention as a possible primitive garden ruin; it was incontestably British, and was associated with the Celtic twilight made so fashionable by the Ossianic poems (translated by many Europeans, including Goethe); it appears in the background of Barry's 1787 painting of King Lear weeping over Cordelia. In 1790 'an imitation of an ancient British monument' was recommended as 'a pretty device' which 'may be raised at small expense; the materials may be brick or timber plastered over'.[27] It is fortunate that the use of Stonehenge as a garden ornament did not presage the use of a Stonehenge style in 'serious' architecture; it might well have followed

**18** 'Sketch of a Hutt . . . at the upper end of Garden at Kedleston', by Robert Adam, c.1760–70

20 'Apiary for John Allnutt Esqr. Clapham Common', 1813, a design by Joseph Gwilt

19 'Larder or Dairy', a design by Thomas Elison, c.1800–10

21 'Danse des Femmes d'Otateiti', after G. B. Cipriani

precedent and done so (Fig. 45). Its appeal may have been assisted by the growing interest in basic geometrical shapes and in primitivism, in stones as stones;[28] to Alison, nothing was 'more sublime than Rocks, which seem to be coeval with Creation'.[29] Such primitivism was hardly advanced by plastered timber or by the gardening practices of Mr Bertie Greatheed (described by the poet Gray as a 'fat young man with a head and face much bigger than they are usually worn'), who, no doubt beguiled by Burke's definition of the Beautiful, had cut up the rock at Guy's Cliff 'till it is as smooth and sleek as sattin'.[30]

## The exotic

The oriental also beckoned. To the meandering curves of 'sharawaggi', so fashionable in the earlier eighteenth century, Chambers had added the possibility of formality; the Chinese, he said, 'have no aversion to strait lines; because they are . . . productive of grandeur'; nor do they have 'any aversion to regular geometrical figures, which they say are beautiful in themselves, and well suited to small compositions';[31] the last point may have influenced Repton. The acceptance of straight lines in Chinese-style gardening was associated with some shift of English interest from the visionary landscape gardens of Peking and Jehol to the smaller town gardens made accessible after the establishment of a trading base at Canton — 'a little world of insignificant intricacy'.[32] The former, incidentally, sometimes resemble the fantastic landscapes seen in Roman wall paintings, which not infrequently contain both classical garden buildings and buildings with upturned roofs that look remarkably like a Roman form of 'chinoiserie'.[33]

Chinese garden buildings had appeared in England in the 1740s. Chinese architecture was neat and lacked melancholic associations; it was therefore not built in ruin, and where it was combined with Gothic the result was cheerful rococo fantasy; not infrequently, Chinese and Gothic were perfectly integrated in garden buildings (Fig. 22) and in furniture; in a way that presaged the Regency synthesis. Sometimes the Regency was remarkably anticipated; the Chinese Fishing Pavilion of 1765 at Alresford, for example, with its octagon roof and swept out verandah, could easily be mistaken as early nineteenth century. Turkish tents, which were to spread their wings at Virginia Water, had appeared by 1750,[34] as had Chinese Parasols, later to bloom under another name for Papworth (Pl. XIX). Kew spawned a numerous brood of exotic buildings; an ornate Moorish Alhambra, probably by Müntz, with strongly coloured proto-Regency decoration within, was erected in 1750; between 1757 and 1763 Chambers added a group of buildings in exotic styles varied enough to be used later by Soane for comparative purposes in a lecture to his Academy students.

Few Regency gardens did more than include the occasional chinoiserie structure. It seems anomalous that George IV, the royal

amateur of the Chinese style, never indulged in a Chinese garden; even the extravagant Chinese Fishing Temple at Windsor (Fig. 23), which revived rococo architectural chinoiserie (compare with Fig. 24; see p.196), was placed in an unadventurously charming garden compounded of the usual ornaments of the later Regency period disposed in a Picturesque way — fountains, tubs, shrubs in the lawns. The more elaborate cottage orné often had a garden of the same type, with Chinese tubs and vases a fashionable ornament for the verandahs (Pl. LIII; see p.217).

Sir George Staunton, who as a page had accompanied Lord Macartney on the 1793 embassy to China, and who read and wrote Chinese, created a Chinese landscape garden at Leigh Park near Portsmouth, acquired in 1820. He equipped the house with Chinese paintings, wallpaper, and lanterns; the garden was landscaped between 1820 and 1840, with a lake, begun in 1828, that had on it three islands based on those in Peking; there were Chinese garden buildings, including a summer-house, and a Chinese bridge and boathouse with authentic Chinese inscriptions; on Fort Island stood a battery of guns, beneath the Chinese imperial flag.[35] A Chinese garden was numbered amongst the manifold delights of Cassiobury; it was described in 1826 as 'inclosed by high trees and walls, and [containing] a number of vases, benches, fountains, and a third green-house, — all in the genuine Chinese style. Here were beds surrounded by circles of white, blue, and red sand, fantastic dwarf plants, and many dozens of large China vases placed on pedestals, thickly overgrown with trailing evergreens and exotics. The windows of the house [the greenhouse] were painted like Chinese hangings, and convex mirrors placed in the interior, which reflected us as in a "camera obscura".'[36]

The Indian style in gardens did not appear until the 1790s; even then, Hindu or Moghul decorations were merely used as decoration in settings that made no attempt at an Indian idiom. In 1793 (the same year in which S. P. Cockerell gave Daylesford an Indian dome), an octagonal temple was built in Indian style to the design of James Forbes at Stanmore Park, Middlesex. It was followed in 1800 by a Temple at Melchet Park, built of Coade stone by Rossi and imitating an aquatint by the Daniells, with a slight Chinese concavity added to the verandah of the porch. Garden artefacts evoked the Indian at Sezincote, the Moghul-style house built in 1805 to the designs of S. P. Cockerell (Pl. XVI; see p.198); the gardens contained Indian-style garden buildings and ornaments, designed by Thomas and William Daniell, set in a wonderfully lush Picturesque landscape. The choice of the Hindu, rather than Moghul, style for Indian garden buildings probably arose from the association of the Hindu style with buildings hewn from the cavern. Particularly delightful was the dell at Sezincote with its water-garden, where beside a pool stood a temple containing a Coade stone figure of the Hindu deity 'Suryah' (Fig. 25); beneath it was a bridge

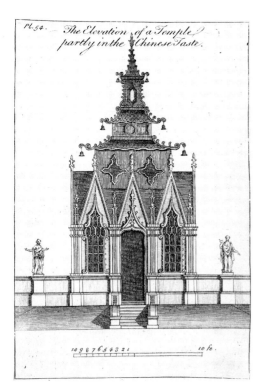
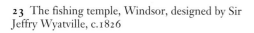

22 'The Elevation of a Temple partly in the Chinese Taste', a design by William Halfpenny, 1750–2

23 The fishing temple, Windsor, designed by Sir Jeffry Wyatville, c.1826

24 'A Decorative Temple for Park or Grounds in the Chinese Style', a design by E. Gyfford, 1807

25 Sezincote House, Gloucs., 'View of the Temple of Suryah & Fountain of Maha Dao', 1817

26 'The General view from the Pavilion', a design by Humphry Repton, 1805

supported on octagonal shafts copied from the Elephanta Caves, and another pool where a three-headed serpent spurted water from its fangs.

There is no doubt that, had it materialised, Repton's Indian-style garden at Brighton would have surpassed all others in the style. The garden buildings and ornaments were designed in both Hindu and Moghul style, the Aviary (Fig. 26) being primarily Hindu, the Pheasantry (Pl. XVIII) primarily Moghul (see p.198); the ambiguous resemblances between Gothic and Moghul ornament are as present in the garden design as in Nash's later Pavilion. The gardens were planned in a more controlled, less Picturesque style than those at Sezincote; square pools and symmetry were juxtaposed with carefully casual groups of trees and circular beds in the lawn.

## Garden seats and alcoves

Garden seats came in various guises. Repton was fond of placing in his designs one or two seats in unpretentious, vaguely rustic style (Pl. XXI); they have the appearance of being made of wood, although many garden seats were produced commercially in iron. Four designs of 1800

27 Garden seats, designs by W. Robertson, 1800

28 Design for a garden seat, by James Trubshaw, c.1833

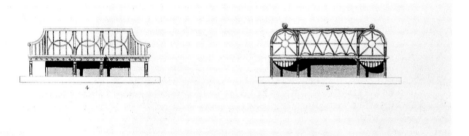
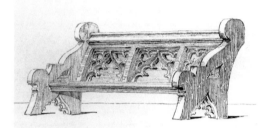

(Fig. 27) are more sophisticated; offered by W. Robertson together with 'Small Gates for Villas . . . Park Entrances, Aviarys, Temples, Boat Houses, Mausoleums and Bridges . . .', they are all painted green, no doubt 'invisible green' as recommended. They are described thus: 'No. 1 and 2 are forms in general use: No. 3 and 4 are singular, in having seats at the extremities, and centre [with arms] for a single person'.[37] They are raised on a stone step to exclude damp.

Papworth's designs are all that is most attractive in Regency garden artefacts. Witty, refined, charming, an allusive blend of motifs drawn from a variety of sources (Fig. 143), they speak clearly of their designer's personality. Nowhere does it come through more sunnily than in two ideas for garden seats (Pl. XIX). The upper design is 'an imitation of those buildings in India that . . . very nearly resemble an umbrella: the stems and beams of it are intended to be made of light work in iron, and the roof filled in with copper sheeting'.[38] It had been anticipated in a design for an 'Umbrello seat in the Indian manner' by Charles Over in 1758.[39] The Indian reference has sufficient similarities to certain classical forms to allow hints of other associations (Figs 17, 140); Hope's Greek umbrella[40] and the Pompeian 'piccolo padiglione, o baldacchino'[41] seem not far away. The lower design is 'of a marquee character' with a cloth cover, the 'devices being either woven in the cloth itself, or Painted upon it. This is supported upon an iron framing . . . and in winter it could be put away. . . .'[42] These designs were not just delightful conceits on paper, at which people looked and smiled. A depiction of Ireland's Royal Grounds in Brighton of the 1820s shows

an 'umbrella' exactly like that of Papworth; according to the text it was in the company of a castellated structure in treillage, a 'Merlin's' swing, a Gothic aviary, a grotto, a maze, and a battery of six pieces of cannon.[43]

Papworth shows other garden seats, including a classical seat of which the ceiling and various ornaments were to be gilded; a Venetian Tent, very splendid and Turkish looking; a Polish Hut 'similar to many of the cottages of Poland, and not unlike those of Switzerland' (see p.217); a bath, an apiary, and an aviary that makes obeisance to a pagoda. He also has a 'garden seat' (Pl. XXII), designed so that foliage could be trained 'in a light and playful manner: the construction is very simple, consisting of oak pillars and iron rods to form the arcades and trellises. The basket like ornaments on the pillars may be formed either of light-iron or wicker-work into which the creeper could be trained'.[44] He produced no designs in the Gothic taste, although there was a demand for Gothic garden furniture, as is shown in the large number of cast-iron 'ecclesiastical' Gothic garden chairs that survive. Soane had one at Lincoln's Inn Fields.

Several chair designs from the later 1830s by James Trubshaw for Elizabeth, Duchess of Sutherland, markedly contrast with those of Papworth, although by that time Papworth himself was designing Jacobean garden seats. Trubshaw produced two neo-classical designs, another in the Elizabethan style, and several in the Gothic.[45] The neo-classical chair, a bench with winged lions as arm rests, is much in the 'Tatham' tradition (Fig. 331; see p.412); the Gothic one is more forward-looking (Fig. 28).

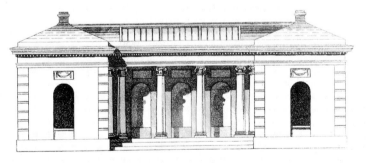

**29** 'A Pavilion or Summer-House in the Egyptian, or Turkish taste', a design by Robert Lugar, 1805

**30** A swimming bath, a design by W. Robertson, 1800

**31** 'Design No. 8. The Bath', a design by P. F. Robinson, 1826

**32** 'Elevation of a Temple with a Greenhouse on each Side', a design by George Richardson, 1792

'Alcoves' were popular, and could be simple or elaborate. A design by George Stanley Repton, for instance, in Reptonian treillage with a tiled roof,[46] contrasts with a domed and swagged design by Thomas Elison, curiously 'indoor', and not unlike some of the earlier designs of Sheraton. Papworth, as one might expect, managed to produce a design of charm and sophistication that is, nevertheless, indubitably 'outdoor' (Pl. XXIV). 'The stile of this little building is light and elegant but of no specific architectural character' (it is a perfect example of a Regency synthesis); it 'should be rather splendid in its finishing. . . . The pillars are of iron, and from them are suspended China pattera of rich colours; the chains are gilt, as is also the terminal of the roof. The scale-like forms of the roof covering are of thin lead, and might be richly painted; indeed, the whole should be so decorated as to become highly ornamental, and be in splendid harmony with its accompanying parterres and flower beds.'[47] The building has a colour and festivity that produce an effect not unlike that of the rococo.

Gilding, also a prominent feature of rococo gardens, now returned as early as 1805, Repton's design for the Orangery at Brighton had shown gilded pillars, a synthesis of Indian detail and Pompeian candelabraform shapes; by the 1820s gilding was high fashion.[48] Repton said that whenever cast iron was used, it should be gilded or bronzed; it would otherwise appear 'unequal to its office' (see p.316).

The tradition of architectural experiment in the garden was continued in an eccentrically exotic design of 1805 for a 'Pavilion or Summer-House' by Robert Lugar (Fig. 29); it was reissued in 1823, immediately after Nash's Pavilion at Brighton had arrived fully blown on the scene. The pavilion, which followed a chinoiserie design 'of a light fanciful form', was described by Lugar as 'in a bolder style, and better suited for a romantic retreat in an extensive park. This is in the Egyptian, or Turkish taste . . . The prospect tower is in the style of a Turkish minarett, and if built in an appropriate situation could prove an excellent landmark'.[49] So it could. The antithesis of the Papworth alcove, the design is a perfect example of an unsuccessful synthesis.

Another type of building that was beginning to appear in gardens was the swimming pool. 'The painful consequences too frequently resulting to youth, from bathing, and learning to swim in rivers, ponds, etc. seems to point out a necessity of erecting buildings expressly for this purpose . . .'.[50] As usual, the English were late arrivals when it came to pleasure; Pliny had enjoyed his heated swimming pool at his Laurentinum villa, with its view over the sea, long before the Anglo-Saxons had left their European forests.[51] The top-lit bath of the design by Robertson was to be 34 feet long, and 4 feet deep (Fig. 30); its graceful portico, glimpsed in a park, would have struck something of a 'Grecian' note (see p.129). Twenty-six years later, P. F. Robinson produced a design for a swimming bath in the French Romantic Classical idiom (Fig. 31).

## The conservatory

The grand orangeries or conservatories of the seventeenth and eighteenth centuries had been built expressly for the purposes of entertainment. They were free-standing buildings, set apart from the mansion; that tradition continued and was revived in the 1820s — Nash's conservatories at Buckingham Palace and Fowler's Indian conservatory at Syon, for example, stood apart from, although near to, the main mass of building. This type is ambitiously shown in Richardson's design of 1792 for a 'Temple with a Greenhouse on each Side' (Fig. 32), one of 'several elegant and extensive designs of Greenhouses and Orangeries, with rooms adjoining, for the purpose of reading, eating fruit, and drinking tea': the desire to be magnificent is expressed in the comment that the 'additional rooms make the whole designs appear with much greater importance and advantage than if they were to stand alone . . . it would be in character to decorate the inside with rural scenes, prints, or paintings'.[52]

Repton had pointed out that when greenhouses had contained only orange trees and myrtles, no overhead light had been needed; however,

**XX** 'Pavilion & Green House for a Gothic Mansion', a design by Humphry Repton for Plas Newydd, Anglesey, 1798

**XXI** 'View from my own cottage in Essex', Hare Street, after improvement, by Humphry Repton, 1816

XXII 'A Garden Seat', a design by J. B. Papworth, published in 1823

XXIII Blaise Hamlet, near Bristol, c.1822, designed by John Nash, 1810

*Opposite* XXIV 'An Alcove', a design by J. B. Papworth, c.1823

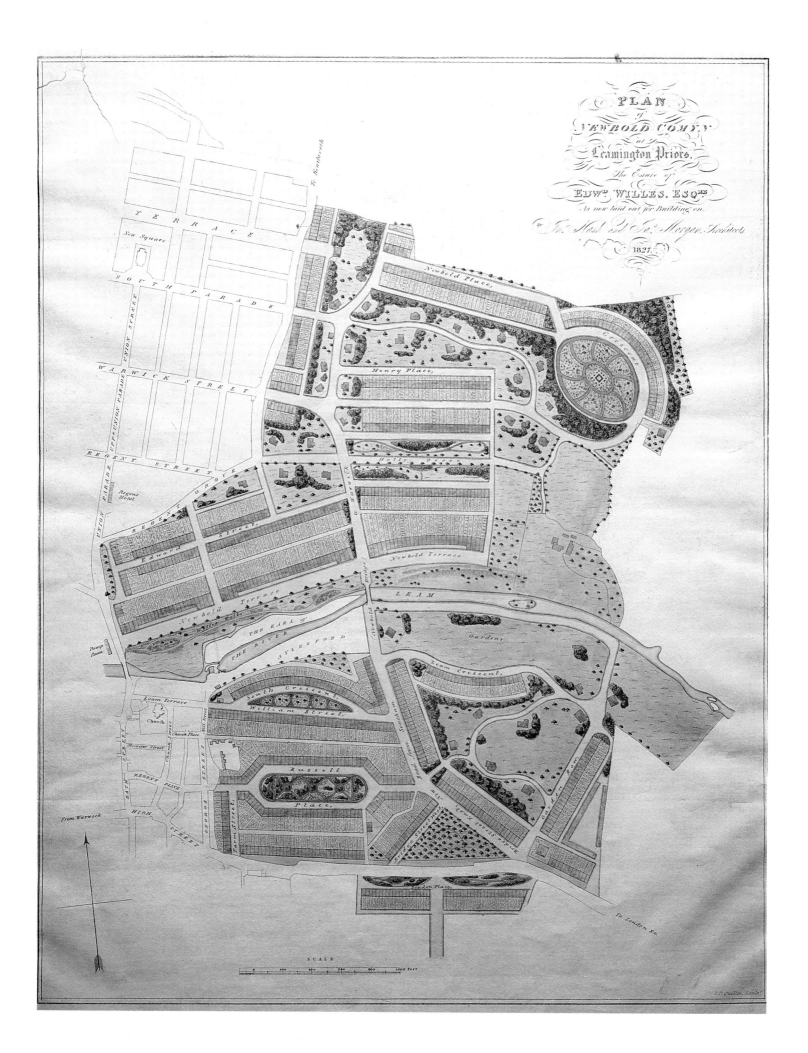

PLAN
of
NEWBOLD COMYN
at
Leamington Priors,
The Estate of
EDWD. WILLES, ESQRE.
As now laid out for Building on.
by Jno. Hosd and Jno. Morgan, Architects.
1827.

New Square

TERRACE

SOUTH PARADE

UPPER UNION PARADE    UNION STREET

WARWICK STREET

REGENT STREET

UNION PARADE

Regent Hotel

REGENT GROVE

Edward Street

Newbold Place,

Henry Place,

Holly Grove,

Newbold Terrace,

Crescent

Newbold Terrace

Newbold Walk

THE EARL OF

THE RIVER

LEAM

Gardens

AYLESFORD

Newbold Bridge

Leam Crescent,

Pump Room

Leam Terrace

Church

Church Place

WILLIAM STREET

BATH STREET    REGENT PLACE    HIGH STREET

GEORGE STREET

Regent Place

Leam Street

South Crescent

William Street,

Russell

Place,

Newbold Street

Newbold Street

Avenue Road

Gardens

Garden Road

From Warwick

To Kenilworth

To London &c.

London Place,

SCALE

To Kenilworth

F.P. Owellen Sculpt.

the new geraniums and ericas needed a glass roof, which 'will never add to the external ornament of a house of regular architecture'. He advised that the glasshouse should be in the flower garden, its glass roof disguised with treillage (Pl. XV).⁵³ Despite the problems of the roof, the conservatory left the parterres and the park at the beginning of the Regency period to become part of the house; nothing better illustrates the changes brought by the Picturesque into the pattern of domestic living. Repton himself contributed to the development; most of the houses designed by himself and Nash included conservatories within the structure (e.g. see pp.165, 179).

The desire for splendour did not disappear with the change from the detached to the integrated conservatory; the grand enfilade survived in a less overbearing, and more romantic form. Speaking of the library, drawing room, breakfast room, and dining room, Repton said: 'of late, especially since the central hall, or vestibule, has been in some degree given up, these rooms have been opened into each other, ensuite, by large folding doors . . . this enfilade . . . is occasionally increased, by a conservatory at one end and repeated by a large mirror at the opposite end' (Fig. 3).⁵⁴ He added an injunction to set a large mirror at an angle of 45° at the end of the enfilade, an expedient that gives an illimitable perspective; this device was suggested for the conservatory designed in 1805 for Brighton Pavilion. Repton also designed for that scheme an Orangery that would have been open in summer, glazed in winter, a course he recommended for the 'Pavilion and Greenhouse' at Plas Newydd, Anglesey (Pl. XX), 'where the house partakes of a Gothic character'. This would have imparted grandeur: 'I suggested the addition of a green-house, terminating a magnificent enfilade through a long line of principal apartments. The hint for this model is taken from the chapter rooms to some of our cathedrals . . .'.⁵⁵

Thomas Hopper's attached conservatory at Carlton House (Fig. 34; see pp.165, 316–17) was designed for entertainment, plants constantly being moved in and out. The construction was of iron, with plaster ornaments;⁵⁶ the extraordinary curved roof of the aisles demonstrates

how the plastic qualities of the new material introduced new forms into a design in 'ecclesiastical' Gothic. The Carlton House Conservatory contravened Repton's principle that a lobby should intervene between conservatory and house in order to restrict the smell of earth;⁵⁷ Papworth made something of the same point in 1818, saying that the conservatory had become an apartment and that it was unhealthy to attach it to a drawing or dining room, due to the plants' absorption of 'vital air' during the evening.⁵⁸ In some cases it became more than an apartment; the conservatory designed by Robinson in 1825, apparently without a glass roof, approaches in its grandiosity the 'winter garden' of an Edwardian hotel. Its Doric has been tamed, given slender proportions, bases, and arches, and every surface is covered in treillage (Fig. 35).

The attempt in the early 1800s to establish the Egyptian style led to Charles Heathcote Tatham's 'Design for an Egyptian Temple proposed to be used as a Greenhouse' for Trentham Hall, Staffordshire (Fig. 33). The proposal (see p.192) is ingenious and not unimposing, but there is an inherent contradiction in attempting to use, as models for a greenhouse, temples that attempted to exclude the light.

Loudon's invention in 1816 of the iron 'ridge and furrow' construction and a wrought-iron sash bar that could be bent in any direction without reducing its strength made possible the voluminous later glasshouses of Decimus Burton and Joseph Paxton, which echo the curves of the crinolines flaunted within them. The first curvilinear hothouses were built in Bayswater Gardens by the ironmongers, W. D. Bailey; ironmongers became to greenhouses what engineers became to bridges; the technical possibilities encouraged new designs, although at first some caution was shown: 'In . . . modern houses, where columns, pediments, cornices and other architectural finishings, present themselves, something of the same kind should enter into the architecture of a greenhouse; but always in a subordinate degree and not to interfere with utility'.⁵⁹ The greenhouse built in 1824 for Lord St. Vincent by Baileys (Fig. 36) shows just such a compromise between

XXV Design by John Nash for the development of the Willes estate, Leamington Spa, 1827

33 'A Design for an Egyptian Temple proposed to be used as a Greenhouse' for Trentham Hall, Staffs., by C. H. Tatham, 1804

34 'The Interior of the Prince of Wales's Conservatory at Carlton House', designed by Thomas Hopper, 1807

35 'Design No. 4 Conservatory', 1825, by P. F. Robinson

classicism and the new technology. Ironwork proved a convenient way of reproducing Gothic ornament on greenhouses, and facilitated the construction of orientalising cupolas, as in the delightful conservatory attached to Decimus Burton's Colosseum in Regent's Park, built in 1823–7 (Pl. XVII).

The sense of adventure banished timidity; in 1827 a 'glass dome', 60 feet high and a hundred in diameter, was erected at a cost of £14,000 for Mrs. Beaumont of Bretton Hall, Yorkshire. Beneath the gilt coronet that surmounted it lay a magazine of advanced technology. The structure was heated by steam; ventilation was supplied by a skylight opened by weights immediately below the coronet, and supplemented by inwardly opening windows at the base of the upper dome and by horizontal shutters in the low iron screen. So nicely judged was the engineering, that before the insertion of the glass 'the slightest wind put the whole of it in motion from the base to the summit'.[60] The makers guaranteed it for several years; in 1832 it was taken down for reasons other than safety and auctioned.

Iron and glass encouraged enterprise. In 1825 Henry Phillips, a Brighton botanist and landscape gardener, joined forces with Amon Wilds the architect; the scheme was for a princely street, with ammonite capitals topping its pilasters, that would lead from the sea to a large garden in the centre of which would arise the Athenaeum, a conservatory in the shape of an oriental dome heated by steam; it was to contain a library, reading room and museum, plus a school for the sciences and the liberal arts, a constellation that expressed in a typical way the Regency faith in cultural and scientific values. Amon Wilds's own house in Gothic style lay beyond the site, alongside his domed orientalising 'mini-Pavilion'.[61] Lack of finance killed the project; perhaps a mercy, considering the fate of its successor in Hove,

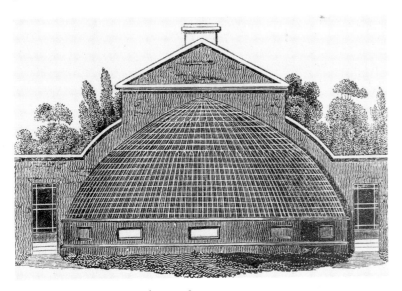

**36** Lord St. Vincent's greenhouse, 1824

which collapsed in dramatic fashion when the supporting scaffolding was removed.

## Profusion

The expressive Regency term 'profusion', usually employed to describe over-indulgence in rich decoration or expenditure, is nowhere more appropriate than when used of the more elaborate gardens. Even Repton's schemes were invaded by the fashion for miscellaneous ornament, as is apparent in a depiction of 1818 of a garden designed in about 1808; an aviary is accompanied by a conservatory or orangery, a strangely castellated structure of indeterminate purpose, and a cottage complete with Reptonian smoke (Pl. XIV).

The medley that could accumulate is vividly presented in an account, written in 1802 by an impressionable clergyman, of the famous Hawkestone Park, one of the earliest tourist spots — some time later Prince Pückler-Muskau gave it 'the preference over all I have seen'.[62] The Reverend Richard Warner had thoroughly assimilated the tenets of the Picturesque; he admired Wordsworth, and his half-fascinated, half-condemnatory account of the garden buildings is punctuated by exclamations on the graces of the landscape.[63]

The first structure encountered was a 'little fantastical cottage (fitted up in the Dutch style) called Neptune's Whim', surrounded on every side by numerous 'mottos, stanzas, and copies of verses'; this the clergyman's party thought 'childishly artificial'. Behind it was a colossal statue of Neptune, with attendant Naiads. 'With these injudicious ornaments may be classed another — equally objectionable'; this was a windmill 'painted in the Dutch manner, to keep up the idea of a North-Holland picture' (presumably by Ruysdael or some such painter).

Thence a path led to a deep and sequestered glen, denominated 'a scene in Otaheite . . . imagination is assisted in her flight to the South-Sea islands by a cottage constructed in the manner and fitted up with the furniture of their inhabitants; a canoe lying in front of it is introduced to aid the delusion'. This is probably the same structure wickedly described over twenty-five years later by Prince Pückler-Muskau as 'a New Zealander's hut . . . built many years ago from a drawing of Captain Cook's, and furnished with arrows, spears, tomahawks, skulls of eaten enemies, and such-like pretty trifles, the innocent luxuries of these children of nature'.[64] As a contrast, there was a small chapel, and 'whilst contemplating there, a venerable figure, clothed in the stole of a Druid, slowly passing from a dark recess in the apartment, crossed before us to the altar, made his obeisance, and departed; leaving us much more surprised at, and almost ashamed of, the very singular impression which our minds could be made to experience'. On to the Hermitage, and another denizen; 'A venerable figure is seen in a sitting posture, who (by means of a servant previously

**37** 'The Church Way' at Broomwell House, Brislington, 1826–7

placed behind him) rises up as the stranger approaches; asked questions; returns answers; and repeats poetry'. The Hermit was stuffed.

Other attractions included a 'Pont de Suisse', an obelisk, a Roman wall, a cave where an ancestor of the family had hidden in the Civil War, and an 'Elysian-hill' with neat parterres and clumps of exotics; it had a menagerie near by, and a 'pretty cottage . . . furnished with a good collection of stuffed birds. The green-house is built in the Gothic style . . .'. Mr. Warner, whose enjoyment of these incidents beams through an assumed condescension, reflected that 'the astonishment' excited by the majestic rocks and groves was of too intense a nature to bear long without pain, and that the frivolous objects refreshed and relieved the mind: 'I know not whether I be right in my reasoning; but if not, I fear I have no other excuse to offer for the Druid, the Hermit, and the Dutch cottage'. It is obvious that fashion was beginning to quiz the Hawkestone devices; however, they remained popular throughout the period, albeit descending the social scale.

'Profusion' in garden buildings is seen in its most uninhibited form at Alton Towers, Staffordshire, where Charles, fifteenth Earl of Shrewsbury, began work on the garden in 1814 and employed a regiment of workers until his death; his main agents were Thomas Allason, a pupil of William Atkinson, and Robert Abraham. The site was a richly picturesque valley, 'naturally in a high degree romantic'. The result was questionable; even Loudon found 'the greater part of [the garden] in excessively bad taste . . . the work of a morbid imagination, joined to the command of unlimited resources'.[65] There was 'such a labyrinth of terraces, curious architectural walls, trelliswork arbours, vases, statues, stone stairs, wooden stairs, turf stairs, pavements, gravel and grass walks, ornamental buildings, bridges, porticoes, temples, pagodas, gates, iron railings, parterres, jets, ponds, streams, seats, fountains, caves, flower-baskets, waterfalls, rocks, cottages, trees, shrubs, beds of flowers, ivied walls, rockwork, shellwork, rootwork, moss-houses, old trunks of trees, entire dead trees, etc. that it is utterly impossible for words to give an idea of the effect.'

Oddities included an imitation cottage roof, formed by sticking dormer windows, chimneys, and heather imitating thatch, on to the 'sloping surface of a large grey mass of solid rock'; and a projecting rock; 'formed into a huge serpent, with a spear-shaped iron tongue and glass eyes'. There were Gothic temples, Grecian temples, and Indian temples, some cut out of the solid rock; there was an octagon Chinese pagoda, intended to be eighty-eight feet high, but unfinished at the Earl's death (a gasometer housed in the lower storey was to fuel Chinese lamps in order to illuminate the water spouting from its monsters and from its apex). Beside a 'dry Gothic bridge' was a 'huge imitation of Stonehenge'; it was given a rudimentary pediment. Behind it lay a mass of castellated stables, and in front a 'range of architectural conservatories, with seven elegant glass domes, designed by Mr. Abrahams, richly gilt'.

The Earl of Shrewsbury seems to have neglected few forms of expression in his garden, but there is no mention of antiquarian woodwork such as that used by the collector Mr. Braikenridge at Broomwell House. 'The Church Way' (Fig. 37) was only one of at least six similar concoctions in the garden, half of which were used as doors and half of which had no practical function; the earliest existed by October 1823. They were made up of 'ancient' miscellaneous woodcarvings, of which a good many came from the Continent; the arrangements have a primitive symmetry.[66] It is difficult to believe that the age that nurtured the delicate art of Papworth could produce the ornaments of Mr. Braikenridge's garden at Brislington. Horace Walpole's warning had been amply justified.

Chapter five

# Town and Village Planning

## Regularity and regular landscaping

The idea that a town should be regularly disposed was deeply rooted by the beginning of the eighteenth century. It was thought essential that the plan of a town should be regular on paper, whatever tricks the lie of the land might play, or might allow to be played. When the rapid expansion of Bath began, geometry ruled; there was no attempt to exploit the hilly terrain for Picturesque purposes; the new streets climbed the steep slopes undeviatingly, and the crescents were placed to lie on one plane at right angles to the slope. The buildings were tied to the streets, or followed the regular shapes assumed by squares and crescents.

Regularity applied as equally to the planning of villages as to that of towns. The opportunity to plan either afresh did not often occur; if on occasion a landowner decided to obliterate a village from his prospect, the new village that resulted was built in a symmetrical manner. When Capability Brown rebuilt Milton Abbas for Lord Milton in the 1770s, he erected identical thatched cottages facing each other along a straight street. His employment for such a purpose was in itself a sign of change; the use of an architect for a village would have been rare before 1760. The result of Brown's employment was that he landscaped Lord Milton's village in a Brownian manner.

Regular planning of villages was approved even by William Gilpin, the missionary of the Picturesque; he wrote of Nuneham Courtenay in the 1770s, a rebuilt village that had 'two rows of low neat houses built close to each other and as regular and uniform as a London street', that regularity 'perhaps gives the most convenience to the dwellings of men. For this we readily relinquish the picturesque idea. Indeed I question whether it were possible for a single hand to build a picturesque village. Nothing contributes to it more than the various styles in building'.[1]

This passage has its ambiguities, but Gilpin's disbelief in the compatibility of irregularity and utility, or in the possibility of Picturesque variety emanating from one hand, is clear. He was quickly to be proved wrong on both counts.

The regular disposition of buildings in towns meant that landscape incorporated within a town was also regularly disposed. The association of landscape and towns was not new; at Bath, for instance, new fashions in landscape gardening had prompted the incorporation of large tracts of green into the mid-eighteenth century town, green that was confined rigorously within square and crescents, or that existed as views from the ordered confines of the city. Architecture dominated nature, and not vice versa; no trees were to be grown on the green of Bath's Queen's Square, to assure perpetual pre-eminence to the obelisk. The cult of the Picturesque changed this attitude; in 1813, during discussions on the planning of the New Town at Edinburgh, allusion was made to Queen's Square in Bath, and to the 'former prejudice, that trees and town buildings are incongruous objects'.[2] Two powerful authorities invoked to contest this view were Claude and Poussin; William Stark, the planner of the New Town (see p.84), wrote that: '. . . our best landscape painters, Claude and the Poussins, never tired of painting (trees). . . . From the practice of these great masters, whom we must regard as unerring authorities, of constantly combining trees and architecture, it might be inferred to have been their opinion that there could be no beauty where either of these objects was wanting.'[3]

As the eighteenth century advanced, the influences of Rousseau and of sentimental pastoralism made themselves felt. An ill-judged attempt to import rurality into the metropolis is attested by the scornful reaction of John Stewart to sheep penned in Cavendish Square; he alluded to 'the poor things starting at every coach', adding that 'it requires a warm imagination, indeed, to connect the scene with that of

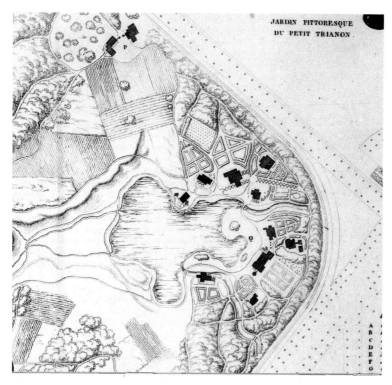

**38** 'Jardin Pittoresque du Petit Trianon', designed for Queen Marie-Antoinette, published 1800

flocks ranging the field, with all the concomitant ideas of innocence and a pastoral life'.[4] It is obvious that the incarceration of sheep in a formal square signalled an attitude that would soon prejudice the formality of the square itself, and by the beginning of the nineteenth century opinion was ready to accept the incorporation of large tracts of informally planned landscape in towns.

## Irregularity and irregular landscaping

Despite the prevalence of regularity, other traditions existed. Alberti had differentiated between the planning of large and small towns; there was nothing to stop his readers, especially when bolstered by the theories of the Picturesque, from extending his views on the planning of small towns to larger ones: 'if the City is noble and powerful, the streets shou'd be strait and broad, which carries an air of greatness and majesty; but if it is only a small town . . . it will be better . . . to have them wind about . . . and within the heart of the town, it will be handsomer not to have them strait, but winding about several ways, backwards and forwards like the course of a river . . . they will add to the idea of the greatness of a town, they will likewise conduce very much to beauty and convenience. . . . Moreover, this winding of the streets will make the passenger at every step discover a new structure. . . .'[5] Given such a precedent, and there are others, Sir Joshua Reynolds'

comment on the charms of irregularity made in 1786 seems less startling; he remarked that 'the turnings of the streets of London and other old Towns' were attractive, and that had the grand Wren plan been followed, the result would probably have been 'rather unpleasing; the uniformity might have produced weariness and a slight degree of disgust'.[6] Reynolds, apparently the embodiment of academic conservation, was here, as on other occasions, preaching aesthetic revolution.

The invasion of the principle of Picturesque irregularity into urban planning was resisted; the architectural publicist Elsam, at the time that Nash's work in London was getting under way, sounded a warning: 'the present taste, or rather predilection for the picturesque, should not be indulged . . . to the prejudice of the pure and genuine principles of architecture. The most correct forms and beautiful proportions are only to be found in works which unite simplicity with regularity. Buildings, therefore, which are regular in all their parts, but irregularly disposed, whether in streets, squares, or elsewhere, may create for a few seconds new and extraordinary effects, combined with the surrounding circumstances; but where designs are carried into effect, which are manifestly calculated to destroy the beautiful symmetry of our best and most regular streets, we cannot help thinking that the genius of architecture has taken an excursion into the realms of fancy, intoxicated with the charms of variety'.[7]

As far as villages were concerned, custom sanctioned irregular plans that had not been the act of a 'single hand', to use Gilpin's phrase. Uvedale Price did not share Gilpin's preference for regularity in new villages, and condemned their formal planning on aesthetic grounds; he thought it better to copy the characteristic beauties of old villages which, as opposed to those of a city (this was before Nash took a hand), were those of 'intricacy, variety, and play of outline'.[8] Even Elsam had to concede that in villages, cottages 'if arranged with judgment . . . never cease to produce the most pleasing effects, particularly when studded among plantations of underwood or coppice scenery'.[9] The adoption of the Speenhamland system (from 1795) produced a shortage of labourers' cottages; landlords were led to build new houses and groups of houses, many of which were designed and situated according to Picturesque principles.

The Picturesque ideal of the irregular village, old or new, had triumphed by 1816, the date of the neat view from Repton's cottage in Hare Street, Essex (Pl. XXI). Beyond the dandified garden stretches the Picturesque asymmetry of the village street; the large joints of meat that hang in the sun outside the butcher's shop, within sight in the 'unimproved' view, are carefully concealed by a Dutch seventeenth-century style pergola. And asymmetry reigns in the historicist jumble of Robinson's 'Village Street' of 1830 (Fig. 39), intended explicitly to illustrate Uvedale Price's theories.

**39** 'The Village Street', a design by P. F. Robinson, 1830

Deliberate irregularity of plan combined with incorporated landscape appeared earlier in villages than in towns, and it is significant that the villages concerned were often connected with gardens and parks. In this sense one of the most picturesque of all housing estates, if such it can be called — the houses were not inhabited — and one that attracted much notice, was created in France, in the gardens of Versailles, in the 1770s; this was the 'Jardin Pittoresque du Petit Trianon', with its famous 'Hameau' (Fig. 38). Not the first of its kind,[10] it was the most famous, and the fate of its owner gave it a penumbra of mournful romance. The 'picturesque' arrangement of the buildings in the Hameau — the very name is significant — preceded those of Nash's Blaise Hamlet by almost thirty years (Pl. XXIII).

The building of Blaise Hamlet in 1810, with its cottages grouped in

tranquil asymmetry around a green (see pp.214, 215), united utility with Picturesque form and plan; only four years earlier, George Dance had designed a village at East Stratton where cottages that copied the local vernacular had been placed in total symmetry. The glory of Blaise Hamlet, celebrated in innumerable decorative china cottages, made it difficult for those who in their hearts preferred symmetrical plans to hold their own. Blaise Hamlet amalgamated the shaggy picturesque of Morland and the Dutch with that prime Regency attribute, neatness; united, they were irresistible. It influenced the village of Edensor at Chatsworth, planned and built by Paxton and the sixth Duke of Devonshire from 1838; Edensor became, to all intents and purposes, part of the Picturesque ensemble of palace, park and village. In 1835, Duke and architect had together seen Blaise Hamlet; the Duke wrote in his diary; 'The most perfect cottages . . . I ever saw . . . Paxton was struck with the chimneys'.[11] They visited the regular village of Nuneham Courtenay two days later; no comment and no imitation.

## Urban landscape and geometry

The geometrically planned and landscaped town persisted throughout the Regency, despite the fashionable appeal of irregularity. When Edward Willes of Leamington called in P. F. Robinson to design the incorporation into the town of part of the Willes estate, he was given such a plan in May 1823; it approaches the scheme eventually approved (Fig. 40). Unfortunately the project hung fire and was never completed. The design is formal, with much use of large gardens and two impressive tree-lined thoroughfares; it employs a crescent and a square, the latter containing a church, a well-tried device for instilling a sense of community. The church, an extraordinary affair in 'Anglo-Norman style', closed the view from the parade.[12] Robinson also designed a cottage orné at the edge of the developed area, Binswood Cottage (Fig. 160; see p.217). The prospectus for the scheme makes clear the picturesque rurality of the surrounding countryside. The Picturesque clearly influenced Robinson's plan, but as clearly the plan is of a traditional nature.

Picturesque ideas deeply affected the development of Edinburgh, which achieved both symmetry and the Picturesque. Despite Gilpin's unappreciative comment: 'Arthur's seat presents an unpleasing view from every situation',[13] the natives early saw the advantages of their city's topography; in 1786, for example, a proposed new road was described as 'the most picturesque and elegant approach that possibly can be to any city whatsoever'.[14] By 1825 a different adjective was being used, an adjective that signified an enrichment of the concept of the Picturesque — 'our own romantic town'.[15] This vision subjugated the quarrels, the controversies, the financial limitations, the meannesses, and produced the grandly beautiful city that partly stands today.

The development would have begun earlier, had not the combination of bad harvests and Pitt's war halted expensive public works; before those misfortunes, Robert Adam had been instructed to design Charlotte Square on a scale that eschewed frugality.[16] The war ended, and in January 1813 the Commissioners for the New Town received competition plans. One came from William Stark, whose observations were published in June 1814 as a remarkably distinguished *Report . . . on the Plans for laying out the Grounds between Edinburgh and Leith*;[17] the report might be called 'modern' were that not grossly to flatter present-day planning.

Stark considered that the architect's task was to appreciate and exploit the merits of his site, not to impose something alien upon it. He advanced two principles; that symmetry of plan was of little value, and

that convenience and scenic effect were all important. Streets should follow the natural contours of the ground; trees were of prime consequence. One reason for preserving trees was that 'Beauty of site will be found most likely a vendible commodity'. To prevent any misunderstanding of the motives of these hard-headed burghers, two facts should be mentioned: no buildings were to be erected on the bridge over Calton Hill, a restriction that reduced profits, and the owners of new buildings on Prince's Street were paid £3,500 to persuade them to reduce the height of their buildings and preserve the view.[18] From 1825 it became axiomatic that the picturesque valley between Prince's Street and the Old Town should remain open. The beauty of Edinburgh is enhanced by contrast, 'the convenience of a rectangular distribution of the buildings, uniting with the elegance of the encurved street and the circus, and the regular outline of the whole finely contrasted with the crowded and shapeless masses of the Old Town and the bold ruggedness of the natural scenery'.[19] Even Elsam might have been satisfied with the effect of Playfair's Royal Circus, of which the 'unequal height' was said to enhance the 'singular and picturesque grouping of the elegant streets . . . the blemish . . . essential to the general beauty of the whole' (Fig. 41).[20]

## The synthesis

Masterly as was the planning of Edinburgh, Nash's vision, whether in the Picturesque urban landscape of Regent Street (Fig. 42) — no trees — or in the villa landscape of Regent's Park, was more strikingly original.

In the Regent Street area, the buildings were released from the straitjacket of parallel roads; the roads themselves had a new function, that of providing viewpoints of the type thought beautiful over three centuries earlier by Alberti. Earlier plans by Leverton and Chawner had been dictated by geometry, with few concessions to the Picturesque and little attention paid to levels; the plan by John White, the Duke of Rutland's architect, had serpentine avenues articulating the site in an old-fashioned manner, with landscape included as a gesture. They lacked the vitality and integrated views of Nash's plans; had the latter's 'Grand Approach from Charing Cross to the British Museum' been executed, the West End would have been united.

Nash's effects in the Park were achieved by combining garden geometry with the informalities of the landscape garden and with Picturesque devices. The priorities were demonstrated when he planted ahead of building in order to establish maturity as quickly as possible; as early as 1812 it was said that 'Regent's Park will in a few years afford a notable example of the union of the ancient and modern styles of planting', that it would combine the 'grandeur of avenues, open groves, and circular platoons of wood' with 'the variety of light groups, close thickets, and single trees', episodes of 'wildness and rude scenery' with 'the most refined elegance', glades of 'smoothly mown turf' with the 'most elegant, delicate, and showy exotics'.[21]

Such joys would doubtless have been exhibited also in Nash's masterly plan, alas largely unexecuted, for Leamington Spa. The differences between the Picturesque of the New Town at Edinburgh, that of Nash as shown in Regent's Street and Regent's Park in London, and that of the projected but unfulfilled development at Leamington, are instructive.

Recently fashionable spa towns such as Cheltenham, Leamington and Tunbridge Wells had grown apace. The same improved roads that encouraged 'tourists' in search of the Picturesque encouraged other excursions: 'Those pilgrimages which our ancestors took to gratify their love of change under the mask of devotion, we now take from the same

motives, under the equally specious pretence of pursuing health, or more sincere avowal of pleasure'. The Leamington Priors of 1801, with three hundred and fifteen souls, had by 1841 been rechristened 'Royal Leamington Spa', and had become the haunt of 'dukes and their duchesses, marquesses, earls and barons, with their coroneted partners — not to mention the many Ladies Augustas and Louisas, baronets and their spouses, besides military knights and their ladies . . .'.[22] Such fine folk provided fine fare for the building speculator.

Nash's plan was produced for Edward Willes, who had previously received three plans for an area bisected by the River Leam from P. F. Robinson, who had worked for Willes in another part of the town (Fig. 40). The dates of Robinson's plans (October 17th, 21st and 23rd, 1826) probably reflect Willes' speedy rejections. All three plans were based on a tight grid street system surrounded by 'villa land'; there was no

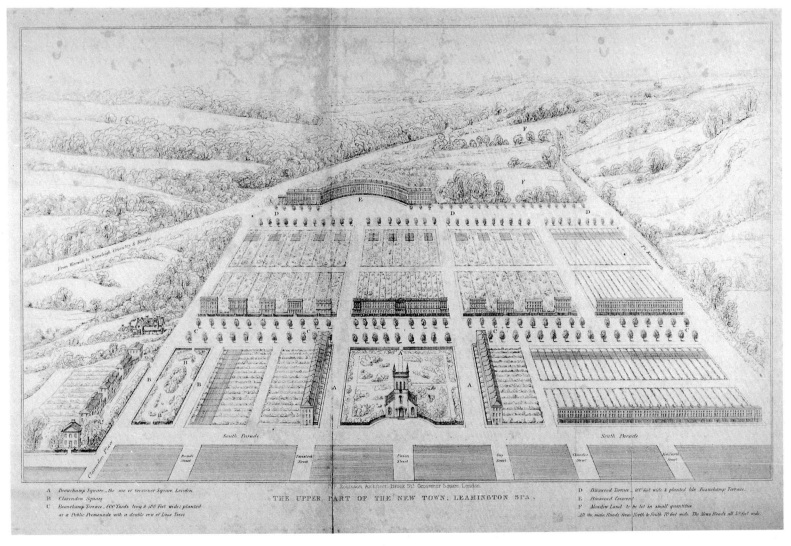

40 'The Upper Part of the New Town, Leamington Spa', designed by P. F. Robinson, 1825

41 'Part of Royal Circus Edinburgh', by Thomas Shepherd, 1830

42 'Harmonic Institution, Regent Street', London, 1827

integration of houses and park. The second plan introduced three crescents, plus two curved streets, but the rows of houses to the south were set sideways to the park, missing the possibilities of the terrain. All three plans lacked flexibility and flair.[23]

Willes turned to the most flexible and poetic of English Picturesque architects, who produced a plan of effortless brilliance (Pl. XXV). There can hardly be a more poignant illustration of the difference between a worthy but pedestrian planner, and one of genius, than that afforded by the Robinson and Nash plans for Leamington. Had the former been implemented (and, in the teeth of architects, developers, and local and national government officers and politicians, preserved), we would exclaim at the beauty of Regency Leamington. Had the latter been implemented, we would think Leamington an earthly Paradise (although the large amount of green would have made its destruction more certain).

The Nash plan carried further the Picturesque integration of buildings and landscape dazzlingly displayed in the Regent's Park. If the Regent's Park project was 'rus in urbe', the plan for Leamington was 'urbs in rure'. Rather than a plan for a metropolis, it is a plan for a provincial town adjacent to open countryside. The urban spaces are concentrated on the west side of the development, next to the older parts of the town; here the streets tend to be straight or geometrical; even the paths in squares and crescents are subdivided geometrically. Despite the urbanism, almost every range of building faces park or greenery. In the vicinity of the villas, the streets become informal and serpentine; the villas, cunningly placed, are shielded with belts of trees

to suggest boundless grounds. The river and its meadows remain as a green thread running through the whole. Particularly happy is the way 'Leam Crescent' presents a geometrical curve that becomes a longer, serpentine road, an idea used in a different way by Decimus Burton in Palmyra Square in Brighton. An ambiguous structure in the centre of the radial plantation adjacent to 'Newbold Crescent' is revealed by a later rough sketch to have been intended as a temple; the antique gods were still to be admitted.

Nash himself came to Leamington and stayed at the Regent's Hotel, perhaps to encourage an already flagging scheme. It all came to very little; the concept was diluted beyond retrieval. A few attractive fragments of what was actually built remain in a town ravaged by modern development.[24]

## The urban park

Another interpretation of the Picturesque survives at Tunbridge Wells, a spa that, like Leamington, grew from a 'fashionable hamlet'.[25] The Calverley Estate was designed by Decimus Burton, who had been closely associated with Nash. The Estate never attained its proposed size; had it done so, it would have been a perfectly controlled small development which, though lacking the brilliance and sophistication of the Nash plan for Leamington, shows something of Nash's influence. Especially felicitous is the 'Park', which was built as a miniature park to contain twenty-four villas rather than one large mansion; they faced south and south-west before a broad crescent-shaped drive. Its lodges were in

**43** 'Villas in Calverley Park', Tunbridge Wells, designed by Decimus Burton, 1829

diverse styles: Farnborough Lodge and Baston Lodge were cottages ornés — the former with a cross above the gable — Keston Lodge was Italianate; Victoria Lodge (named after the Princess, not the Queen) was Doric. The villas were not stucco, but of local sandstone; most had plain and dignified Italianate façades and compact, 'unPicturesque' plans; the effect of the group as a whole was completely Picturesque (Fig. 43). Adjacent was the Crescent, a dignified composition with shops and a colonnade; the intention was to provide convenient shopping facilities, but the attractions of the lively Pantiles district proved too strong and most of the shops were converted to houses.[26]

A similar Picturesque development, Park Crescent in Brighton, lined up Italianate villas in horseshoe formation around a large park with serpentine paths and Picturesque planting contained within the horseshoe; the houses present a plain façade to the street but picturesquely broken shapes towards the park, which on the south side is enclosed by a wall and a gateway which has (or had until very recently) a fine pair of piers surmounted by a lion and lioness.[27] The whole was designed by Amon Wilds in 1829. The sea gave Brighton and Hove further Picturesque possibilities; the three largest (three-sided) squares either continue as crescents, or open themselves up in a way that seems to take the sea into their embrace.

A handful of such urban assemblages, greatly reduced through ignorance and greed, still survive in Britain. They adorn the land; they blend in perfect balance the delights of town and countryside, constituting one of the most beguiling manifestations of the aesthetic values of the Picturesque.

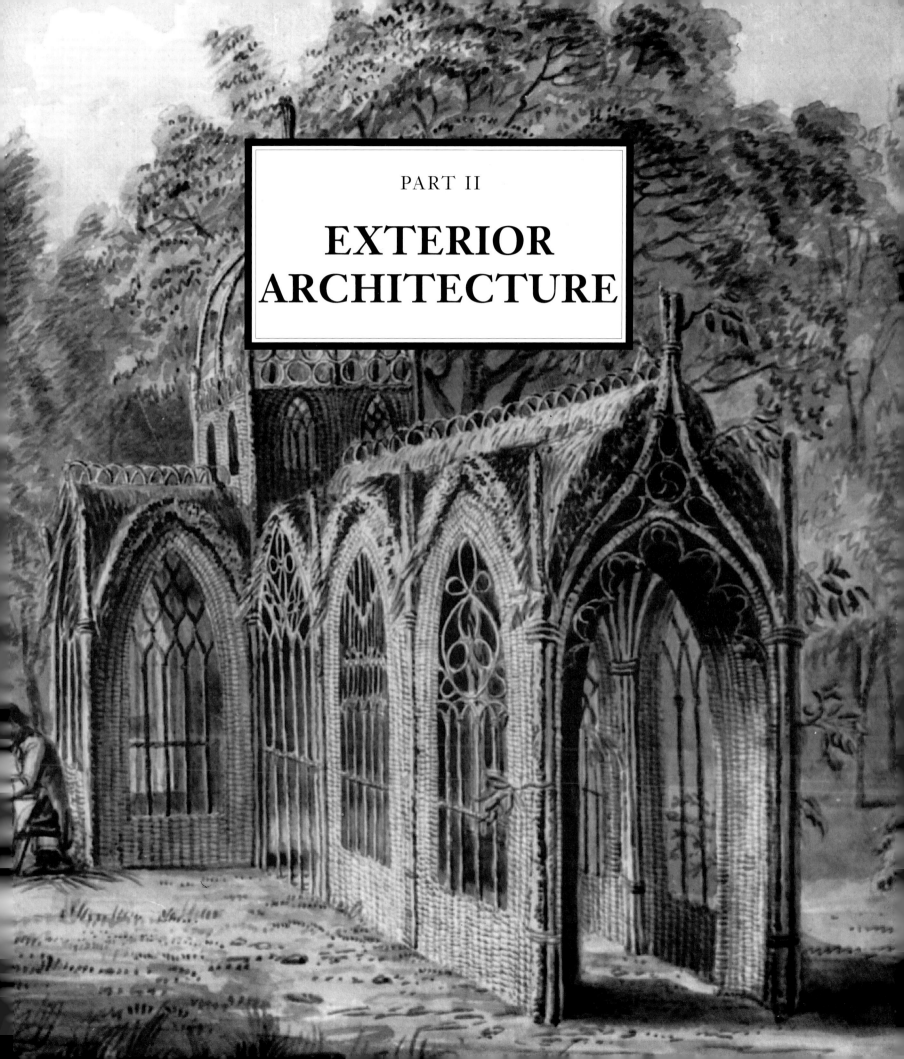

# PART II

# EXTERIOR ARCHITECTURE

# Chapter one

# Formative Influences

## The stylistic quandary

The architects of the Regency were confronted with a majestic body of instruction, opinion and prejudice; it was not infrequently contradictory. Inconsistencies clouded the issue; in taking one path, architects might declare that they were taking another. The deciding factor was, no doubt, temperament.

There were three principal ways in which architects responded to this formidable mass of theory. The first was to discover and follow the rules of a favoured style — but not slavishly. Both sides of this equation — the rules, and their imaginative interpretation — were repeatedly emphasised by theorists (beginning with Vitruvius). Sir John Soane, for instance, in the first of the conscientiously earnest series of lectures given in his capacity as Professor of Architecture at the Royal Academy, said in 1809: 'We must be intimately acquainted with not only what the Ancients have done, but endeavour to learn from the Works what they would have done. We shall thereby become Artists not mere Copyists: we shall avoid servile imitation and . . . improper application.'[1] It is true that Soane, having stressed the importance of avoiding mechanical copying, later in the same lecture told his students that the Greeks 'cultivated Architecture so successfully that they left to succeeding ages only the humble task of imitating their works', which will 'perhaps never be equalled'.[2] If their Professor was so confused in his counsels, what were the poor students to do? Such contradictions were common. To put this in context, one should recall that it was thought no disgrace to copy either paintings or buildings, especially in the process of learning; the exaggerated homage paid to mediocre originality is a modern whim. Nash had no hesitation in allowing a copy of old Somerset House, thought to be the work of Inigo Jones, to be placed in a most prominent part of his new Regent Street; the only change made

was to replace the pilasters of the original with columns, perhaps in homage to Laugierian theory.

The second response was to adopt a style and to follow its rules — when they were known — implicitly, or as implicitly as possible given the constraints of modern life and the English climate. This course was attempted by the more pedantic Greek Revival architects, sometimes with arid and forbidding results; C. R. Cockerell, who began as a Greek revivalist,[3] expressed a general reaction in his comment: 'The great end in view seems to have been attainment of the negative merit of avoiding errors, to what purpose have the Elgin and Grecian discoveries, the purchases of fine painting for the ornament of our country and the travels of individuals tended if we are to be quakers in architecture'.[4]

The third possibility was to follow not the rules of one style, be it with servility or originality, but to take the ingredients of various styles and make an original synthesis, as Repton had done with gardens. The options increased with the addition of Egyptian, Gothic, and oriental styles to the classical repertoire, but the method could be used with more limited means.

A striking example of the last approach — in architecture, interior decoration, and furniture — is seen in the style created by Thomas Hope. The Roman, Greek and Egyptian motifs which provide most of his chosen ingredients are usually archaeologically correct, but the result is a novel synthesis. Dance, himself less original only than his pupil, Soane, appreciated the originality of Hope; he remarked in 1804 of Hope's house in Duchess Street that he thought it 'better than he expected, and that by the singularity of it good might be done as it might contribute to emancipate the public from that rigid adherence to a certain style of architecture and of furnishing and unshacle the Artists . . . [he] derided the prejudice of Uniting Designs in Architecture within certain rules, which in art though held out as laws had never been satisfactorily explained . . . architecture unshacled would afford to the greatest genius the greatest opportunities of producing the most powerful effects of the human mind. . . .'[5] It is clear from Dance's own work that he construed this freedom as the freedom to make a synthesis. The lack of any overriding rigid orthodoxy and the box of architectural delights to hand meant that the patron in Regency times had more scope in choice than ever before.[6]

An important influence on both patron and (if he could manage it) architect, was that of the 'travels of individuals', which usually took the form of the Grand Tour. By the beginning of the Regency period this had been a well established custom for a century or so; the tastes of the upper classes had been cradled in France and, more especially, in Italy, at the most generous and impressionable time of life. The tourists returned laden with objects and ideas, eager, where circumstances allowed, to profit at home by their experiences. They saw, especially in Italy, buildings and objects, antique and modern, of a variety, a magnificence and a sophistication that hardly existed at home. The modern palaces of Rome, for instance, were packed with antique sculpture and paintings of the highest quality, some of which the noble owners were willing to sell — 'the palaces of the Barberini, Borghese, Pamfili, Falconieri, Lancelotti, and Spada princes, were despoiled by English gold. . . . One stands amazed at the number of pictures introduced by the enterprise of private picture dealers in England between 1795 and 1815, during the hottest time of the war'[7] — and they themselves were overwhelmingly impressive examples of much of the most accomplished Renaissance and post-Renaissance architecture in Europe. If anything could teach humility to the proud aristocracy of England, at that date the proudest in Europe, it would have been the sight of the Roman palaces. Their interior decoration was unsurpassed: it included the richest and most developed forms of arabesque, from Renaissance to neo-classical, far beyond anything ever developed in England (see pp.233, 234, 235): exquisitely sensitive ornaments in the stucco re-invented in the early sixteenth century, including the admired proto-neoclassical decorations of Algardi (see p.230) at the Palazzo Pamphili; the 'antique drapery' (see pp.261–2) in the 'loggia di Galatea' at the Farnesina, beneath Raphael's godlike frescoes; the luxurious neo-classical decorations of the Palazzo Borghese — the riches were inexhaustible. The Roman palaces influenced the English both directly and through Percier and Fontaine, themselves a fount of inspiration for the Regency. And although Rome was the goal of the Grand Tour, it did not stop there. Italy was full of Renaissance architecture and works of art, which frequently display a combined delicacy and virility that is nearer to the antique than anything produced by neo-classicism.

It was a tragedy that the tradition of the Grand Tour was interrupted by the Napoleonic wars, which over long periods, long enough for a generation to grow up that lacked the cosmopolitan education of its fathers, rendered continental Europe impassable; by 1816, when the fourth and last volume of the *Antiquities of Athens* was published, the author of its preface could write 'every youth who had the means, made *what was then* [author's italics] called the grand tour'.[8] This isolation may help to explain increasing symptoms of provincial insularity, most evident in the eccentricities of aesthetic antiquarianism. Be that as it may, taste was deeply affected by the cargo of ideas imported from the Grand Tour, the influence of which lay primarily in its transmission of an antique and Renaissance culture absorbed whilst the youthful pores were open.

## Laugier: the column

The influence of the Abbé Laugier was of quite another order; primarily intellectual in its nature, it affected even those architects who did not succumb to it, and it 'operated very powerfully on the superficial part of European connoisseurs'.[9] Laugier's functionalist and rationalist theories were published in his *Essaie* and *Observations* of 1753 and 1765 respectively; Soane, one of the most deeply impressed, possessed eleven copies of the *Essaie*.[10]

Laugier was a Jesuit priest who rejected the Counter-Reformation baroque of his Order in favour of the purest antique style, a style he saw as based on materials and function. In reading his works, it becomes clear that his theories, couched as they were in rationalist and logical terms, sprang from observations made in the light of an exact and refined taste that is peculiarly French; he expressed the characteristics of French taste, its combination of elegance and power, in an extreme form.[11] His approval of the French architects Perrault and Soufflot demonstrated this. Readers who might not be convinced by his minimalism might well be convinced by his taste. Restrictive as his theories were, he was not opposed to rational innovation: 'Hé! qu'importe que ce soit une nouveauté, pourvu qu'elle soit raisonnable'.[12]

Beginning with the primitive hut (Fig. 44), to which he attributed a high significance, Laugier analysed the forms of Greek architecture — the column, the entablature, the pediment, etc. — in the light of their evolution from a pristine construction in wood (Pls IX, XXVI) to a later reproduction in stone.[13] He urged that all form that was not based on the logic of primitive construction, and all decoration that did not have an origin in construction or nature (the triglyphs that had evolved from rafters, the drops of water that were formalised as guttae), should ruthlessly be expunged.

The most beautiful architectural member was the free-standing column. Columns were not to be attached to walls;[14] they should stand on the pavement, not on pedestals;[15] they should be given 'la diminution ordinaire', not an entasis, 'un renflement vers le tiers de la

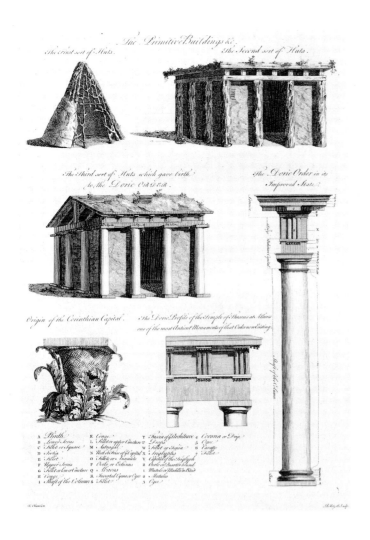

hauteur de leur fust'; they should not be carved 'à bosses';[16] they should not be replaced with pilasters, which are never necessary (although they had been used by the Greeks).[17] They should never have arcades placed above them: 'Ces arcades sont vicieuses . . . un usage contre nature . . . elles sont absolutment inutiles'.[18] Laugier's strong language on the last architectural solecism may have been prompted by the strength of its attractions, which had good classical precedent, as in the Temple of Bacchus at Rome, illustrated by Desgodetz;[19] such arcades had been used in some of the most beautiful buildings of the Renaissance.

This revolutionary emphasis on the beauty of the utilitarian column contradicted the aesthetic theory of the column accepted since the Renaissance. Alberti had laid down that the 'pleasure and delight which we feel on the view of any Building, arise from nothing else but Beauty and Ornament', and defined 'Beauty' as a 'harmony of the parts . . . nothing cou'd be added, diminished or altered, but for the worse'. The column belonged to the category of 'Ornament' — 'The principal ornament in all Architecture certainly lies in Columns', and Ornament was a 'kind of auxiliary brightness and improvement to Beauty . . . somewhat added or fastened on, rather than proper and innate'.[20] This conception of the column as auxiliary ornament, derived from Roman rather than Greek architecture, was adopted by the architects who succeeded Alberti, including the venerated Palladio.

Laugier's enthronement of the load-bearing column as the most beautiful architectural member encouraged its employment in a way different from that which had become traditional, even where some of his strictures were ignored, as for example by Ledoux, who was fond of 'vicieuses' arcades. Without this new attitude to the column, such buildings as Joseph Bonomi's Rosneath (Pl. XXXII) or Fowler's

**44** 'The Primitive Buildings', by Sir William Chambers, 1759

**45** A survey of Stonehenge, 23rd September, 1817

**XXVI** A primitive temple in wood

**XXVII** Blenheim Palace, designed by Sir John Vanbrugh and Nicholas Hawksmoor

**XXVIII** Detail of stucco from 'The Entrance Portico and West Front' of Brighton Pavilion, c.1820

**46** 'View of a design for the lodge at Bentley Priory', Mddx., 1790, by Sir John Soane

**XXIX** A shepherd's hut between Naples and Portici, c.1783, by J. R. Cozens

*Overleaf* **XXX** Lansdown Tower, Bath, designed by H. E. Goodridge, 1824–7

Hungerford Market (Pl. XXXIV) would probably have looked quite different.[21] One wonders what wistful pre-Laugierian longings might have been in Soane's mind when he wrote in one of his three copies of Colonna's *Hynerotomachia*, beside a passage that ran 'Mais les Corinthiennes, & Ioniques, qui sont grailes, estoient là mises pour parement & beauté', the words 'Corinthian & Ionic used for ornament'.[22]

Regarded simplistically, the effect of Laugier's doctrine on Regency architects was to divide them into those who followed him and concentrated upon the full column, and those who disregarded his prohibitions and guiltlessly used pilasters; again simplistically, it divided them into 'Greeks' such as Soane and 'Italians' such as Nash, those who saw buildings structurally and those who saw them scenically. Of course, even those most influenced by Laugier often disobeyed him, including Soane; no architect who was an artist would have allowed himself to be totally so restricted.

For Laugier's strictures extended well beyond the column. Entablatures should always be straight;[23] pediments should always be triangular;[24] they should never be placed one upon the other, which could not be surpassed for absurdity.[25] When Soane taught his students, as in 1813, the 'impropriety and absurdity of "Domes, Blocking Courses, Arches, Pediments, Pedestals under Columns, Pilasters and Columns used together in the same composition — Caryatides, etc."'[26] he was paraphrasing Laugier: thence came his 'Cistercian' attitudes.

Laugier's rules gave a logical basis to the Greek Revival. As late as 1826 Mrs. Cresy found it worthwhile to translate Milizia's *Lives of Celebrated Architects*, which repeated Laugier's teachings with added refinements: fluted columns 'are not proper in the interior of edifices where rain cannot enter', because flutes are a rationalization of the channels caused by rain. Milizia in some details relaxed a little; he allowed statues to stand on pediments (Laugier thought it illogical to put them where real people would suffer vertigo) but not to sprawl on them.[27]

Laugier was alive to the attacks that would be made on his reductionism (as Sir William Chambers said, 'it is only by special favour that he condescends to tolerate doors or windows, or even walls')[28] and admitted that it would perhaps be objected 'que je réduis l'Architecture presqu'à rien'. His reply to the charge was to enthrone genius and geometry; they held the key, and they would give infinite variety: 'Avec le peu que je lui mets en main, s'il a du génie, et une légère teinture de Géométrie, il trouvera le secret de varier ses plans à l'infini, et de regagner par la diversité des formes, ce qu'il perd du côté des superfluités que je lui retranche'.[29] Elsewhere he declared that there were only two ways of creating new architecture. The first was 'd'inventer des moulures dont la forme n'ait pas été connue.' The second was 'de combiner d'une manière nouvelle les moulures

anciennes'.[30] Dance and Hope followed the second course and invented novel ways of using ancient forms; the possibility that distinct styles might be combined to create a new architecture appears not to have crossed Laugier's mind, although his proposals for Gothic come near it.

## French Romantic Classicism: primitivism

Geometry . . . Laugier's advice chimed in with the growing interest, even in England, in elementary geometric forms and primitivism. In 1715 Colen Campbell in his *Vitruvius Britannicus* had praised, with reference to the 'Simplicity of the Ancients', the square and the circle.[31] Kent and Roger Morris had proposed to use the cube and cubic forms as the basic element in composition;[32] the interest in cubes is clear in Kent's work, which has affinities with some Regency architecture. The tendency manifested itself more uncompromisingly in France, in reaction against a rococo more uninhibited than anything that England had seen; by a natural association of ideas, the virtues of primitive architecture were equated with the virtues of the primitive — and republican — society from which it sprang, and the new style assumed a moral (and ultimately a revolutionary) dimension.

This new French style, engendered by the union of primitivism and elementary geometry with Laugierian doctrine, has been christened 'French Romantic Classicism'. Strong, at times forceful to the point of brutality, it was in French hands capable of great refinement (and co-existed with a suave and civilised French classicism unaffected by primitivism). It relied much on cubical and cylindrical forms, the column and the pyramid (Fig. 80). It much affected Regency architecture; in 1825 Thomas Hardwick wrote that 'the names of Le Roy, Dewailly, Peyre, Le Doux, Antoine, Perronet, Soufflot, and others . . . will ever reflect the greatest credit on the state of the art in France at that period'. His comment was made in a memoir on Chambers, who in 1774 went to Paris and 'afterwards expressed himself particularly struck with the great improvement in the French architecture which had taken place in a few years'.[33] In the words of a modern critic, Boullée, de Wailly, Peyre, Antoine, Ledoux, Gondoin, Brogniart, Chalgrin, represent 'one style, which is, broadly speaking, the Dance style'.[34] They represent also prominent aspects of the Soane and Smirke styles.

The romantic primitivism that permeated 'French Romantic Classicism' also affected the English attitude towards Gothic; (at times classical and Gothic primitivism were felt almost to be one; Bishop Hurd, for example, thought that 'Greek antiquity much resembles the Gothic').[35] Primitivism found sophisticated realisation in the classical idiom earlier than in the Gothic — as was only to be expected, since the classical vocabulary had been highly developed as a language, whereas the Gothic 'language' was unparsed (see pp.160–1).

# New techniques: cast iron, stone, stucco

There is yet another implication in the work of Laugier that had a meaning for the Regency. His identification of function with beauty had a significance for engineering; it helped to make feats of engineering acceptable as works of art (Piranesi had something of the same attitude) as, at the other end of the scale, it helped to make huts and primitivism acceptable. A building much praised by Laugier, the church of St. Geneviève by Soufflot, had a good deal of iron concealed in its construction; it would have been interesting to know Laugier's opinion of the proper use of this material. The opportunity his theories offered of sympathetically including engineering within the discipline of architecture was missed by English architects, and the two professions developed separately.

This raises another issue with which Regency architects had to cope; that of proliferating technical resources, which made the task of choosing materials more complex and created uncertainties as to where the peculiar characteristics of the new materials might lead stylistically. At the beginning of the period, it might have seemed possible to preserve in architecture the intellectual homogeneity of earlier epochs, when art and science were one. The imminent division between aestheticism and the new technology might not have been inevitable, as was indicated by such tokens as the aesthetic awareness apparent in Regency engineering drawings,[36] the invention by the painter Alexander Naysmith of the 'bow and string' method of construction for bridges and roofs,[37] and the architectural interests of prominent engineers and the engineering interest of prominent architects. However, no British architect emulated Schinkel, who, fascinated by the English Industrial Revolution, by the machine, the factory, cast iron, zinc, and papier mâché,[38] turned to the 'radical abstraction' of developing buildings out of construction and function — although he did not forsake 'archaeological' forms.

During the first two decades of the nineteenth century the gap in Britain between architects and engineers became too wide to cross. The architects had neglected such basic requirements of their profession as mathematics: 'The consequence has been the establishment of a new branch of art whose professors are called "civil engineers"' who should, complained the architects, confine themselves to their own vocations: 'In their designs, even the best . . . there are many violations of architectural propriety . . .'.[39] After 1815, the only British architect who materially added to building technology was Robert Smirke, with his extensive use of concrete for foundations and iron girders.[40]

Cast iron, one of the major new techniques available, was widely adopted by architects. Bridges were obvious early candidates for its use, and cast-iron bridges such as those at Coalbrookdale and Sunderland were quickly adopted into the Picturesque canon (although Lady Holland said of the bridge at Coalbrookdale that it was 'more curious from its novelty and use than beautiful . . . the dull black of the iron assorts ill with limpid streams and verdant banks').[41] It was inevitable that a substance that could span rivers would be used to span large interiors; the Mill at Castle Foregate in Shrewsbury, built in 1796–7, was perhaps the first structure in Europe held together by an internal metal frame of iron columns and iron beams.[42] Cast iron entered non-industrial architecture through its use in conservatories (Fig. 34, Pl. XVII), and was rapidly adopted for other buildings; in 1813–14 Rickman's St. George's Church at Everton was built almost entirely of cast iron. C. R. Cockerell recommended cast-iron beams to support long stretches of unsupported entablature — he liked the 'agreeably wide intercolumniation' of the Tuscan Order as seen in paintings by Poussin:[43] in 1819 he designed a Gothic hammer-beam roof in cast iron.[44]

Nash used cast iron habitually. In 1795 he built a cast-iron bridge at Stanford, Worcestershire, which collapsed. Undeterred, he employed cast iron extensively in his London developments — the Doric columns at Carlton House Terrace, for example, have cast iron cores covered with stucco. At Buckingham Palace, his use of cast iron to support the floors led to acrimonious controversy. Consciousness of the dangers of fire helped to encourage the use of cast iron: Hartley's patent system of nailing iron plates to the structural carpentry of houses was thought to inhibit it. Smirke habitually used cast iron as fireproofing. The Pavilion at Brighton has domes made of cast-iron plates covered with stucco; the upper part of the towers is in the same material, with no brick used, and the Bath stone minarets have cores of cast iron covered with bitumen. It was used decoratively, as in the Corridor of the Pavilion, where it simulates bamboo. And it became an essential part of that beguiling

47 Design for canopies and balconies by C. A. Busby, 1810

Regency invention, the house with cast iron verandahs, balconies, and railings, allowing a veil of fantasy to be thrown, at little cost, over what was often a cut-price façade (Fig. 47).

Improved techniques in the handling of stone gave opportunities for virtuosity to architects sensitive to materials, a merit by no means ubiquitous during the Regency (although even Nash could show it when working for the King). The interest in primitivism had drawn attention to megalithic virtues (Fig. 45), praised by Vitruvius and Alberti.[45] Le Roy and James Stuart, the rival French and British delineators of Greek architecture, both drew attention to Athenian skills in handling large stones, although the comedy of their disagreements extended to this subject; the editor of Stuart's 1794 volume mentioned that the angular block of the architrave of the temple of Jupiter Olympus 'must measure nearly twenty-one feet six inches long, about three feet thick, and not less than six feet six inches high . . .' — bigger than the stone in the Propylaea lauded by Le Roy and others.[46] It was noted by Wood that no cement had been used in the construction of the Great Temple at Baalbek, although iron pins had been used to join the shafts of the columns.[47]

One of the most famous of all engineers, Rennie, was noted for the accuracy of his jointed stone. As was Thomas Harrison, who attracted encomiums for his work at Chester Castle; another architect noted for his love of large stones, C. R. Cockerell, praised Harrison as 'undoubtedly the noblest genius in arche. we ever had' and said of Chester Castle: 'certainly a great hand is visible . . . it is in the great merit of the masonry that Harrison's merit lies . . .'. At Chester 'six monoliths of ten tons each were placed on their pedestals one night by Mr Harrison'.[48] Cockerell commended Smirke, another architect interested in industrial methods: 'Since the days of Trajan and Hadrian no such stones have been used as have recently been employed at the British Museum where eight hundred stones from 5–9 tons form the front'.[49] Before an unfortunate economy of the recent restoration, the minarets of the Royal Pavilion were composed of several large stones slipped over the cast-iron core like a collar. John Foulston prided himself that every stone of the commemorative column erected in 1824 as part of his motley group at Devonport (Fig. 136), 101 feet high, was hoisted and set in place without scaffolding.[50]

There was an alternative to stone — stucco. This was applied over the local building material, be it flint or brick, or a composite mixture, or, as was not infrequent, mere lathe and plaster; this last method was common with bow windows. The contrast between stone and stucco, between the monolithic stones of Chester Castle and the stucco façades of Regent's Park, illustrates the tensions present in Regency creativity.

Stucco had been advocated in England since the middle of the eighteenth century. Patents for oil-bound stucco had been taken out in 1765 (by David Wark) and in 1773 (by Liardet). Both were bought out by the inexorable opportunist Robert Adam, who had first used 'Adam's new invented patent stucco' at Kenwood in 1767–9 (Lord Mansfield, the client, said that marble would have been cheaper in the end). In 1778–9 Adam made a contract to stucco new houses in Bloomsbury Square, of which the architect was John Nash — probably his first use of the material. In 1796 a patent was taken out for Parker's Stucco, which used water as a medium; this was the 'natural water cement . . . of England, since most improperly and absurdly termed Roman Cement . . . for the purpose of mystery or for enhancing their value . . .'.[51] When that patent expired in 1810, the market was flooded; by 1819, forty different preparations were available. Another invention, 'Portland' cement, made of chalk and blue clay, was widely used. In 1819 'Hamlin's Mastic', used for moulded ornament, was patented. New methods of roofing appeared, including 'Lord Stanhope's Composition', which used tar, chalk, and slates.[52]

Stucco had an ancient and honourable history; it was used by the Greeks and the Romans, the Renaissance and the Baroque. In the hands of Regency architects, it lost respectability. A description of Fonthill after the collapse suggests a reason: 'The appearance of the ruins, as they now stand, produces an appearance of meanness mixed with grandeur that it is impossible to describe. The greatness of the parts which still exist, and which, from being covered with cement [stucco] have the appearance of stone; and the shattered remains of lath and plaster, studwork, and bricks, and bond timber; and above all, the long strings of tarred packthread hanging from the nails and other remains of what were once mouldings worked in Roman cement, have a tattered appearance. . . . We feel as if we had discovered that what, at a distance, we had supposed to be a marble statue, was, in reality, a mere bundle of rags and straw . . . .'.[53] People had begun to dislike what they saw as the deceptions of stucco. Cockerell rejected Wyatt's stucco even in its unimpaired state: 'nothing can be so dull unsightly as the great stuccoed wall. The rusty brown colour. The flimsy unsatisfactorily substitute for stone . . .'.[54] It was not peeling paint that aroused disgust; in the Regency period the surface was usually treated with transparent washes to resemble stone (see pp.150, 217). One theory held that stucco was unsuited to the English climate: 'Palladio who invented, and so happily adopted intonaco or plaster in the palaces which he built at Vicenza, had the advantage of climate. . . . But in England, and in a great city, this substitution had to resist the effects of an atmosphere perpetually charged with damps and the smoke of sea-coal'.[55] Perhaps its use accentuates what one feels to be a certain meanness of aspect in much of the architecture of the period, not only in England; similar deficiencies are evident in the stucco architecture of early nineteenth century Brussels.

These drawbacks apart, stucco had an individual character that marked the buildings that employed it. It has been mentioned above that it was washed to imitate stone, the preferred choice as a model usually being Bath stone. The few buildings that remain uncovered with glaring white paint (one can imagine how different the Regent's Park Terraces, for instance, or, at the other end of the scale, Cronkhill (see p.110), would have looked in their original state) show, even with the washes worn away, how illusionistic it could be. Some stuccos were more stonelike than others; Portland cement tended to be too pink. Stucco was 'lined out' — incised with lines to simulate stone blocks (Fig. 47, Pl. XXVIII); the blocks thus formed were, in high quality work, washed in slightly different tints to increase the illusion of stonework (at the Marine Pavilion in Brighton, the painter Louis Barzago, who created sky ceilings within the building, painted the exterior in 'fresco'). The incised lines tended to be thinner and shallower than would have been the case had real stone been used; this gives façades a paper-thin character which has a specific aesthetic quality peculiar to itself.

Not only did technical innovation influence architectural materials; the architect's vision of the world was, like everybody else's, affected by industrialism and science, especially where these reinforced Picturesque imagery. Claude, the Poussins and Salvator Rosa had interpreted landscape in a way that came to be used by the gardeners; Wright of Derby and Loutherbourg interpreted light in a way that came to be used by architects. The latter's immensely popular 'Eidophusikon' (a miniature theatre that imitated natural phenomena) transformed perception; it may also have helped the growing interest in stained glass: 'Before the line of brilliant lamps . . . were strips of stained glass; yellow, red, green, purple, and the blue [which] could throw a tint upon the scenery'.[56] Soane saw in such light effects 'The Poetry of Architecture'. The 'sublime' qualities perceived by Burkean aesthetics in industrial activity — vastness, power, obscurity, danger, pain, flaring light and fire, plus 'excessive bitters and intolerable stenches'[57] — enlarged sensibility and added a relish for the portentousness often perceptible in the architecture of the engineers; they used the Egyptian style not only because it was functionally appropriate, but because its Stygian gloom reinforced the qualities of industrial sublimity. John Martin, who had had practical experience in the coal-mines, and who in 1835 drew up a plan for 'Working and Ventilating Coal Mines' for submission to a Select Committee on Accidents in mines,[58] illustrated 'Paradise Lost' using images drawn from open-cast coal mines, salt mines, the Thames Tunnel, and Piranesi's etchings of Roman sewers; his images powerfully affected Regency imagination.

The sensibility that appreciated the sublimity of industrial illuminations is evident in a proposal of 1827 to install a 'flaring light' at Windsor Castle. A novelty 'of striking effect' was planned: 'When His Majesty is there, a flag is to fly on one of the towers during the day, and during the night a blaze of gas light will occupy the same station'.[59]

It never happened; one of George IV's ideas that Queen Adelaide did not have to undo.

## The Vanbrughian synthesis

The propagandists of the Picturesque had a great deal to say about architecture, with decided effect on architectural style (see pp.81–8 for the effect on planning). One particular architect was singled out for special praise, an architect from the past who had been subject to more facetious ridicule than any other great architect working in England — Vanbrugh. As Gilbert Laing Meason said in 1828: 'Vanbrugh as an architect was not understood for nearly a century'.[60] The qualities for which he was now praised are enlightening; they varied according to the eulogist.

Reynolds, for instance, asked of architecture: 'has it not in its power to address itself to the imagination with effect, by more ways than one generally employed by architects?' His reply, which anticipated Alison, was that the imagination should be affected 'by means of association of ideas', a facility 'shared with poetry and painting'. He went on to say that: 'it is from hence, in a great degree, that, in the buildings of Vanbrugh, who was a poet as well as an architect, there is a greater degree of imagination than we shall find perhaps in any other. . . . For this purpose, Vanbrugh appears to have had resource to some of the principles of the Gothic architecture . . .'. The famous injunction that follows, concerning the 'barbaric splendour of those Asiatic buildings' (see p.196), has been frequently misunderstood; it was not an injunction to architects to copy Asiatic buildings, but to use them in the same manner as Vanbrugh had used the Gothic — to subsume them.[61] It was a direct invitation to a synthesis; amongst the people who heeded it were Hope, Dance, and Soane.

Uvedale Price, probably taking his cue from Reynolds, said much the same thing; Blenheim (Pl. XXVII) united in one building 'the beauty and magnificence of Grecian architecture, the picturesqueness of the Gothic, and the massive grandeur of a castle'; Vanbrugh 'as an author, and an architect . . . boldly set rules at defiance, and . . . completely disregarded all purity of style: yet . . . Blenheim and Castle Howard, the Provoked Wife and the Relapse will probably be admired, as long as the English language or nation shall continue to exist'.[62]

Payne Knight picked out from Vanbrugh's work a feature, irregular planning, that he himself advocated; the 'only architect, I know of, who has either planned or placed his houses according to the principle here recommended'.[63] Soane spoke of him as 'the Shakespeare of Architects'[64] and recommended the young architect to study the picturesque effect of his works. Vanbrugh, he said, 'for Invention, has had no equal in this Country. Boldness of Fancy, unlimited Variety, and Discrimination of Character mark all his productions. He had all the fire and power of Michael Angelo, and Bernini, without any of the elegant softness and classical delicacy of Palladio and his follows'.[65] The comment has in it a touch of the eighteenth-century reservation with which Voltaire regarded Shakespeare.

It was now that Vanbrugh, the architect who was the pioneer of the Elizabethan and castellated revivals; whose skylines attained the utmost in Picturesque effect (he has 'converted his chimnies into castles'[66] said Price); whose buildings look like towns in themselves (Price said a mansion in the country should be as a city in itself, with the variety of skyline seen in a city); who had assembled the stables and the 'meanest offices' around the house with the 'grand and picturesque effect' of the mediaeval castle, an effect that Price and Repton said modern houses should emulate; Vanbrugh had at last won full and triumphant acceptance. He had already accomplished the subtle and allusive synthesis towards which the theorists of the Picturesque groped.

## Architectural miscegenations

A synthesis of a different kind, yet one which had qualities in common with the buildings of Vanbrugh, was recommended by Payne Knight — the deliberate re-creation of architectural miscegenations brought

**48** An architectural fantasy, by Robert Adam

about by the vicissitudes of time. It is a pity that he did not conceive this idea before building Downton: 'in the pictures of Claude (Pl. X) and Gaspar [and, one might add, in the fantasy paintings of Robert Adam (Fig. 48)] we perpetually see a mixture of Grecian and Gothic architecture employed with the happiest effect in the same building; and no critic has ever yet objected to the incongruity of it: for, as the temples, tombs, and palaces of the Greeks and Romans in Italy were fortified with towers and battlements by the Goths and Lombards . . . such combinations have been naturalised. . . .' The same process, says Knight, occurred in England, but in stylistic reverse — Gothic preceded Grecian — and 'perhaps, we are becoming too rigid in rejecting such combinations in the buildings of our own country'. The effect of both processes was similar: the fortresses of our ancestors 'were transformed into Italianized villas, and decked with the porticos,

balustrades, and terraces of Jones and Palladio, affording, in many instances, the most beautiful compositions; especially when mellowed by time and neglect. . .'.[67] Here is echoed the romantic predilection for ruins that led Soane to have his own buildings depicted in grandiloquent decay.

In a later passage, Knight explicitly advised for 'irregular and picturesque houses' that 'mixed style, which characterizes the buildings of Claude and the Poussins', which admits all ornaments, from 'a plain wall or buttress, of the roughest masonry, to the most highly wrought Corinthian capital'.[68] This fragmentation of architecture was not only highly romantic; it was the romanticism of a collector of fragments; associationalism itself was constituted of the collection of fragments. It was the product of an intensely cultivated society, whose terms of reference are largely lost to the modern world.

## Chapter two

# The Sources of Architectural Vocabulary

## Classical pattern books

Theorists such as Laugier and Knight influenced architectural style, as did technical advance, but neither provided specific examples or measured drawings from which architects — and decorators and furniture makers — could extract a practical working vocabulary. This vocabulary was taken from pattern books published by other architects, and from scholarly works on the antique published by collectors and connoisseurs; these were supplemented by individual engravings, which were in some cases the same as those published between hard covers. Archaeological discoveries and the expansion of interest beyond ancient Rome to comprehend Greece, Egypt, and the Orient led to the rapid growth in the literature available. For an eighteenth and nineteenth-century architect, professional or amateur, such publications were as essential as tools to a carpenter. Towards the end of the eighteenth century they were supplemented by publications that presented the gentlemanly amateur with ready-made designs; these proliferated during the Regency.

It is at first sight surprising to discover that changes in architectural fashions did not make these books obsolete (apart, of course, from the later ready-made publications). The reason is that they were used as quarries from which constructions according to the current fashion could be assembled. There were limits to this; one could not build a Greek Revival building by consulting Desgodetz on Rome, but fashion was sufficiently omnivorous for most publications to remain in demand. The books recorded the rules, the eternal architectural verities.

One important source, the treatise of Vitruvius, was ancient; for long it was the architect's Bible, or at least the architect's Old Testament. Since no original illustrations survived, the latitude of interpretation was wide, and interpretation varied, in the manner of Holy Writ, according to the inclinations of the interpreter. A manuscript copy had been discovered early in the fifteenth century and was first printed in 1486; it was continuously reissued. Various versions were published in England during the eighteenth century, and the demand remained constant; for example, Dean Aldrich's version (he died in 1710), not published until 1789, was then republished in 1818 and 1824. William Newton's version, the first to give an English text, was published between 1771 and 1791.[1] In 1812 the Greek Revivalist William Wilkins translated Books III to VI, which he thought the most corrupted by early editors; not unexpectedly, he argued that Vitruvius had based his observations primarily upon Greek, not Roman, monuments, and illustrated his book accordingly.[2] Another and complete translation was published by Joseph Gwilt in 1826, and in 1831 Peter Legh produced *Essays on the principles of the beauty and perfection of architecture, as founded on and deduced from reason and analogy, and adapted to what may be traced of the ancient theories of taste, in the first three chapters of Vitruvius. Written with a view to restore architecture to the dignity it had in ancient Greece*.[3] By then, it was a little too late.

Then came the great textbooks of the Renaissance. Alberti's *De Re Aedificatoria*, commended to his students by Soane, much liked by C. R. Cockerell, and highly influential,[4] had been translated into English by Leoni in 1726 and reprinted in 1739. Serlio and Palladio were important — the latter had been supreme in the early eighteenth century, and although under something of a theoretical cloud during the Regency period remained influential. Nash, for instance, owed more, ultimately, to Palladio than to any other architect, and even C. H. Tatham, whose tastes were for unadorned mass, found the Basilica at Vicenza 'worthy of the ancients for magnificence and grandeur' and Villa Capra 'the chef d'oeuvre of modern architecture of any kind, and . . . in point of invention as much as the Art itself is capable of . . .';[5] the editor of the 1826 translation (dedicated to Soane) of the most rigorous of Laugierian disciples, Milizia, declared that Palladio was 'the Raphael of architecture and most justly deserves to be studied above every other'.[6] Palladio's *Quattro Libri*, first partly translated into English in 1663,[7] was translated by Leoni in 1715 and hence intermittently retranslated; a splendid edition appeared in 1738 by Isaac Ware, whose formulation of the Orders was constantly used. The first major British eighteenth-century treatise on the Orders, that of Gibbs of 1732, accepted Palladio as the principal authority, and Palladio supplied the basis of Ware's exposition of the Orders in his 1756 *A Complete Body of Architecture*, a comprehensive work that was twice reissued, and that 'remained a respected and authoritative reference at least until the end of the century'.[8] Other books specifically on the Orders, such as Vignola's *Regola*, Fréart de Chambray's *Parallèle*, and Perrault's *Ordonnance* were in constant use; all dated from the seventeenth century. The prestige of Perrault, praised by Laugier, was high. .

With Colen Campbell one arrives at the native product. His *Vitruvius Britannicus*, issued in various editions between 1715 and 1731, with a subsequent undated edition, was the first British book to include its author's executed designs. It declared a special mission to direct British architectural taste. It lauded Inigo Jones and Palladio, and indicated that the modern country house would be the principle vehicle of Britain's return to 'Ancient' — more or less equated with non-baroque — design. It was influential and imitated; subsequent volumes with the same title included two by George Richardson in 1802 and 1808, containing mostly classical designs, and five by P. F. Robinson in 1827–44, which included mediaeval and Tudor buildings. Inigo Jones was praised by William Kent in volumes that contained both Jones' and Kent's designs; first published in 1727, they were reissued in 1770 and 1835; another book of Jones and Vardy designs was published in 1744 by John Vardy. Kent did not receive much praise during the Regency but his influence is apparent, and it grew.

In 1759 came Chambers' *Treatise on Civil Architecture*, reissued in various guises nine times up to 1862, two of the editions being produced in the 1820s. Joseph Gwilt, in 1825, called it 'the only text book in our language which has yet appeared worthy of being put in the hands of the student'.[9] Chambers was rallying to the defence of Roman as against Greek architecture, although Roman archaeology continued to receive its fair share of publicity; Robert Wood and James Dawkins published their books on the ruins of Palmyra and Baalbec, the source of much rich Regency architectural ornament, in 1753 and 1757. Piranesi, despite his immoderate championship of Rome and denigration of Greece, illustrated both Roman and Greek architecture with a romantic force and glamour that deeply moved contemporaries; Soane told his Academy students that 'Piranesi alone will afford a mine of information'.[10]

The hegemony of Rome was being challenged by Greece, a challenge supported by the theories of Laugier and by some connoisseurs. In 1762 appeared the first volume of *The Antiquities of Athens* by Stuart and Revett; sponsored by the powerful Society of Dilettanti, which thus became a group interested in propagating the new style, it supplied the first accurate record of the remains of Greek classical architecture. The efforts of the Society were supplemented by the powerful propaganda in favour of Greek sculpture and architecture that emanated from Rome itself, betrayed by another Teutonic invader, the Abbé Winckelmann. In 1789 the second volume of Stuart and Revett appeared, containing the major buildings of the Acropolis; others followed in 1794, 1814, and 1830. These, together with such publications on Paestum as Thomas Major's of 1768, were the sources of the Greek Revival.

In addition to publications on ancient architecture, many miscellaneous compilations were produced that served as a mine for all engaged in the visual arts, architects, painters, decorators, furniture makers and so on. One of the most constantly used sources was one of the earliest, the various works on the art and antiquities of Rome published during the seventeenth century by Pietro Santi Bartoli, a pupil of Poussin, and G. P. Bellori, a well known antiquarian. Their publications were constantly reproduced during the eighteenth century, and remained one of the most important repertoires of design for the Regency. Another publication, the monumental series of fifteen volumes of *L'Antiquité Expliquée*, produced from 1715 by Bernard de Montfaucon, illustrated the whole range of antique artefacts, drawing freely from the work of other engravers such as Santi Bartoli. Connoisseurs who published their collections made a most important contribution; pre-eminent amongst these were the Comte de Caylus, whose collection of Egyptian, Etruscan and Roman antiquities appeared (in somewhat scratchy guise) in seven volumes between 1752 and 1757, and Sir William Hamilton, whose first collection of Greek vases was published in 1766 and 1767, his second collection between 1791 and 1795. Architects then had wide interests and wide sympathies, and sought inspiration widely.

The excavations at Pompeii and Herculaneum, the results of which appeared between 1757 and 1792 in the splendid volumes of the *Pitture Antiche d'Ercolano*, proved an inexhaustible source. Many other publications, such as Cameron's *Baths of the Romans*, of 1772, dealt with specific sites. The richness of the published sources is astonishing.[11]

Taken as a whole, these and similar books supplied the basic grammar of the classical language of architecture. They could not satisfy the need to keep abreast of such modern developments as that of French Romantic Classicism, which interested some of the most talented younger British architects. For that, French publications had to be consulted.

## Modern French sources

The Prince of Wales' Marine Pavilion of 1787 (Fig. 66) was a notable example of avant-garde French style in England; it had two elementary and disconnected projecting half cylinders (the bow windows), attached to two cubes on either side of a cylinder. It was the work of a francophile architect, Henry Holland, for a francophile Prince.

Holland did not go to France until just before the Revolution, and must have depended on French publications such as those by Peyre, Patte and Gondoin (Figs 73, 220). Most architects hoped to go to Paris. Otherwise, they had to rely on printed sources, especially during the turmoil of the 1790s and early 1800s. One of the most influential of the earlier advanced neo-classical publications was the eight volumes of the *Recueil élémentaire d'Architecture*, published between 1750 and 1780, of J. F. Neufforge. A widely used treatise was J.–L.–N. Durand's *Recueil et Parallèle des Edifices de Tout Genre Anciens et Modernes* of 1800, many times reprinted and retranslated. Durand had been the draughtsman for one of the most visionary of French Romantic Classical architects, Boullée, and had imbibed many of his principles, including opposition to any form of 'masquerade' and any attempt to disguise the essential parts of a structure. He thought classical proportion unessential, decoration superfluous, and diluted his utilitarianism only in conceding the most fitting forms to lie in those of fashionable elementary geometry. Any resultant austerity could be softened by the natural ameliorations of water and foliage.[12] The *Recueil* contains abundant antique, Egyptian, Chinese and Moresque detail; there is little Gothic. Durand modified well-known buildings of all styles to conform with his theories of modular proportion; he made available an architectural vocabulary that was to be called upon for the next quarter of a century. Particular motifs, such as loggias, colonnades, pergolas, and skylines varied with centre and corner towers, constantly recur.[13]

Another much used textbook was Krafft and Ransonette's *Maisons et hôtels construits à Paris et dans les Environs de 1771 à 1802*, with a text in English, French and German; it was a good source for the most fashionable Parisian architecture by the most advanced architects, and included interiors as well as exteriors. L. A. Dubut's *Architecture Civile* of 1803 was another important book; the exteriors remind one of some features of English Regency architecture, including those of Thomas Hope's Deepdene. Dubut maintained the virtues of regularity of plan and rooms, at the same time stressing the flexibility of his designs: 'ils sont conçus de manière, à supporter beaucoup de changemens sans rien perdre de leur symétrie et conserver toujours les pièces très-régulières'.[14] He may have encouraged those English architects who resisted the Picturesque straggle. In other ways he pointed (as did others) the way to the future; his designs use a feature — elevated loggias — he had noticed in Italy: 'il est peu de leurs Maisons qui

n'aient une galérie ou une loge par le haut; l'une sert à prendre l'air à couvert ou à mettre des fleurs, et l'autre sert d'observatoire'.[15] Soane made a collection of his drawings.

Yet another notable architect was C. N. Ledoux, whose *L'Architecture considerée* was published in 1804 and his *Monumens Français* in 1806 (Figs 80, 83). Such was the interest in European architecture that Robert Smirke published in 1806 his own *Specimens of Continental Architecture*, a half-hearted production that, interestingly, concentrated heavily on the Italians. Smirke's book, by a convinced Greek Revivalist, contains truths that were to work like a leaven as the Greek Revival revealed its limitations; the first, prompted by Genoa: 'there is something in magnificence, however produced, which overawes the prejudices of fashion, and enforces approbation'; the second, as a corollary: 'Though an admirer of the unaffected majesty of Grecian architecture may be offended with the luxurious productions of Italy, we cannot refuse them the praise that is due to genius. . . .'[16] C. R. Cockerell in later years would have whole-heartedly agreed.

Notwithstanding the interest in Italy shown later in the Regency period, French Romantic Classicism retained an influence into the 1830s, as is evident from the work of such an architect as Fowler (Pl. XXXIV). By then architects had also become interested in the French seventeenth century — and in French Gothic.

## Practising British architects c.1790

An architect working in Britain thus carried with him as ballast a weighty mass of theory and instruction. He was not shackled to it; he could cast it overboard and take on something new, according to fashion or caprice; after 1810 the pattern books of the baroque and rococo began to be reused. And the more eclectic the period, the wider the choice open to the architect — and to the patron.

Architects themselves began to complain of the cacophony of voices.[17] One senses vertigo in Repton's comical attempt to define style: 'there are only two categories of buildings; the one may be called perpendicular, and the other horizontal'. The 'perpendicular' included all buildings erected before and during the early part of the reign of Queen Elizabeth I, whether 'deemed Saracenic, Saxon, Norman, or the Gothic of the thirteenth and fourteenth centuries'; 'Gothic' included the mixed gothic, and classic 'Queen Elizabeth's Gothic', in which 'turrets prevailed, though battlements were discarded, and Grecian columns occasionally introduced'. The 'horizontal' category included 'all edifices built since the introduction of a more regular architecture, whether it copies the remains of Grecian or Roman models'. Repton could not keep this up; a third category was introduced, in which neither 'the horizontal nor perpendicular lines prevail, but which consists of a confused mixture of both: this is called CHINESE'.[18] These comments came ten years before he expressed his Indian enthusiasms.

The examples provided by the accomplished work of established British architects were a steadying influence. The two most distinguished elder architects in 1790 were Robert Adam and William Chambers who, born in the 1720s, were to die in 1792 and 1796. One should add James 'Athenian' Stuart (important as an influence although too disorganised, too indolent, and too rich to have left many buildings when he died in 1788) and Sir Robert Taylor, who also died in 1788; the latter's interest in the Italian vernacular was retained by Regency architects, and his Palladianism continued in Nash up to the 1830s.

Adam and Chambers had been lifelong rivals. The latter had consistently disapproved of the former, and had used his dominant position in the Academy, dominant even over Sir Joshua, to exclude him. Adam's reputation had declined before his death; to the waspish comments of Horace Walpole was added the material fact that his star fell from the zenith as that of James Wyatt rose. The Regency saw Adam primarily as a decorator; Soane acknowledged his reform of rococo decoration, adding that although his style was 'well adapted . . . to internal embellishment, it was ill-suited to external grandeur'; he did not form his taste on the best examples of antiquity.[19] Cockerell thought his 'ideas first assembled in ornament and decoration', and considered him a bad planner.[20] His art was only again to become fashionable with the hostesses of the late nineteenth and early twentieth centuries.

None the less, Adam's influence continued. He had remarkably anticipated some Regency developments, such as the association of Gothic with the extreme Picturesque. In addition to publishing Diocletian's Palace, he produced in 1773 and 1779 two volumes of the *Works in Architecture of Robert and James Adam*, a third volume appearing as late as 1822. In 1833 Soane was interested enough to buy nearly nine thousand architectural drawings of the two brothers. Others preserved the Adam influence. It lingers in designs for ornament published by Pergolesi in 1801 with plates dated from 1781 to 1801[21] and in a further volume of 1814, showing the 'Etruscan' and 'Grotesque' styles. George Richardson, a former draughtsman who had worked eighteen years in the Adams' office, perpetuated what was more or less the Adam style in his publications until 1816; the early style of Thomas Leverton was influenced by that of Adam, as was that of Bonomi, although the latter had a strongly individual bent.

In abstract architectural terms the Adam style continued to be influential; the brothers had claimed to have brought back the principle of movement, abandoned by the Palladians, which selected features 'meant to express the rise and fall, the advance and recess with other diversity of form, in the different parts of a building, so as to add greatly to the picturesque of the composition'.[22] They claimed to have increased the variety of room shapes (a principle adumbrated by

Alberti[23] and seen in Roman planning), noticing at Spalatro 'a remarkable diversity of form . . . conspicuous in other parts of the Palace. . . . Modern Architects . . . are apt to fatigue us with a dull succession of familiar apartments'.[24] This concern for variety was carried to excess during the Regency (Fig. 87).

Chambers fared better than Adam; respect for him never diminished. Trained in Blondel's Ecole des Arts in Paris, and later exposed, as was Adam, to the fructifying influences of Clérisseau and Piranesi in Rome, he was attracted to the neo-classicism of such French designers as Le Geay and Le Lorrain — although he felt constrained to accommodate his style to the temper of his English clients with a strong dash of Palladianism. It was a style that outlasted fashion. Soane thought highly of Chambers; he referred to the demolished staircase of Melbourne House as 'worthy of being placed in competition with the finest productions of Italy'.[25] Chambers disliked contemporary Gothic, disliking equally his own solitary essay in that style, Milton Abbey.

Three younger architects, George Dance, James Wyatt, and Henry Holland, all born in the 1740s, had established careers by 1790, but were to continue as important 'Regency' architects. The oldest, Dance, lived until 1825, although he retired in 1815. In some ways he can hardly be separated from his pupil, John Soane. Both Dance and Soane were followers of Laugier, in the pursuance of whose doctrines Dance produced architectural innovations that became part of Soane's lexicon. Already, in 1765–7, Dance had used an enriched architrave rather than an entablature above the Ionic order of the nave of All Hallows, London Wall, a device that at first shocked Soane but which he later accepted — justifying it, however, by reference not to Laugier but to the Greeks, whose authority was less questioned.[26] Another Dance invention, to be constantly employed by Soane, was used for the first time in 1777–9 at Dance's London Guildhall, where the four pendentives were continued into the dome without interruption; the dome was lit by an oculus, and decorated with a three-dimensional velarium, another constant Soane motif. M.–J. Peyre has been cited as a possible source of the pendentive motif;[27] Byzantium might also have contributed. For Dance had a bent towards synthesis, and practised what Reynolds preached; no other Regency architect so successfully assimilated alien forms to produce something new, save Soane himself. One wonders whether Dance had consciously imbibed the positive aspect of Laugier's message, as distinct from its inhibiting catalogue of prohibitions — the belief that infinite variety could be achieved through combining the components of architecture as the 'sept tons de la Musique' have been combined through the centuries, and that 'Scavoir saisir ces combinaisons différentes, sources d'une agréable variété, c'est l'effet du génie'.[28]

Henry Holland had begun by becoming the architectural partner of 'Capability Brown', a precedent followed by Nash with Repton; it cannot have escaped the beady-eyed Nash that the arrangement had introduced Holland first to the Whig grandees, and ultimately to the grandest of grandees, the ultra-fashionable Prince of Wales; Repton was to do exactly the same for Nash. Holland's French entourage illustrates the chauvinistic remark made by Lord Warwick, who was a 'John Bull', to the effect that foreigners 'hung together like prawns, if you take up one others are attached to it'.[29] C. H. Tatham, who joined Holland's office in about 1789, has himself been seen as a formative influence on the style of the Regency; his book (see p.373) certainly proved of great use.

The third of this group, the brilliant James Wyatt, who could 'draw circles and strait lines without the aid of compasses or ruler — as correctly as with them',[30] died in 1813 in full harness, leaving the Prince of Wales in tears for the loss of his Gothic Pavilion. Wyatt was responsible for the most renowned, and perhaps the most unsatisfactory, of all great Regency buildings — Fonthill. His style varies, ranging from a cool but decorative classicism with temperate and sensitively placed ornament to the Gothic of Fonthill and the early Ashridge. He told George III that 'there had been no regular architecture since Sir William Chambers — that when he came from Italy he found the public taste corrupted by the Adams, and he was obliged to comply with it'.[31] His Gothic was successful in its day, approved by the arch-Goth, Horace Walpole, and attracting numerous, too numerous, clients. Looking at these three architects, Dance, Holland, and Wyatt, one notices how different each was from the other

and how each embodied tendencies that were to continue. One should perhaps add to their number Thomas Harrison of Liverpool, also born in the 1740s; less influential, he produced some of the noblest buildings of the Regency period.

The architects considered so far had been decisively shaped by the eighteenth century, and, no matter how long they lived and worked, they retained something of it. We now arrive at a group — Nash and Soane, born in 1752 and 1753, and as antipathetic to each other as Adam and Chambers had been — and such younger men as William Wilkins (born in 1778), Robert Smirke (born in 1780) and C. R. Cockerell (born in 1788), all of whom emerged as fully-blown 'Regency' architects. Soane was established by 1790, since he had by 1788 won the surveyorship of the Bank of England in competition with, amongst others, James Wyatt, Holland, and S. P. Cockerell; he survived until 1837 as one of the most original of all British architects.

Regency style in architecture veers from 'a style professedly miscellaneous',[32] as advocated by Payne Knight (see pp.101–2), to the strict Greek archaeological accuracy attempted by Wilkins, with all variants between. Despite the fact that one Regency theorist declared that 'there never has existed, in any age or nation, but three styles of architecture, the Grecian, the Roman, and the Gothic'[33] it remains convenient to discuss the architectural styles of the Regency in three groups: classical, Gothic, and exotic, the last to include Chinese, Indian, and Egyptian (although there is a case for including Egyptian with classical).

## Chapter three

# Classical Styles

Buildings in a 'classical' Regency style tend to separate into groups with their own individualities, although there was much cross-fertilisation from which no group, not even that of the doctrinaire Greek Revival, was immune. One of the most innovatory of these groups was interested in ideas connected with primitive classicism, and in forms drawn from the Italian vernacular, used sometimes in union and sometimes apart. Its productions fall more or less within the 'Picturesque' category.

## Primitive classicism

Although the primitive proved something of a cul-de-sac — the eccentricity of actually reproducing primitive buildings other than in the garden would have been excessive — its tenets often exerted an influence even when not overtly followed. The movement was given a coherent theory by Laugier's analysis of Greek architecture as a stone version of the primitive hut, and by his reiteration of the hut's significance: 'ne perdons point de vue notre petite cabane rustique';[1] as convinced an anti-Laugierian as Chambers absorbed the doctrine (Fig. 44). It was a form of architectural Darwinism, and grew complex ramifications. Amongst other things, the idea cast an enchanted light upon primitivism, the power of which cannot be understood without taking associationalism into account. Hope himself was subject to this form of teleological romanticism: 'The hut of Pelagius, the last entirely wooden cottage in Arcadia, remained the unvarying model of every subsequent fabric in stone or marble, however stupendous, which arose throughout Greece'.[2] It was inevitable that an attempt would be made to incorporate such emotionally charged associations into more formal architecture, both in France and England; the influence of French Romantic Classicism is often perceptible in British attempts.

It was fairly easy to impose on the ordinary cottage, the habitation of 'domestics and dependants', allusions to the Greek primitive hut: 'the thatched covering of the Porch is supported by trunks of trees fashioned like columns'.[3] Gardens also provided opportunities (Pl. IX). Soane strikingly embodied the idea in a series of designs for dairies. The first, of about 1780, was for Lady Craven, an eccentric personage with bucolic tendencies who had chosen thatch for Craven Cottage at Fulham (at about the same date the French architect Brogniart built a thatched cottage with unfluted Greek Doric columns).[4] Lady Craven's dairy remained a design; its successor, a dairy of 1783 for Hamels in Hertfordshire, was built (Pl. XIII). It had a portico of unfluted timber Doric columns with rudimentary bases, the columns wreathed in creepers; a primitive Doric entablature had open triglyphs, as rafters supporting the roof. The steep slope of the pediment indicated Soane's acknowledgment of Laugier's remark that had pediments been invented in a cold climate, the abundance of snow would have introduced 'l'usage des toits haut et aigus' and that 'leurs proportions seroient comme on les voit dans les édifices gothiques'.[5] The roof was thatched, and the dairy had stained glass in its windows. Despite the primitivism, the result was sophisticated, pretty, and not a little French; the dairymaid of the design (whose pose comes ultimately from an antique figure of Ceres) has, of course, just escaped from Raphael's fire in the Borgo.

Another Soane dairy design, for Betchworth Castle, is more solemn (as were the unexecuted designs for Lady Craven). Two wooden Doric columns, completely baseless, and possibly fluted in an irregular style to indicate the channels caused by rainwater, stand in antis, with two pilasters on either side apparently faced in flint (a motif occasionally used thereafter by Soane to indicate rusticity). Only the inner pilasters have capitals, and none has a base. The triglyphs are again open rafters, supporting a thatched roof.[6] Even more solemn, not to say portentous, is a design that forcefully expresses the union of primitivism (Pl. XXIX) and the vernacular, Soane's project of 1790 for a lodge at Bentley Priory (Fig. 46); the arches convey the same impression of weight sunk into the ground as those at Cairness (see p.131), and the thatched roof has the gravity of a pyramid; French influence is obvious.

In 1790 Soane took primitivism from the park to the house in a design for the Hon. Wilbraham Tollemache, of Steephill at Ventnor in the Isle of Wight (Fig. 49); the result has a farouche charm. The house is austere, a rectangular block articulated only by a string course; its ground floor windows extend to the ground. The porch, with thatch and primitive Doric columns, assorts oddly with the house; the illogical juxtaposition of primitive porch and less primitive house — illogical because no imagined sequence of development can be read into such a juxtaposition — suggests that the porch is there for its associational meaning only, a piece of evocative artifice the resonances of which are now lost. The attempt had no future; the repertoire of extreme primitivism was to find no place in the Regency synthesis, and remained confined to garden constructions such as the apiary by Gwilt (Fig. 20) and Repton's charming 'rustic thatched hovel suitable for a promontory in a forest', which he regarded as a thatched equivalent of the Temple of Vesta at Tivoli.[7] Repton used the same theme for one face of the entrance to the Menagerie at Woburn, where the circular temple became semi-circular and was given thatched wings with wooden columns and festoons of pine cones; John Adey Repton designed a rustic pavilion with its pediment crowned with large pine cones as acroteria, with smaller cones forming a decorative row to the apex.[8] The attempt to establish a similar primitivism for Gothic was unsuccessful (Fig. 107).

## The Italian vernacular and the domestic Italianate

A type of primitivism which could easily be related to the Greek primitivism of Laugier existed in Italian vernacular buildings. There is evidence of much interest in them, an interest apparent, for example, in a letter of 29th August 1800 from Mario Asprucci to C. H. Tatham, enclosing a drawing and plan (Fig. 50) of a simple Italian hermitage opposite the Villa Aldobrandini; Asprucci's complementary comments indicate that Tatham's interest was certainly practical: 'L'idea [referring to the design of the hermitage] è molto semplice, ma da questro con la vostra immaginazione son sicuro che potrete fare qualche cosa molto bella'.[9]

49 'Elevation of Entrance Front', Steephill, Ventnor, Isle of Wight, designed by Sir John Soane, c.1790

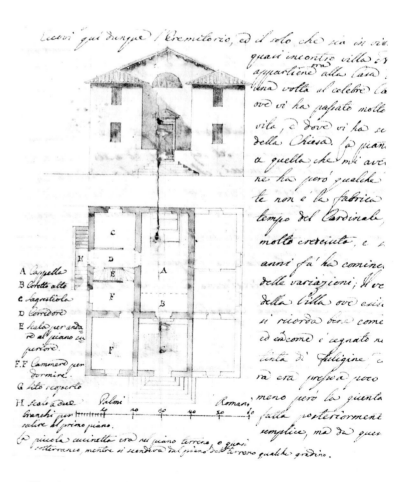

50 Hermitage opposite the Villa Aldobrandini, August 1800

**51** 'Prospetto, e veduta dell'antico Sepolcro creduto de Scipioni', published by Pietro Santi Bartoli, 1697

Italian vernacular architecture was well suited to the design of smaller buildings. It often carried antique associations, as in the 'Prospetto e veduta dell'antico Sepolcro creduto de Scipioni', illustrated by Pietro Santi Bartoli in his *Gli Antichi Sepolcri* (Fig. 51); first published in 1693, the book was a main source for Regency designers, for which reason the connoisseur George Cumberland showed anxiety about Bartoli's standards of accuracy.[10] Such buildings were common in Italy; P. F. Robinson in 1830 included in his *Designs for Farm Buildings* a tower on an arched base very similar to that illustrated by Santi Bartoli; he thought it would remind travellers of the Temple of Venus

in the Kingdom of Naples; its roof was copied from the Temple of Vesta at Tivoli.[11] Similar towers and temples frequently appear in the paintings of Claude.

Santi Bartoli's illustration of Scipio's tomb may have been a source for a design by Soane published in 1793 (Fig. 52), and for one of Nash's most famous and beautiful houses — Cronkhill (Fig. 53); the tower and arcade are both constituents of Cronkhill, and Cronkhill's stucco in its original state would have looked more rustic. There are no round rooms at Cronkhill; the tower is used for its Picturesque qualities alone; the same ingredients were employed by Nash at Sandridge. The original design for Cronkhill shows outbuildings not unlike Gandy's designs of 1805 (see p.131), which in turn have something in common with Gyfford's design of 1807 for a hunting or shooting box (Fig. 54). This contains a kitchen, a parlour, and four bedrooms, and was meant to constitute a picturesque feature in a park. The combination of cube and cylinder strongly recalls French Romantic Classicism; the imposition of a Gothic 'French' window on an astylar temple façade and the use of fluted decorative panels on the towers make an incongruous whole. Other designs by Gyfford (Fig. 24) also show French Romantic Classical influence.

The type of domestic Italianate house that is usually associated with the later Regency period appeared fairly early: when Turner, devotee of Claude and the most Picturesque of Regency painters, made designs in various styles for a house at Twickenham in 1810–12 he finally chose an Italianate version with broad overhanging eaves and two side wings with recessed panels (Fig. 55). Italian vernacular characteristics were frequently conjoined with sophisticated classical ornament, ranging from Greek Revival key patterns and paterae to rich late classical shell motifs, the last often drawn from Wood's Baalbek and Palmyra; this combination became ubiquitous in the later Regency, and lasted well into Victorian times. Nash's Park Village East typifies the Italianate 1820s vernacular villa, where basic Italianism is combined with balconies and canopies in a characteristic Regency synthesis (Fig. 56; see pp.203–12); the modest vernacular is probably a deliberate contrast with the palatial Italian rhetoric of the grander buildings of Regent's Park (see pp.150–1).

The Italian vernacular style itself could be expanded into the palatial — it had associations with Palladio and Inigo Jones. It was used in a palatial way by Asprucci's countryman Joseph Bonomi, one of the most imaginative of architects and decorators in England at this period (Reynolds temporarily resigned from his presidency of the Academy following its refusal to elect Bonomi Professor of Perspective in 1790).[12] Longford House in Shropshire (Fig. 57), built 1789–94 (a drawing was exhibited at the Academy in 1797), uncompromisingly presents a widely-spaced Tuscan porch with a blank pediment and flattened triglyphs masquerading as rafters to uphold the roof; the beauty of the

**52** Design for a Prospect Tower for Ossington Hall, Notts., c.1786, by Sir John Soane

**53** Design for Cronkhill, Salop., by John Nash, c.1802

54 'A Hunting or Shooting Box', a design by
E. Gyfford, 1807

55 'Sandycombe lodge, Twickenham, villa of
J. M. W. Turner, Esq. R.A.', 1814

columnar form, of which Laugier was so sensible,[13] is allowed full expression both in the portico and in the columns on either side of the door. The façade, which was of white stone 'like Portland',[14] is blank of decoration; only the Diocletian window above the doorway is allowed a curve (something like the arrangement in the drawing sent by Asprucci to Tatham).

The Tuscan order, the order of Italian bucolicism, attracted some attention in these years: in 1802 Henry Holland used it at Wimbledon Park. There may have been political inhibitions; it was the 'characteristic order of Republican Rome'[15] and was much used in French Romantic Classicism. None the less it was recommended, as in a design of 1806 for a Casino by James Randall. The text declares that 'the roof is after the Italian manner'; the boldly projecting hollow pediments clearly show the rafters that form the 'dentils'; the pillars, with vestigial bases, stand on a platform in accordance with Laugierian principles, as do those at Longford; the depressed rectangles above the windows are void of sculpture (Fig. 58). The bay at the side resembles those in Sir Robert Taylor's Italianate villas.

The influence of Laugier recurs in the pared-down style of the gaunt Eastwell Park in Kent, another house by Bonomi (Fig. 59). This was designed as a huge rectangular block, connected to a servants' wing on one side and a greenhouse on the other by curving wings on the Palladian pattern (Palladian plans occur in unexpected places). Only the

**56** 'Park Village East, Regent's Park', 1827

**57** 'Principal Elevation of Longford House in Shropshire', designed by Joseph Bonomi, 1789–94

Scale of

58 'Perspective View of a Casino', a design by James Randall, 1806

59 'Design of a House and offices built at Eastwell Park in Kent', by Joseph Bonomi, 1794

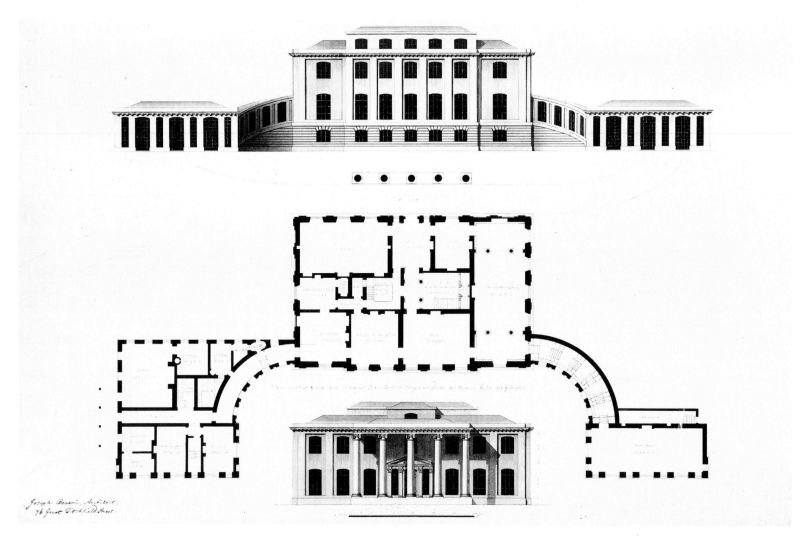

plan of Eastwell is Palladian; the elevations are boldly novel. The façade, apart from its free-standing Ionic portico of five columns, is plain; the windows have no mouldings; the 'pilasters', similar to those on the south elevation, lack bases or capitals. The south elevation is plainer still; again no mouldings, apart from dentils that signal the rafters of the roof, and an attic that somewhat resembles certain attics by Soane. The strangest feature is the extensive use of 'strip pilasters', which in three-dimensional form were to be employed later in Egyptianising and extreme classicising styles, both in Britain and in Europe; Schinkel used them, and they entered twentieth-century 'Fascist' architecture. The strip pilaster was frequently used by Soane; incised decoration in the Soane manner would make the Bonomi façade look quite Soanean. They occur in Egyptian architecture, and may be seen in Denon and in Norden (see p.190). However, there was another source of squared-off pillars and pilasters that could have contributed not only that motif but also the curiously dissociated disposition of the masses of Eastwell — the minor pavilions of greenhouse and servants' quarters are connected to the main block by singular sloping corridors. This source was the fanciful villas depicted in the murals at Herculaneum and elsewhere (Figs 61, 97).

These odd little pictures were well known and were looked at with more interest than their merit would seem to warrant, no doubt because they were, unquestionably, ancient depictions of ancient, albeit capricious, houses. Since the middle of the century disquiet had been expressed, as by the painter Allan Ramsay in 1751, at the founding of modern domestic architecture not upon the palaces and dwelling places of the ancient Greeks and Romans but upon their temples, 'from which the ornamented part has been borrowed and applied to domestic use, in a manner abundantly absurd, for the most part; and which, nevertheless, custom has rendered agreeable to the sight'.[16] Robert Adam had made much of this criticism, and others had followed. French architects had looked at the plans of Roman houses; for example, the single-storied court of Rousseau's hôtel de Salm of 1782 shows their influence.[17] The pictured Pompeian villa may later have animated a much grander building than Eastwell (see pp.151, 152, 155).

One of the most inventive, exciting, and romantic of all Regency country houses — Thomas Hope's Deepdene — was called by Loudon an 'Italian villa' and such it undoubtedly was, albeit of a most sophisticated and eclectic kind. The Italian ingredient came from the vernacular and from Roman antiquity; it provided the basis of a brilliant synthesis that fused elements taken from various countries and periods into an harmonious whole. It is a thousand pities that the proposed illustrated book on the house was never issued, since apart from providing a record, it might have exerted a beneficial influence similar to that of his *Household Furniture and Decoration* (1807) (see p.381 et seq.).

The foundations on which Hope based his architectural ideas were described in his credentials as arbiter on the style of Downing College (see p.138); through the studiously precise words glows a picaresque romanticism not unlike that (with, it is true, a different quest) of Byron's Don Juan: 'Egyptian architecture I went to investigate on the banks of the Nile; Grecian, on the shores of Ionia, Sicily, Attica, and the Peloponesus. Four different times I visited Italy, to render familiar to me all the shades of the infinitely varied styles of building, peculiar to that interesting country, from the most rude attempts of the Etruscans to the last degraded ones of the Lombards; Moorish edifices I examined on the coast of Africa, and among the ruins of Grenada, of Seville, and of Cordova; the principle of the Tartar and Persian constructions I studied in Turkey and in Syria; finally, the youngest branch of the oldest of the arts, that erroneously called Gothic, I investigated the most approved specimens of throughout England, and most of the provinces of France, Germany, Spain, and Portugal'.[18] As a statement of Regency eclecticism, this could hardly be bettered.

More light is cast on Hope's architectural ideas by the posthumously published *Essay on Architecture*, which shows a great admiration not only for Gothic but also for some of the productions of late Roman and 'Lombard' architecture; a large number of the proposed illustrations were drawn from these periods. Hope's predilections, as displayed on the exteriors of the Deepdene, seem to have moved towards a combination of plain surfaces and impeccable, frigid, minimal detail. There was more than a hint of the barn, which seems to have attracted him; he said of the interiors of late Roman basilicas that they 'resembled huge barns of the most splendid materials; but huge barns which from their simplicity, the distinctness, the magnificence, of their component parts, had a grandeur which we in vain seek in the complicated architecture of modern churches'.[19]

The Deepdene was converted from an older building between 1818 and 1823, with Thomas Atkinson as supervising architect; it is evident that, as with his furniture and decoration (see. pp.272–3, 381 et seq.), the inspiration was Hope's. The building managed to be both casual and sophisticated. The deliberate disjointedness of its plan, the diverse structures that lay at different levels and that broke the skyline in variously shaped forms; the terraces and loggias, the integration of house and landscape that recalls assemblages of buildings in paintings such as those of Claude and Poussin without copying them, made up an eclectic whole that has also a hint of French designs such as those of Dubut. The Deepdene emerged as a virtually astylar building, in an architectural language full of unorthodox adventure. The forecourt (Fig. 60) had Pompeian-type square pillars on the elevated loggia — Cockerell recognised the Pompeian influence on the building[20] — and pilasters set into a curved wall that was a backdrop, containing no rooms beyond; beside the loggia an apparently Egyptian figure

**60** 'A commemorative Seat on the Terrace', the Deepdene, Surrey

(perhaps in Coade stone) was seated against the wall. The tower had set into it a tabernacle, resting on corbels, that looked like an Italian shrine; it contained a statue. Near the 'Italian Stairs to Mrs. Hope's apartment from the Pine Grove'[21] was a projecting bay window almost in Alhambra style, with diamond panes of stained glass; beneath were Gothic windows.

The amphitheatre façade, with its strange triangular-headed openings, was strikingly original (Pl. VI). Hope illustrated in his *Essay on Architecture* two works of art that suggest triangular openings. One, the tomb of Honorius at Rome, has a lamb beneath a triangular pediment that has no horizontal member, giving the effect of a triangular opening; the other illustrates an unquestionable triangular arch, set on pillars, from the cloisters of Zürich, a building Hope admired. An antique sarcophagus illustrated full page in the catalogue

of the Museo Pio-Clementino, one of Hope's listed sources, has triangular arches alternating with round arches.[22] The triangular arch also had primitivist associations; it appears in Egyptian architecture, notably in the entrance doorway to the Great Pyramid, where the form helps to withstand the crushing weight from above, and also in the megalithic structure (which has a corbelled 'dome') at Mycenae of the 'Treasury of the House of Atreus', a name that would raise the hair at the back of the neck of any amateur of Greece. The suggestive nature of this last exalted association, plus the fact that Hope may have been looking for a primitive dome, might persuade one that this last building influenced his adoption of the triangular arch.

The house was not without frivolities. The pink and blue glass in the conservatory pediment had a sun-ray pattern, with obvious emblematic meaning. The chimney-stack over the dining room was

**61** A scene with buildings, from an antique Roman wallpainting, published by Pietro Santi Bartoli, 1750

disguised as a tower, carrying chimney pots disguised as jars, a device used earlier by Soane and subsequently taken up by Loudon. Chimney stacks above a loggia were joined by an arch in the Vanbrugh manner, simplified. Exotic touches included Chinese polychromatic garden seats and aloes. Ancillary buildings included an Italianate lodge; a 'Castellated Archway of Approach', a strange minaret-like tower topped by a cross; a spire; loggias; and pediments. Visitors felt both the exoticism and the ambiguities; Maria Edgeworth was reminded of 'some of the views in Athenian Stuart of Turkish buildings, grotesque and confused among trees in no particular taste'.[23]

A brilliant combination of the Italian vernacular with the castle style is seen in Hope's design for 'Proposed conversion of tower kitchen garden into a gardener's house' at the Deepdene. The design for the gardener's house is as sophisticated as was the Deepdene itself, but

subtly rustic, including an allusion to late Roman or mediaeval corbelling, with another use of the triangular arch, the triangle echoed in the chimney pot. A doorway on the side of the house (Fig. 62) has a simple porch, with an arch rising from vestigial flat pilasters, and a pitched roof with the rafters showing; of a type sometimes given a curved roof, as in a lodge to the Deepdene, it occurs commonly in late Regency and early Victorian architecture. Again, there is a French flavour in the design; in fact it reminds one of a simplified Lequeu, although the possibility that Hope had any knowledge of the latter is remote.[24]

Loudon described the Deepdene as 'an example of what the Germans call the ecstatic in architecture. There is not one English architect who would of his own accord have designed such a house; nor, if he had designed it, could he have found more country gentlemen by

**62** 'Proposed conversion of tower kitchen garden into a gardener's house', the Deepdene, Surrey

whom it would have been understood or carried into execution'.[25] Did Schinkel see the Deepdene on his English visit? It is reminiscent of certain of his villas.[26]

A distinctive feature of Italian vernacular architecture, to be seen at the Deepdene and elsewhere, was the campanile. It offered a great deal to the Picturesque; it had Italian and Claudian associations, it made a feature in the landscape, it gave a vantage point for viewing the prospect, and it faced every aspect; one could hardly ask for more, since lifts lay in the future. Sometimes combined with a loggia and in more stumpy form than its Italian prototype, it became part of the vocabulary of English urban design, both in single houses and in larger combinations such as crescents; a fine example is Park Crescent in Brighton, mentioned above (p.88) for its Picturesque planning; its Italianate campaniles break the skyline.[27] And the campanile gave the impoverished Caliph, William Beckford, his final opportunity to build a lofty tower, the romantic Lansdown Tower, built in 1824–7 by Henry Goodridge 'from designs arranged according to the classic taste of the owner' (Pl. XXX).[28] The lantern, 'after a pure Grecian model'[29] is cast iron; save for that, the building is virtually astylar, with a strong Italian character complemented by the interior (see p.278 et seq.).

The interest in Italian vernacular architecture continued; Gilbert Laing Meason, who recommended great Italian paintings as a source of architectural inspiration, drew attention in 1828 to the 'picturesque elegance' of the Italian village and town,[30] a union of two favourite Regency epithets that would have favoured anything to which it could be applied. In 1827 T. F. Hunt's *Architettura Campestre* advocated the

use of Italian roof tiles as 'light and economical, most beautiful in form, and secure as a covering, affording no harbour either for birds or vermin';[31] he disliked slate, increasingly popular: 'its cold blue colour is so out of harmony with verdant scenery, that landscape painters have often on that account omitted buildings, which would otherwise have formed prominent objects in their pictures'.[32] Tiles are used in Hunt's design for a 'Prospect Tower and Garden Seat' (Fig. 63); the building was intended to include a small reading room and apartments for a gamekeeper or other outdoor servant, for 'Beauty scorns to dwell, Where Use is exil'd'. Once again, the design blends the Italianate with French style;[33] the 'Pink Lodge' is given a loggia. The design was altered in realisation; unfortunate changes in proportion and fenestration eliminated sophistication and 'manner', and the building is coarse and lumpish.[34]

The Italianate style found fine expression in a villa built by Charles Barry for Mr. Attree at Brighton in 1829–30; known locally as 'the Italian villa', it was intended to form part of a large development (Fig. 65).[35] To the vernacular idiom Barry added allusions to the Renaissance palazzo in which he was so interested; with its Italian garden, Attree Villa expressed the latest manifestation of a taste that had interested the English for three centuries, now adapted to the needs of a prosperous Brighton solicitor.

## 'Grecian'

The styles derived from Laugierian primitivism and the Italian vernacular fall more or less into the 'Picturesque' category. Another detectable style — although one cannot force styles, in such a fluid period, into too much of a strait jacket — belonged more, in Burke's

**63** 'Prospect Tower and Garden Seat', designed by T. F. Hunt, 1827

**64** 'The whole Building from South to West', the Deepdene, Surrey

**65** The Italian Villa, Queen's Park, Brighton, designed by Sir Charles Barry, 1827

sense, to the 'Beautiful'. Perhaps the most convenient, albeit imperfect, term with which to denote it is 'Grecian', a word used loosely by contemporaries to denote architecture, decoration and furniture that comprehended both Greek and Roman; it shaded off into the Greek Revival and to a lesser extent into the 'palatial Italianate', both discussed below. One of the most constant marks of 'Grecian' is the use of the column, often unfluted. 'Grecian' was traditionalist, reassuring and popular, sometimes delicate and sensitive, and without the politically disreputable associations with which primitivism and the doctrinaire Greek Revival were at first tainted; it used features taken from later eighteenth-century French architecture but rejected the eccentric and grandiloquent aspects of French Romantic Classicism. It was favoured not only by the great Whigs but by the greatest of the Whigs, the Prince of Wales. Its major early Regency exponent was Henry Holland, but it was practised, not exclusively, by the Wyatts, by Nash, by Decimus Burton and by Papworth.

Holland's style has the refinement and restraint of 'Louis XVI', with a dash of the 'goût grec'. It was probably this sophisticated moderation that appealed to his aristocratic patrons. He habitually used strong but harmonious Greek versions of the Ionic Order, such as that of the Temple on the Illisus; the graceful and congruous style that he achieved survived, somewhat coarsened, as an important strain in Regency architecture, seen for example in some of the work of Decimus Burton.

Holland was both speculator and architect: his own house at Sloane Place, built in 1789 as part of his development of the area, illustrates his domestic style, seemly and pleasing; the house has paired Ionic columns, plain windows without mouldings, and a delicate iron balcony

on the first floor.[36] It may show the influence of a well-known design for a 'Maison de Plaisance' by M.–J. Peyre, published in 1765, a design that has features in common with those of many Regency houses including Bonomi's project for Burwood Park (Fig. 73; see p.128). Some of the motifs of the Sloane Place house had been previously used by Holland in the Prince of Wales' Marine Pavilion at Brighton of 1787 (Fig. 66), which combined French Romantic Classical 'cubism' (see p.105) in its massing, with shallow bow windows in the fashionable 'French' form along the whole façade; it had a domed semi-circular centrally placed exedra (encircled with Holland's favourite Ionic order), of which the ultimate source (despite the Pavilion's use of the Ionic rather than the Corinthian order) was the Temple of Vesta at Tivoli. The dome was fashionably pantheon-shaped, encircled with Coade stone statues, the last apparently an afterthought, perhaps an idea of the Prince's rather than Holland's. The building has been seen as influenced by Rousseau's hôtel de Salm;[37] the exedra motif, used by Vanbrugh but rejected by the Burlingtonians, had begun to reappear in England from about 1760 onwards; used by Adam, Carr, Dance, James and Samuel Wyatt, Soane, Cockerell and Holland,[38] it was often fused with what became the Regency bow, as in the grand 1820s terraces of Busby at Brighton (Fig. 148).

The 1787 Pavilion was, unlike its ultimate successor, generally admired, providing the obvious source of a Busby design for a single-storied villa of 1808; Busby added verandahs at the sides. The servants' apartments were at the back, the hall, parlour, and dining room at the front; there were two lavatories. A simpler version (Fig. 67) employs merely the central exedra and dome. Busby did a good deal of work in Brighton, and his imitation of the 1787 Pavilion (he also imitated that

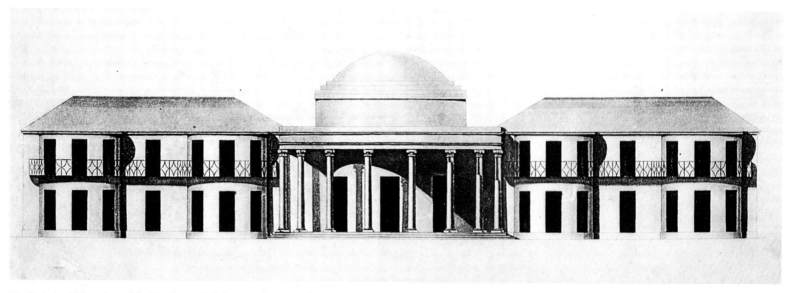

**66** 'Principal Elevation of the Pavilion at Brighton in Sussex', c.1800, designed by Henry Holland

XXXI 'Design for a Theatre in a Provincial Town', by J. B. Papworth, 1814

XXXII Rosneath, Dunbartonshire, 1806, the garden front, designed by Joseph Bonomi

**XXXIII** Dinton Park, Wilts., 1812–14, designed by Sir Jeffry Wyatville

of 1801 with the influential trim added by Holland and P. F. Robinson), testifies to the continued influence of the earlier version.

The work that gave Holland fame was his masterly remodelling of Carlton House for the Prince of Wales between 1783 and 1796; its richly classical interiors were set off by a restrained but impressive exterior, with a grand unfluted Ionic screen set before the house in the manner of a Parisian *hôtel particulier*; the most notable example of such a screen in Paris was that of the hôtel Condé by M.–J. Peyre, published in 1765.[39] Holland's screen, and the Corinthian columned façade behind, were applauded by the cognoscenti. The screen influenced the three-bay unfluted Ionic portico of Nash's own house of 1797–8 at 29 Dover Street. When Carlton House was demolished in 1826 there was a proposal to use the portico columns as a memorial to the Duke of York;[40] they were eventually incorporated in the façade of Wilkins' National Gallery.

Something of the Holland style shows in the work of an interesting and somewhat unfulfilled architect, Michael Searles; born five years after Holland, he died in 1813. The evolution of a Searles design is exhibited in a series of drawings for the Paragon at Blackheath, built between 1793 and 1805. The Blackheath Paragon, the Paragon at Southwark and the Circus at Greenwich (the last two designed by

Searles during the late 1780s to the early 1790s), were all designed in the form of taller blocks united by single-storey links. An early design for Blackheath is somewhat old-fashioned (Fig. 68); an Ionic portico much in the Holland manner provides a central feature, and it has round and square-headed windows; balustrades surmount both the cornice and the slender Doric loggias. These features recall both Holland and Peyre, but the juxtaposition of the portico in some designs with the curving, loggia-linked units of the crescent produces an effect that suggests a Palladian country house indefinitely extended. In later designs the Blackheath crescent grew simpler, marking the way taste was travelling: the portico, which in an early design had a flamboyant sunburst, was omitted, and the Paragon became a simple curve linked by colonnades. Searles' designs for other projects show the same process; the early stages are sometimes clumsy and even grotesque.[41]

Socially and architecturally, Brighton played in the first thirty years of the nineteenth century the role that Bath had played earlier; despite continuing demolitions and the white paint that now covers most of its stucco buildings, some areas still convey the impression of a Regency town. Holland's 1787 Marine Pavilion and its 1801 remodelling (Figs 66, 147) set fashions followed in Royal Crescent, begun in 1798 and completed, after financial vacillations, in 1807. This was the first

**67** Design for a villa, by C. A. Busby, 1808

**68** Design for the Paragon, Blackheath, by Michael Searles, c.1793

group of houses planned in Brighton as a single architectural composition. Faced in black glazed mathematical tiles, a medium used in white by Holland on various buildings including the Marine Pavilion, the curve of the crescent was given a rippling effect by a combination of bow windows, balconies, and canopies similar to that seen on the Pavilion; this combination is now accepted as constituting the most typical Regency ensemble of all (see p.203 et seq.). At Royal Crescent the bow windows were criticised: 'bow windows in a crescent destroy, in a great measure, the elegance of the curve'.[42] Other provincial towns were by the turn of the century beginning to acquire crescents, in different styles according to architect and locality. There was no standardisation.

## Stylistic variants: the villa

The discriminating and charming versatility of the style of the early Regency is demonstrated by the various ways in which certain problems posed in designing the 'villa' were met; in Regency hands the villa achieved a polite and affable sophistication that, without reaching the heights, is civilised and attractive. It usually made a virtue of understatement, possibly another manifestation — like the understatement in men's clothes incarnated in the person of Beau Brummell — of the way in which the fashion for 'parade' was in speedy decline; the decline preceded political democratisation. By 1825, the lack of parade even at the centre of the system itself — Windsor — was

noticed, and was reflected in the way the castle was rebuilt; to C. R. Cockerell the castle was 'like an ordinary County Gents Ho. . . . but nothing like chambre, antichambre, waiting chamber, ministers' Rooms, salle de Huissiers with all the parade & pomp & circumstance of a court . . . nothing chevalresque, high or striking, poetical, literary, imaginative or gentlemanly . . . nothing that affects the imagination'.[43] There were attempts to 'affect the imagination' in the villa, but classical villas tended not to pursue the 'chevalresque'.

The term 'villa' underwent much contemporary examination (as it has undergone much modern examination).[44] The villa evolved with the Picturesque; the house of parade reigned over an avenued and organized park, whilst the villa sat pictorially in a romantic landscape. Contemporaries, in true English fashion, were obsessed by the social implications of the villa; these changed as the period wore on. Charles Middleton, in 1793, gave a practical working definition expressed in terms of the social hierarchy: 'First, as the occasional and temporary seats of the nobility and persons of fortune from what may be called their town residence, and . . . of course . . . in the vicinity of the metropolis. Secondly, as the country houses of wealthy citizens and people in official stations, who also cannot be far removed from the capital: and thirdly, the smaller kind of provincial edifices, considered either as hunting seats, or the habitations of country gentlemen of moderate fortune.' All villas were to be small and convenient: 'Elegance, compactness, and convenience, are the characteristics of such buildings, either separate or combined, in contradistinction to the magnificence and extensive range of the country seats of our noble and opulent gentry'.[45] Middleton's designs show an up-to-date vocabulary — shallow relieving arches, paired pilasters, parapets, porticos — much in the vein of other fashionable architects.

By the end of the period the villa had descended the social scale. Although James Elmes, writing in 1829, on one page describes the villa as an 'Italian palace in the country', on another he makes the true picture clear: 'The term is never more properly applied than when given to such urban structures as those which are rising around us, serving as well as they may do from situation as to the town, and from position as to rural beauty . . .'. These were, of course, 'Quite unlike those merchants' and sugar-bakers' boxes which crowd the sides of Clapham Road and Kennington Common . . .'.[46] The pejorative social aspects of the suburbanised villa are summarised in Peacock's term, 'Mainchance Villa'.[47]

In the 1790s and the early years of the new century, the villa had not yet lost its bloom. The most fashionable practitioners were the brothers James and Samuel Wyatt, with Nash a fast rising star. The Adam style influenced both Wyatts; they used the same team of craftsmen as that engaged on Kedleston, of which the most notable were the painter (and architect) Biagio Rebecca, the stuccoist Joseph Rose II, and the scagliola maker Domenico Bartoli; this Italian-based team contrasts with Holland's French contingent, although both Samuel and James were enamoured of contemporary French design, having been infected with the enthusiasm by Matthew Boulton.[48]

The elder of the Wyatts was Samuel; born in 1737, he had been appointed clerk of works at Kedleston by Robert Adam and in 1774 settled in London. A natural classicist, as was Chambers, he made only five Gothic designs in his career. His style was individual and distinguished: his houses are often astylar, composed in the cubes and half-cylinders of French Romantic Classicism; geometry was allowed full expression. Certain of his forms, such as those of the Octagon Cottage at Holkham, hint at C. N. Ledoux — although Kentian cubism can at times have an effect similar to that of French geometry. Some of the estate buildings at Holkham, where he worked from 1780–1807, have the same motifs that attracted Kent, Tatham and Bonomi — Italian vernacular details such as Tuscan columns, overhanging eaves and Diocletian windows;[49] they would have seemed especially appropriate in the rural and agricultural context.

His plans were flexible and geometrically ingenious, often sacrificing exterior symmetry to practicality; he was the first architect to incorporate an orangery in the main structure. Technically, he was adventurous; his early training as a carpenter perhaps reinforced a naturally practical bent. He used Coade stone ornament, mathematical tiles, copper sheeting on roofs, and a metal composition for window astragals. He was amongst those who early used cast iron for structural purposes, as at the Winnington poultry yard of about 1782 to 1785.[50] He speculated in slate quarries; according to Repton, 'even the buttons of his coat' were slate.[51]

Doddington Hall, Cheshire (Fig. 69), completed in 1798, exemplifies Samuel Wyatt's mature style; it has the 'Wyatt' window, a modified Venetian window constantly employed during the Regency

**69** 'South Elevation of Doddington Hall in Cheshire', designed by Samuel Wyatt, 1798

**70** 'Principal Elevation of Bowden Park in Wiltshire', designed by James Wyatt, 1796

period. Here the window is given Corinthian columns, and putti in Coade stone roundels; the plaques with garlands are also in Coade stone. Doddington resembles some houses by Bonomi in its lack of window mouldings and use of the Diocletian window, but the effect is totally different. Austerity is replaced by a dandified, rather feminine elegance, restrained by strong geometrical shapes and the plain curve of the dome. The house is remarkable for the excellence of the jointing and the size of the stone blocks. The north façade is similar to that of the main front, with the addition of an outward curving staircase; this motif had been used in England, by Chambers and Adam amongst others, but it also had a French connotation; at the Maison Epinnée in Paris of 1796, by Olivier, it was combined with an 'English' garden.[52]

Samuel Wyatt's later designs were often completely astylar, in what was acidly defined by Repton as the 'Modern Style': 'The numerous difficulties in reconciling the internal convenience of a house to the external application of Grecian columns of any order, at length banished columns altogether, and introduced a new style, which is strictly of no character. This consists of a plain building, with rows of square windows at equal distances; and if to these be added a Grecian Cornice, it is called a GRECIAN BUILDING: if instead of the Cornice, certain Notches are cut in the top of the wall, it is called a GOTHIC BUILDING. Thus has the rage for simplicity, the dread of mixing dates, and the difficulty of adding ornament to utility, alike corrupted and exploded both the Grecian and Gothic style in our modern buildings'.[53]

James Wyatt was a character, perhaps a 'card'. Opinions of him varied. Many were dazzled: 'The first instance of a regularly bred and genuine architect was the classical and scientific Wyatt . . . richer and more learned in his art than either Jones, Wren, or Vanbrugh';[54] 'to no individual architect will the English school be so much indebted as to James Wyatt, for purity and beauty of style'.[55] To C. R. Cockerell, he was 'a secondary star'.[56] His lack of system and disregard for clients were notorious. He first found fame in 1772 with the Pantheon in Oxford Street; by 1776 he was 'as difficult of access as a Prime Minister'. His classical domestic architecture 'began in the late Palladian tradition and ended with some acknowledgments to the Greek Revival'.[57]

Like his brother Samuel, James was fond of strongly bowed

**71** 'North Front of Southgate Grove', Middx., designed by John Nash, 1797

windows and the flat Pantheon type dome; not so attracted to astylar façades, he often used the Orders. These characteristics are evident at Bowden Park in Wiltshire, built in 1796 (Fig. 70). Beneath the dome is an unfluted Ionic portico, not dissimilar to that of the Marine Pavilion at Brighton; 'Wyatt' windows, down to the ground, have Coade stone plaques above; at the corners, in place of the usual pilasters, are niches and blind ovals. The house is understated and, to use that overworked Regency word, 'elegant'. The plan is somewhat unusual, in that the entrance façade presents the short side of the house, which extends behind in a long line. Behind the pillared bow lies the entrance hall, a sensible arrangement which avoids the overshadowing of the drawing room by columns, a solecism deprecated by, amongst others, Laugier and the painter Ramsay.[58] Either side of the Hall are the Dining and Drawing Rooms, with the Library behind the former and the Breakfast Room behind the latter; fashion was observed by the Breakfast Room leading directly into a long 'Greenhouse', integral to the main block. This type of house was the classical alternative to the Picturesque castellated or Gothic house of the kind popularised by Nash (see p.174 et seq.).

The Wyatt style was popular, and was reflected in the work of other architects; it influenced some of the designs in John Plaw's *Rural Architecture*, first published in 1785 and reissued five times up to 1802. Plaw's book was the first example of the 'villa book'; it was the first British architectural book to be illustrated in aquatint, and the first in which architecture and landscape were depicted together in a Picturesque composition; tubs of shrubs are displayed before the houses. It was to have numerous issue. Plaw, a practising architect, presumably knew his clients' predilections; the designs are a curious mixture with little individuality; they show, besides the Wyatt influence, some traces of primitivism; one design (Pl. XLIII) is oddly Kentian, another (Pls LII and LIII) recalls Bonomi; yet another (Pls XLVIII and XLVIX) explicitly acknowledges the influence of Soane. The total effect is of an assemblage of undigested elements.

Nash's Southgate Grove of 1797 had a Picturesque enfilade of the type depicted in Repton's plan (Fig. 71); the 'doors from the library to the conservatory are of looking glass, to reflect the prospect of the end window of the drawing room; besides this, the bookcases . . . of the library fold back into the recesses . . . and by that means lay the whole end of the library into the conservatory. . . .' Built in the year that Nash returned to London, his bankruptcy behind him, it has sphinxes, urns, and *oeil de boeuf* windows; the last first appeared in Nash's work at Llynsnewydd, Henllan Bridge, in about 1794,[59] and were to become a favourite motif. The ground floor 'Wyatt' windows have decorative tympana with radial fluting around a Palmyra-type shell; beneath the restraint lies bravura, quite distinct from the reticence of the Wyatts.

Different again was the Casina at Dulwich, built by Nash in the same year as Southgate. A familiar flat dome, circumscribed by a balustrade, formed the central feature of a semi-circular ground floor extended by a single storied loggia on either side; the loggias had flat roofs edged by a balcony of the same design as that around the dome. There were reminiscences of Holland, but it may be that, despite the many differences, both the Casina and Holland's house at Sloane Place (see p.120); and Bonomi's design for Burwood Park (Fig. 72) were influenced by the frequently engraved *Maison de Plaisance* by Peyre (Fig. 73). Peyre's text explained that 'J'ai orné la Façade de Colomnes formant le Pérystile, comme le sont la plûpart des Cazins Italiens . . . on en voit un très grand nombre d'exemples dans Palladio';[60] the connexion with the Italian vernacular is clearer in Peyre's design than in Nash's Casina, despite the latter's Italian name. Peyre added that 'La Terrasse au-dessus du Perystile augmente les communications'; it seems possible that the English writer James Dallaway recognised the affiliations between the Peyre and Nash designs, since he commented of the latter that it 'introduced a new style of country house, by combining the advantages of an English arrangement, with the beauty of a Palladian plan'; the delphic statement becomes clearer when one looks at the house. The 'new style' may have owed something to Repton, who claimed that the 'Casino' was 'a house built from the joint designs of Nash and myself'.[61]

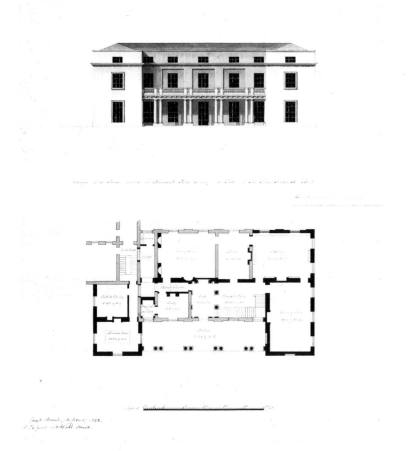

**72** 'Design of a House erected in Burwood Park, Surrey', by Joseph Bonomi

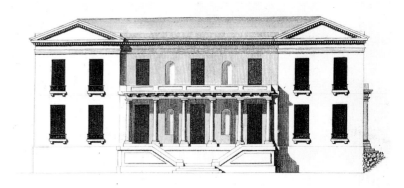

**73** 'Maison de Plaisance', by M.-J. Peyre, published in 1765

All these classical houses presented an ordered and symmetrical front to the world, unlike the sprawling assemblages favoured by the theories of the Picturesque, which were usually in the Gothic style (Fig. 123). Some disliked this plain regularity, especially where the building was large. C. R. Cockerell referred to James Wyatt's houses as having a 'cold and old stateliness which appalls and awes me'; his late houses 'rise . . . like a great box dropt upon the ground'.[62] Others defended it; Busby, for instance, denied the doctrine of Payne Knight and Repton that the house had to fit into the landscape; he thought instead that, 'all the beautiful effects of light and shade, of colour and outline, are produced by the contrast of the regularity of the building with the picturesque variety of nature . . . in such situations the most simple building will be the most pleasing'.[63] Regency taste was supple enough to encompass both positions with ease.

The James Wyatt domestic classical style could be appropriately adapted for palatial buildings, as it is in the design for Downing College at Cambridge, which was subjected to the implacable and catastrophically damaging criticism of Thomas Hope (see p.138). Jeffry Wyatville, nephew of Samuel and James, who worked for them in succession before setting up on his own in 1799, continued the Wyatt classical style for a time; his design of 1812–14 for Dinton Park (Pl. XXXIII) in Wiltshire, in the Wyatt manner and with typical 'Wyatt' windows, is also touched by the Greek Revival (Wyatville had shown an early interest in that style); its Ionic portico and unadorned windows combine 'Grecian' suavity with Greek Revival austerity to fine effect. The basic formula could be adapted to express individuality with ease.

A design of 1814 for a theatre by J. B. Papworth, placed in an agreeable provincial circus, is in that undemanding vein of gentle classicism into which the more clear cut style of Holland settled (Pl. XXXI). Well mannered and perhaps a little genteel, its 'Grecian' charm, which seems almost to anticipate the pastiche architecture of Rex Whistler, wears well. The ease with which styles could be switched

**74** 'Autre Vue de la Facade du Pronaes', Paestum, by G. B. Piranesi, published in 1778

is illustrated by the note to Robertson's swimming-bath (Fig. 30); its graceful Ionic portico could, if thought 'out of character for such a building' be replaced by 'plain rusticated Tuscan columns' and the pavilion 'covered with vermiculated rustics'.[64] The Beautiful could be swapped for the Picturesque.

## The Greek Revival and French Romantic Classicism

Homère chanta les dieux, les héros; pourquoi l'Architecte, ce Titan de la terre . . . dédaigneroit-il le conseil des dieux avec lesquels il peut communiquer, pour expliquer aux humains, un langage élevé . . .
*C. N. Ledoux:* L'Architecte Considérée (1804)

By 1814, the year of Papworth's circus, a classical style of a different genre, that known as 'Greek Revival', had become fashionable (see p.104). In England it displayed two aspects, which reflected separate origins in England and France. One, originating in French Romantic Classicism, took over a measure of the French style's freedom and imagination; the other, the English-born Greek Revival, was archaeological to the point of sterility. The two types frequently intermingled, but can as frequently be distinguished; an architect might use both manners distinctly, as did Robert Smirke. The French style preceded the English in attaining mature expression (despite the early English use of archaeological Greek forms in garden ornaments (see p.59)), and its British offshoots will precede the native-born product in these pages.

French Romantic Classicism (see p.97) united Piranesian romanticism and the classical primitivism of Laugier with a desire for moral and political regeneration. It will be perceived that the division of Laugierian primitivism into an academic and a free interpretation would readily occur, given the tensions between the 'archaeological' spirit and romanticism, both of which were gaining strength at the same time.

During the Regency, romanticism became recognised as a force. According to an article in the *Quarterly Review* of 1814, probably by Coleridge, Mme. de Stael had introduced to the British public the system of distinguishing 'the productions of antiquity by the appellation of classic, those of modern times by that of romantic'.[65] This concept was elaborated; as put by Hazlitt, 'the principle of the one is simplicity and harmony, that of the other richness and power. The one relies on form and proportion; the other on quantity and variety . . .'.[66] In 1832 a further definition stated that: 'Classicality produces rigidity: Romanticism encourages affectation. . . . The one is a chastely formed vessel . . . the other a female of exuberant charms';[67] no doubt the fame of Lady Hamilton's 'attitudes' had derived from her union of both in one person, as Goethe, who was susceptible to both qualities, appreciated.

The appeal of romantic primitivism to the sensibilities of the later eighteenth century is demonstrated in attitudes to Rome and Paestum. Piranesi had admired the forceful, the primitive, and the stupendous in Roman architecture. This was not a new taste; his praise of the Cloaca Maxima in Rome, for instance, (preferred by Milizia to the 'over-decorated' sacristy of St. Peter's)[68] had been anticipated in the fifteenth century by Alberti, who said as if of a general opinion that 'Among all the wonderful things in the City of Rome, the Drains are accounted the noblest . . .'.[69] But even Piranesi, the arch-romantic, whose delineations of Roman 'magnificence' cannot be surpassed for 'richness and power', and who had ardently defended Rome against Greek usurpations (placing a Greek Doric column in the inferno of his 'Carceri'), even he yielded when in 1777–8 he produced images of the temples at Paestum that movingly capture their 'terribilità'; in so doing he helped to transform 'an archaeological interest into an emotional understanding' (Fig. 74).[70]

Paestum lost its isolation and became famous. Soane visited it in 1778 (he never went to Greece), and in 1780 submitted a re-worked triumphal bridge design to the Parma Academy in which the Corinthian order had been replaced by Greek Doric, the whole being permeated by French Romantic Classicism. In 1777 Payne Knight went to Paestum and found the ruins Picturesque. In 1786 Goethe spent a day there and called it 'the most noble image I could take intact with me northwards';[71] he described his initiation into its beauties in enlightening terms; the columns were at first offensive and 'even terrifying', but 'I pulled myself together, remembered the history of art, called up images in my mind of the austere style of sculpture' and was reconciled to them.[72] This sounds more like the attitude of mind that led to the English academic Greek Revival than that which informed French Romantic Classicism. Joseph Forsyth in 1813 expressed a more spontaneous reaction; he 'felt all the religion of the place' and thought the ruins 'the most impressive monuments I ever beheld on earth'; their 'peculiarities create an exaggeration of mass which awes every eye', and although 'they reverse the first principles of Vitruvius they do so with advantage'.[73]

**75** Designs for lodges, by J. M. Gandy, 1805

Such sentiments must have inspired the work of the elder Playfair, the most advanced neo-classicist in Britain in the early 1790s. Playfair was keenly interested in classical primitivism and in French Romantic Classicism; his primitivism differed from that of Bonomi, which had an Italian and vernacular bias. Playfair was in Paris in 1787, and in Italy in 1792–3; his library included the *Ruines de Pestum* and '4 French books on building. . . . A portfolio with architectural designs and the Halles aux Grains'[74] (the last was the 'Halle au Blé' by Le Camus, an outstanding monument of French Romantic Classicism). Another influence on Playfair was that of Soane, himself influenced by Laugier; all the roads lead back to primitivism and Greece. Aspects of Playfair's work display Regency taste at its most extreme, more extreme than most of that which followed. Had Playfair not died in 1794 at the age of thirty-nine, and had he come to London, there might have been an imaginative talent in British Greek Revival architecture of an order that was lacking.

Playfair's interests are reflected in his designs and works, such as the design for a villa with pyramidal outhouses which shows the influence of C. N. Ledoux, in the unexecuted designs for a house at Ardkinglas in Argyllshire, the tower of which anticipates Bonomi's Rosneath (Pl. XXXII),[75] and most of all in the house at Cairness, which was built. Cairness exhibits the distinct geometrical forms of Romantic Classicism; the house has forceful primitive classical detail on the exterior, most of all on the wings of the office block; the half-buried unfluted columns, with a strong entasis as if crushed out of shape by the arch that presses relentlessly down on them, have affinities with the squat Doric of Ehrensward or Gilly: they may be influenced by the work of Ledoux at Bourneville.[76]

Amongst other serious early examples of primitivist architecture certainly or probably influenced by French Romantic Classicism were Great Packington Church by Bonomi, and Hammerwood Lodge in Sussex by Latrobe; the order chosen for the latter was Delian Doric (the austerely distinguished manner of Latrobe was carried in 1796 to the republican congenialities of the United States, where it became the official style). However, one of the age's most forceful creations was Chester Castle, 'the finest group of Greek Revival buildings in Britain',[77] begun in 1788 by Thomas Harrison. He, who must be numbered amongst the most impressive of Regency architects, had spent much time in Italy in the 1770s; the Grand Prix style, columned and grandiloquent, is manifest in his earlier designs. The building of Chester Castle evolved over thirty-five years, from 1788 to 1822, and the style changed from one influenced by French Romantic Classicism to an undiluted archaeological Greek of a force that has prompted speculation that he might have seen designs by Weinbrenner or Gilly.[78] The development is seen clearly in the radical change proposed in the entrance gateway; a design of about 1793 is much in the Romantic

Classical idiom, a triumphal arch with lions atop unfluted Doric columns, and a flat-domed pavilion at either end, with obelisks beyond that effectively lack bases (the junction is marked by a string course, but the line of the obelisk is uninterrupted) (Fig. 76). This design was replaced in 1810 with a distinguished 'archaeological' propylaeum (Fig. 77).

Gandy was amongst those who showed an interest in the elementary forms of Romantic Classicism; his strange projects for cottages and other rural buildings were published in 1805, the year after the appearance of Ledoux's *L'Architecture Considerée*. Gandy's designs are an eccentric combination of utility, the Picturesque, and French Romantic Classicism. His design for lodge gates is odd but effective (Fig. 75); he described it as 'Two Cones, as Lodges, to be thatched down to the ground: this would have a singular and not unpleasing effect'; the thatch was to be supported by an iron frame,[79] a union of primitivism and advanced technology; what a distance from William Morris! The gate carries a simplified 'Etruscan' motif (see p.239), an idiom that appears elsewhere in Gandy's work at this period. The design has obviously been influenced not only by the latest and most sophisticated French publication but by the humble English oast-house, a source made acceptable by the new dignity attributed to the primitive.

Robert Smirke had early been influenced by French Romantic Classicism, as is shown clearly by a grand design produced in about 1798–1800, before he went to Europe, for Augustus Square, Hyde Park (Fig. 78). A magnificent, plainly coffered semi-sunken arch, that recalls Ledoux's archway at the hôtel de Thélusson of 1778–81, itself inspired by the unexcavated arch of the Circus of Maxentius as pictured by Piranesi, frames the view in the style of Piranesi's 'Ponte Magnifico' of 1743. The arches penetrate a square in which unpedimented temple façades relieve an insistent repetition of windows that creates the impression almost of a grid. The drawing, with its strong contrasts, suggests the same trance-like stillness as that extracted by de Chirico from French Romantic Classical architectural drawings.

Robert Smirke's Covent Garden Theatre of 1808–09 (Fig. 79) was inspired by Ledoux's design for a gaol in Aix-en-Provence (Fig. 80). The fluted baseless Doric of the portico sets the tone of the whole building; its uncompromising character caused a 'fever'. Liked by Gandy, Henry Blundell and the painter Lawrence, it drew a comment from Soane that blew up a considerable tempest. Smirke had visited Greece; Soane had not, and he always adhered to the baroque architectural tradition which drew the various parts that make up a building into a composed whole. This gave a unity utterly different from the disjointed effect of Smirke's 'graeco-cubic' manner (called by the younger Pugin the 'square style'), which derived vigour from the juxtaposition of individually treated blocks. So that when Soane told

the Royal Academy students that he deplored the 'practice of sacrificing everything to one front of a building . . . a more recent work points out the glaring impropriety of this defect'[80] the apparently mild allusion caused a perfect tumult. The row did not prevent Soane from repeating his strictures in a later lecture: 'The Ichnography of many of our Buildings consists of a series of squares and parallelograms, and the exterior is formed of discordant parts without that due connection, so necessary to constitute an entire and perfect whole'.[81] Despite Soane's opinion, one regrets that Smirke was to put aside the majestic force of Augustus Square and Covent Garden in favour of a tepidly academic Greek Revival style.

The unporticoed façade of the Theatre Royal, Drury Lane, designed by James Wyatt's son Benjamin Dean Wyatt, in 1812, was far less uncompromising (Fig. 81), and was much liked by the Prince Regent, who seems to have disliked Smirke's style (he rejected his

*Opposite top* **76** Design for Chester Castle, c.1793, by Thomas Harrison

*Opposite below* **77** 'North East View of the Gateway to Chester Castle', c.1810, designed by Thomas Harrison

*Above right* **78** Design for Augustus Square, Hyde Park, c.1798–1800, by Sir Robert Smirke

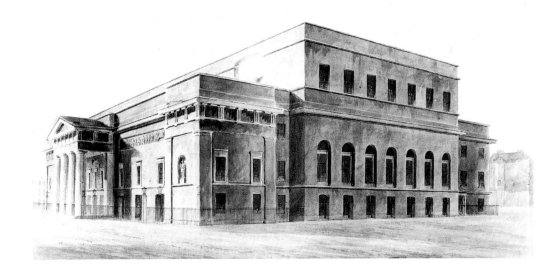

**79** Covent Garden Theatre, 1809, designed by Sir Robert Smirke

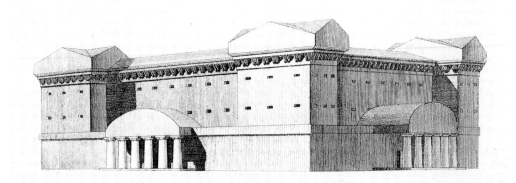

**80** Gaol in Aix-en-Provence, designed by Claude Ledoux, 1785

design for York House). It was accepted by a committee that declared that Philip Wyatt's model 'appears to surpass in execution anything that has ever been produced of the same nature'.[82] Influenced by the more polite and less avant-garde French architecture of the later eighteenth century, the unornamented flat horizontal lines of the façade are articulated by four unfluted Doric pilasters alone, their bases almost high enough to be pedestals — less offensive to the conservative than Smirke's fluted and baseless Doric columns. The four tripod gas burners would have been dramatically lit at night, their archaic flames emphasising the antique references of their forms, a perfect example of ancient design given a thoroughly appropriate modern use. Such lamps were used extensively for clubs and public buildings; less frequently for churches, where their pagan associations would have seemed sacrilegious.

Bonomi's Rosneath in Dunbartonshire of 1803–06 (Pl. XXXII) showed how various, and how distinguished, available manners could be. It was designed for the fifth Duke of Argyll, who had squabbled with Mylne, his usual architect. His son persuaded him to employ Bonomi and the painter Alexander Nasmyth, the latter having achieved a good reputation, in accordance with Picturesque principles, for landscape gardening. The Duke had misgivings; he wrote to his son: 'Your display of Taste, and Bonomi's fame are secur'd [but] I hope you will not associate too much with Bonomi and Nasmith. You will find

them expensive pets — They will not consult your Pecuniary interest as poor old Mylne us'd to do mine'.[83] So it proved; the house was never finished.

Rosneath was a building of a different kind from Bonomi's Tuscan porticoed Longford (Fig. 57; see pp.110–11), although the same theoretical basis — Laugier — could have given rise to both. At Rosneath Laugier's obsession with the beauty of the free-standing column was given full rein, although his condemnation of the error of placing columns where they obscured windows was ignored. The design is reminiscent of such buildings as the Parisian hôtel de Galliflet of 1775 by E.–F. Legrand, which has an Ionic colonnade along the whole of the front; it is also oddly reminiscent, despite the use of the Ionic rather than the Corinthian order, of the parade of unfluted columns as pictured by Robert Wood at Palmyra and Baalbek; one is reminded that Robert Wood had two copies of Laugier's *Essaie* in his library.[84] The Ledoux-like belvedere resembles both an early design of Thomas Harrison[85] and Mario Asprucci's design for Ickworth.

Full Corinthian columns appear in a design for an 'ornamental villa' of 1825 by P. F. Robinson (Fig. 82); they are accompanied by an extensive panoply of bas-reliefs, balustrades, vases, and armorial trophies; windows appear to have been sacrificed to architectural considerations. The style was extended to the terrace and to the garden; the terrace, like the house, was given powerful submerged arches of the

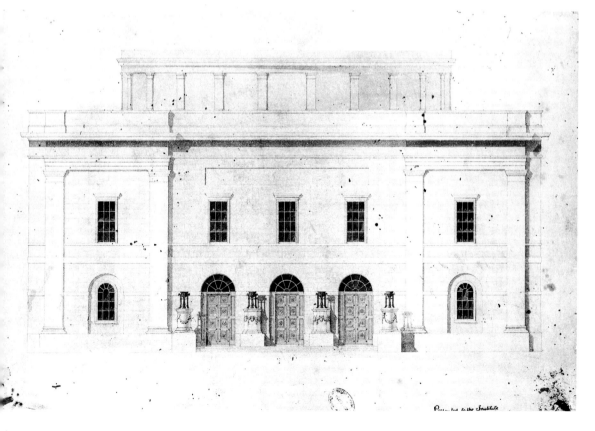

**81** Design for the Theatre Royal, Drury Lane, 1812, by Benjamin Dean Wyatt

Piranesi/Ledoux type, together with obelisks, vases, niches with statues, and a Piranesian key-stone. The style is portentous and overweening; Robinson remarks that the house appears large because it has galleries of one storey only. Details of the design bear strong resemblances to those of Ledoux's 'Maison de Mdle. Guimard' (Fig. 83).

French Romantic Classicism allowed an eccentricity and originality self-denied to the doctrinaire Greek Revivalists. A design of 1817–20

for High House, West Acre, by William Donthorn (born in 1799), who began as a pupil of Wyatville, is asymmetrical to the point of derangement (Fig. 84). The wing on the left has an almost catacomb-like air, with an extraordinarily depressed pavilion adjacent to the portico. The placing of the disparate cubic shapes resembles an assemblage made with a child's set of building blocks (relieved by the cylinders of columns and 'towers'); the design anticipates the work of

82 Entrance court to a villa, 1825, a design by P. F. Robinson

83 'Maison de Mdle. Guimard', designed by Claude Ledoux, 1783

*Maison de M^lle Guimard située à la chaussée d'Antin.*

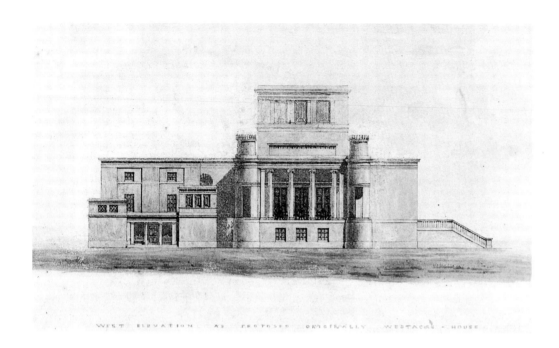

**84** 'West Elevation', High House, West Acre, design by William Donthorn

**85** 'The Principal Park Lodge Entrance to Lissadell Court', County Sligo, by Francis Goodwin, 1833

'Greek' Alexander Thomson. Another design constructed on the 'building block' principle is that of the well-known 'Irregular house' published in 1827 by James Thomson,[86] in which unintegrated shapes were assembled in a variety that would have given Soane apoplexy; lacking that intuition for simplicity and balance without which coherence and grandeur are unattainable, Thomson's design merely conveys unease.

The style's peculiarities are evident also in Francis Goodwin's idea for the lodge at Lissadell Court in County Sligo, where he worked from 1830 to 1835 (Fig. 85). Goodwin was explicit about his intention to produce an unintegrated design, explaining that the watch tower offered 'a striking contrast with the lodge . . . being as much detached from, as united with, the latter by the gate, and the ornamental railing . . .'.[87] The design has an embattled look; its square-set pilasters lack bases but have the vestige of a capital, there is a campanile with a shape like a truncated obelisk atop it and stepped gate piers. Could such a structure have given the owner any great sense of domestic joy as he approached it, despite the reassuringly Picturesque hills?

One of the most impressive buildings to be influenced by French Romantic Classicism was Charles Fowler's Hungerford Market of 1831–3 (Pl. XXXIV). Fowler, one of the few architects who was an expert engineer, had built the Indian-style conservatory at Syon and Covent Garden Market, both still extant; Hungerford, alas, has disappeared. The French influence at Hungerford was strong; the natural alliance between Laugierian theory, engineering, and Romantic Classicism was again demonstrated;[88] probably influenced by Ledoux, Fowler defied Laugier by placing 'arcades vicieuses' above columns. The unfluted Doric columns, without bases, were placed in colonnades one above the other; the upper arcade had plain iron railings. Dignity and fitness united to produce beauty.

## The archaeological Greek Revival

Side by side with a revival of classical primitivism that allowed adventure and originality flourished a pedantic revivalism that discouraged any deviation from usages established two millennia ago. The search for an antique style of undisputed authority, authenticity, purity, and beauty ended in Athens and Paestum. It may seem strange that such a rigidity accompanied the licentious eclecticisms seen elsewhere during the Regency period, but the style in question — the Greek Revival — gathered together and expressed in an extreme form 'archaeological' inclinations that had been growing in strength over a lengthy period. In modern application, two flaws quickly became apparent: the buildings imitated had been created for a hot and dry climate; and people had erected them as temples, not as houses. For a time at least idealism ignored the drawbacks.

The new forms were early seen in ancient settings in the works of painters; Mengs and Gavin Hamilton were followed by David and Benjamin West, the last the favourite painter of George III who, less apprehensive and less perceptive than Louis xv, told West that the Doric Order was his favourite order of architecture;[89] he was, however, referring to the unfluted Tuscan order, appropriate with cows and general bucolicism. The 'goût grec' went hand in hand with the cult of nature, the noble savageries of the latter reinforcing the political resonances of the former. Similar affiliations worked in music, in the reformed and 'natural' operas of Gluck, for example; the preface of *Alceste* of 1767 has been called 'a neo-classical manifesto'.[90] In 1802 John Flaxman, speaking of the superiority of the antique over Michelangelo, said that: 'The ancients copied Nature, the moderns, Art',[91] an assertion triumphantly repeated by Hazlitt when he discovered veins in the musculature of the Elgin marbles.[92] The Greek buildings admired and taken as models had been remoulded by Nature; all were in a state of advanced and Picturesque decay; created anew, their Picturesque quality receded. Many that had been 'beautiful' in the Burkean sense when new had become 'sublime' with age. When the Regency took on the task of recreating the Sublime, usually in modern materials and always for modern purposes, it was taking on quite a lot; a sublime temple in decay is not the same as a sublime spanking new Bank or Opera House. Some buildings, such as Decimus Burton's Colosseum in Regent's Park, were treated to look old.

In 1789 the second volume of Stuart and Revett's *Antiquities of Athens*, containing the grandest monuments of the Acropolis, was published; those in the volume of 1762 had been minor, mostly Hellenistic, of 'a sort of slight and finical elegance'.[93] The influential Society of Dilettanti signalled its switch of allegiance from Rome to Greece by a symbolic change in dress; in 1790 the scarlet toga, the Roman garment ceremonially assumed by the Society's President, was discarded for a vestment designed by Payne Knight based on the Greek chlamys. Rome had been dethroned.

The archaeological Greek style was not immediately accepted, despite the interest of architects; one of the earliest to design in it was, oddly enough, Jeffry Wyatville, not normally thought of in connexion with the Greek Revival; in 1794 he produced a design for a screen at Hyde Park Corner in a powerful archaeological Greek style, with fluted and baseless heavy Doric columns, and no pediment above the entablature. Any remaining vestiges of the jacobinical associations of Greek primitivism must have been dispelled by sight of the Emperor's architectural new clothes, chosen with a new Roman Empire in mind; in Paris, meant to be its capital, Greek republican severity receded before an heroic magnificence of a distinctly Roman imperial character. The favourite imperial order, the florid Corinthian, was combined with cubic clarity at the Madeleine in 1806 and the Bourse in 1808; a Roman triumphal arch, the Arc du Carrousel, appeared in 1808, It is an irony that the old imperial and monarchical capitals — St. Petersburg, Berlin, Munich — were at this time venturing into neo-classical austerity. London did not become a 'Greek' city; when Napoleon fell, it was on the point of being transformed by Nash into an urban panorama of Italianate palaces. The British ascendancy in Europe was political, not cultural (despite English literary successes); London's specious stucco façades are not inappropriate to the ephemeral nature of commercial dominance.

In 1804 Thomas Hope wrote a letter to the Master of Downing, 'Observations on the Plans and Elevations Designed by James Wyatt for Downing College, Cambridge'. It bitterly criticised Wyatt's 'Grecian' design for the new college, first made in 1783 and reworked in 1800, and recommended the use of Doric; its language combined a messianic vision with a self-assurance, unmixed with the hypocritical diffidence of the English, that explains Hope's tendency to anger self-important people. He declared that the knowledge gained from his travels had freed him from prejudice, and that if he 'should manifest a partiality for any particular style, it will only proceed from the beauties of that style being really greater and more numerous than those of any other'.[94] From the heights of that self-confidence, he gave his opinion. He rejoiced that Downing had rejected Gothic, making a side-swipe at Fonthill of which Beckford admitted the justice; regretting it was not Grecian, Hope said that 'a style had on the contrary been adopted, which subjected every one of its details to disadvantageous comparison with the cathedral at Salisbury'.[95] He said that at Downing, 'I could wish that, instead of the degraded architecture of the Romans, the purest style of the Greeks had been exclusively adhibited', a style not only the best, but 'hitherto, unfortunately, the rarest'.[96]

He considered the superiority of Greek Doric both aesthetic and associational: 'the real Doric, through the simplicity and yet contrast of its forms, produces on the outward sense a vibration, infinitely more rapid, more general, more intense, and leaves on the inward sense an impression infinitely more forcible, more distinct, and thus more lasting, than any its feeble rival can operate'.[97] Given the depth and fervour of this aesthetic response, Hope's words on associationalism are doubly memorable: 'If we regard that *still infinitely higher species of beauty* [author's italics] which, inherent entirely in association of ideas, acknowledges the mind alone as the scene worthy of its delights, the attributes of that sort of beauty adorn the Grecian order in the same proportion, in which the opposite defects blemish that of the Romans'.[98] The Greek Doric evoked all the beauties of Homer, of Greek tragedy and philosophy, and the miraculous achievements of Greek civilisation in thought and art; the associations with Rome, on the other hand, were, as expressed in the words of one whose volumes were continuously republished throughout the Regency period, with

'the dark unrelenting Tiberius, the furious Caligula, the feeble Claudius, the profligate and cruel Nero, the beastly Vitellius, and the timid inhuman Domitian . . .'.[99] Such subtleties of aesthetic appreciation are now largely lost, but they must be taken into account in comprehending the success of the Greek Revival. One sees them at work, for example, in Aberdeen's proselytising 'Inquiry' of 1822, into the 'Principles of Beauty in Greek Architecture', which is constantly illustrated with quotations from Greek poetry.

Many of Hope's observations, such as the remark that the only two modern buildings fit for corrected imitation were the Louvre façade by Perrault and the Porte St. Denis, reflect the teachings of Laugier, both being amongst the few commended by him. Hope referred to the wooden hut, saying that the Greek imitation in stone pleases as a portrait, the Roman offends as a caricature.[100] He forbade plinths and pilasters: 'All pilasters I would proscribe without remission'. He praised modern French style: 'while the French are beginning to make most rapid strides towards the purest style of the antique, shall we obstinately lag behind [and adhere to an architecture] . . . vitiated and corrupt?'[101] He went on to criticise Wyatt's design in words that caused lasting affront, adding to offensive detailed criticisms of Wyatt's proposals — 'the proportions of the entablature . . . are almost burlesque. . . . No partial alterations could bring [the steeple] within the reach of my ideas of taste and elegance',[102] a general conclusion that annihilated: 'Neither elevations nor section display a single instance of fancy, a single spark of genius. . . . Everything alike in them is trite, common place, nay, often vulgar. . . .'[103] Poor Wyatt; what a change from the hyperbolic chorus of praise that had greeted the Pantheon!

Excellent as were his maxims, Hope was less happy in his recommendations: 'Mr. Wilkins has lately brought home, and intends to publish, designs of a Greek temple, in the cella of which Doric columns rise on distinct bases':[104] Mr. Wilkins was his preferred choice as architect. The bases were probably intended as a compromise, since Doric columns that rose direct from the ground were brutish to unaccustomed eyes; Elmes, writing in 1823, spoke of those who had hated 'the new-fangled "Doric" without a base, as much as they did a shirt without ruffles', even preferring 'the rusticated and twisted columns of Batty Langley'; they had 'lamented the shocking innovations of Wyatt and Soane, the more dreadful importations of Stuart, and were nearly going into a fever when the portico at Covent Garden [Fig. 79] was opened'.[105] The intrigue succeeded, if intrigue it were, and Wilkins was appointed architect to Downing College. The Greek Revival was in, and it must for a short time have seemed that the prospects for 'Grecian' were dim; in 1805 Wilkins defeated Holland in

XXXIV 'Galleries, Hungerford Market', 1829–32, designed by Charles Fowler

Galleries. Hungerford Mark I.

XXXV The proposed Grand National Cemetery,
c.1830, by Francis Goodwin

XXXVI 'St. Pancras Church', London, designed by
H. W. Inwood, 1819–22

the commission for the East India Company College at Haileybury (Holland had been given a passing blow in Hope's letter as the designer of 'the awkward screen that hides Carlton-House').[106]

Wilkins had spent four years from 1801 in Greece, Asia Minor, and Italy; his first executed work, Osberton House in Nottinghamshire of about 1805, had a full-scale Doric portico. But at Downing, somebody's nerve failed, and fluted Greek Ionic was substituted for Greek Doric; the propylaeum and the library were never built. The college buildings were placed in an open 'campus' rather than organised around a quadrangle in the old manner, an idea soon afterwards employed by Jefferson at Virginia with happier results; it became common in America. The effect at Downing was bleak; it diminished the architecture. Cockerell disliked Downing, and Miss Edgeworth was 'Sadly disappointed. It will never bear comparison with King's College Chapel'.[107] One regrets the loss of the suavities of James Wyatt.

The kind of compromise adopted at Downing was common, and compromise extended to the type of Doric chosen. In 1810 the architect Edmund Aikin wrote that although the hypaethral temple at Paestum 'appears to possess the characteristic energy of the primitive style in the highest degree', he himself thought the 'perfection of the Doric order' was in the Temples of 'Minerva' at Sunium and Athens (he retained Roman nomenclature) and in the Temple of Theseus at Athens; there 'something is taken from the massive bulk, something from the asperity of the primitive style, without sacrificing a particle of real grandeur; the attributes of force are united with those of dignity, and strength is crowned with grace'.[108] The more doctrinaire revivalists disliked compromise or inaccuracy, and were slow to bless and quick to chide even the better architects; when in 1806 the first pure Greek Ionic portico in London appeared on the front of Dance's College of Surgeons (the columns were unfluted, they were fluted in 1834 by Barry) it was commended by Cockerell as 'the Ionic portico the gravest I have seen and the most severe' but condemned (a Laugierian criticism) as 'ill applied to the thin paper form of a Ho. with wh. it has no connection'.[109]

In practice, many British Greek Revival architects reduced Greek Revival motifs to a decorative trim; a Doric column here, a 'battered' doorway there; enough to give a little fashionable astringency. The kind of thing that happened may be seen in Charles Middleton's use in 1799 of the Tower of the Winds, much employed since its publication by Stuart and Revett in 1762; it lent itself to incorporation in less strait-laced structures (Figs 86, 87). Middleton used it as a basis but made an obeisance to the nascent Greek Revival by substituting Doric columns without a pediment for the original pedimented Corinthian doorway; the result remains 'finical'. The central chimney is taken from an antique altar; Greekness is diluted by such Italianate features as the

balustrades. The total effect is nearer to Wyatt than to the Greek Revival. Inside, the peculiarly shaped rooms carry the fashion for variety to awkward excess.

The curious tension that existed between the severities of the Greek Revival and the general tendencies of the period is perceptible in the dissonance between the sculpture used on Greek Revival buildings — unless it be a straight copy of such subjects as the Parthenon frieze — and the architecture itself. Winckelmann's praise of 'noble simplicity and sedate grandeur' had referred to the 'Gesture and Expression' of Greek sculpture — 'a great soul lies sedate beneath the strife of passions in Greek figures'[110] — but he had been greatly influenced by Hellenistic copies. The result was to nourish in neo-classical sculpture a disturbing combination of impassivity and sweetness, encouraged by contemporary interest in Mannerist painting (see pp.358–9) and perhaps by Burke's definition of 'beauty'; as Aberdeen pointed out, the influence of the 'sexual affections' in Burke's definition 'appears to have been in a great measure overlooked'; it is 'evident that the properties and qualities considered by Mr. Burke as essential to every species of beauty have been principally, if not entirely, collected from the female form'.[111] The general appeal of this sweetness, exhibited in the work of sculptors such as Flaxman and Canova and in the 'poésie' of influential designers such as Prud'hon, helps to explain why a Greek austerity so far removed from it was antipathetic to so many.

Grange Park in Hampshire (Fig. 88), the only English country house that Wilkins was allowed to build in the image of a Greek temple (his other country houses were all Gothic) is much more impressive than Downing College. Wilkins remodelled the existing seventeenth-century house in 1805–09 for Henry Drummond; it was enlarged by C. R. Cockerell in 1823–5. The scholarly Wilkins compromised a little in tolerating windows — 'there is nothing to confirm the conjecture that windows were ever introduced in temples for the purpose of giving light to the interior'[112] — but not much. The choice of the Grange's style was said to have been prompted by the sight of Dance's unfluted Doric portico of 1803–06 at Stratton Park,[113] which 'roused the ire and contempt of Mr. Drummond . . . [who] determined coute-que coute [a serious threat from a banker] to show the country a real portico'.[114] So the Theseion at Athens, a building that Hope had 'lived in sight of' for three months, without wearying of it,[115] was recreated in brick and Roman cement in the damps of Hampshire.

C. R. Cockerell, who visited the Grange in January 1823, was, despite some 'incorrect' and 'vulgar' details, entranced; significantly, he used a pictorial comparison: 'Nothing . . . can be finer, more classical or more like the finest Poussins . . . There is nothing like it on this side of Arcadia.' In May of the same year he was struck by the 'sunshine upon the building', with 'as clear a sky, the lights and reflections, as Greece'.[116] He had the advantage of a day that matched the

**86** The Tower of the Winds, Athens, published by Stuart and Revett in 1762

**87** An octagonal house, a design by Charles Middleton, 1799

architecture, when sunlight and shadow emphasised the columns and the geometrical shapes of the entablature.

The design of the Grange had been anticipated in the architect Robert Mitchell's publication of 1801: *Plans and Views . . . and an Essay to elucidate the Grecian, Roman and Gothic Architecture*. The most interesting engraving in the book, designed 'to elucidate the Grecian architecture', is uncommonly like Grange Park (begun in 1805). Given the limited number of models for an academic Greek design, it is not impossible that the two designs were arrived at independently.

Other Greek Revival houses followed. The most sublime, in the Burkean sense and in any sense, is Belsay Castle in Northumberland, designed and built by an amateur, Sir Charles Monck (with the assistance of the architect William Dobson), who in 1804 had gone to Greece with Sir William Gell. It combines the archaeological precision of Greek temple detail with a plan, arranged around a peristyle, derived

**88** The Grange, Hants., c.1809, designed by William Wilkins

from that of the Graeco-Roman villa; this came perhaps via France or, possibly, via Pompeii. Such a plan provided more domestic amenities than one based on the temple. There is no vestige of the Picturesque; like Dance's Stratton and Wilkins' Osberton, Belsay confronts the world as a cube. Monck relinquished the strict classicism of Belsay and displayed the virtuosity of his age in designing the stable block with a belfry based on the Tower of the Winds; for a nearby row of arcaded houses an Italian vernacular style was chosen; in 1842 he added a Gothic school.

In Scotland, the spirit of the Greek Revival permeated an entire town. Edinburgh, called from its philosophic and literary fame the 'Athens of the North', became so in appearance also; masterly planning (see p.84) was supported by masterly architecture. In place of Nash's metropolitan Italianate stucco, Edinburgh was given fine Greek Revival stone (Fig. 41). There is no sense of penny pinching, as there always has been with the politicians and merchants of the English capital; the material, a hard grey limestone, is magnificent; the designs are imposing, well suited to the unyielding material. There was much concern for uniformity, expressed in 1806 in the contract between the city of Edinburgh and the owners and architects of the land north of Queen Street; it contained the first detailed regulations for building over a large area in Edinburgh. Precise details were stipulated; basements were to be of 'broached ashlar, or rock work, and above all to be polished, droved, or broached ashlar, and . . . [to] have blocking courses fifteen inches high'.[117] Most detailed were the 'Articles and Conditions of Sale of the Grounds of Drumsheugh' by the Earl of Moray. These laid down that James Gillespie or another architect named by the Earl would supply elevations for the front and back of the houses, with full-size drawings of the mouldings, and drawings of the stables; Gillespie was to give drawings for walls and iron railings; included in the stipulations was the width of the pavements and the height of the garden walls. No expense was to be incurred by the Earl. The result was splendid and powerful.

One Edinburgh enterprise, conceived in a spirit reverential if not sacred (a memorial to those killed in the Napoleonic Wars), would if pursued have produced one of the most remarkable monuments of the Greek Revival, nothing less than a facsimile of the Parthenon sited on Calton Hill. The enterprise was launched in 1822; various manoeuvrings were followed by the appointment in 1822 of C. R. Cockerell as architect, with the younger Playfair as resident architect. The money ran out and only a tremendous fragment materialised, more poignantly expressive unfinished than completed.

## Decline of the archaeological Greek Revival

By the 1820s the Greek Revival was under attack. Doubts began early; they were forcefully expressed by Charles Kelsall in 1814. A natural iconoclast — he argued against the teaching of Greek and Latin in the

ancient universities, his arguments illustrated by copious quotations in both languages — he cited as happy examples of the revival of Greek architecture Smirke's Covent Garden Theatre (Fig. 79), Benjamin Dean Wyatt's Drury Lane (Fig. 81), Hertford and Downing Colleges, Foulston's Assembly Rooms and Theatre at Plymouth, and Thomas Harrison's County Gaol at Chester (Fig. 77). However, he went on to say that a 'too servile imitation of Grecian architecture is likely to become a stumbling block', adding that 'the artist who takes the spirit of the Grecian taste as his groundwork, at the same time engrafting with judgment the best parts of the Italian style on his designs, will bid fair to attain perfection in his art'.[118] Kelsall was eclectic — he thought Borromini's interiors unequalled — but erratic; whilst admitting Italo-Grecian, Saxon, and 'Norman' (Gothic) into his designs, he excluded arches as incompatible with the best Grecian taste, and implied that the Greeks might have had true domes.

Others agreed with his reservations on the Greek Revival. Utilitarian and aesthetic arguments moved in unison against the use of the Greek Revival style in houses. An early opinion of the Grange had opined that 'a Temple instead of a house' had arisen, and that a 'good family house' had been turned into 'a very bad one'.[119] In 1823 Cockerell was assailed by double doubts. He became disillusioned with a Greek Revival house he had designed at Lough Crew, County Meath, which he found 'sadly plain. will never again use Athenian order except in small scale . . . in its squareness left me an unpleasant expression'.[120] And seeing Downing, 'his feeling for the Greek received a shock from which it never recovered. Downing College struck him as utterly poor and ineffective.'[121] Cockerell, again in 1823 (obviously a climactic year for him), said of the Grange that 'as to the propriety of making a Grecian Temple a domestic habitation, that is a question admitting of much doubt'.[122] Loudon followed in questioning 'how far those cumbersome proportions and that Doric severity which according to Vitruvius were reserved to honor the major deities, are applicable to the purposes of villa architecture'.[123] Such doubts were increasingly voiced.

The usual charge against Greek Revival architecture was that it was dull. Some was vulgar. One of the most striking monuments was H. W. Inwood's St. Pancras New Church, designed in 1819 immediately after the architect's return from Greece (Pl. XXXVI). St. Pancras, the most expensive church of its day, is a compendium of Greek architectural motifs, the caryatids of the Erechtheion being prominent; the disposition of the masses is taken from St. Martin-in-the-Fields. According to Inwood, the church was liked by Hope: 'I am most proud to acknowledge hearing from the late learned and illustrious connoisseur, R. P. Knight, that you had been pleased to express much approbation of the church lately completed on the model of Erechtheus'.[124] Cockerell did not share that approbation; in 1821 he wrote: 'simple Greek Greek Greek — radiates bad taste thro' the

whole, ignorance and presumption . . .', and in 1822 'Mr. Inwood and his boys . . . wherever their authorities have ceased they have as usual been aground'.[125] If the unity of taste described by Price and Knight is a valid concept, Inwood's writing and architecture may be an example of it: his *The Erechtheion at Athens*, a lavish publication of 1827, is remarkable (in its period) for an illiterate text. Gwilt probably intended St. Pancras when he questioned the good taste of using caryatids in modern buildings: 'Their exclusion from sacred buildings at least appears absolutely necessary'.[126]

Three major critical charges were made against the Greek Revival. The first alleged barrenness and pedantry: 'Generally, whatever is truly Greek in taste and conception appears to our northern judgments too severe, too naked, too devoid of ornament'.[127] This comment reflected general opinion in 1836; by 1847 Elmes could say of Wilkins, one of the high priests of the movement, that 'His was the very mummy of the art — as cold, as lifeless, and as much bound up in the bands of precedent'.[128] It is not surprising that Greek architecture should have been rejected when unbridled ornament was becoming fashionable — Mr. Pinmoney would have turned from it long before.

The second charge was that Greek architecture had been created for a hot, dry and bright climate and had been injudiciously transposed to northern latitudes; this had both aesthetic and practical implications. Columns stopped the light, the slope of pediments and roofs was not steep enough to cope with rain, the style disregarded windows, and so on. Hope had written perceptively of Greek buildings in his letter on Downing that 'no adequate idea can be obtained of that variety of effect produced by particular site, by perspective, a change of aspect, and a change of light'.[129] The underlining was Soane's, who wrote beside this passage in his copy of the pamphlet: 'true, worthy of the most serious consideration of him who wishes to distinguish himself in the higher beauties of Architecture'.[130]

The third charge was not without aesthetic implications, but sprang from the need for practicality; the Greek style was much more restricted in application than the Roman. Even Hope recanted. He did not use the Greek style at the Deepdene — it is, in fact, everything except Greek — and coupled aesthetic and practical criticisms in what amounts to a complete renunciation: 'To the last their [the Greeks'] want of science produced an enormous consumption of materials in proportion to the space obtained. To the last the internal forms of their edifices must, with all the elegance that could be applied to their limited combinations of outlines, have displayed a want of height, an angularity, an absence of that curve and swell which enables the arch, and cupola, and vault, to produce equal variety, connection, and harmony'.[131] Meason put it succinctly in 1828, when he said that the arch, the vault and the dome 'have been a hundred-fold of more utility to modern nations than all the remains of Grecian architecture' and that, although Greece held first place in architectural rank, 'for domestic application, the Italian is decidedly more useful, and within the reach of our customs and habits'.[132] By that time, the Italian was well on the way to replacing Greek.

## Soane

Gwilt classed Soane and Smirke as 'Grecian' architects (see p.150), and it is true that both ultimately owed much of their architectural language to the Greek fundamentalism of Laugier. However, they were different from each other as architects and as people (Smirke had spent a few months in Soane's office in 1796 but had left because of mutual dislike). And as a contemporary journal remarked, the architecture of Soane compared with that of Smirke and Wilkins was 'like the Arabian Nights Entertainments opposed to Cocker's Arithmetic'[133] (Nash combined both).

Soane shows a clear inheritance from his former master Dance. In both the pulse of French Romantic Classicism beat strongly; both were serious, imbued with a sense of destiny; both heeded Reynolds' injunction to imitate Vanbrugh and utilise the spirit rather than the form of other styles and civilisations; both at times failed to distinguish caprice from inspiration. Dance showed an especial interest in assimilating Gothic and Asiatic forms (see pp.201, 202). Soane was intrigued by Gothic, but seems to have had more temperamental affinity with the classical antique; his art, more than that of any other Regency architect, has the echo of the vault, the sepulchral resonances that banish gaiety from the work of so many of those architects and decorators imbued with the archaeological antique, including Hope (see pp.385, 388–9, 391). Nothing could differ more in spirit from the classically inspired elegancies of the later eighteenth century.

Tyringham Hall and Chapel (Fig. 89, Pl. XXXVII) display Soane's version of Romantic Classicism. A design of 1793 for the house has

**89** Tyringham Hall, Bucks., 1793, designed by Sir John Soane

some likeness to F.–J. Belanger's Bagatelle of 1777, built for the Comte d'Artois. Soane gave Tyringham a full-scale portico of unfluted giant Ionic columns forming a shallow bow, with idiosyncratic double pilasters (defying Laugier) at either end of the façade. The incised band of Greek key decoration that runs across the façade is a device later to be used extensively, by Soane and others; it occurs in classical architecture, and can be seen for example at Baalbek.[134] The house is four-square, with the basement used as offices in the pre-Picturesque way. The impressive triangular design of 1800 for the sepulchral chapel has fluted Doric columns that carry heavy Doric entablatures and jutting pediments, topped with sarcophagi that proclaim the building's purpose. Again, Laugier is not followed to the letter; the statues in niches and the construction of the dome both disobey his dicta,[135] although he was an advocate of variety in plans and liked the idea of triangular churches.

For his own house, Pitzhanger Manor in Ealing, Soane produced in 1800–03 a façade that showed both how far he had left behind the Romantic Classicism of Tyringham, and how inconsistent he must have appeared to any student who cared to compare his house with his teaching (Pl. XXXIX). Based on a Roman triumphal arch, the front is orchestrated by four fluted Ionic columns that stand in bold relief before the rest of the design, which is articulated by strip pilasters. Laugier was doubly flouted, since he had declared against columns on pedestals and had objected to statues placed where humans would fear to tread;[136] perhaps Soane had been convinced by the dry common

sense of Chambers: 'whenever the image is so different from the original it represents, as not to leave the least probability of its being mistaken for the real object, this strict adherence to propriety is very superfluous'.[137] Soane later used such statues on the front of his Lincoln's Inn house.

The Pitzhanger façade has much in common with the inside of the entrance gateway to Lothbury Court at the Bank of England (1798–9); here the arch was explicit, and the columns, not on pedestals but two by two on an elevated base (another motif condemned by Laugier), were richly Corinthian; unlike Lothbury Court, the Pitzhanger front exhibits a tension between the finical flatness of the incised pilaster strips, the bas-reliefs, and the garlands — all placed with mannerist precision — and the bold volume of the projecting columns. The use of low Coade stone reliefs on the Pitzhanger façade was paralleled in and about Rome by the decorative use of real antique sculpture on façades — as, for example, at the Villa Medici — and the occasional oddness of proportion, as here between the central bas-relief above the columns and its surround, may have imitated the sometimes inconsequential placement of fragments in Italy.

The rich façade of the windowless Lothbury front of the Bank of England, as completed in 1805, is a wonderful invention in which an august classicism unites with the Picturesque (Fig. 90); the skyline is especially effective, with the bold scrolled motif beloved of Soane (Fig. 91) that appears on so many of his buildings (Figs 92, 229). Elmes noted that 'Mr. Soane . . . introduced into this country the manly and

**90** The Bank of England, the Lothbury Front, 1805, designed by Sir John Soane

beautiful order of the circular temple of Vesta at Tivoli, which he measured . . . in Italy with praiseworthy care and accuracy. In this grand edifice [the Lothbury front] the architect has given a beautiful adaptation of this exquisite architectural gem (which Claude has introduced for its endless beauties in many of his works) . . . and has carried his bold design upon a lofty base, emulating the beauties of his predecessor Vanbrugh'.[138] It is indicative of the increased care for accuracy that Soane himself had measured the temple at Tivoli, already published by Desgodetz in plates 'dessinés et mesurés très exactement'. Soane's feeling for the Corinthian order is lyrically recorded in his lectures: 'Art cannot go beyond the Corinthian Order . . .'; it is 'of peculiar and enchanting beauty'; his romanticism deprecated any attempt to dismiss the delightful fable of its invention by Callimachus: 'we must lament that any attempt should be made to shake its authenticity'.[139] The use of a Corinthian order taken from a circular temple as a device for rounding a corner would immediately have recalled the original at Tivoli to an educated contemporary and all its associations — with Italy, with the emperor Hadrian, with Claude and the Picturesque — would have been invoked in modern metropolitan London. It is easy to see why associationalism had such an appeal.

Soane's compelling design for a block of houses on Regent Street, bare apart from the strip pilasters and the familiar double scroll

91  A well in the cloister of San Pietro in Vincoli, pictured by Percier and Fontaine, 1798

92  Design for houses for John Robins, Regent Street, by Sir John Soane

(Fig. 92), gives the impression, accentuated by the non-depiction of glazing bars, of a flat wall punctuated by holes. Did the inspiration possibly come from ruined Roman façades such as those at Ostia, where the insistent repetition of utilitarian windows set in an unornamented space has a similar effect? Soane was a mysterious and convoluted man, and might have found a poetic fitness in thus placing, in the heart of commercial London, a reminiscence of the vanished mercantilism of Ostia. The design has a lowering power: only the presence of astragals in the windows, a sign of present life, relieves the utter melancholy. Soane annotated a passage in his edition of Horace which ran in translation, 'The magnificent Structures which are nowadays erected will, in a little Time, scarce leave a Sufficiency of Ground to be tilled', with the words: 'Horace wrote this with a Design to oppose the Luxury and Prodigality of the Age in which he lived'.[140] What street more epitomised the luxury of the Regency than Regent Street?

A sinister romanticism broods over the tomb designed for his wife (and himself) in 1816 (Pl. XXXVIII). A structure based on Roman sepulchres of the type pictured in Montfaucon and other sources is placed beneath his own peculiar motif of a pendentive dome of which the interior contour repeats that of the exterior (see pp.245, 246). This carapace, its wavy line perhaps taken from 'Etruscan' pottery, increases the solemnity of feeling, which is given a touch of the macabre by the expressionistic gesture of the skeleton set at the base. This last motif existed in England, notably in the Nightingale monument in Westminster Abbey, but it seems as likely that Soane took the idea

94 'View of the Lodge', Pellwall House, 1822–8, design by Sir John Soane

straight from Bernini, for whom he had some admiration.[141] Such an image, associated with the baroque and the perfervid excesses of Counter-Reformation emotionalism, was far removed from the placid neo-classical pieties of customary Regency grief.

Soane's expressionism is manifest in another form in designs of 1805 for the Barrack Building for the Bank of England; they may reflect his admiration for the masterpiece of his master Dance, Newgate Prison, itself one of the most expressionistic of all English eighteenth-century buildings; they carry also reminiscences of Piranesi, Giulio Romano, and perhaps Palladio (Fig. 93), all brought up to date with a Doric portico. Repton could not have complained that these designs did not convey the purpose of the structure (see p.292); belligerence is implicit in the architecture and explicit in the pyramids of cannon balls and spears. These last references were much in the French spirit of 'architecture parlante'; the bedroom at Bagatelle designed by Belanger as a military tent had stoves formed of a heap of cannon balls and grenades.

Another aspect of Soane's allusionism is shown in the design for a triangular lodge at Pellwall House (Fig. 94). The proportions are Gothic, but the details are classical; one detects the presence of Vanbrugh, and indeed the way in which the building has assimilated Gothicism reminds one of Vanbrugh; it is no coincidence that it resembles Dance's essays in Gothicism. The chimneys have an especially Vanbrugh-like flavour, placed above the walls with the air of battlements. The triangular arches are interesting; used also by

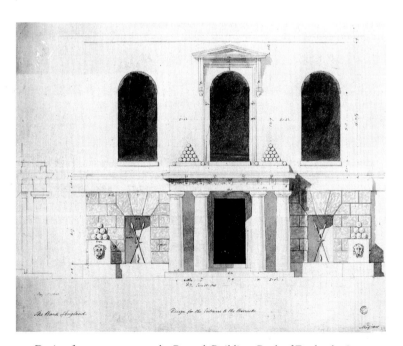

93 Design for an entrance to the Barrack Building, Bank of England, 1805, by Sir John Soane

Hope at the Deepdene (see p.116), they here probably have primitivist Gothic associations. The peculiar turret has hints of the Italian vernacular.

Soane's late design for the gallery at Dulwich, which proposed the repetition of the mausoleum motif as an entrance porch (Pl. XL), again paid homage to Vanbrugh, but beneath the classical guise there may be other influences at work. The dramatic tall arches of the two end pavilions recall, despite the differences of detail, the great Moghul gateways of India depicted by the Daniells and used by Dance; the long repetition of the arcades, coupled with the change in level between these and the main roof of the gallery, has something in common with the nave of a Gothic church. If these influences are present, they are completely absorbed. The effect, especially as given in the watercolour, is of a wild romanticism.

Soane's mannerisms were taken up by other Regency architects, and appeared up and down the country. Even Nash essayed his style (Fig. 95); numbers 224–40 Regent Street, on the highway of Nashdom, had the incised lines, the vases, the acroteria, of Soane; however Nash, the master of the Picturesque, completely missed the expressionistic

96 St. Andrew's Chapel, Devonport, 1823, designed by John Foulston

95 'Part of the East Side of Regent Street', nos. 224–40 Regent Street, 1822, designed by John Nash

and romantic aspects of Soane's style; the Picturesque and the romantic were not identical, although frequently in alliance.

One of Soane's closest imitators was John Foulston. He had migrated from London to Plymouth on winning the competition for the Royal Hotel there; the design united 'the distinct purposes of an Hotel, Assembly Rooms, and Theatre', containing hotel, assembly rooms, theatre, billiard room, coffee rooms, and bars, all in Greek Revival style. Constructionally it was advanced, making extensive use of rolled iron in the theatre roof as a fire-proofing expedient.[142]

Foulston's uninspired version of the Soane style was exemplified in St. Andrew's Chapel at Plymouth of 1823, built of Dartmoor granite (Fig. 96). The exterior has Soanean detail of pilasters, doorway, acroteria, and urns upon the tower; the interior has Soanean incisions on the pilasters (especially popular, perhaps because they were cheaper than capitals and fluting), a Greek key pattern on the pulpit, and the flat arch. Foulston said 'its character is intended to be severely Greek, not abounding, but choice in ornament. The Gallery fronts, instead of being cut up by a series of panels, are decorated with a continuous honeysuckle enrichment, and rests on candelabra columns'.[143] The altar was painted to resemble porphyry. One wonders what a mildly Greek chapel might have looked like.

## The palatial Italianate: Palladian

With the decline of the 'archaeological' Greek Revival, everything pointed to Italy as the source of new architectural ventures. Cockerell, one of the most perceptive critics, had shown the way the wind was blowing as early as August 1815, when he wrote to his father from Rome and observed of Italian architecture (he was thinking of Italian palace architecture) that 'tho' out of fashion it is most particularly necessary for all the purposes of practice in arche. and by no means to be neglected in any point of view'.[144] In this he was not exceptional. Many architects who went to Italy after Waterloo were interested in Italian palaces, especially those of Florence, Venice, and Rome; Palladian Vicenza was already well known.

In 1825 Gwilt prefaced his re-publication (itself a sign of the times) of Chambers' *Treatise* with the comment: 'With the greatest submission to those who are better informed . . . I cannot help acknowledging my bias towards what may properly be called the Italian school of Architecture, as it is found in the works of Palladio, Sanmichele, and others, who formed their style from the resources which the remaining antiquities of Rome afforded'. The Italian offered everything that the Greek did not. Elmes said, in classifying Nash, Gwilt, and Ware (the architect of the Burlington Arcade) as Italian architects, and Soane and Smirke as Grecian, that the Italian style 'had all the vices of beauty, and is too rich, too redolent of charms, too redundant in variety . . .'.[145] His

prim disapprobation made it sound attractive but dangerous; post-Laugierian Palladianism suffered for some time from puritan guilt. However, Palladio had been of all Italian architects the one most favoured by the English, and one cannot be surprised that he emerged from eclipse.

Nash, named by Elmes as an 'Italian' architect, had as we have seen shared the general interest in Italian vernacular architecture (Fig. 53), an interest that he retained throughout his life. He had also inherited from his master, Sir Robert Taylor, a Palladianism that remained a staple ingredient in his work, albeit often given a French flavour, especially after his visit to Paris in 1814. He picked up a constituent in Palladio's genius that in Palladio was present without being dominant, and that was in accordance with a strain in Nash's own personality — the bravura element; unless used with taste this can lead to vulgarity, and Nash's taste was erratic. Uvedale Price noticed this bravura quality in the background architecture, Palladian in type, depicted in the paintings of Veronese, and described it as 'the picturesque of regular and entire architecture';[146] this attribute is strikingly similar to a certain quality in Nash's architecture. It was probably this that was in Cockerell's mind when he commented: 'The architecture of the Regent's Park may be compared to the Poetry of an improvisatore — one is surprised and even captivated at first sight with the profusion of splendid images, the variety of the scenery and the readiness of the fiction. But if as many were versed in the Grecian rules of this science as there are in those of Homer and Virgil this trumpery would be less popular'.[147]

Palladio used stucco; the Basilica at Vicenza is his only work entirely in stone.[148] When Nash covered London with stucco palaces (many, like his own house at 14–16 Regent Street, devoted partly to commercial uses), he was following in the footsteps of the master, and may have felt he was doing so. Two groups of largely extant buildings in London show his talents to fine effect — Carlton House Terrace and the terraces of Regent's Park. Their present appearance is a solecism; the leases for Regent's Park stipulated that tenants were to 'clean, colour and rejoint in imitation of Bath Stone the outside stucco or mastic work . . . in the month of August', to paint the outside sashes fronting the Park 'in imitation of oak', and the iron railings of the areas and balconies 'of the colour of Bronze' once every four years.[149] The gleam of white amongst the trees was not part of the original idea.

Bearing this in mind, one realises why Nash's contemporaries thought it proper to subject his architecture to criticism, instead of treating it as a theatrical backdrop. They found grave faults. Elmes' judgment of Chester Terrace, made in 1821, may be taken as typical. Chester Terrace, he said, 'like most of that gentleman's works, combines genius and carelessness. Genius, and powerful conception in the composition, and a grasp of mind equalled by no other artist of the day in the design: and carelessness, sometimes degenerating to littleness, with a deficiency of elegance in the details'. The Terrace, he said, had a Corinthian Order 'of a feeble and effeminate character in its details, surmounted by a balustrade of lanky proportions and tasteless forms. The capitals do not spread sufficiently . . . and the volutes are too small, and are pinched up, as if the acanthus, when the Callimachus of Chester Terrace gathered them to decorate his order, had been withered by a frost'. But, it was 'a grand, bold, and commanding row of mansions . . . a noble composition. The Corinthian arches at each end are novel in idea, grand in conception, imposing in effect' and the pavilion-like houses at each end make 'a fine and novel effect'.[150]

The most flamboyant and theatrical of all the terraces was Cumberland Terrace, placed originally to face the King's 'guingette' (never built) in the Park; the Terrace resembles the most unreal of Veronese's backgrounds. Unreal or not, the terraces were a popular success; this was far from the case with the 'trumpery' of the first structure of Buckingham Palace, which provoked a storm of disapproval; the odium was concentrated on the façade to St. James' Park (Fig. 98), the garden front being found more acceptable.

The background to the building of the palace was the victorious triumphalism of the years after Waterloo; the feeling of competition with imperial Paris was strong. The sense of London's unworthiness was not new; Lady Holland had in March 1800 written in prophetic terms: 'In future times when this little island shall have fallen into its natural insignificancy, by being no longer possessed of a fictitious power founded upon commerce, distant colonies, and other artificial sources of wealth, how puzzled will the curious antiquary be when seeking amid the ruins of London vestiges of its past grandeur . . . the bridges alone would strike the eye as fine remains'.[151] Foreigners were amazed at London's provincialism: Delacroix, for instance, in the early 1820s (at a time when improvements had been effected), was shocked at the absence of 'all, that we call architecture'.[152] Farnborough, one of the King's intimates who, urged on by him, were working for the improvement of the capital, would have felt chagrin at Delacroix's observation. He expressed his ideas in a pamphlet of 1826 that emphasised the grand gesture and the grand plan, and harked back to the seventeenth century in so doing. He said with immoderate pride of Regent Street that 'to say that there are not some architectural freaks displayed . . . would be absurd, but as a whole it is the finest street in Europe';[153] he applauded the practice of building houses and shops in a terrace and thus transforming them into palaces, and declared with truth that 'In the person of George IV are united the discriminating judge and the liberal patron of the arts . . . may his reign form an era in the annals of taste, as it ever will in the annals of glory'.[154] The glory has departed; the taste (partially) remains.

In a period when shops became palaces, palaces should look like palaces: the King's London house was felt as a national disgrace. A foreign prince had expressed reproach for the mean English royal palaces, and had been told that 'our magnificence was to be seen in our subsidies not in our palaces'; the retort had excited Farnborough's contempt but had been reported with glee by Mrs. Arbuthnot, the Duke of Wellington's intimate.[155] The Duke himself was of that order common in British politicians who have no conception of 'la gloire' in cultural terms; it was sad that, at a time when opinion ran strongly for architectural magnificence, so much power should be in the hands of a penny-pinching person who, rather than build another Blenheim, chose to patch up his banal house at Stratfield Saye. Mrs. Arbuthnot's opposition to the plan of Sir Frederick Trench and his Committee to build a royal palace in Hyde Park is recorded in her journal for October 1825: 'the worst plan of a house I ever saw and quite colossal, for he proposes a statue gallery 500 feet long, a drawing room 190 and the other rooms in proportion. It is the most ridiculous plan I ever saw for added to it is the idea of a street 200 feet wide extending from the end of Hyde Park opposite the new palace to St. Pauls!! . . . The King and Duke of York are madly eager for this plan . . . all the rest of us laughed at Colonel Trench and his plans . . .'.[156]

It was in this atmosphere that Nash designed and built Buckingham Palace. The façade that fronted St. James' Park was execrated (Fig. 98). It was unlike anything anybody had seen before, extraordinarily loose-limbed; the ground floor colonnade and the main bulk of the façade hardly tied together the disparate elements of the composition. Especially eccentric were the upstanding blocks on the wings, looking like separate buildings erected upon the stories below; also disconnected were the temple-like structures at either end of the garden façades; precedents existed for these, but taken together with the rest the disconnectedness appears part of a deliberate system. When Nash experienced the humiliation of the demolition and redesigning of the St. James' façade, his comment was that 'I was not at first aware that the effect would have been so bad, but now I think that any wings would take from the dignity of a palace'.[157] This sounds unconsidered; many palaces have wings on the entrance front, including Versailles and Blenheim.

What prompted so practised an architect to involve himself in such a fiasco? The accepted opinion of Nash was that his detail was bad, but that he was a master of composition; as Elmes said in the passage quoted above, 'Genius, and powerful conception in the composition, and a grasp of mind equalled by no other artist of the day in the design'. Nash's detail, where the King's sharp eye was upon him, was good; the faults of the first Buckingham Palace façade, if faults they were, were compositional, but it can hardly be supposed that the composition was unintentional. Critics seem to have been perplexed; one spoke of 'a house, of which the front is blocked up by its own wings

**97** 'Painting in the House called the Vestals', Pompeii, as published in 1817–19

— of which the portico consists of the heaviest Doric columns without bases below, and of the most ornamented Corinthian above, and of which the whole is surmounted by a little Cupola resembling in shape and size an egg in an egg-cup. . . .'[158] In fact, were the disconnected and sprawling composition deliberate, an under-played dome would be essential, since a large one would have drawn the whole together.

A clue may lie in the way building evolved, as explained by Nash to the Select Committee on Windsor Castle and Buckingham Palace in July 1831. He said that 'his late Majesty's intentions and commands were to convert Buckingham House into a private residence for himself'. A plan was made adding merely a few rooms: 'I continually urged his Majesty to build in some other situation, and made several Plans for that purpose . . . without any effect. . . . I then urged His Majesty to pull down the house and rebuild it . . . in a line with Pall Mall . . . one day, either at Buckingham House or Kensington, HM took me to Lord Farnborough, and said good humouredly "Long, now remember I tell Nash before you, at his peril ever to advise me to build a Palace. I am too old to build a Palace. If the Public wish to have a Palace, I have no objection to build one [not difficult to believe!] but I must have a pied à terre. I do not like Carlton House standing in a street . . . if he pulls it [Buckingham House] down he shall rebuild it in the same place, there are early associations that endear me to the spot". . . . From that moment I never presumed to press HM on the subject of building a Palace . . .'.

The building was enlarged to Nash's design, and the King, to Nash's indignation, recanted his denials that he would hold his Courts there: 'After the Building was covered in, HM sent for me to Carlton House, and said "Nash, the State Rooms you have made me are so handsome, that I think I shall hold my Courts there". I took the liberty to submit to him how unfair such a determination was to me as his Architect.'[159] If this account be true — and Farnborough is mentioned as a witness — it might help to explain the nature of the unsuccessful façade.

The palace was obviously first intended as a private house; it would not have been untoward for it to have been conceived as a palatial villa, of the Italian type — Elmes had remarked that the villas of the modern Romans were in fact palaces.[160] But the peculiarities of the unsuccessful version gave it something of the air of a quite different type of building, of those seen in the mural decorations of Pompeii and Herculaneum, the little depictions of what appear to be architectural whimsies but which were in fact the *villae maritimae*, the *porticus* villas that, often on the most princely scale, lined the Campanian littoral and the sea coast of Latium. The magnificent series of the *Pitture Antiche d'Ercolano* was one of the most frequently used source books of the period; the subject was of contemporary interest, given the recurring dissatisfaction — which was gaining impetus in the 1820s, intensified by the failure of the Greek Revival — with the use of temple architecture for domestic habitations. And the little Pompeian paintings provided a possible basis for the imaginary reconstruction of one of the most celebrated of ancient buildings, a building that had had a profound influence on Renaissance gardens and hence on English gardens — Pliny's villa at Laurentinum. As Meason wrote in 1828, 'The representation of a marine villa on the wall of a room at Pompeii [Fig. 97], may be likened to the splendid villa of Pliny. All the rooms are behind ranges of covered porticos . . . These may be found in the Pompeian painting, which in number of porticos is perhaps exaggerated; but in Pliny's day they were created to an extravagant extent'. He referred elsewhere to 'The immense quantity of these pillars, which the ruins of these ancient villas afforded'.[161]

Attempts were made to reconstruct Pliny's villa; at Rome in 1786 Percier 'avait imaginé . . . de reconstituer une demeure antique en restaurant une maison de campagne de Pline, "Le Laurentin".'[162] A drawing in the Soane Museum (Fig. 99) is a Regency effort. A version by Schinkel[163] has the 'front blocked up by its own wings', the fault alleged of Buckingham Palace.

The St. James' façade of Buckingham Palace has an eccentric and capricious composition, a disconnectedness, in common with the wall paintings and with the reconstructions. Perhaps Nash had been inspired to try something new; one can see, in his later work, an advance into fantasy and he might well have taken chances with a

**98** 'New Palace, St. James's Park', Buckingham Palace, 1827, designed by John Nash

**99** Reconstruction of Pliny's Villa, by E. Stevens

**100** State Paper Office, 1829–34, designed by Sir John Soane

**101** 'View of The Reform Club House in Pall Mall now Building by Charles Barry Architect', 1838–41

**102** Design for Combe Bank, by George Dance

*Above* **103** Design for the Royal Exchange, 1839, by C. R. Cockerell

private house that he would not have taken with the focus of the British Court. This sense of fantasy can be seen in the Pavilion at Brighton, in the Regent's Park Terraces, in Carlton House Terrace and even in Regent Street (Fig. 42, Pl. XLIX). It is regrettable that its manifestation at Buckingham Palace was stifled.

## The palatial Italianate: 'Tuscan'

In 1825 Gwilt had added a note to his misgivings concerning modern imitations of Greek architecture: 'The Tuscan school for grandeur and

exhibition of the picturesque is without parallel. My reasons for this preference arise from the fact that it is more plastic, that is, more capable of being submitted to the wants and habits of this country'.[164] The curious thing about Gwilt's statement is that the Tuscan palaces to which he appears to have been referring were not particularly 'Picturesque' in the accepted sense, since they were four-square, cubic and had flat, uninterrupted cornices. Since taste was moving towards them, they became, ipso facto, Picturesque.

Taste was becoming more eclectic, or eclectic in a different way: it was inclining even towards the baroque (see p.182). Both Soane and

Charles Barry designed buildings influenced by the Italian Renaissance style in the 1820s; the latter had visited France, Italy, Greece, Turkey, Egypt, and Syria, and had made studies in Rome and Florence of the Renaissance buildings upon which he was to draw. Barry and Soane were in friendly communication, and the former's interest in Renaissance buildings may have rubbed off on the latter. Barry's Attree Villa of 1827 (Fig. 65) preceded Soane's New State Paper Office of 1829, but there is no hint of vernacular Italian influence on the latter's firmly Renaissance design (Fig. 100). The astylar façade has something in common with that of Barry's Travellers' Club, of the same year. The Italian Renaissance palazzo reached London in all its gloomy grandeur in 1838–41 in Barry's Reform Club, which both set the seal on the new style and presented its most splendid embodiment (Fig. 101). Exterior and interior pomp here united to usher in Victorian clubdom in its most imposing aspect.

Also imposing, but in a quite different way, was the palatial Italianism of Cockerell, as seen in the New Ashmolean Museum and Taylor Institution of the early 1840s, and in the design for the Royal Exchange of 1839 (Fig. 103). Mingled with the Italianate elements are traces of the baroque and even of French Romantic Classicism; Cockerell had travelled a long way from the Greek purity of his early career. The ostentatious magnificence of the Royal Exchange design

casts its shadow forward, even as far as the new Regent Street that was to replace Nash's civilised stucco with the commercial bombast of the twentieth century.

## 'Classical' ineptitudes

Regency classicism came in many guises; the choice was large, involving not only varieties of antique classicism, including the Egyptian, but the classical styles that developed during and after the Renaissance. The best synthesists were astonishingly successful, especially Dance and Soane; they were capable of abandoning synthesis in favour of an earlier manner, as did Dance's Kentian Palladian design for Combe Bank (Fig. 102). It looks deceptively easy, but where the restraint of taste was removed, the result could be uncomfortable or comical. Two projects will suffice; the first (admittedly by a student) combines the Italian vernacular, Giulio Romano-type Renaissance, and a Palladian-type hybrid in a design both ludicrous and disgusting (Fig. 105); the second, somewhat more literate, fuses French Romantic and Italian interpretations of classicism with a strong dash of Vanbrugh, especially in the gateway on the left (Fig. 104). It is a tribute to Regency taste that this kind of thing occurred comparatively rarely.

**104** Design for an 'Italian' villa, 1834, by E. H. Browne

**105** 'Sketch for a Summer House & Dairy Combined', 1834, design by David Brandon

XXXVII 'Design for a Sepulchral Chapel',
Tyringham, Bucks., 1800, by Sir John Soane

XXXVIII Design for the monument to Mrs. Soane,
1816, by Sir John Soane

157

XXXIX Pitzhanger Manor, Mddx., the entrance front, 1800–03, designed by Sir John Soane

XL Design for the Dulwich Gallery, 1811–14, by Sir John Soane

# Gothic Styles

A bit of Gothic is all the rage now. They will put a crooked top to a cottage window, as if they could not make a strait one; and they will say it is tasty: it is Gothic: . . . Pray, sir, can you tell me what Gothic rightly means? For it seems to me often only another word for nonsense.
*William Mitford*[1]

## The Gothic predicament

### Sublimity and patriotism

The testy comment quoted above posed a conundrum discomforting to the architectural gothicists, who encountered considerable difficulties in their attempt to resuscitate a defunct style; indeed, the versatility of the classical vocabulary and the magnificent achievements of architects working within the confines of the classical style might make one wonder why architects bothered to venture amongst the reefs and shoals of Gothic. The principal answer is, of course, that they and their clients were entranced by it.

Few escaped its spell. Soane and Hope, for example, neither of whom moved easily in the Gothic style — Hope virtually ignored it — were obviously deeply affected by its emotional power. Soane told his students that 'our great Cathedrals' have 'qualities which are the great sources of true sublimity'. Can, he asked of Westminster and Salisbury, 'the most unobservant spectator . . . fail to be impressed by their magnitude and solemn appearance?' through which the eye 'wanders with inexpressible delight . . .'.[2] When Hope embarked on a rhapsodic and visionary description of the beauties of Gothic in his *Historical Essay on Architecture*, the passion of the author of *Anastasius*, hardly perceptible in the 'furniture book', was drawn forth.[3] It was the sublimity of Gothic, more than its decorative richness or its variety, that inspired Regency attempts at imitation, the more inevitably since aesthetic delight in ecclesiastical Gothic had been fostered by an associated literary romanticism. It was useless to apply eighteenth-century rationalism to this new enthusiasm; when Alison wrote in 1790 that 'the same relation of Breadth and Height which is so wonderfully affecting in the Gothic Cathedral, although at variance with all the classic rules of Proportion, would be both absurd and painful, in the

Forms of any common apartment',[4] he misjudged the temper of his times; only a decade later the famous fête in honour of Nelson was to be held in the uncommon apartments of Fonthill Abbey.

Gothic emotion had its perils, as was clearly perceived by Walpole: 'one must have taste to be sensible of the beauties of classic architecture; one only wants passions to feel Gothic'.[5] The consequences of this passion have been noted by architectural historians: architectural standards were 'confused and debilitated' by literary antiquarianism, which 'is much easier to acquire than an eye for classical proportion'.[6] The success of Gothic left the broad road to Abbotsford open.

The emotional force of Gothic architecture was heightened by the appeal of a patriotism that was not less powerful in being founded on fallacies. The first fallacy was the nationalistic claim made by the antiquarian John Carter and others that England had invented the Gothic style (Hope, true to form, not only said that the English had not invented Gothic, but that they had 'displayed it with less vastness and less variety' than the Europeans).[7] The second, equally fallacious, was that the Goths or Franks who invaded Rome had bequeathed freedom to the English (in Gibbon's words, 'they deserved, they assumed, they maintained the honourable epithet of Franks or Freemen'); the preface of Batty Langley's book on Gothic architecture of 1742 had equated Gothicism with British freedom.

The falsity of ideas has never hindered their adoption, and patriotic ideas endeared Gothic style; in 1820 they prompted those proposing a national monument to Shakespeare not only to suggest Chantrey as one 'fitted to mould the figure with true English feeling', but also that the style should be Gothic: 'It would be quite heathenish to erect an edifice to the memory of Shakespere, after Egyptian, Grecian, or Roman models'.[8] The equation between Shakespeare and Gothic — 'an ancient majestic piece of Gothic architecture' — was an old one; it had been made by Alexander Pope.[9] The idea that Gothic architecture, freedom, and Britishness went together helped to ensure that the new Houses of Parliament designed in the 1830s wore Gothic dress; it is a happy fact that the two bulwarks of the Constitution, at Windsor and Westminster, became in rebuilding the two greatest triumphs of Regency 'Picturesque' Gothic — architectural fancy dress apotheosised.

## Gothic construction

In order to revive the Gothic style as contemporary architecture, it was necessary to understand the principles of Gothic construction, which were intimately linked with aesthetic effect. This proved extremely difficult. Much has been written in the present day about the survival of a continuous, almost 'underground' Gothic in England since the Middle Ages; it is clear that the 'survival' was skin deep; structural principles had to be rediscovered. One eighteenth-century architect,

James Essex, had understood Gothic detail and Gothic structure in a manner unique in his time; unfortunately, his *History of Gothic Architecture in England* was never published. Antiquarianism alone did not answer; when John Carter, the scourge of Wyatt, produced one of the earliest churches to attempt academic Gothic, a Roman Catholic Chapel of 1792 at Winchester for Bishop John Milner, the result was lean and arid.

Comprehension of Gothic as a complete and coherent style was rare; many architects had a deep interest in ecclesiastical Gothic, and a more limited interest in mediaeval castles (which, as engines of war, could not adopt the architectural felicities of the cathedrals); there, however, their interest stopped, to the extent of saying that Gothic domestic buildings had not existed. As Hope pointed out, this was hardly true, and if few examples of Gothic domestic architecture remained in England there were numerous Gothic secular buildings extant on the Continent.

**106** The probable origin of Gothic architecture, a Royal Academy lecture drawing used by Sir John Soane

Admiration of Gothic construction led Chambers, a classicist if ever there was one, to deplore the faulty construction of the Greeks and Romans and to assert that Gothic architects had 'a lightness in their works, an art and boldness of execution; to which the ancients never arrived: and which the moderns comprehend and imitate with difficulty'.[10] Given this lack of comprehension and difficulty of imitation, most architects used the Gothic style principally as decoration. As antiquarian depictions of Gothic increased in availability and accuracy, the complaint was made that architects combined accurate detail with inaccuracy of structure; this situation persisted well into the nineteenth century.

An essay published in 1797 illustrates the 'very deep obscurity which still surrounds this curious subject'. Its author, Sir James Hall, Bart., identified the three characteristics of Gothic as the pointed arch, the clustered column, and the branching roof[11] (he ignored the flying buttress). He was inspired to understand the origin of Gothic forms in a manner tinged with Laugierian primitivism: 'It happened that the peasants of the country through which I was travelling were then employed in collecting and carrying home the long rods or poles which they make use of to support their vines . . . these were to be seen, in every village, standing in bundles, or waving, partly loose, upon carts. It occurred to me, that a rustic dwelling might be composed of such rods, bearing a resemblance to works of Gothic architecture, and from which the peculiar forms of that style might have been derived'.[12]

The theory is charming; that it vindicates the author's argument that all the forms of Gothic 'are connected together by a regular system' and that 'its authors have been guided by principle and not, as many have alleged, by mere fancy and caprice'[13] is less certain. Not only did Hall derive Gothic construction from the properties of willow (Fig. 107 Pl. XLIII); he found analogies for ornamental details, including those of window tracery, in the same medium (he had noticed at Batalha (Fig. 108), a Portuguese Gothic building much admired by the late eighteenth and early nineteenth-century Gothicists, crocket ornaments that resembled willow leaves). In 1792 he went into his garden and built a 'Gothic Cathedral' of willow; it struck root and throve, and to his joy completely vindicated his theories, producing buds and tufts of leaves on the rods, crockets and cusps from decaying bark, all ready for imitation in stone. Nothing could more clearly illustrate the primitive nature of Gothic studies at the turn of the century than Sir James's essay.

### Destruction and conservation

Eighteenth-century ignorance of the principles of Gothic construction had been fostered by a preoccupation with the idea that Gothic architecture must have depended upon a system analogous to the classical orders; it is easy to see why the concept of Gothic as an inert

107 A Gothic nave in stone, and in willow, from an essay by Sir James Hall, 1797

rather than a dynamic architecture would have veiled its true qualities. A notorious attempt to give Gothic architecture order and proportion equivalent to those of classical architecture had been made by Batty Langley; ambiguously, the first edition of 1742 had been entitled *Ancient Architecture*, being changed in subsequent editions to *Gothic Architecture*. Despite critical scorn, the volume was used well into the nineteenth century, long after close observation of existing buildings and Thomas Rickman's analysis (see p.163) had invalidated the 'system' set up by Langley. Walpole had perceived that Gothic had no system analogous to that of the orders, but did not feel that it suffered from the lack: 'the men who had not the happiness of lighting on the simplicity and proportion of the Greek orders were, however, so lucky as to strike out a thousand graces and effects, magnificent and yet genteel, vast yet light, vulnerable and picturesque. It is difficult for the noblest Grecian temple to convey so many impressions to the mind as a cathedral does of the best Gothic taste'.[14]

Laugier had written on Gothic, and his words had been heeded in England. He had been moved by Gothic, and had bestowed on it high praise — and blame. He believed, as one would expect, in the forest origins of the style: 'ces grands berceaux formés par deux rangées d'arbres de haut futaye ont fourni le modèle de l'Architecture de nos Eglises gothiques' (Fig. 106).[15] Pursuing this idea, he suggested it might be better to imitate Gothic architecture inside churches, reserving Greek for the exteriors — an extraordinarily bizarre proposal from a rationalist and structuralist. He conjured up a vision anticipating Gaudí, in which palm trees would masquerade as Gothic columns.[16] He rhapsodised on the beauties of Gothic in words that may have influenced those spoken by Soane quoted above (see p.159): 'l'oeil plonge délicieusement à travers plusieurs files de colonnes . . . un mélange, un mouvement, un tumulte de percés et de massifs, qui jouent, qui contrastent et dont l'éffet est ravissant.' However, he condemned the detail of these wonderful churches, which he considered full of 'sots ornemens que le goût du 14e et du 15e siècle leur a prodigués. Un affreux jubé se présente. . . .'[17]

His remedy was ruthless: 'Ecartez d'abord tous les obstacles qui diminuent, qui offusquent la variété et la bizarrerie de ses aspects. Détruisez tous les faux ornements qui surchargent les massifs ou qui bouchent les percés. . . .'[18] As for the tombs, that in many churches jostled for the best place: 'tous ces monumens seront enlevés. Ou on les détruira, ou on leur assignera des places plus convenables'.[19] What does the radical programme of this impious clergyman bring to mind? None other than that carried out by James Wyatt at Salisbury Cathedral, who followed it to the letter. Moreover, the same aesthetic concepts that ruled the 'restoration' of Salisbury ruled the design of Fonthill; 'variety' and 'intricacy', constituents of the 'beautiful' as defined by Burke, were rejected in favour of uninterrupted vistas of the sublime; as in 'les Eglises gothiques', the 'grande élévation se fait sentir sans interruption et sans trouble'[20] — not even chandeliers impeded the grand progression of Gothic spaces (see p.314). The result was far removed from the rococo prettinesses of Strawberry Hill.

Laugier had had no hesitation in suggesting that mediaeval buildings should be altered to conform with eighteenth-century aesthetic ideals; this attitude was common. However, there is evidence of other attitudes, informed by the wish to preserve. This sentiment had manifested itself on occasion for centuries (at the dawn of the Gothic period, the monks of Canterbury had wished to preserve Norman work). But conservation joined forces with the revival of interest in Gothic as a style and its success as a literary form to gain strength, and the preservation of old and picturesque churches and houses was increasingly advocated. The vegetable growth of antiquarian sentiment put on leaf, nourished by a general sense of tradition and propriety. The wish to preserve had appeared in the eighteenth century in unmistakable form. In 1740, for instance, the Countess of Hartford had regretted 'the modern rage for pulling down the venerable castles and abbeys . . . there always appears to me more grandeur in these piles, than in any of the new-fashioned edifices'. This feeling can be taken back further; she recalled, in reference to Longleat, that 'when my father died [in 1708] I still remember his lamenting that my grandfather had taken down the Gothic windows on the first floor, on one of the fronts, and put up sashes . . . the present Lord Weymouth

. . . ordered the sashes to be pulled down, and the old windows to be restored'.[21]

Uvedale Price shared such opinions, and had warned against rashness in repairing old mansions: 'too much caution cannot be used'.[22] Repton shows many instances of such sensitivity; his *Observations* of 1803 contains a general plea for the retention of old buildings 'if a single fragment remains of the grandeur of former times',[23] and when in 1805 he worked on Barningham Hall in Norfolk, the east front was 'preserved most scrupulously. . . . There is something so venerable and picturesque in many houses of this date [Elizabethan], that I have always endeavoured to preserve as much of them as could be adapted to modern uses. . . .'[24] In the same decade Lord Mansfield sacked all the workmen at Scone Palace and suspended operations for a year when a misunderstanding resulted in those parts of the fabric that were to be retained being torn down.[25]

Draconian as Wyatville's work at Windsor seems to modern eyes, to destroy entirely the ancient seat of the English monarchs had become almost (not quite; see pp.169–70) unthinkable; as it was, his wholesale destructions aroused protests.

Interest in authenticity at times acted against the interests of conservation. Old Gothic detail was re-used in new structures. Continental Gothic buildings were rifled not only as sources of design; they were rifled. The most startling example was the incorporation in the 1820s of large bits from Les Andelys and Jumièges, both in Normandy, in the new Highcliffe Castle; this and other depredations led to a vigorous protest by Victor Hugo in 1825, whose eulogy of Gothic architecture in *The Hunchback of Notre Dame* of 1831 must be the most poetically eloquent and sustained in any language. His protest was followed by effective protective measures by the French government, over a hundred years in advance of much weaker legislation in England.

## Design sources

Laugier's attitude towards Gothic left no place for historical authenticity, but the fiery controversies provoked by the destructive 'restorations' at Salisbury and elsewhere that had followed his precepts helped to encourage careful antiquarian publications of the glories of Gothic architecture. John Carter's and, to a lesser extent. Richard Gough's impassioned invective against vandalism and 'Wyatt the Destroyer', beginning in 1789 and continuing for thirty years, rendered the pages of *The Gentleman's Magazine* a seething crucible in which the standards of Gothic restorations were tested and found wanting. The controversy resulted in Carter's exclusion by Wyatt from the restorations at Westminster Abbey. Interest in authenticity had been growing steadily: Chambers had written that 'one cannot refrain from wishing, that the Gothic structures were more considered, better understood. . . . Would our dilettanti instead of importing the gleanings of Greece [a hit at the Greek lobby] or our antiquaries, instead of publishing loose incoherent prints; encourage persons duly qualified, to undertake a correct elegant production of our own cathedrals, and other buildings called Gothic, before they totally fall to ruin; it would be of real service to the arts of design.'[26] The last phrase indicates a concern for practical use, not for antiquarian study.

A step towards satisfying Chambers' requirements was taken by John Britton, who from 1805 to 1814 produced *Architectural Antiquities of Great Britain* in forty quarterly parts. His stated object was 'To preserve correct delineation and accurate accounts' of the ancient edifices;[27] the publication was cheap, and found ready buyers. The editor of Britton's autobiography commented: 'The great success and popularity which attended this work was, doubtless, chiefly owing to the superiority of its graphic illustrations, which far surpassed any architectural engravings previously published'; these were not all that might be desired, since they were still 'general views, with but few plans, geometrical elevations, or architectural details'. None the less, their effect was profound, and 'In the nine years which elapsed during the publication of the *Architectural Antiquities* a taste for ancient church-architecture was widely diffused, with a desire to imitate it in modern edifices: Architects were led to measure and examine the buildings illustrated . . . as well as others in all parts of Europe'. The conclusion was that 'it is not too much to assert, that the successful application of the so-called "Gothic" Architecture of our ancestors to modern Ecclesiastical or Domestic purposes, may, to a large extent, be attributed to this and other works simultaneously produced by Mr. Britton'.[28]

The lack of architectural precision in Britton's publications was supplied; from 1820 to 1823 *Specimens of Gothic Architecture*, produced by Augustus Pugin, Josiah Taylor, and Britton himself, published prints 'entirely different in style and character to those in Mr. Britton's contemporary publications, being exclusively geometrical elevations and sections, with a scale to each subject'.[29] In 1830 it was agreed by Le Queux, Longman, and Britton, that an architectural dictionary of mediaeval architecture be produced; it was ultimately to be dedicated to Queen Victoria.

### Chronology of Gothic

The lengthy period of time over which the great majority of English cathedrals were built made their analysis difficult; the uncertain chronology of English Gothic made its 'thousand graces and effects' infinitely perplexing to those confronted with the usual magnificent jumble of an English Gothic cathedral. This problem was in the mind of Robert Mitchell when he stated in 1801, in his *Essay to elucidate the Greek, Roman and Gothic Architecture*, that few English Gothic buildings existed 'which, in all their parts, can be offered as adequate examples of pure Gothic Architecture. It is, therefore, only by strictly investigating the whole that the principles of Gothic Architecture can be acquired, and by judicious selections, what constitutes the pure style can be defined.' Acute enough to see that Gothic should be considered as 'an original style of Architecture' and that 'its principles . . . must be sought in itself', he found it impossible to discover them; he provided only one Gothic illustration, and the text demonstrated his inability to 'read' Gothic structure. He thought that the 'most striking difference between the Grecian and Gothic Architecture arises from the former possessing the entablature and the latter the pointed arch'.[30] He felt the old Batty Langley unease at the lack of system and rules appertaining to Gothic columns, on which his attention was fixed, obviously as the equivalent to the classical orders; he never mentioned buttresses, stresses, or the true principles of Gothic structure.

Difficulties are evident in the designs of L. N. Cottingham, whose lifetime (1787–1847) spanned the transition from decorative to structural Gothic. He repaired Rochester Cathedral in 1825, which included rebuilding the central tower, and was employed during the 1830s and 1840s in restoring many mediaeval churches, including Hereford Cathedral, 'with the most scrupulous regard for evidence, and with the least possible displacement of old stone', according to Giles Gilbert Scott.[31] A book of working drawings now in the British Library illustrates his care and accuracy in recording detail; the named sources include Westminster Abbey, York Minster, St. Peter's at Ipswich, and Lichfield Cathedral. Despite all his experience, when he came to invent he assembled accurate detail into a thoroughly early nineteenth-century whole.

This combination of accurately reproduced detail and fancifully reproduced structure was common. Guidance was to come from the establishment of a correct Gothic chronology. As might be expected, the doyen of eighteenth-century gothicism, Horace Walpole, had been concerned with an attempt to establish it; a letter sent to him in June 1783 described such a project in terms of archaeological exactitude: 'il faut que la datte des monumens que l'on choisirait, soit apurée d'une manière autentique et qu'il soit également certain que l'estampe représente le monument dans l'état où il était à cette époque'.[32] Nothing came of it. Over thirty years was to pass before Thomas Rickman's *Attempt to discriminate the styles of Architecture in England* was published, in 1819.

This established the chronology of the different phases of English Gothic — Early English, Decorated, and Perpendicular; convenient labels which have been employed ever since. Gothic was given a temporal correctness, as opposed to the correctness of proportion and detail used in the classical styles; in future, accuracy would be judged according to whether a modern Gothic building were true to the period it purported to reproduce. The worm of sterility lay within the apple of

**108** The monastery church of Batalha, Portugal, by James Wyatt

knowledge, similar to that which afflicted the Greek Revival, although Rickman said that renewal, not imitation, was required. Oddly enough, despite his acuteness — he recognised, for example, Earls Barton as a Saxon building[33] — Rickman was still dominated by the orders; columns, he said, were 'essential parts' in architecture, and 'to them and their proportions all other arrangements must be made subservient'.[34] He saw in Gothic, as did others, an Englishness denied to the classical styles; Wren was a man 'whose powers, confessedly great, lead us to regret he had not studied the architecture of his English ancestors with the success he did that of Rome'.[35]

Despite his insistence on Englishness, Rickman did not scruple to pillage French Gothic as a source for design (Fig. 244), and his contemporaries constantly used it. Hope's recommendation of European secular Gothic has been mentioned above. Admired and imitated examples included the cathedrals and churches of Normandy, especially those of Rouen; Strasbourg, hallowed by Goethe and impressively towering above all else in Durand's treatise; and Batalha in Portugal (Fig. 108), the rich architecture of which was used by James Wyatt at Lee Priory (the favourite child of Strawberry, according to Walpole), taken as a model by Sir James Hall, much esteemed by Beckford and used for Fonthill, as well as being recorded by Beckford in twelve letters that breathe the skittish intoxication of his youth.[36]

## Domestic 'cathedral' or 'ecclesiastical' Gothic

Mediaeval Gothic architecture was most marvellously and conspicuously displayed in the cathedrals, and ecclesiastical Gothic was widely used as a source for domestic architecture and decoration. Typical of the practice was a design by James Malton of 1803 for a gateway in the Gothic style (Fig. 109); he did not attempt to copy a genuine Gothic gateway, of which many examples existed up and down the country, and his gateway aptly illustrates the misunderstandings of Gothic structure that prevailed. The charming lodges, the proportions of which indicate a probable use of cast iron, present 'four similar fronts to view, and from being octangular, under a square entablature, would at all times form a pleasing diversity of light and shade';[37] the ornament, Malton added, could be abridged. It was in the picturesque and decorative qualities of Gothic ornament that his real interest lay; structurally, the façades have very much the appearance of a classical temple, with pillars and pediment, its statues having been replaced by crockets — it will have been noticed that he uses the term 'entablature'. The effect of the whole is eighteenth century, hardly even 'Strawberry Hill'; no baron or monk, rusty or not, ever came within a mile of this structure. There is no hint of accuracy or of archaeological pedantry, despite correct detail.

It was not unusual for a cathedral to provide a model for a greenhouse, as in Repton's design for Plas Newydd (Pl. XX; see p.77), which may in turn have influenced a pretty Gothic greenhouse by Papworth, built to accord with the style of a Gothic house.[38] There was no attempt to harmonise Hopper's cast-iron conservatory at Carlton House (Fig. 110), which had obvious ecclesiastical ancestry (see p.77), with the classical elegancies of Holland's building; the Prince of Wales was then influenced by Walsh Porter, whose taste was notoriously liberal.

'Ecclesiastical' Gothic was used not only for gatehouses and conservatories, but for villas and mansions. James Malton, who gave several designs for villas in the Gothic style, expressed, in relation to a design for a 'hunting or shooting box',[39] doubts that were equally applicable to his 'inland villa' (Fig. 111): he was 'not without apprehension it may be considered by many as overcharged with decoration, and more resembling a church than a dwelling. This air it certainly has. . . . Notwithstanding, the design, as it is, might be suitable as a dwelling'. Hardly the words to encourage waverers. The flowers on the balcony may be an attempt at the homely, but more readily suggest flowers on a Gothic ruin. Malton made some concessions to domesticity; the windows, for example, were to be perforated only to the height of the spring of the arch, and would appear internally to have a square head. This subterfuge is not infrequently discovered in Regency Gothic mansions. Gothic, especially the ecclesiastical variety in its 'full luxuriance of gothic embellishment',

**109** Design for a gateway in Gothic style, by James Malton, 1803

**110** 'The Exterior of the Prince of Wales's Conservatory at Carleton House', designed by Thomas Hopper, 1807

**111** Design for 'An inland villa', by James Malton, 1803

*DESIGN. 14.*

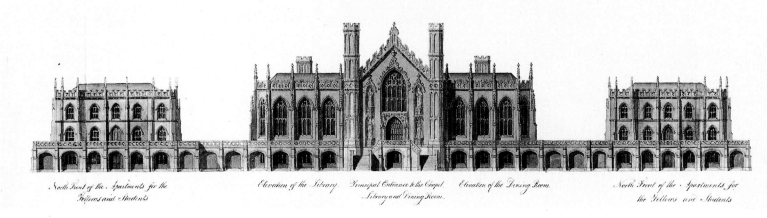

*North Front of the design for Downing College.*

*North Front of the Apartments for the Fellows and Students* — *Elevation of the Library.* — *Principal Entrance to the Chapel Library and Dining Room.* — *Elevation of the Dining Room.* — *North Front of the Apartments for the Fellows and Students*

**112** 'North Front of the design for Downing College', Cambridge, by William Porden, 1805

tended to be expensive; James Malton, in proposing that his designs would be 'of very easy execution in artificial stone',[40] was repeating advice given by others. It is paradoxical that these complex fancies were contemporary with the elegant plainness of Samuel Wyatt's houses and with the forceful asceticisms of the Greek Revival.

'Ecclesiastical' Gothic on a small scale seems more anomalous than on a large, possibly because whilst mediaeval religious communities inhabited buildings not so dissimilar from, for example, Porden's design for Downing College (Fig. 112), mediaeval ladies and gentlemen did not live in chantry chapels. The style somehow becomes more credible when the house concerned is large, as was Eaton Hall, the apogee of domestic ecclesiastical Gothic (see pp.62, 317, 318). Nevertheless, contemporaries found it difficult to feel at ease with ecclesiastical Gothic applied to domestic uses. And there was a certain sameness about examples of 'ecclesiastical' Gothic, whoever the architect, unlike the strongly individual styles produced by different architects working in the classical modes. Variety could be achieved by mixing 'ecclesiastical' Gothic with other styles, as was done at the charming Fern Hill in the Isle of Wight (Fig. 113), built for the Duke of Bolton. It combined an airy Gothic arcade, two stories high and perhaps inspired by the west front of Peterborough Cathedral, with a tower that managed to recall both a castle and a campanile. Far less ambitious and accurate in its detail than such a house as Ashridge (Pl. XLIV; see p.180), it retained something of eighteenth-century charm and insouciance.

Current misgivings concerning 'ecclesiastical' Gothic were expressed by Repton — whose taste, common sense, and perception of what was and was not reasonable are advantageously seen in the Picturesque controversies — in his analysis of the various Gothic styles available (see p.174). Had there been any one architect devoted heart and soul to 'ecclesiastical' Gothic the story might have been different, but there was not; Gothic was practised by all, or almost all, as an ancillary to classical styles rather than as a substitute for them. The 'mixed' and not the 'ecclesiastical' style was to become the most commonly accepted Gothic mode for domestic architecture.

**113** Fern Hill, Isle of Wight, 1834

## Modern Gothic churches

The use of the 'ecclesiastical' Gothic style in modern churches might well have been considered indisputably appropriate, and so it was, in the sense that it was the style used originally for such a purpose — although modern Gothic churches tended to employ in small buildings the decorative panoply that was more usually reserved in mediaeval times for larger buildings. Objections were felt on the grounds not of architectural but of religious propriety. The smell of popery hung around Gothic, and it is hardly surprising that protestant Anglicans, versed in Alisonian associationalism, viewed the increasing use of Gothic forms in churches with suspicion. Associationalism is a type of adult play; play can become serious; the difference between the Gothic of Horace Walpole and that of the younger Pugin is that the former wished to surround himself with Gothic play whilst the latter wished to recreate Gothic civilisation. Suspicions were to be confirmed, in that Gothicism and Tractarianism were to have a close emotional connection.

The great opportunity for building Gothic churches came with an Act of 1818 intended to provide churches for enlarged populations: of 214 churches built in London as a result, 174 were Gothic. Most were cheap; Soane estimated the average cost of a new church at £30,000, using St. James, Piccadilly, as an example, but the Commissioners preferred £20,000; the churches were to be capable of holding 2,000 people. The variety of forms of Gothic presented to the Church Commissioners revealed the predilections of individual architects. Neither Nash, nor Soane, nor Smirke had built a church anew in their lives before 1819, and each had to find an idiom. Nash proposed as Gothic six of his ten designs: one, in Tudor Gothic (Fig. 114), has good detail, perhaps helped along by Augustus Pugin; it has some affinities with Nash's Aqualate Hall, Staffordshire, of 1808. The distance that separates this Gothic style from that of Smirke (Fig. 115) shows what might have been accomplished with the style; the cubic preoccupations of French Romantic Classicism and the Greek Revival dominate Smirke's forceful design, which is an implicit denial of the Regency concept of ecclesiastical Gothic and the 'thousand graces and effects' of Walpole. Not a single pinnacle interrupts the long line of the nave roof; they are sparse enough over the aisles. The effect is curiously akin to some early twentieth-century essays in pared down Gothic. Soane produced several Gothic designs,[41] and one semi-Norman design, which look paper-thin compared with his classical buildings. Some results were surprising; whereas Rickman, the codifier of historic Gothic styles, had used much iron in his church at Everton near Liverpool in 1813–14, James Savage, an engineer by inclination if not by training, produced in 1824 in St. Luke's at Chelsea a church that, with flying buttresses and stone vaulting, is one of the earliest thoroughgoing revivals of mediaeval structural method.

Ecclesiastical Gothic as used for churches and public buildings was to have an interesting future, in which the limitations of pedantic historicism were to be experienced and in some cases transcended. However, ecclesiastical Gothic was not the only string to the Gothic bow; at least two other Gothic modes added to the variety of Regency Picturesque. One was the castle style, and the other the castellated or mixed style, the latter comprehending the Elizabethan, Tudor, or Old English styles. The former was the earlier to be adopted.

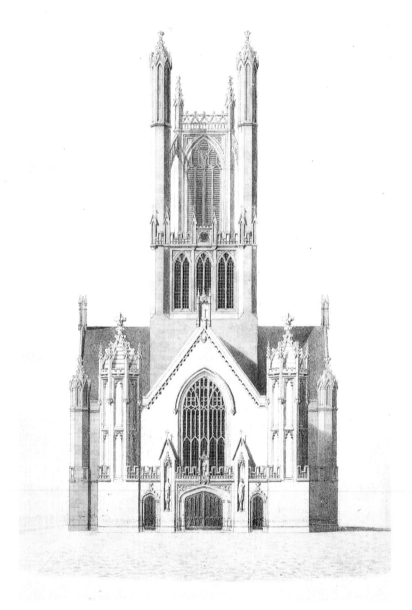

**114** Design for the Church Commissioners, 1818, by John Nash

## The 'castle' style

The revival of castle building in the late eighteenth and early nineteenth centuries is one of the more remarkable instances of human irrationality; harmless because it was an aesthetic adventure, it demonstrates that the springs of style lie deeper than utilitarian definitions of 'fitness for purpose'. For an age and a nation that was moving towards utilitarianism, to revive an aesthetic language based on

a system of defence that had been powerless against assault for two hundred years was absurd. People were aware of this contradiction. C. R. Cockerell, confronted with Eastnor (Fig. 118), complained that although Smirke had done it, 'with more judgmt than any one, the effect is great. a character of force is given. a defence might possibly be made', at the same time, 'a castellated mansion in these days [is] an anomaly, contradiction in terms . . . it is to make a play scene of your house . . .'. He thought it 'lamentable that men of taste Adams, Wyat, Smirke should give in to such miserable affections which can realy only arise in family pride of possessors and in nonsensical fanciful notions drawn from novels or blue books'.[42] This puts it in a nutshell.

An extreme statement of such views on incongruity is set out in violent polemic produced by Charles Kelsall in 1827; 'A Letter to the Society of the Dilettanti on the Works in Progress at Windsor'. Kelsall did not unreservedly condemn the quality of the work done: 'the materials employed are good, . . . the windows are Gothic, essentially Gothic . . . [some are essentially classical] several of the towers are not ill-corbelled'.[43] But he roundly condemned the principle: 'may we not conclude that the plan already advanced in execution, would be more appropriate to the scene of a melodrama at the Coburg Theatre than at Windsor?'[44] — exactly the same grounds on which Cockerell had objected to Eastnor. Kelsall's solution was radical; apart from preserving the Lower Ward and the Chapel (the interior of the latter was 'so beautiful, as almost to baffle criticism') the rest was to be flattened; 'the Round Tower, its tumulus, and all the surrounding

**115** Design for the Church Commissioners, 1818, by Robert Smirke

**116** Downton Castle, Herefordshire, built from 1772

169

buildings to the East levelled, in short, complete rase campagne on the TERRACE'.[45] Anticipated protest was met with jacobin mockery: '"But", cries the bigotted antiquarian: "what would you have proposed to raze to the ground that pile, which has been consecrated by the Edwards, the Henrys, and Elizabeth, which is identified with all the chivalrous recollections of the Holy Land, and which was so deservedly appreciated by George III and his family?" I assert boldly, Yes.' In its place, Kelsall proposed grandiloquent buildings in 'Graeco-Palladian' style.

A reason that prompted people to build modern castles was that they found the old ones beautiful. Apart from associational beauties, the forms of castles presented an unrivalled opportunity to deal without offence in the pure geometric shapes — the cube, the cylinder, the cone — that taste found so attractive in the late eighteenth and early nineteenth centuries. The associational beauties themselves were manifold; Regency castles may at times recall to us the world of Kemble and Kean rather than that of the Edwards and the Henrys; Regency romanticism may to us verge on the comic: 'How were my ears gratified to hear the workmen talk of the East tower, its hanging turret and buttress; the Saxon entrance . . . the galleries, etc., etc.! and to crown the whole I heard the Duke enquire, "When will they begin my Bower window?"'[46] This does not invalidate the more profound associations attached to castles, of a depth that moved Vanbrugh and Adam. Especially important were their grandeur and sublimity; in this they were the mediaeval counterparts of Paestum; rough, primitive, durable, ancient, and majestic: 'The Sublimest of all the Mechanical Arts is Architecture, principally from the durableness of its productions; and these productions are in themselves sublime, in proportion to their antiquity. . . . The Gothic Castle is still more sublime than all; because, beside the desolation of Time, it seems also to have withstood the assaults of War'.[47]

Some seem to have been drawn into Gothic and even into castle building almost against their will. The most notable example was the prosaic King George III himself, who spent huge sums on the Castle designed and built for him (never completed) at Kew. It became part of his mania: 'Wyatt is expected down this day — a string will thus be touched which will affect the brain'.[48] In 1804 the King 'talked abt. His new building at Kew, and said He shd. have thought it impossible 30 years ago that He should ever encourage Gothic architecture — Wyatt He sd. was now in the habit of it — At Fonthill He had done a great work.'[49] A motive that impelled his subjects in building castles could not have been imputed to the King — romantic snobbery, 'family pride of possessors', as Cockerell put it. The very term 'castle' conjured up antiquity and ancestors; many of the newly rich followed a course similar to that of Peacock's Mr. Ebenezer MacCrotchet, who christened his villa Crotchet Castle, and determined to hand down to

posterity the honours of Crotchet and Crotchet.[50] There were real life versions of Mr. Crotchet; the number of fictional variants, in and out of the 'silver fork' novels, shows the ubiquity of the phenomenon.

In judging the castles themselves, it should be remembered that Gothic archaeology was less developed than classical, and that except in a few cases that occurred towards the end of the period, authenticity tended to be less important than the joys of creation and of association. The age was not exact. It is not surprising that Jane Austen could conceive a James II chapel furnished in mahogany;[51] it is surprising, at first sight, that Sir Walter Scott, an antiquarian whose novels carry something of the burden of the modern footnote, could give a 'Gothic' castle a latticed window, and a Franciscan friar a grey gown, all in the reign of Richard I![52] Abbotsford tells all (see pp.327 et seq., 423); the freedoms exercised (to be fair, usually consciously) by the novelist were not to be denied to the architect and decorator.

Freedoms of a different and more intellectual kind are exercised in the castles of Robert Adam, precursors of those of the Regency, both those that he drew as phantasms of his leisure hours and those that he designed and built as part of his business. These last buildings impress the understanding as castles, although they are nothing like mediaeval castles. They have none of the mediaeval sprawl imitated in the plan of Downton (Fig. 116), and are much more sophisticated in elevation, paying homage not only to the Middle Ages but to Vanbrugh and to late antiquity; the cubes and cylinders of the structures are given full, symmetrical expression (Fig. 117). Wedderburn, of the early 1770s, has battlements and label mouldings; it also has rustication. Mauldsley in Lanarkshire displays the seventeenth-century influence of Holy-roodhouse. A design for the south front of Culzean of about 1777 is, apart from four exaggerated cross-shaped windows, almost as much late Roman as mediaeval. The affiliations between Roman and mediaeval defensive architecture were noticed; Knight, for example, identified battlements and corbels as having been used in Roman architecture: 'The overhanging battlements, now called Gothic, were certainly known to the Romans, as early as the reign of Titus; . . . as there are, among the paintings of Herculaneum . . . walls and towers entirely finished in this way. . . .'[53]

The ghost of Diocletian's palace at Spalatro haunts many of Adam's designs; its exterior, with its quadrangular form flanked with sixteen towers, was as much military as palatial, and Adam, who had seen the building, recognised and imitated a strength that was darkening into the primitive: 'the awful ruins of Spalatro are not less expressive of the decline of the arts, than of the greatness of the Roman empire in the time of Diocletian'.[54] The influence of Spalatro and late Roman forms are evident in a design, romantic and powerful, for Culzean Castle (Fig. 117). At Seton Castle, of 1791–2, elementary geometric forms are combined with the Scottish crow-stepped gable and towers that recall

**117** Culzean Castle, Ayrshire, 1777–92, a design by Robert Adam

the native Scottish house.[55] Despite the difference in conception and quality, elements are here prefigured that were to reappear in Blore's Abbotsford. One wonders whether the Greek Revivalist, Smirke, in designing castles and city gates that are not without nobility (Fig. 119), was not as conscious as was Adam of the ambiguities of forms that were at once Roman and mediaeval.

James Wyatt's castle style was less distinguished and original than Adam's. Besides doing a good deal of work at Windsor for George III, he was commissioned in 1801 by the fifth Duke of Rutland to redesign Belvoir; in place of the embattled Romano-Scottish manner of Adam arose a romantic castellated Gothic vision, supplemented in 1816, after a fire, by the more sober Gothic of the Duke's chaplain John Thoroton, the antiquary. The fantasy does not disguise contemporary predilections; the round tower on the south-west front, for example, with its battlements and round-headed windows, has at first-floor level the air of an enormous Regency bow window in the shape of a semi-

cylinder. The moving spirit in the rebuilding was an energetic woman with strong ideas on architecture and decoration, Lady Elizabeth Howard, whose home before becoming Duchess of Rutland had been Vanbrugh's Castle Howard. The new Belvoir, blessed in its picturesque site, attracted a good deal of attention: in certain ways it anticipated Wyatville's Windsor, and was visited en fête by the Prince Regent in 1813. He had already recorded romantic susceptibilities aroused by a visit of 1799, before the remodellings began: 'I really figured to myself what with the ancient appearance of the Castle, the prodigious concourse of the natives without, and the numbers of the bettermost sort within doors, together with the illuminations, the music, the noise and the bustle, that I was transported in a dream to some of those scenes which we have read the description of having existed in the days of chivalry'.[56]

Two of the best known later Regency castles were designed by Smirke: Lowther and Eastnor. These buildings were basically

118 Eastnor Castle, Herefordshire, 1812–20, designed by Sir Robert Smirke

119 Design for a grand entrance to Carlisle, by Sir Robert Smirke

symmetrical, as had been Wyatt's castle at Kew for George III. Eastnor, especially, has a dramatic grandeur (Fig. 118); it lacks the toy fort quality that Wyatt's castles tend to have; there is nothing pasteboard about its large, plain, and solid forms, with splendidly handled masonry. It is extensive, with an entrance hall sixty feet high that would have appeared eminently absurd to Alison. Despite the eight years that the castle took to build, Smirke's final account of just under £86,000 was not so far removed from his estimate of £82,000, made in November 1811.[57] No doubt the patron was as orderly as the architect, but the comparison with Nash and George IV provokes reflection. The forceful elementary forms of Eastnor are seen in Smirke's magnificent design for a grand entrance to the city of Carlisle (Fig. 119), appropriate for a city associated with the Edwardian conquest of Scotland.

According to an awkwardly expressed manuscript,[58] Wyatville's designs for the remodelling of Windsor Castle were 'made under a most ardent impression to add to the magnificence of the Castle, and at the same time it has been considered as the best feeling not to entertain any vain notions of destroying the existing parts merely for the purpose of shewing a presumed ability to make better, but in such few changes as are made to have in view the original character of this construction, though it would be perfectly ridiculous to restore the whole to the appearance of a dungeon like residence. Though Windsor Castle is altogether an imposing and grand mass of building, it does not abound with picturesque parts, and those who have made such buildings their study will not think it any great stretch of vanity in the declaration that

no great difficulty would occur in designing a building of the same magnitude, possessing both qualities in a superior degree'.

The exterior that arose in the 1820s, conjured up by the combined efforts of architect, King and Sir Charles Long, is unforgettably grand, unsymmetrical but perfectly composed. The detail, such as the flint galletting between the stones (observable in other buildings of the period) has been criticised: 'he has committed some gross faults, such as machicolations over inclined bases and over inferior buildings, and the sameness and meanness of the masonry has a bad effect on so large a front'.[59] An attempt was made to assimilate new and old: 'all the external work has been done so exactly in the old style, and with stone and mortar so stained to assimilate, that there is no great show of new work'.[60] The architect's imagination encompassed wild life; he called jackdaws and starlings to aid in providing the Picturesque, leaving holes for them to build nests: a 'very tasteful provision . . . by which the Castle has been made to retain its ancient effect, with some of the associations of its antiquity'.[61] The castle shrank to a villa in P. F. Robinson's bijou version of the East Front of the Upper Ward (Fig. 120); this design is dated August 1825, indicating that Robinson had been quick off the mark. Such reductions were built up and down the country, attracting satirists in the process.

An extraordinary castle described in 1833 as 'almost the only modern castle . . . equalling the solid magnitude of those which have descended to us from our forefathers'[62] is Penrhyn Castle in Gwynedd, designed by Thomas Hopper, the architect of the cast-iron conservatory at Carlton House. Penrhyn is a far cry from such

**120** Design for a villa in castle style, 1825, by P. F. Robinson

**121** Goodrich Court, 1828–31, designed by Edward Blore

frivolities, or seems so at first sight — the style is a massive and four-square Romanesque; Hopper had previously used Romanesque at Gosford Castle in County Armagh. Penrhyn's stonework, from local quarries and worked by Welsh masons, was hewn and laid with precision. Prince Pückler–Muskau, who visited the castle in July 1828, understood the English social scene; describing the eating-hall as an imitation of Rochester Castle, he added, 'What could then be accomplished only by a mighty monarch, is now executed, as a plaything — only with increased size, magnificence, and expense — by a simple country-gentleman, whose father very likely sold cheeses. So do times change.' The castle, with Norman windows, has two keeps, one reminiscent of Castle Hedingham. Pückler-Muskau emphasised its forbidding nature, equating it with the contemporary social climate: 'at every entrance' in the park wall 'a fortress-like gate with a portcullis frowns on the intruder — no inapt symbol, by the by, of the illiberality of the present race of Englishmen, who shut their parks and gardens more closely than we do our sitting-rooms'.[63]

Goodrich Court in Herefordshire, designed by Edward Blore and built between 1828 and 1831, was yet another new castle (Fig. 121): for its antiquarian builder, Samuel Rush Meyrick, being new meant being second-best. Meyrick's first idea had been to find a ruin and restore it. George IV might have said that he did precisely that at Windsor, but Meyrick's attitude, as expressed in a letter sent to Sir Walter Scott in 1822, was more purist: 'Notwithstanding what you say in that beautiful work on Scottish Scenery and Castles [*The Provincial Antiquities and Picturesque Scenery of Scotland*] . . . respecting rendering an old ruin habitable, I am now fully in pursuit of that object, hoping to attain it within a year's time. But I assure you you need not dread demolition for unless I would make it fit to live in without the slightest alteration,

even cutting an additional window, I would forbear and build my residence within view. If therefore I succeed in making such a purchase it will be with perfectly antiquarian motives'.[64]

Associational pleasure could no longer so easily be obtained by imitating the real thing: possession of the thing itself was preferred. Beckford had wanted to build a ruin and live in it (see pp.179–80); Meyrick wanted to make a ruin habitable and, if he could not do so without alterations, to build a new house and look at the old, as Vanbrugh had intended with Woodstock at Blenheim. Having failed in 1827 to buy the ruined castle at Goodrich, he built his own castle on the opposite hill. In 1828 he wrote: 'am about to build instantly a dwelling in the style of Edward 2nd under the superintendence of the first gothic architect of the age my friend Edward Blore . . . I will show you the plans of what will be termed "Goodrich Court"'.[65]

Edward Blore had begun as an antiquarian draughtsman, the alternative, for early Gothicists, to the classicist's study of artefacts in books and collections; he had drawn the cathedrals of York and Peterborough for John Britton and helped to illustrate Hall's essay on the origins of Gothic. He had made numerous studies of fifteenth and sixteenth-century domestic architecture, using the knowledge gained to design the 'Tudor' buildings that became his speciality. Introduced in 1816 to Sir Walter Scott, he assisted in designing Abbotsford and in drawing Scottish antiquities for Scott's book mentioned above. There are traces of Scottish influence at Goodrich, especially in the use of the cone-shaped spire. The inner courtyard had something of a collegiate flavour; Ackermann's publications on the colleges of Oxford and

Cambridge had popularised their charms. It is noticeable that the Court stood not in formal gardens with terraces and balustrades; it stood on a terrace, but in contrast with George IV's Windsor the terrace was a rude bank, and the surroundings were of the wild and Picturesque variety that Payne Knight had urged in the 1790s.

## The 'Gothic and Roman' mixed castle style

As we have seen, the castle style was not confined to large buildings; it found expression in villas, like Crotchet Castle, or in the design after Windsor by P. F. Robinson. There were other stylistic possibilities, as seen in a design by James Malton (Pl. XLI) of 1802, which was published in his book of 1803. It shows a building 'founded entirely on the castle construction, and designed as a hunting lodge'. In his text, Malton made two interesting observations. He remarked that, 'Those truly noble modern mansions of our opulent nobility and gentry, that like brilliant gems bespangle our delightful isle . . . are very incongruous with the scenery of nature. If huge edifices be raised among woods, and lawn, and water, then is Sir John Vanbrugh's style of architecture better suited to combine with the natural objects of the country, than the elegant, but formal forms of Graeco-Roman architecture.' Elsewhere he spoke of 'intermediate or mixed styles of architecture; such as, what may not improperly be termed Vanbrughian, and justly appreciated by Sir Joshua Reynolds'.[66] And, of course, urged by Payne Knight.

It seems likely that Malton's design, which has a triangular plan ('neither new nor singular', as he says) was specifically compiled according to the Reynolds/Payne Knight recipe for the 'mixed' style. It combines the castle form with details that recall the seventeenth century (had he seen Bolsover?), and Inigo Jones; these details may be an attempt at late Roman in the style of Adam's miscegenations, especially the rusticated Doric portico with its balustrade above and statues in the niches, which wear Roman armour much in the Jacobean style; these are accompanied by Gothic 'Venetian' windows, coats of arms and corbels. Such ideas were in the air; Farington recorded in 1798 how James Wyatt had suggested that the design for a monument to Sir Edward Coke, the great Jacobean lawyer, at Stoke Poges, should be 'agreeable to the Architecture of that day — something like the designs of Inigo Jones before he went to Italy — a mixture of Gothic and Roman manners'.[67]

## The 'castellated' or 'mixed style of Queen Elizabeth's Gothic'

Popular as the idea of the castle was, replete with agreeable associations of romantic mediaevalism — old families, chivalry, armour, and torture — it suffered as a domestic building style from disadvantages similar to those of 'cathedral' Gothic. It was equally as odd to live in a modern fortified house as in a church pretending to be a dwelling. People wanted the fashionable conveniences; French windows, loggias, conservatories, easy access to garden and park, hardly possible over a drawbridge. As Repton put it: 'The CASTLE CHARACTER requires massive walls, with very small windows. . . . The correct imitation . . . must produce the effect of a prison'.[68] He equally rejected the cathedral, or 'ABBEY CHARACTER'; it 'requires lofty and large apertures, almost equally inapplicable to a house, although in some few rooms the excess of light may be subdued by coloured glass'; only the mediaeval Chapel, Church, Hall, and Library furnished proper models, the other rooms, the 'mean habitation of monks and students' being too small and low.

Repton also rejected James Wyatt's form of Gothic; he said that Wyatt preferred to use Gothic rather than Grecian because it was better suited to the English weather, but that his Grecian inclinations showed through; climate 'required the weather mouldings, or labels . . . rather than the bolder projections of the Grecian cornices, which he often found necessary to make more flat than the models from which they were taken . . . he introduced a style which is neither Grecian nor Gothic, but modern Gothic. The details are often correctly Gothic, but the outline is Grecian, being just the reverse of the houses in the reign of Queen Elizabeth and King James, in which the details are often Grecian, while the general outlines is Gothic.' Repton returned to the charge in his memoirs in a way that hints at an obsession. He described Wyatt's Sheffield Place (1776–90) as 'one of his earliest attempts at Modern Gothic — by which I mean that heterogenous mixture of Abbey, Castle, and Manor House, for which a taste had been introduced by the experiments of Horace Walpole at Strawberry Hill. The Public had pronounced this new style to be "vastly pretty" — and the same mongrel breed of architecture had been propagated ever since by buildings of all dimensions from the Palace to the Pigsty'.[69]

Repton concluded that the 'mixed style of Queen Elizabeth's Gothic' was to be preferred: 'Yet a mixed style is generally imperfect: the mind . . . feels an incongruity of character, like an anachronism in the confusion of dates; it is like uniting in one object infancy with old age, life with death, or things present with things past'[70] — to some, this would sound like a definition of poetry, and mixed styles can indeed be intensely poetic. Repton's reluctance may have been partly assumed; his object at the time was to persuade the Prince of Wales to adopt the Indian style. Elsewhere he was more direct: 'It may seem a bold thing to suggest a house in a style which some may call the worst species of Gothic, yet I know no other kind . . . that is perfectly applicable to a house. . . . [We are] driven to the date of Queen Elizabeth'.[71] So in addition to cathedral or castle Gothic, and the 'Gothic and Roman' mixed style, there was the possibility of yet

XLI Design for a hunting lodge in castle style,
1802, by James Malton

XLII Luscombe Castle, Devon, 1799, designed by
John Nash

XLIII A Gothic 'cathedral' made out of willow, c.1792

XLIV 'South East view of Ashridge, Buckinghamshire', Ashridge Park, Herts., 1808–13, designed by James Wyatt and Sir Jeffry Wyatville

another 'mixed' style, called also 'castellated' (battlements were usually in evidence), 'collegiate', 'Tudor', 'Old English', and in modern times 'Jacobethan'.

The 'castellated' style of the Regency was not unheralded; there were signs from quite early in the eighteenth century of a growing taste for it and for the Elizabethan/Jacobean motifs often associated with it. It might not have been utterly unexpected that Kent would build at Hampton Court in Tudor style, where the same wish for conformity prevailed as with Wren's Tom Tower at Oxford or Hawksmoor's towers at Westminster Abbey; Kent went so far, however, as to insert Jacobean style interiors, which indicates more than a mere wish for decent conformity. At Rousham, Kent gave the existing Jacobean house a Gothic castellated dress; at Burghley and at Corsham, Capability Brown built Jacobean bath-houses, strapwork being employed as a decorative motif. The same avant-garde predilections appeared in interior decoration, usually in old houses (see p.275).

Tudor and Jacobean styles grew in favour because of their associations and antiquarian appeal; as the eighteenth century wore on, they were increasingly appreciated for aesthetic reasons. They had been completely accepted by the time that Cockerell, visiting the Elizabethan 'prodigy house' Burleigh, found its 'aspect grand . . . chimneys in 2 cols with entablature in regular. looks like the ruins of

Palmyra or Baalbek. Vanbrugh must have taken his notion of chimnies from this . . . the Elizabethan is truly a romantic style of architecture'.[72] Repton had given his approval to the Elizabethan style by the early 1790s, and it was probably he, rather than Nash, who first forwarded its use; the unaccepted designs for Magdalen College at Oxford of about 1801, by the Reptons and by Nash, exhibit the chasm between the Reptons' collegiate Gothic and Nash's fantastically pinnacled stage-set.[73]

The Reptons' first joint venture with Nash, at Corsham in 1797, produced a design — for which Humphry Repton claimed the credit — that mixed secular and 'ecclesiastical' Gothic (Fig. 122). The north front was basically Elizabethan, with 'turrets, chimney shafts, and oriels' copied from 'Burleigh, Blickling, Hampton Court, Hatfield, etc.'; the central apartment, however, took as its model the Chapel of Henry VII at Westminster. In justifying this choice, Repton said that modern Gothic buildings should imitate some genuine fragment, and that since it was desired to build an octagonal room that would project beyond the line of the façade, Henry VII's Chapel 'though not an octagon, was the only projecting regular polygon' available.[74] The reasoning seems mechanistic, and it is hardly surprising that the composition lacks unity, adding substance to Repton's claim to the design; Nash had grave faults, but was unlikely to have made that particular error.

122 Corsham Court, Wilts., 1797–8, designed by John Nash and Humphry Repton

**123** Plans and elevations, by George Dance

**124** 'Fonthill Abbey S.E. View', designed by James Wyatt, 1796–1812

The castellated style first found perfect expression at Luscombe, produced by the Nash/Repton partnership in 1799; it has a spontaneous and easy charm (Pl. XLII). In the Red Book, Repton applied the term 'castle' to the building, recommending the castle style as one which 'by blending a chaste correctness of proportion with bold irregularity of outline, its deep recesses and projections producing broad masses of light and shadow, while its roof is enriched by turrets, battlements, corbles, and lofty chimneys; has infinitely more picturesque effect than any other style of building'.[75] It also provided all the conveniences — direct access to the gardens; French windows; conservatory; an irregular plan that allowed full advantage to be taken of the views — that were totally lacking at Corsham. The style perfectly lent itself to the vagaries of Picturesque planning (Fig. 123).

Charm was hardly a quality that could be ascribed to Beckford's magnificent and irrational Fonthill (Fig. 124). It may seem capricious to include Fonthill in a group of 'castellated' houses, rather than placing it with the 'ecclesiastical' Gothic group with which its name alone would warrant its location. Its form certainly produced the 'large and lofty apertures', almost 'inapplicable to a house', which Repton saw as a quality of 'Abbey Gothic', and its 'interior is in the ecclesiastical manner, as decidedly as that of any Abbey existing',[76] especially in the Entrance Hall and Octagon (Fig. 236). Yet a comparison of its exterior with such ecclesiastical Gothic designs as those by James Malton

(Fig. 111) shows how much it had departed from the cathedral to the castellated style, a departure justified by the domestic buildings of old cathedrals and monasteries. These were commonly in a style used also by secular colleges; when Rickman in 1827–31 built the New Court of St. John's at Cambridge, a completely appropriate Gothic collegiate style was at hand.

One wonders what modern opinion of Fonthill would have been had the building survived. The astonishment and approval of contemporaries was generally expressed in quoting its dimensions; its stupendous size was magnified by its plan which, apart from the wing to the east that contained the habitable drawing rooms, was much like that of an elongated and narrow church with cloisters but without transepts or aisles. However, one catches beneath the overwrought superlatives of laudatory publications a whiff of criticism that hints at deeper misgivings. Rutter, for instance, mentioned that its mixture of styles 'has been generally visited with condemnation' by the better informed, although in its defence he protested that its mediaeval sources had not, and should not have been, faithfully copied: 'The Abbey is not *Frankenstein*, built up of the actual head of one individual, the arms of another, and the body of a third, forming a disquieting and unnatural whole'.[77] He made a curious defence: 'Among other reasons why the discrepancy of style is really so little felt by all, and so gently censured by the best judges, is the fact, that each division is of itself large enough to fill the eye and the mind of the spectator; and that where discordant styles occur in the same view, that in the foreground is so decided and overpowering, as to throw the distant and subordinate one out of immediate consideration'.[78] The exterior of the wing containing St. Michael's Gallery was, especially in its lower parts, noticeably unpicturesque in its flatness and lack of buttresses (presumably to ensure maximum light to the windows). There were doubts about materials as well as design; the busts on the South Arcade, for example, were 'in cement, but no symptom of dilapidation yet appears, and we hope will not'.[79]

The genesis of the building was hardly likely to encourage consistency. The idea was first prompted by the idyllic beauty of the site, which commanded wonderful views on all sides. The architect employed by Beckford was James Wyatt, who had acquired an early reputation as the expert in Gothic design; his restoration work had given his office a wide acquaintance with mediaeval buildings, and he had worked at Strawberry and Windsor. His Gothic was not academic; his attitude to it can be deduced from his work and from a remark made in 1798: 'Grecian must be Grecian — but fancies — such as Gothic, Moorish Chinese Etc. might be imitated — some of them capable of being reduced to rules'.[80] In 1796 he had been instructed to make 'a Convent, partly in ruins and partly perfect' with 'a suite of rooms, small but amply sufficient'. A depiction shows the Chapel prominent with buildings beyond in a nondescript castellated style, not so unlike the Lugar design for an inhabited ruin (Fig. 14). The eager impatience of Beckford hurried on the structure; timber and cement were the principal materials: 'notwithstanding the magnitude of the plan, no idea of the durability which attaches to a permanent dwelling was ever entertained'.[81] The consequence was that the first tower had reached its summit when, 'a smart gust of wind acting suddenly on a large flag' the whole collapsed, in a 'tremendous and sublime' manner. Beckford's only reaction was to wish he had seen it.[82] He also missed the second collapse, accomplished without a flag, when in 1825 another and stronger gust brought down the inadequately supported central tower.

It is instructive to compare Fonthill with Ashridge, another enormous Gothic house, and one in which stucco was used extensively (Pl. XLIV). James Wyatt was again the architect; he built it for the Earl of Bridgewater from 1808 onwards, and incorporated the relics of refectory and cloisters already on the site; presumably these influenced the choice of style, which is castellated Tudor, with the huge bay windows that were regarded as such an asset. The most determinedly Gothic part of the structure is the chapel and its spire, connected with the house by a conservatory. Apart from hall and chapel, the interior is not Gothic, and until Wyatville took over from his uncle on the latter's death in 1813, the plan of the house was more or less symmetrical; it was he who gave it the Picturesque sprawl. The elaborate formal

gardens, small and enclosed, were by Repton and quite unlike Beckford's version of the Picturesque; they included a cast-iron Gothic Conduit and a 'Rosary'.[83]

Prince Pückler-Muskau found Ashridge tiresome. This 'modern gothic castellated style, which looks so fairy-like on paper, in reality often strikes one not only as tasteless, but even somewhat absurd . . . you see a sort of fortress, with turrets, loopholes, and battlements, not one of which has the slightest purpose or utility, and, moreover, many of them standing on no firmer basis than glass walls [the greenhouses and conservatories connected with the apartments], — it is just as ridiculous and incongruous, as if you were to meet the possessor of these pretty flower-gardens walking about in helm and harness'.[84] This is of course exactly what they longed to do, and what they did do at the Firle Games and Eglintoun Tournament.

## Later 'castellated' houses

'Newstede. The convent, much as it was'; so Horace Walpole noted of Newstead Abbey,[85] which of all Regency houses most perfectly fulfilled the beau ideal of a romantic dwelling. A 'sort of castellated Abbey',[86] the home of a famous and wicked poet, it was in a picturesque state of dilapidation: 'Newstead! fast-falling, once resplendent dome!' as Byron put it, in a remarkable and not very good poem that combines the feudal array of Scott — and more — with ill-omened birds that shriek their dirge as they do in the more extravagant parts of Chambers' essay on Chinese gardens; the poet described himself as 'the last and youngest of a noble line' who 'now holds thy mouldering turrets in his sway'. Byron was to modernise his Gothic language; the old-fashioned terminology of this early poem — 'dome' used for church or temple, in the sense that Pope endowed Homer's Greece with 'domes' — was replaced by the more up to date 'rich and rare mixed Gothic', in 'Don Juan'.[87]

When the poet relaxed his sway in favour of the military, in the person of Colonel Wildman, Newstead Abbey was restored; Wildman called in John Shaw. Byron had satirised the kind of architect who:

> produced a plan whereby to erect
> New buildings of correctest conformation,
> And throw down old, which he called restoration.[88]

Shaw was not of this type, or only moderately so; a Fellow of the Royal Society, the Linnaean Society, and the Society of Antiquaries, he began in 1818 a restrained remodelling (Fig. 126), which contrasts with the radical work done a little later at Windsor. He did not impose a uniform style on the house. The entrance porch, originally reached by a steep flight of steps, was replaced by a ground floor porch in a vaguely Decorated style, perhaps as a compliment to the ruined West Front of the Abbey church; the old porch was used elsewhere. To the south of it a new tower was built in Norman style, inspired by a genuine Norman doorway at its foot;[89] it balances the west front of the church better than did the lower buildings formerly on the site. An octagonal kitchen, based on that at Glastonbury, which was popular with Regency architects as a model, was added to the east façade. The result, taken as a whole, has great beauty, with associations comprehensible even to the modern observer. Ilam Hall in Staffordshire, another Shaw house, of 1821–6 (Fig. 125) was given terraces in the same style as Newstead. As was Mamhead in Devon (Pl. VII) by Anthony Salvin.

Mamhead (1828–39), in beautifully handled Bath stone, was the work of an architect who was also an accomplished painter in the Picturesque manner; the grounds were enlivened by a mock castle, also designed by Salvin, high on the slope; it contained the laundry and brewhouse. Salvin, a pupil of Nash, had a good command of late

**125** Ilam Hall, Staffs., 1821–6, designed by John Shaw

**126** 'Newstead Abbey 1829', 'West Front' and 'South Front', Notts., a design by John Shaw

**127** Lenten Lodge, Wollaton Hall, Notts., 1823–4, designed by Sir Jeffry Wyatville

mediaeval detail — perhaps from contact with Augustus Pugin in Nash's office — and employed it with individual style and vitality. The accuracy of the detail, especially in the greenhouse pavilion, may reflect the influence of such nearby Tudor houses as Montacute and Bingham. Salvin must have looked at Ashridge; the echoes are obvious (Pls VII, XLIV). The plan of Mamhead is symmetrical, probably as a result of Salvin's inheritance of a classical plan made by Charles Fowler in 1822.[90] The symmetry does not inhibit a pronounced sense of Picturesque movement.

The use of the Renaissance variety of Tudor increased in frequency as the century wore on. It had appeared early, principally in connection with remodellings. An aborted example was Scone, where in 1802 George Saunders had produced elevations for remodelling the Elizabethan/Jacobean house which 'show a sensitivity in their handling of Scots Jacobean forms without parallel until David Hamilton's Dunlop House, Ayrshire, built new thirty years later'.[91] In England, Wyatville worked on the restoration of Longleat from 1806, and in 1801 and 1823 restored and extended one of the most flamboyant Elizabethan houses in England, Wollaton Hall in Nottinghamshire; in 1823–4 he built the Lenten Lodge for Wollaton (Fig. 127) in a style analogous to that of the house, using details from the Hall's central tower. It cost £6–7,000 to build;[92] the result was princely; it now announces a housing estate.

The apothesis of 'Jacobethan', with a baroque admixture, may be seen still at Harlaxton Manor (Pl. XLV); for once the epithet 'astonishing' is fully justified. The respective parts played by those concerned in its creation — the owner Gregory Gregory, the architects Salvin and William Burn, and Burn's assistant, David Bryce — are uncertain.[93] The house has an obsessional character; as assertive as Blenheim; provincial (despite eclectic detail within) where Blenheim is European, it illustrates the tendencies of the period in an extreme and advanced form. Building began in 1832, after ten year's genesis. Gregory told Loudon that 'there being, at the time he commenced, few or no books on the subject' he studied, amongst other buildings, Bramhill, Hardwick, Hatfield, Knole, Burghley (clearly echoed in the entrance front), Wollaton, Kirby, Longleat, Temple Newsam, and the colleges at Oxford and Cambridge. Salvin's architectural drawings lack the baroque ingredient prominent within the house, the originator of which is open to speculation. It takes over in the entrance hall, which has altantes, putti, festoons and tassels, effective but coarse; it has been likened to a stage set. The house indeed reminds one of a stage set, a stage set in the glare of daylight. The cost was said to have been £200,000.

## School Gothic

Schools and learning had been long associated with the Gothic and Elizabethan styles, especially evident in the venerable universities of Oxford and Cambridge; it became natural to turn to it when new scholastic buildings were contemplated. When, for example, Rugby School was rebuilt between 1809 and 1816, a quadrangle in Tudor Gothic was designed by Henry Hakewill; care was taken to retain the fine trees. In 1819, Harrow chose to add as an extra block a copy of an original building of 1615, despite the latter's description by a writer of 1818 as 'a building little calculated to call forth the admiration of the casual spectator by any architectural embellishment';[94] the architect, C. R. Cockerell, may have increased the attractions of both original and copy by adding 'Dutch' gables. The lower classes were also admitted to the influences of Gothic; by the 1820s Gothic had begun to displace the utilitarian classical style hitherto used in most elementary schools, and was employed in many of the new National Schools. An enchanting example of 1829 by Stroud and Mew, in flint faced with stucco (Fig. 128), stood in Brighton next to the Royal Pavilion estate until its

**128** The National School, Church Street, Brighton, 1829, built by Stroud and Mew

wanton destruction in 1971 (hoardings still occupy the site); it had within it a superb cast-iron Gothic staircase.[95]

A school in collegiate Gothic was designed by Blore for Bedford (Pl. XLVI); it was opened in 1834. It owed its size to the incorporation of an 'English or commercial' school, a boys' and girls' National School, and a hospital school. The Trustees in 1828 told the architects that they were 'resolved that the buildings shall be of stone and as they wish them to be in the style of what may be called the Collegiate, conventional and domestic English architecture of the period comprising the reigns of Edward VI, Mary, and Elizabeth, they request that no plans be sent in imitation of the Grecian, Roman, or Anglo Italian styles. The only deviation that could be allowed would be the admission of the perpendicular or Florid style of the purely English architecture of the reign of Henry VIII. The Trustees are anxious that the buildings should (if it be practicable) present such features as may

recall the era of the dawn of Reformation, the foundation of Endowed Public Schools, and the memory of Sir William Harpur'.[96] Piety and associationalism united could hardly go further.

Associationalism could as easily thwart the use of Gothic as encourage it. The message conveyed by the mayor of Leicester's statement at the opening of a school in the Greek Revival style in 1837 was that the tenets of Benthamite utilitarianism were intended to prevail over the classics; Greek and Latin were not to be taught; Mr. Montgomery (see p.3) would have applauded. Hardly, it would seem, a sound reason for adopting a classical style of architecture, but the negative reasons were stronger than the positive; the mayor, it was reported, 'rejoiced greatly that they had adopted the Grecian style of Architecture in preference to the Gothic — the former, simple, chaste, and beautiful and suitable to every species of building. . . . To those whose associations fondly clung to the dark Monastic exploded institutions of our country, who love to dwell rather on the gloomy periods of our history, than to contemplate the blaze of light and knowledge which has since burst upon the world — to such persons he was aware the Gothic style of architecture has great charms . . .'.[97] The school, designed by J. A. Hansom, was, as might have been expected, non-conformist; by this date, Anglicans tended to prefer Gothic.

## Tudor vernacular: Norman

The domestic Elizabethan style is pictured in a scholarly publication by T. F. Hunt, whose *Exemplars of Tudor Architecture adapted to modern habitations . . . selected from Ancient Edifices* appeared in 1830. The publication is redolent of the antiquary; a quotation in the crabbed quaintness of black letter is used on the title page, luring the romantically inclined towards the delights of Tudor chambers:

> Towris hie, full plesant shal ye finde,
> With fannis fresh, turning with every winde,
> The chambris and parlers of a sorte,
> With bay-wyndows goodlie, as may be thoughte.

Black letter is used frequently in the publication, although the author's sense of the appropriate led him to use modern types when quoting eighteenth and nineteenth-century authors; several of the most sumptuously picturesque verses from Keats's 'Eve of St. Agnes' set the emotional scene for an essay on stained glass by Willement. Hunt made concessions to modern comfort; nothing, he observed, could be more

inconvenient than the 'ecclesiastical features' of pointed windows in ordinary sitting rooms;[98] he suggested of a cloister that by 'filling the arches with frames of glass in winter, a conservatory would be added to the luxury of a promenade at all seasons . . .'.[99]

Hunt was concerned with colour and patina in an earnest way utterly at variance with the gay inconsequence of the cottage orné: 'Barge-boards, pendants, pinnacles, and brackets . . . should always be made of strong oak, and left to acquire, by age, a gray hue; and not of slight deal painted'.[100] He quotes Payne Knight and Price, taking up the latter's dislike of white in the landscape, and adds the stricture that 'Even very white teeth . . . if seen too much, often give a kind of silly look'.[101] The book shows examples of door handles and key escutcheons taken from Westminster Abbey, King's College Cambridge, and St. Michael's, Coventry; these robust forms were quickly taken up and vulgarised by Loudon, and are still stocked by iron-mongers. Hunt also delineated Tudor furniture of an academically correct kind (see p.425).

Hunt's design for a 'dowry-house' (Fig. 129) has a seemly and understated 'Old Englishness' that anticipates William Morris. The decoration on the ridge of the roof was justified by reference to Payne Knight; it was 'only by breaking the outline that an ornamental variety can be produced';[102] such ornament, in terracotta or cast iron, became common in Victorian buildings. As did triangular and other patterns on brickwork. often rendered in glazed and coloured bricks.

The Norman style did not have the appeal of the Gothic, but was used to a limited extent, in domestic as well as ecclesiastical architecture. A house in Norman style was offered in 1826 by the determinedly many-sided P. F. Robinson (Fig. 130); this is

**129** Design for a dowry-house, 1829, by T. F. Hunt

**130** A villa in the Norman style, 1827, a design by P. F. Robinson

XLV Harlaxton Manor, Lincs., designed by Anthony Salvin, 1831–7

XLVI Bedford School, 1833–7, designed by Edward Blore

XLVII Aloupka Palace, the Crimea,
1836–7, designed by Edward Blore

contemporary with his design for a 'Norman' church at Leamington Spa (see p.84). The rich surface texture of the house is undoubtedly of Norman origin, but there is something faintly primitivistic Italian about the roof on the extreme right, with its beams that hint at an entablature. The latticed windows are far removed from the plate glass of Beckford and the gothicists, and there is no hint of any compromise that might supply Norman 'French' windows, verandahs, or conservatories.

The same renunciations were not required with churches; a design by Soane for the entrance portico of Marylebone Church in Norman style shows how much easier it was to use it with advantage in an ecclesiastical context (Fig. 131). The interest in chiaroscuro is typical of Soane; he may have become aware of Daguerre's experiments shown in London from June 1827, to one of which this design bears a curious resemblance.[103]

**131** The entrance portico of Marylebone Church, a design by Sir John Soane, c.1818

*Opposite top* **XLVIII** 'North East View of the Cotsen Bhang, on the River Jumna, Delhi', India, published by Thomas and William Daniell, 1795–1808

*Opposite below* **XLIX** The East Front of Brighton Pavilion, designed by John Nash, 1815–21

Chapter five

# Exotic Styles

## Egyptian: influences on design

The style which demonstrated the 'wild enormities of ancient magnaminity' at their most powerful was undoubtedly the Egyptian. It had primitivist associations with Greek and Roman architecture that made it significant to the classicists, although the tincture of classicism that European draughtsmen unconsciously imparted to their renderings of Egyptian artefacts had ameliorated original harshnesses. Many Egyptian motifs — pyramids, sphinxes, obelisks — had been incorporated into Roman, and thence into Renaissance and baroque art; these had to be purged of later civilties before they appeared again truly Egyptian. Commentaries and pictorial representations went back further in time than they did for the Indian style, as did understanding. Piranesi repeated with approval Buonarroti's opinion of Egyptian art: 'if [it] seems to us rude, it is not for want of art, but out of a veneration to antiquity, and out of the great respect which the Egyptians had to sacred things'.[1]

The post-antique use of Egyptian motifs does not imply ready access to Egyptian architecture. Those who managed to see it were overwhelmed; in 1739 the explorer Frederick Norden exclaimed: 'Let them talk to me no more of Rome; let Greece be silent. What magnificence! . . .'[2] But his pictorial records were limited. Many people were vague about Egyptian art; for instance, the omnivorous collector and connoisseur the Comte de Caylus showed no Egyptian architecture, and some uncertainty on attributions. He realised the importance of Egypt, saying that the Greeks wished to forget what they owed to it and to persuade the world that they themselves had invented their arts, 'Cependent ils n'en ont pas imposé à la Postérité' (he himself mistook as Egyptian what is obviously an early Greek bronze kouros, which he called 'embarrassing').[3]

Piranesi, in the brilliant and congested Egyptian designs illustrated in the *Diverse Maniere* of 1769 (Figs 263, 300), first exploited the possibilities of the style, using Egyptian motifs in a manner influenced by 'Pompeian' fantasy architecture. His designs were for decorations, not architecture, but were used as a source for both. His work influenced the Egyptian-style decorations by Antonio Asprucci at the Villa Borghese in Rome; these were published by Parisi in 1782[4] and were seen by many English visitors, including architects.

The Egyptian sources available to architects such as the elder Playfair (see p.131) were greatly augmented by the pictorial spoils of Napoleon's journey to Egypt; the stony grandiosities of Vivant Denon's famous and superbly illustrated *Voyage dans la Basse et la Haute Egypte* impressed the whole of informed Europe; published in 1802, it was immediately reprinted in London (Fig. 132). In the same year the scene painters of the Lyceum Theatre produced 'Aegyptica', a moving panorama based on Denon.[5] In June 1803 the *Edinburgh Review* commented that 'Few publications, we believe, have ever obtained so extensive a circulation in the same space of time as these travels'.[6] In 1806 the diplomat William Hamilton published *Aegyptiaca*, the most accurate guide to Egyptian antiquities after Denon.

The success of the *Voyage* and public fascination with the Egyptian style aroused apprehensions. In 1803 the powerful French theorist and scholar Quatremère de Quincy issued a stern warning in his *De l'Architecture Egyptienne* against the solecism of imitating Egyptian architecture in inferior materials; the Greeks, he said, 'dans le système imitatif de leur Architecture, substituèrent une matière à une autre matière. Il y eut en Egypte *identité de matière et de goût*' (author's italics). He continued: 'Dès-lors absence de ce plaisir qu'on prouve à voir une chose représentée par une autre chose. L'Architecture Egyptienne fut par conséquent en ce genre aussi peu imitative qu'il fut possible', and

132 'Porte intérieure du Temple de Tentyris',
Egypt, published by D. V. Denon, 1802

exculpated the copyist from the unfortunate effects of the copy: 'A la verité cet effet, provient moins ici du défaut de l'art imitateur que du défaut du modèle inimitable'. Moreover, unlike Greek ornament, organically derived from primitive wooden construction, Egyptian ornament was imposed on the structure; decoration on Egyptian buildings can therefore be only like that of 'une broderie sur une étoffe'. The 'luxe' of Egyptian architecture lay not in ornament, but in its 'genre de construction colossale et à grand appareil'. Soane's gloss on this passage in his copy of the text is 'Strength or solidity is the only quality in the Egyptian buildings'. In short, 'L'Architecture égyptienne ne connut et ne put connoître la variété. Elle fut essentiellement monotone'.[7] These stern words were supplemented by observations on the meaningless nature of hieroglyphs in modern use.[8]

This weighty opposition to the fascinations of Denon may have been amongst the reasons for the limited success of the Egyptian as an architectural (as opposed to an interior-decorative) style in Regency England. The interest in architectural primitivism should have favoured it, as should the widely accepted opinion that the ancestry of Greek Doric lay in Egypt. But English authorities promulgated the French interdict; Hope repeated de Quincy's strictures virtually word for word in his *Household Furniture* (see pp.343–5, 384), and Soane told his students that although Egyptian architecture had 'prodigious solidity and wonderful magnitude . . . grandeur and unaffected

simplicity', it lacked the virtues of correct design, having a 'uniformity and tiresome monotony' in both its general forms and in its details.[9] Greek and Roman architecture was historically and aesthetically acceptable in stucco; Egyptian was not. It became ridiculous used in trivial contexts; Soane denounced the use of the Egyptian style in shop fronts: 'what can be more puerile and unsuccessful than the paltry attempt to imitate the character and form of their works in small and confined spaces?' (Fig. 133).[10]

The bias against Egyptian artefacts extended to sculpture. Although Sir Joseph Banks had urged Henry Salt, the British consul in Cairo, to acquire Egyptian antiquities for the British Museum, he wrote snubbingly to Salt in 1819 to say of one of his most wonderfully beautiful acquisitions that, 'Though in truth we are here much satisfied with the Memnon, and consider it as a chef-d'oeuvre of Egyptian sculpture; yet we have not placed that statue among the works of *Fine Art*. It stands in the Egyptian Rooms.'[11]

Most against the Egyptian style, perhaps, was the portentous gloom of the temple architecture; it seemed to speak (it was in fact symbolic of eternal life) too eloquently of death and coercion; many contemporaries discovered no trace 'either of a pleasing fancy, or of indulgence and respect for the softer emotions of humanity'.[12] It was apparent to all that, as Hope said, the Egyptian style was 'the most fully extinct':[13] most architects seem to have agreed with Busby that 'of all the vanities which

**133** A shop front in Egyptian style

the hope that 'it has beauties not inapplicable to this climate, when combined with taste and judgment. . . . There is a boldness of outline and a grandeur of parts in this Elevation characteristic of the original style . . .'. He proposed that 'to preserve a complete uniformity of character . . . many parts of the interior should be finished and furnished in the same style with the exterior, according to the present prevailing fashion. Sphinxes, Chimeras, etc. may be introduced as supporters, or as ornaments'.[15] Randall, a practising architect, fell into the old and deprecated habit of using temple architecture as a model for domestic dwellings; his adaptation of Dendera and other sources for a house which has the full pageant of pylons, graffiti-like hieroglyphs, and Hathor-headed pillars, its windows punctuated by grim glazing bars, makes for a dwelling more intractable even than one derived from the Greek Doric temple. Had an architect of genius been committed to the Egyptian style, the story might have been different.

The style was easier to accept in public buildings. The conspicuously sited Egyptian Hall in Piccadilly (Fig. 135), designed by P. F. Robinson and opened in 1812, was said (incorrectly) by Elmes to have been modelled on the temple at Tentyra (Dendera).[16] The primitive figures were modelled by Sebastian Gahagan and cast in Coade stone.[17] The building's Hall, which housed exhibitions, became a well-known feature of London (it was remodelled in Egyptian style in 1819 by J. B. Papworth; see p.346), and in 1821–2 housed an exhibition of high quality Egyptian artefacts brought together by the illustrious explorer G. B. Belzoni. London was bewitched; on the opening day of the exhibition, 1,900 people paid half a crown to see it.[18]

An attempt was made to use the Egyptian style in garden buildings. A distinguished greenhouse design by C. H. Tatham (Fig. 33; see p.77) contrasts, in its austere academicism, with the free-wheeling attitude of Randall and Robinson. Tatham showed the interest in Egyptian art that might have been expected from one of his bent; he had copied a design by J. N. Sobre of 1795 in which an obelisk supported on an elephant had been decorated with 'hieroglyphs' consisting of symbolic — and meaningful — triumphal and military motifs in classical style.[19] Greek primitivism had succeeded in the garden; Egyptian did not, in part because no Egyptian poetry supplied alluring associations.

The synthesising tendencies of the Regency were rejected by John Foulston, an architect of little imagination; he congratulated himself on being 'free from the abomination of having exhibited a combination of styles in the same building'. He preferred the opposite method: 'Notwithstanding the grandeur and exquisite proportions of the Grecian orders, the author has never been insensible to the distinguishing beauties of the other original styles; and it occurred to him that if a series of edifices, exhibiting the various features of the architectural world, were erected in conjunction, and skilfully grouped, a happy result might be obtained. Under this impression, he is induced

a sickly fashion has produced, the Egyptian style in modern Architecture appears the most absurd'.[14] It was left to the engineers, to whom prodigious solidity was often essential, and to whom 'matière et goût' were inseparable.

## Egyptian style buildings

Egyptian motifs were used successfully and ubiquitously in interior decoration and furniture, and it is clear that the style's popularity in that sphere encouraged efforts to make it popular as an architectural form. James Randall's 'Perspective view of a Mansion in the Egyptian Style' of 1806 (Fig. 134) is accompanied by a text that explains that since the Egyptian style 'has been adopted in many articles of interior decoration with general approbation', he offers 'an Elevation for an English Mansion, founded on the style of Egyptian Architecture' with

134 'Perspective view of a Mansion in the
Egyptian Style', a design by James Randall, 1806

135 Egyptian Hall or Bullock's Museum,
Piccadilly, 1811–12, designed by P. F. Robinson

ON STONE BY T J RICAUTI.                                                                PRINTED BY G LEE

TOWN HALL . COMMEMORATIVE COLUMN . MOUNT ZION CHAPEL . CIVIL AND MILITARY LIBRARY KER ST DEVONPORT.

JOHN FOULSTON ARCH!

**136** Town Hall, Commemorative Column, Mount Zion Chapel, Civil and Militia Library, Ker Street, Devonport, 1821–4, designed by John Foulston

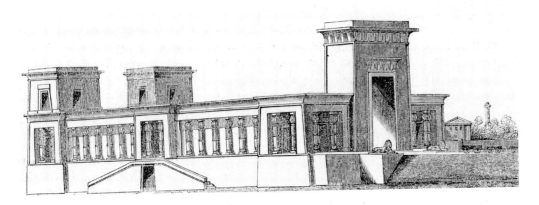

**137** 'Design for a Termination to a Railway', 1835, by W. J. Short

to try an experiment . . . for producing a picturesque effect, by combining, in one view, the Grecian, Egyptian, and a variety of the Oriental. . .'.[20] It is curious the Foulston did not perceive that whilst it might be difficult to obtain harmony by combining different styles in one building, it would be impossible to obtain it by placing deliberate contrasts of style contiguous to each other.

The result of his experiment, the extraordinary Ker-Street parade of styles, makes sense only in terms of the museum or of the entertainment industry (not the same thing, *pace* some modern museum directors) (Fig. 136). The architecture is uninspired; the Egyptianism of the Civil and Militia Library is simplistic, the same zig-zag detail being used on the façade as around the bookcases in the library interior; the pillars remind one of Martin's paintings, probably having a common source in Denon. The paucity of his Egyptian invention, and the

similarity of the Indian-style Mount Zion Chapel to the recently completed Pavilion at Brighton, suggests that Foulston did not venture far in search of inspiration.

The failure of the Egyptian style in architecture was summed up by *The Mirror* in 1827: 'It is somewhat surprising, that among the crowd of novelties . . . the "Egyptian" has not taken its share. It is true that some very partial attempts have been made: in the metropolis, we believe, not exceeding two; and if we add to these a school recently erected at Devonport [Foulston] . . . a mausoleum at Trentham for the Stafford family [Tatham] . . . and an iron-manufactory now erecting in Wales, we have probably enumerated the whole . . . they have scarcely attracted any notice, whether for good or evil.' The article went on to blame architects for neglecting the style's possibilities, and concluded: 'as to the specimens where it has been thought fit to introduce the

Egyptian window or doorway in churches of a Greek design, we consider the attempt faulty and censurable'.[21]

The allusion to the 'iron-manufactory' is a reminder that the primaeval force of the Egyptian style was attractive to engineers and industrialists (Fig. 137). Not only was it an aesthetically appropriate style: the form of the pylon was functionally ideal to withstand tensions exerted by suspension bridges and pressures endured by railway viaducts. Captain Samuel Brown, who designed the Egyptian-style Chain Pier at Brighton on the suspension principle, had helped to develop the techniques that enabled stronger suspension chains to be made; his innovations were used by Thomas Telford in the design for the Menai Straits bridge of 1825.[22] Erected in less than twelve months in 1823, the Chain Pier lasted for almost three-quarters of a century before breaking up in a great storm, by which it was no dishonour to be destroyed. Its towers were drawn after the pylons at Luxor, pictured by Norden as early as 1755. The Egyptian style was used by Brunel in his suspension bridge at Bristol, preferred to the Gothic design submitted by Telford. Brunel had intended to decorate the surface of the towers with 'Egyptian' cast-iron reliefs illustrating the building of the bridge by John Horsley;[23] the use of the new material for 'art' is significant.

Brunel was a friend of John Martin, who had an interest in industrial problems (see p.100). The architectural backgrounds of Martin's apocalyptic architectural dreams, or rather nightmares, considered by Charles Lamb to be of 'the highest order of the material sublime'[24] (despite the 'vulgar fright' and 'animal anxiety for the preservation of their persons'[25] that animates his figures), are often tinged with the Egyptian manner; the popularity of the paintings reflects a contemporary liking for sensationally portentous architecture which may have struck some chord in Brunel and other engineers. It seems poetically appropriate that the forms employed by the Industrial Revolution, explicitly identified by Blake with Satan, were taken from an ancient and mysterious civilisation that had for centuries instilled a sense of terror and awe.

The Egyptian style found fitting use in funerary monuments; the associations are too obvious to be stated. The most grandiose plan was that of Thomas Willson in 1824 to create a funerary Pyramid, planned to hold five million corpses; the Pyramid, obviously influenced by French Romantic Classicism, was claimed to be compact, ornamental, vandal-proof (the royal mummies that littered Europe should have dispelled this optimism) and hygienic. It would 'go far towards completing the glory of London'.[26] In the event, it did not.

## Chinese and Indian design sources

During the course of the eighteenth century a frivolous or esoteric use had been made of Chinese styles, usually in garden buildings or in the more sophisticated and mannered forms of interior decoration. A sustained attempt was now made to press them, and Indian styles, into 'serious' service.

The 'rules' of the Chinese style, often treated by eighteenth-century architects, decorators and writers as if it had some affiliation with Gothic, were to be found in a book by Chambers which, first published in 1757, became a major source of architectural and decorative chinoiserie in Europe and served the Regency period and beyond (Fig. 255). *Designs of Chinese buildings, furniture, dresses, machines and utensils*, collected according to the author in China, included elevations and plans of Chinese buildings, with six examples of Chinese columns palladianised; the proportions were specified as if the columns were classical. Knight, who liked neither the Chinese nor the Indian style, rebuked Chambers: 'nor have I seen or hear of curved roofs on this side of China, except in imitations introduced into this country principally by a person, who gave equal proofs of the purity of his taste when he censured the temples of Athens, and designed those of Kew'.[27] In about 1815 chinoiserie began again to be tinged with the rococo, and motifs and styles resembling those of earlier rococo pattern books emerged (Pl. LXXXVI), quite distinct from the 'classical' Regency chinoiserie derived from Chambers.

The first pattern book, if such it can be called, for the Indian style did not appear until Repton published his proposals for the Pavilion at Brighton in Indian style in 1808 (see pp.69, 198). But the way had been prepared, intellectually and pictorially. The English in India, led by Warren Hastings, had interested themselves in Indian art, philosophy, and literature; Sanskrit and Persian were studied, Sir William Jones leading the translations in 1785 and 1790 of two major Hindu works;[28] the common roots of Indo-European languages had been demonstrated (this preceded the growth of nineteenth-century racialism). The interest aroused is shown in such theories as those advanced by Thomas Maurice in 1806; he postulated that Brahmin priests, gradually mingling with the 'Celtic tribes who pursued their journey to the extremity of Europe, finally established the Druid, that is, Brahmin, system of superstition in ancient Britain. This, I contend, was the first Oriental colony settled in these islands' (this again was before the nineteenth-century growth of racial prejudice). Maurice thought also that, solar devotion having originated under Belus on the plains of Babylon, his posterity, the Belidae, had emigrated to Britain and built Stonehenge.[29] The theory in some ways parallels the attempt to equate Gothicism with freedom.

Other commentators pursued other chimera: Cathedral Gothic was 'a corruption of the sacred architecture of the Greeks and the Romans, by a mixture of the Moorish or Saracenic, which is formed out of a combination of the Aegyptian, Persian, and Hindoo',[30] perhaps not so outrageous a theory as first appears. Such architectural theorising, whether by Maurice or Knight, was sympathetically open-minded and had a sense of common inheritance that makes the promiscuous massing of styles in such concoctions as Alton Towers more understandable. Maurice's account is spiced with an extract from a 1638 description of the palace of Akbar at Agra that demonstrates another aspect of Regency interest in India — the appetite for the fabulous, reflected in such works as William Beckford's *Vathek* and the orientalisms of Byron, Southey, and Moore: 'the palace was altogether the grandest object he had ever beheld . . . a row of silver pillars under a piazza . . . beyond . . . the presence chamber; and this more spacious apartment was adorned with a row of golden pillars of a smaller size, and within the balustrade was the royal throne of massy gold, almost encrusted over with diamonds, pearls, and other precious stones'.[31] The Regency taste that produced the Golden Drawing Room at Carlton House (Pl. LXXXIII) and the Banqueting Room of Brighton Pavilion (Pl. CII) must have fed on such opulent descriptions.

Reynolds' reaction to such exoticisms as those pictured in Hodges' *Select Views in India*, published in 1785 to 1788, has been mentioned above (see p.100); in his Discourse of December 1786 he said: 'The Barbaric Splendour of those Asiatic Buildings which are now publishing . . . may . . . furnish an architect not with models to copy, but with hints of composition and general effect. . . .' Reynolds was more open to new ideas than Knight, who, contesting Burke's definition of the beautiful, remarked that, 'The buildings most consonant to the above definitions of beauty are the Hindoo [he meant Moghul] domes. . . . Their undulating flow of outline tapered to a point; their frail and delicate structure; their clear bright colours. . . . Yet I do not believe that either Mr. Burke or his commentator ever found such a building beautiful: for . . . their natural good taste triumphed over their theories'.[32] Many people did find such buildings beautiful, not only as depicted by Hodges, who bathed palaces and landscape in a golden Claudian vapour, but as they appeared, accompanied by waving palms and exotic inhabitants, in the splendidly picturesque aquatints published between 1795 and 1808 by Thomas and William Daniell, whose six large folio volumes were the principal quarry for those seeking to design buildings in Indian style.

## Chinese style

Regency chinoiserie is so familiar in furniture and decoration, and Brighton Pavilion has so conspicuous a place in the popular image of the Regency, that it comes as a surprise to find that apart from garden buildings few Regency buildings with complete Chinese-style exteriors exist. Motifs drawn from Chinese architecture were used extensively in that remarkable synthesis of styles, the Regency house (see p.203), but that is another matter. The Chinese element in the exterior of the Pavilion is virtually restricted to the two pagoda roofs, forms only unambiguously Chinese when used in tiers. And chinoiserie based on Chambers is usually a sober affair compared with rococo interpretations (Fig. 22); this restraint may be seen clearly in Holland's modest Dairy of the late 1780s at Woburn Abbey. Porden produced a series of designs in about 1805 for Brighton Pavilion in a Chinese style drawn from Chambers; glittering in gold, red, and blue, they none the less failed to entice the Prince of Wales.[33]

It is difficult to account for the neglect of the Chinese style in architecture, when the appetite for novelty was so greedy and so often accused of lack of discrimination. The Chinese style might have been alien to the temper of the early years of the century, when Hope and other cognoscenti were seeking to advance the cause of an architecture and a type of furniture derived from weighty and enduring stone; massiveness was in fashion. Chinese architecture was quite the reverse, being based, according to Hope, on the tent: 'The palaces only look like a number of collected awnings, and the very pagodas . . . are nothing more than a number of tents, piled on the top. . . .'[34] Hope thought Chinese architecture limited by its nature; it 'appears with the tenacity of life, of the lichen, and the moss, also to possess their low vital energy', and it 'is never seen to grow into new, and finer, and more stately forms'.[35]

Another factor in this disregard may have been the influence of French Romantic Classicism, hardly tolerant of any style that could not be pressed into its service; it found the Egyptian style sympathetic and encouraged its acceptance, but when it sought to assimilate the Chinese style to its grave and disciplined rhythms, its cubic solidity and vestigial ornament, it produced something which completely missed the point (Fig. 24), or at least missed the point of most chinoiserie. Decorative chinoiserie returned in rococo guise; first in the short-lived interior decorations of 1815 to 1817 at Brighton Pavilion (see p.339) — at almost the same time that Duchess Elizabeth was reviving 'Louis Quatorze' in the Saloon at Belvoir Castle — and then in the context of a general acceptance of 'revived rococo'. Even then it returned as architecture only in parks and gardens, and principally as the result of George IV's activities (Fig. 23).

## Indian style

The Indian style was in reality two styles, the Hindu and the Islamic. Hope was quite clear in separating them; that of the Hindus, he said, everywhere affords 'traces of the void cut in the live rock';[36] the Islamic was the style of the Mughal princes of India who, 'instead of the patterns immediately under their eyes' — the 'heavy indestructible pagoda of the idolatrous native' — imitated instead 'the airy arches and the lofty cupolas of the Persians and the Greeks'.[37] Hope considered

**138** Design for a 'Villa in the Eastern Style', by Robert Lugar, 1805

**139** Design for the West Front of Brighton Pavilion, by Humphry Repton, c.1805

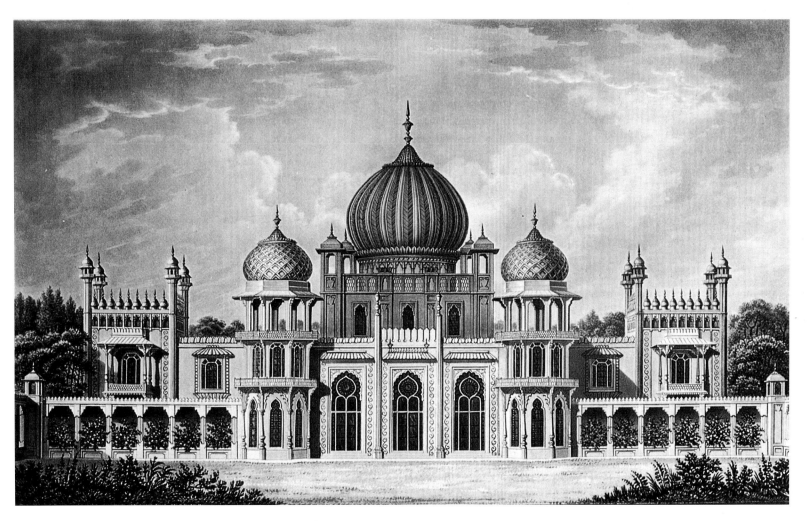

that Islamic architecture, in rejecting the dark and choosing the light, had, together with that of the Saracens, the Moors, and, indeed, the Gothic itself, the noblest lineage possible — 'that ancient and primitive Greek Architecture itself'.[38]

Most unusually for a new style, the Mughal was first used in England in a public building, George Dance's Guildhall of 1787–9, where it was combined with Gothic; some surviving unused designs are more strongly Indian, with scalloped windows, than the realised building. It appeared in domestic architecture in 1788, in S. P. Cockerell's Daylesford, built for Warren Hastings, where it had obvious associational meaning for the calumniated owner; at Hafod, in 1794, an Islamic cupola was combined with Gothic. At Sezincote in 1806 (Pl. XVI) the Mughal style was used undiluted for house and stables, as opposed to the more barbaric Hindu style adopted for the garden ornaments (Fig. 25); the architect was again S. P. Cockerell, who worked on mansion and gardens with Thomas and William Daniell. The Mughal style was combined with a Palladian plan; the outward curving wing that contains a conservatory was meant to be balanced by a wing on the other side. The cupola (as Hope put it, Islam had caused the cupola to 'belly out like an onion')[39] gives the composition a central weight and emphasis. The architectural detail is of high quality, and the whole ensemble is extremely beautiful; a honey-coloured local stone was used.

In 1797, William Porden had exhibited at the Royal Academy a 'design for a place of amusement in the style of the Mohametan architecture of Hindustan';[40] in the same year Daniell had published the Jami' Masjid at Delhi, which Porden drew upon in designing the Indian-style 'stupendous and magnificent' (Fig. 26) Stables at Brighton, begun in 1804. Farington said the Stables were influenced by the 'Corn Market' at Paris[41] (by Le Camus, and a major monument of French Romantic Classicism). Crowned by a mighty dome, its shape more neo-classical than onion-like, with a gilded finial, the Stables provoked some tedious humour.[42]

The Indian style attracted a popular following in these years. In 1805 Robert Lugar published an uncompromising 'Villa in the Eastern Style' (Fig. 138), and it must have been about this time that the Bath House at Arno's Castle near Bristol, first built about 1760 in the Gothick style,[43] was 'Indianised' with domes, finials, and a central lantern that may possibly have owed something to Porden's cupola. In 1808 Repton attempted to capture royal favour by publishing new designs for Brighton Pavilion in Mughal style; he was prompted by the positive enthusiasm of the Prince of Wales, with whom he had had prolonged discussions in 1805.

The result was a beautiful series of drawings in which the garden, with its aviary modelled on Daniell's 'Hindoo Temples at Bindrabund', its Pheasantry with a lantern drawn from Daniell's Mughal 'Palace in

the Fort at Allahabad',[44] its Orangery and other buildings in a variety of Indian styles, made a ravishing whole with the Pavilion (Fig. 26, Pl. XVIII). The last was to be in academic Mughal style, less harmonious than Sezincote (Fig. 139); it had an octagon at the end of the private apartments which, apparently meant to be clad in blue and white tiles, was inspired by the upper storey of the eastern bastions of Daniell's 'View of the Cotsen Bhang' (Pl. XLVIII). The beauty of the designs did not persuade the Prince, although he had a moment of delighted acceptance. The gardens were the most convincing part of the scheme. The Prince turned to Wyatt, but plans for a Gothic Pavilion were cut short by Wyatt's carriage accident; the Prince then instructed Nash to prepare designs. It would be interesting to know how their discussions ran.

## Exotic syntheses

For, when funds allowed, Nash began in 1815 to build to a design that was in no way 'correct' — a brilliant amalgamation of Indian, Chinese, and not a little Gothick (Pl. XLIX). The result impresses itself on the mind as perhaps the most immediately recognisable Regency building of all; a rejected design reveals that this was achieved by a

140 'Un piccolo padiglione, o baldacchino', from a Pompeian wall decoration, published in 1765

multiplication of domes and minarets in a manner that borders on the reckless, the same intemperate use of motifs as was to be seen, in a classical style, on the vilified façade of Buckingham Palace (see pp.151–6).

Nash's Pavilion incorporated Holland's existing building. The latter's rippling bow-windowed front was clothed by Nash in Mughal forms, the lacy screen of the 'jalis' uniting the central bow with the two great rooms which Nash added at either end; Mughal domes and minarets crown the whole, with minarets surrounding the two 'Chinese' pagoda roofs at either end; the eventful silhouette distracts one from sensing any oddness arising from the use of Holland's Marine Pavilion as a core. Nash's Pavilion does not lack Gothic touches; the 'Strawberry Hill' towers, glimpsed behind the central dome, are next to a chimney stack with two ogee-shaped flying buttresses (completely unfunctional); the water tower, also flavoured with Gothic, has, alas, disappeared, leaving a serious gap in the composition. The window

astragals are ambiguous. The materials used are Bath stone and stucco, the latter as usual imitating stone. Designs exist for a Mughal-style conservatory;[45] it was to have been a free-standing building, for which the fashion was growing.

The 'pagoda' roofs have been called 'Chinese', but ambiguities surround such forms. During the eighteenth century classical antiquities of an outlandish kind were often classed as 'oriental' or 'Chinese' (see pp.67, 243); Greek key patterns taken from 'Etruscan' vases could often, if divorced from their context, be taken for Chinese. The 'baldacchino' from Herculaneum (Fig. 140), which is described in the text as 'un piccolo padiglione', a 'little pavilion', is a piquant example of the web of ambiguities that envelops the brilliant synthesis of styles at Brighton. Taken from a classical site, the Herculaneum *padiglione* reminds one not only of the pagoda roofs of the Royal Pavilion but also of such items as Papworth's garden seat (Pl. XIX), called by him 'Indian', and the 'Chinese' canopies so often found above

**141** Design for Mrs. Jennings' house, Windsor Park, by John Nash (?)

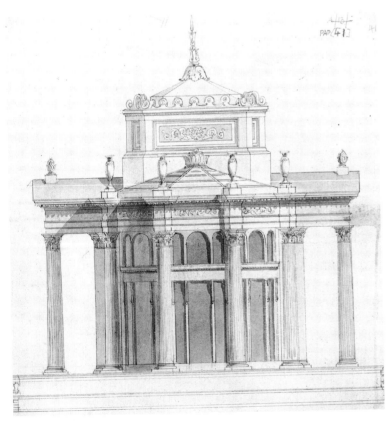

**142** Design for Ashburnham Place, Sussex, before 1813, by George Dance

**143** Design for an aviary or conservatory, by J. B. Papworth

Regency doorways and balconies. Given the classical affiliations of these motifs (Pompeian murals also show 'pagoda' roofs on classical buildings), the ease with which they were incorporated into a domestic architecture primarily classical in origin is easy to understand (see p.203).

The example of Brighton Pavilion was too outré to be followed on any scale in England, although the Brighton architect Amon Wilds built in 1833 as his own house a 'Western Pavilion' in which a Mughal dome is allied with a Regency bow and Italianate detail. A Mughal dome acted as a conservatory adjacent to Decimus Burton's Doric porticoed Colosseum in Regent's Park (Pl. XVII). And the abortive Brighton Athenaeum (see p.79) was to have contained beneath its oriental dome an 'Oriental Garden', and to have stood on a street called 'Oriental Place' leading down to the sea; scalloped Indian detail is still to be seen on the adjacent Silwood Terrace.

For Windsor, the seat of the Great Exotic himself, Nash made a design for 'Mrs. Jennings' House' that brings together pagoda and domes in Pavilion style (Fig. 141); the first floor portico is supported by columns derived from the classical fasces, and panelled treillage introduces yet another Frenchified element; a possible source for fasces and trellis may be seen in the *Oeuvres d'Architecture* of M.-J. Peyre, published in 1765, a source probably used by Nash (see p.128). The design suggests an existing building dressed up.

The Pavilion style was imitated throughout the world in that festive form of seaside architecture that began with Brighton's splendid West Pier, now almost beyond repair.[46] The Pavilion itself had offspring in the shape of the fanciful Aloupka Palace in the Crimea, designed by Blore, the pupil of Nash (Pl. XLVII); the exotic synthesis was enriched with Tudor Gothic, castellated Gothic, and with formal terraces and gardens, the whole set in a hilly landscape. Begun in 1828, Aloupka Palace was designed not only to follow the shape of the Ai Petri Mountain that lay behind it; its façade was faced with green diorite marble, imported from Italy, intended to echo the mountain's colour.[47] At the behest of a Russian prince, the Regency Picturesque was here transported, as if on a magic carpet, to the confines of Asia.

Nash was not the only person to indulge in syntheses of Mughal style with other styles. George Dance has been mentioned above as the first architect to use Indian motifs, and he remained the most consistently assiduous in doing so, driven by principle rather than opportunism. Dance, the 'most complete Poet Architect of his day',[48]

had strong views on the necessity of 'unshacling' architecture (see p.90) in order to create new styles. Some fascinating designs show his experiments in combining Gothic and Indian. Encouraging resemblances between the two forms of architecture had been remarked by many, including Hodges, who had written of the 'perfect similarity between the Architecture of India, brought there from Persia by the Descendants of Timur, & that brought into Europe by the Moors seated in Spain . . . known by the name of Gothic Architecture. . . . In all this the ornaments are perfectly the same — the Lozenge Square filled with Roses, the ornaments in the Spandrels of the Arches, the little pannelling, and their mouldings . . .'.[49]

A design by Dance for Ashburnham Place, which he altered between 1813 and 1817, combines eclectic motifs in princely fashion, the windows being given pediments and the porte-cochère columns capped with coronets (Fig. 142); other designs for the house blend Indian with Gothic. A design for Norman Court combines Indian turrets, again capped with coronets, with a cupola that may carry reminiscences of the Tower of the Winds; at the left a Vanbrugh-like coat of arms breaks the skyline. A more faithful interpretation of Reynolds' adjuration to use the spirit and not the forms of alien styles would be difficult to find. Might Papworth have had access to Dance's

**144** Coleorton Hall, Leics., designed by George Dance

designs? A strange pavilion-like conceit by Papworth is much in Dance's manner, using Indian detail together with Corinthian pillars and odd round arches: again, the Tower of the Winds is quoted (Fig. 143). This design appears to be have been for a garden building; other Papworth garden buildings are, to use his own words, of the same 'no specific architectural character' (Pl. XXIV; see p.70).

The stylistic evolution of Coleorton Hall in Leicestershire, built for Sir George Beaumont by Dance between 1804 and 1808, illustrates the magical mystery tour that a Regency architect might take. One of the most adventurous of architects was here working for an exacting patron who was also a fast friend; other members of Beaumont's group included Uvedale Price, Payne Knight, Hope, Coleridge, and Wordsworth, the last of whom designed Coleorton's winter garden. Beaumont rejected Price's recommendation of Nash, and in the autumn of 1801 asked Dance to make designs to be sent for comment to Price and to William Mitford.[50] The intermediate stages produced intriguing ideas; a design with giant Corinthian pillars and a lantern with an Indian flavour was offered; also a dandified castellated design (Fig. 144), vaguely recalling Seton Castle. Dance clearly felt free to venture with a patron of Beaumont's calibre. In the event, the entrance front was built in a form of Gothic tinged with Indian, with minaret-like turrets not unrelated to the Indian detail of Dance's 1777–8 London Guildhall. The south front has windows with moulded drip stones that, Tudor in derivation, are so simplified as to become an abstract grid that has been likened to Schinkel's 1827 project for a bazaar in Berlin.[51] The polygonal Gothic hall within, rising to the full height of the house, was borrowed from Soane's Tyringham design (Fig. 89), which was lent to Dance at the latter's request.[52] The porte-cochère may have been influenced by Nash's Luscombe (Pl. XLII). Coleorton was cold, despite Dance's central heating.[53] Using Dance, Beaumont obtained not a castle or castellated mansion, as he might well have done with Nash, but a sophisticated synthesis composed in accordance with those ideals that animated Hope at the Deepdene (see pp.115–17). The divergent results at Coleorton and the Deepdene exhibit the vitality of the synthetic ideal and of the culture that produced it.

Chapter six

# The Regency Synthesis

## The 'picaresque' house

In the concluding pages of his encyclopaedic essay on architecture, written at the end of his career, Hope criticised the architecture of his time on two principal grounds: inappropriateness of form and inferiority of material. Some, he said, 'by building houses in the shape of temples, have contrived for themselves most inappropriate and uncomfortable dwellings'; some, 'instead of a temple, have lodged themselves in a church'; others 'have, in [times of] profound peace, or at least of internal security and refinement, affected to raise rude and embattled castles, as if they expected a siege'. He thus disposed of the Greek Revival, 'ecclesiastical' Gothic, and modern castles.

Hope then turned his attack against the flimsy materials and dullness of ordinary houses: 'In England, government, by taxing alike heavily, brick and stone, which form the solid walls; and the apertures . . . for the admission of light; discourages . . . both solidity of construction and variety of form; copyhold tenures, short leases, and the custom of building whole streets by contract, still increase the slightness, the uniformity, the poverty of the general architecture. Here the exterior shell of most edifices is designed by a surveyor who has little science, and no knowledge of the fine arts; and the internal finishing . . . is left to a mere upholder, still more ignorant. . . .' The final paragraph of his work, and therefore in a sense the last word he left posterity, was an eloquent appeal for a new kind of architecture, which for him lay purely in the future: 'No one seems yet to have conceived the smallest wish or idea of only borrowing of every former style whatever it might present of useful or ornamental, of scientific or tasteful; of adding thereto whatever other new dispositions or forms might afford conveniences or elegancies not yet processed . . . and thus of composing an architecture which, born in our country, grown on our

soil, and in harmony with our climate, institutions, and habits, at once elegant, appropriate, and original, should truly deserve the appellation of "Our Own".'[1]

These seem extraordinary words, born perhaps of the browner tinge given to life by advancing years and disillusion. For setting aside his own noble achievements, and those of some of his peers; setting aside the work of synthesising architects of genius such as Dance and Soane — had the great connoisseur no eyes? The artefact in which the Regency urge towards eclecticism and synthesis was most successfully and ubiquitously displayed stood all around him; true, often flimsily built, but beguiling for all that, and to us one of the period's most attractive legacies — the typical Regency house.

Eclecticism was the breath of life to Regency architecture, the oxygen that regenerated debilitated tissues. The eagerness with which the components of various styles were grasped and discarded, the readiness of most architects to attempt any style, indicate a feverish desire for novelty shared by architect and client; it was much remarked by contemporaries. The plain shell of the house created by the various building acts, with the inherited harmony of eighteenth-century proportions, made an ideal ground for various embellishments culled from Europe and Asia. To it were added classical porches in different Orders, from smooth Tuscan to crisp Ionic, ornate Corinthian, and uncompromising baseless Greek Doric; bay and bow windows, the latter often shallow in the earlier period and curvaceous in the later; rectangular windows, often capped with voluptuous curled shells from Palmyra, Baalbek, and other antique sources, or even with sunflowers. Applied to the façades were balconies and balustrades from Italy and France, verandahs from India, treillage from France and from antiquity, ironwork of every fashion, from Gothic to Chinese to Saracenic to Etruscan to Pompeian, and most characteristic of all, the instantly

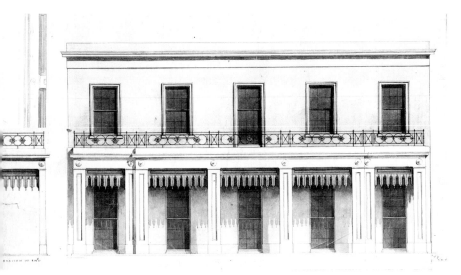

**145** Design for a verandah, 1828, by J. B. Papworth

**147** 'A View of the Pavilion at Brighton as it formerly stood', the Marine Pavilion, Brighton, the East Front, 1801, designed by Henry Holland and P. F. Robinson

**146** Design for the addition of canopies and verandahs, No. 1 Bath Place, London, by J. B. Papworth

recognisable Regency canopy, usually in lead or copper, convex or concave, and ambiguously Indian, Chinese, or classical (Fig. 47). The surface of the house was decorated with patterns ranging from Greek key to incised Soanean devices and arabesque. The origin of these motifs, and the associations they bore with them, were usually well known, if occasionally confused. As James Malton wrote in 1803: 'The rude ornaments of Indostan supersede those of Greece; and the returned Nabob, heated in his pursuit of wealth, imagines he imports the *chaleur* of the East with its riches; and we behold the stretched awning to form the cool shade . . .; the new fashioned windows of Italy, opening to the floor, with lengthened balcony, originally intended to survey the lawns, the vista and the groves of Claude . . . or the canals of Venice; are now to be seen in every confined street of London'.[2] These 'stretched awnings' of canvas were in common use (the lead canopies were often painted to simulate them (Figs 148, 150, 152, 153)); Loudon recommended blue and white striped gingham.[3]

This particular mixed style, the style of what one might call the 'picaresque' Regency house, betokened the same interest in the foreign and exotic as was seen in Regency drama, theatrical spectacle, poetry and journalism, and even dress. It was deservedly popular, and is especially evident in those parts of the country that had a sophisticated local population: it has a gaiety and light-heartedness that accommodated it to spa and seaside towns such as Cheltenham, Leamington, and Brighton, where it continued in favour up to the middle of the century (Fig. 151). In good examples, the synthesis is perfect, and the alien origin of the various elements does not obtrude; it is only in the later examples that the balance is upset, and heavy Italianate detail — even Jacobethan detail — overweights delicate railings and canopies.

L  Cottages for Attingham Park, late 1790s, by Humphry Repton (?)

LI  Cowdray Lodge, Sussex, designed by C. H. Tatham, c.1800

LII 'A Cottage Orné', design for a cottage for two ladies, by J. B. Papworth, 1818

LIII Knowle Cottage, Sidmouth, c.1818

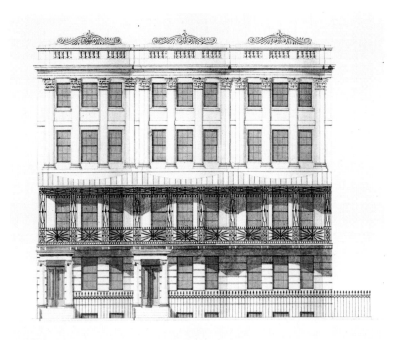

**148** Design for houses on the 'West Cliff', Brighton, by C. A. Busby, c.1825

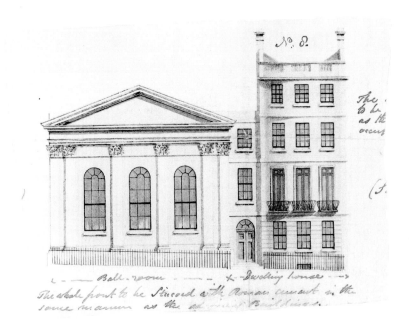

**149** Design for a ballroom and dwelling house, by C. A. Busby

One of the most important catalysts, perhaps the most important, in the creation of the style was the transformation of the Marine Pavilion at Brighton. Balconies had been added in the 1790s to the bow windows inherited from the Frenchified Holland design of 1787 (see p.120); in 1801 an enchanting chinoiserie trim of green copper canopies and treillage was given to the façade by Holland and P. F. Robinson (Fig. 147). The Marine Pavilion was the haunt of the brilliant and illustrious society that trailed after the Prince of Wales; one can be sure that fashion looked hard at its style. It influenced both the picaresque house and the cottage orné (the Marine Pavilion of 1801 was very like a large cottage orné) and the style could be extended without difficulty into terraces, squares, and crescents.

It quickly took over Brighton; in his *Designs for Modern Embellishments* of 1810 Busby gives schemes for typical balconies and canopies (Fig. 47). Busby's designs convey the essence of the style; behind the ornamental frippery in iron and lead the house has a sense of form and volume, displayed in the architect's liking for the deep bow front (Fig. 148). The latter could be accompanied by ironwork and striped canopies (Fig. 152) or, for greater grandeur, could be articulated by Ionic or Corinthian pilasters (Fig. 148) or pillars. A late design by Thomas Cubitt shows verandahs and striped canopies combined with plate-glass windows serving the important 'reception' rooms of the first floor, whilst smaller and therefore cheaper panes are used for the ground-floor windows (Fig. 150). The large sheets of plate glass that

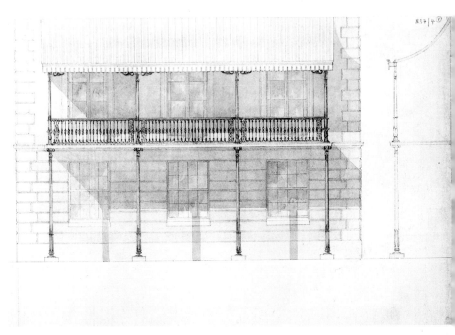

**150** Design for a town house, by Thomas Cubitt

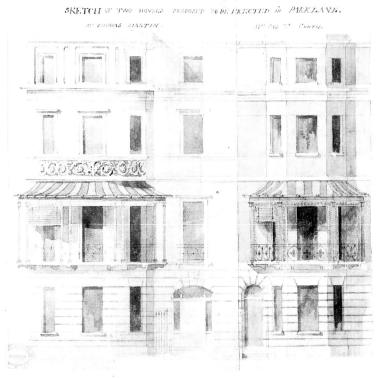

**151** 'Lansdowne Crescent, Victoria House, Elizabethan Place, Royal Leamington Spa', 1835, designed by William Thomas

**152** Sketch of two houses proposed to be erected in Park Lane, design by John Goldicutt

came in during the later 1820s imparted a solemnity alien to the blither versions of the 'picaresque' house. Balconies and canopies were often added to older houses, as seen in a design by Papworth (Fig. 146) where verandahs that display his happy touch are applied to a staid façade. A design by Goldicutt shows canopies painted in stripes attached to a façade with a bay and a bow; the front has a heavily rusticated ground floor and a panel of arabesque decoration; Venetian blinds are at the verandah windows (Fig. 152).

Or more could be added; a truly composite house of 1825 (Fig. 153) has verandahs, ironwork, striped canopies, an Italianate circular door head, a 'Tudor' porch, scalloped barge boards and various 'battered' gables. Next door to this disorderly assemblage sits purity incarnate in the shape of a classical villa. Similarly disarmingly inconsequential juxtapositions were (and are, albeit strangled by traffic) seen at Leamington, where Lansdowne Crescent, designed in 1835 by William Thomas, its palace façade enlivened by canopies and verandahs, sits next to 'Victoria House' (mixed Grecian and Italian), and 'Elizabethan Place' (Jacobethan semi-detached) (Fig. 151). The larger town developments of the later Regency period were usually a matter of choosing between the 'canopy and verandah' style and an Italianate palace style that was often touched by French Romantic Classicism; Brunswick Square in Brighton of about 1825, by C. A. Busby, is of the latter type. There was every opportunity for variety.

The 'picaresque' style was of service in shop front design, as seen in an attractive example by C. A. Busby (Fig. 154), probably meant for Brighton. Such small panes on shop windows were, like those of

153 'Group of Villas on Herne Hill, Camberwell', in 1825

154 Design for a shop front, by C. A. Busby

domestic windows, soon to give way to large expanses of plate glass, used extensively by J. B. Papworth, who made something of a speciality of shop design. Oddly enough, there seem to have been few Gothic designs for shops, perhaps owing to a lingering feeling concerning the sale of indulgences.

An arresting feature of such Regency houses was the fine design of the ironwork, seen even on the most routine. There is a reason for this; the ironwork was as often as not designed by eminent architects. As Cottingham said in 1823, of a collection of ironwork designs republished in 1824, 'many . . . have been executed from the designs of the most eminent artists. . .'.[4] In 1841, John Weale[5] acknowledged as designers of ironwork not only Burton but Nash, Smirke, Soane, Stevenson, Vanbrugh and Wren; the inclusion of the last two displays the growing historicism of the period. Often the designer was not acknowledged; the Burton gate design was reproduced in a pattern book by Henry Shaw, unattributed.[6]

The methods of manufacture allowed plagiarism; all patterns for iron were first carved in wood, the patterns remaining with the producer after the clients' castings had been supplied; they thus entered the public domain. Refined detail was made possible by improved techniques; the development of the refractory furnace fuelled by coke produced a highly liquid metal. The excellence of design extended to the street lamps in front of the houses; a lamp designed for Hyde Park Corner, for example, which bears the cipher of King George IV, owed its form to its high descent from an antique candelabrum base (Figs 155, 286[c]), with a modified Pompeian candelabraform shaft wittily adapted to carry the modern medium of gas, a variant on the more sacrificial type of tripod seen in front of Drury Lane Theatre (Fig. 81). The model was to be used in various guises throughout the nineteenth and early twentieth centuries, and still survives in a hopelessly impoverished modern form.

Ultimately, the motifs that decorated the 'picaresque' house were taken from publications that illustrated the stateliest European and Asian monuments of the antique, exotic and modern world; domesticated, they showed clear traces of a lofty origin. As they did when added to the unadorned shell of the cottage orné, which in its most typical form was taken from the humblest type of native peasant dwelling, the cottage; ornamental accoutrements were added to this foundation, resulting in many cases in sophisticated whimsies far removed from the original. The 'picaresque' house and the cottage orné, starting from different points and originally distinct types, became almost indistinguishable towards the end of the period.

## The cottage orné

'Ah, zur!' said the old man . . . 'every now and then came a queer zort o' chap dropped out o' the sky like . . . and bought a bit o' ground vor a handvul o' peaper, and built a cottage horny, as they call it. . . nothing in the world to do, as we could zee, but to eat and drink, and make little bits o' shrubberies, o' quashies, and brutuses, and zelies, and cubies, and filigrees, and ruddydunderums, instead o' the oak plantations the old landlords use to plant; and the Squire could never abide the zight o' one o' they gimcrack boxes . . .'.

*Thomas Love Peacock*[7]

The term invented in the eighteenth century to describe the English 'decorated' cottage, 'cottage orné', is hybrid; 'cottage' was unknown as a French word in the eighteenth century (although since adopted as a masculine noun) and the term 'cottage orné' appears indiscriminately with masculine or feminine ending. The union may reflect mixed parentage.[8]

Painters had for long been interested in the cottage. Seventeenth and eighteenth-century painters, Dutch and Flemish, French and English, depicted cottages in rural scenes (Pl. X) of which the subjects ranged from the peasant carousals of Van Ostade to the artificial pastorals of Boucher and the low life sentimental dramas of Greuze. Thatched buildings appear in the Chinese and Japanese gardens depicted on lacquer that influenced the rococo landscape garden, and thatched buildings such as Kent's 'Merlin's Cottage' (or 'Cave') began to be seen in English gardens (Fig. 15): Adam drew thatched and tiled cottages beside classical fantasies, of which some were architectural miscegenations of the type that attracted Knight. And he designed cottages for English parks; one has a thatched, parachute-like roof.[9] Another, for the park at Kedleston, where he worked between 1760 and 1770, is an extraordinary confection, mainly northern European

**155** Roman bas-relief, detail as pictured by Pietro Santi Bartoli, 1693

in character but with a fugitive Italianate air that anticipates P. F. Robinson (Fig. 18; see p.65). Horace Walpole built a charming 'Rustic Cottage' at Strawberry Hill in 1765; it contained a tea room and library, and was both thatched and tiled, with a bay window. Dr. Johnson sat awesomely in a tiny thatched summer-house at Kenwood. The vogue reached English and French royalty; George III built a thatched cottage at Kew in 1772 for Queen Charlotte, and the buildings of the Hameau at Versailles served as backgrounds for theatrical *paysanneries*. Unlike most of the English buildings, the latter had no utilitarian function, and their studied artifice, not only thatched or reeded but decorated with *trompe l'oeil* cracks by the painters Tolède and Dardignac, is unparalleled in England.[10]

Towards the end of the century, Morland and Gainsborough became well known for bucolic subjects. The last struck a special chord; there are many contemporary references to his rustic fancy pictures; he gave 'distinct characteristics and original variety to his cottagery, and to the furniture and circumstances with which his best works are so eminently enriched. His woodmen, shepherds, dairy-maids, cottage-children, pigs, dogs, fallen timber, leafless stumps, thorns and bramble fences, and other incidents of rural oeconomy, have the full merit of originality'.[11] Gainsborough's cottages were realistic. The Picturesque theorists took up the cottage theme in a way that presented difficulties to the architects; Price liked Gainsborough's cottage paintings[12] (he went with Gainsborough on country excursions) and mentioned Greuze and the Dutch with approval. These all depicted hirsute and unkempt thatch, and although Price said that neatness and regularity on a small scale always pleased,[13] he took a view on cottages that was determinedly painterly and inconvenient. New and old thatch were both attractive; middle-period thatch looked damp and dirty: 'the best instructions may be gained from the works of the Dutch and Flemish masters . . .'.[14]

J. T. Smith, who declared himself in 1797 to be 'by no means cottage-mad' preferred 'the neglected fast-ruinating cottage . . . the weather-beaten thatch . . . the paper-pasted casement . . . the decayed bee-hive and the broken basket . . .'.[15] He disdained prudish neatness, abominating 'the regular, white-washed' (anathema to the Picturesque theorists: Uvedale Price deprecated the 'perpetual glare' of undiluted lime-wash; Wordsworth rather liked it) 'or new brick wall — the glaring red chimney pot — the even thatch'd roof — the equi-distant groups of sweet pea — and the jasmine prudishly trimm'd up into solid columns and cubes, stiff as a chimney, and hiding perhaps some picturesque feature. . . .'[16] Knight, who disliked 'dress cottages', would have agreed. Neatness was nevertheless to triumph; neglected thatch was consigned to the same limbo as Knight's thistles, and the ideal was recognised in Blaise Hamlet (Pl. XXIII), not Dame Battey's cottage (Fig. 156).

The vogue for the cottage orné in England was signalled by the publication in 1785 of a design manual by John Plaw: *Rural Architecture: consisting of designs, from the simple cottage, to the more decorated villa*. Most of the designs were classical and orthodox, but the author scored a number of significant 'firsts'. It was the first 'villa' book, the first British architectural book to include aquatints, and the first to place designs in a picturesque landscape.[17] The frontispiece depicts not architecture but landscape; the wide horizons of lake and mountains dominate the scene. On the extreme right stand two figures representing Taste and Rural Simplicity, the former clad in a Vandyck collar and 'rustic' dress, not unlike that in which the speculator's daughter, Miss Susannah Touchandgo, made 'dreadful havoc amongst the rustic mountaineers',[18] and the latter plainly attired; Taste is drawing the attention of Rural Simplicity to a small house on an island.

The partnership thus asserted was to prove influential, punctuated by attempts to keep it equal; Rural Simplicity had the worst of it, although she was occasionally given grim support by Utility, a parvenue deity in the eighteenth century. The cottage orné became during the Regency period a favourite toy of the middle and upper classes, garbed, like many favourite toys, in scraps of finery taken from more resplendent uses. Taken all in all, it is surprising that the result was so attractive; perhaps the substratum of humour that lay beneath both the creation and the appreciation of the cottage orné helped. It is difficult to be pompous about such a disarming activity; to be both pretty and funny cannot be altogether bad.

Henry Holland may have contributed to the cottage fancy, as several drawings in an album of C. H. Tatham's work testify. One drawing for cottages built for Southill in 1797 shows tall 'Elizabethan' chimneys, above deeply folded thatch, of the type favoured by Repton and Nash; another shows a quite large cottage with primitive rustic pillars.[19] But the great creative figure was Nash, perhaps with help from Repton. In the late 1790s a project had been mooted to create a picturesque hamlet on the Berwick estate at Attingham, as the existence

of panel paintings dated by Nash's Dover Street address indicates (Pl. L).[20] These paintings have been attributed to Nash, but they have mannerisms, from the character of the buildings (in some cases hardly Picturesque enough) to that of the foliage and the birds in the sky, that appear in watercolour paintings by Repton (seen also, it is true, in other paintings of the period). There was nothing to prevent Repton from using oil, and he was still working with Nash at the time. In 1803 he wrote that 'perhaps there is no form more picturesque for a cottage than buildings of that [Henry VIII] date . . . especially as their lofty perforated chimneys . . . contribute to the beauty of the outline'.[21]

The concept of the cottage orné was refined in 1798 in James Malton's *Essay on British Cottage Architecture*. Subtitled, 'an attempt to perpetuate on principle, that peculiar mode of building, which was originally the effect of chance', Malton repudiated Dr. Johnson's definition of a cottage as a 'mean habitation', redefining it in Picturesque terms as 'a small house in the country; of odd, irregular form, with various, harmonious colouring, the effect of weather, time, and accident; the whole environed with smiling verdure, having a contented, chearful, inviting aspect . . .'.[22] Contentment was to extend from the appearance of the cottage to the life lived in it; rural arcady was to banish care, an old dream.

**156** Cottage, 'On Merrow Common, Surrey. The residence of Dame Battey, aged 102', 1797

**157** Design for a cottage, by James Malton, 1798

Malton described the features that distinguished the cottage as 'A porch at entrance; irregular breaks in the direction of the walls; one part higher than another; various roofing of different materials, thatch particularly, boldly projecting; fronts partly built of walls or brick, partly weather boarded and partly brick-noggin dashed; casement window lights . . .'. However, it was necessary 'to unite rusticity with elegance'; the need for elegance led to such expedients as carving and painting heart of oak to look like 'oak stumps . . . with the bark on'. Rustic Simplicity suffered, despite Malton's expressed dislike of 'the affected cottage'.[23] His designs are interesting; not like the developed form of the British cottage orné, they have some resemblance both to certain features of the buildings of Marie-Antoinette's Hameau and, surprisingly, to certain late nineteenth and early twentieth-century 'cottages' (Fig. 157).

The books that fostered the fashion multiplied; each attempted to introduce variations. D. Laing, for example, produced designs, of which some are ugly, which used flint or pebbles as a band along the 'plinth' in something of the way that Soane used flint strips decoratively in country buildings. The plants that clothed cottages received attention, and Lugar in 1805 introduced botanical class-consciousness into the cottage scene: 'If creepers are set to embower the trellis work, plant the monthly rose, and clymatis or virgin bower . . . but no common creepers or honeysuckles should be seen near the Cottage Orné; their province is to shade and enrich the peasant's cot'.[24] Such attitudes, and the general emphasis on ornament, provoked a reaction; the more utilitarian publications tended to dismiss ornamented cottages. One such, by Richard Elsam on rural architecture (1803), was subtitled 'an attempt, also, to refute, by analogy, the principles of Mr James

Malton's essay on "British Cottage Architecture".'[25] Elsam supported regularity and symmetry, oddly enough admitting the opposite into London squares and buildings; he thought irregularity in cottages built for the rich suggested only 'poverty' and 'the grotesque'.[26] His pattern book of 1816, plainly entitled 'Hints for Improving the condition of the Peasantry in all parts of the United Kingdom' shows cottages that lack frills and furbelows (the text makes clear his emphasis on 'the sister country', Ireland). The movement towards ornament proved more popular. Rustic Simplicity had to stand by and watch the gentry bedecking the cottages of their tenantry, dashing the self-indulgent urge to ornament with a touch of philanthropy.

An enchantingly pretty hamlet, built between 1810 and 1811 at Blaise Hamlet near Bristol for John Harford, a Quaker banker, displayed the perfect compromise. God and Mammon, assisted by Nash, produced a place of pilgrimage for the devotees of the Picturesque; Blaise Hamlet (Pl. XXIII) was described in 1828 as the 'beau ideal' of a village: 'A beautiful green space in the midst of the wood is surrounded by a winding road; on it are built nine cottages, all of different form and materials: — stone, brick, wood, etc., and roofed with thatch, tiles, and slate; each . . . enwreathed with various sorts of clematis, rose, honeysuckle and vine. The dwellings, which are perfectly detached though they form a whole, have separate gardens, and a common fountain, which stands in the centre of the green, overshadowed by old trees. The gardens, divided by neat hedges, form a pretty garland of flowers and herbs around the whole village . . . the inhabitants are all poor families, whom the generous proprietor allows to live in the houses rent-free. No more delightful or well-chosen spot could be found as a refuge for misfortune: its perfect seclusion and snugness breathe only peace and forgetfulness of the world'.[27]

This idyllic hamlet, as much a triumph of the Picturesque as Windsor Castle and Westminster Palace, was nothing other than a collection of almshouses: Nash had suggested that they should be built individually rather than in the customary block. The form of the cottages is infinitely various, helped by the 'two-tiered effect' of the roofs and the appendages nestling up to the main block of the cottage and supporting it; the seductive thatch or tile on porches and bay windows adds to the sense of the cottages having grown, rather than having been made in a single operation. The tall 'Elizabethan' chimneys, one of the few consciously archaistic touches, were constructed of bricks especially moulded to patterns sent to Harford by John Adey Repton.[28] The cost of the hamlet exceeded the estimate, emerging at £3,800, despite the noticeable lack of the fashionable appurtenances of the cottage orné — French windows, verandahs, conservatories, etc.

Nash insisted on the utilitarian nature of the appendages, the pigeon-houses, privies, ovens, etc.; his attitude is revealed in a letter of

1804 (to a different client): '. . . I have the mortification daily to see these minutiae of cottages misunderstood and very much of their good effect depends on the right understanding of their details. They are meant to be essential parts of the construction and growing out of the necessity of the things themselves. When this principle is lost sight of they become pretensious and mere appliques, than which nothing is more disgusting'.[29] Did Nash direct Laugierian principles towards cottages; is this the apotheosis of the 'petite cabane rustique'? Taste and Rustic Simplicity here join hands in a perfect expression of idealised, yet real, rusticity. Dame Battey, aged 102 (Fig. 156), might easily have ended her days in one of these cottages, should she not already have died of draughts.

As Cockerell said: 'Nash has always original ideas . . . he built therefore irregular cottages with all those little penthouses for beehives, ovens, etc. and irregularities which he found in peasants' cottages and they are so beautiful that it is a sight visited from Clifton and I have always called it sweet'.[30] Sweet! Is this yet another category of the Picturesque? The word encompasses a great deal.

A cottage designed and built by Papworth for 'two ladies in the neighbourhood of the Lakes' (Pl. LII) is, albeit simple, indisputably of the 'ornamental' variety with its floor-length, diamond-paned windows, one of them a bay; its rustic, vaguely Tuscan colonnade; and its Gothic scalloped barge-boards. The peculiar outward-leaning fence was perhaps meant to repel animals (see pp.348–51 for the interior). A cottage designed by Malton has a primitive Tuscan order, with a pediment containing a Diocletian window, all very Italianate and rustic (see p.108) and applied to what can only be called a bungalow (Fig. 158). Described as 'perfectly novel, and I may say, singular in its construction', the building is a rustic classical cottage orné, lacking the usual trim; it has Laugierian and perhaps Soanean antecedents. A more usual type was offered by Busby in 1825 for Sidmouth, where cottages ornés appear to have flourished (Jane Austen had prepared the ground for a jibe in her, alas, unfinished novel *Sanditon*); Gothic with square-framed windows, or an alternative with canopies and diamond-paned windows; the whole was to face south. The plan shows a spine corridor between family and service areas.

One could inhabit a ruin; such was an 'ornamented Cottage with ruins' (Fig. 14), which represented the last stages of elegiac decline; this example of 1805, republished in 1815 and 1823, is a direct descendant of Sanderson Miller's sham castle at Edgehill of 1746–7. Or one could employ oriental detail, as in a thatched cottage designed by George Adey Repton in about 1800 for Liphook in Hampshire; the Indian-style domed porch is combined with windows that also attempt an orientalising manner, the whole done with that taste and restraint that characterised the work of the Reptons.[31]

Taste and restraint are not qualities which could be assigned to the cottage orné of two ladies slightly more whimsical than Papworth's ladies of the Lakes — the famous Ladies of Llangollen, Lady Eleanor Butler and Miss Ponsonby, who gave their cottage a terrifying antiquarian trim. The gothic canopies were decorated with an

**158** Design for a cottage, by James Malton, 1798

159 Cottage of the Ladies of Llangollen, Plas Newydd

160 Binswood Cottage, Leamington Spa, 1824, designed by P. F. Robinson

outlandish jumble of turned, faceted, and carved woodwork, much of it apparently Elizabethan and Jacobean (Fig. 159); strange faces grimace beneath the canopies, freakish animals cavort on the railings, the whole being illuminated at night by the classical lamp that hung in the central porch. One sees what Loudon might have meant when he wrote in 1833 that 'Whoever wishes to furnish and fit up a house in such a manner as to produce a new and strange effect . . . cannot attain his end at less expense than by having recourse to Elizabethan fragments'.[32] The woodwork was supplemented by stained glass retrieved by the ladies' own labour from the ruins of nearby Vale Crucis Abbey. Cost was ever a consideration with the Ladies of Llangollen.

P. F. Robinson, who in his work at Brighton Pavilion and elsewhere may have played a larger part in the development of the 'picaresque' house and the cottage orné than he has been credited with, built in 1824 at Leamington a large thatched cottage orné in Tudor style for Edward Willes (Figs 40, 160; see p.84). Robinson advocated 'Old English' styles for practical reasons and despite its thatched bay windows, Gothic barge-board and finials, Binswood Cottage, as it was called, was robust enough to survive until today, albeit robbed of embellishments. The diamond-paned windows, mullioned windows, and decorated roof ridge added to its attractions. A cottage by George Stanley Repton, designed for Sarsgrove in Oxfordshire in 1829 and 'excessively' — a favourite Regency adjective — pretty, manages to combine Grecian columned bow windows with barge-boards and Tudor chimneys (Fig. 161).

Yet another type was the Swiss Cottage (Fig. 162), born of Alpine romanticism; supposed to be built entirely, or almost entirely, of wood, it proliferated, especially in gardens. Loudon said that its woodwork should imitate larch or silver fir, and that it need not have large stones on the roof, since the English climate did not require them.[33]

Treatments for the exterior surfaces of the cottage orné were debated. One possibility was a single coat of stucco 'laid on with an uneven surface, to give it the appearance of undressed stone'; another was to have the cottage 'plastered and stuck with small pebbles, as large as hazel nuts, which presented a very agreeable appearance' — in other words, a Regency form of pebbledash.[34] Stone lime was used, coloured with lamp or ivory black and yellow ochre; Edmund Bartell advised that 'every material of a strong harsh colour should be rejected. The fierce red of some kinds of bricks, and the perfect white of a wash of lime are equally disgusting.'[35] There was a general prejudice in the period against both red brick as well as white paint. Loudon gives recipes for adding bullock's blood, with or without ochre, to lime, an ancient way of colouring; also a receipt for a mixture of lime, charcoal, yellow ochre, and copperas, as used generally on London stucco to imitate stone.[36] He also gives a method of 'splashing', the object of which was 'either to imitate the lichens and weather stains of an old wall, or some

particular kind of stone'.[37] His other, general injunctions included making decorative patterns on plastered cottage walls with wickerwork, or impressing them with 'hieroglyphics, with sculptures of various kinds . . . with memorable or instructive sayings, or chronological facts';[38] a 'marine character may be given by shells; a rustic one by bark of trees; and a grotesque one by roots of trees; that of a Dutch cottage by glazed tiles'.[39]

The cottage orné could become quite grand. Endsleigh in Devon (see p.46) was a large house, or rather two houses connected by a cloister, built by Wyatville in 1810. The architect's work in the earlier part of the decade on Longleat and Wollaton may explain why Endsleigh, despite the low eaves, barge-boards, verandahs (cobbled in pattern with knuckle bones and pebbles — another old peasant method) and rustic columns, gives the impression of being a small castellated manor rather than a cottage orné (contemporaries regarded it as a cottage orné). Part of this effect may come from the local granite used to build it; hardly the stone best chosen to convey the emollient rusticities of the ornamented cottage. Nor does the cost — £70,000 to £80,000[40] — sound rustic, especially compared to the £3,800 of Blaise Hamlet. At Endsleigh picturesque rurality was pursued in a way reminiscent of Marie-Antoinette's Hameau; it had an elaborate dairy (which, like the Hameau, had its own ware; not Sèvres, but Wedgwood creamware painted with grapevines — for milk! — and 'Endsleigh Dairy'),[41] a Swiss cottage, grotto, etc., and, in accordance with Repton's advice that 'the view from the house would be enlivened by the smoke of a cottage on the opposite side of the water', a fire was lit in that cottage every morning, a custom that endured until 1940.[42]

Another grand cottage was Knowle Cottage at Sidmouth, which was opened to the public every Monday during 'the season' (Pl. LIII). As the 1837 Guide to the 'Illustrations and Views of Knowle Cottage, Sidmouth, the elegant Marine Villa Orné of Thomas L. Fish Esq.' said, a stranger who did not know that the 'magnificent proprietor of Knowle Cottage was accustomed to exhibit his splendid, unique, and beautiful cottage, to myriads of persons . . . would be absolutely astonished at the constant and rapid influx of persons in every kind of vehicle, who are straining forward with an ardour no obstacle can impede, and no impediments overcome'. There was 'the struggle for admission — the crash of bonnets, and the destruction of millinery'.[43] It was no bijou residence that people fought to see. The verandah alone was 315 feet long and twelve feet wide, supported 'at equal distances, by immense oak pollards'; the 'gothic' arches appear to be virtually triangular, a form of primitivism. The verandah contained flower stands bearing 3,500 plants and thirty-four 'splendid china vases'; it had a rustic seat in the centre with versions of Canova's *Homer* and *Hebe*. From it one could see the 'Gardenesque' disposition of the garden, decorated with 'rich Conch and other valuable large shells', greenhouse

**161** Design for a cottage orné, Sarsgrove, Oxon.,
by George Stanley Repton

and hot-house plants, and globes containing gold and silver fish. Beyond lay the outer park, with kangaroo, Cape sheep, buffalo, llamas, gazelles, pelicans and emu (see p.351 for the interior).

King George IV had his menagerie, with his favourite animal, the giraffe; he had also his Cottage: Royal Lodge, Windsor. He had been often entertained at Craven Cottage, Fulham, the extravagantly bizarre cottage orné of his crony Walsh Porter (see pp.270–1, 326, 345–6), which may have influenced him in building his own cottage orné. Accident may have played a part; he decided to have a 'cottage' at Windsor repaired as a temporary *pied à terre*, and in 1812 Nash replaced the tiled roof with thatch; the career of Royal Lodge had begun.[44] In 1816 Wyatville took over, continuing until 1830. The building grew hugely, fully justifying the assertions of the 'irregular' Picturesque school that it would be easy to add to a building erected according to their principles; it became 'a kind of cottage ornée, too large perhaps for the stile but yet so managed that in the walks you only see parts of it at once and these well composed and grouping with the immense trees'.[45] Its style was a palatial version of Nash's double-layered Blaise Hamlet idiom, with thatch over the ground floor windows and over an extensive verandah, and innumerable tall Tudor chimneys that betrayed the size of the building; one view of the entrance shows seven windows and twenty-seven chimneys. In one view (Fig. 163) it appears very small, with an embowered Gothic loggia and a Gothic balustrade above a ground-floor 'conservatory'. The windows had small panes, and there was an enormous glass conservatory, quite outvying Mr. Fish's.

It was infinitely luxurious and damp; in it George IV spent many sybaritic hours with his cherry-brandy and elderly houris, and it pleased

even the captious Princess Lieven: 'a dwelling place at once royal and rustic, on the outside the simplicity of a cottage, within the rarest reunion of comfort, elegance, and unspoiled magnificence, which left behind a sentiment of une charmante béatitude'.[46] The building, like most of George IV's enterprises, attracted its share of ridicule: 'a sort of thatched Henry the Seventh's chapel'.[47]

Royal Lodge was rivalled by Cowdray Lodge in Sussex, built about 1800 for W. S. Poyntz by C. H. Tatham (Pl. LI);[48] and exhibited at the Royal Academy in 1801. It was a fully blown cottage orné, and if built entire at that early date was a precocious example. If it were entirely the brain-child of the stern Tatham, nothing would more plainly declare the catholicity of Regency taste; Tatham's talents were not exactly the kind that one would expect to see blossom in such frivolities. One wonders whether Holland played any part in its genesis; the Holland cottages in the Tatham album have been mentioned above (p.213), and the 1801 form of the Marine Pavilion at Brighton (Fig. 147) has affinities with the most elaborate form of cottage orné. Cowdray is not far from Brighton.

As time passed, the distinction between the cottage orné and the 'picaresque' villa became blurred, due perhaps to the over-large size of the more opulent examples of the former. Moreover, a cottage orné situated in town or suburb was regarded by many as a solecism. Elmes described in 1829 a house called 'Albany Cottage', belonging to a Mr. Thomas Raikes, declaring that 'as a specimen of the English cottage ornée, it is scarcely to be surpassed'. To us, there is little to distinguish Albany Cottage from any other 'picaresque' villa, and Elmes' description of his ideal cottage shows how far bucolics had receded; it is hard not to suspect parody, although none seems to have been intended. Of the garden, for example, he wrote: 'in front of this verandah, the windows under which, should all open as French sashes down to the floor . . . should be a wide gravel walk, as yellow and as smooth as a Limerick glove; then a lawn, as level and as shorn as the cloth of a billiard table; interspersed with a few irregularly shaped patches, like a slashed doublet, filled with nature's embroidery, half hardy annuals, geraniums sunk in pots . . . the . . . Dahlia.' Gloves, billiard tables, doublets? After this, one is not surprised that the thatch should not be 'that rough sort of thatch like an Irishman's wig', but 'combed wheat straw, laid thick and smooth, and trimmed at the eaves, with compact ornamented ridges and verges'.[49] The Picturesque had been suburbanised.

Loudon reveals the degeneration of the cottage ideal in all its squalor. He takes, for instance, a small single-storey cottage, which he says quite truly is unfitted to the English climate — its origin obviously lies in Italian vernacular building — and subjects it to 'alterations and improvements' designed to introduce more light and space. He dresses it in turn in 'castellated Gothic, monastic Gothic, Indian Gothic, Italian

162 'Swiss Cottage, Cassiobury', Herts., 1837

163 The Royal Cottage, Windsor, designed by
John Nash and Sir Jeffry Wyatville, 1812–30

97

**164** 'An improved design of a single storey dwelling', by J. C. Loudon, 1833

style [Pl. LI], or Elizabethan style'.[50] The results have absurdity without charm. One feels the nonsense of Mr. Jorrock's visit to 'Rosalinda Castle', a castellated cottage orné, not far away: a fiery-red brick castellated cottage . . . combining almost every absurdity a cockney imagination can be capable of. Nosey, who was his own 'Nash,' set out with the intention of making it a castle and nothing but a castle, and accordingly the windows were made in the loophole fashion, and the door occupied a third of the whole frontage . . . the light was almost excluded from the rooms, [but] 'rude Boreas' had the complete run of the castle whenever the door was opened. To remedy this . . . the Gothic oak-painted windows and door flew from their positions to make way for modern plate-glass in rich pea-green casements, and a door of similar hue. The battlements, however, remained, and two wooden guns guarded a brace of chimney-pots and commanded the wings of the castle, one whereof was formed into a green-, the other into a gig-house. The peals of a bright brass-handled bell at a garden-gate, surmounted by a holly-bush with the top cut into the shape of a fox, announced their arrival to the inhabitants of 'Rosalinda Castle,' and on entering, they discovered young Nosey in the act of bobbing for gold-fish, in a pond about the size of a soup-basin; while Nosey senior . . . was reposing, 'sub tegmine fagi,' in a sort of tea-garden arbour, overlooking a dung-heap. . . . At one end of the garden was a sort of temple, composed of oyster-shells, containing a couple of carrier-pigeons, with which Nosey had intended making his fortune, by the early information to be acquired by them; but 'there is many a slip', etc., as Jorrocks would say.

This has everything; a cottage at Streatham[51] with battlements and plate glass, a conservatory, topiary and a shell temple for pigeons, all reeking of fashion having sunk to a lower social stratum. Even the cottage orné, with its continuing vitality, would find it hard to survive Nosey and his dung-heap.

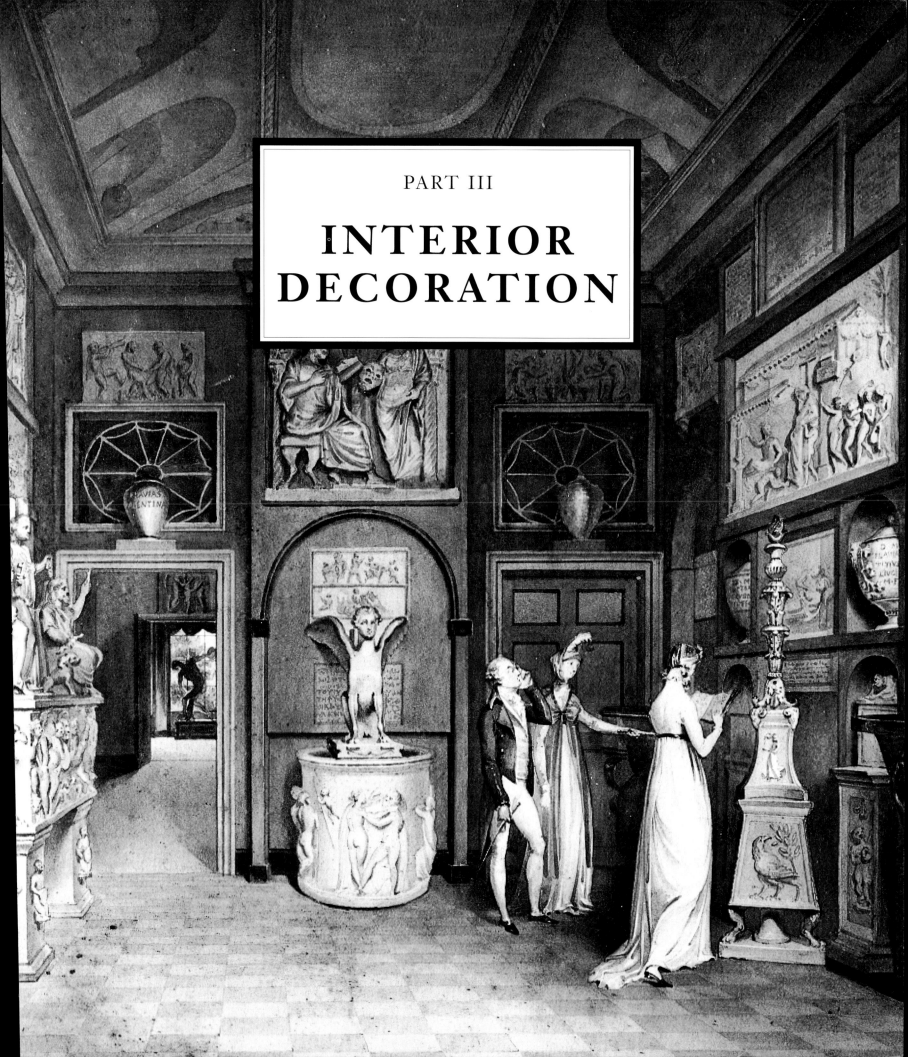

# PART III

# INTERIOR DECORATION

Chapter one

# Formative Influences

## Conflicting modes: picturesque disorder versus the domestic museum

Two observations made by Repton recorded changes in social habits that had a pronounced effect on interior decoration. In 1803 he recollected that in the past 'the best room in the house was opened only a few days in each year, where the guests sat in a formal circle . . .'; his illustration shows chairs arranged almost as rigidly as if seated in order of precedence around a non-existent dining table (Fig. 165). He went on to say that this formality had become unfashionable, for guests now gathered in casually scattered groups[1] (this for many years had been the practice in the fashionable French salons, often as crammed to the doors as a modern cocktail party). In 1816 Repton noted that the most

recent modern custom was to use the library, which now often opened directly into the drawing room, as a 'general living-room', the two rooms being united by having the same carpet and curtains; 'and the comfort of that which has books, or musical instruments, is extended in its space to that which has only sofa, chairs and card-tables'.[2] His two illustrations, which compared the stately aridity of the ancient cedar parlour with the luxurious informality of the modern living room (Figs 165, 166), say all. Not only had the habits of the denizens of the rooms changed; the rooms themselves had altered out of all recognition.

When formal was replaced by informal intercourse the social setting changed in sympathy. Separate spaces were integrated, and the informal grouping of people was accompanied by the informal redisposition of furniture. One result was that the 'architectural' as

**165** 'The old Cedar Parlour', by Humphry Repton, 1816

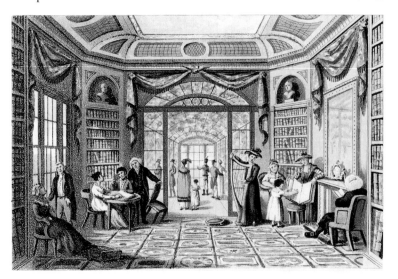

**166** 'The Modern Living-Room', by Humphry Repton, 1816

opposed to the 'decorated' interior went partially out of fashion; partially, because manners had become only partially informal. Etiquette still had a place, but wealth had become as important as rank and was no longer to be snubbed by polite usage. Wealth had, moreover, to be displayed; garish ostentation became the order of the day. The lordly formality and restrained richness of decoration that had once characterised high society lingered only in elderly or conservative circles; the revived rococo style was adopted by dukes and gaming houses alike.

These changes existed side by side with another and opposite phenomenon — the impulse to turn a house into a museum (Fig. 169, Pl. LVII). It was the great age of private classical museums, and they were created and embellished in every place that had pretensions to culture; the lead was given by Rome itself, where the popes vied with each other in housing their antiquities in the most sumptuous surroundings. Others, kings such as Gustavus III of Sweden, and private people such as Goethe in Weimar and Soane and Hope in London, followed suit. Fashion played its part, but the initial motive was veneration for classical antiquity. The intensifying exactitude with which ancient modes of decoration were reproduced created settings perfectly suited to the exhibition of classical antiquities; furniture took on antique forms, sometimes reproduced with startling and un-congenial accuracy. These interiors were filled not only with genuine antiques but, more frequently, with copies and adaptations mixed. Copies were thought perfectly adequate to communicate the associa-tions of the original, and domestic interiors everywhere contained versions in plaster, bronze and ceramic of famous classical sculpture and Greek vases; by the end of the period, the diffusion of the taste down the social scale had introduced Apollos and Venuses into the humblest home (Fig. 267). 'Archaeological' interiors, extremely beautiful though they often were, were not liked by everybody, and the irreverent or the sybaritic, such as Sydney Smith or Lady Holland, criticised them for their self-conscious archaisms and lack of comfort.

## The Theatre

It might seem at first sight that a society deeply moved by the abiding idealisms of archaeology and museology was hardly likely to be influenced by the transient illusionism of the theatre, in which the element of play came into the open. However the theatre, and organised spectacles and fêtes, were highly popular and aesthetically persuasive; private theatricals were also fashionable, sometimes becoming very elaborate; such illusionists as Nash and the painter Lawrence were devotees. The theatre both reflected and initiated fashion; it had the advantage of being ephemeral and cheap, and could play the same enterprising role in introducing styles in interior decoration as did garden buildings in architecture. It attracted outstanding talent, both in design and acting. Fancies could be indulged, exotic and singular schemes could be created without fear of ridicule or waste, archaisms could be recreated within the sanctuary of historical drama (Figs 167–8).

One of the most talented of the formative spirits was Loutherbourg — yet again, a painter shaped the future. In 1779 his pantomime *The Wonders of Derbyshire* helped to popularise the Picturesque; in 1781 he was recruited by the young William Beckford to organise a mysterious Christmas performance at Fonthill in which the performers played in masquerade for three days and nights; the house was transformed into a 'negromantic' environment that bore many allusions to Egypt and the Orient.[3] Loutherbourg's *Omai: or, a Trip around the World*, first played in 1785, was based on Cook's voyages, with scenery influenced by the pictorial records of John Webber and William Hodges; it became one of the longest running productions of the English eighteenth-century stage.[4] The East was often called upon by the theatre; oriental and exotic delights had been aired in *Sethona* in 1774, which had an Egyptian setting, and in 1782 the scene-painter John Inigo Richards used the Asiatic drawings of Tilly Kettle for *The Choice of Harlequin or the Indian Chief*; for *Ramah Droog* he used the Indian drawings of the Daniells. The common Regency practise of employing scene painters to decorate the floors of rooms with designs in chalk for gala occasions brought them frequently into houses, where their ideas and activities might be extended; Walsh Porter, the Prince Regent's friend and a leader of taste, was in a good position to use theatrical decorating talents (see pp.345–6).

When Drury Lane theatre was rebuilt in 1791–4 by Henry Holland, the manager Kemble appointed William Capon, who shared his passion for mediaevalism and who had the zeal of an antiquary, to design the scenery.[5] Every effort was made to ensure authenticity: for instance, the Gothic Library in *The Iron Chest* was given vaulting copied from St. Stephen's, Westminster; in 1809 Kemble moved to Covent Garden, and there Capon painted six wings of old English streets with startling exactitude; 'Gothic' interiors were given the same care (Fig. 168). Costume was designed with a concern for authenticity. From 1809, the scene painters Grieve, Phillips, Whitmore and Lupino added their talents; Samuel Rush Meyrick (see pp.173, 330) advised the manager Planché on historical accuracy in the 1820s. It was in the theatre that the nationalism that accompanied the revival of Gothic was most clearly seen; the pageant of George IV's coronation, in the Tudor dress that owed much to the stage, was celebrated by the pageant of the coronation of Henry V (from *Henry IV*, part 2) in the theatre. Authenticity reached the point where in 1827 a critic said of a production of *Cymbeline* that 'We expect next to see legitimate authority produced for the dressing of Puck, and authenticated wings

**167** Gothic hall, theatre design by Inigo Richards

allotted to Mustardseed'. Did the younger Pugin imbibe Gothic authenticity from Covent Garden, where he worked as a theatrical designer from 1829–32?

Theatrical experiences deeply influenced the way people thought, as is evident from their appearance in unexpected contexts. James Christie, for instance, published in 1825 a theory that the paintings upon Greek vases were copied from transparencies used as scenery in the Eleusinian Mysteries, which must have looked like 'the Eidouranian of our scientific countryman, Mr. Walker' or the transparencies of Java.[6] At another extreme, when the whimsical Charles Lamb portrayed George IV, feasting in the oriental delights of the Pavilion, as teasing his guests by simulating circumstances of horror and affright analogous to those in which the guilty Belshazzar started from the writing on the walls, he described the catastrophe as a pantomimic transformation scene organised by an employee of Covent Garden (did this actually happen?). In so doing Lamb drew on an imagery common to all his readers, an imagery reinforced by memories of John Martin's paintings which were themselves influenced by theatre, and in their turn influenced architecture:

> The guests were select and admiring: the banquet profuse and admirable; the lights lustrous and oriental; the eye was perfectly dazzled with the display of plate, among which the great gold salt-cellar, brought from the regalia in the Tower for this especial purpose, itself a tower! stood conspicuous for its magnitude. And now the Rev. XXXX the then admired Court Chaplain, was

**168** 'A New Way to Pay Old Debts', by George Clint

**LIV** *The Artist and His Family*, 1813, by Adam Buck

LV  The Deepdene, Surrey, the Small Drawing Room

*Opposite* LVI  Carlton House, the Saloon, c.1818

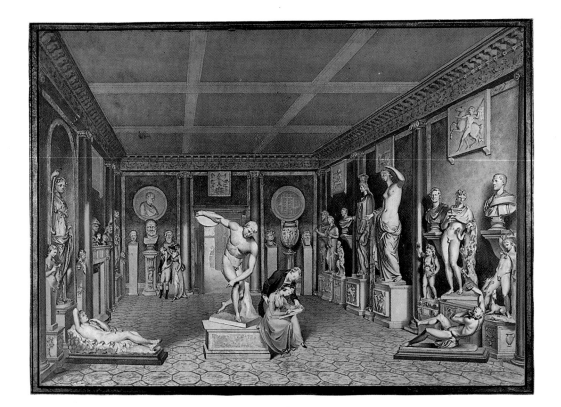

LVII Charles Towneley's collection at Park Street, Westminster, by Maria Cosway, c.1800

169 Entrance hall of Charles Towneley's house, Park Street, Westminster, c.1800

proceeding with the grace, when at a signal given, the lights were suddenly overcast, and a huge transparency was discovered, in which glittered in gold letters —
'BRIGHTON — EARTHQUAKE — SWALLOW-UP- ALIVE!'
Imagine the confusion of the guests; the Georges and garters, jewels, bracelets, moulted upon the occasion! The fans dropped, and picked up next day by the sly court pages! Mrs Fitz-what's-her-name fainting, and the Countess of XXX holding the smelling bottle, till the good-humoured Prince caused harmony to be restored by calling in fresh candles, and declaring that the whole was nothing but a pantomine hoax, got up by the ingenious Mr. Farley, of Covent Garden, from hints which his Royal Highness himself had furnished.[7]

It hardly needed the transparency; the Banqueting Room at Brighton (Pl. CII), one of the two most extravagantly inventive examples of Regency decoration in existence, was in itself a transformation scene, with Nash as stage manager and the Prince Regent as producer.

## The 'decorated' and the 'architectural' interior

Those who discussed decoration during the Regency period often distinguished between the architectural and the non-architectural interior. The emphasis varied according to the speaker, but 'architectural' generally denoted an interior that displayed moulded ceilings and entablatures with or without the orders; 'non-architectural' (or 'decorated', a term that also occurs) meant an interior decorated principally by flat painting, wallpapers, or fabrics, sometimes accompanied by restrained architectural detail such as pilasters and mouldings.

The client would make a choice depending on predilection and use; if a 'decorated' rather than an 'architectural' interior were preferred it was usual to employ an 'upholsterer' rather than an architect, if only because the reluctance of the architect was a constraint. There was an element of aesthetic snobbery in this, and indeed one can understand the architects' reluctance to become identified with some clients' decorative fancies. The King himself was not exempted from this disdain; Wyatville, encouraged by George IV and William IV to produce a book of engravings of Windsor Castle, wished it to be confined to pictures of the exterior, since he 'considered internal decorations as something of a comparatively temporary nature . . . he felt no inclination to perpetuate by the graver some works which he knew to be the result of circumstances, the introduction for instance of old French boiserie of the age of Louis xv, which would never have appeared in the Castle had the architect been guided solely by his own judgment'.[8] Wyatville was right in thinking that 'something of a comparatively temporary nature' attached to the internal decorations at

Windsor; were George IV in questionable shape ever with martial stalk to walk the Terrace at midnight, he would no doubt be bewailing subsequent mutilations of his resplendent and considered interiors.

It was a constant lament that later Regency architects, unlike Adam, Chambers, and Holland, were not sufficiently interested in interiors. Critics thought that taste would greatly improve were architects to cease regarding interior decoration as beneath them, were they not to leave decoration entirely in the hands of such powerful upholsterers as the Craces, Morel and Seddon, Bullock, etc.; even scene painters were employed as decorators directly by the client. Architects never entirely withdrew from interior decoration, but their intervention became rare enough to be counted exceptional; towards the end of the period, it was remarked that they had begun again to design interiors. In 1828, in 'several houses recently built, both in town and country, the taste of the architect has been called in, to give designs for arrangement of curtains, for grates, pier tables, chairs and sophas. In every instance, we have remarked the superior chasteness of the designs, and the harmony of the whole with the architectural style of the rooms . . .'.[9]

Strong opinions were voiced on the merits and disadvantages of the 'architectural' versus the 'decorated' interior. Those who disliked the former were able to call upon the long-held prejudice against the use of exterior 'temple' architecture inside a building. This argument was reiterated in 1825 by the architect John Goldicutt in a publication that advocated the use of (mostly painted) Pompeian decoration; the book was 'made to assist the Artist in the interior decoration of houses, as well in what regards figure as colour. It was formerly a general notion, that the same species of Architecture which was used on the outside of houses was as applicable to the inside of them, and hence the same heavy forms, the massy column, and cumbrous architrave and pediment, etc. were adopted in rooms as in porticos. . . . The discovery of an ancient Town . . . shows that the Ancients had not committed the same blunder . . . and opened to us the view of a more festive and imaginative species of decoration'.[10] Another Pompeian enthusiast, Sir William Gell, reproached Vitruvius for his diatribe against 'Pompeian' caprice; he had 'inveighed in vain against thus adorning the walls of houses . . . he liked not the substitution of the slender reed, or candelabraform pillar, in the place of the more regular but massive column; . . . and . . . could not approve of that mixture of foliage and volutes with semi-animals, the remains of which are amongst the most admired fragments of architectural antiquity'.[11] The comments of Vitruvius on this kind of decoration were famous;[12] his strictures were extended in modern times to the combination of intricate light stucco ornament and painted decoration used by Adam, a mode held in contempt by Chambers and by most of those Regency aesthetes who preferred 'architectural' interiors.

One view advanced, not unexpectedly in an age that flaunted the costliness of display, was that all painted architecture 'evinces far more of ambitious economy than real beauty'.[13] This comment occurs in an account of Soane's house, but Soane may not have shared this view; he employed painters himself, and mentioned Thornhill, Verrio, and even Kent with approval.[14] However, he upbraided the 'decorated' taste of his day, commending as alternative models a baroque and a neo-classical decorator, both Italian; 'we have a present fashion of crowding on to flat monotonous ceilings . . . plaster ornaments and small compartments, spotted occasionally with an unimportant picture. . . . Our walls are now covered with fine papers, with a portrait or a bust interspersed, according to the whim of the fashionable decorator of the day. Instead of all these colifichets, we should have had Decorations that would have done honour to an Algardi, or an Albertolli. We ought to see the walls of the principal rooms of the Mansions of our Nobility dressed with rich hangings, and enriched with all the charms of Historical Painting, and with all the powers of the Sculptor's breathing marble masterpieces . . .'.[15] Soane's preferred decorations were of an august quality; Algardi's stucco decorations at the Palazzo Pamphili in Rome, greatly admired by connoisseurs, had to an extent anticipated in the seventeenth century the archaeological arabesque of the later eighteenth century; Albertolli's rich contemporary neo-classicism had been made available to all in publications of the 1780s (see p.235).

Soane, who thought so much in 'architectural' terms that he converted the wayward flat-painted architectural fantasies of Pompeian decoration into three dimensions (see p.243 et seq.), none the less wished to add to the components of 'architectural' decoration the less architectonic resources of interior decoration, including paintings and sculpture. The distinctions he drew were fine; he declared, in an obvious reference to Hope's Picture Gallery at Duchess Street (see p.286), that 'although the Greek Doric column, with its massive entablature . . . is occasionally seen in the dwelling rooms and galleries

of men, in many respects distinguished for classical knowledge and correctness of taste, yet such practise is contrary to every rational principle of internal decoration, and also to the Text of Vitruvius, who expressly directs . . . columns in such situations to have been of a light gay character'.[16]

Soane and others may have been influenced by Laugier, who thought the use of the orders in rooms inappropriate because 'de sa nature elle doive être une des parties principales qui constituent le bâtiment'; they must never be used 'pour la décoration seule'. They also make decoration 'lourd et massif'; columns restrict space and 'augmentent la profondeur des embrasures'. Laugier's declaration that these disadvantages were removed if the columns were painted on to the walls encouraged painted decoration and illusionism. He prohibited the intermixture of columns with 'tapisserie', and preferred bed alcoves hung with fabric to those embellished with columns and balustrades; the best method was 'former cette alcove en manière de pavillon avec des rideaux retroussés et soutenus par des cordons' — in other words, a tented alcove. It is intriguing to hear the stern dogmatist advocate the voluptuous tent; oddly but consistently, Laugier's theories favoured the 'decorated' approach within doors.[17] His opinions can never be ignored in this period.

Bearing in mind this broad distinction between the decorated and architectural treatment of interiors, what options were available? The first was, naturally, the antique: 'There is but one way for the moderns to become great, and perhaps unequalled: I mean, by imitating the ancients', said Winckelmann,[18] a statement the application of which was broadened by his contemporaries. To imitate the ancients was not so simple; the choice was multifarious. It was agreed that a knowledge of archaeology was essential; the better the understanding of antique forms the greater the likelihood of both their correct use and their modification, where modification was necessary or desirable, with propriety.

## Chapter two

# The Decorated Interior: Classical Styles

For those who wished to avoid using the orders and entablatures in internal decoration, or who preferred painted decoration for other reasons, three principal decorative modes that had antique sanction offered themselves: the arabesque or grotesque; the 'Etruscan'; and the 'Pompeian'. They could be used undiluted; they could be combined in a composite form; they could be mingled with three-dimensional architectural components, or with decorative stucco; they could, if so desired, be rendered entirely in flat painting. They were a perfectly respectable antique alternative to 'temple' architecture.

## Varieties of 'arabesque'/'grotesque'

From the Renaissance to the beginning of the twentieth century, arabesque in its various forms was, together with the Orders and their components, the most important single ingredient of high-style interior decoration. It could be executed in divers media, including stone, stucco, paint, mosaic and wooden and metal veneers: it was not lightly to be undertaken, being laborious in production, exacting in invention, time-consuming and expensive; it is usually seen only in work of metropolitan standard, and is uncommon in provincial societies such as that of eighteenth-century America. Its quality depended upon the craftsman, who was often the designer also, especially where painted arabesque was concerned. It was dignified by an ineffaceable association with antiquity and with Raphael.

A word should be said about the term 'arabesque' itself. It originally denoted, as it implies, a style of ornament that orginated in the Near East — 'moresque' was an alternative word. This was an intricate foliate decoration used notably on 'damascened' engraved metalwork; the main vehicle for its entry into Europe was Venice. The patterns of arabesque or moresque were of a type easily integrated into the

fashionable Renaissance ornament that was derived from the delicate interior decorations in paint and stucco of ancient Rome (Figs 173, 234); these latter decorations were often called 'grotesque', a word that originally referred to their subterranean 'grotto' sites, buried beneath the accumulated debris of centuries, but they came, confusingly, to be called 'arabesque' also, and this is the sense in which the word was used in the eighteenth century. The word 'grotesque' became eventually more specifically applied to the fanciful and exaggerated nature of some of the ornaments employed in arabesque, an extended meaning still in current use.

Robert Adam described the confusion that had arisen in a condescending footnote to his *Works in Architecture* of 1778: 'By grotesque is meant that beautiful light stile of ornament used by the ancient Romans found in "grotte", which was imitated in the Renaissance in the loggias of the Vatican, and in the villas Madama, Pamphili, and Caprarola'. However, 'the French, who till of late never adopted the ornaments of the ancients . . . have branded those ornaments with the vague and fantastical appellation of arabesque, a stile which, though entirely distinct from the grotesque, has, notwithstanding, been most universally confounded with it by the ignorant'.[1] Unfortunately, we have to condone that ignorance by using the term 'arabesque' as Adam's contemporaries used it, bearing in mind that they occasionally observed the distinction noted by him.

Not all ancient arabesque was subterranean; the Arch of the Goldsmiths at Rome, for instance, a building illustrated by Desgodetz in 1682,[2] had pilasters that were decorated with carved arabesques contained within a frame contiguous with the edge of the pilaster, in exactly the same manner as pilasters designed by such architects as Athenian Stuart, Chambers, and Adam, amongst many others. However, by far the richest source of ancient arabesque or grotesque decoration known in the early Renaissance was the excavated 'Domus Aurea' of Nero,[3] supplemented by and sometimes confused with the Baths of Titus, erected at a later period on part of the same ground. Despite the discovery of new and exciting examples of antique decoration, the site as a whole retained its primacy. As late as 1789, after all the new discoveries, Nicholas Ponce wrote that 'De tous ces monuments, les Thermes de Titus sont . . . celui qui peut offrir le plus de ressources aux artistes; ses peintures, très-supérieures à celles d'Herculanum, offrent, surtout dans le genre arabesque, les dessins les plus précieux'.[4] Besides arabesque and other motifs, the 'Domus Aurea' supplied little landscapes and *natures mortes* and influential examples of the system of confining the arabesque within a pilaster.

**170** Arabesques by Raphael, published in 1772

**171** 'Pilasters for Commodes', by Thomas Sheraton, 1793

Normally the term 'arabesque' was used in the late eighteenth and early nineteenth centuries to include both the ancient Roman style and its modern variants. Modern arabesque as used by the designers of the Regency came in at least five guises.

The most famous was that of Raphael (Fig. 170); he had been preceded in adapting ancient arabesque by Pinturicchio, Crivelli and many others, and when towards the end of the Regency period people began to show a serious interest in the early Renaissance they looked at pre-Raphaelite arabesque — even in the 1790s, C. H. Tatham was intrigued by the fifteenth-century sculpted arabesque of the Lombardis, which has a pure and simple quality.[5] Raphael's arabesque never lost its renown, even at the height of the neo-classical period.

Another variant of arabesque, used extensively during the classical revival of Louis XIV, was that associated with the designer and engraver Bérain. Perhaps partly because it was used so often with boulle inlay, a technique of inlaid metal that has something in common with damascening, Bérainesque arabesque has a tincture of the character of the original Near Eastern 'arabesque' or 'moresque'; it also resembles a certain type of light and intricate Italian mannerist arabesque, with which it may share Eastern antecedents. Be that as it may, Bérainesque arabesque is lighter and more intricate than antique arabesque. It added to the Renaissance repertoire the characters of the Commedia dell'Arte, chinoiseries, Turqueries, singeries, and opulent Dutch flowers; the rococo period supplied shot taffeta effects, derived from Watteau (and ultimately from Rubens and the Venetians), garlands and exotic birds. Bérainesque arabesque was to be revived in the middle of the Regency period, and became popular with the amateur of 'pen-work'.

The English architects who immediately preceded the Regency period evolved their own versions of arabesque; much of this was 'architectural' in character, executed in stucco rather than paint. The most remarkable was that of Robert Adam, who drew on both Raphaelesque and antique arabesque, adapting them to his own idiom; Stuart and Chambers employed arabesque on pilasters in place of fluting, a motif employed in grand interiors during the Regency period.

French and Italian neo-classicism stiffened modern arabesque and gave prominence to antique motifs such as sphinxes, griffins, peacocks, swans, and little neo-classical temples; these motifs occur in the long-known arabesques discovered in Rome, but their use must have been encouraged by their frequent appearance in the decorations of Herculaneum and Pompeii. This arabesque was employed by the French and English artists associated with George Sheringham and Henry Holland, such as Lignereux and Trécourt, and by furniture designers such as Sheraton (Fig. 172) and Hepplewhite.

As if these varieties were not enough, yet another and quite distinct form of arabesque appeared in the late eighteenth century; this, often found associated with 'Etruscan' decoration (see p.236 et seq.), was taken from Greek vases (Fig. 268); it is usually made up of sparse and lucid scrolls, with the anthemion occupying a prominent place. Its chaste outlines were easier of execution than more complicated varieties, and it became extremely popular during the Regency period, although since it was usually painted examples are now rare.

The variants of arabesque available at the dawn of the Regency therefore included: the antique Roman, painted or in light relief; the Renaissance, painted or in relief; the Louis XIV or Bérainesque; the high rococo, which was revived in the 1820s; the neo-classical; and the 'Etruscan'. Further variants were to occur or to be revived, such as the use of arabesque on a gilded background as practised in the seventeenth century. An eclectic period like the Regency saw no reason to deny itself; it used arabesque according to preference. Sheraton, for instance, employed a simplified Raphaelesque type confined within a pilaster for his 'Pilasters for Commodes' (Fig. 171) and a French (or Italian) neo-classical type for an 'Ornament for a Painted Panel' (Fig. 172); he averred that arabesque 'still, and ever will be retained in ornament less or more. The most tasty of these were selected by Raphael, and painted by his pupils on the walls and ceilings of the Vatican Library at Rome, and which are handed down to us, by the Italians, in masterly engravings: which, in the course of this work, I have consulted, and from which I have extracted some of my ideas, as well as from some French works'.[6]

The antique world provided models for combining arabesque with small paintings on a round, rectangular, or other straight-sided figure (Fig. 173); these paintings could if desired be executed in either a 'Pompeian' or 'Etruscan' manner. Dance's design for the Library of Lansdowne House of 1788–93 has Roman arabesque (Fig. 174) combined with dancing maidens of the Herculaneum type.[7] A similar decorative idiom was used for the front of the boxes at the Haymarket Theatre of 1793 by Novosielski (Fig. 175); the theatre, with a horseshoe auditorium inspired by that of Bordeaux, was the second largest in Europe.[8] Flat painting for theatre decoration was probably thought suitable for utilitarian reasons; a well known treatise of 1790 had emphasised the importance of theatre acoustics, recommending both that 'wood, being of all materials the most favourable to sound, should be adopted in a theatre, in preference to any other, not only in the divisions, but in the walls' — a fine recipe for a bonfire — and that there should be 'No carved work, projecting ornaments, modillions, dentils etc. or festoons of silk or damask'.[9]

The eager interest taken by Holland in arabesque and in 'Pompeian' decoration is explicit in Tatham's correspondence with him; a letter from Rome of 4th April 1796 shows both Tatham's opinion of the primacy of the Italians in this field, and the readiness of some Italians to adopt unsuitable English fashions: 'Your Postscript on undertaking a Work at my return upon the subject of "external & internal decorations used by the ancients to their buildings both private and public", would be I think but a replication of what is for the most part already done (especially in this country). The only examples we can trace are those of frises arabesque ornaments, and Relieved Stuccos, as to the internal; the former of which varying and complicated as the nature of the style so generally admits — and At the Baths of Titus & the Villa Negroni

[Pl. LVIII] here, may be seen ample documents that this method of painting was mostly used in their nobler buildings — The Ruins of the Ancient Cities of Pompeia and Herculaneum, evince a most luxurious prospect of the decorations in question, employed both inside and outside. . . . The light stucco you mention rendered necessary to be aided by the pencil, as depending on colours in shades for their relief, is seen mostly upon the vaulted Roofs of existing Ruins of Sepulchres, a method adopted in the earlier times. — The best example I know in stucco'd ornaments is in a Vaulted room said to have been a bath amongst the vast ruins of Adrian's Villa at Tivoli, the principal enrichment of which I formerly sent you a sketch — The Baths of Livia here, have a Ceiling exactly as you describe, the ornaments coloured and gilt, and decorated with compartments of figures very rich profuse and complicated . . . to this day an Italian never modernizes his House without arabesque being the principal decoration; although sometimes nowadays for the sake of aping his Neighbours (I mean those of a

172 'Girandoles' and 'Ornament for a Painted Panel', by Thomas Sheraton, 1793

173 Ceiling of a Roman Sepulchral Chamber, pictured by Pietro Santi Bartoli

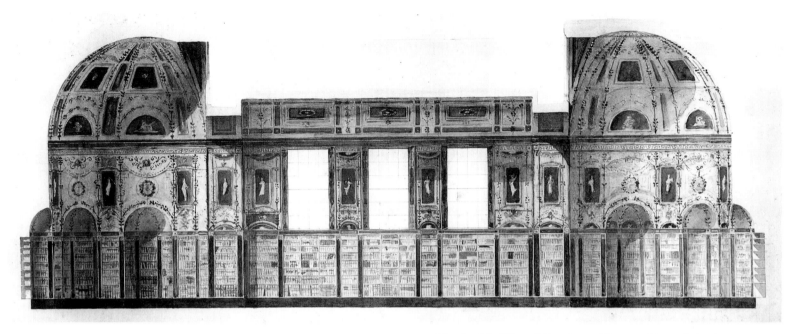

**174** 'Sketch of the Library', Lansdowne House, 1788–93, design by George Dance

prevailing Nation such as the English are at present) hang their Gala Rooms with red hot damask and the like colours . . .'. After mentioning 'Raphael's Logia's' as a fertile source for 'original and applicable subjects', Tatham went on to declare that, 'The late Messrs. Adams' were the children of the Arabesque, yet I do not scarcely recollect one instance in which they successfully employed it, it is a style productive of great fatigue to the designer, more to the Artist, and an infinite expence to the purse of the Employer . . .'.[10]

A later letter, of 8th July 1796, returned to arabesque: 'I have much attended to your hints of the study of arabesque Ornaments, I have made a large Collection of drawings on this Account . . . you have been the happy cause of my giving much more attention to the immediate class of Ornament in question than I should otherwise have done — I hope to evince the fruits of it hereafter'.[11] Holland's incitement of Tatham to study arabesque in Italy evinces an interest unconfined to French fashions in interior decoration; like Percier and Fontaine, he was profoundly attracted by what was available in Italy, and a publication of 1782 by Albertolli shows ceiling decorations at Milan that remind one in detail of Holland's work at Carlton House.[12] Perhaps significantly, Albertolli refers to this arabesque as 'Grottesco'.[13]

The flexibility of arabesque assisted its popularity. Pergolesi, for example, incorporated a decussated and Greek key motif in his arabesque which, ambiguously 'Etruscan' or Chinese (see pp.239, 336, 338),[14] was ripe for adaptation by the Craces in Brighton Pavilion.[15] Cockerell, as might have been expected from his Italian proclivities, records having spent 'half the day in looking over the loggia of Raphael and other motives of ornaments for his ceilings — on the idea of

**175** The Auditorium, the Opera House, Haymarket, 1791, designed by Michael Novosielski

selecting such as would have character of antique, simple but speaking & characteristic & new — or old in a new light'.[16] The versatility of arabesque is repeatedly demonstrated: an example by George Smith of 1828 displays 'Decorative Pilasters' which could be painted with arabesque in colours, 'such are the Pilasters in the Vatican at Rome'; carved and gilded, or painted to imitate bas-reliefs; or, yet another possibility, such arabesque was 'frequently executed by the French in a style which they term Rehaussée D'or; which is done by a species of hatching in gold on a dark ground, where the gold itself forms the high light; or where such species of hatching in gold is relieved by dark shadows on a light ground'.[17]

## 'Etruscan'

Arabesque was complemented by, and from the 1780s was often mingled with, another form of 'non-architectural' decoration which was called 'Etruscan'. The term was founded on an error, the misapplication of the term 'Etruscan' to Greek vases; had this not happened, the style would have been called 'Greek', which is more enlightening.

The growing vogue for Greek vases reached its height in the last decade of the eighteenth century and the first of the nineteenth (Figs 176, 183; Pl. LIV); few fashionable houses neglected them. They enjoyed immense prestige. They served at least three purposes. First, they were beautiful as ornaments in themselves; as d'Hancarville said, they had been discovered in areas where the Romans had established

their 'maisons de plaisance', and 'il est naturel de croire qu'ils y avoient rassemblé ce qu'ils trouvoient de plus élégant, de plus fins et de plus précieux en tout genre'.[18] Second, they provided more than two hundred new forms for pottery, porcelain, silver, copper, glass, and furniture, and, moreover, forms from 'la source la plus pure'.[19] Finally, the quality of the pictorial designs was such that 'ils pourroient être placés parmi les plus belles compositions de Raphael' and with them 'on peut réunir les styles de tous les temps de l'art des anciens'.[20] This last remark went to the heart of the matter; the synthesis that resulted was remarkably distinguished. Quite apart from the influence of the motifs seen on the vases, the Greek emphasis on outline revolutionised both the fine and the applied arts.[21]

When the Irish artist Adam Buck painted himself with his young family he placed his figures in a setting drawn from the Greek vases ranged at the back in a majestic row (Pl. LIV).[22] The mother's chair and stool are copied from such vases; her hair style, dress, and posture are all to be seen in them (Raphael himself had imitated Greek poses); the arabesque on the wall and the back of the chair are of an 'Etruscan' type. The use of 'Etruscan' decoration indoors was particularly happy when associated with the Greek Revival style. The imitation of the antique reached unprecedented heights; one might add in parenthesis that the story that women attempted to reproduce a particular type of clinging drapery seen in Greek statues by wearing wet dresses is, *pace* the fashion historians, perfectly true; Lady Louisa Stuart in 1798 objected to the practice not only on the grounds of indecency, but, perhaps a more reasonable objection, because of the age of those who

**176** 'Third Room containing Greek Vases', from the Duchess Street house of Thomas Hope, 1807

LVIII Antique wall-painting from
the Villa Negroni, Rome, published
in 1778

LIX A wall with doorway, a design
for the Library, the Marine Pavilion,
Brighton, by the Crace firm, c.1802

LX  The Blue Velvet Room, Carlton House, c.1818

indulged in it: 'Don't imagine me an old maid growling at the young people, for some of the most remarkable statues in wet drapery are very fully my contemporaries at least'.[23] The concern of men that their lower limbs should be clad in tight, light garments that gave the illusion of nakedness stemmed from the same antique source; like 'wet drapery', this was carried to extraordinary lengths; the dandy Lord Alvaney is recorded 'in great delight at some Paris pantaloons — peau de pendu [i.e. skin of a hanged man]; and if the Pendu was the right size the pantaloons fitted without a wrinkle and without a seam of course'.[24]

The vases supplied simple but beautiful motifs, usually abstract, which were more important for the purposes of interior decoration than were the wonderful drawings of gods, heroes, and humans. The motifs, usually already arranged as the borders of panels, were easily assimilated into the 'panelling out' system of the Pompeian and other styles. They included the 'Etruscan' arabesque mentioned above; linear representations of architectural detail (Fig. 268); Greek key patterns in varying degrees of complication (Fig. 177); the anthemion (Fig. 178); strings of bay leaves and rosettes; interlaced ovals, circles, and arches (Fig. 177), and decussated squares and diamonds (Fig. 178) all of which can, like the frets, look very Chinese; and the little squares, sometimes with other squares within them, that were to be later used by Charles Rennie Mackintosh and the Wiener Werkstätte to such exquisite effect.

The vases also gave a palette, the black, red, ochre and white of 'Etruscan' decoration. Quite frequently it is the palette that stamps a decoration as 'Etruscan'.

The 1770s was the period when both 'Etruscan' and 'Pompeian' decoration, which became staple ingredients of Regency style, appeared decisively on the scene. The French designer Dugourc, who worked at Bagatelle, claimed in his autobiography to have introduced 'Etruscan' decoration into France.[25] Robert Adam asserted that he had introduced the 'Etruscan' style to England in the Countess of Derby's dressing room (1770) and at Osterley (1776);[26] the former is in 'the colouring of the Etruscans' but in fact contains no 'Etruscan' motifs, the latter has 'Etruscan' colours and various 'Etruscan' motifs such as anthemion surrounds to the paintings, but the arabesque disposition of the ornament on walls and ceiling is thoroughly Roman.[27] James Wyatt designed an 'Etruscan' interior at Heveningham in c.1784.[28]

Despite these and other early essays, it is quite clear from the indefatigable Tatham's letters to Holland that as late as 1796 the 'Etruscan' style in interior decoration was virtually unknown in England (it seems possible that Tatham himself played a part in disseminating the easily applied form in which it became so popular in England in the early nineteenth century). Writing to Holland from Rome in April 1796, Tatham mentioned: 'I had almost forgot a modern

**177** Decoration from a Greek vase, published by P. F. d'Hancarville, 1766

**178** Decoration from a Greek vase, published by P. F. d'Hancarville, 1766

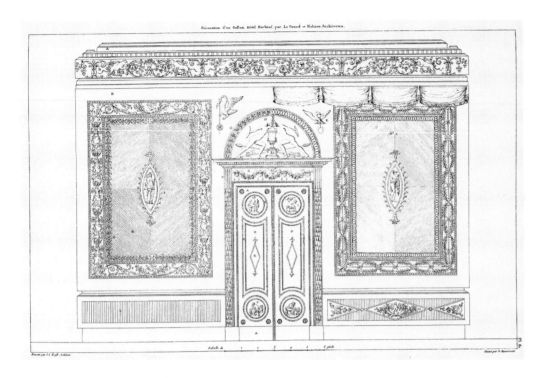

**179** 'Décoration d'un Sallon, Hôtel Marbeuf', 1790, designed by Le Grand and Molinos

**180** 'Decoration', 1804, by George Smith

**181** '. . . un candelabro capriccioso . . .' and 'un pezzo di obelisco', from a Pompeian wall-decoration, published in 1779

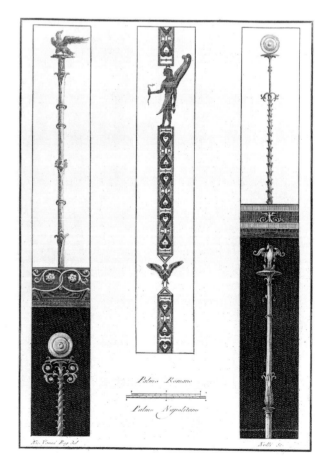

invention set on foot by a man at Naples of the name of Tichbein who has published certain prints, bordures hangings & such like in the Etruscan style, precisely copied from Sir Wm. Hamiltons Vases & adapted to small rooms and Cabinets, he has himself fitted up a room as a specimen with which I was so much pleased, that I procured of him specimens of the ornaments with their prices, you can scarce imagine how successful and new such ornaments appear — they are used in the way of our modern paper hangings, & are suited as well to the walls of a room as to the whole furniture throughout — figures, ornaments, symbols of every kind are copied from the real vases, representing them in their exact colours — the bordures are for pannelling etc, (as I have sent you a scrap) and the figures are destined for the centre of pannells in a wide open field of dark colour — I will write you more details of this new & tasty method of fitting up rooms hereafter'.[29]

The French had produced highly original 'Etruscan' furniture designed by Hubert Robert in 1787 (see p.363), and by 1790 a decoration proposed for the hôtel Marbeuf (that could have been entirely flat painted) contained unmistakable elements drawn from 'Etruscan' borders (Fig. 179). It was probably from such French sources that George Smith drew ideas for an eclectic 'Decoration' published in

1804 (Fig. 180); this design is not called 'Etruscan', but it employs a frequently reproduced motif from d' Hancarville placed within a panel edged with 'Etruscan' diamond-shaped motifs; on each side is 'un candelabro capriccioso con sopra un Aquila' inspired by an illustration in Volume Four of *Le Pitture Antiche d'Ercolano* (Fig. 181). The marbled dado is 'Pompeian'. This eclectic mixture is typical of many decorations.

Charles Augustine Busby published in 1810 a little book containing designs for interiors of the type that, executed in transitory materials, were to be seen everywhere in Regency England. The 'Etruscan' influence was strong. One design[30] looks like a simplified version of a more sophisticated decoration such as that proposed for the hôtel Marbeuf; the schematic nature of the detail was probably partly a matter of scale and partly because decorators knew the motifs well enough to supply the details (exactly the same 'Etruscan' shorthand was used on the 'Etruscan' details of Bullock designs shown in Ackermann's *Repository* (see p.403)). Another Busby design (Fig. 182) is entirely composed of 'Etruscan' motifs, including the arabesque; the round panel in the centre is of a type seen on 'Etruscan' vases, but such round shapes had oriental connections also, and the disposition of the

**182** Design for a room, by C. A. Busby, 1810

ornament makes one wonder whether Busby were not hinting at an 'Etruscan'/Chinese synthesis of the kind ventured on by French designers. A Crace design in 'ethnic' chinoiserie of 1802–04 with a similar roundel was possibly installed at Brighton Pavilion (Pl. LIX); Busby was a native of Brighton.[31]

The 'Etruscan' style was seen at its grandest in the Saloon (or Dining Room) at Carlton House (Pl. LVI), created as part of the extensive remodelling undertaken by the Prince of Wales in the first decade of the nineteenth century with the assistance of the egregious Walsh Porter (see p.345). The predominantly red, black, and silver colours of the wall ornaments[32] and the character of the wall and door paintings class the decoration as 'Etruscan' despite the strong architectural emphasis of the room with its dome and imposing Ionic columns, in scagliola imitating 'red granite' (porphyry), that survived from the decoration by Holland. The dome was painted with a sky, the curtains were in blue silk, the predominant impression was blue and silver.[33] A contemporary described the room as 'one of the most splendid apartments in Europe; the walls are entirely covered with silver, on which are painted Etruscan ornaments in relief, with vine leaves [the 'Etruscan' simple arabesque] trellis work etc. . . . the capitals and bases are silver, as are also the enrichments, moulding etc. of the architrave and cornice; the latter is surmounted by an ornament that is somewhat Turkish in its character [it is in fact 'Etruscan', and is the same motif that surrounds the circular paintings in the 'Etruscan' room at Osterley] and which if it does not belong to the Ionic order [that is, is not an Ionic entablature] nevertheless adds to the splendour of the room'.[34] The whole is richly eclectic, with chandeliers as massive and as architectural as the columns, a chimney-piece and mirror frame studded with Piranesian Egyptian stars, and Garter stars glittering on the draperies.

The 'profusion' of the Regent's taste may have provoked a reaction perceptible in the commentaries of the *Repository* on the designs of George Bullock, who associated a modest 'Etruscan' wall decoration with the chaste folds of 'antique drapery' (Fig. 198; see pp.402–03). Bullock's 'Etruscan' formula closely resembles that illustrated in Nathaniel Whittock's *Decorative Painters' and Glaziers' Guide* of 1827; Whittock described the 'Etruscan or Italian' as 'a more chastened style', in which 'the ornaments are not so bold, and the scrolls are formed by serpentine graceful lines, intermixed with a single leaf or flower. The heavy columns and ornamental frieze is entirely abandoned . . . and the panels are formed by single lines, or narrow plain mouldings, and ornamented at the angles with a single leaf or flower pointing towards the centre' (Fig. 198, Pl. CXXIV). He emphasised the style's delicacy, and said that the colours 'are as light as the ornaments and are generally the lightest tints of blue, pink, and a grey called in colouring neutral tint'.[35] This last extraordinary statement may derive from a mistaken

identification of the Etruscan black, red, ochre, and scarlet palette with the brilliant 'Pompeian' palette such as conceived by Gell (see p.243), but it was a peculiar thing for a decorator to say, and it is possible that Whittock had been influenced by a recent decoration that had used 'Etruscan' motifs with those colours (see pp.340, 341). Whittock illustrated the 'Etruscan' 'Inner Hall' at Carlton House with the comment that 'this style of decoration is not much used at present'.[36]

Papers in 'Etruscan' style were used to decorate the Small Drawing Room (Pl. LV) and the Library at the Deepdene. Apart from the ceiling cove, the Small Drawing Room was without 'architectural' detail; the walls were completely flat, the printed paper having a dado and frieze with a classical arabesque and garlands in 'Etruscan' terracotta pink, brown and black; the pattern of circles was also taken from 'Etruscan' vases. Architectural emphasis came from the green Mona marble chimney-piece and the architectonic overmantel mirror and silk-hung baldacchino that housed the ottoman, with its curious silk recesses — what was behind them? — the crimson curtains hung from a gilt-bronze rail. The 'Empire' tincture was softened by the domestic wallpaper; carpet, hearthrug, and low upholstered seats instilled a proto-Victorian stuffiness belied by the angry Regency swans; the effect was very different from that of the Duchess Street house. The monopodium table is similar to one illustrated in plate 39 of Hope's book, although it differs in detail.

The 'Old Library' wallpaper had an arabesque frieze; the deep-set mirror was in advanced taste, not unlike those installed by Beckford in Lansdown Tower; another mirror opposite reflected into infinity. The chimney-piece may be French[37] or it may have been designed by Hope.

## 'Pompeian'

The eighteenth and early nineteenth century 'Pompeian' style took its name from the excavations that began systematically at Pompeii from 1748 (and at Herculaneum from 1738); the term comprehended decorations in 'Pompeian' style found in places other than Pompeii, such as the Villa Negroni murals at Rome (Pl. LVIII). The intense interest in excavations continued throughout the period; in 1814, for instance, the King and Queen of Naples gave a reception at Pompeii during which an excavation was carried out to the sound of music.[38] The 'Pompeian' style was based on painted Roman wall decorations that in their most extreme form indulged in every architectural and ornamental fantasy and caprice, freed by the liberty given by flat painting from constraints of gravity and practicality. The style employed panelled compartments (often orchestrated by pilasters), candelabraform pillars (often imitating bronze), 'airy pergolas' (to use Sir John Summerson's happy phrase), and it manufactured fathomless spatial ambiguities. Rational perspective was defied; the lack of a common vanishing point was essential to the decorative effect. The colours, when unfaded, were often bright and strong, of a type associated in the later eighteenth-century mind with orientalism — the colours of the interior of Müntz's 'Alhambra' at Kew, for example, were much in this range.

The association of neo-classicism with strong colour and strong contrasts, as displayed in 'Etruscan vases' and Roman villa decoration, must have encouraged what was probably a natural reaction against the delicate colours of the 1780s and early 1790s; Regency taste preferred vivid colours, increasingly vivid as the period wore on and with lavish use of gold. Sir William Gell referred in 1817 to the 'most brilliant and endless variety of colours' seen in Pompeian murals, saying that although the Romans had been censured for gaudiness, 'no nation ever exhibited a greater passion for gaudy colours' than the Greeks; they had almost all the colours of the Renaissance, plus Egyptian azure and Tyrian purple'.[39] In Rome, he painted his sitting room in 1828 'in all the bright staring colours I could get, a sort of thing between Etruscan and Pompeii'.[40]

People were struck by the allusiveness of 'Pompeian' decorations, which seemed open to almost any interpretation. When the Villa Negroni frescoes in Rome were unearthed in 1777, the painter Thomas Jones referred to 'the painted ornaments much in the Chinese taste'.[41] Payne Knight wrote: 'The oriental style of building, with columns extravagantly slender and high, was well known to the Romans, as appears from the grotesque paintings found in Herculaneum and Pompeii, which have . . . a near resemblance . . . with those executed in the semi-gothic church of Monreale'.[42] In modern times, Payne Knight's 'gothic' and 'oriental' analogy has been carried further; Gothic has been seen as the 'recaptured inheritance' of 'Pompeian' aedicular fresco art: 'The pointed-arch system was, I believe, adopted' because 'it had an air of fantasy — perhaps, dare one guess, of Oriental fantasy? — which went along with the realisation of the "Pompeian" idea'.[43]

In 1827 Whittock subdivided 'Pompeian' decoration into Grecian, Egyptian — Piranesi had used 'Pompeian' constructions as a basis for some of his decorations in the Egyptian style at the Caffè Inglese (Fig. 263) — and oriental types; the last were defined as 'distinguished by their disproportioned, though not inelegant columns; the capitals and bases of which differ in every way from the Greek and Roman architecture'.[44] Transmutation of the Pompeian candelabraform motif into exotic styles was easy; examples are seen in the cast-iron columns in Indian style designed by Repton for the Pheasantry at Brighton (Pl. XVIII). Chinese, Gothic, Indian, Grecian, Egyptian — this suggestive painted architecture was well suited to the process of creative synthesis (see Pl. CIII).

An Italian, Joseph Bonomi, created in the Gallery at Packington Hall in Warwickshire an early and thoroughgoing example of a 'Pompeian' room. Decorated between 1785 and 1788 for the fourth Earl of Aylesford, the source was the Baths of Titus in Rome,[45] and the Warwickshire version was rendered in the original black and red. An archaeological touch was that the decoration, executed by the Turinese J. G. Rigaud assisted by two other Italians, Pastorini and Borgnis,[46] was painted in 'antique' encaustic, a technique previously essayed by Caylus, Vien and Le Lorrain;[47] the first known English revival of the 'klismos' chair (see p.355) accompanied this early 'archaeological' ensemble.

The creators of Packington were mainly Italians; Holland's interest in Italian arabesque has been mentioned above. He was not alone; contemporary Italian neo-classical decoration in general was viewed with great interest by the English. The Palazzo Borghese, for instance — its fame paralleled that of the (somewhat later) house of Mme. Récamier in Paris — was seen by many English visitors; its ceilings, by the two Aspruccis, were drawn by Tatham, its furniture by Hope and (perhaps) Smirke. Italian influence on Regency style should not be regarded as weaker than that of the French, despite such influences as the French workmen employed by Holland, and despite the power and prestige of the French style of Percier and Fontaine. The latter were themselves a conduit for Italian ideas; when Napoleon asked Fontaine; 'Quel est le plus beau palais connu?', the answer was: 'Le plus imposant, mais aussi le moins commode, c'est le palais Farnèse, à Rome; les plus grands, ceux de Gênes; les plus vastes, ceux d'Allemagne, et les plus habitables, ceux de France'.[48] The reply of the courtier hardly conceals the Italian bias of the artist, a bias elsewhere freely admitted.[49] In England during the 1790s French and Italian influences, to judge from the decoration at Carlton House, ran in tandem; it was then that Mario Asprucci was commissioned by the notorious Earl-Bishop of Bristol to design Ickworth, thus beginning a story that unfolded over many years.

## Soane and the Villa Negroni

Soane, amongst others, was fascinated by the 'Pompeian' style; themes drawn from it occur prominently within his houses at Ealing and in Lincoln's Inn Fields. In his Breakfast Room at the latter house he hung a series of coloured etchings by Angelo Campanella of the Villa Negroni; discovered in 1777 (Pl. LVIII), the villa afforded splendid examples of the 'Pompeian' style, rendered in the prints in unfaded bright colours, with the pictorial parts of the decoration modernised in a way that made them look like a neo-classical version of seventeenth-century Roman baroque painting. Soane had been in Rome in 1778 when the discovery was new and when the first of Campanella's plates were being published; he acquired several sets for his library.

These were used as sources for the decoration of the Front Parlour at Pitzhanger Manor at Ealing, his first house (Fig. 183). Many of the room's architectural components derive from Roman columbaria, but

**183** Pitzhanger Manor: the Front Parlour, designed by Sir John Soane

its painted blue-and-buff decoration is to be seen in Plates I and III of the Campanella etchings. The Parlour has 'Pompeian' 'panelling out' (see below); the deep skirting was painted to imitate porphyry.[50] The chairs are in severe 'klismos' style. The prominent place given to the splendid 'Etruscan' vase is appropriate; Soane knew that the Romans decorated their villas with Greek works of art.

The Breakfast Room at Lincoln's Inn Fields (Fig. 184) demonstrates Soane's 'Pompeian' interests as clearly as any of his interiors; here he hung the etchings on deep red walls in what must have been a conscious allusion to their surroundings. He wrote of the Breakfast Room that the 'views from this room into the Monument Court and into the Museum, the Mirrors in the Ceiling, and the Looking Glasses,

combined with the variety of outline and general arrangement in the design and decoration of this limited space, present an almost infinite succession of those fanciful effects which constitute the poetry of Architecture'.[51] Is there any better description of the bewildering caprices of antique painted 'Pompeian' architecture, which approach the metaphysical, than this last phrase? An essential element in the 'fanciful effects' of the Breakfast Room is ambiguity, an ambiguity akin to the ambiguities of space and plane seen in the Pompeian murals. Mirror is a way of dissolving a solid surface, a wall or pilaster, into air, into thin air.

Soane's plentiful use of mirror was not unique to him; as Britton said in his description of Soane's house, 'Percier has given the design of

**184** Sir John Soane's house, Lincoln's Inn Fields, the Breakfast Room

a gallery, the end wall of which consists almost entirely of mirror, placed between the columns' (Fig. 233);[52] Percier's *Cabinet pour le Roi d'Espagne* at Aranjuez has a ceiling reflected into infinity in a way similar to that employed by Soane, as for example in the Lincoln's Inn Fields Library.[53] Large mirrors became a hallmark of Regency taste; the Prince of Wales was conspicuously fond of mirrors placed to produce infinite recession (Pl. LXXXIII); in the 'Etruscan' Circular Dining Room at Carlton House the mirrors reflected each other and the chandeliers to give 'the appearance of repetition in endless continuity, which gives a magical effect and splendour to the apartment'.[54]

In 1814 Gandy, the artist who entered the Soanean magic world and depicted Soane's interiors in a way that intensifies their eerie power, revealed in a letter of 1814 to Soane (a letter which suggests the apprentice writing to the Sorcerer) the fascination with mirrors that he shared with his master. The subject was Prince Eugène's dressing room in Paris. Gandy wrote: 'The whole of the walls and doors were lined with mirrors. The columns detached [?] hid the joints of the Glass . . . . the Ceiling painted like the Baths of Titus, a deep gold fringe under the cornice hid the upper part of the Mirrors. . . . This complete Catoptric Room from its reverberating reflections produced a wonderful effect of artificial space. The columns were reflected to infinity in each direction. The mind fancied a Fairy Hall and an Enchantment.'[55] Once again, the ideal of Regency decoration approached the pantomime transformation scene, which also presented an 'Enchantment'.

If the lavish use of mirror is not unique to Soane, his method of use is unusual; the usual Regency mirror-induced splendour differs in kind from Soane's metaphysical tease. He employed mirrors not to impart grandeur — indeed, not to give beauty — but in a sly manner in which the most obvious intention is to deceive, to produce spatial enigmas. The Breakfast Room at Lincoln's Inn Fields in its final form has convex mirrors in the ceiling[56] — Britton said that mirrors could be effective placed high 'for instance, in the semicircular part of an arcade, so as to convey the appearance of it being perforated'[57] — and mirrors in thin vertical panels both in the bookcases and, significantly, within the flat pilasters that appear to support the dome. The effect of these last approaches that of the pilasters in plate VI of the Villa Negroni series, pierced in a form corresponding to that of Soane's inset mirror. Such spatial ambiguities are everywhere in the house; especially 'Pompeian' is the view of the narrow gallery that runs along the window side of the drawing room, with its peculiar 'bridges' and candelabraform pillars (Fig. 185; the latter not shown).

Spatial equivocations are apparent in the Breakfast Room dome, which hangs suspended over the central space like a canopy, with light breaking in at either side — a total contradiction of the way a dome is expected to behave. The effect has some correspondence with that of the canopies in the Villa Negroni and in other 'Pompeian' architectural murals. If one stands in the Breakfast Room and looks up towards the skylights which lie on two sides of the dome, the vertical plane

185 Sir John Soane's house, Lincoln's Inn Fields, the gallery adjacent to the Drawing Room

186 Sir John Soane's house, Lincoln's Inn Fields, design for the Plaister Room

presented by the section of the dome gives an impression much like that of the Negroni 'canopy', above which a similar illogical solidity presents itself in the vertical plane (Fig. 184, Pl. LVIII). That plane can as easily be seen as being behind the canopy, at one with the walls, in which case the thin curved shell looks something like a baldacchino in a Renaissance painting, or like the dome of the Soane family tomb (Pl. XXXVIII).[58] Above the 'canopy' in the Campanella etching is a curved panel enclosed by lines that begin to approach a Greek key pattern; such lines are commonly used in various patterns in Pompeian decoration. They somewhat resemble the painted and incised lines so common in Soanean decoration, as seen for example on the ceiling of the Breakfast Room.

The candelabraform pillars of Pompeian decoration are plentiful in Soane's house at Lincoln's Inn Fields; usually bronzed, as in antique murals, they are sometimes furnished with forms that recall Gothic pendants or fan vaulting — although such forms appear also in the 'Pompeian' originals and in late Roman architectural detail. They may be seen in the Eating Room and Library, where the walls are 'painted of a deep red colour, in imitation of the walls at Herculaneum and Pompeii . . . the mouldings are of a light bronze colour';[59] all have classical detail save two, which are unequivocally Gothic. A strange design for the Plaister Room (Fig. 186), through which a chill wind from antiquity seems to be blowing, has simplified candelabraform pillars, combined with a lantern and with an ironwork balcony showing

LXI A ceiling at Frogmore House, decorated by Mary Moser

LXII Floral wallpaper in Chinese style with blue and silver panels, from the Royal Pavilion, Brighton, c.1815

LXIII The Saloon in 1817, Brighton Pavilion, designed by John Nash and the Crace firm

LXIV Windsor Castle, design, c.1826–8, for a carpet,
by J. J. Boileau

LXV 'Design for Parquet floor', by James White,
c.1820–30

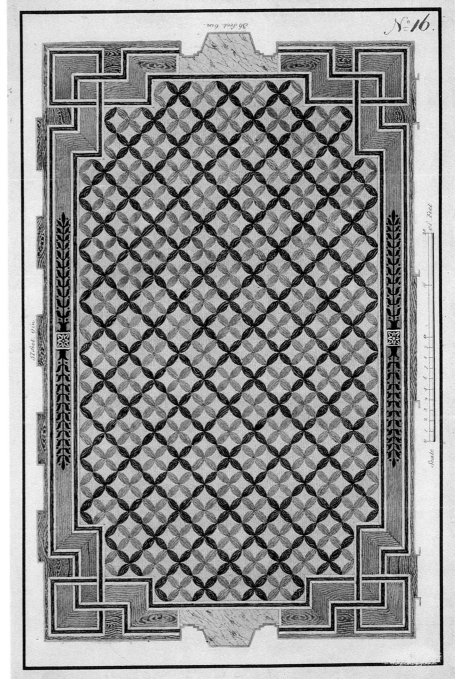

LXVI The Bedroom of Mme. Récamier, Paris, 1802, by Sir Robert Smirke

LXVII Design for 'His Majesty's Bedroom', Windsor Castle, as approved by George IV, 1827

LXVIII 'A Small Bed', from the *Repository*, 1816

LXIX Design for the Boudoir, the east wall, Windsor Castle, as approved by George IV, c.1826

LXX  The 'Rose Satin Drawing Room', Carlton House, c.1817

LXXI  'Crimson Drawing Room', Carlton House, c.1816

LXXII 'Octangular Tent Room', by George Smith, 1826

LXXIII The King's Boudoir, Brighton Pavilion, 1826

a favourite Soanean motif that renders in line the sculptured grooves of such Roman sarcophagi as the 'Cassa Sepolcrale di Cecilia Metella' (that tomb is topped with a Soanean motif, a Greek key pattern and two opposing scrolls). The motif had been used by Adam and other neo-classical decorators, but Soane pushed it to an abstract extreme.

## 'Panelling out'

Roman arabesque was combined with 'Etruscan' motifs, as in the Osterley Dressing Room; both were often organised in panels — 'panelling out' — increasingly often as the period wore on. Panels are an ancient form of decoration, arising originally from techniques evolved to cover a large area with wood and to counteract movements caused by variations in humidity. In some form or other, panels had always been in fashion; Roman panelled doors, for example, were essentially similar to modern panelled doors; Fragonard in 1774 mentioned the 'plusieurs maisons bourgeoises' of Pompeii 'dont les murailles sont peint à panneaux, comme de notre tems, avec beaucoup d'arabesques'.⁶⁰ It was therefore easy to integrate the panelled compartments of 'Pompeian' murals and 'Etruscan' vases with other fashionable modes of decoration. 'Panelling out' was an abstract framework on which any treatment in any style could be based; it was often affiliated with the proportions of the orders.

The treatment could be simple or elaborate; a lead in elaboration was given by Paris. Alternative proposals for the late eighteenth-century decoration of a Parisian saloon at the hôtel Marbeuf by Le Grand and Molinos (Fig. 179), a building that was praised by C. R. Cockerell, use motifs taken from Greek and Roman sources to delineate and ornament a framework of panels. This kind of French decoration was to be taken up in England in the more costly and cosmopolitan schemes installed after about 1800; in the meantime, the prevailing fashionable style was Holland's version of Louis XVI decoration, again largely articulated with 'panelling out'. Panels could as easily be filled with damask or other fabrics as with painted or stucco decoration.

Sheraton's 'Plan & Section of a Drawing Room' of 1793 (Fig. 187) gives his interpretation of the Holland style. The room is no particular room, but a compendium of the 'the Prince of Wales's [at Carlton House] the Duke of York's, and other noblemen's drawing-rooms'. Wallpaper was being used more frequently: in Sheraton's scheme the 'pannelling on the walls are done in paper, with ornamental borders' in arabesque 'of various colours'.⁶¹ Wallpaper in a drawing room would at this date have been regarded in some quarters with reserve; the Prince of Wales's Drawing Room would have been executed in the more expensive — and expressive — medium of paint.

The arabesques in Sheraton's depiction appear less complex than those in the hôtel Marbeuf, and probably would have been so; it is not just a matter of scale.⁶² None the less, Sheraton thought the room he depicted overstated; 'not, however, a proper precedent for drawing-rooms in general, as it partakes principally of the character and ordinance of a state saloon room'.⁶³ Adjacent to the two end windows are long panels like pilasters, decorated with arabesque; these also would have been in paper. Above the mirrors are paintings in 'clair-obscure'. Sheraton says that the Prince's room, which had five windows, did not have mirrors between the windows as in his illustration, but had instead 'richly furnished Corinthian pilasters' (his mirror frames have the simpler Ionic) and 'the cove and ceiling are richly ornamented in paintings and gold'.⁶⁴ Sheraton's curtains, with the sun-ray pleat above, are typical of his style, so different in their disciplined forms from the opulent folds or the 'antique drapery' soon to come into fashion — although his method of hanging, which he described as a new technique using rings and 'French rods' that allowed the material of the curtain to be contracted or expanded at pleasure, made much of the later opulence possible. It also quickly eliminated the

**187** Details of 'A Plan & Section of a Drawing Room', 1793, by Thomas Sheraton

eighteenth-century festoon, with its stiff formality. The Prince's dining room appears at this date to have been comparatively simple, again with 'panelled-out' walls and with a panelled ceiling.

The 'panelled out' style was susceptible to any degree of elaboration; it early became a formula, often used without finesse or discrimination. It could as easily form a base for exotic as for classical decorations, and may be seen in an unused design in the Chinese style of 1802 for the Pavilion at Brighton (Pl. LIX); the marbling in cornice and dado is 'Pompeian' inspired. 'Panelling out' is conspicuous in the grander schemes installed in the Pavilion after its remodelling by Nash (Pls XCIX, CI, CII).

An exceedingly sumptuous form of 'panelling out' is displayed in the Blue Velvet Room at Carlton House (Pl. LX), redecorated between 1806 and 1814; little if anything from the Holland period was allowed to survive.[65] Between 1811 and 1814 the gilded woodwork was progressively enriched. The rich Garter blue velvet on the walls, in conjunction with the resplendently ornate gilding, is unmistakably 'high Regency' in effect. The panels alone articulate the walls; there are no columns, pilasters, or other forms of architectural decoration; however magnificently dressed, the walls are flat. The elaborately carved panels were the work of Edward Wyatt, who also provided the frames and pier glasses; he carved and gilded 'in burnished gold twenty four emblematical door panels', later moved to the Crimson Drawing Room at Windsor Castle.[66]

The banal level to which the subtle art of Holland had fallen by 1826 is seen in George Smith's illustration of 'panelling out', which he calls 'English Decoration'. Smith explained that the 'style of decoration exhibited in this plate may properly be termed French [!] inasmuch as it was first introduced into this country by certain French artists, brought over from France by Messrs. G. and F. Eckhardts'; their methods (painting) were too expensive, but 'what before was only effected by the hand, has now been accomplished by the art of printing' (wallpapers).[67]

In 1827 Whittock summarised the available styles which employed decorative panelling in words that show that, despite the inevitable confusion between modes of decoration that had been so generally intermingled, a perception of the original differences had survived; this is less surprising in that he, like others, expected the decorative painter to study antique origins at first hand, in the shape of the ancient sculpture and ornament in the British Museum: 'the museum is open to all persons decently attired, and . . . not the slightest expense can be incurred . . .'.[68] Enlightened times. The indispensability of the antique was insisted upon over and over again; Britton repeated accepted wisdom in saying that the more an artist understood antique forms, the more likely he would be to catch their spirit and be able to judge how far to modify them.[69]

Whittock declared that for Grecian, Roman and Gothic decoration — Gothic is included, which shows what a fundamental part of the decorative vocabulary 'panelling out' had become — it would first 'be necessary for the student to know how to divide the panels or compartments'.[70] He defined the classical styles as the Greek, the 'Pompeian' (which he equates with arabesque), and the 'Etruscan' or Italian. The decoration of the Greeks 'is marked with a light elegance of style; the ornaments principally taken from the implements, vessels, and sacrifices [tripods and altars] used in their religious ceremonies' (the vases were excluded). 'It is supposed that the walls were divided into compartments or panels, and that these were filled with paintings. . . . The walls were divided by pilasters, either formed in the building or imitated by painting, and the cornice of the ceiling was made to correspond with the style of the architecture; and between the pilasters hung painted representations of festoons of flowers . . . in some instances, intermixed with medallions'.

Much of this was art-historical conjecture; the practical reality was given on the next page: 'most of the patterns given in this work in furniture painting and decoration, are taken from the engraved representations of the walls in the interior of the houses at Pompeii'. And compartmentalism or 'panelling out', and flat pilasters, were identified as the basic characteristics of 'Pompeian' decoration. Whittock also emphasised the freedoms indulged in by the 'Pompeian' style; ' a mixture of the ornaments of the various styles, so as to blend the beauties of each . . . this style has obtained the name of the Arabesque, which is certainly best adapted for the interior of dwellings, and the Greek and Roman style of decoration for public buildings'. The last phrase refers to what has been called here the 'architectural' as opposed to the 'decorated' style. Arabesque was defined by Whittock as 'fancifully flowing circular lines with every object in nature, without caring for their connection, otherwise than as they tend to form the scroll'. Whittock included the 'Etruscan' style as one articulated by panels (see p.242).

Such a mixture as Whittock described is seen in a design of about 1818 by John Goldicutt possibly for Grundimore, near Christchurch in Hampshire (Fig. 188). The wall is panelled in buff and brown in Pompeian style, with a marbled skirting; it has 'Tuscan' pilasters, a panelled door, and a panel of arabesque of the Renaissance type; a Vitruvian scroll above the panels has above it a mural decoration with a sky background and naturalistic vines with grapes and birds; all charming in an underplayed way. Far more rigorous is a design for a dining room by Gillow & Company of about 1820 (Fig. 189), in which both panelled-out walls and ceiling are in a richly congested late neo-classical style with a strong 'Etruscan' tincture; the motifs, including vine leaves, anthemion, fir cones etc. are similar to those employed by George Bullock.

**188** Design for interior decoration, possibly for Grundimore, Hants., 1818, by John Goldicutt

**189** Design for a Dining Room, by Gillow and Co., c.1820

## Trellis and foliage

The 'Casa Pseudourbana' at Pompeii, which had a room adorned with trellis and foliage arranged in compartments, is an instance of the ancient fashion (Fig. 190) for using painted trellis or pergolas in interior decoration. The trellis was usually accompanied by leaves, flowers, or garden scenes, sometimes by garden statues as at the 'House of Venus' at Pompeii. Numerous Roman decorations that employed such themes survive, including examples in mosaic on the vaults of Santa Costanza in Rome. These motifs were revived in the Renaissance, and from then on constantly recur; they were popular in European rococo decorations of the middle of the eighteenth century. In England, for example, Horace Walpole had the China Room at Strawberry Hill decorated by J. H Müntz with a copy of a Renaissance pergola taken from the Borghese villa at Frascati.[71]

At the dawn of the 'Regency' period a design for the Countess of Pembroke by John Soane clothed the walls of a room in Pembroke Lodge with lattice, from which spindly blue and green growths reached up towards the ceiling (Fig. 191). The simple treatment avoids such rococo exuberances as parrots and monkeys and is reminiscent of genuine ancient decorations like that of the 'Casa Pseudourbana'; the restraint betrays the design's neo-classical antecedents. Soane retained a liking for such fresh and spring-like decorations throughout his life;

**191** Design for interior at Pembroke Lodge, Richmond, by Sir John Soane, 1788

the ceilings of the Back Parlour at Pitzhanger of about 1802, and the Breakfast Room at Lincoln's Inn Fields of 1798, united trellis, leaves, flowers, festoons and sky with the star-shaped motif, also taken from an antique source, that he so favoured (see p.303).[72]

In two such designs of 1801 (or slightly earlier) for the Pavilion at Brighton, Pompeian doves flutter, flown to England by way of France.[73] At Southgate Grove in Middlesex, the Birdcage Room of about 1798 was wreathed in vegetation; in Queen Charlotte's Cottage at Kew, convolvolus grew up trellis, all probably painted by royalty.[74] The artist Mary Moser, famed for her flowers, was extensively employed by members of the royal family; she painted a ceiling at Frogmore with a splendidly be-flowered decoration (Pl. LXI). Towards the end of the period, flowers painted on walls and ceilings were sometimes given a gold background, which brought them closer to earlier styles.

The trellis and flowers combination was occasionally tinged with chinoiserie; Chinese wallpaper provided a genuine oriental alternative, and was used in 'panelled-out' decoration combined with chinoiserie detail; one of the most charming manifestations of this was the short-lived 'rococo' decoration of 1817 of the Saloon at Brighton (Pl. LXIII). A wallpaper from a vanished decoration in the same palace combined orientalising flowers and oval chinoiserie paintings in blue and silver to exquisite effect (Pl. LXII); this kind of decoration came to be thought particularly suitable for cottages ornés (see p.348).

**190** Detail of a wall 'In Casa Pseudourbana di Pompeii, piano superiore', 1796

## 'Landscape'

Whittock mentioned in 1827 another type of decoration seen in ancient murals; in the upper panels (above the dado) of Pompeian compartments were 'sometimes seen landscapes without figures'. These were not uncommon in antique times, and more examples have been uncovered since Whittock's day; they sometimes have a domestic flavour, as at the 'House of the Orchard' at Pompeii, which displays fig, plum, pear, apple, cherry and lemon trees organised in compartments. A famous example of such a Roman landscape room, in the House of Livia at Rome, combines landscape with compartmentalism. More elaborate landscapes were described by Vitruvius in a passage which, preceding his famous condemnation of 'Pompeian' fantasy, would have been known to everybody: 'ambulatories, being of a great length' (did this description and others inspire the long galleries of the Elizabethans?) were 'ornamented with landscapes . . . harbours, promontories, sea-coasts, rivers, fountains, canals, temples, groves, mountains, cattle and shepherds . . .'.[75] Whittock added that in Italian palaces 'at a later period' the panels were filled with landscape paintings; he may have been thinking of such decorations as those recorded of Claude (see p.21). The ravishing wall paintings by Fragonard (rejected by Mme. Dubarry) at the Frick Collection, which place dalliance in a luxuriously floriferous garden setting, the whole organised in compartments, are in essence a sophisticated development of the ancient tradition of landscape wall decoration. In about 1771 the dining room of Mlle. Guimard in Paris was entirely covered in a continuous and uncompartmented landscape with trees, clouds, and deities, all much in the feathery Fragonard style except that one detects neo-classicism in the formal trellis of the window walls.[76]

Landscape as interior decoration became popular in later eighteenth-century England, probably assisted by the interest in landscape nurtured by the Picturesque — Anna Seward said that the perspective of the Drakelowe Hall room painted in landscape by Thomas Sandby in 1793 was 'so well preserved as to produce a landscape deception little inferior to the watery illusion of the celebrated Panorama'.[77] The kind of landscape depicted on walls could be varied according to taste; after the growth of romanticism a choice existed between the neo-classical and romantic landscape.

An example well in the classical tradition is the 'Design for the Door side of the Little Drawing room for R. Burdon Esq. Grosvenor Square Dec. 1799' by William Atkinson; an idealised countryside, complete with treillage and classical temples, is brought into the town (Fig. 192). At Woolley Hall in Yorkshire the Drawing Room was decorated by the Italian Agostino Aglio (Fig. 193), who also painted the Hall and Staircase. The decorations throughout the Hall are called in the book commemorating them 'temporary',[78] connecting them with specific festivities, and there seems a distinct possibility that those for the Drawing Room were as temporary as the others and were regarded as temporary scene-painting (see p.223); the lack of a dado and the total absence of wall furniture points to a room organised for a fête rather than for ordinary domestic life (even Mlle. Guimard's room had a dado). The panels are topped with an arabesque frieze, with motifs at the corners of the panels; there are no pilasters, nor are there any pronounced three-dimensional architectural features. The plants and flowers in the window continue the vegetable theme.

Panoramic landscape rooms transposed into Gothic, Chinese, or Egyptian taste (Figs 243, 259, 262) also existed or were proposed; they shared much the same formula of compartmentalism and landscape

**192** 'Design for the Door side of the Little Drawing Room for R. Burdon Esq. Grosvenor Square Dec. 1799', by William Atkinson

**193** 'Drawing Room of Woolley Hall', 1821, decorated by Agostino Aglio
**194** Window blinds, 1803, designs by Paul Sandby

whatever the idiom. Wallpaper was used extensively to give the effect; especially splendid were the luxurious imported wallpapers of Dufour, which depicted vividly coloured and often exotic continuous landscapes, and which carried their oriental burden (1816) into a cottage orné in distant Ireland (see p.351).

Landscapes were used to decorate transparent blinds (Fig. 194), a natural extension of the idiom. Whittock devoted a whole section to them in his book of 1827, explaining the method of painting in transparent colours on fine Scotch cambric or lawn; he thought architectural scenes unfit subjects for such decoration, though if architecture were required, picturesque ruins and broken columns, obviously with an accompanying landscape, would be the most appropriate.

## Parquet

Interest in Pompeii and the antique may have helped to revive the fashion for parquet in the 1820s (Pl. LXV); the designs were commonly influenced (as were carpets)[79] by the magnificent mosaic pavements

**195** 'Mosaic pavement', published by John Goldicutt, 1825

that, surviving from Roman antiquity, included in their various motifs inventive arabesques, rectilinear patterns that played with illusionistic perspective, labyrinths, and fabulous and real creatures; the floors were extensively published (Fig. 195). Parquet had never entirely gone out of fashion; George Dance, for instance, designed inlaid floors in a neo-classical manner; one was made for the Music Room of Mount Stewart in County Down in 1805.[80] The fashion arose of having a parquetry border around the carpet, as at Apsley House in the 1820s; some of the patterns may have been inspired by the 'Etruscan' borders to the compartments on Greek vases. Sheraton in 1803 had asserted that 'since the introduction of carpets, fitted all over the floor of a room, the nicety of flooring anciently practised in the best houses, is now laid aside',[81] a complaint anticipated by Isaac Ware in 1756. There may have been truth in this. Mr. George Seddon, interrogated in 1831 by the Parliamentary Commission into Buckingham Palace and Windsor Castle (the financial chickens coming home to roost after the death of George IV), was asked about the satin wood and white holly floor of the 'bay drawing-room' at Buckingham Palace. It cost £1,986 plus the labour of laying it, and Seddon explained that the work had not been done by contract because he had told Nash it was impossible to estimate; he had never laid a wainscot floor before. He would not undertake another. The floor had been 'taken up and down once or twice'; £53.16s had been incurred — 'the extra expense of laying it down that His Majesty might see the effect of it'.[82] It is remarkable that major decorators such as Seddon and Company had no experience of laying parquet.

The sumptuous designs of James White, who laid his own floors, must have required expert handling (Pl. LXV). The strong colours show the intention before impairment by fading. White's inspiration was antique and architectural, with *trompe l'oeil* and illusionism enjoying the same popularity as in past centuries. In certain designs the type of continuous leaf design employed by George Bullock was used; the immediate source of inspiration may have been 'Etruscan', although the motif occurs in other antique contexts. The fashion for parquet grew steadily; by 1837 Peter Nicholson could write that 'the fashion of laying floors with various coloured woods, disposed in patterns, seems now to become more general in this country'.[83]

## 'Antique drapery'

A favourite neo-classical way of decorating a room without using pronounced three-dimensional architectural features was to drape it with fabric in an antique manner. This fashion, called by George Smith 'antique drapery',[84] originated in Greek and Roman decoration; it is seen on Greek vases, is used in Roman murals of scenes from everyday life, and appears, over and over again, in tombs (Fig. 196), on arabesque ceilings, and in domestic wall decorations. The drapery seen in ancient sources usually hangs in formal folds; these possibly originated from the use of unseamed widths of cloth, which would have articulated the drapery in a manner similar to that seen in the 'velarium' (Figs 225, 227; Pls LXXIX, LXXX; see p.292). Such ancient drapery occasionally assumes an air astonishingly 'high Regency' in effect, as is seen in a painting from Herculaneum (Figs 197, 198).

'Antique drapery' was revived as a motif in the fifteenth century; one sees it, for example, in works of the Central Italian school influenced by Mantegna; it was occasionally used by Raphael as a background to scenes depicting ancient life[85] and as a decoration. It appears as decorative detail in the arabesques of the Vatican Loggie.[86] Poussin frequently used it; one sees it in his recreation of Roman life in the *Sacrament of Penitence*. It became a commonplace in eighteenth-century paintings of ancient life, replacing baroque draperies as the neo-classical interest in archaeological accuracy increased.

The motif first became a constituent of advanced neo-classical interior decoration in the late 1770s and early 1780s; it was seized upon by the French, and in its early days was particularly associated with French style (although its revival probably originated in Italy). Percier and Fontaine often employed it. Sometimes, especially in bedrooms or boudoirs, the walls were virtually covered with fabric (Fig. 199;

**196** 'Roman Columbaria', published by Thomas Hope, 1809

Pls LXVI, LXVII). In tent rooms both walls and ceilings were concealed. It was a quick way of decorating, and in revolutionary and Napoleonic France speed, and sometimes portability, were not infrequently a consideration.

An early English example of 'antique drapery' may have existed in the francophile and fashionable young William Beckford's 'Turkish Room' at Fonthill Splendens. Created before Percier and Fontaine got into their stride, it was in *le dernier cri*, and most luxurious: 'The ground of the vaulted ceiling is entirely gold, upon which the most beautiful arabesques, and wreaths of flowers, are delineated in the vivid colours of nature, by . . . Boileau and Feuglet. The whole room is hung around with ample curtains of the richest orange satin, with deep fringes of silk

and gold. Between the folds of this drapery, mirrors of large size appeared to resemble openings leading to other apartments. . . . The windows are screened by blinds of orange silk, admitting a warm glow of summer light. Opposite to these apertures, an altar of the finest verd-antique contains the fireplace, secured by a grate-work of gilt bronze. On each side are two cabinets of elegant and novel form, sculptural and gilt in a magnificent style, the upper panels painted by Smirke, and the drawers by Hamilton. Candelabra, vases of Japan, cassolets, and piles of cushions, are distributed about the apartment.'[87]

The room was obviously in the latest (orientalising) French fashion. The ceiling, flower-painted in colour upon gold, sounds akin to the slightly later Percier and Fontaine version of a Renaissance and seventeenth-century idiom, and it anticipated later Regency taste; the plentiful use of mirror was common in France. Britton's mention of the 'warm glow of summer light' in reference to orange silk must have come from Beckford himself, who whilst on the Grand Tour wrote of embellishing his windows in Chinese style with transparent curtains to 'admit the glow of perpetual summer'[88] (at Lansdown Tower a square room beneath the lantern was hung with orange drapery). Also anticipating the later style was the use of pieces of lacquer together with furniture especially designed for (and perhaps partly by) Beckford; the two cabinets mentioned were decorated by Smirke and Hamilton in imitation of ancient cameos.[89] One cannot tell how 'antique' the draperies were in Beckford's Turkish Room at Fonthill Splendens, but the association of antique drapery with 'Turkish' ottomans, as in that room, was to become a Regency commonplace, and Beckford was always 'advanced'. Sheraton's drapery was *retardataire*. In 1793 he showed a 'Turkey Sofa' or ottoman within a draped alcove, probably based on a memory of what he had seen at Carlton House; despite its elevated origins, the drapery was in Sheraton's usual early manner (his drapery did not become 'antique' until the early 1800s (see p.376)). The undraped part of the wall is painted with arabesque.

Throughout the short Peace of Amiens, in 1802, the English swarmed on to the Continent; one of the principal sights was the house of Mme. Récamier, redecorated by Berthault in 1798 with the assistance of Percier. Maria Edgeworth gave the lay reaction to the bedroom: 'a room where are united wealth and taste, all of modern execution and ancient design that can contribute to its ornament'.[90] Farington, who visited the house in September 1802, said: 'Her House is furnished with singular elegance . . . evidently not in the way which any Upholsterer would propose but from the designs of an Architect of high and cultivated taste. There is also that uniformity in all the parts of the furniture [the term then included textiles] according properly to the design of the whole that shows that everything was done under the direction of one uniform plan . . . it is in the bedchamber of Mme. Récamier (Pl. LXVI) that the Artist has endeavoured to exhibit the

LXXIV  The Small Drawing Room, Windsor Castle, design for the west wall, c.1826–8

LXXV  Design for 'His Majesty's Closet', Windsor Castle, c.1826–8

**LXXVI** The Library, Windsor Castle, design for the east wall, c.1826–8, as approved by George IV

**197** 'Roman drapery', from a Pompeian wall decoration, 1765

**198** 'Drawing Room Window Curtains', from the *Repository*, 1816

highest proofs of his taste. It appears more like the design of a painter . . . than as intended or proper for mortal use. The whole is so ideal, that is so little similar to any fashion which prevails, that it certainly has the same effect on the mind that looking at a beautiful design in painting would have. The rich and costly appearance of the furniture is only a second consideration; it is the taste and elegance which most delight the eye'.[91] The bedchamber combined 'antique drapery' and arabesque, and appeared to Farington like a painting brought to life; his remark on the mode being so unlike any current fashion shows how long it took fashions to reach England.

Samuel Rogers also admired Mme. Récamier's house; however, he thought the Percier and Fontaine rooms at St. Cloud 'bad taste', a view echoed by Lady Holland, whose words help to explain why acceptance of the French style was limited in England. She described the apartments at St. Cloud in August 1802 as 'in le goût sévère, which, in other words, means a dark and dingy style. The walls are hung with cloth, and draperies of cloth edged with magnificent parti-coloured fringes are festooned over it. The colours being generally dark green and brown produce a solemn effect, and the whole has a sombre military appearance; the rods of the curtains are finely polished spears. Where the Queen's [Marie-Antoinette's] apartments have been preserved, I admire them far beyond those in the goût sévère, and prefer bright gilding to the heavy mahogany, and a well stuffed sofa to a small, hard one. In short, the exchange is a bad one, les ris et les amours please me, broad cloth and sphinxes do not.'[92] The way to the 'Louis Quatorze' revival was well prepared. It is fair to add that Fontaine himself had thought the scheme at Malmaison too sombre; 'Les lambris en acajou plein, les encadrements en velours et les draperies en étoffe sur les portes paraissent d'un effect triste'.[93] This last ensemble had been executed by Jacob in ten days.

Fully developed 'antique drapery' in the French manner is seen in George Smith's 'Boudoir with Ottomans' of 1804 (Fig. 199). Here the 'whole decoration is after the antique. The mantles on the wall are meant to be real, and of satin, muslin, or superfine cassimere; the borders worked in needlework or printed'. Alternatively, the 'whole of this ornamental Design may be executed in water-colour, on the walls,

**199** Boudoir with Ottomans, 1804, by George Smith

by a skilful artist'.[94] Or, Smith says, it could be executed in wallpaper. The staffs supporting the drapery were to be in matt gold. Unlike those shown by Sheraton, the ottomans are undraped. Fabrics, apart from borders, were often plain in the early Regency period, or only lightly patterned; stripes, although not as common as often supposed, were also used; they were sanctioned by antiquity, especially in the form of coverings for couch bolsters; the *Pitture Antiche d'Ercolano* shows several examples.

The use of 'antique drapery' thereafter became increasingly common (Fig. 228); it especially lent itself to curtains (Fig. 198) and bed-hangings (Pl. LXVIII), and its flat formalised folds were to be seen on sofas and other pieces of furniture (Pl. CXVII). It proved an alternative to the voluptuous swags that contributed so materially to the Regency upholsterer's ideal of 'profusion'; it appears to have been taken up by Ackermann's *Repository* and George Bullock as part of a campaign to improve taste (see pp.402–03). That campaign may have been provoked by the taste of which Carlton House, as redecorated under the hands of Walsh Porter, was the pre-eminent example.

The luxurious elaboration of the draperies of walls and curtains put up by Porter at Carlton House takes them far beyond the republican austerity of the original antique drapery. Paintings added to the richness of the effect; a plate in Percier and Fontaine's *Recueil* of 1802 showed a bedroom in which the 'antique drapery' on the walls had been partially obscured by 'tableaux de prix', a method adopted at Carlton House. The 'Rose Satin Drawing Room' (Pl. LXX) was comparatively simply hung, although the effect must have been sumptuous. The walls have no architectural features, save for the gilded pilasters that frame the swagged curtains; the same satin as on the walls covered the seat furniture. The ceiling largely survived from Holland's time. Splendid as the room was, it paled beside the 'Crimson Drawing Room' (Pl. LXXI); beneath the Italianate Holland ceiling, studiously 'antique', the walls are heavily draped in damask; the developed flounces and furbelows, with their heavy fringe, almost approach a late sevententh or early eighteenth-century manner.[95] The walls were progressively hung at intervals between 1805 and 1813, which would have allowed stylistic development. Dutch and Flemish paintings played a major part, as in the Rose Satin Drawing Room; those above the doors in the Crimson Drawing Room, of which three may be seen in the view, were identically framed in 'Louis Quatorze' frames. Was Carlton House the place where the 'Louis Quatorze' revival began (see p.305)? The Prince's self identification with the Grand Monarque is well known; he walked on blue carpets strewn with gold fleurs-de-lis; association-alism at this period was two steps towards re-creation. The black and gold doors and the black marble and gilt-bronze satyr chimney-pieces, supplied by the Vulliamys in 1807, emphasise the weighty sumptuosity.[96]

The King's Bedroom at Windsor was decorated with 'antique drapery' in austere mode at a surprisingly late date for England — the Continent enjoyed a late flowering of 'antique drapery' in the designs of Schinkel and others, and it lent simple charm to many a Biedermeier window, but it appears to have been less common in England. The work at Windsor, completed before the King's death in 1830, was executed by Morel and Seddon, a firm which, apart from a large commision to supply furniture worth over £15,000 for Stafford House, seems to have worked principally for the royal family. The bill for Windsor was settled at £179,300.18s.9d. in 1831 after one of over £200,000 had been disputed. The assistants used included Bogaerts; J.-J. Boileau; F. H. G. Jacob-Desmalter; and A. W. N. Pugin;[97] the French contingent was dominant. The King's Bedroom is much in the French style of thirty years earlier (Pl. LXVII); the walls are draped in pale hyacinth silk hangings edged with gold, with cream silk in the bed alcove. The strong accents of *pietra dura* on the commodes, which have tops of white marble, contrast with the plain silk in much the same way as did the Percier and Fontaine furniture in Mme. Récamier's bedroom (Pl. LXVI). The bed, which stands on a marble plinth, is in the style of Jacob-Desmalter; an alternative design shows the bed alcove simply framed in giltwood, as was also the recess for the bath; a sun-ray pleat spread its rays behind the bed. The bath, 'the vapours of which when heated must prove rather an inconvenience',[98] stands within a recess backed with mirror and hung with fluted cream fabric behind blue silk curtains; the bath cover, of oak veneered with rosewood, satinwood, and purplewood, and mounted in gilt bronze, with twenty-two *pietra dura* plaques ('old Florentine tablets') may have been designed by

Jacob-Desmalter; it was made by Morel and Seddon.[99] The general effect of the placing of the plaques on the bath cover, combined with the character of its decoration, is reminiscent of Roman arabesque. The window curtains, *en suite* with the blue hangings, were hung in the same style, and when closed looked exactly like them (Pl. LXVII extreme right); their simplicity strongly contrasts with the ornate arrangements characteristic of mainstream late Regency taste. The giltwood chairs and sofa designed for the room share the same rich restraint. This exquisite ensemble is remarkable as an exercise in an outmoded style; it demonstrates the versatility and the conservatism of George IV's taste.

The design for the Boudoir is in much the same idiom (Pl. LXIX). The walls were hung with flat rather than draped damask; the curtains were draped simply, although not with quite the antique austerity of those in the Bedroom. Two fine Louis XVI side tables are by Carlin, inlaid with blue and white Wedgwood plaques; next to them were chairs by Morel and Seddon in a style favoured by the early Empire; 'Six Gondola chairs ornamented & gilt as designed, stuffed back and seats, covered with the office silk, & furnished with gimp etc.' Of carved and gilt walnut, they had sabre legs, down swept side rails ending in a dolphin's head, and delicate vertical rails that form the lower part of the back.[100] The Boudoir contained also candelabra that had come from the Throne Room at Carlton House, the gilt wood pedestals perhaps having been designed by Daguerre in about 1794.[101] The general impression of the room must, once again, have been of a return to an earlier period.

## The tent room

One could, by going just a little further, entirely envelop the room in fabric, thus creating the 'tent room'. The tent room had antique, oriental and military associations and was thus trebly attractive; originally a French fashion — a bedroom hung as a military tent, designed by Belanger, was installed at Bagatelle in the 1770s — it later appeared in French publications. Stripes were thought appropriate for tents and tented canopies, and had for example been used for the tented constructions erected at L'Isle Adam for the famous alfresco banquet given in 1766 by the Prince de Conti; such tents were similar to Roman examples depicted on Trajan's column and elsewhere. Napoleon's 'Salle de conseil' at Malmaison, where he and his ministers and generals conferred surrounded by Percier and Fontaine's authentic decor, was constructed as a military tent; it seems to have been striped.[102] The Prince of Wales planned and perhaps erected a 'Silk Tent' or 'Military Tent Room' at Carlton House, and sarsenet hangings of pale blue and white stripes were purchased.[103] The tent form was thought also highly appropriate for the boudoir; the association here was probably with the seraglio, and the ottoman, with its Turkish associations, was often to be

200 'Boudoir de la Princesse de Courlande', Paris, 1802

found in tented boudoirs. Perhaps the boudoir and the military tent have more in common than appears at first sight.

A typical French example of the former was the boudoir of Queen Hortense in the rue Cerutti, which also had an ottoman;[104] it had mirrors behind curtains in the manner of Hope's Flaxman Room (see p.273); the material was pleated, and the room had triangular lambrequins, which had both Turkish and mediaeval associations. Despite the greater 'luxe', something of a military air remained, plainly to be seen also in the Boudoir of the Princesse de Courlande as pictured by Krafft and Ransonette (Fig. 200). This last room had pleated pink silk that opened on to a mirror behind an ottoman; it also had triangular lambrequins, decorated with Turkish crescents, with stars, and fringes in gold. Mme. de Courlande's Boudoir was published in 1802; George Smith's 'Octangular Tent Room' of 1826 had similarities (Pl. LXXII), especially in the lambrequins with crescents. Like the Boudoir, the Octangular Tent Room was of pleated material: 'The face of each side is covered with calico gathered in plaits, which may be of one plain colour, or these plaits may vary alternately in colour viz. green and white, white and pink, lilac and yellow or otherwise, as choice and taste may dictate'.[105] The exotic note sounded in tent and crescents appears to be continued in the fitted carpet, which was probably meant to suggest tiles; similar unused designs exist for the Corridor of the Pavilion at Brighton.[106] Smith shows the fabric as green and white, with gold cords and tassels (a trim like that in the Boudoir of the Princesse de Courlande) and crimson curtains, window ottomans, chairs and sofa. An up-to-date note is struck by the 'Louis Quatorze' clock on the chimney-piece.

The Prince of Wales adopted the new fashion early; his bedroom of 1787 at the Marine Pavilion was hung in quilted chintz; probably a tent room, it was certainly a draped room. At a slightly later period his bed was indisputably 'fitted up as a tent' and in 1802–04 a design was made for an alcove with a tent ceiling, either for the bedroom or, more probably, the boudoir; it also had an ottoman.[107] Apparently again designed for chintz, the form of the draperies is not that of 'antique drapery'; it is more like the festoons commonly used in the 1790s, as in Sheraton's 'Turkey Sofa' of 1793. And the King, with that extraordinary mixture of adventurousness and conservatism so typical of him, remained faithful to the idea of his boudoir at Brighton as a tent room through all the exotic transformations of the next twenty-five years. In the early 1830s 'His Majesty's (old) Boudoir' was described as having 'fluted blue silk on the walls and ceiling (entirely decaded/festooned and fringed with same silk, and white ground blue pattern convolvolus, calico blue silk ropes, tuft fringe — white silk ropes, bell tassels and tufted fringe — the centre compartment having four fasces or standards . . .' (Pl. LXXIII).[108]

Thomas Hope had his tent room at Duchess Street, a 'closet or boudoir' (Fig. 265).[109] The exotic note was again struck; the room was 'fitted up for the reception of a few Egyptian, Hindoo, and Chinese idols and curiosities'. The draped walls and tent ceiling, of cotton with a heavy fringe, were articulated with bamboo pillars and laths; an undisturbed surface of mirror was placed behind the chimney-piece, which was designed from an Egyptian pylon; the superstructure on which the ornaments stand suggests a simplification of more elaborate inventions in Piranesi's *Diverse Maniere*. The disparate ingredients were integrated with masterly judgment and astonishing success.

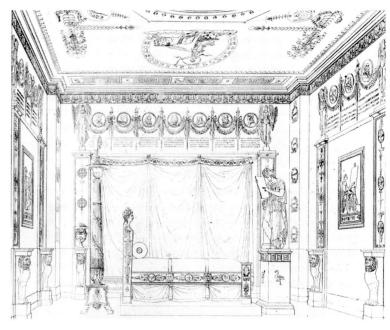

201 'Vue perspective de l'Atelier de Peinture du C. I. xxx à Paris', 1812, designed by Percier and Fontaine

202 The Flaxman Room at the Duchess Street house of Thomas Hope, 1807

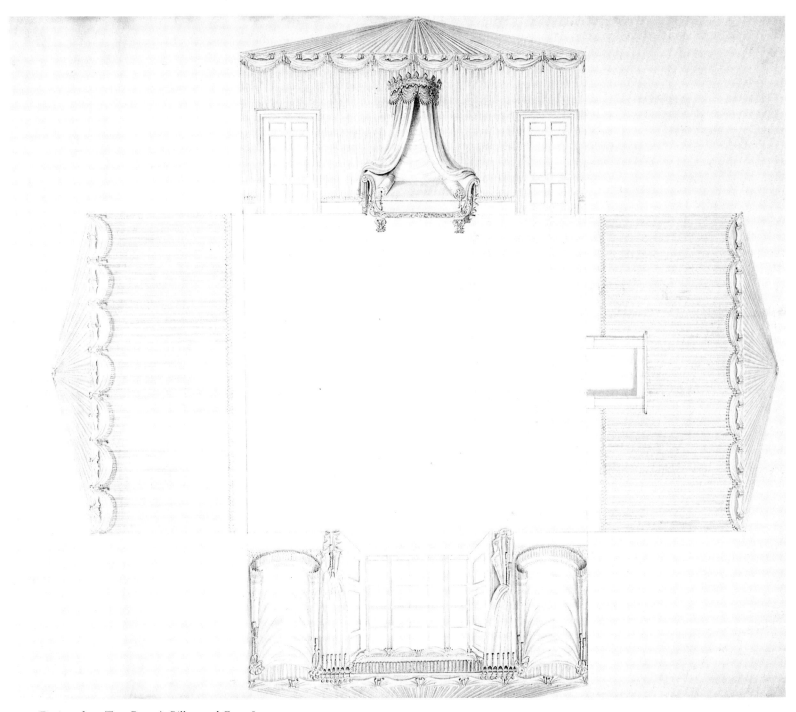

**203** 'Designs for a Tent Room', Gillow and Co., 1820s

Walsh Porter's palace of varieties at Craven Cottage had a 'Tartar's or Persian chieftain's tent, very complete, ornamented with panels of looking glass, which between the blue striped linings of the tent' — blue stripes — had the Prince of Wales's Carlton House project some connection with this (a little spare material)? — 'had a peculiar effect: it was lighted from the top by a window in the form of a crescent'.[110] The

**204** 'Monsr. J. Isabey's Exhibition Rooms
61 Pall Mall', June 1820

tent remained popular throughout the period; a design for a tent room by Gillow and Company from the 1820s shows a room made up of pleated silk with elaborate swags and draped panels; its 'Frenchness' is accentuated by a 'French' bed with a domed canopy (Fig. 203). The tent ceiling was employed not exclusively in high-style decoration; its ease and cheapness made it as popular for exhibition use in the Regency period as today; a typical example was that of the gallery in Pall Mall of the French artist Isabey, whose delicate touch had itself depicted so many charming interiors (Fig. 204).

## Percier and Fontaine

The Percier and Fontaine style was much studied by the English. Had it not been for the wars, it might well have been directly commissioned by them. Percier and Fontaine designed no house in England (unlike the Italians Asprucci and Bonomi), although a letter exists in the Tatham sketchbook (an interesting provenance) at the R.I.B.A. from Percier to a Colonel Graham concerning the designing of a 'Maison de Campagne', proposed as a single-storey house with 'Venetian' windows and a treillage walk; the date was 1802, during the Peace of Amiens.[111]

The Percier and Fontaine style had a distinctive character. It was a highly accomplished and sophisticated fusion of all available antique and Renaissance sources,[112] uniting a rigid geometrical framework with a luxuriant, meticulous, and frigid arabesque; 'Pompeian', 'Etruscan' and Raphaelesque arabesque were intimately integrated with each other. Tatham had called the Adam brothers the 'children of the Arabesque' (see p.235); but how much more true this was of Percier and Fontaine! The line engravings, exquisite as they are, give a false idea of the reality; colour cancels the occasional finickiness, and, often accompanied by lavish gilding, produces a harmonious magnificence. It was a new style; it could be serene and congenial, well fitted for lofty domesticity, or it could be overpoweringly magnificent and vibrantly rich, suited to imperial pretensions. It could be executed mainly in flat painting (Fig. 201), in which case the arabesque was the most frequently employed motif,[112] or it could be architectural (Fig. 232), when the inspiration often came from Italian palaces. When used in a grand manner the style impressed with glitter, strong colour, and complexity; as Fontaine said of their redecoration of the Tuileries: 'des glaces répétant la décoration; des arcades . . . multiplient l'effet des pilastres, qui reçoivent les corniches et réfléchissent la lumière . . .'; he spoke of the arabesques 'dont les ornements légers et dont les couleurs brillantes peuvent, par leurs reflets, ajouter encore à l'effet des glaces qui sont répétées sur toutes les faces'.[113] The English equivalent of this aspect of the Percier and Fontaine style is to be found (despite differences) in the brilliant colour, congested decoration, and profuse gilding of certain apartments at Carlton House and Windsor Castle.

**205** 'A Hall Chimney Piece & Lights', a design by G. Cooper, 1807

Some found it much to their taste. Of these the most eminent was Hope, who knew Percier and Fontaine well. His own sense of style was too strong for slavish imitation, but the Flaxman Room at Duchess Street closely approached the Percier style (Figs 201, 202); certain features had been prefigured in the earlier Turkish Room at Fonthill Splendens, including the orange satin drapery; the Flaxman Room had orange satin 'draped in ample folds over pannels of looking-glass'.[114] The curtains were of 'the fiery hue which fringes the clouds just before sunrise'; they were edged with black velvet, hung over looking-glass. The sky was decorated with roses and stars, 'still unextinguished luminaries of the night'; the table tops and chimney-piece were black marble; the furniture was 'chiefly gilt'; the Flaxman *Aurora visiting Cephalus* and other sculptures were white marble.[115] Orange, blue, black, white and gold — a strongly conceived and contrasting colour scheme, absent from the chilly line engraving. The frieze adds to the likeness to Percier and Fontaine.

Despite the similarities intensified by the common use of outline, nobody would confuse the style of Hope with that of Percier. Hope's style, equally sophisticated, is simpler, stronger, even brutal. One can discern the cast of his mind and his method by looking at a few designs for chimney-pieces. The first, published in 1807, the same year as his *Household Furniture*, is by George Cooper (Fig. 205). It is undigested Percier and Fontaine, its martial symbolism influenced by perhaps two

of their designs, the bed 'pour un guerrier grand chasseur' and the tent room at Malmaison.[116] Another design by Cooper shows elaborate patriotic marine symbolism. Few English clients would have found attractions in such highly wrought designs. If one now looks at two French designs for chimney-pieces, not from Percier but from Krafft and Ransonette (Fig. 206), and compares them with Plate 58 of Hope's 1807 book, one can see what Hope made of them (Fig. 207). The French examples, shown adjacent in Krafft's book, are classical (Jove's thunderbolt, laurel wreaths, Victories) and Egyptian (the winged serpent, the sistrum, sphinxes). From the first Hope took the semi-circular opening, the high plinth (adding to it the 'step' from above the plinth of the second), and the general outline; from the second he took the fender and the sphinxes, the latter metamorphosed into griffins. Selective elimination of the subdivisions and ornament has rendered the synthesis immeasurably more distinguished than its prototypes.

John Nash went to Paris for the first time in October 1814; when he built his house in Regent Street between 1819 and 1823, it was given shops on the ground floor, as in Paris; the interiors also displayed French influence. 'The principal story is . . . a most generous affair of gilding, ultra-marine, and the newly invented Mosaic gold [a patented alloy] in the richest Parisian style imaginable. The Cafe de mille colonnes, or Napoleon's Salle des Marechales, are nothing to it, for flutter, multiplicity of mouldings, filigrain, and leaf gold. Mr. Nash

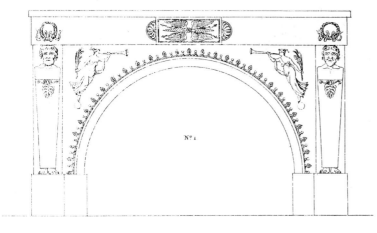

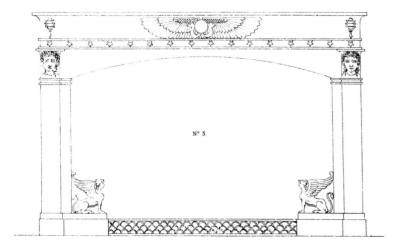

206 'Diverses cheminées', published by Krafft and Ransonette, 1802

Plate 58

207 A chimney-piece, Duchess Street, designed by Thomas Hope, published 1807

seems to have emulated in these apartments the laboured elaborateness of finish that characterizes the works of M. Percier'.[117] The Library or Gallery (Fig. 208) — liked by Nash enough to be re-erected at East Cowes Castle on his retirement — seems simpler than Percier (although recorded detail is omitted in the print), and the mouldings are typical Nash, reappearing, for instance, in the King's Library at Brighton; apart from that, the resemblance to Percier is close. The 'arabesques . . . copied from those in the Vatican, admirably executed in fresco, adorn the broad pilasters between the niches';[118] these are much of the Percier type. In each niche was an oculus, and in the lunette below a 'fresco' copy of a painting from the 'Logge di Rafaelle'; these copies by Richard Evans, an assistant of Lawrence, were painted in Rome and may have been executed in the technique that Evans used for his fakes of Pompeian paintings. The Renaissance-style arabesque confirmed the direction in which taste was then moving — towards the Italy of palaces. The arabesque was complemented by 'casts of the best antique statues', and copies after Titian, Guido, Caravaggio and Guercino.[119] The walls and pilasters were closely decorated with 'a pale red stucco, with small gold mouldings',[120] and it looks from the print as if the pilaster side on the window bay may have been filled with mirror; all very Percier and Fontaine.

## Classical revivalism

Classical styles that attempted 'archaeological' accuracy, and were based more or less directly on the antique without the employment of intermediary interpretations, in other words 'neo-classical' styles, were supplemented in the 1820s and 1830s by styles based on the earlier classical revivals of the Italian Renaissance and the French and English seventeenth centuries. During the Regency period the term 'Louis Quatorze' was used of a classical revival style that was often more than touched with eighteenth-century rococo (which historically had begun to appear before the end of Louis XIV's reign); to avoid confusion the term 'Louis Quartorze' is used in these pages in that sense; it is applied only to the French revival style that displayed a strong rococo influence; this is dealt with as a separate style, distinct from the grand seventeenth-century revivalism that was only slightly, if at all, affected by the rococo. Another complication is that some English (rather than French) seventeenth-century revivalism was in a sense involuntary, in that its creators imagined they were producing a sixteenth-century effect; the source of error was the fact that certain favourite 'antiquarian' objects that were in reality seventeenth century were thought in the Regency period to be Tudor or earlier (the best known example of this is the seventeenth-century East India ebony furniture that was so popular in antiquarian furnishings). In cases where the antiquarian element is paramount the result is dealt with below under

**208** The Library, or 'Gallery in the house of John Nash Esqr.', Regent Street, 1822–4

the heading 'Gothic', as is the Regency amalgam of Tudor and Jacobean known today as 'Jacobethan' (associated as both so often were with Gothic architectural detail). In fine, this section will treat of Renaissance and seventeenth-century classical revivalism; 'Louis Quatorze' and antiquarian revivalism will be treated elsewhere.

### 'Seventeenth century'

Signs of an interest in English seventeenth-century interior decoration and a sympathetic attitude towards old houses became evident quite early in the eighteenth century. An instance occurred at Blickling Hall in the 1760s, when the second Earl of Buckinghamshire installed a new Eating Room within the shell of the old Jacobean parlour, retaining the ancient wooden chimney-piece (despite the threats of wife and sister to burn it during his absence), and panelling the new room in wainscot; the new doorcases imitated the Jacobean detail of the chimney-piece, although there was more than a hint of eighteenth-century arabesque. New woodwork on the staircase, by the Ivorys of Norwich, was also 'Jacobean'.[121] Such a pastiche of seventeenth-century work, although early, had had precursors.

It was not unprecedented that old decoration should be preserved or imitated, but the scale on which this was done in the Regency period was new. One of the pioneers was Lewis Wyatt, who at Lyme Park (1814–17) and Hackwood (1807–13 and later), produced Wren, Jacobean, and Tudor interiors (including Gibbons pastiches carved by Edward Wyatt) twenty or so years before Salvin and Blore.[122] The intention to preserve was explicit in the words written by Wyatville in

1818 on the title-page of his designs for the rejuvenation of Chatsworth, grandest of English late seventeenth-century houses: 'These designs are formed on the principle of adhering to the Character of the present building, of gaining all the required advantages and adding to the grandeur of the place'.[123]

William Beckford appears to have revived seventeenth-century styles on an extensive scale at Fonthill Abbey, intentionally and unintentionally. Unfortunately, save for the 'Western Yellow Drawing Room' ('so called from the hangings of an apartment which, though open to the south and west, are yellow!')[124] the rooms in the castellated eastern wing of the Abbey, the habitable apartments, were not illustrated, and we depend on written accounts. In certain rooms an English seventeenth-century taste appears to have prevailed. The 'Oak Parlour' had walls which, 'where not covered with tapestry, are wainscoted with a fine deep brown oak; the doors and the fittings of the windows are the same. They have the regular bold mouldings and raised panels of the Anglo-Italian manner, which prevailed at the beginning of the last century, and are not gothic'. The marble chimney-piece 'without mantel' was 'of the same manner as the wainscoting'. There is no mention of carpet on the 'very fine' oak floor. The contents included girandoles said to be from Fontainebleau, with 'oak branches, horns, deers' feet, and other emblems of hunting' introduced into the design. In 'the centre of the east end is a pile of massy decorative gilt plate of various styles and ages', including seventeenth-century pieces; such a piling-up of accoutrements was an ancient habit.

Of the 'same style of fitting up as the oak parlour' was the Oak Library, which contained an 'extensive and costly' collection of historical books for the use of artists and architects engaged on the Abbey. This room was carpeted with a lozenge pattern in black and scarlet; it had a massive library table 'covered with purple velvet', an antique or antiquarian mode according to emphasis. The walls were covered in oak wainscot, in 'large raised panels and deep bolection mouldings', with doors and closet doors concealed; the effect was marred for Rutter by the inclusion of 'imitation oak' and mahogany. The next room, the 'Cedar Boudoir', was an octagonal room entirely furnished in cedar, including the ceiling;[125] cedar had been fashionable in the later seventeenth century, and for Repton in 1816 was synonymous with out-moded antiquity (see p.222).

Two other rooms at Fonthill should be mentioned. One, the 'Lancaster State Bed Chamber', seems to have been much in the 'Tudor' (really seventeenth-century) style; the ceiling was oak, and the dado wainscot, above which the walls were crimson. The furniture was wholly of ebony 'studded with ivory'; it included an 'ebony and marble robe cabinet', a 'carved ebony Persian cabinet', and 'an ebony state bedstead, with crimson damask hangings';[126] the last, now at Charlecote,

is seventeenth-century East India trade furniture. The Bed Chamber sounds pure Edgar Allan Poe (one wonders, incidentally, whether Poe's insistence on the need for 'aristocracy' was any reflection of Beckford's pathological snobbery).

'Seventeenth century' proclivities were not confined to the great and the eccentric. Joseph Potter of Lichfield, who had worked with James Wyatt on Lichfield and Hereford Cathedrals, and who became cathedral architect at Lichfield, designed a dining room in something of a 'Wren' style for Grendon Hall, Warwickshire, which he rebuilt in Elizabethan style in about 1825 (Fig. 209).[127] The wooden panelling, probably meant to be grained, entirely covers the chimney-breast, and bears a carved acanthus wreath and bust; above the panelled dado the walls are painted red. The chimney-piece, a simple black marble Gothic design, was probably thought appropriate with the wainscot.

There was much mingling of Tudor and seventeenth century; the Elizabethan period had a romantic and patriotic aura that gave it popularity up to the mid-century and beyond (the publication in 1855 of Kingsley's *Westward Ho!* was to place it within the reach of every schoolboy). A grandiose design of 1840 (Fig. 210) for an 'Elizabethan Library' is representative of what found its way into many of the more aspirant 'Jacobethan' horses that were being built at this period; the brown panelling would probably have been grained, in a graining that still survives in the back passages of many old country houses. Or 'the old oak carvings may be imitated in deal, which when stained and waxed, will have a handsome appearance'.[128] Other, humbler designs provided the kind of 'respectable' library in which Archdeacon Grantly might have written his sermons and read his Rabelais.

The finest interiors in England in grand seventeenth-century revival style were those created by that master impresario George IV at Windsor; this revivalism was by no means academic, in contrast to the archaeological bent of neo-classicism. The Windsor interiors were created by the upholsterer rather than the architect, and the intention appears to have been to emulate seventeenth-century pomp: 'nothing can conceal the dazzling splendour of the gilding, which seems to be much overdone, as Mr. W-ville said it was "His Majesty's Taste". The ceilings are a mass of gilding and panelling, pilasters etc. the same'.[129] The interiors were antipathetic to Cockerell: 'the eternal set of Lib, draw Ro and ding Ros. but scarcely a gentn. he understands much less what is royal [it is not quite clear whether 'scarcely a gentn.' refers to the King or to his architect!] ceilings without skill or beauty, especially drawg. Ro proportion of which is quite spoilt. disapprove style of Louis 14th . . . no sculpture but of the lowest carvers, no painting but house painting, absolutely mechanical throughout the whole building . . .'.[130] Cockerell's father must have realised he was going against the grain when in May 1817 he advised his son to make his way in the world through interior decoration: 'You will be surprised to find more

**209** 'Chimney side of the Dining room',
Grendon Hall, design by Joseph Potter, c.1825

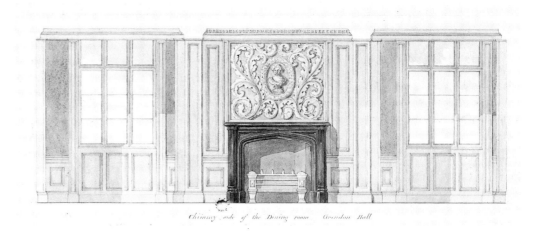

*Chimney side of the Dining room    Grendon Hall*

**210** Design for an 'Elizabethan Library',
by H. W. Arrowsmith, 1840

importance attached to the decorations of a Saloon than to the building of a Temple: if you can therefore bend to the consideration of what is called the fittings up of the best Hotels and Palaces of Paris, the graces of Their Meubles and the harmony of their Colours in Hangings painting and Gilding You may be the general Arbiter of Taste here'; he mentioned Percier as the first architect and Desmalter and Jacob as the first 'decorators in furniture'.[131] It was good advice as far as the world went, as the Windsor interiors testify.

The panelled ceilings and the lambrequin pelmets of the Library curtains (Pl. LXXVI) — no Regency swags — have obvious seventeenth-century affiliations; the baroque scrolls of the lambrequins are in the Marot style. The panelled doors, not shown in the illustration, have carved and gilded Louis XVI pearwood trophies. The scroll on the coving is similar to that on four six-light candelabra on tripod stands by the Vulliamy firm, originally delivered to Carlton House between 1810 and 1814.[132] Within the compartments on the walls is flat green damask trimmed with gold; the material supplied for the curtains and chair coverings included 'Green Flowered Tissue' at 38/- a yard, and 'Green Gros de Naple all boil'd Silk' at 6/10d a yard (in September 1827 the *Windsor and Eton Express* declared that £80,000 worth of the richest British silk drapery had been supplied for the State Apartments, including 1,600 yards at four guineas a yard). Morel and Seddon charged £300[133] for an Axminster carpet by Boileau, its design drawn from antique sources (Pl. LXXIV). The chimney-piece, a sumptuous confection with bronze satyrs, came from the Crimson Drawing Room at Carlton House (Pl. LXXI).

Seven of the bookcases, made by Tatham, Bailey and Saunders in 1814, had been in the Gilt Column Room at Carlton House; five more were now made to match by Morel and Seddon.[134] Other furniture from Carlton House included the gilt-bronze tripod stands 'after those found in the ruins of Herculaneum'[135] supplied by Rundells in 1811, and two carved and gilded tripod crane stands, probably made in 1811[136] after the well known candelabrum from Hadrian's Villa. Added to twelve chairs from Carlton House was a set of fifty-three new sofas, armchairs, chairs, stools, and screens. These included X-frame chairs (not those in the illustration), a shape which carried associations with the antique, with the Renaissance, with the English seventeenth century, and with Kent. The Library also contained boulle tables, probably French. In sum, the room and its contents, although inclining to the antique and the seventeenth century, were thoroughly miscellaneous, the tenor of the whole being contradicted by the glimpse of Gothic glazing bars beneath the pelmets. All was held together by a strong ruling taste, and there is no hint in the design of the coarse vivacity of 'Louis Quatorze'.

The design for the Small Drawing Room (Pl. LXXIV) has strongly patterned green and gold damask in compartmented walls set in white and gold; the arabesque of the Library is absent. The curtains, in rich green and gold fringed with gold (not illustrated), were hung in the 'antique drapery' mode and completely concealed the Gothic glazing bars. The framework of the doors is strongly architectural, unlike those in the Library; the doors finally used were probably not those shown on the design. Another scheme (not illustrated) has 'Ebony Cabinet Door(s), richly ornamented in Ormolu', probably by F. H. G. Jacob-Desmalter;[137] these would have echoed the ebony, gilt-bronze and *pietra dura* cabinets that came from Carlton House. The splendid armorial trophies framed above doors and mirror came probably from the same source. In execution, some detail in the room — the corner pieces to the panels, the coving — acquired a rococo air. The furniture included the neo-Kentian chairs illustrated, X-framed stools in Versailles fashion, and Holland candelabra from Carlton House.

Compartmented red and gold damask in a white and gold room was proposed for 'His Majesty's Closet' (Pl. LXXV). There are arabesque panels on either side of the glass; the chimney-piece is in marble and ormolu. On either side of Louis XVI boulle cabinets are X-framed giltwood chairs by Morel and Seddon. The boulle torchères are in seventeenth-century style; the *Windsor and Eton Express* in November 1828 mentioned furniture moved from the despoiled and neglected palaces of Brighton, Hampton Court and Kensington to the Castle, and seventeenth-century furniture was probably included. Damask was not the only wall covering used; the paper hangers Robson & Hale supplied paper described by Princess Augusta in September 1827, when she went to see the papers made 'to fit up the Private or Company Apartments. They really are magnificent. Robson . . . is a very clever man. He has produced a flock paper with gold; and by a process with oil the flock loses its roughness and looks like a velvet ground. All the paper done in that way has the perfect effect of silk or velvet according to which it is to resemble'.[138]

## 'Renaissance revival'

Beckford ventured early on 'Renaissance Revival'; a group of rooms at Fonthill — the Great Dining Room, Crimson Drawing Room, and Grand Drawing Room (Fig. 238) — introduced something of this character. The first two were crimson, the last was hung with garter-blue and gold silk damask. All had beamed ceilings in early Renaissance style; 'not quite free from an air of rudeness . . . their shadows are deep and powerful . . . painted in imitation of oak';[139] that in the Crimson Drawing Room had carved and gilt corbels. The first two rooms were furnished almost exclusively in French, Italian and East Indian ebony, boulle, and lacquer; eighteenth-century artefacts were employed in the third (see pp.401–02). The last contained paintings by Claude, Veronese, Vandyck, Philippe de Champaigne, Rubens, Cuyp, Bronzino, and Watteau.

These particular Fonthill interiors shared some features with the intriguing series of late Regency interiors designed by Beckford for Lansdown Tower (Fig. 211; Pls LXXVII, LXXVIII), which seem to represent an 'old age' style, in which the frills have been discarded for a powerful simplicity. Beckford was more subtle here than at Fonthill; the historicism is evident, but has been absorbed. As in the work of George IV and his decorators at Windsor, one sees the distance which separates a brilliant and controlled creation based on taste from antiquarian miscellanies such as those of Scott and Meyrick (see pp.327, 328, 330, 423). Beckford died in 1844, designing, acquiring, and quarrelling to the last; in the year of his death a volume by Maddox and English was published that records these last interiors.

Certain ingredients are found elsewhere, but nowhere else was the ensemble so distinguished. The essential components are heavily timbered ceilings, plain in profile, albeit 'enriched with scarlet, purple and gold'[140] (one should mention in parenthesis that such beamed ceilings were not free from ambiguity, in that Sir William Gell's reconstructions of Pompeian interiors, for instance, show similar heavy beams).[141] There were flat walls either with a dado, or quite plain, and massive furniture, usually in oak or ebony, which had a pronounced 'Renaissance' flavour. There was an extensive use of marble and various hardstones. The colour schemes, in scarlet, blue and gold, were simple, to an extent that perhaps made even Beckford pause: 'To tell you the truth, I am rather afraid of the lumpish effect of so much scarlet en masse — I do not wish to change the hanging, until I have fixed upon a colour more to my mind'.[142]

The preface to the text of English's book tells us that 'the first embellishments of this charming edifice were sold a few years ago, with the view of finishing the whole more classically, as it now stands'. This sounds like information from Beckford, and one wonders what exactly he then understood by 'classically'. The classicism of Lansdown Tower is not what was usually meant by the term; it is more like the 'classicism' of the early Renaissance.[143] The heavy beamed ceilings; the flat walls with architectural furniture, often in the form of hanging cupboards;[144] even the shape of the arched windows, recall interiors such as those in fifteenth-century Flemish paintings or in the Carpaccio *St. Ursula* series. The windows are especially telling; in many fifteenth-century paintings they lack glass, their optical effect resembling that of the round-headed windows of the Belvedere of Lansdown, each of which is filled with a single sheet of plate glass without glazing bars; or they have small round panes of blown glass similar in effect to that of the roundels within the door at the end of the Ante Room (Fig. 211). The red and blue colour schemes recall the symbolic use of red and blue robes in Italian paintings of the Virgin and Child; lunettes in the Sanctuary painted by Maddox illustrating the life of Christ employ red and blue in the robes. Rhetorical though it was, Beckford had a strong

**211** The Ante Room, Lansdown Tower, Bath, published in 1844

streak of religiosity; a statue of the Virgin and Child stood in the Lansdown Tower Oratory. Was the decoration of Lansdown Tower partly inspired by fifteenth-century interiors as depicted in paintings? There may have been other contemporary influences tending to the same result.[145] We have seen at Fonthill earlier examples of Beckford's feeling for beamed ceilings, and Charles Kelsall included what could have been Renaissance-type ceilings in his vision of a classical Windsor Castle of 1827; two large folding doors of richly carved oak were to lead to the principal apartments, lined with American cedar and furnished in crimson silk: 'if you take 4 or 500 Venetian sequins, and hammer them into fine leaf gold, setting off these with cedar roofs, composed of beams laid transversely, and exhibiting carved roses, richly gilt, in design receding hexagons, you will have a ceiling as notable perhaps, as can reasonably be imagined'.[146]

The stairway of Lansdown Tower announced the style. Circular, with ascetically unadorned walls and a plain staircase of archaic form,

**212** Design for a drawing room by Gillow and Co., 1820s

it had at its foot a monumentally 'noble vase of polished granite'[147] decorated with bronzes of a bare simplicity that allowed the volumetric qualities of the stone full expression. The aquatint of the ante room to the dining room (Fig. 211) shows the first of the beamed ceilings, with a simple egg and dart fillet; the architectural features are simple and Italianate; a triple-arched mirror, shaped like an early Renaissance window but with modern French affiliations also, stands over a massive Siena marble side table almost Romanesque in its severity; the table bears three antique 'Etruscan' vases. The benches, with their weighty volutes and crossed rails, have an air of the Renaissance version of the antique. The door, unadorned apart from bolts, has similarities to antique motifs used at the Deepdene. The colours are restrained; brown wood and a pinkish terracotta, with a red carpet that is employed in other rooms.

The depiction of the Scarlet Drawing Room (Pl. LXXVII) shows plain scarlet moreen walls[148] without architectural embellishments, and a carpet of the same tone; the plain scarlet and blue curtains hang from rods without draping, as at Fonthill (see p.314). The oak furniture is strongly architectural in character (Pl. CXXV; see p.412); the wall cabinets carry coffers, beneath which stand vases of porphyry, verd-antique, and Egyptian granite. The table is boldly modelled of contrasting scrolls, and has a granite top. The fireplace is of 'Brocatelli' marble, over which hangs a painting by Hondecoeter, obviously chosen because that painter's magnificent reds and scarlets harmonised with the colour scheme; most of the other paintings are Dutch and Flemish. The oak chairs, admirably suited to the room, combine front legs of Roman origin with backs that show the influence of the klismos[149]; their stretchers and upholstery, carrying deep fringes and spaced nails, recall the seventeenth century.

The Crimson Drawing Room (Pl. LXXVIII), suffused wholly with crimson, is in the same manner; it has a novel architectural chimney glass; both here and in the Scarlet Drawing Room the chimney-board seems to have been plain. The furniture again is massive and architectural in form, with a strong Renaissance flavour, the hanging cabinets echoing a Renaissance practice. The chairs, black with a gilt rim, are of the same form as in the Scarlet Drawing Room. There is a cloth on the centre table in a manner resembling that used in the seventeenth century, although it has to be remembered that such draped tables did not necessarily betoken antiquarian influence; Roman tables were draped and are often seen so pictured in neo-classical paintings. The table in the window is mosaic, with a Florentine mosaic coffer reputed to have belonged once to Mazarin. The room contained a Giovanni Bologna bronze, two candlesticks by Vulliamy 'of pure standard gold' after a design by Holbein, a pair of candlesticks 'from the Alhambra' with 'characteristic arabesque ornament', candelabra of 'polished granite', and vases of rare china, jasper, agate, jade, chalcedony, and cornelian.[150] Also in the room was a splendid but not over-elaborate ebony cabinet of seventeenth-century form, bearing lacquer and porcelain; there were two ebony stools. The Belvedere had ebony X-framed stools and a strongly coffered dome. These little rooms had an effortless brilliance; they were as excellent as those of Hope and less alien; in his last years, the cadaverous old aesthete in his Tower had triumphed.

## 'Simplicity'

The interiors discussed above have been virtually all of a type where the upholsterer, not the architect, had held sway or, in the case of Carlton House, where the architect had been overwhelmed by later 'upholstery'. In none did the architectonic element predominate; in the Deepdene and Lansdown Tower the rooms were given volumetric furniture and, in the latter case, vigorous mouldings. There were, however, a large number of rooms in 'respectable' houses where certain factors — the picturesque interest in 'intricacy', the lack of the hand of a distinguished decorator, the liking for plainness (probably encouraged by the puritanism of the Greek Revival and by such building styles as that of Samuel Wyatt (see p.126), for if one has a house with an astylar exterior it is an anomaly to have pillars and entablatures within) — produced an unfortunate juxtaposition of austere wall and ceiling surfaces with a jumble of contents.

Repton deprecated the effect of this in 1808; after praising the irregularities of Gothic rooms, by which the eye was 'amused, entangled by a degree of intricacy unknown in modern rooms', he proceeded to condemn the 'rage for what is called SIMPLICITY', which produced 'plain walls without the smallest break or projection, and plain ceilings without the smallest enrichments of painting or sculpture'. He said that the 'large windows, and large piers, and doors too large for common use, [which] have been made the criterion of GRANDEUR' in fact only lessened the apparent space. 'To remedy this defect in modern rooms, it has of late become the fashion to cover the ceilings with lustres, and to crowd the floor with tables and sophas, and musical instruments, which in some degree create separate compartments and recesses. . . . The plainness, or simplicity (as it is called) in modern Houses, has been extended to every room alike, and often causes in Dining Rooms an excess of echo and noise which is intolerable'.[151] Prince Pückler-Muskau made a similar complaint about miscellanies of furniture, and it is probable that the search for intricacy and interest was responsible for the deliberate use even of miscellaneous chairs (Fig. 166), as mentioned in an advertisement of 1814: 'The fashion now is with many Gentlemen to have every chair of a different pattern in the same apartment'.[152]

Gilbert Laing Meason repeated the accusation in 1828: 'Nothing strikes foreigners more than the great want of architectural designs in

213 Design for window furnishings by Gillow and Co., c.1825

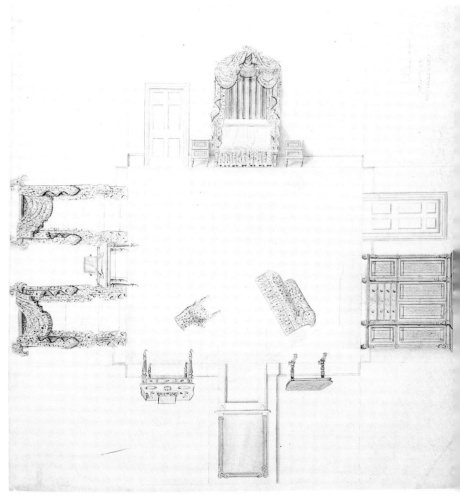

214 Design for a bedroom by Gillow and Co., 1820s

**215** The Library at Binfield, Berks., 1836–7

LXXIX Design for the vestibule, Aynho Park, Northants., 1800, by Sir John Soane

our living rooms. A flat white ceiling with a stucco cornice prevails in all. Some little decoration around the doors and windows are given; but the walls in the dining room are painted and plain colour; and in the drawing room, an unmeaning gaudy-coloured paper, or pale scroll figured one, occupies the wall from the ceiling to the floor . . . few architects propose interior decoration, and but few have made it their study. The walls in our rooms are therefore never in harmony with the ceiling, which appears to have no support, nor united in effect with the floor. Strip our rooms of their gaudy carpets, of the tables, and chairs, and sophas, crowded together like an upholsterer's shop, and there is not a more wretched looking appearance than the empty rooms of a fashionable house'.[153]

Architectural nullity extended to the chimney-pieces; in May 1815 Farington said that the sculptor Rossi 'complained of Architects having made such a change in their designs for chimney-pieces leaving out ornaments and making them so plain that they could now be executed for from four pounds to fifteen, while formerly a chimney piece would have cost 50 or £60, the Sculptors He said had greatly suffered by this alteration. I asked Him who had introduced this change, and he mentioned Robt. Smirke as being the Leader of it'.[154] Greek Revival aridity had reached the interior. This aridity, incidentally, was not confined to Britain.

The truth of these strictures is confirmed by such designs as that for a drawing room (Fig. 212) by Gillows, the epitome of middle range taste; the attempt is made to substitute an 'interesting' arrangement of furniture for architectural incident. The floor space is carefully separated into two areas by two ottomans (the ubiquity of the completely upholstered ottoman during the Regency period has been obscured by the disappearance of most examples). The inner area has two sofas, each with its own sofa table; the outer has chairs facing the windows.

The 'rage for what is called SIMPLICITY' may have encouraged a compensating fashion for elaborate curtains and pelmets, and for the practice of continuing the curtains across the walls. A design by Gillows (Fig. 213) has the acanthus decoration which became so fashionable in the 1820s; the type was vigorous, influenced by Tatham's rendering of it (in which he himself followed Piranesi); here it is uncomfortably powerful, as are the oversized ropes and tassels. The acanthus would have been finished in burnished gilding. It seems less over-nitrogenized in the design for a bedroom (Fig. 214), where the furnishings are chintz, a common bedroom choice. The furniture includes a wash-hand stand, night cupboards, and a dressing table. More middle-class furniture of the Gillows type is seen in a painting of the Library at Binfield (Fig. 215); there is no gilding in sight, apart from the curtain poles, and the placing of sofas and armchairs next to the fireplace, with a sofa table next to two loose chintz covered armchairs, and two tables in the window area each with two chairs, is typical of the attempt at 'intricacy', and much in accordance with the Gillows plan (Fig. 212). Without the chintz draped curtains the walls and ceiling, which have no relieving pictures, would look barren; as it is, the fireplace wall, which has a meagre overmantel glass, is chaste to the point of desolation.

Chapter three

# The Architectural Interior: Classical Styles

## Semi-public areas; picture and sculpture galleries; theatres

Any consideration of 'architectural' as opposed to 'decorated' interiors should take into account two inter-related factors. The first was practical and utilitarian; it is evident that upholsterers' contrivances such as 'antique drapery' were hardly suitable for public buildings (or only for public buildings devoted to entertainment of certain kinds). Public buildings therefore tended to have 'architectural' interiors. The early nineteenth century saw many more public buildings erected, often on a grand scale, than ever before; apart from clubs, these were buildings in which people might expect to meet others whom they were not prepared to accept as social equals. The second factor was the desire to impress, and here the decline in the emphasis on 'parade' as practised in the great eighteenth-century houses meant that as time went on more and more rooms became private, and were decorated accordingly; Laugier had, as we have seen, frowned on the use of pompous architectural elements in private rooms. There was therefore an increasing rift between domestic and public interiors, although a feeling remained, atavistic yet obstinately lingering, that some rooms in a domestic house such as the entrance hall, galleries for sculpture or pictures, music rooms, grand saloons, were more 'public' than others, and could be decorated in a more public manner.

These considerations affected the decision on whether to employ an 'architectural' or 'decorated' style, but others governing the choice were inherent in the characters of the styles themselves. One can well see that the frivolities of rococo or of neo-classical arabesque were perfectly suited to the intimacies of daily life. This was hardly true of

the archaeological classical taste, an important component of Regency architectural style, in which a virility emerged that bordered on the uncivil; we have seen it affect even such a graceful motif as the acanthus. Hope encouraged this trend, as did the fashion for ancient sculpture (Figs 217, 219; Pl. LXXXII), which no longer was confined to smooth and often over-restored Roman versions of Greek sculpture; the liking for broadly handled and often battered architectural fragments, hitherto a special taste, became more general. Canova, whose own style was based on smooth Roman copies, refused to restore the Elgin marbles. The architectural style that complemented this extension of taste was suited to public or semi-public rooms.

Most great houses had their sculpture galleries; the orderly ladies seen in Charles Towneley's entrance hall (Fig. 169), which was really the overture to a private museum, have not abandoned decorum as did guests at the height of a ball at Lansdowne House, when the ladies 'hung shawls and other articles of dress on the statues, which dreadfully shocked one's feeling for art'.[1] Towneley's guests dined in a remarkably stony ambience (Pl. LVII). Bonomi had designed a magnificent gallery for Towneley's sculpture in 1789, a domed central space supported on a system of pillars and alcoves, the dome decorated with antique arabesque such as that in the Baths of Titus, the walls decorated with bas-reliefs.[2] Some of the most splendid architectural creations of the period were sculpture galleries, like the unparalleled example at Woburn, the result of the successive talents of Holland and Wyatville.[3] Soane acquired the classical fragments of sculpture formerly procured for Holland by Tatham, and arranged them in his own study where they were forever before his eyes, a kind of private meditation on the mutability of empires; adjacent was his grandiloquent invention of the domed crypt (Pl. LXXXII), in which Piranesian assemblages of mutilated stone towered from floor to ceiling. Soane's use of ancient

LXXX Interior perspective of the Sepulchral Chapel, Tyringham Hall, Bucks., designed by Sir John Soane

216 'The Chimney-Piece &c in the Gallery at Castle Howard', design by C. H. Tatham, 1800–01

217 The Statue Gallery, the Duchess Street house of Thomas Hope, 1807

218 The Picture Gallery, the Duchess Street house of Thomas Hope, 1807

plunder to create a romantic interior, ruins brought in from the park to the house, appears to be unique in the period, perhaps surprisingly so.

In 1800–01 C. H. Tatham designed the gallery at Castle Howard in a style of austere splendour (Fig. 216); the sense of clarity, weight, and force, emphasised by the battered pilasters and primitivism, make a powerful whole; different though it is in form from Vanbrugh's work, the feeling it provokes is not so distant from that of Vanbrugh's walls and monuments in the park. The gallery is well judged for its purpose; Smirke's solecisms in his Lansdowne House gallery of 1816–19 are avoided — Cockerell commented in 1822 that the antique statues at Lansdowne House were rough in texture and best seen at a distance 'but positively not as P. Knight says to be considered as furniture, to regard them otherwise — or [to maintain] that uninstructed persons ought to feel pleasure in beholding them, is affectation and cant . . . the incongruity holds throughout, the marble plinths pose on a parquet floor, a most distressing circumstance. The statues discoloured are opposed to highly finish walls of stuccoe painted and gilt of tender colour in which a spot would have lost the Tradesman his employment, their coarse texture is backed by red drapery of delicate texture.'[4]

Architectural austerity rules in Hope's 'Statue Gallery' at Duchess Street (Fig. 217); this room and the Picture Gallery (Fig. 218) were the only 'architectural' interiors in the house, since apart from minor mouldings, the other rooms appear to have been adorned by the art of the painter-decorator. Hope explained of the Statue Gallery that 'as this room is destined solely for the reception of ancient marbles, the walls are left perfectly plain, in order that the back-ground, against which are placed statues, might offer no inferior ornaments, or breaks, capable of interfering, through their outline, with the contrast of more important works of art'.[5] The trabeated ceiling, strict Greek Revival in manner, was probably painted with *trompe l'oeil* graining; 'The ceiling . . . is divided into cassoons by means of rafters, which imitate a light timber covering'.[6] It seems possible that despite its archaeological appearance in the engraving, Hope's Statue Gallery may in reality have looked more 'decorated' than did Tatham's; the colour of the walls is unknown. There may have been coloured glass in the lanterns, as in the Ampitheatre at the Deepdene.

The ceiling of the Picture Gallery may have had simulated woodwork also, since Hope remarks that the small columns in the lantern (imitated from those on the Temple of the Winds (Fig. 86), rest on 'massy beams, *similar to those in marble* [author's italics], which lie across the peristyle of the temple of Theseus' at Athens.[7] This may imply that the beams, and the lantern columns (it would have been a solecism to rest 'marble' columns on wooden beams) were wooden, perhaps painted also in *trompe l'oeil* graining; if so, what of the entablatures and larger columns? Were they also 'wooden'? It is not impossible; there was great interest in the wooden Doric temple, which

would have been viewed as correctly primitive in a way that wooden Ionic or Corinthian would not. Wood would have toned with the walls, likely to have been the red usually used in picture galleries (no nineteenth-century connoisseur would have been so obtuse as to place paintings on a white background). The question remains open; Hope described the sphinx ended seats as 'stone seats' (Fig. 218),[8] which perhaps militates against the 'wooden' theory. The paintings seem to have been protected by curtains; Regency collectors were careful. Beckford kept his Raphael *St. Catherine* glazed; he admitted that the reflections obscured the painting, but opened the glazing with a key for visitors[9] — as did the Duke of Wellington his Correggio, refusing the key to anybody else.[10]

The beautiful 'Ampitheatre' at the Deepdene (Fig. 219) was, as its name indicates, imitated from ancient theatres; the interior shows possible reminiscences of the anatomy theatre at Gondoin's famous 'Ecole de Chirurgie' of 1780, also known as the 'ampitheatre' and like Hope's building influenced by the Pantheon (Fig. 220). On the tiered steps of the former are ranged sculpture, funerary vases and coffers. The half dome is coffered in primitive manner, the allusion to the beam being clear. A dandified pink and blue lamp, probably glass, was designed by Hope in a lotus shape; a marble floor, imitating the antique in buff, blue, pink and white, echoes its colour. Polychromatic Chinese porcelain garden seats stand on the steps. Windows and doorways have triangular openings (see also p.116).

Theatres came in as many styles as any other building. The Greek Revival might seem a chilly manner for a theatre, but Smirke gave the interior of his monumentally austere Covent Garden (Fig. 221) a matching interior, described by Britton as 'very imposing; the colour is a subdued yellow, relieved by white, and superbly enriched with gilding'.[11] The dome, primitive in a character not unlike that of Hope's Ampitheatre — the Greek Revivalists found domes difficult, since the Greeks did not provide examples — is matched by a proscenium arch painted to simulate coffering; behind it is a curtain of antique drapery and Greek scenery. In contrast was the Frenchified, Percier and Fontaine style interior of Drury Lane by B. D. Wyatt, noted for its splendour and much admired by the Prince Regent; it made unrestrained use of strong colour and rich materials: and, yet again a contrast, the interior by Nash of the Haymarket Theatre, built in 1820–1 (Fig. 222), when the Pavilion was completed, and with a strong whiff of its outlandish splendours; its pillars are related to those of the Red Drawing Room at Brighton.

## The 'Palladian' formula

It was not necessary for an 'architectural' interior to be elaborate; quite often it was simple, and the restraint that marks many late eighteenth-

**219** The 'Ampitheatre', the Deepdene, Surrey

**220** The anatomy theatre, Ecole de Chirurgie, Paris, 1780, designed by J. Gondoin

**221** Interior of the Theatre Royal, Covent Garden, designed by Sir Robert Smirke, 1808–09

222 'Interior of the New Theatre Royal
Haymarket as it appeared on the Night of its
opening 4 July 1821', designed by John Nash

century interiors was fortified by the puritanical inhibitions of the Greek Revival. A typical understated architect-designed interior that combines simplicity with architectural form is provided in George Richardson's design of 1792 for the 'Section of the Chimney Side of the best Drawing Room' (Fig. 223). This plain but dignified scheme was meant to be completed by framed paintings hung upon the walls; the Palladian formula, old-fashioned even in 1792 in that it was nothing

like contemporary English or French avant-garde decoration, persisted throughout the Regency and into the early Victorian period, accompanied by first a simplification and then a coarsening of detail. An associated design for a Music Room is slightly more advanced; it has 'Pompeian' dancing maidens on the walls. The looking glass in the drawing-room — an instance of architect-designed furniture — was to be 'partly gilt in burnished gold', and the walls 'from the top of the surface moulding to the astragal under the frieze, may be . . . hung with fine paper or light figured silk'.[12]

## Stylistic variants

As would be expected, the most interesting 'architectural' interiors were produced by the most interesting architects. Bonomi's design for the dining room at Lambton Hall, County Durham, of about 1800 (Fig. 224) is impressive and original, weighty and serious; the vaulted roof in Italian palace style is supported on heavy consoles. Included in the design are landscape paintings on the walls, similar in general effect to those of another Italian, Agostino Aglio, on the staircase at Bretton Park. The double chimney-piece adds to the measured solemnity, as does the advanced neo-classical furniture, also presumably designed by Bonomi; based on the stone fluted leg, it has an antique weight. The

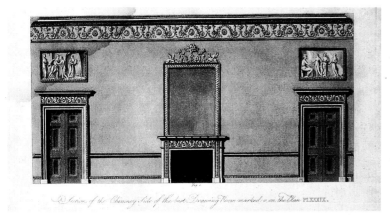

223 'Section of the Chimney Side of the best Drawing Room',
by George Richardson, 1792

224 Design for the Dining Room, Lambton Hall, Durham, 1800, by Joseph Bonomi

225 Sepulchral Ruins near Torre di Schiavi, etched by G. B. Piranesi, 1756

room is shown without the upholsterers' contribution, carpets and curtains. The design for the drawing room (not illustrated) has plain walls and a most magnificent vaulted ceiling with idiosyncratic detail. Once again architect-designed furniture (console tables and wall seats) is shown on bare boards; the architect also designed the mirrors above the chimney piece and between the windows.[13]

Bonomi was an original architect, but not as original as Soane. By the 1790s Soane was well on his way towards the mannerisms of his later style. The entrance hall of Bentley Priory of 1798 is as strongly architectural as an entrance hall could well be (Fig. 226), looking somewhat like a section of eccentric cloister; the associations suggested by the name 'Priory' may have led Soane to attempt one of the syntheses of classical and Gothic by which he achieved extraordinarily suggestive effects. This forceful composition, which has walls coloured to represent Siena marble, and yellow glass in the windows, uses Delian Doric columns without bases[14] to support, at a remove, groined vaulting; the influence of Dance is not far away. The Gothic allusion is overt in the singular Don Giovanni-like stove, a suit of armour complete with helmet in which the breastplate conceals fire, a grim conceit that must have looked especially daunting when opened. It would be a bold client who would build this stern entrance hall, hyperborean despite the yellow colouring.

Bentley Priory offers also a resolutely 'architectural' design for a Music Room;[15] one imagines that the various apertures and embrasures might have produced a 'decided resonance', as Miss Niphet said of Lord Curryfin's attempt at acoustic Greek vases.[16] The triple arch of the balcony, which recalls Vanbrugh's staircases, allows one of those mysterious lighting effects so dear to Soane, supplemented by light from windows on both sides. The balcony in front of the organ is of the Cecilia Metella pattern seen in Soane's designs for his own house (Fig. 186; see pp.246–7). The Ionic columns are large enough to avoid Soane's stricture that; 'A column should never be really small, as in chimney pieces, door dressings and such like . . . or it will become puerile and trifling'.[17] Soane thought the relative magnitude of columns on smaller buildings, whether internal or external, an important consideration; they could be made to look too small, or their bulk could become a nuisance, especially when it stopped light; 'This will in a great measure justify the opinion of some fashionable builders of the present day who speak of columns now out of fashion'.[18] He had strong views about folding doors, in common use in the now fashionable 'suites' of rooms; they should not be too wide for their height. He thought English doors tended to be 'extremely offensive to the eye', an error not seen in 'the French architects, from whom we have borrowed the idea of large Folding Doors'.[19]

Soane's designs for the staircase and vestibule for Aynho Park carry antique architectural grandeur as far as it could be carried in a house

226 Design for the Vestibule, Bentley Priory, Mddx., 1798, by Sir John Soane

227 Coffee Room, 1808, designed by John Walters

**228** 'Wellington Rooms Liverpool', Mount Pleasant, 1814, design by Thomas Rickman

that was not a palace. The staircase design is wonderfully stony,[20] with a heavily coffered and decorated barrel vault; it has full, fluted Ionic columns, life-size statues on pedestals, and a simple 'Pompeian' iron balustrade; it is complete in itself — it would be inadmissible to add paintings or any other decoration. The same is true of the vestibule (Pl. LXXIX); here, however, austerity retreats before a polychromatic Roman dazzle. The design has an imperial air with its marble or scagliola free-standing Ionic pillars, heavily pedimented doorways, and dome, the last echoed in the elaborately inlaid floor. The window wall is decorated in something of a different idiom, flat painted with a lunette resembling the little landscape scenes from Herculaneum, and a maiden in Herculaneum style.

The dome of the Aynho Park vestibule (Fig. 226) bears a three-dimensional decoration based on the 'velarium', an antique motif (Fig. 225) employed in Western art from the Renaissance onwards and a favourite resource of Soane's; it had been used in something of the same way by the younger Dance in his Council Chamber at the Guildhall of 1777–8. The velarium was based on the canvas awnings used to shield audiences from the sun in classical theatres and circuses;[21] they were sometimes coloured with magical effect. In its original form the velarium has an affinity with 'antique drapery' (see p.261 et seq.); its petrification into a fluted dome does not disguise the common harmonies of the two forms of decoration, drawn from a common source in textile hangings. It was a favoured antique motif in painted decorations on walls and ceilings and appears, together with 'antique drapery', amongst the luxuriant fancies of the arabesques in the Vatican loggie.

Soane's use of the velarium in a domestic setting did not prevent him from proposing it for the dome of the sepulchral chapel at

Tyringham (Pl. LXXX); in this he also followed antiquity (Fig. 196). At Tyringham the velarium is taken a step further towards its antique architectural three-dimensional form in that it is itself the dome; it is not confined within another shape. The whole design is heavily indebted to antique tomb architecture. The velarium is used for another kind of interior in the 'Coffee Room' from the Auction Mart designed by John Walters in 1808 (Fig. 227), where it is accompanied by 'Etruscan' decoration on the walls. We therefore have the same dominant motif used in the entrance hall of a house, in a sepulchral chapel, and in a coffee room; one can see what Repton meant by his general complaint that 'characteristic architecture' — by which he meant architecture that clearly declared the 'character', that is, the purpose of a particular building — was neglected: 'our hospitals resemble palaces, and our palaces may be mistaken for hospitals; our modern churches look like theatres, and our theatres appear like warehouses'.[22] The melancholic origins of much classicising interior decoration declared themselves obtrusively; more than one of Repton's contemporaries thought modern domestic decoration tomb-like, and this objection can with justice be urged against Soane; such repugnant associations may have encouraged the use of the upholsterer. Any congenial source appears to have been grist to Soane's mill; the extraordinary ceiling designed in concentric whirls for the Lady's Dressing Room at Pellwall House, for example, resembles a form of ancient Greek pottery decorated in circles with white, terracotta, and black clays,[23] and one wonders whether that was the source.

The ingredients commonly used in classical 'architectural' interiors

**229** The Privy Council Chamber, Downing Street, 1824–7, a design by Sir John Soane

LXXXI Freemasons' Hall, 1828–31, designed by Sir John Soane

*Opposite* LXXXII 'The Museum as arranged in 1813', Lincoln's Inn Fields, by J. Gandy: designed by Sir John Soane

*Opposite* **LXXXIII** The Alcove, the Golden Drawing
Room, Carlton House, designed by John Nash

**LXXXIV** The Elizabeth Saloon, Belvoir Castle,
Rutland, designed by Matthew Cotes Wyatt in
1824

**LXXXV** Apsley House, the Gallery, 1853

LXXXVI The Yellow (North) Drawing Room, Brighton Pavilion, c.1818

LXXXVII 'The Auditorium of St. James's Theatre', design by Frederick Crace

LXXXVIII The Drawing Room, Selsdon House, c.1830

LXXXIX Fonthill Abbey, South End of
St. Michael's Gallery, 1823

XC Gothic Dining Room, Carlton House,
designed by John Nash, 1814, c.1817

**230** Design for interior decoration, by Sir Robert Smirke, after 1820

— columns, pilasters, entablatures, coffered ceilings, bas-reliefs — are deployed in characteristic designs by Rickman, Smirke, Cockerell, and Robinson (Figs 228, 230, 231). Rickman designed in 1814 for the Wellington Club, Mount Pleasant, a suite of rooms in classical vein with unfluted Corinthian columns, antique drapery, and acroteria; the seemly ironwork and lamps were also designed by the architect. Smirke's pencil sketch of the 1820s shows bas-reliefs and damask-filled compartments articulated by pilasters, with acanthus-decorated corbels on the ceiling. Well-mannered as it is, the scheme lacks the excitement and fire of Soane — or, for that matter, Nash. Cockerell, in a sketch for the Dining Room at the Grange (not illustrated), ranged further afield for inspiration than did Smirke, bound as the latter was in Greek Revival fetters. On 23rd April 1823 Cockerell wrote: 'On Baring's dining Ro: turned over every book of decoration I have', a process repeated the next day: 'searched all my books [for] novelty, originality of conception — yet appropriate';[24] architects did not then believe that imitation and use of authorities precluded originality. The result was highly architectural; Ionic pillars, entablature, and coffered ceiling, with a hint of the late seventeenth or early eighteenth centuries; the architect was perhaps influenced by seventeenth-century work in the house itself.

A design of May 1825 for the Saloon of an ornamental villa by P. F. Robinson (Fig. 231) shows an elaborate Greek Revival interior with a gesticulating Hercules in the distance; the room has coffered ceiling, bas-reliefs, pilasters and pillars; devices such as the joining of the pillars on the same base are found in contemporary French decoration. The design begins in other ways to approach the Continental manner, belied by the kilted figure in the painting on the right; the paintings are

set on the walls in architectural style. The draped windows are curiously incongruous in proportion and detail. The chair on the right, with its flowing back, is derived from antique marble prototypes (Fig. 272). Robinson's design is perfectly proper, despite a few infelicities, but one sees why so many people preferred the 'decorated' to the 'architectural' look.

## Nash 'Empire'

Nash has, unjustly, hardly been taken seriously as a designer of interiors. The architectural form of the two great rooms added after 1815 to Brighton Pavilion is undoubtedly of his design; they are wonderfully exhilarating, with their huge French windows, domes and swagged ceilings, a brilliant synthesis of the dome and the tent. The rooms perfectly combine architecture and decoration, the strong forms holding their own against the profusion of ornament applied to the extensive flat surfaces provided by the architect (Pls C, CII); the orientalisms of the decoration do not disguise the 'Empire' character of the whole. The rooms have much bold three-dimensional decoration, especially in the overdoors and in the splendid free-standing pillars that originally stood at the angles of both rooms.[25]

Some of this detail was designed by Robert Jones, some by Nash: 'To a Canopy made to Mr. Nash's design formed into an octagon with Ropes up each rib';[26] this canopy has, in its relationship with the dome, more than a passing similarity to that of the gallery and the area above

**231** Design for a Saloon, by P. F. Robinson, 1825

232 The Royal Gallery, House of Lords, designed by Sir John Soane

233 'Cheminée exécutée sur un fond en glace dans la Galérie du Pce S. . . en Pologne', designed by Percier and Fontaine

of Soane's Court of Chancery built in 1822–5. It is probable that Nash contributed other details at Brighton, such as the Pompeian 'fan vaulting' in the South Drawing Room, similar in its details to that in Gothic form in the Gothic Dining Room at Carlton House (Pl. XC); mouldings in the King's Library resemble those in Nash's Library at Regent Street (Fig. 208); the bamboo staircases in the Corridor resemble other Nash staircases.[27] It seems unlikely that common details in so many different places were contributed by decorators, or even by draughtsmen from Nash's office.

## The Soanean synthesis

Nash's repetition of detail is not evidence of limited imagination; if it were, Soane, reproached for repeating his architectural effects, let alone his detail, must stand accused of it. Soane's obstinacies did not extend to an unwillingness to adapt his style to differing requirements. When called upon to design stately ceremonial spaces for the House of Lords the result has some similarity with the grander interiors of Percier and Fontaine (Figs 232, 233); Soane's interior was strong, somewhat more spare than Percier and Fontaine, and employs the familiar starry ornament in the vaulted ceilings that he drew from Pietro Santi Bartoli's *Gli Antichi Sepolcri*, originally published in 1693 (Fig. 234). There was some resemblance in these designs to the Italian Renaissance and to the baroque; Soane was not unsympathetic to the latter; he did not despise Bernini, a bête-noire of the neo-classicists, saying of the 'Fontana nella Piazza Navona' that 'it is impossible not to be pleased with this mighty flight of genius';[28] he also admired the Scala Regia in the Vatican.

One of Soane's most wonderfully expressive interiors, albeit not on a large scale, was that of the Privy Council Chamber in Downing Street, of 1824–7 (Fig. 229). Rich and imposing, with heavily grand doorways and window frames which bear versions of his favourite double-scroll motif (see Fig. 92) that look like antique fragments weighing down Ionic columns, the chamber was given a canopy designed and supported on principles similar to those employed in the Breakfast Room in Soane's house (Fig. 184). The light spills in from skylights and windows on either side. The Privy Council Chamber canopy is quite differently shaped from the domed canopy of the Breakfast Room; it is much longer than it is wide, and uses the star ceiling motif. This motif, utilised by Adam, Chambers, and Dance, and a favourite device of Soane's, is here turned into something that resembles a Gothic vault, a resemblance accentuated by the spring of the vault from the pilasters in a form similar to that seen in some Continental Gothic churches, where the line from pillar to vault rises with hardly an interruption. The theme here reaches an apex of suggestive power, evoking the simulacrum of some creature that has extended huge wings across the room; the expressiveness is heightened by the proportions of the room, much higher than they are wide. The concept is remarkable, and it is hardly surprising that the Privy Councillors were disquieted. The room did not survive long unaltered.

Soane produced other unnerving vaults during the 1820s, such as those of the Court of Exchequer and the Court of King's Bench and, perhaps strangest of all, that of the Freemasons' Hall, built from 1828–31 (Pl. LXXXI). In all, one senses the ghost of Gothic, flying above at a great height without stopping. It is difficult to believe that Soane, in these daring exercises, was not subject to two especial influences. The first was the adjuration of Reynolds to follow Vanbrugh in reproducing spirit rather than copying form (see p.100); the second was the precise advice of Laugier, who offered a constant encouragement towards experiment, in form and in the mixing of styles. He had praised the vaults in which 'l'Architecture gothique déploie ses plus brillantes ressources'; St. Eustache in Paris, a Renaissance Gothic vault in mixed style (did such vaults influence the Privy Council Chamber vault?), was unsurpassed: 'rien de plus élégant . . . par la bizarrerie de ses contours'. Laugier had condemned all vaults built since the Renais-

**234** Ceiling decoration from a Roman tomb, published by Pietro Santi Bartoli

sance as 'lourde et massive', and had counselled: 'varions les formes de nos voûtes, répandons y de sages ornemens'. He emphasised the value of light and advocated the piercing of vaults with lanterns, rather than with lunettes; he said that one could 'dans le plan circulaire d'un dôme trouver une voûte en façon de rose gothique'. Speaking of difficulties connected with 'les voûtes à arêtes', he said that 'Le mieux est d'effacer ces arêtes en y substituant des pendentifs et en les racordant à un tableau rond dans le milieu'. A summary of his advice on vaults sounds like Soane's own practice: 'varier leurs formes en mélangeant les berceaux, les pendentifs, les voûtes sphériques, et en enrichissant ce mélange précieux, d'ornemens qui nos Sculpteurs y taillent bien plus correctement et de plus grand goût que tout ce qu'on voit dans les anciennes voûtes'.[29]

This 'mélange précieux' is exemplified in the Freemasons' Hall (one wonders, in parenthesis, whether Soane, a mason himself, knew and shared Hope's theories on the profound importance of freemasonry to design in the mediaeval period).[30] In the foreground is a flattened variant of the 'berceau'; beyond is a flat ceiling in the centre of which is a 'voûte sphérique', illuminated by a lantern and cut-off square in a way that recalls the Breakfast Room suspended dome-canopy and that here creates corners with 'pendentifs'; the last are emphasised by the chandeliers that depend from them. The pronounced moulding that runs along the wall, at the lower level of the pediments over the doors, separates the ceiling area as a whole from that which lies beneath. The surface decoration of walls, ceiling, pilasters, chimney-pieces, the grid-like division of the apertures above the chimney-pieces, give a general impression of a panelled room.

Soane was a strange character, as his own house demonstrates; strange as that is, however, it is no stranger, and less economical and consistent, than the Freemasons' Hall. In the latter, the underworld element in Soane's art is seen at its most haunted.

## 'Louis Quatorze' or rococo revival

We turn from the most architectonically constructed of Regency interiors to the style most notoriously licentious — 'Louis Quatorze', or the revived rococo. The two styles were no doubt so confounded because rococo had appeared before the death of Louis XIV; as styles they were historically distinct, rococo freedoms being a reaction against the classical grandeur of the original Louis XIV style — a grandeur that, through the French neo-classical conduit, entered the mainstream of Regency furniture design. Papworth clearly saw the difference; he lamented that the 'Classic style of Art . . . as designed by Le Pautre and others [which he considered the true "Louis Quatorze"] . . . is almost lost to the country'.[31] The name of Le Pautre, the greatest of French late seventeenth-century designers, was held in respect; as early as 1799 Tatham wrote that 'Great praise has been bestowed by many on the works of LE POTRE and so far as praise is due to richness of invention, and variety of execution, he certainly deserves it, but his designs must never be set in competition with those of the Ancients. . . .'.[32] Le Pautre was increasingly mentioned in the 1820s; there is visual evidence of the increased use of his designs. George Smith said in 1826 that 'the works of Jean le Pautre, who flourished in the age of Louis XIV of France (although this period was productive of a bad style) are distinguished by their variety and peculiar happiness of invention'.[33] It sounds as if Smith

himself may have confused 'Louis XIV' and the rococo, although it is true that the later designs of Le Pautre begin to approach rococo.

Papworth firmly attributed the confusion to commercial activity; he said that many manufacturers had sought 'a style of ornament capable of being executed with facility by workmen unpossessed of theoretical knowledge and of practical accuracy. This style has been fostered to a great extent and erroneously termed that of Louis XIV, but . . . in fact is the debased manner of . . . Louis XV. . . . Designers and Workmen of many mediocre talents are preferred to better Artists in this kind of work, for it is little amenable to the criticism of the judicious . . .'.[34] He blamed its use for begetting a race of workmen incapable of producing Grecian, Roman, or Italian ornament.

The manufacturers of whom Papworth speaks tended to use composition, especially papier-mâché, to reproduce 'Louis XIV' ornament. The use of composition of divers kinds had existed for a long time, as had forms of papier-mâché, but it is evident that in the 1820s fashion, technique, and need came together. Nathaniel Whittock in 1827 attributed the origin of papier-mâché ornaments to their use in the theatre, with the comment that 'the intelligent decorator will see that any clever boy may produce them' — a striking confirmation of Papworth's lament for lost skills: he called it 'a species of decoration which is at present confined to theatrical ornaments, but from the ease with which it may be produced, and its beautiful effect, joined with its great durability and lightness, it might be introduced into the decoration of apartments with great advantage'.[35] Whittock was a craftsman, and knew of what he spoke; it seems likely that yet again the theatre influenced decoration. He added that papier-mâché would be better for gold and bronze ornaments than carvers' and gilders' composition, which tends to crack. The most usual composition was 'Jackson's Putty' which does crack; Earl Gower had intended Bernasconi to execute the stucco at Stafford House, until Benjamin Dean Wyatt persuaded him to use Jackson's Putty.[36] Cracked wood is august; cracked composition is shoddy.

George Smith told a different tale from Whittock, although the two may possibly be reconciled; he said that papier-mâché had been recently introduced from France, but that the English variety was more durable and a better imitation of real carving, 'from its sharpness of edge and depth in cast'. He added that, 'with respect to the elegance and phantasy of design in paper decoration, the French offer patterns very far superior to all others'.[37]

'Louis Quatorze' was entirely restricted to interiors; the classical façades gave no hint of the decorative tumult within (as had often been the case with real, especially German, rococo). It is not surprising that it was disliked by perceptive judges. It was grossly inferior to the animated style it purported to imitate, although the revulsion expressed by more sensitive critics was generally extended to the real thing; Cockerell was unprejudiced enough to describe how he had united 'the richness of rococo and the breadth and merit of Greek' in ornament he had designed for plate.[38] Soane, who as we have seen liked some baroque art, disapproved of 'a most strange and preposterous attempt at something new in internal Decoration imported from France. This species of Decoration consisted of flat surfaces scrawled over with short arched lines and twisted curves, with single and inverted C's and tangled semicircles. These poor, fantastic and awkward conceits' made up a style 'well adapted to internal embellishment' but 'ill-suited to external grandeur'.[39] This description of rococo, which employs such geometrical imagery as 'tangled semi-circles', implies that Soane had no conception of the irregularity and spontaneity which lay at its heart; had he seen the work of Cuvilliés he might have had a better opinion of it.

Hope, whose tastes included neither the baroque — 'a Fontana, a Bernini, and a Borromini . . . far outstripped in bad taste the worst examples of the worst era of pagan Rome'[40] — nor the rococo: 'Its proper name should be the inane or frippery style'[41] — saw the movement towards rococo as the bankruptcy of taste: 'Finally, as if in utter despair, some have relapsed into an admiration of the old scrollwork . . . of which the French had become ashamed'. He despised the fashion for rococo works of art, which had been the channel through which the style itself had returned: 'Not content with ransacking every pawnbroker's shop in London and in Paris, for old buhl, old porcelain, old plate, old tapestry, and old frames, they even set every manufacturer at work, and corrupted the taste of every modern artist, by the renovation of this wretched style'.[42]

The revival of the 'Louis Quatorze' style probably came partly in the wake of English historical revivalism. The restorations at Windsor carried out for George III, who seems to have had more reverence for the work of his predecessors than did George IV, may have made a contribution. Some of the remodelled interiors were given the 'Grinling Gibbons' carvings in wood[43] which became one of the specialities of the versatile Edward Wyatt. Between 1805 and 1812 Rigaud and Matthew Cotes Wyatt added to, or created, ceiling paintings at Windsor Castle in the manner of Verrio;[44] decorative painting of this kind had been out of fashion for many years. By 1810 such enterprises as the huge panorama in 'fresco' of the Crucifixion at St. Mary Moorfields, by Aglio, had become acceptable. It was a short step from Verrio to the ceilings painted by Matthew Cotes Wyatt in the mid-1820s at Belvoir Castle (Pl. LXXXIV).

It seems likely that the Prince Regent was one of the earliest to dabble in the 'Louis Quatorze' style. Carlton House has been mentioned above in this connection (see p.268); the 'Golden Drawing Room' (Pl. LXXXIII), created by Nash in 1813, in which the Prince Regent's known love of gilding manifested itself on virtually every surface (Percier and Fontaine did much the same in the ballroom at Compiègne) shows 'Louis Quatorze' tendencies in its mirror frames, furniture, and *objets d'art*. The mirror frames particularly, interestingly called 'picture frames' by Pyne,[45] were decidedly 'Louis Quatorze' in character. A different kind of revivalism was to be seen in the Pavilion at Brighton, where between 1815 and 1817 interiors were created by Nash and Robert Jones that can only be described as 'revived rococo', albeit in chinoiserie vein. This was seen strikingly in the Yellow Drawing Room (Pl. LXXXVI) which had chinoiserie furniture and ornaments (see p.339), and chinoiserie paintings stuck directly on to the walls in painted frames that recalled the work of John Linnell himself. Linnell, the veteran of late rococo in England, was well within living memory; mentioned in 1796 by his son-in-law Tatham as 'drooping into second childishness',[46] he was respected enough for Tatham to propose designing his monument. Robert Jones, and other craftsmen concerned, may have been old enough to have worked in the ebbing rococo style; expert craftsmen tend to live and work long. Unused designs for the Banqueting and Music Rooms[47] are in an enchanting chinoiserie high rococo style, without the coarseness that pervaded 'Louis Quatorze' elsewhere.

The Wyatts had a good deal to do with the 'Louis Quatorze' fashion. J. D. Paine, an architect who worked on the Windsor interiors with Wyatville between 1828 and 1832, said that Benjamin Dean Wyatt was 'generally considered as the introducer of the style'.[48] Philip and Matthew Cotes Wyatt trafficked in French furniture and *boiseries* from Paris; in March 1819 Beckford informed his general factotum, Franchi, that Philip had 'brought treasures of the most capital Buhl, ebony carvings after your own heart'.[49] At Hawkestone, where Lewis Wyatt 'showed the same expertise as his cousins Benjamin and Philip in recreating the decor of the age of Louis XIV',[50] the work was combined with careful conservation; in 1826 it was stipulated that, 'The plan of a new House and offices shall be so form'd as to bring in every part of the old house worth preserving. That the Saloon and Chapel shall be the same size and form and everything transformed or copied . . . that casts be taken of all the plaster mouldings or ornaments of good taste and character, that the chimney-pieces and other furnishings be selected and appropriate'.[51] This contrasts with the ruthless swathe cut by George IV through the Restoration interiors at Windsor.

One of the leading revivalists was Elizabeth, Duchess of Rutland, who painted landscapes in the manner of Claude — or Beaumont — drew buildings, and landscaped Belvoir Park. She was an enthusiast for French decoration and furniture, one of those women biliously defined by Soane as 'Lady Patronesses'; the first of his five categories of modern architect was the 'Heaven-Born Architect (The Pictorial Architecture, or Architecture A la Mode)' whose 'designs have been made from the hints and ideas of Lady Patronesses'. Soane wrote

**235** Design for a Music Room by Gillow and Co., 1820s

bitterly in 1830 that the name of Vitruvius was seldom heard 'and his principles were considered as mere dreams of dotage'; he thought that the 'causes that have reduced the Queen of Fine Arts to her present degraded state, will be found rather in those arbiters of taste who, from their rank and situation, compel the Architect to incorporate their sometimes crude conceptions into his best-digested composition'.[52] He may well have been correct, although the 'Heaven-Born Architect' was no doubt willing to accept the largesse that Heaven bestowed.

The Elizabeth Saloon at Belvoir Castle, designed in 1824 by Matthew Cotes Wyatt, combines a 'Louis Quatorze' ceiling, heavily articulated in circles and semi-circles, with rococo decoration on the walls; some of the *boiseries* are French (Pl. LXXXIV).[53] The ceiling paintings, by Matthew Cotes Wyatt, remind one of Romanelli, a pupil of Pietro da Cortona who helped to decorate the Louvre. The carpet is Aubusson; the furniture included *pietra dura* cabinets. The essay at Belvoir was followed by the costly use of 'Louis Quatorze' at Crockford's Club in 1827 by Benjamin Dean Wyatt, singularly appropriate in view of the gambling that had taken place in the rococo apartments of the *ancien régime*. Crockford's aroused comment. George Smith said acidly in 1826 that 'perhaps such a taste may be in union with the wasteful transfer of property made in such establishments'.[54] The club had 'a truly Asiatic splendour almost surpassing that of

royalty. Everything is in the now revived taste of the time of Louis the Fourteenth: decorated with tasteless excrescences, excess of gilding, confused mixture of stucco painting, etc., — a turn of fashion very consistent in a country where the nobility grows more and more like that of Louis the Fourteenth'.[55]

'Louis Quatorze' was used at Apsley House in 1828 by the Duke of Wellington, by the Castlereaghs at Wynyard and at Londonderry House, and, most grandly and flamboyantly, at Stafford House by the Sutherlands. A Lady Patroness came into action at Apsley House (Pl. LXXXV); in November 1828, Mrs. Arbuthnot noted that the Duke of Wellington 'has quarrelled with the architect, Mr. Wyatt [Benjamin Dean Wyatt], and begs I will manage it all with him. . . . I dare say Mr. Wyatt and I will go on very well together, and the plan is, I think, as good as it can be . . . when his [the Duke's] house is the admiration of all London . . . I shall consider the merit all due to me'.[56] In September 1829 she said that she had made 'the drawings for the doors and windows, which I thought Mr. Wyatt had proposed in a shape and design that was frightful. I made the drawings for the skirting board and added the ceiling etc.' Both she and Dowbiggin, the upholsterers, disliked the yellow damask of the Gallery; Dowbiggin thought it would 'entirely destroy the effect of the gilding in the room' but the Duke insisted on it.[57] Was he influenced by the memory of Beckford's

Drawing Room at Fonthill (Fig. 238) with its yellow damask, a room that he had greatly liked and that had incurred similar censure? The ornament at Apsley House, estimated to cost £2,000 if carved, in the event cost under £400; the saving had been achieved by using paste composition applied to straight wooden mouldings, a method fit for the essentially mechanical nature of much revived rococo design.

Another possible method of decorating in the 'Louis Quatorze' style would have been, as Wyatt wrote in 1833, to buy and alter old *boiserie*, which was extremely expensive.[58] People knew that the old work was better; Wyatt wrote in August 1829 that he had seen 'three very fine old carved oak picture frames, for the whole length portraits, and a pair of very fine French pier tables, exactly suited to the style of decoration intended for the Gallery'.[59] Old decoration had more individuality than the new; the decorative detail at Apsley House is frequently virtually identical with that at Stafford House.

The most thoroughly rococo of the Windsor interiors was the Ballroom. In this room the rectilinear discipline that holds together the historicist elements in the other apartments was maintained, being especially present in the frames and compartments in which the Gobelins tapestries were placed and in the strong compartmentalism of the ceiling; the ornament, however, especially in the rich gilded plasterwork of the ceilings, attempts to capture the capricious vivacity of eighteenth-century high rococo, and does not entirely fail.

George Smith tepidly endorsed the Louis XIV style by saying that despite its 'bad taste', it had never been surpassed for richness and splendour of effect; he also made clear that it was 'in no way answerable to the dwellings of persons of small fortune'.[60] Unfortunately, this was a double recommendation in a competitive and showy society. He described its characteristics in familiar terms: walls compartmented and divided by pilasters painted to imitate marble; walls panelled and carved; he recommended the use of 'Norman oak', often parcel gilt, as appropriate. He illustrates a style without finesse.[61] His representation of a Louis XIV curtain cornice has, like those at Windsor, no Regency swagged drapery; the vallance is instead gathered into flutes,[62] which 'is sometimes termed petticoat, and at other times, hammercloth drapery', a term drawn from its use on carriages.[63]

Smith's reference to the exorbitant cost of Louis XIV decoration — 'extravagant expense . . . cannot be recommended' — may account for Gillows' expedient, in their design for a Music Room (Fig. 235), of combining revived rococo furniture with the fashionable acanthus and with fluted silk on the walls. Fabrics were costly, but this treatment was economical compared with the cost of other rich forms of decoration. The room may have been intended also as a ballroom; the furniture includes torchères, ottomans, and sofas. A rococo drawing room at Selsdon House (Pl. LXXXVIII), designed and built in 1829 by its owner, carries the Regency tate for lavish use of looking glass to extremes; compartmentalism is combined with rococo detail, which stops abruptly at the cornice. Either the chandelier was not hung, or it was omitted to give a good view of the extravagant use of mirror. The room displays the characteristics that recommended revived rococo to grand hotels and theatres (Pl. LXXXVII), where its coarse festiveness found ideal application.

Chapter four

# Gothic Styles

## Gothicism

The varieties of classical interior decoration discussed above had matured over a long period. Whatever the nature of their antique origins, the motifs had been adapted to the exigencies of modern life; incongruities had been ironed out or assimilated. People might inveigh against the solecism of living in saloons and drawing rooms put together from parts of ancient temple exteriors, but they were in practice completely accustomed to it. Not so with Gothic; the amateurs of the style who first used church architecture inside their houses were being self-consciously outrageous; the flippant tone in which Horace Walpole referred to Strawberry Hill and Gothicism was pre-emptive of the mockery of others. As soon as the propagandists of Gothic began to take it seriously — it is difficult to be both romantic and flippant, although Byron managed it — so was the case against it made seriously (and, by the Catherine Morlands and Scythrops, comically).

Many people, including Payne Knight, rejected Gothic as unsuitable for interiors — the Downton interiors were all classical. One of the charges against it was impracticality; upholsterers imperilled their reason attempting to reconcile modern draped curtains with pointed Gothic windows. It was difficult to find appropriate furniture; not everybody could design their own, or wished to pay an architect to do so. It was probably this kind of problem — supplemented by Laugierian ideas of fitness — that led Repton to declare 'the only rooms of a house which can, with propriety, be Gothic, are the hall, the chapel, and those long passages which lead to the several apartments'.[1] He may have been influenced also by the theory of 'character', by which a building, and presumably a room, should declare its purpose; the purpose declared to most people by Gothic might be thought to be too ecclesiastical for a drawing room; it was a period when society still

prayed. However, other factors favoured Gothic. In the age of the parvenu, old families wished to assert their old status and new wished to flaunt their heraldic credentials, often based on optimistic pedigrees. The opportunity of emblazoning coats of arms in glass was a leading motive of many who chose the Gothic style; Beckford of Fonthill, arch-gothicist and arch-snob, answered Hope's criticisms by thus identifying his motive for adopting the Gothic style.[2] He may well have been speaking the truth.

The use of an outmoded style for contemporary living presented considerable problems, aesthetic and practical. One solution was so to 'decorate' Gothic that it became modishly contemporary; Walpole filled Strawberry Hill with damask, wallpaper, and painted and gilded Gothick tracery filled with glittering mirror glass; he perceived the compound character of the result: 'The designs of the inside and outside are strictly ancient, but the decorations are modern; and the mixture may be denominated in some words of Pope, "A Gothic Vatican of Greece and Rome"'.[3] Another solution was to turn it into romantic scenery of the kind associated with theatrical performances (Fig. 167), a blend of literary and architectural extravagance, as did Beckford at Fonthill (Fig. 236); the penalty was that the vast spaces of Fonthill were virtually uninhabitable. Another was to synthesise it with other decorative styles, as did George IV at Windsor (Pl. XCIV). None of these expedients was mutually exclusive.

Gothicism affected not only buildings, inside and outside; its effect on dress was a measure of its pervasive influence. Ackermann supported classical antiquity against antiquarianism in dress; in March 1809 the *Repository* congratulated itself that, 'By following . . . antiquity . . . the

XCI 'Library of Sir C. T. Staunton Bar.', at Leigh Park', Hants., designed by Lewis Vulliamy, 1832–3

LIBRARY OF SIR G. T. STAUNTON BAR.T AT LEIGH PARK.

XCII 'Gothic Bedroom', from the *Repository*, 1813

XCIII Design for the south wall, the Dining Room, Windsor Castle, c.1826–8

present taste has happily emancipated the ladies from . . . ridiculous lumber . . . systems and powder, whalebone and cork, flounces and furbelows, and pockets and pincushions . . .'.⁴ However, by March 1811 the *Repository* feared that 'the monotonous forms, discordant colours, and ostentatious display of ornament, which distinguishes the dresses of the fourteenth and fifteenth centuries, are really more admired by ladies in their hearts, than the prime taste and modest elegance of the Grecian costume'. The Gothic movement threatened even the high waist, the most obvious of classical influences on female dress; a dread symptom appeared: 'the disposition which has lately manifested itself among many ladies to enter again upon all the horrors of long waists'.⁵

The ladies would have seen many long waists upon the stage (Fig. 168); romantic novels had familiarised them with the idea of Gothic, and the stage accustomed them to Gothic scenes inhabited by Gothic people. With George IV's coronation, the stage became real life and Cockerell, for one, found it utterly convincing: 'One seemed transported into history. I never once associated a modern note with it'.⁶

Gothic interior decoration in the early nineteenth century suffered from being ignored by some of the most creative designers. Thomas Hope, despite his high opinion of Gothic architecture, despite his eclecticism and encyclopaedic knowledge, never attempted Gothic as a style. His opinion that architecture 'is essentially an art of direct utility; its productions must be ruled . . . by fitness'⁷ may have excluded Gothic, but it was more likely to have been a matter of inclination. As it was with Percier and Fontaine, the fountain-head of much Regency design; the latter said dismissively of mediaeval art that 'celui-ci est trop éloigné de nos moeurs'; the former, with more than a touch of hauteur, 'cela n'est pas fait pour nous', regretting the English export of 'le goût des ogives, des petites colonnes, des vitraux . . .'.⁸ The interest in mediaevalism shown in French late eighteenth-century history painting,⁹ the mediaeval dress and decorations used at the marriage of Napoleon and Marie Louise, led to little French gothicism before the reign of Charles X. The lack of interest of Hope and the French — not to mention the Italians, who had but a sparse Gothic heritage on which to build — deprived Regency designers in this instance of two of their major sources of inspiration.

## Beckford of Fonthill

In these circumstances the activities of Beckford, who was reputed the richest commoner in England and who played the part in the early nineteenth-century Gothic movement that Horace Walpole had played in the later eighteenth century, were of crucial importance. Beckford, who appears in the perspective of time as one of the three greatest creative connoisseurs of the Regency period (the others being Hope

and George IV) found his vocation early. In 1781, before attaining his majority, he defined with sinister accuracy his path for the next seventy years; he should never be 'good for anything in this world, but composing airs, building towers, forming gardens, collecting old Japan, and writing a journey to China or the moon'.¹⁰ He omitted his considerable talent for invective.

Beckford had a surfeit of accomplishments: musician, architect, gardener, collector, writer and, he might have added, bibliophile, designer, and interior decorator. His brilliance was flourished before the world. He 'caught a sentence at a look' and 'could easily read and understand a goodly-sized octavo volume during his breakfast'.¹¹ He was learned; besides the 'classical languages of antiquity, he spoke four modern European tongues, writing three of them with great elegance'.¹² As an exercise he translated, from Arabic into French, excerpts from the cruel and splendid world of the *Arabian Nights*; in 1814 he rejoiced in the impression that his pronunciation of Arabic and Persian had made on Langlès, the French orientalist.¹³ He saw into the darker recesses of his soul; in 1780 or earlier, he wrote in a large and unformed hand a thinly disguised self-portrait: 'The pride of Ancestry and a haughty consciousness of his descent . . . rendered him obnoxious to the World in general. And finding himself disliked and dreaded, he had retired from court to the solitude of an ancient castle in the midst of his Duchy, where he employed himself in literary pursuits and forgot his ennuis and ill-humours . . . [sometimes] Architecture engaged his attention, and he built lofty Towers in the morisco style, and added magnificent Corinthian porticos to the gothic abodes of his ancestors. When this rage was subsided, the form of antiquities began to predominate . . . medals and tesselated pavements . . . rusty helmets, tattered shields, inscriptions and broken monuments . . .'.¹⁴

The passage prophesies his career, up to his retirement in a 'lofty Tower'. In the words of his famous aphorism 'I do not drink, I build'. Like George IV and Hope, he took an active part in designing; Rutter asserted of a 'panoramic survey' of the interior of Fonthill, that 'it was executed from a sketch made by Mr. Beckford himself. The colossal height . . . the defiance of all common-place or ordinary arrangement, and the daring originality of its design, were probably far beyond the range of his professional architect'.¹⁵ He sought refuge from 'ennuis' in his Gothic sanctuary with its amazing enfilade, at the end of which was his half-burlesque — and only half-burlesque — oratory. His 'literary pursuits' supplied vital incentives; Fonthill was born of literature, and, despite its Gothic form, partly of the literature of the Orient. *Vathek*, begun in 1782, was thirty years later praised in high language by Byron as a '"sublime Tale" . . . for correctness of costume, beauty of description, and power of imagination it far surpasses all European imitations' of oriental tales;¹⁶ it has retained its extraordinary power. Beckford's letters are of a captivating vitality and spite. He had the self-

sufficiency of the complete narcissist. 'His daily meals, whether alone or in company, were always served up in rare and fine china, whilst all the appendages were silver, gold, or gilt'.[17] The one thing on the list which he ignored was the antiquarianism of 'rusty helmets, tattered shields, inscriptions and broken monuments'; as with George IV and Hope, the aesthetic impulse predominated. Opera, the total, and totally irrational, aesthetic experience, was one of his favourite delights.

His eclecticism appeared early; on the Grand Tour he enjoyed, at Pisa in the Campo Santo, the 'mixture of antique sarcophagi with Gothic sepulchres', and the cathedral itself impressed with its blend of Grecian design, Gothic proportion and general Orientalism of appearance. Portugal seized his imagination; he did not return after 1798, but 'in a sense, he never left' the '. . . fabulous, crazy loveliness of that lotus-eating, comic-opera, devout, ridiculous moonish world . . .'.[18]

Fonthill Abbey (built 1796–1812) disappeared in 1825 in a way that Aladdin himself might have engineered, but its memory lingers in the six different publications that celebrated it and in the fiction of Edgar Allan Poe.[19] Its interiors displayed several styles. The first and most defiantly undomestic was the completely uncompromising Gothic of the Entrance Hall and the Octagon (Fig. 236). The dimensions were stupendous; the Entrance Hall was seventy-eight feet high with doors

thirty feet high (always opened by a dwarf,[20] a conceit that belonged to an earlier age); the Octagon, not as high as the lantern at Ely by which it was inspired, was at 128 feet almost thirty feet higher than the loftiest mediaeval nave in England, and the comparatively confined floor space exaggerated the height. These astounding spaces would probably have been extended into the projected 'grand baronial hall' had it materialised. The effect must have been quite unmediaeval, with simulated graining on the woodwork, 'chalky and cold'[21] stucco on the walls, crimson and scarlet curtains, and, in the Octagon, 'brilliant stained glass of purple, crimson and yellow, in a tesselated pattern' in the lower windows, and frosted glass in lozenge shaped panes edged with yellow in the lantern.

A different style is displayed in the rooms of the grand enfilade — over three hundred feet[22] — which extended either side of the Octagon; these were St. Michael's Gallery (Pl. LXXXIX), King Edward's Gallery (Fig. 237), the Vaulted Corridor, and the Oratory. The first two rooms made up the longest uninterrupted space in the building; a large window was placed at the south end of St. Michael's Gallery, whilst a long sequence of tall windows marched along the western wall, the books opposite veiled by scarlet and blue curtains from the sun. The rooms were in fact enormous libraries that contained about twenty

**236** 'Fonthill Abbey, Octagon, looking S.E.', 1823

**237** 'Fonthill Abbey, King Edward's Gallery looking N', 1823

thousand books, many distinguished by sumptuous bindings, whether original or Beckford's. His attention to detail was unremitting: 'to be bound in plain, chaste, fragrant russia, as pure and simple as possible, gilt leaves kept large and roughish'.[23] He boasted: 'The cabinets (in St. Michael's Gallery) contain some six 100 volumes of the greatest beauty, interest, and curiosity. . . . The rarest & finest travel books (those of the C15th and C16th) are now in full view and available: in short 'tis a marvel. An intelligent connoisseur could not take a step in this gallery without exclaiming "indeed, there is nothing like this in the world".'[24]

These rooms had large Gothic windows, but the stained glass was confined to their upper parts, the lower being filled with huge sheets of expensive plate glass — when Fonthill fell, the largest amount of plate glass in any house in the kingdom fell with it. Only the three windows at the south end of St. Michael's Gallery were entirely glazed with stained glass, perhaps to protect the books from the strong morning sun. The glass was by the Egintons, father and son. The fan-vaulted stucco of St. Michael's Gallery vault was of a delicate stone colour, 'jointed and party coloured',[25] that of the ceiling of King Edward's Gallery of oak, flat and composed of reticulated Gothic compartments. The curtains of both apartments were simply hung, without a single contrived Regency fold; the decorative resources of the upholsterer were restricted to the gold fringes in St. Michael's Gallery and totally

renounced in King Edward's Gallery, although the curtains in both had 'heraldic borders',[26] discreet enough to be undiscernible in the prints. The simplicity is a studied effect.

The furniture in these two galleries is uncommonly interesting (see p.422); it includes 'Renaissance Revival' pieces, ebony, lacquer, and boulle. Beckford appears to have attempted to create a 'Tudor' impression, and the curtains may have been designed to further this, much as the 'Marot' curtains at Windsor were associated with seventeenth-century revivalism. Whatever the intention, the association of lacquer, boulle, and ebony is very much a later seventeenth-century taste, and whatever the date Beckford imagined the old furniture in these rooms to be, it was mostly seventeenth century.[27] This (probably unintended) seventeenth-century character was strongest in King Edward's Gallery — an impression heightened by red damask walls and the ranges of oriental porcelain in the cabinets. The pieces on the Borghese table were of a kind associated with seventeenth-century princely collections — a 'mounted nautilus, upon an ivory plinth, carved by Benvenuto Cellini'[28] and a silver-gilt and ivory vase, one of a pair by Willaume, the Huguenot silversmith.[29] The numerous candlesticks were 'executed by Vulliamy, after designs by Holbein';[30] they were actually designed by Beckford and Franchi. Other objects in St. Michael's Gallery included a seventeenth-century German amber cabinet and an 'ancient reliquary' said to have been brought by St. Denis from Palestine; it is a mediaeval Limoges enamel *châsse*. The walls of St. Michael's Gallery, pink in Rutter's and Britton's illustrations, are described as 'a plain buff'.[31]

All the Gothic rooms at Fonthill of which an illustration exists eschewed chandeliers, or any illumination save single candles; nothing of the massed candelabra or massy chandeliers so popular in the period. Abundant candles were a contemporary example of conspicuous consumption, and Beckford was never averse to being regarded as a conspicuous consumer; the crime of 'lèse-économie'[32] was not capital. The single candles were as much part of stylistic consistency as were the simple curtains.

The Galleries led to the Oratory, similar in intention to Walpole's Tribune but more stately and more dramatically situated. The hush of the preceding Vaulted Corridor and Sanctuary — 'an involuntary silence falls upon every visitor'[33] — prepared one, as one passed through bronze doors modelled upon those of Henry VII's Chapel, for a 'Portuguese' experience: 'When dimly illuminated by the rays of its own simply elegant lamp . . . when the windows of the adjoining gallery are shrouded by their crimson, purple, and gold draperies, and the soft solemn organ sends its mellow tones through the echoing galleries, whilst the odours of eastern perfumes contribute their fragrance to feast another sense, it is more easy to fancy than to depict the seraphic influence of such a scene'.[34] Beckford and the seraphs had created a

**238** Fonthill Abbey, the Grand Drawing Room, 1823

setting that astounded all in the most gratifying manner. The drawback was that these rooms were rendered almost completely uninhabitable by cold and noise; the height and situation of the building made it at times a kind of Wuthering Heights, which had an effect on Beckford not far removed from torment. Practicalities were ignored: 'All the Abbey, with all its Towers, furnishes but about 18 bed-rooms, thirteen of which, from their almost inaccessible height, their smallness, their want of light and ventilation, from one or all of these causes combined, are scarcely fit for their intended use; and of the other five, not one has a dressing room'.[35] This architectural silliness parallels the literary silliness of 'Gothic' novels.

Another room, the 'Gothic Cabinet', sounds as if it came from a different world, Strawberry Hill and Mme. Récamier's bedroom combined: 'A highly ornamented and elegant little room; the ceiling covered with architectural decorations'; it was vaulted, ornamented with Gothic 'tracery' and the 'walls hidden by mirrors, by plate glass, or by silk. In the embowed recess are three windows, each of one piece of plate glass; an instance in which the effect of that superb article of modern luxury is carried as far as possible'.[36] This room was at one time Beckford's dressing room.

To the pomp of the decorations was added the boast of heraldry. The fanciful Beckfordian 'extraordinary accumulation of descents from royal and illustrious families',[37] which provoked a savage sneer from Cobbett, was stamped on every available surface, ranging from vast areas of ceiling to the tiny and incessantly repeated motifs of the arabesques which Beckford designed for artefacts in silver and gold. His absorption in the subject reached the point of mania.[38] The Entrance Hall contained seventy-four coats of arms on the frieze of the roof; King Edward's Gallery had portraits of King Edward and six 'royal and most distinguished knights' whose arms blazed in the windows opposite; on the frieze of the entablature were placed the arms of Edward III and seventy-one knights of the Garter 'from all of whom Mr. Beckford is lineally descended';[39] the ceiling was embellished with Beckford's Latimer Cross, as were the cabinets and other furniture, including the base of the Borghese Table. The King himself at Windsor did not go so far. He had no need to.

## 'Ecclesiastical' Gothic

The paucity of published sources on Gothic architecture (pp.162, 163) affected the art of interior decoration, and all the more so since the popular pattern books were hardly forthcoming with information. George Smith, for example, showed only one example of Gothic decoration, an engraving of 1807 for a 'Drawing Room decoration'.[40] It consists of a wall punctuated by three Tudor arched Gothic bays, with sofas in the two outer recesses and a table in the middle; belonging

239 The Grand Hall, Corsham Court, Wilts., designed by John Nash, 1797–8

decisively to the 'architectural' rather than to the 'decorated' type of interior, it is neither imaginative nor interesting.

The easiest thing for those who wished to use Gothic and had the means was to commission designs from an architect. The most obvious source for Gothic detail were the great ecclesiastical edifices, and it is not surprising that much domestic Gothic bore clear traces of ecclesiastical origins; such was the Grand Hall at Corsham, designed in Nash's business-like Gothic in 1797–8 (Fig. 239; see p.317). This

**240** 'The Monks Room' or 'Parloir of Padre Giovanni', the house of Sir John Soane, Lincoln's Inn Fields

Gothic is of a type he resorted to elsewhere (Pl. XC); thin, wiry, angular and hard, with a good deal of cusping and a mechanistic look probably influenced by the use of cast iron; the balustrades and supports at Corsham were cast at Coalbrookdale. The form of the staircase and treads, probably also of cast iron, perhaps trimmed with brass, is typical Nash. He was at this time in harness with Repton, whose excellent taste led him to have strong views on cast iron; Repton

thought it should be gilded or bronzed, to acknowledge its nature: 'otherwise it will appear unequal to its office'.[41] If 'iron columns be made to represent stone, they will appear too light and weak. . . . This remark is every day confirmed by the too slender groins of Gothic Arches, to imitate stone, in plaster or cast-iron . . .'.[42] The columns at the end of the hall at Corsham, which are not over thin, may have been of iron enclosed in wood, a method Nash later used for the 'Pompeian' columns in the Drawing Rooms at Brighton (Pl. XCIX).

'Brother' Soane — a term mockingly applied by his fellow freemason Nash — contemplated the Middle Ages with some awe, a notion that one can be sure never crossed Nash's mind. Soane assembled in his own house the 'Parloir of Padre Giovanni' (Fig. 240), supposed to 'impress the spectator with reverence for the Monk' (a far cry from the ironic rationality of the eighteenth century: 'Egypt, the fruitful home of superstition, affords the first example of the monastic life').[43] Soane's description of his 'Parloir' reveals the spell of Gothic associations, perhaps even of Gothic novels: 'The interest created in the mind of the spectator, on visiting the abode of the Monk, will not be weakened by wandering among the ruins of his once noble monastery. The rich Canopy, and other Decorations of this venerable spot, are objects which cannot fail to produce the most powerful sensations in the mind of the piety of our forefathers, who raised such structures for the worship of the Almighty Disposer of Events'.[44]

Libraries were often associated with the learning of the Middle Ages, and hence thought appropriate in Gothic; Soane, whose Gothic was more memorably applied in more subtle ways (see p.303), designed a fully fledged Gothic Library for Stowe in 1805; it had a fan-vaulted and panelled ceiling, constructed by the plasterers on site from casts taken from the rich late Perpendicular decoration of Henry VII's Chapel in Westminster Abbey, perhaps the most frequently raided of all Regency Gothic sources. The library had elaborate Gothic bookcase doors, and a fully fledged Gothic canopy — all curiously at variance with the simple ebonised and bone Regency Gothic furniture that stood in the room, and that has been attributed to Soane (see p.415).[45]

The first Gothic interior at the Prince Regent's Carlton House, the Conservatory, was designed by Hopper and begun in 1807 (Fig. 34; see pp.77, 165). It had free-standing columns forming a 'nave' and two 'aisles'; free-standing columns were fairly rare in domestic Gothic other than in entrance halls, no doubt because they gave too church-like an air. It was hardly a conservatory in the true sense of the term; more a long Tudor Gothic gallery, elaborately decorated in ironwork painted to simulate stone. 'A great deal of cheerfulness pervades the whole', said the *Repository*, describing a fête held in June 1811, for which two thousand guests were asked to come dressed in articles of British manufacture; a fountain was installed, with green moss and artifical flowers.[46] In 1812 a mat that imitated grass was introduced to cover the

Portland stone pavement.[47] The interstices of the fan-vaulting were filled with armorial stained glass; this, together with the glass from the sky light of the staircase at Carlton House, was later removed to Windsor Castle; on January 13th, 1827, George IV wrote in an imitation of his architect's accent: 'the whole of it must be kept, and paid for by the Publick, for Windsor Castle, I shall find where to place it, although Wyatville hum'd and haw'd at first a good deal about it, however, I brought him at last to say, that "he cud pleace soom of 't to advantage' though E ad not joust thin fix'd where"'.[48] The statues were of Coade stone. Beyond lay the Dining Room and the Golden Drawing Room.

Nash's brand of Gothic was seen at Carlton House, in the Dining Room for which estimates were drawn up in 1814 (Pl. XC). It is pretty but prosaic; odd, because Nash was capable of poetry, not least when he was being fantastical. The panelling was in varnished oak with burnished water gilding; the Gothic ornaments were partly in oak and partly in plaster simulating oak. Nash gilded *his* monks' heads — the eight that terminated the brackets from which hung the lustres.

A series of Gothic designs shown in 1813 in Ackermann's *Repository* have the overweening quality of Fonthill Gothic; that for a staircase particularly evokes Fonthill, and to judge from the figure that stands on

it the staircase was intended to be at least thirty-five feet high; the text speaks of it as 'not calculated for very large dimensions', a measure of how far behind taste had left sobriety. The designs are neither inventive nor interesting; perhaps the most characterful is the 'Gothic Bedchamber and State Bed' shown in April 1813 (Pl. XCII), which has a Schinkel or Caspar David Friedrich-like spookiness. The bed is 'formed on the principle of the Gothic crosses of Queen Eleanor' and was to have hangings of orange silk lined with blue, with blue ropes and tassels.

The interiors of Fonthill compare with those of another great Gothic house of the period — Eaton Hall, rebuilt by Porden from 1804 to 1812, and greatly enlarged by Benjamin Gummow in the same style from 1823 to 1825 (Fig. 241). Fonthill had a measured artistry denied to Eaton. The difference was that between two architects and two patrons. James Wyatt, whatever his shortcomings, was a more refined and original architect than Porden; Beckford, whatever his misdemeanours, was a patron of rarer sensitivity than the Grosvenors. The Fonthill interiors have a controlled grandeur that comes from an understood purpose; the rich mixture of furniture and objects is perfectly harmonious. Eaton, splendid and imposing as it appeared, with admirably designed and substantial furniture (see p.416), yet had

**241** The Drawing Room, Eaton Hall, Cheshire, 1826

the air of Gothic confectionery, without the wayward and delicate charm of its eighteenth-century counterparts. Eaton lacked antiques of the type housed at Fonthill; mingled with its Gothic were 'Louis Quatorze' picture frames, probably new.

The great Gothic windows of Eaton displayed the Grosvenor family tree in resplendent leaf; one of Porden's reasons for recommending Gothic was to preserve 'that distinction to Rank and Fortune, which it is the habit of the age to diminish . . . with regard to splendour it [Gothic] is far superior'[49] — the same reason that commended 'Louis Quatorze'. Porden's intention was defeated by the upholsterer; Mrs. Arbuthnot's judgement in 1826 was that Eaton was 'the most gaudy concern I ever saw. It looks like the new bought and new built place of a rich manufacturer . . . there is something much more imposing in the solemn dignity of Lowther, where nothing appears parvenu and all is

oak and stonework'.[50] Mrs. Arbuthnot no doubt had a keen social nose, although her criticism did not extend to the gaudy 'Louis Quatorze' interiors of Apsley House. The extensive use of cast iron at Eaton may not have helped; it was used for detail throughout the house, from the Gothic tracery of the windows to the forest of Gothic pinnacles; cast iron was said by Porden to be 'more desirable than Stone and He gets that for 14 shillings which wd. cost in Stone, £9'.[51]

This variety of Gothic continued to be employed throughout the period, as in the Library at Leigh Park of 1832–3 by Lewis Vulliamy (Pl. XCI), and the Boudoir at Bretby Park of 1838 by Samuel Beazley (Fig. 242). The Library, an octagon with a central pendant, derives its form from a chapter-house; the Boudoir also has a pendant, with fan vaulting and pilasters. Both are architectural and three-dimensional, architects' Gothic.

There was an alternative — decorators' Gothic, the painted illusionistic wall shown by Whittock (Fig. 243), which is really the antique compartmented landscape room in Gothic dress. The whole was to be executed in distemper. Whittock thought Gothic the most beautiful and varied of all decorative styles; suited to all rooms, it was particularly appropriate for halls, dining rooms, and concert rooms — and rooms used for divine worship. One hears an echo of Repton's insistence on 'character'. Whittock added that there was another excellence in Gothic — it had clear rules; without naming Rickman, he quoted Rickman's categories (see p.163).

This signals a new approach to Gothic towards which architects, assisted by various publications, had been feeling their way; the age of Gothic archaeology and the younger Pugin was about to dawn. Whittock himself, who knew the rules, found it difficult to leave old ways; his design for Gothic decoration is based on Perpendicular Gothic, but believing that Perpendicular 'continued lines have an unpicturesque effect in painting' he has mixed them with the 'Ornamented arches of the third style, or florid Gothic', which he thought the most beautiful.[52] Styles continued to be mixed, and Rickman's rules did not prevent Continental Gothic from continuing to be employed in English designs; Rickman himself, in his design for a staircase for the University Library at Cambridge (Fig. 244) used as inspiration the most amazing and flamboyant of all French Gothic-Renaissance staircases, that in the Parisian church of St. Etienne-du-Mont (in Rickman's time it was attributed to Philibert de l'Orme).

The idea that Gothic was appropriate for halls and dining rooms may have influenced the pattern at Windsor, where George IV's new Dining Room and Coffee Room were Gothic (Figs 245, 246; Pls XCIII, XCIV). Morel and Seddon applied for assistance to Augustus Pugin, whose designs for Gothic furniture were published in Ackermann's *Repository* between June 1825 and October 1827 (see pp.416, 421). 'This was just the opportunity calculated to draw forth the abilities of the

242  The Boudoir, Bretby Park, Derby., designed by Samuel Beazley, 1838

XCIV Design for the north wall, the Coffee Room,
Windsor Castle, c.1826–8

XCV The Entrance Hall, Abbotsford, 1831

*Opposite* **XCVI** The Staircase, Corehouse, Lanark, designed by Edward Blore, c.1824

**XCVII** Window Alcove, the Marine Pavilion, Brighton, by John Crace (?), c.1802

**XCVIII** Design for a room in the Chinese style, by G. Landi, 1810

*Opposite* **XCIX** The North Drawing Room, Brighton Pavilion, c.1819

**C** The Music Room, Brighton Pavilion, designed by John Nash, Frederick Crace and Robert Jones, c.1820

**243** 'Gothic style, Landscape in Distemper', wall decoration, by Nathaniel Whittock, 1827

son, to whom his father immediately transferred the business'.[53] It has been conjectured that the furniture in the design for the Dining Room is in the younger Pugin's hand, but that the rest of the drawing is by somebody else, perhaps by Augustus Pugin.[54] A companion design has been attributed to George Morant.[55]

The Dining Room design is a curious mixture. Beneath a Gothic timber ceiling, simply panelled without cusps or curlicues, and a Gothic frieze, are walls divided by strip pilasters and decorated with a peculiar form of stiff Gothic arabesque; the walls are marbled in 'Pompeian' fashion, a mixture of idioms that is seen also in some Regency chinoiserie. Above the doors, which are panelled in Perpendicular Gothic with mirror in the panels, are overdoor paintings of martial mediaeval scenes. In realisation, the arabesque was omitted, and the marbling replaced by large mirrors, with Tudor arches within the compartments. The Pugins designed candelabra for the Dining Room (Fig. 245) (the two on the right); eight were made by William and George Perry.[56] The others, in cast iron, were for the Gallery. The curtains and seat fabrics were in 'Crimson Figured Damask'.[57] An anomalous feature was a large equestrian figure of Louis XIV, on a base of ebony and gilt-bronze in the style of P. P. Thomire.

The design for the Coffee Room (Pl. XCIV), although Gothic, is more enterprising than that for the Dining Room. The Gothic

ornament on the mirror decorates a round arch, and that on the frame of the tapestries is constrained into a rectangular form. The effect is not unlike that of some French Renaissance Gothic. The Gobelins tapestries, woven in 1768 and purchased by George IV in 1825, have fantastic Bérainesque designs in a style which is more 'Pompeian' than anything else; the lambrequins are not unlike those elsewhere in the Castle. The designs for the tapestries, by Claude Audran, were commissioned in 1699.[58] One can see why George IV thought they went with Gothic; they are ambiguous enough to have been described by a Sotheby's cataloguer in 1970 as 'fantastic panels showing the influence of the Chinese style'[59] — one hears again Thomas Jones's comment on the Villa Negroni frescoes (see p.243). The problem of draping Gothic windows is solved (Fig. 246) by putting them within a gilded architectural framework and by keeping the draperies simple; the result is harmonious, with some resemblance to a Pugin reredos. The design illustrated is one of several variants. The torchères are those made by Coade in 1810 for the Gothic Conservatory at Carlton House, now gilded by Morel and Seddon. Apart from the Gothic furniture, the room contained two mahogany and two oriental lacquer cabinets; the last may have picked up the capricious 'Chinese' element in the tapestries.

Some architects, such as Salvin, could express their own strong personalities whilst using more or less historically accurate detail. His

**244** Design for a Grand Staircase, 1834, by Thomas Rickman

**245** Design for candelabra for the Dining Room and Gallery, Windsor Castle, c.1826–8

**246** Design for the east wall, the Coffee Room, Windsor Castle, as approved by George IV

**247** The Sculpture Gallery, Mamhead, Devon, 1838, designed by Anthony Salvin

## Romantic antiquarianism

Tudor and seventeenth-century styles became popular with those whose imagination was stirred by associational antiquarianism. Soane's associationalism was as whimsical as the man himself, but it seems clear that the contents of the Monk's Parlour (Fig. 240), which included a plaster-cast of an Elizabethan chimney-piece from the Palace of Westminster, were not chosen only for the sake of their associations; the room, said Britton, 'has an air of elegance, and displays a taste that we can hardly imagine belongs to the cell of a religious recluse'.[60] 'Elegance' and 'taste' would not today be the first adjectives to spring to mind.

The equilibrium between aestheticism and associationalism was fragile. Two forces encouraged the acquisition of objects with few, if any, aesthetic attractions. One was romanticism: 'In the study . . . stood a pair of light fancy stands, each supporting a couple of the most perfect and finely polished skulls I ever saw. . . . Between them hung a gilt crucifix . . . in one corner of the servants' hall lay a stone coffin, in which were fencing gloves and foils. . . . If I was astonished at the heterogeneous mixture of splendour and ruin within, I was more so at the perfect unanimity of wildness throughout . . . it was the spirit of the wilderness'.[61] Not Nightmare Abbey, but Newstead Abbey; the 'spirit of the wilderness' is seldom considered a desired ingredient of interior decoration, and it contradicted the conventional nature of Byron's refurbishment of the Abbey's interiors.[62] The second force was an antiquarianism that held aesthetic quality of small account, or that was ignorant of aesthetic quality. Romanticism and an aesthetically undiscriminating antiquarianism often went together; collectors of this kind must be distinguished strictly from the connoisseurs and dilettanti who collected for aesthetic reasons. Beckford was a connoisseur and dilettante with exquisite visual taste; Walter Scott was a romantic antiquarian with no visual taste at all. Any collector of antiques and *objets d'art* would be gratified to have a lacquer cabinet that had belonged to Cardinal Mazarin; few would wish to have a cooking pot picked up on the Scottish moors, no matter what its associational interest might be.

Veneration for the antique and the fine arts had filled the houses of the rich with ancient sculpture and modern paintings; these had been placed in rooms decorated to accord, and the museological idea, although it *had* comprehended the natural sciences, had not been incompatible with grandeur and taste. Associational antiquarianism was more refractory; more difficult to accommodate in interiors based on classical sources than were sculpture, paintings, and *objets d'art*, it was easier domiciled in Gothic, Tudor, or seventeenth-century style interiors, not least because pieces of old woodwork — and stonework — found a home there as naturally as did an ancient bas-relief or

'Sculpture Gallery' at Mamhead (Fig. 247) displays, beneath a fan-vaulted ceiling, a series of 'Tudor' statues by Charles Raymond Smith, which includes Lord and Lady Daubeny, Henry VII and Elizabeth of York, Henry VIII and Lady Jane Seymour, Queen Elizabeth and Sir Walter Raleigh, Cardinal Wolsey and a bishop; the sculpture is accompanied by English chairs of a type of about 1680, probably genuine, and modern sofas. The whole was lit by gas. The purpose of such an assemblage differed from that of the traditional grand sculpture gallery; in place of an ordered arrangement of the real and supposed masterpieces of antique schools, resonant with echoes of Mediterranean civilisation and of the literary, political, and philosophical achievements of the ancient world, is a completely modern collection with no great aesthetic pretension but a romantic appeal based on picturesque patriotism. The result has attractions, but the final effect is provincial.

sarcophagus in a classical entrance hall or sculpture gallery. Moreover, those inclined towards antiquarian objects tended to favour the associations of antiquarian architecture and interior decoration. Because such collectors were led primarily by antiquarian and not aesthetic motives, their assemblages frequently lacked aesthetic distinction, and with the general decay of taste this lack went uncensured and often unperceived. Although even Loudon was moved to say of the taste for Elizabethan furniture that it was 'more that of an antiquary, or of a collector of curiosities, than that of a man of cultivated mind'.[63]

An early and famous example of make-believe romanticism, without any true antiquarian content, was Walsh Porter's Craven Cottage (see pp.108, 270, 345–6). Taking over Lady Craven's cottage orné, he raised the building by an additional storey, replaced its latticed compartments with stained glass, and 'fitted the interior with grotesque embellishments and theatrical decorations. The entrance hall was called the robber's cave, for it was constructed of material made to look like large projecting rocks, with a winding staircase, and mysterious in-and-out passages ['intricacy'!]. . . . One of the bedrooms was called, not inaptly, the lion's den. The dining room represented, on a small scale, the ruins of Tintern Abbey; and here Mr. Porter had frequently the honour of entertaining . . . [the] Prince of Wales.'[64] The Cottage at this stage, approved or ridiculed, was undoubtedly an 'aesthetic' compilation.

Its fate in 1834 is a perfect illustration of the way romantic dilettantism developed into antiquarianism (Horace Walpole's interests developed in the same way). It was taken over by Messrs. Baylis and Lechmere Williams, in whose hands it became 'a museum, arranged with a view to pictorial effect'.[65] This 'modern antique' house, given the new name of 'Pryors Bank', was filled with Continental and English antiquities; in extending its boundaries a 'rich harvest from the lumber of brokers' shops' was freely used. Such brokers' shops are mentioned frequently from the 1820s; Loudon speaks of 'upholsterers in London who collect, both in foreign countries and in England, whatever they can find of curious and ancient furniture, including fragments of fitting up of rooms, altars, and religious houses; and rearrange these curious specimens, and adapt them to modern uses'. He says of the Elizabethan style that it is 'seldom necessary to manufacture objects in this manner, further than by putting together ancient fragments'; the brokers included Wilkinson of Oxford Street, Hanson of John Street, and Nixon of Great Portland Street.[66]

Baylis and Williams used panelling from Magdalen College, Oxford in their Dining Room, together with two pendants from above the tomb of Shakespeare, 'inverted and used . . . as footstools'; more panelling came from Canterbury Cathedral, York Minster, and St. Mary's, Coventry. The staircase of Winchester House provided balusters, and a bay window from the same source made a summer-house, probably somewhat in the manner of Mr. Braikenridge (see p.80). There were fragments from the old Royal Exchange; a Gothic chimney-piece from Carlton House, probably that designed by Nash for the Gothic Dining Room (Pl. XC), stood in the drawing room. The furniture included seventeenth-century baroque furniture from the Gradenigo Palace in Venice.[67] The decoration and contents were, in short, a free-for-all; the guests, who often got up 'some piece of fanciful mummery' in antique costume (the stage brought to life), must at times have seen themselves as in a dream, since 'the senses are often deceived, from mirrors . . . being so judiciously arranged', a Soane-like expedient.

Amongst the earliest in the antiquarian field were the Ladies of Llangollen, sat in pathetic elderly contemplation of their fame amidst a heap of old oak, mementoes, Gothic clocks and hour glasses (Fig. 338); the chairs in which they sit, not old, imitate a seventeenth-century type. Their cottage had begun by being painted a warm white (see p.348), much as recommended for cottages in 1804 by Bartell — white walls and woodwork left 'as from the hands of the carpenter'.[68] By 1814 Gothic was being replaced by Tudor, and the ladies were 'Seized . . . with the Oak carving mania', as Sarah Ponsonby put it. The hall, staircase, and a living room were covered in oak, to the extent that twenty years later the interior of the house gave one visitor the sensation of being in a large cupboard.[69] The exterior of the house (Fig. 159; see pp.215, 217) is a case of interior decoration sallying outside; as a contemporary account put it, 'an elegant doorway or ENTRANCE, composed of turned wood columns, in the style of the furniture of the sixteenth century. The whole is ornamented with highly finished carvings, which have been collected from ancient houses in different parts of the kingdom, and fitted together with ingenuity and taste. These decorate almost every part of the interior as well as the exterior of the house.'[70] It may seem a long step from the exterior of the Palazzo Borghese, decorated with ancient bas-reliefs, to the Ladies of Llangollen and their ancient oak, but it can hardly be denied that the step was logical.

The glamour of the Great Hall, with its armour and antiquarian paraphernalia, bewitched the Regency mind, which busied itself in both devising new and renovating old. A quaint example was (it has been recently stripped of its embellishments) at Cholmondeley Castle, where, 'It is intended that the new Hall shall in every Respect have the appearance of an old Gothic Castle, as much as possible consistent with neatness';[71] the 'spirit of the wilderness' was not required; Austen rather than Byron. Built between 1801 and 1805, largely to the sketched-out ideas of Lord Cholmondeley, the Castle was furnished by George Bullock, who supplied and bedecked the Hall with 'mediaeval' armour (Fig. 248); this armour was as much a part of interior decoration as were the stucco trophies (drawn from antique sources)[72] in an Adam

**248** 'Entrance Hall, Cholmondeley Castle', 1801–05, decorated by George Bullock with ceramic armour, 1805

entrance hall; most of it was made from painted ceramic, some of the shields were of painted pine; the prototypes included oriental armour thought then to be Norman. The origin of one helmet was purely heraldic; it never existed in reality. The manufactured 'armour' was supplemented by modern arms, including swords of a pattern issued in 1796 for the British Light Cavalry.[73] One feels the inexorable approach of *Ruddigore*. This decorative approach contrasts with the almost contemporary Browsholme Hall, where the contents of the old but rearranged hall included not only armour but such items as 'the skull found in the west wing . . . a very curious and ancient Scotch piggin'.[74]

An essential link in the chain that connected Cholmondeley Castle with the authentically renovated Hardwick (see pp.333, 426) is provided by the works of Sir Walter Scott. Scott occupies more than a special place in the history of antiquarianism; the magnitude of his

vision of the historical process, expressed in powerfully romantic novels, changed the way in which the past was viewed; he 'did more than any professional historian to alter mankind's vision of its past'; he established 'the fact of change'; his 'great insight is that we are all men of our time'.[75] He was a man of <u>his</u> time, which accounts for Abbotsford.

Scott's Abbotsford was a new building stuffed with supposedly genuine relics. He collected for many years before he built; as his fame grew, people gave him things. He collected not only old objects; he was interested in history in the making, as manifested in armour worn at Waterloo or in a glass drunk from by George IV, which he put in his back pocket and promptly sat upon. Aesthetic quality tended to be irrelevant. The collections largely determined the nature of Abbotsford's interiors; when he moved to the house in 1812, 'we had twenty-four cartloads of the veriest trash in nature':[76] it is hardly surprising that the interior became, as he predicted, 'full of Rusty Iron coats and jingling jackets'.[77] Iron coats were abroad in Edinburgh; at a fancy dress party a 'very gay cavalier with a broad bright battle axe was pointed out to me as an eminent distiller and another knight . . . in black corse armour . . . was the son of an eminent upholsterer so might claim the broad axe from more titles than one'.[78] Theatrical influence helped directly in forming Abbotsford; those involved included, besides William Atkinson and George Bullock, one Daniel Terry, who had trained in James Wyatt's office for five years and then joined the theatre, first as actor and then as actor-manager. All had, in different ways, made illusionism their trade. It can be seen how far away this was from, say, Burlington and Kent; it is not to be wondered at that the results were so different.

The exterior of Abbotsford had been enriched with 'grotesque antiquities'; ancient woodwork was incorporated within. The decoration of the interior was carried out by D. R. Hay of Edinburgh, who was something of a theorist; he produced a volume in 1828 on colour as used in decorative painting. The nub of his argument was that success depended upon a skilful arrangement of complementary colours, harmonised by the addition of diluted versions of the complementary colours and neutralised by a colour that possessed the 'properties of both contrast and harmony'.[79] This was in effect a codification of what had been done for centuries.

At Abbotsford there were no inhibitions against using imitative techniques, and there were no pretensions to truth of material. Thus the Gothic reticulated ceiling of the Dining Room, with its decoration influenced by casts taken by Bullock of mediaeval sculpture ('the ceiling of the dining-room will be superb. I have got I know not how many casts, from Melrose and other place, of pure Gothic antiquity'.)[80] was of plaster, grained by Hay to imitate oak. Hay wrote that Scott 'abominated the commonplace daubing of walls, panels, doors, and window-boards, with coats of white, blue, or grey. . . . He desired . . . rich, though not gaudy hangings, or substantial old-fashioned wainscot work, with no ornament but that of carving, and where the wood was to be painted at all, it was done in strict imitation of oak or cedar . . .'. Four pictures, fixed on the dining room wall, with a narrow oak moulding, were 'surrounded with an imitation of a carved frame of the same material, painted in light and shade upon the flat plaster'.[81]

The more illusionistic the better; a contemporary recorded that the ceilings were 'all encrusted with roses, leaves, fruit, groups of figures, imitated in plaister, and painted like oak with such exactness that it is impossible to detect it without scraping it: an operation in which Sir Walter found a sceptical Swiss Baron engaged one morning, when he came down earlier than his guest expected'.[82] This pleasure in deception is at variance with the notion that exact imitation was not the purpose of illusionistic painting, an opinion which may owe something to

Pliny's well-known diatribe against the deceptions of *trompe l'oeil*; the illusionistic painting in Brighton Pavilion, where complete realism in graining is combined with colours impossible in nature, is at the opposite extreme from that at Abbotsford.

A glance at two rooms will give an idea of the decoration. The Entrance Hall (Pl. XCV) was described by Scott himself towards the end of his life: 'The walls from the floor to the height of eight feet are panelled with black oak which was once the panelling of the pews belonging to the church of Dunfermline. . . . In this panelling are inserted many pieces of carved oak of the same work. The west side of the hall is furnished with long windows, which are filled with painted glass representing the arms of different families of the name Scott. . . . [all the glass at Abbotsford was modern] The ceiling of the hall . . . is vaulted and ribbed [in plaster, painted to imitate oak by Hay] and decorated with a line of escutcheons going round both sides of the hall,

**249** The Library, Abbotsford

with the following inscription in black letter "These be the Coat Armouries of ye Clannis and men of name keepit the Scottish marches in ye days of auld . . ." . . . a large range of schields running east and west along the top of this hall, understood to be the various escutcheons belonging to the proprietor [an arch ambiguity]'. Above the carved panelling was about four feet of 'strong fir painted the colour of oak . . . easily penetrated with nails or hooks of iron, and the space is reserved for . . . arms both Gothic and modern, offensive and defensive, together with the spoils of wild animals, mineralogical specimens and other articles . . . the massive chimney piece . . . modelled in freestone from what is called the Abbots seat in the cloister of Melrose'.[83]

The armour, coated with copal by Hay, dominated the hall; Samuel Rush Meyrick (see p.330) had helped Scott to acquire it. Three casts of human skulls were present; two of Shaw, a then famous lifeguardsman who had killed six men at Waterloo, and a cast of that of Robert the Bruce, disinterred in 1818. The table at the left had a mosaic slab, purchased from the broker Swaby, on a modern Gothic base. An old bronze pot stood before the fire.

The Library (Fig. 249), fitted up in about 1822, was planned by Terry, Atkinson and Scott. The ceiling, of plaster grained by Hay to simulate cedar, was decorated with adaptations of mediaeval ornament, including the 'Roslin Drop', taken from the florid Gothic of Roslin chapel and placed in the ceiling of Scott's bay window. Above the

bookcases is what Hay described as 'painted imitation drapery . . . of a sombre hue of green, in order to relieve the red hue of the cedar . . . that it might also partake of the richness of the backs of the books with which the cases underneath were filled, it was embellished with devices in gold colour'.[84] The drapery is 'antique drapery' mediaevalised with looser swags and lambrequins; there were genuine mediaeval precedents. The bookcases and the Breccia marble chimney-piece are Gothic; the restrained curtains — no swags ('simple useful pattern, without that puling trash of drapery') — were in 'superfine crimson cloth from Galashiels'; they had an inventive trimming 'packthread gilt in oil gold which washes with soap and water'. The whole house was lit by gas.[85] A Turkey carpet was recommended, but the fitted carpet shown in the drawing was chosen. The furniture was extraordinarily mixed (see p.423). Hay thought that the effect of a library should be 'solemn and grave'.[86]

Interiors that were first cousins to those of Abbotsford existed at Broomwell House, Brislington, the residence of Mr. George Braikenridge, Fellow of the Society of Antiquaries, who retired from business in 1820, with an 'ample fortune', at the felicitous age of forty six.[87] An ardent collector, Braikenridge was more concerned with quality than was Scott — his collection included the twelfth-century 'Malmesbury Abbey' ciborium and the 'cradle of Henry v' — but he was remarkably in advance of his time in his interest in ephemera, including such recorded items as an 1852 printed paper biscuit bag.

250  The Library, Broomwell House, Brislington, c.1825

*Bracket and Pendant of the Roof in Christ Church Hall, Oxford.*

*Published by J. Taylor High Holborn London.*

**251** Bracket and pendant of the roof in Christ Church Hall, Oxford, by A. Pugin, 1821

He bought the eighteenth-century Broomwell House in 1823 and Gothicised it, the Venetian window of the room that became the Library being replaced by Gothic (Fig. 250). In the library were the 1821 and 1823 volumes of Augustus Pugin's *Specimens of Gothic Architecture*, and Braikenridge used the engraved illustrations; his doorway, for instance, is copied from that of St. George's Chapel at Windsor. The ceiling supports are also Puginesque; probably drawn from Christ Church in Oxford, they display a motif used also in furniture (Fig. 251). The ceiling was ornamented in 1830 with forty-five carved and painted coats of arms of eminent Bristolians, following advice given by Sir George Nayler, Garter Principal King of Arms. The Tudor stone chimney-piece came from a burnt-out Bristol house; it had seventeenth-century royal associations, perhaps emphasised by the painting of Edward VI placed over it; it was fitted with a modern Gothic grate. The windows were given ancient stained glass. The

furniture consisted of a mixture of Regency Gothic, seventeenth century, and pieces made up from fragments of old woodwork (see p.425). Like the Ladies of Llangollen, Braikenridge was greatly taken with old woodwork.

## A Gothic museum

The museum idea had been so much a part of the neo-classical movement that it is not surprising that the same impulse affected the Goths. In the houses of such collectors as Braikenridge or Messrs. Baylis and Williams it was subsumed in interior decoration; at Goodrich Court, which (Fig. 121; see p.173) was described in 1837 as prompting dreams of 'Froissart and his chronicles of arms and chivalry',[88] it was expressed in the most direct way possible: the house was opened to the public as a museum, with labelled displays of the armour and other historical objects belonging to the armour expert Samuel Rush Meyrick. Meyrick's scholarly collection, which had become a loadstone for artists and antiquarians, had given him a reputation that prompted his commission to reorganise the armour at the Tower and at Windsor, for which he was knighted in 1832. At Goodrich the collection was arranged from the beginning with didactic aim, and less with a 'view to pictorial effect' than that of Messrs. Baylis and Williams at Pryors Bank (see p.326).

Contemplation of the Goodrich interiors illustrates the distances traversed since Horace Walpole opened Strawberry Hill to visitors; the playful and luxurious allusiveness has vanished, to be replaced by a serious and occasionally grim attempt at authenticity. There was little possibility of inspired improvisation; the plates illustrated in Skelton's book of the house were engraved from drawings made by Meyrick several years before the interiors came into existence.

The domestic rooms — Library, Dining Room, Breakfast Room, and Drawing Room — were not open to visitors, and were never illustrated. The Library had a sixteenth-century ceiling said to have come from Breda in Holland; the Dining Room contained modern oak furniture in antiquarian style. The Breakfast Room was described in about 1842 as being furnished in the 'gorgeous style of Queen Anne's time', with paintings by H. P. Briggs R.A. imitating those of Verrio; since the writer included 'Seve and Dresden porcelain' as 'originals of the time of Queen Anne', the description was perhaps not exact. It sounds, with its 'ceiling rich in pattern and highly ornamented with gilding'[89] as if it might have been a variant of 'Louis Quatorze', high in fashion at that moment. The octagonal drawing room was decorated with 'mediaeval' wall paintings by John Coke Smith. Had Meyrick heard of the Nazarenes? He had continental connections.

The most impressive of the public rooms was the Grand Armoury (Fig. 252). It was large, 86 feet by 25 feet, and had what appears to be a

CI The Saloon, Brighton Pavilion, designed by John Nash and Robert Jones, c.1820

CII The Banqueting Room, Brighton Pavilion, designed by John Nash and Robert Jones, 1821

CIII  Design for a 'Grand Egyptian Hall', by G. Landi, 1810

CIV  The South Gallery, Brighton Pavilion, c.1815

deliberately primitive character, perhaps thought suitable to the wild locality; the columns that support the gallery are especially rudimentary, not unlike some seen on Gothic cottages ornés. It sounds as if minor additions followed the execution of the engraving: 'the antient British arms and the first unbroken series of guns from the first invention to the fire-lock are absolutely unique, while the Greek and Roman armour cannot fail to be highly interesting. Above these glass-cases are the emblazoned banners of Edward II . . . in the niches, are placed ten suits on horseback, and several on foot, from the time of Edward III to that of James II'. The figure at the end is 'King Charles 1st in an original buff jacket and gorget, with his armour on the floor of a tent, and his crown and helmet on the table attended by his standard bearer. . . . The face and hand of King Charles which rests on a rapier, were painted by H. P. Briggs R.A.'

One's apprehensions are realised by the reports: 'a splendid collection seriously injured by the puerile style of its arrangement: such as the introduction of dilapidated doll faces into the visors . . . numberless tickets and placards scattered through all the public rooms, reiterating the request, "Don't touch anything". It is pinned to banners, wafered to walls, stitched on hero's garments.' A visitor in 1838 found that the figures and drapery destroyed 'solemnity', but were instructive.[90] This is the world of the didactic museum, with its educational high-mindedness and its aesthetic philistinism. As a substitute for the stately sculpture galleries of Dance or Tatham, it has its unsatisfactory aspects.

The Gothic interiors so far mentioned fall broadly into two categories. The first includes those designed for clients who simply wanted Gothic interiors, more or less grand, sometimes to house coherent collections of furniture, paintings and *objets d'art*, sometimes not; such were Corsham, Fonthill, Eaton Hall, Ashridge, Windsor and so on. The second includes those interiors created for antiquarians of various degrees of avidity, such as Broomwell, Abbotsford and Goodrich. These were, however, not all. There is a third category, which comprises the interiors of genuine old houses that were 'restored' sometimes sympathetically, sometimes not, ranging from the discretion observed at Hardwick to the wholesale re-creation of Charlecote. And yet another category is that of the more or less scholarly re-creations of Tudor and Jacobean interiors for houses that were built in that style in large numbers from the 1820s onwards.

## Scholarly restorations and re-creations

In certain great houses a sympathy with old decoration, plus knowledge, facilitated tactful and understanding renovation. The sixth Duke of Devonshire treated Hardwick Hall with an admirable understanding and restraint that could be imitated with profit today by

**252** 'Grand Armoury at Goodrich Court', by Joseph Skelton, 1830

those who administer old houses; the leap in understanding from Horace Walpole's 'Vast rooms, no taste'[91] to the Duke's sensitivity should not be underestimated. Cothele also received sympathetic attention. At Audley End a more radical policy was undertaken (from 1825), but the result was harmonious and pleasing. The third Lord Braybroke published in 1836 a *History of Audley End* which reveals the scholarly antiquarianism that informed his reparations; he condemned the alterations effected by the first Lord Howard de Walden, when Adam had been employed to modernise the house. He may not have realised that much of the woodwork in the Saloon had been either newly made in Jacobean style, or replenished from elsewhere in the house, during the 1770s and 1780s.[92] His antiquarianism was tinged with the usual genealogical romanticism; after the Great Hall had been restored it was hung with an armorial record of its history: 'From the

**253** Design for chimney-piece, by James Trubshaw, c.1830

brackets silken banners have recently been suspended, upon which are emblazoned the heraldic bearings of the different possessors of the manor of Walden, commencing with Geoffrey of Mandeville, and brought down to the present time'.[93]

Helped by the architect Henry Harrison, who 'designed some poorly detailed Tudor or Jacobean houses',[94] and by the antiquary Henry Shaw, Braybroke attempted authenticity, remarking contemptuously of the eighteenth-century Gothic chapel, newly fitted in about 1770, that 'it was in the style called after its patron, Strawberry Hill Gothic, a mode of decoration sufficiently objectionable under any circumstances, but perhaps never adopted with less judgement or a worse effect'.[95] He used existing decoration in the house as a source for his new work. For the new Library, made from an area occupied previously by bedrooms, 'the ceiling, as well as the compartments containing the books, together with the friezes and cornices, and the pilasters, were carefully imitated from examples in different parts of the house'; the chimney-piece came from the north wing.[96] The drawings for ceilings, friezes, and fittings were 'designed by Mr. Henry Shaw'.[97] When the Dining Room was created from two bedrooms, anxiety to preserve original ceilings led to the retention of old friezes above the demolished separating wall.[98]

Creative antiquarianism was not absent; the treatment of the Great Hall combined invention and conservation. The great oak screen, wainscot and chimney-piece, painted white in about 1740 in the teeth of remonstrances, were stripped with soft soap; the panelling was largely replaced, the ceiling timbers furnished with typical Regency graining, and the old chimney-piece, doubled in size by Henry Shaw, was 'enriched with ancient carvings', which included neo-classical

statues from the Adam Library.[99] Some Charles II style chairs, a Jacobean inlaid buffet, armour and portraits were introduced. The whole was supervised by Henry Shaw.

Certain new houses were accomplished scholarly re-creations. Many betray their true period by detail and surface finish rather than by general inaccuracy of form; the grand staircase at Corehouse, Lanarkshire, for instance, of 1824–7 by Blore, is quite a good shot at the original (Pl. XCVI), furnished as it is with what may be a real late Elizabethan or Jacobean table, a modern Gothic lantern, antiquarian chairs and ancestral portraits. Detail often tells a tale, such as in a design by James Trubshaw for a chimney-piece (Fig. 253) which, with its combination of strapwork, cabuchons, and garlands, gives a somewhat baroque overall impression; it illustrates the way in which designers absorbed the manners of past working experiences and re-expressed them, betraying eclecticism even in attempts at authenticity. Trubshaw had been employed at Fonthill, Windsor, and Buckingham Palace, and had worked for Blore, Henry Shaw and Barry. An architect, no matter how exacting, would find it difficult to control detail produced by such a subordinate.

## Norman and Swiss

Another style essayed for interiors in the 1820s and beyond was the Norman. P. F. Robinson gave several Norman designs, including a drawing room with a flat beamed ceiling and wall tracery of the type (round arches interlacing) that had been thought to have contributed to the genesis of the pointed arch.[100] The arches spring from a dado. This dreary interior, with its round-arched 'Norman' furniture and severe little chandelier, has an arid archaic austerity, slightly mitigated by a large 'Norman' overmantel mirror. The accompanying Hall[101] has a barrel vault and simple unornamented arches; the way in which the staircase ascends from the centre of the back of the hall and divides as it leads to an arched gallery, thus giving two tiers of arches, is pure Regency, a 'Norman' version of the Italianate hall based on such Renaissance examples as that of the Palazzo Lancellotti, from which Regency collectors carried off so many treasures, as recorded by Mrs. Jameson.[102] Given the Italian round arches, the transition was easy.

Far removed from such Mediterranean antecedents was the barbaric opulence of the Grand Staircase at Penrhyn Castle, completed by Welsh masons in 1832 (Fig. 254). The lantern, reminiscent of the Gothic lantern at Ely, surmounts an overcharged richness of decoration that recalls Hindu ornament. A characteristic of some later Regency design is a gouty swelling of the forms, and this seems to have affected Penrhyn. The living apartments at the Castle displayed rich fabrics and 'Norman' furniture. The Norman style had a limited following, although George Smith thought it worth while to include in his 1826

254  The Grand Staircase, Penrhyn Castle, 1832

book a design for a cornice that is 'cabled, fluted, and ornamented with beads, after a Saxon invention'.[103]

Not Norman, but 'Swiss', the interior of the Swiss Cottage designed by P. F. Robinson for Regent's Park[104] had none the less curious affinities with the Norman style. On the one hand some details recall 'Norman' decoration, on the other they appear to anticipate Voysey or even the Wiener Werkstätte. The ornament of walls and fireplace is based on the structural forms of wooden buildings, as indeed is that of some genuine Saxon architecture; the points of resemblance with Norman could be fortuitous, they could arise from the strong synthesising tendencies of the period, or they could be distant effects of Laugierian functionalism. The interestingly ambiguous furniture, almost 'Arts and Crafts', pictured by Robinson was rejected in the real Swiss Cottage for 'twig' furniture of eighteenth-century antecedents.

Chapter five

# Exotic Styles

Exotic or oriental styles — Chinese, Indian, Egyptian, Turkish and Saracenic — attracted architects and craftsmen throughout the Regency period. Their motifs and associations were glamorous; the idea of Eastern magnificence was general enough to be metaphorically extended to classical decoration; the Arabian Nights came naturally to the mind of the journalist who in 1822 likened the splendours of Carlton House to those of the palace of Aladdin, of he who desired 'nothing but gilding, nothing but what looks glittering.'[1]

This being so, it is odd that exotic forms were not much used other than as decorative trim, even in interior decoration; individual rooms that carried through an exotic style in a full-blooded way were rare. This hesitancy perhaps had something to do with social change, with the reluctance of the parvenu to do anything that might attract ridicule; an opulently conventional display was safer. Perhaps the self-confident narrow-minded puritanism of the merchant felt that Athens could offer nothing to Sheffield, or Canton to Russell Square. The growth of racial prejudice may have played a part; when Whittock in 1827 said of the Chinese style that 'the civilised mind revolts',[2] the novel sentiment repudiated a beauty that had captivated the civilised and the rich for over two hundred years.

## Chinoiserie — 'Etruscan', 'ethnic', and 'rococo'

The Prince of Wales, whose tastes, although receptive to new influences, bore the indelible impress of the eighteenth century, remained fascinated by chinoiserie throughout his life. Fortunately he had the will and acquired the means (at the cost of the bankruptcies and even suicides of tradesman) to give that fascination material form; Brighton Pavilion in its final form displayed the decorative resources of the period on a scale unparalleled elsewhere. It had its humbler predecessors.

The Prince's first essay in the Chinese style, the Chinese Drawing Room at Carlton House, was completed in 1792 (Figs 256, 257). It was eighteenth-century in character; in it Holland amalgamated Chambers' Chinese idiom (Fig. 255) with the manner of the French decorators who carried out the scheme from 1789 onwards. The latter included J.-J. Boileau, who painted the Chinese panels and arabesques, probably assisted by L.-A. Delabrière and A.-J. de Chantepie (see p.363).[3] It seems likely that Holland did not have overall control, but that the main protagonists were equal; it is highly probable that the Prince orchestrated the whole, as was his custom throughout his life. The Carlton House formula of compartments bearing scenes of oriental life, separated from each other by pilasters and mirrors and placed above a dado decorated with Chinese fret and other abstract designs, with doors bearing chinoiserie arabesques, was to be used over and over again by the Prince of Wales, finding its rhapsodic consummation in the Music and Banqueting Rooms of the Pavilion at Brighton.

Sheraton's prints of the Chinese Drawing Room give enough clues to make one wonder whether the room had not an 'Etruscan' tinge influenced by the furniture within it (see p.427). Certain motifs such as intersected circles and fret patterns appear in both Chinese decoration and on 'Etruscan' vases,[4] and the intersected circles on the dado and on the frames around the chinoiserie panels, the 'Greek key' atop the pilasters,[5] and the pattern around the door frames have their ambiguities. It is a pity that there are no other and less schematic visual records of the room than Sheraton's, who did not take to the 'Etruscan' style in the 1790s and may not have acquired an eye for 'Etruscan' ornament; it is difficult to recall ornament in a strange idiom, especially if seen fleetingly. If a teleological argument has any weight, one might add that when the furniture and ornaments were reunited at Brighton Pavilion in 1821 in what appears to have approached a re-creation of the Chinese Drawing Room (even the

**255** A Cantonese Room, by Sir William Chambers, 1759

**256** 'A View of the South End of the Prince of Wales's Chinese Drawing Room', Carlton House, by Thomas Sheraton, 1793

257 'A View of the Prince of Wales's Chinese Drawing Room', Carlton House, by Thomas Sheraton, 1793

yellow fabric was re-used), they were indubitably given a Chinese/'Etruscan' setting (see pp.340–1).

In 1802–04 the Prince installed the first chinoiserie interiors at the Pavilion, in harmony with its chinoiserie — or rather composite — exterior (see p.209). The character of the remodelled building had much in common with that of the cottage orné, and the association of chinoiserie interiors with the cottage orné was to continue (see pp.348–51). Not that the style of these first chinoiserie interiors at the Pavilion, installed by the decorators John and Frederick Crace, was to find imitators; it was far removed from both that of eighteenth-century chinoiserie and that of the chinoiserie decorations installed after 1815. Contemporaries called these interiors 'barbaric'; Lady Bessborough in 1805 categorised them as 'like Concetti in Poetry, in outré and false taste, but for the kind of thing as perfect as it can be . . .'.[6] The style had much of a quality that would nowadays be called 'ethnic' (one wonders whether the Laugierian interest in primitivism, so evident in these years, had possibly spilled over into chinoiserie interior decoration (Pl. XCVII)). It is evident that the source for many of the motifs used was not Chambers (although his influence is seen) but the brightly coloured little gouaches of scenes from Chinese life that were exported to the West in large numbers; from these came the rockwork, tea-woods, and the great variety of complicated frets.

The tale that the catalyst was a gift of Chinese wallpapers is almost certainly false, but real Chinese wallpapers were indeed used; their effect differs from that of the Gallic chinoiserie wall decorations used at Carlton House. The Prince also used real Chinese costume on life-size three-dimensional figures, masses of miscellaneous and exceedingly curious Chinese curiosities, and a good deal of Chinese export furniture. There appears to have been no gilding, and surviving remnants of the decoration are of fairground quality, in contrast with the exquisite touch of the French painters who were used at Carlton House. This roughness must have been part of a deliberate effect; there is absolutely no question of the Prince accepting a rough finish for the sake of cheapness, or merely because the Pavilion was supposed to be an informal seaside villa.

There was much stained and painted glass, the chinoiserie equivalent of the stained glass that was appearing elsewhere. Most of the decoration was flat painted; three-dimensional ornament tended to be flat fret-work, with little carving. All was highly varnished with copal. Several ceilings were painted to simulate clouded skies; skies occasionally appeared on the wall, with surrealistic effect; marbling and rockwork were ubiquitous. The surfaces of woodwork and occasionally walls were painted to simulate Chinese 'tea-wood', glazed in unlikely colours. The colours in general were vivid, brilliant, and boldly contrasted.

**258** 'Decoration for a Drawing Room in the Chinese Taste', 1807, by George Smith

The design for a window alcove along the East Front (Pl. XCVII) shows many of these characteristics, such as the bold and primitive patterns, the Chinese wallpaper (behind the curtains), rockwork on cornice and dado, tea-wood on the alcove ceiling. The rudimentary free standing bamboo structure from which the curtains hang is a peculiar and deliberately primitivist construction; another design shows fabric hanging over a similar device placed in front of a mirrored wall. Only in the decoration of the main drawing room, the Saloon, which had blue and silver wallpaper and decorations in which appears a hint of the 'Etruscan', did a more delicate taste appear. These schemes disappeared after 1815, obliterating an unusual episode in the history of chinoiserie. The 'ethnic' lead set by the Marine Pavilion was to a certain extent followed by George Smith's 'Decoration for a Drawing Room in the Chinese Taste' (Fig. 258) published in 1807; the design suggests a compendium of the Entrance Hall, the Dining Room, and the Conservatory/Music Room of 1802–04.[7] Their fresh and original barbarism in Smith's hands became crudity; he has missed the point.

The eventful design by Gaetano Landi for a room in the Chinese style, published in London in 1810 (Pl. XCVIII) is as extravagant as the interiors given to the pavilion after 1815, but is in a quite different hybrid 'Pompeian'/Chinese idiom; the 'Pompeian' element is seen in the multiplicity of slender columns, the suspended apses (it was obviously a regular building, with two apses, two entrances, and two gates) the velaria, the spatial recesses and ambiguities. The room is a puzzle; either the landscape, the shutters, and other features are *trompe l'oeil*, which seems unlikely — the side of the apse, with its caryatid pillars and garlands, can be seen through the window on the extreme left — or the openings were designed to be without glass, with the shutters probably intended to give shade. The source of light in the

room is depicted as coming from the landscape and sky, and falling on to the walls and floor. It seems, although published as a Drawing Room, most probably to have been designed as a luxurious garden room, perhaps, to judge from the landscape, to stand as an eye-catcher on an eminence; it would be more at home in Landi's native Italy than in the English climate.

The development of the Pavilion interiors followed another course. A unique and enchanting blend of chinoiserie and virtuoso marbling in complementary colours, rapidly installed and as rapidly removed, was followed by a series of interiors in 'revived rococo' style (Pl. LXIII) of which the Yellow Drawing Room was the most unrestrained example (Pl. LXXXVI). The flat paintings that decorated its walls were topped by a three-dimensional drop-hung coving, in bright yellow with a 'purple enrichment', probably contributed by Nash, and by fantastical banners next to windows and chimney-piece. These were painted in transparent glazes over silver leaf, a technique used elsewhere in the building. The centre window was ornamented with 'various Chinese ornaments in colours'. The guiding spirit in these decorations was almost certainly Robert Jones, an artist superior in invention and handling to Frederick Crace; Jones had probably worked in the manufactory of Frederick Eckhardt with Boileau, Feuglet, and Joinot,[8] and his style shows French influence; his paintings in the Pavilion's Banqueting Room are influenced by Boucher and Pillement. Wonderful high-keyed rococo chinoiserie designs were produced for the Music Room, which were rejected for the new manner of Frederick Crace.[9] In 1821 the rococo decorations followed the 'ethnic' interiors into oblivion, surviving only in the sobered Corridor.

The North Drawing Room of 1821 that replaced the Yellow Drawing Room was larger, extended to the east; the line of the old window wall is marked by two cast-iron supports concealed by carved and gilded pillars, 'Pompeian' with a touch of India; these are enwreathed with serpents, perhaps originally those of Hygeia, and have at their top the Chinese/'Etruscan' fret (Pl. XCIX). The new decorations, designed to harmonise with the furniture and ornaments from the old Chinese Drawing Room at Carlton House now installed here, were a blend of chinoiserie, 'Etruscan', and 'Pompeian' motifs. They were executed in flat painting and gilding, the walls being separated into compartments in the 'Pompeian' manner but without pilasters and without wall-paintings. Large mirrors in flat fret-cut frames were put into the returns of the bay and elsewhere; the panels of the door frames also contained mirror. The details of the ornament that marks out the compartments in the North Drawing Room are taken from the Chinoiserie/'Etruscan' details of the pier tables (Pl. CVI), clock and candelabra that furnished the room — interlaced circles, Greek key fret, and so on. Even the eastern looking 'lambrequin' motifs over the panels have their counterpart in decorations from Herculaneum. The colours of flake white and gold (gilding was admitted in unbridled quantity) were intended to contrast with the vivid red and gold of the adjacent Music Room (Pl. C) and Saloon (Pl. CI), as the reticent ornament was chosen to contrast with the riot on either side; the pink ceilings are plain.

Whittock in 1827 made it clear that he did not like the Chinese style, saying that 'If the Chinese style is ever used with effect it must be in large summer apartments, devoted to public amusements. But the painter will never find it in his interest to recommend this style of decoration, as it is attended with endless trouble and expense'.[10] Whittock's chinoiserie (Fig. 259) was appreciably more domestic than either Landi's palatial pleasure hall or the overwhelming richness of the palace at Brighton; he recommended the use of old china as a source for motifs.

Whittock proposed a chinoiserie scheme much like that of any compartmented landscape room: 'If the room is to be divided into panels, make it form an open viranda, with bamboo sticks, forming any Grecian or Egyptian fret ornaments; and if the line is continued parallel with the ceiling, let it be broken with small bells or flowers . . . the landscape seen through the viranda cannot be too faint, nor the sky too serene.'[11] However, certain features in the design encourage speculation about Whittock's sources, especially given his peculiar statement quoted above (see p.242) that defined the 'Etruscan' colour scheme as pale, so at variance with the traditional terracotta, black, and white. The tassel-hung curtain, especially in the side-panels, reminds one of that on the pier table removed from the Chinese Drawing Room at Carlton House to the North Drawing Room at Brighton (Fig. 256); the central dado motif of interconnected elongated lozenges is not unlike a motif on the Chinese Drawing Room chimney-piece, also moved to the

Plate XL.

**259** 'Chinese Decoration', by Nathaniel Whittock, 1827

260 Carlton House, the Armoury, 1814

261 The 'Drawing-Room', the Duchess Street house of Thomas Hope, 1807

redecorated North Drawing Room of the Pavilion; even the round motifs in the dado are broadly reminiscent of the exquisitely refined 'Etruscan' chinoiserie motifs used in the Chinese Drawing Room pier tables (Pl. CVI) and *objets d'art*. Taken separately, these would mean nothing; taken together, it seems likely that Whittock had taken a stroll in the North Drawing Room at Brighton.

Whittock, as a professional painter, did not mention the easiest of decorations, Chinese wallpaper. This remained in fashion throughout the period; Scott at Abbotsford, for instance, in the midst of the antiquarian hugger-mugger, found room for 'twenty-four pieces of the most splendid Chinese paper, 12′ high × 4′ wide, a present . . . enough to furnish the drawing room and 2 bed-rooms'.[12]

## The apotheosis of chinoiserie, and the Indian taste

Whittock wrote that he was 'aware that he is running counter to the prevailing taste in the highest quarter, by condemning the introduction of the Chinese style. The Chinese apartment at the pavilion at Brighton [this must mean the Music Room] may be cited as an instance of elegant decoration, and such it indisputably is . . . but even in the room above mentioned this style will find few admirers, and time has shown but a few imitators.'[13] The Music Room (Pl. C) contains a chinoiserie of dazzling extravagance. One says 'chinoiserie', but the room is a synthesis; the red and gold paintings on the walls, organised

in the familiar compartments, are taken from Indian scenes by William Alexander, and there is much eclectic detail.[14] Nash provided the basic shape; the dome, the octagon canopy, and most probably the details of the dome, with its cockleshells diminishing in size towards the apex, are his work. The King drew the first design for the bamboo wreathed in ribbons which makes up the tent ceiling at either end of the room. Frederick Crace provided the details; his designs, significantly enough, were executed in colourful opaque gouache heightened with Chinese white, unlike the limpid watercolour in which the rejected 'rococo' proposals had been painted.

The curtains, in rich curved swags that echo the swags of the tent ceilings, are at the opposite extreme to the thin folds of 'antique drapery'; they were composed of six separate layers of 'blue and crimson satins, and yellow silks richly fringed', and bore ornaments by Crace, Bailey, and King that cost £3554.11s.4d., which compares with the £1,517 paid to Bailey for the '4 Elbow and 12 Single Chairs, and 18 Runners'. This lilac and gold seat furniture, designed by Robert Jones, was sumptuously carved with dragons' wings and monsters (see p.428).[15] The huge yellow and blue carpet, the largest in the kingdom, was designed by Crace; the eccentric lustres, of frosted and stained glass painted with chinoiserie motifs, edged with blown and frosted 'pearls' — a conceit that may have originated as drops of water on the flower-like forms — were lit by gas. The obsessive richness of the Music Room, the uncanny liveliness of its serpents and dragons — the effect under flickering gas-light (it flickered in the early days) must have been somewhat unnerving — the colour scheme of 'Carmine, Lake, Vermilion, Crome, Yellow and other expensive colours',[16] made up a disturbing world into which English chinoiserie did not again venture.

If a consistent use of the Chinese style was uncommon, that of the Indian was rare. There was a strong Indian element in Hope's Drawing Room at Duchess Street (Fig. 261), which he said was 'principally fitted up for four large paintings by Daniel' of 'buildings in India, of Moorish architecture'; the use of the word 'Moorish' in that context bespeaks a phase of Hope's understanding that he was to progress beyond. The engraving does not show the Persian carpets that covered the floor nor does it reveal the colours, which 'in compliance with the oriental taste' were 'everywhere very vivid, and very strongly contrasted'; they lightened from skirting to cornice, the sofa being deep crimson, the walls sky blue, and the ceiling pale yellow, with azure and sea green; there was a good deal of gilding. 'Some part' of the decoration was 'borrowed from the Saracenic style', although Hope said that the presence of alien objects made it 'impossible to adhere to the Moorish style in the greater part of the detail'.[17] In fact the decoration was a brilliant synthesis, as was Hope's custom. The ceiling is described as imitated from those in Turkish palaces; the peacocks' feathers would not have appeared exclusively eastern to Hope, since he would have been aware of their frequent use in Roman decoration;[18] the bay leaves that edged the ceiling and cornice are seen in 'Etruscan' and other classical decoration; the furniture derived from mainly Roman sources. Hope described the sofa as 'low, after the eastern fashion'; it was an ottoman. The eastern character may have been intensified by emanations from the 'incense urns, cassolettes, flower baskets, and other vehicles of natural and artificial perfumes'.

From one highly charged interior to another, and one in which the Indian style was brought to its highest level in Regency England — the Saloon at Brighton in its latest form, not finished until 1823 (Pl. CI). The designer of this, perhaps the most brilliantly harmonious room in the building, appears to have been Robert Jones working alone. A magnificent unused design by Jones[19] shows Indian three-dimensional ornament combined with chinoiserie paintings; in the event Indian ornament dominated, although the doors were decorated with magnificent English lacquer in the Chinese manner, Chinese bells are included in the decoration, and a gorgeous dragon, probably endowed with painted glass wings, rode above the lustre. The motif of the sky ceiling had survived from the 1802–04 decorations, when the dome had been skied by Louis Barzago.

The compartmented walls and the mirrors in the Saloon are surrounded with burnished giltwood; their Indian canopies are repeated in the marble and ormolu chimney-piece made by Parker, which adopts the formula first seen in the Chinese Drawing Room chimney-piece (as

do the chimney-pieces in the Banqueting Room). The canopies occur again in the wonderful Indian-style wall cabinets (not shown on the aquatint) which are perhaps the most splendid and individualistic pieces, in design and execution, of surviving Regency furniture (Pl. CVII; see p.428). The curtains were in 'His Majesty's Geranium and Gold Colour Silk', as was the upholstery; the wall panels, fluted in the aquatint, were finally to be covered in flat crimson silk, heavily decorated in gold; the painted decoration on which the panels were placed was in brown and silver. The Axminster carpet, also designed by Jones, was a pile carpet as were those in the Music and Banqueting Rooms, whereas the rest of the ground floor was carpeted with Brussels weave; the aim was obviously to contrast the two grandest rooms with the others. The Saloon carpet included sunflowers in its design, a motif that appears in gilded wood on the walls and that was added by Vulliamy to the 'Kylin Clock' on the chimney-piece; the sunflower had oriental connotations, but was perhaps also connected with George IV's self-identification with Louis XIV. The Egyptian winged solar disk, a device here associated iconographically with the sunflower,[20] caps the foliage of the pilasters in the apses.

Indian and Chinese allusions intermingle in the Banqueting Room (Pl. CII). Chinese dragons abound on chandeliers, on painted decoration and on the furniture; the painted panels on the walls are of scenes from Chinese life. Once again, they are set in formal compartments with a dado of Chinese frets. However, the spectacular plantain leaves of the dome, partially *trompe l'oeil* and partially in painted copper, have a precise Indian reference, albeit not to Indian architecture; they are seen in the rich and exotically green landscapes pictured by the Daniells, and it was a stroke of Picturesque genius to bring them within doors; was the idea born from some flamboyant plant housed in the Conservatory that preceded Nash's Banqueting Room on the same site? The dome decoration may also have a reminiscence of the well-known soffit from the Temple of the Sun at Palmyra, which had been used by Adam and others; it shows feathers encircling a sunflower within a dome, and is not so far removed in conception from the Brighton ceiling (Robert Wood's publication, in which it appears, was much in use during the later Regency). The overdoors and the lotus shapes of the gasoliers, tinted sea green, have Indian origins. Robert Jones appears to have been in charge; the room is nowhere mentioned in the surviving Crace ledgers.

The appetite for exotic impedimenta was omnivorous. An example is the 'Armoury' at Carlton House, which occupied five rooms on the attic storey. It was 'a museum, not of arms only, but of various works of art, dresses, etc. . . . arranged . . . under the immediate inspection of His Royal Highness'. The dresses and uniforms formed an 'immense collection'; they were held in presses, and the uniforms were in sets 'from a general to a private, of all countries which had adopted uniforms' — an archive that no doubt served the Prince when engaged in one of his favourite avocations, that of designing military uniforms. Another room (Fig. 260) contained 'some Asiatic chain armour, and an effigy of Tippoo Sutann on horseback, in a dress that he wore. Here are also a model of a cannon and a mortar on new principles; some delicate and curious Chinese works of art in ivory, many rich eastern dresses, and a palanquin of very costly materials.'[21] There is no doubt that these objects were used by the Prince's designers; an unused design of about 1820 for the Entrance Hall of the Pavilion, for example, shows Tippoo Sahib, in the same armour and on horseback, on a panel surrounded by trophies of oriental armour including shields, arrows, spears, and maces, very like those in the Carlton House Armoury.[22]

The fashion was not confined to Carlton House; Goodrich Castle had an Asiatic Armoury which displayed Islamic decoration, with elements from Spain, India, and China. On either side of the doorway stood a Chinese garden seat and what may have been some variety of export Chinese cabinet; within were an Indian mounted soldier and a reclining Rajah. It appears to have had more in common with the displays at the old Imperial Institute than with the imaginative confections of Regency exoticism.

## The Egyptian taste

British designers who wished to use Chinese or Indian decoration suffered from the same disadvantage as with the Gothic — the indifference of the French. This could not be said of the other major exotic style, the Egyptian, drawn by Napoleon's vain-glorious Egyptian adventure within the orbit of French patriotism. In point of fact, the first Egyptianising interior recorded in Britain, that of the Billiard Room at Cairness, was created in 1793, well before the Egyptian campaign and before the appearance of the convenient references provided by Denon's *Voyage dans la Basse et la Haute Egypte*. The room, designed by the elder Playfair was, like the house itself (see p.131), uncompromisingly primitivistic, and it seems obvious that it was Playfair's interest in primitivism and French Romantic Classicism that led him to Egypt; current theory saw Egyptian architecture as a primitive version of Greek.[23] The room had pale yellow masonry walls with painted granite architraves; the ceiling was based on the Baths of Nero at Baia.[24] It may be of significance that Playfair was in Italy in 1792–3, and probably saw not only the decorations of Piranesi (available of course in printed form)[25] but also Antonio Asprucci's Sala Egizia at the Palazzo Borghese.

Robert Smirke saw the Palazzo Borghese on his visit to Rome in 1802 and must have seen the Sala Egizia — and it seems possible that it influenced his splendidly brooding design for a room in the Egyptian taste (Fig. 262); the influence of Piranesi's decorations for the Caffè Inglese is perceptible.[26] The room is, in reality, a landscape room translated into Egyptian. Landi provided his version of a 'Grand Egyptian Hall' in 1810 (Pl. CIII); this also recalls the neo-classical Egyptian taste of the Sala Egizia, which itself owed a debt to Piranesi (Figs 263, 300).

Although earlier, Italian influences were outweighed by the importance of Denon as a source for designers. However, admiration of Denon's powerful images was counterbalanced by the hostility expressed by a powerful French scholar to the modern use of the Egyptian style. Quatremère de Quincy (and earlier the Comte de Caylus) had given it the thumbs down as a subject for imitation (see p.190), and Hope followed Quatremère; he urged young artists 'never to adopt, except from motives more weighty than a mere attempt at novelty, the Egyptian style of ornament',[27] and repeated De Quincy's

**262** Design for a room in the Egyptian style, by Sir Robert Smirke

**263** Design in the Egyptian style, by G. B. Piranesi, 1769

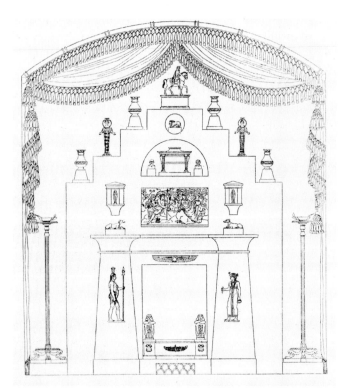

**264** Drawing Room with Egyptian decoration, the Duchess Street house of Thomas Hope, 1807

**265** The 'Closet or Boudoir', the Duchess Street house of Thomas Hope, 1807

comments on the meaninglessness of hieroglyphs. He went on to say: 'Modern imitations of those wonders of antiquity, composed of lath and plaster, or callico and of paper, offer not one attribute of solidity or grandeur to compensate for their want of elegance and grace, and can only excite ridicule and contempt'.

The fine sentiments did not prevent him employing the style at Duchess Street; indeed, its 'little canopus' (Fig. 264) was expressly stated to have been decorated in accordance with the Egyptian antiquities, including a mummy case, that it contained. The decoration appears to have been entirely painted, and the effect of the walls is as wholly Egyptian as that of the Picture Gallery and the Flaxman Room is classical. Only the 'antique drapery' above the frieze comes from a different world. The frieze was taken partly from papyrus scrolls; the ceiling was copied from mummy cases, with a hint, in the detail, of the conventions of 'antique drapery' (in fact an identical idiom occurs in Roman decoration); the prevailing colours of walls, ceiling, and furniture (see p.384), 'are that pale yellow and that bluish green which hold so conspicuous a rank among the Egyptian pigments; here and there relieved by masses of black and gold'.[28] 'Meaningless' hieroglyphs were avoided. The paintings on the walls were set in plain frames studded with Piranesian Egyptianising stars.

The stepped structure above the chimney-piece in Hope's 'tent room' (Fig. 265) could have been influenced by the similar stepped forms, scattered with stars, that had appeared in two Piranesi chimney-pieces;[29] Hope's version is much sparer than those of Piranesi, in which a crowded and restless ornament had jostled Egyptian passivity.

In his 1808 book (see p.360) George Smith gave only one Egyptian-influenced decoration; it consists of a simple compartment with a marbled dado and porphyry skirting, a cornice of chaste stars, and two Egyptian figures in the centre of a panel contemplating a cat; no hieroglyphs.[30] The decoration is dated 1804; Egyptian motifs were popular at the time but the design is Egyptian at a remove; all the 'Egyptian' components are in reality Roman, having been taken from 'un pezzo di obelisco' and other mural decorations at Herculaneum published in 1765 (Fig. 181);[31] the humorous cat and general frivolity are typically 'Pompeian', and presented few obstacles to acceptance.

Smith's 'Decoration' makes a pointed contrast with the *chef d'oeuvre* of Egyptian interiors, the 'Egyptian Hall' in Walsh Porter's Craven Cottage, an extraordinary concoction that found itself cheek by jowl with the Robbers' Cave and the Tintern Abbey Dining Room. Porter's Cottage provoked derision; Repton, for instance, went to see it after having heard that the Prince of Wales 'had commended the taste of Mr. Walsh Porter in a cottage near Fulham'. 'There', said Repton 'I had seen many things done out of the common way and with good effect — and others so whimsical and absurd that I dreaded the sort of taste I might have to encounter at Brighton — But . . . the Prince said

there was doubtless much to approve in the ingenuity with which so confined a spot had been treated. . . . But he added "I hope you do not give me credit for admiring his sofa Camel, or his miniature Gothic or his Flaming Chimney piece!" '[32]

The drawing of Porter's 'Egyptian Hall' (Fig. 266) does not reveal how far the decoration was flat painted and how far three dimensional; the main columns stand proud of the walls, as do the palm trees — described as 'exceedingly well executed, with their drooping foliage at the top.'[33] A contemporary account gives additional details: the Egyptian Hall was 'an exact copy from one of the plates in Denon's Travels in Egypt. . . . The two great doors cost two hundred guineas; they are composed of wrought iron work, divided into various compartments, filled with plate glass. . . . The interior is richly painted in the Egyptian style; it is supported by eight immense columns, covered with hieroglyphs, and at each corner of the room is a palm tree. A sphinx and a mummy are painted on each side of the door; the ceiling is painted with hieroglyphics; a female figure in bronze, as large as life, stands near the door, holding up a curtain painted in imitation of a tiger's skin; and a moveable camel, in bronze, stands near the entrance. The whole of this room is striking and characteristic.'[34] The accoutrements were animalistic; 'a lion's skin for a hearth-rug, for a sofa the back of a tiger, the supports of the tables were four twisted serpents or hydras . . .'.[35]

The most anomalous element in this bizarre chamber is that the walls were clearly conceived as those of the outside, not the inside, of an Egyptian building; this is a courtyard rather than a room, with columns, palm trees, camel, and the semblance of roughly hewn stonework. The eccentric manner in which the chandelier is slung on long chains from the entablature reinforces this effect. One would have expected a sky ceiling, but the account given above mentions hieroglyphs (neither they nor the zoomorphic furniture are indicated in the drawing; perhaps the room went through several phases?). The couple on the sofa look as if they had strayed into a temple precinct from an adjacent drawing room; the effect is surrealistic; Joseph and Potiphar's wife would be less surprising in such a context. The carpet shows two stray Egyptian stars, no doubt two of a host. The window on the right looks Gothic.

Walsh Porter composed music, and wrote a comic opera called 'The Chimney Corner';[36] had he theatrical friends or acquaintances on whose talents he called to realise the effects at Craven Cottage? Whittock declared that 'the only difference between the decoration of apartments and scenery is, that the painting in the former is much nearer to the eye than the latter'.[37] And is there a clue in Hope's words, quoted above, concerning 'modern imitations' of 'lath and of plaster, of callico and of paper' of '*Real* Egyptian monuments' (author's italics) exciting 'ridicule and contempt'? This passage is inapplicable to interior

**266** Craven Cottage, Fulham, the Egyptian Hall, c.1805

decoration, unless of the eccentric type of Walsh Porter's Egyptian interior, which does attempt to imitate a real Egyptian monument, and which did excite both ridicule and contempt.

The other rooms of Craven Cottage were equally theatrical. The chapel had groined arches with pendants; ceiling and walls were 'painted in exact imitation' of the Chapel of Henry VII at Westminster Abbey. The stained glass, said to have been procured by Porter in France and Italy at the beginning of the French Revolution (if true, he was early in the field) cost 'above 800 guineas; the doors were painted in bronze in imitation of the two great doors of Henry VII's Chapel', a source used also for the Sanctuary doors at Fonthill. Beyond were 'several other apartments fitting up in the style of different foreign countries' (see pp.270–1).[38] The house combined elements of both the museum idea and the 'travelogue'; the heterogeneous mixture of styles and civilisations carried the picaresque tendencies of the period to an extreme recorded within no other one building. The main aim seems to have been to amaze and amuse, and the fact that all took place in a cottage orné helped to bring it — but only just — within the pale of acceptable behaviour.

The best known of all Regency interiors in the Egyptian style was the Egyptian Hall in Piccadilly, designed in 1819 by J. B. Papworth.[39] Papworth was exceptional, a Regency architect who become a specialist in interior decoration. He was known for his readiness to turn his hand to anything, from pocket handkerchiefs to palaces, a capacity that in 1815 led to his confident assumption of the middle name 'Buonarotti';

his multi-faceted career illuminates the interconnected world of decorators and architects. Inspired[40] to become an architect by a drop-scene of a Corinthian colonnade and Court at the Haymarket Theatre in 1787 (his father was a leading stuccoist, another predisposing factor), he spent a year studying 'Internal Decoration' with George Sheringham; he there met the decorator George Morant, with whom he was to work between 1808 and 1818.

Amongst his productions were the rustic buildings at White-Knights (see p.56); innumerable designs for furniture and interior decoration for various clients; designs for shop fronts, in which he was considered a specialist; a design for No. 94 Holborn Hill in 1829–32, the earliest 'gin-palace'[41] (it is an engaging thought that the designer of excessively pretty garden buildings also devised the glittering and hospitable gin-palace); various accomplished publications (see pp.70, 406); and reputedly the invention of the oblong prismatic shape for lustres — 'the fashion for the small and long oval or diamond-shaped drop was discarded, and so suddenly . . .'.[42]

Knowing Papworth's talents, one is sure that the Egyptian Hall was more refined and whimsical than the coarse illustrations reveal. Once again, the temple at Dendera supplied columns; the cast-iron railing on the gallery appears to have been a flight of fancy on Papworth's part. Near the apex of the cupola floated the signs of the Zodiac; the name of Egypt had long suggested astrology and magic, but the source for the motif may have been the Temple of the Sun at Palmyra, where it was used in an analogous manner.[43]

The Egyptian style, like the Gothic, was associated with learning, and for that reason was used for libraries; the interior of Foulston's Egyptian Library of 1823 at Plymouth provided a perfunctory example.[44] George Smith included an interior in the Egyptian style in the series of comparative illustrations given in his book of 1828; it also is for a library.[45] Smith, explaining that he attempted to employ the Egyptian style without its heaviness, criticised Piranesi for 'too close a copy of a style and manner which in all its parts is massive and colossal'; it is curious that this criticism, French in origin, should be repeated at a time when massiveness was so fashionable. The design owes much to Piranesi, and in its lightness and vivacity — it has palm trees in the corners — approaches an Egyptian version of the rococo. Whittock also showed the Egyptian style, classifying it as suitable only for large apartments, such as an entrance hall, a library or a museum; again, the emphasis on learning. His decoration was to have large pilasters in porphyry, with tablets in white marble and gilt capitals; all these, needless to say, were to be in illusionistic painting, The sphinx and lions' heads were to be bronzed, the bronze dust to be applied sparingly.[46] The vulnerability of such eccentric and quickly outmoded decorations to time and change accounts for their almost complete disappearance.

## 'Profusion'

To many accustomed to eighteenth-century standards, the flamboyant tendencies of high-style decoration in the first decade of the nineteenth century, especially as seen in the work of the Carlton House set, appeared intolerably vulgar; Payne Knight, never one to mince words, spoke for them. In 1814 he attacked the Prince Regent in vituperative and unmistakable terms in a publication — the *Edinburgh Review* — that was read by everybody with cultural pretensions. Referring to Westall's painting, *The Grecian Marriage*, a Regency anticipation of Gérôme, he declared that 'Happy are the subjects of a sovereign, whose taste is gratified by such objects'; he regretted that 'noise, tumult, glitter, and bustle, become the sole objects of taste: and all the quiet elegance of liberal art, and intellectual gratification, sink neglected and expire'. Worse was to come: 'Even the monster Nero, had he occupied a private station of middle rank [the last classification masked too open a reference] in this country, would have been neither more nor less than a well-bred, well-drest, accomplished, and selfish voluptuary'.[47] The association of the character and luxuries of the Prince Regent with such worthies as Nero was not confined to Payne Knight; a little later Byron, another bogey, said that he had once made a list of the different worthies, ancient and modern, with whom he had been compared, and that these included: 'Nero, Apicius, Epicurus, Caligula, Heliogabulus, Henry the VIII, and lastly, the King'.[48]

Hazlitt attacked Beckford on much the same grounds of tasteless ostentation — under, it is true, something of a misapprehension, in that the contents of Fonthill had by then been compromised by the activities of the auctioneer. Hazlitt saw the Fonthill taste as a petty, gaudy, undiscriminating eclecticism: 'a glittering waste of laborious idleness, a cathedral turned into a toy-shop' (not a bad description of the Portuguese churches that had entranced Beckford); 'an immense Museum of all that is most curious and costly, and at the same time most worthless. . . . Ships of pearl and seas of amber are scarce worth a fable here . . . tables of agate, cabinets of ebony and precious stones, painted windows "shedding a gaudy, crimson light", satin borders, marble floors, and lamps of solid gold — Chinese pagodas and Persian tapestry . . . whatever is far-fetched and dear-bought, rich in the material, or rare and difficult in the workmanship — but scarce one genuine work of art, one solid proof of taste, one lofty relic of sentiment or imagination.'[49]

The meretricious and gaudy strain in Regency taste was not confined to high life: it was taken up with enthusiasm by the aspirant to gentility. Exotic styles gave particular licence to excess. 'Mr. Soho' the upholsterer, talking to 'Lady Clonbrony' who was attempting to submerge her Irishness in fashionable 'Lon'on' (was this a dig at Lady Morgan, an Irish compatriot of Miss Edgeworth, the author?), recommended decorations that mingled Europe and Asia: '. . . the Turkish tent drapery . . . in apricot cloth, or crimson velvet . . . or, en flute, in crimson satin draperies fanned and riched, with gold fringes, en suite — intermediate spaces, Apollo's head with gold rays — and here, ma'am, you place four chancelieres [footmuffs or ottomans], with chimeras at the corners, covered with blue silk and velvet fringes, elegantly fanciful — with my STATIRA CANOPY here — light blue silk draperies — aerial tint, with silver balls — and for seats here, the SERAGLIO OTTOMANS, superfine scarlet — your paws — griffin, golden — and golden tripods here, with antique cranes[50] — and oriental alabaster tables here and there . . .'. The other rooms were to be no less exotic: 'Alhambra hangings' with 'TREBISOND TRELLICE PAPER', were a possibility, or a 'Chinese pagoda', or 'the Egyptian hieroglyphic paper, with the ibis border to match — the only objection is, one sees it everywhere — quite antediluvian — gone to the hotels even . . .', the 'MOON CURTAINS, with candlelight draperies . . . sphinx candelabra, and the phoenix argands . . .'.[51] No wonder that some felt that the architects should step in and sort it out. Such unrestrained satire was no more unrestrained than its object, as Walsh Porter's cottage alone would demonstrate.

# The Cottage

## The cottage orné and the artisan's cot

Craven Cottage's interior was an extreme example of the possibilities open to the cottage orné, but other modes were available. Cottage furnishing extended from the most highly wrought decoration to unadorned simplicity. The French had been elaborate; behind the rustic façades of the Hameau, with their *trompe l'oeil* cracks, lay a world of luxurious and studied artifice; rooms were panelled in mirror, painted with neo-classical and chinoiserie decorations, glazed with Bohemian stained glass and furnished by Riesener and Jacob. The English tended in the early days towards cottage simplicity; thus the Ladies of Llangollen in 1789 painted 'the Parlour and Library a beautiful rich white, the Doors varnished skirting boards chocolate colour . . .'; the dining room was white also, with the seats of the chairs decorated in pale blue convolvolus against a white background. These were the days of their spring, when Eleanor Butler 'Got a bundle of Moss Rose buds. Threw them in a careless manner over the Library Table which had a beautiful effect.'[1] Thirty years later the old ladies would have needed the biggest dahlias to make an effect in the welter of old oak and stained glass.

Edmund Bartell, writing in 1804, opted for simplicity, recommending the use of unpainted woodwork, instancing the Gothic library of Felbrigg in Norfolk; he approved of a cottage which had whitewashed walls as far as the 'mouldings' (the dado), beneath which they were covered with fine matting.[2] And the interest in flowery freshness did not disappear; flowers often grew up the trellis that came from both antique and oriental sources. Such decoration must have resembled that of the upper part of the Pavilion (Pl. LXII), which in Nash's time still survived from the beginning of the century; although the Pavilion trellis was interpreted in a primarily oriental spirit, it was

given flowery borders and a flowery carpet lay underfoot. The method of execution was interesting; sheets of repeated trellis designs were printed with wood blocks and then cut up and applied to the wall in the desired pattern.

Papworth, presenting his ideas for the interior of a cottage orné (Pl. LII) occupied by two ladies, recommended real trellis, chintz, cane and real and painted flowers, the whole suffused with a discreet chinoiserie that was obviously of a kind similar to surviving fragments of decoration from the Marine Pavilion of 1802–04; the emphasis on flowering plants, typical of the period, is striking. The style remains current today. It will be noticed that panelling and pilasters are part of Papworth's recipe. The quotation is long, but the charm of the picture redeems the length: 'The entrance is by a rustic porch supported by the stems of elm-trees; the little hall and staircase are decorated with trellising, composed of light lath and wicker basket-work, very neatly executed, and painted a dark-green: this is placed against the papering of the walls and ceilings, which are of a deep buff colour. Flower-stands and brackets are attached at various parts, from the bottom to the top of the staircase. The railing of the stairs being also of basket-work, the strings, etc. are painted buff or green, as the occasion required; for every part is so arranged, that the green may be relieved by buff, or the buff by the green. The most elegantly beautiful flowering plants are selected as embellishments, and are tastefully disposed on the several flower-stands; thus the walls are every where adorned with them, and some are trained over the trellis of the ceilings, whence they hang in festoons . . . the whole arrangement has a light and tasteful effect. On the outside of each step of the stairs a bracket is affixed, on which small and equal-sized green porcelain garden-pots are placed, containing specimens of the most beautiful plants. . . . The parlour, the music-room and the lobby are very simply and neatly decorated by

cv Knowle Cottage, Sidmouth, c.1818

CVI Pier table, designed by Adam Weisweiler, 1787–90

CVII Wall cabinet, designed by Robert Jones for the Royal Pavilion, Brighton, c.1820

compartments coloured in tints resembling an autumnal leaf, the yellow-green of which, forms the pannels, and its mellower and pinky hues compose a very narrow border and stile that surround them. The draperies are of buff chintz in which sage-green leaves, and small pink and blue-and-white flowers prevail: the furniture is cane-coloured. Upright flower stands of basket-work are placed in each angle of the room, and the verandah is constantly dressed with plants of the choicest scents and colours. . . . The drawing-room is fancifully ornamented with paper in imitation of bamboo and basket-work, in the colour of cane, upon a sky-blue ground; each side is divided into compartments by pilasters, which support a sort of roofing and transverse bamboo rods, to which seem to be suspended the most exquisite works of the Chinese pencil . . . of views of their apartments, representations of the costume of the people, and of the natural productions of China. A very able artist has further decorated this room, by painting a variety of Oriental plants, as supported by the pilasters, &c about which they entwine, and arriving at the ceiling, they terminate, after spreading a short distance upon it. The furniture and draperies are the same as in the parlour. The chambers are papered with small and simple trellis pattern, and the draperies white, with a mixture of lavender colour and buff. In the whole of this cottage there is no portion of gilding; . . . even the book-bindings are unornamented by gold, the lettering being merely stamped upon them.'³

The trellis idiom described by Papworth seems to have been adopted at Knowle Cottage (see p.217) where, to judge from a watercolour (Pl. CV), trellis wallpaper (which continues on the ceiling), and a leafy wallpaper were used; the band of classical scrolls belongs to the curtains. A description of the Morning Room, which opened on to the conservatory and had a Dresden chandelier and mirror, no doubt also encrusted with flowers, concluded by noting that: 'We cannot take leave of this splendid room without noticing the papering . . . it harmonises to perfection with the exterior and is in perfect keeping with the interior'.⁴ The 'Grand Suite of Rooms', obviously an enfilade, was a hundred feet long, with bow windows at each end. The windows were fitted with stained glass at the upper level, plate glass at the lower; seventy tables, large and small, stood along the centre and side of the room covered with bijouteries and Dresden porcelain.

Other treatments were possible. The Swiss Cottage at Cahir, in County Tipperary, one of the most charmingly fanciful of all cottages ornés, possibly designed by Nash — it has the typical Nash 'two-tiered' look — and built in 1816,⁵ has a living room that is turned into an exotic landscape by the use of Dufour wallpaper. Above a partly pictorial dado are the 'Rives du Bosphore', which continue without interruption around the corners of the room; above the chimney-piece is a section of the 'Monuments de Paris', exactly where a mirror would

have fitted. The furniture might well have been 'cane-coloured', of the gentle exoticism described by Papworth.

One of the more delightful of cottages ornés was 'A la Ronde' in Devon, the home of yet two more maiden ladies, Miss Jane and Miss Mary Parminter; the cupola above the thatched roof of their sixteen-sided house bore not a weathercock, but a weatherhen — how far all this seems from the garish Regency world of Lady Oxford and Miss Harriette Wilson! The decoration, much of it carried out by the ladies, made lavish use of shells and feathers. The drawing room had a featherwork frieze that was carried also around doorways and fireplace, its pattern based on that of Portuguese tiles; the feathers were from game birds and domestic fowl. Walls and pictures were decorated with shells, feathers, and rolled paper; the ladies used books and journals as inspiration, plus four fine quality Italian shellwork pictures that hung above and around the drawing room fireplace, itself in the form of a grotto of shellwork with a landscape background in paper. The rooms contained sand and seaweed pictures, cut-paper pictures, a small shell-covered doll representing brother James, and two small tables painted with floral decoration by the ladies and set with a miscellaneous collection of intaglios, coloured marbles, scagliola, shells and mosaic, inserted into putty and covered with glass.

The chef d'oeuvre was a shell and feather gallery in the lantern. According to family tradition, the house was modelled on the Baptistery of San Vitale at Ravenna, and the decoration was intended to emulate the San Vitale mosaics. Be that as it may, the walls were covered with a pattern of shells and seaweed set in panels, interspersed with panels of feather and sand designs, each surmounted by a featherwork bird. A painted crown and the date 1810 commemorated the fiftieth jubilee of George III. At both turns of the narrow wooden 'Gothic' staircase were little grottos with shellwork decoration surrounding panels of mirror glass, and small rolled paper pictures, painted and gilded.⁶ The survival of all this to the present day is little short of miraculous.

It would be difficult to conceive more singular decoration, but the Hermit of Louth managed it. Repton records of the Hermitage in 1790 that the Library, reached by a covered way paved with sheeps' bones, was adorned with not only the skeletons of leaves but 'some real skeletons of small birds — mice — and other little animals, the whole being arranged in the most graceful forms'; the furniture was 'of bamboo sent from India'. The Oratory, paved with horses' teeth, was yet more inventive: 'how to account for the glitter from the walls? — No court dress bespangled with Tinsels could reflect the light like that rich pattern of foliage. . . . They (the walls) were hung with Indian matting of the finest kind, on which the fanciful pattern had been wrought by unheard of means! The Hermit explained that having remarked on the leaf of a plant a glittering substance left by a snail . . .

by early rising and late watching he had collected hundreds of these little artificers (and) patiently directed each little workman in the track he should take.'[7] Perhaps it is just as well that this scheme did not survive; it would have set a pretty task for the conservators.

After such poetry, Loudon's views on the artisan's cottage, also a matter of debate, must needs fall flat. Loudon, whose opinion was that 'the most useful is unquestionably the most beautiful'[8] wrote much on the subject. The humblest cottage should have a cornice; ornaments for ceiling centres could be obtained in papier-mâché. The cottage parlour should have a marble chimney-piece, although cast-iron ones were available.[9] The internal woodwork should be grained as oak, 'not with a view to having the imitation mistaken for the original, but rather to create allusion to it . . . to produce . . . variety and intricacy'.

The walls might be stencilled; since contrast was a source of beauty, flowers and plants should be the subject in town cottages, and people, buildings and streets in the country. Plain cottages should have stencils in simple panels, with ornaments at the angles (thus 'Etruscan' decoration reached the workman's cottage). Wallpaper could be used in any cottage; the variety was endless, the fashions changing as often as with printed cottons. Gothic papers and papers with trellis and flowers, sometimes used to cover the ceiling — a 'cottage orné' reference — were available; this last practice, said Loudon, with perhaps a side glance at Papworth, was bad taste in the country. Patterns which attempted closely to imitate nature palled the quickest, whereas architectural and sculptural designs withstood fashion. The entrance hall should have a paper imitating hewn stone (this idea is a variant of the 'lining out' — simulated marble and stone blocks — found in the hallways of the middle classes).

Stair carpets 'give an air of great comfort and finish to a house; and a cottage should never be without one'. Loudon also mentioned that a 'very neat pattern' for carpets, lately introduced for libraries, would suit Gothic cottages; it consisted of 'an imitation of wainscot'. Paper carpets and painted floorcloths were also available. Cottages should have pictures and sculptures, consisting of engravings and plaster casts; the last, of Venus, Cupid, Adonis, etc., should be varnished (Fig. 267).[10]

Loudon suggested that outside wire blinds, transparent from within, could be ornamented with landscapes and figures or, for cottages beside a road, with the owner's name or the implements of his trade. So we have cornices, wallpapers, carpets and Venus and Adonis within, and the artisan's trade sign outside. In 1825 Cobbett lamented the disappearance from the farmhouse (more substantial than the cottage of the artisan) of the old oak furniture; in its place 'the worst of all, there was a parlour. Aye, and a carpet and bell-pull too! . . . there was the

267 The 'March of Intellect': Venus and Apollo for sale, 1831

mahogany table, and the fine chairs, and the fine glass, and all as bare-faced upstart, as any stock-jobber in the kingdom can boast of . . . half a dozen prints in gilt frames hanging up: some swinging book-shelves. . . . The children . . . are all to be gentlefolks!'[11] 'Upward mobility' exacts a price.

# PART IV

# FURNITURE

Chapter one

# Formative Influences

... we confess we are not a little proud of this Roman spirit, which leaves the study of [these] effeminate elegancies to slaves and foreigners, and holds it beneath the dignity of a free man to be eminently skilled in the decoration of couches and the mounting of chandeliers.
*The Rev. Sydney Smith:* Edinburgh Review, *July 1807, p.478*

The variety of styles offered in the Regency period was as perplexing for furniture designers as it was for architects and interior decorators; however, the relative cheapness of furniture allowed more liberty to experiment, permitting design to run to stylistic extremes. This comparative freedom did not mean that furniture designers worked in a vacuum; they were subject to certain constraining influences.

## Stylistic influence of room decoration

The various styles employed in decorating rooms influenced the form and ornament of furniture in at least two ways.

First and most obviously, the style chosen for the room often dictated that of the furniture. For example, Gothic rooms were usually given Gothic furniture; not invariably — Beckford did not have Gothic furniture at Fonthill (Fig. 237; Pl. LXXXIX), and the Gothic boudoir at Bretby (Fig. 242) was furnished in revived rococo style. But the high Roman mode of the 'Corinthian Room' and the 'Golden Drawing Room' (echoes of Nero's 'Domus Aurea'?) at Carlton House in the early 1800s, probably a conscious re-creation of the ostentatious interior decoration of imperial Rome, was accompanied by the grandiose furniture, associated with the name of C. H. Tatham, that was largely based on antique Roman marble originals (Pl. LXX). A novel or striking interior that became well known would often find imitators not only of the style of the room but of that of the furniture, which might well be copied or reproduced in pattern-books or journals and sold commercially (Pl. CXVIII, centre).

Moreover, the decorative details pictured on the walls often found their way on to the furniture. For instance, the 'Etruscan' style, which in its simpler forms was a common vehicle of middle-class wall decoration in the first three decades of the nineteenth century, was

often accompanied by analogous furniture. George Bullock shows painted 'Etruscan' decoration on the walls, 'Etruscan' decorated fabrics hanging in the formalised simple folds of 'antique drapery' (Fig. 198), and furniture that extensively employs 'Etruscan' motifs (see p.403). This last association is not clearly spelt out in publications because increased awareness of the 'Etruscan' misnomenclature led to avoidance of the term; the word 'Grecian' seems frequently to have been used to describe furniture which would earlier have been called 'Etruscan', and which certainly employed 'Etruscan' motifs.

Gothic interior decoration supplied almost all the motifs of Regency Gothic furniture, which completely ignored the real domestic furniture styles of the Middle Ages; the gaudy 1820s Gothic interiors of Eaton Hall were tenanted by furniture that overlaid classical furniture forms with Gothic architectural detail; utter nonsense if it pretended to imitate genuine Gothic furniture, but matched exactly to the interior decoration (Fig. 241) and effective as theatrical properties. Such confections were condemned as unhistorical by George Smith in 1826: 'in those days the furniture for domestic use was massive and heavy, consisting chiefly of bold and highly relieved mouldings, with other members partaking of the round and cable form'.[1] Examples of wall decoration influencing furniture could be multiplied to include Greek Revival, 'Louis Quatorze', and other styles.

Furniture designers took details from wall decoration, whether in fabric, paint, or paper, and re-employed them, often in ways far removed from the original contexts. The painted and stucco arabesques used in neo-classical wall and ceiling decoration were echoed, in paint and in marquetry, on 'Adam', 'Hepplewhite', and early 'Sheraton' furniture; candelabraform and velarium motifs — the Sheraton 'shell' — migrated from 'Pompeian' wall decorations and became common on sophisticated late eighteenth-century furniture. Furniture designers

**268** Decoration from a Greek vase, published by P. F. d'Hancarville in 1766

themselves met the situation half-way; Sheraton, for example, in 1793 recommended that for any effective ornamentation of furniture the designer should make it his business 'particularly to see the painted walls in noblemen's houses . . . and . . . the printed and painted silks executed of late by Mr. Eckhardt . . . adapted for the purpose of ornamenting pannels, and the walls of the most elegant and noble houses'.[2] Towards the end of the period, in 1827, Whittock repeated substantially the same advice as Sheraton, in addition recommending workmen to find patterns for ornament from the ornamental borders sold by paperhangers.[3]

These influences were augmented by the more indirect influence of decorative accessories. For instance, the ubiquitous reproduction on walls, chimney-pieces, furniture and ceramics of motifs taken from bas-reliefs and Greek vases was bound to accustom people to seeing the form of the ancient 'klismos' chair, which was often depicted in them; the much admired vase painting of the *Apotheosis of Homer*, adapted by Flaxman and used by Wedgwood for his jasper ware (Fig. 268), has a fine example of the klismos. Admiration and familiarity would have made three-dimensional imitation less shocking than if the form were previously unknown. The first example of the revived klismos, could it be established, would have a limited significance, since many fashionable people would have been already acquainted with the form and every architect or designer knew and used the publications that illustrated the antique sources; certainly a modern version of an ancient chair in a fashionable context might focus fashionable attention, but the

catalyst for the re-creation of an ancient form was the desire to be consistent in carrying out a new scheme in an ancient style. When Bonomi in the 1780s re-created a decoration from the Baths of Titus for the library of a country house in Warwickshire (see p.243), he revived the klismos chair to accompany it, and the blunt forms of the chair may signify that he intended specifically to imitate the Roman rather than the 'Etruscan' version, influenced rather by the Roman decoration than by Lord Aylesford's fine collection of Greek vases.

## Lightness and heaviness

The appearance of furniture during the Regency period reflected a movement of taste away from lightness and delicacy towards heaviness and amplitude, not to be reversed until after the end of the period. This movement, partly a natural reaction against previous fashion, was assisted by the heaviness of many of the antique artefacts preferred by the leaders of the 'archaeological' style.

The attitude of the early 1790s was succinctly stated by Alison: the terms 'by which we express our contempt or our admiration, are those of Heaviness or Lightness . . .'; it followed that 'all . . . furniture . . . is Beautiful in proportion to the smallness of its quantity of Matter, or the Fineness and Delicacy of the parts of it. Strong and Massy Furniture is everywhere vulgar and unpleasing; and though, in point of utility, we pardon it in general use, yet wherever we expect

Elegance or Beauty, we naturally look for Fineness and Delicacy in it. The actual Progress of Taste in this article is from Strength to Delicacy'.[4] The same held for other artefacts: 'Nothing is less beautiful than thick and massy Glass, which, from its quantity, seems intended to compensate for its Fragility'.[5] Alison also had a predilection for angularity: 'Whoever will look into any of those books, which have made us acquainted with the Forms of Grecian and Roman Furniture . . . will perceive . . . that in scarcely any of them is the winding or serpentine Form observed; and that . . . the lightest and most beautiful of them, are almost universally distinguished by straight or angular Lines, and by the utmost possible diminution of Solidity that is consistent with either Convenience or Use'.[6] The angularity and insubstantiality that Alison thought beautiful in ancient furniture was imitated in the modern, reaching its height in the 1790s at the very moment when it was about to be superseded. The imitation was highly selective, confined to the ancient wooden and metal furniture that pleased early neo-classical taste; for instance Alison thought the tripod, a form idolised by Vien and the early neo-classicists, especially beautiful. Alison's reputation was high and his influence considerable. One finds his creed repeated long after it had been in practice disregarded; Loudon distorted it in his *Encyclopaedia* of 1833: 'Elegance and Grace, in objects of art, are terms generally understood to mean lightness of form, or delicacy of proportion, as contrasted with . . . heaviness of form, or want of proportion. . . .'[7]

Tatham's publication of ancient marble furniture, ponderous and sculptural, as a preferred model, signalled English acceptance at the turn of the century of the revolution in taste that had been led by Piranesi and avant-garde French neo-classical designers. Not everybody was easily reconciled to the weight of the new style; the *Edinburgh Review* of 1807 (in common with others) found Hope's furniture 'too bulky, massive and ponderous to be commodious for general use', an 'assemblage of squared timber and massive brass as would weigh down the floor and crush out the walls of an ordinary London house'.[8] Others liked it; by 1828 fashion had changed enough for another voice from Edinburgh to express a view exactly opposite to that of Alison: 'An ordinary chair, in the most ordinary parlour, has now something of an antique cast — something of Grecian massiveness, at once, and elegance in its forms. That of twenty or thirty years since was mounted on four tapering and tottering legs, resembling four tobacco-pipes; the present supporters of our stools have a curule air curved outwards behind and give a comfortable air of solidity'.[9] Furniture designers of the 1820s noticeably equated comfort with solidity.

Fashionable antique weight was somewhat counter-balanced by an increased liking for mobile furniture. This was necessitated by the fashion for 'intricacy', the wish to give interest to rooms by the deployment of informal groups of furniture (see pp.281, 282). The fashion for mobility was not perhaps as imperative as is sometimes supposed; the more formal and 'designed' an interior, the less the need for 'intricacy' or mobility; the nature of the decoration and furniture in Hope's Duchess Street house or Carlton House indicated that the furniture was perceptibly not meant to be moved about at will. The need or desire to have certain pieces of furniture movable mitigated heaviness; a patron of Papworth, James Morrison, told the architect that he wished him to 'think of a chair that would be easy to sit in and yet not heavy. Remember it is a room constantly in use, and it is of the greatest importance that the chairs be comfortable.'[10]

Two concepts existed, not necessarily in conflict: that of the grand room where order reigned and furniture remained in regulated places, where people were on their best behaviour and did not expect to lounge; and that of the informal room, where disorder was not only permitted but was apropos. Such was the room of Lady Morgan in Dublin, which had an 'air of negligence' (*sprezzatura?*) that 'seemed to declare that the inhabitant of it had made every department of nature and art tributary to her pleasure'.[11] The continued need for light and elegant furniture explains the career of John Mclean who, established in business before 1770, and continuing in it until 1825, preserved a style that owed nothing to Hope or George Smith and that altered little with the times; at the most, a discreet hint of 'Louis XIV' crept in towards the end.[12] Sheraton showed a 'Pouch Table' in his *Cabinet Dictionary* of 1803 (Fig. 269) 'executed by Mr. M'Lean in Mary-le-Bone Street . . . who finishes these small articles in the neatest manner'.[13]

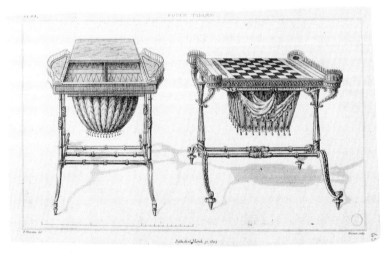

**269** 'Pouch Tables', published by Thomas Sheraton, 1803

Thus, on the one hand, light and delicate chairs, quartetto tables, what-nots, bookstands, and so on, flourished, with the Chinese and Gothic styles contributing their quota of spindly bamboo and fragile frets. On the other hand pier tables, sideboards, large couches, large chairs grew ever more bulky and ponderous. The influences on the two types tend to be distinct; light and mobile furniture was often based on antique wooden or metal furniture as interpreted by the French or English neo-classical designers of the late eighteenth century; the often massive and largely immobile furniture in the classical style was based on classical stone furniture or on Egyptian architecture. It should be remarked *en passant* that it is hardly sensible, when considering furniture, to separate Greek and Roman antique styles from the Egyptian, since motifs drawn from all three were promiscuously intermingled.

## Comfort

Sir Walter Scott and James Morrison (see p.356) equated heaviness with comfort. By this they meant physical comfort; the term 'comfort' occurs also in the sense of 'convenience', or 'les convenables'. A growing interest in comfort in both senses is perceptible in the period, and many innovations, such as the invention of the 'breakfast' room, the 'suite' of living rooms, French windows, etc., increased 'les convenables'. However, the fashionable 'Sheraton' chair of the 1790s was no more physically comfortable, less so indeed, than the French inspired 'Hepplewhite' bergère; no chair, with or without springs, is as luxuriously comfortable as the French upholstered rococo armchair. The ottoman of the 1790s, which became popular and ubiquitous throughout the Regency period, is soft and quite comfortable, but is not so convenient; one observer remarked that it carried the risk of one's falling off backwards, which the sofa did not. The Grecian couch, on which Lady Bertram of Mansfield Park spent most of her time, is much less comfortable (hard-padded with horse hair to keep the shape) than are the softly rounded feather cushions of the Louis XVI style preferred by Lady Holland, who had no doubt of the discomfort of the 'small, hard' sofas of 'le goût sévère' (see p.267). Hope's furniture was vilified both for discomfort and inconvenience.

One should not push the case too far either way, but fashion, whether in furniture or dress, does not make comfort its first priority, and the antique fashions of the early Regency did not make for particularly comfortable furniture. High-style furniture was usually still intimately linked with interior decoration, and comfort was secondary to effect. The rococo revival permitted seat furniture that was both comfortable and comparatively light; the invention of the coiled spring, or rather its general application to seat furniture, has been seen as a further aid to comfort, although the importance of the coiled spring lies in the new shapes it encouraged as much as in the comfort it afforded.

## Emblemism and sweetness

A feature that occurs throughout the period is the application to furniture, especially fashionable furniture, of emblematic symbolism; emblemism was by no means new, but was encouraged by the fashionable associationalism. Sheraton illustrated in 1793, immediately after the publication of Alison's book on the subject, an 'English State Bed' (Fig. 270) that goes just about as far as possible in this direction. Intended to attract the King, the emblematic meaning of the bed took twelve full pages to expound; as a substitute for counting sheep, it could hardly be bettered. 'For ornament to a bed of this kind, it struck me that nothing could be more suitable and characteristic [the last word is used in the sense in which Repton speaks of 'characteristic' buildings where form reflects function] than such as expressed symbolically the different parts of our government, together with those virtues and principles which ought to be the support of regal authority, and the ruling maxims of every good government of whatever kind, whether monarchical, aristocratical, or democratical. Emblems of war have been avoided as much as possible, being inconsistent ornaments for a bed, and because good kings ought not to delight in war, but in peace, unity, and the love of men and their subjects.'[14] A tall order for a bed; and it would take an acute mind to disentangle some of the emblems. The first to be detailed, for instance, 'Democracy', is a woman 'dressed in a homely garment and crowned with vine leaves. In her right hand she holds a pomegranate, which denotes assemblies of the people on matters of importance. In her left hand is a cluster of serpents, which expresses the winding and slow progression of democratic states, owing to the inability of the common people to govern' (because of the vine leaves?). Other emblems include those of Aristocracy, Monarchy, Justice, Clemency, Liberty, Fortitude, Counsel, Law, Obedience, Authority, Tyranny, Love, and Chastity. 'Uneasy lies the head that wears a crown' acquires new meaning in this context.

The defect of Sheraton's emblemism is that his emblems were capricious. Percier and Fontaine, and Hope, used emblems of a more elegant kind, meaningful to everyone familiar with classical mythology; they also used emblems drawn from folklore and poetry that were understandable to everybody. Percier's 'atelier de peinture', for example (Fig. 201), had on its ceiling Apollo, symbol of the day, and at the head of the bed Diana, symbol of the night: 'les ornemens . . . qui composent les détails de cette pièce, sont analogues aux arts de dessein'. Another bedroom had a ceiling similarly ornamented; 'Les compartimens du plafond, les divisions de la corniche, de la frise, sont couvertes d'emblèmes et d'attributs qui en rapport à Diane. Un bas-relief au fond du lit représente cette divinité, conduite par l'Amour dans les bras d'Endymion; les thermes en avant de l'estrade figurent le silence et la nuit'.[15]

**270** 'An English State Bed', 'worthy the notice of a King', by Thomas Sheraton, 1793

The Flaxman ('Aurora') room at Duchess Street was replete with emblemism (Fig. 202; see p.273). 'Round the bottom of the room still reign the emblems of night. In the rail of a black marble table are introduced medallions of the god of sleep and of the goddess of night. The bird consecrated to the latter deity perches on the pillars of a black marble chimney-piece, whose broad frieze is studded with golden

stars'.[16] The giltwood table on the left has 'Females, emblematic of the four horae or parts of the day' supporting the top, on which stands a clock 'carried by a figure of Isis, or the moon, adorned with her crescent'.[17] This allegorising was ridiculed by Sydney Smith: 'after having banished the heathen gods and their attributes pretty well from our poetry, we are to introduce them habitually into our eating-rooms, nurseries, and staircases'.[18] In extending Wordsworthian austerity to furniture, Smith rejected the classical associationalism which, as we have seen, Hope thought more important than visual beauty itself (see p.138).

Defying Smith's philistine wit, emblematic symbolism in furniture continued in use throughout the period, especially by those, such as Richard Brown, who adhered to the classical idiom. A chair for a Library or Withdrawing Room published in his *Rudiments* of 1822 (Fig. 322) has on its back 'two genii striving for the bays and . . . two horned owls' — the emblem of Minerva, or Wisdom; inside is the lyre of Apollo.[19] His 'Pier Commode and Glass' (Pl. CXXIII) has a thyrsus, 'in the centre of which is a water-nymph, that element being first discovered to reflect, and resorted to for viewing the face . . .'. Brown's emblemism was repeated by Stokes, a plagiarist who used Brown's work as a quarry. The emblematic symbolism of heraldry was much used by the gothicists, and was a prime reason for employing the style (see pp.315, 415); Stokes says that hall chairs should bear the family arms. Library chairs should bear such classic ornaments as the laurel wreath (declared by Brown to be absurd on shop fronts) and the owl; card tables, the leaves of tea or coffee plants; drawing room tables, a cornucopia. The combination of stars and flowers is bad: 'a greater perversion of taste can be scarcely conceived'.[20]

When emblemism loses its mythological or folk connotations it becomes trivialised, as with the modern 'logo'; 'There's rosemary, that's for remembrance' is on a different plane from the recommendation for drawing room window seats of the 'Egyptian lotus, or water-lily, or any flower characteristic of rest or composure . . .'.[21] The precise analogies of Percier or Hope were abandoned for meaningless generalisations; the decadent emblematic floriculture of the Great Exhibition loomed. This decadence does not allow us to dismiss emblematic symbolism as naive; when used intelligently it increased the import of the furniture, it added 'a witty allegory', and it influenced or determined the actual form of ornament.

The replacement of the precise associations of classical mythology by a saccharine allusionism is an example of the growing liking for sweetness that is sometimes as developed in Regency as in Victorian art. It is early recognisable in painting, in such important neo-classical artefacts as Vien's *Seller of Cupids* of 1763, which was based on a famous Herculaneum fresco (Vien, incidentally, transformed the costume of the original into one with the high waist that became fashionable during the Regency); it appears in early and in late David, in Angelica

Kauffmann and in some of Reynolds' portraits. It is often combined with archness, not a term of disapprobation in Regency England — Peacock's and Jane Austen's heroines are often called 'arch'. For the modern taste, archness and sweetness mingled, as in Romney's portraits of Lady Hamilton, is discomforting. Sweetness is often accompanied by another quality that also characterises much Regency art — frigidity; the coldness congeals the sweetness and makes it palatable. The coldness of Flaxman's art seems to have made most of his contemporaries unaware of his sweetness, although C. R. Cockerell was not deceived: 'he puts the soft and tender into everything . . . even his grace is meretricious & one sees clearly that his Terpsichore w. conceived at the Palais Royale . . .'.[22]

The 'Palais Royale' allusion points to the continental origin of much of this combination of sweetness and frigidity. The phenomenon was international; its roots lay in Raphael, Guido Reni, Parmigianino (who became more appreciated as the eighteenth century wore on) and in the lesser Mannerists, such as Goltzius and Spranger; the popularity of the last two was deprecated by Fuseli (despite their influence on him).[23] This mannerist sweetness easily went with the suavity of the 'Etruscan' line; a letter to Sir William Hamilton from Sir Joshua Reynolds, commenting on the publication of d'Hancarville's 'Vases', mentioned the 'grace & gentleness of some of the figures . . . much in the Parmegian stile'[24] (not to be wondered at if Raphael and his followers had been influenced by Greek vases). Canova and Prud'hon, powerful influences, were cold and sweet. Archness and sweetness affected the applied arts wherever the human figure appeared, from wall decorations to furniture mounts; it informed the work of Percier and Fontaine. Contemporary English sculpture succumbed to it, although Banks largely escaped. The effect must sometimes have been discordant; one can hardly think that Flaxman's reliefs, for example, harmonised with the severe forms of Smirke's Covent Garden; it is easier to accept a square-set commode decorated with winsome Victories, although the same tensions are present.

## The patron, the upholsterer, and the pattern books

There had been a growing tendency during the eighteenth century for architects who designed interiors to design furniture also, or at least important furniture that held fixed positions such as beds, large sofas, chairs that remained ranged along the walls, mirrors, console tables, and commodes; some of the last were magnificent and hollow shams, useless for any purpose other than decoration. Not every architect was interested in designing furniture, but it became accepted practice; the outstanding example was Robert Adam, whose interiors present a completely coherent taste, the taste of the architect. The Regency period saw this tendency halted, and no architect of the first rank designed whole interiors on the scale practised regularly by Adam; the nearest, perhaps, was Henry Holland at the beginning of the period. Some architects, Papworth for instance, designed middle-class furniture and interiors, but the rarity of architect-designed interiors attracted comment from would-be reformers (see pp.138, 229); only in the 1820s did the practice revive.

In this situation, three factors became more significant. The first was the patron who took an active role in design, whether it were the Prince Regent, Thomas Hope, or Mrs. Holt (see p.388); the sensitivity or obtuseness of the patron might determine the quality of the result, and it could be a hit or miss affair. The patron might call in other lay collaborators, as the Prince of Wales called in Walsh Porter and the Duke of Wellington called in Mrs. Arbuthnot. The second factor was the upholsterer, who supplied decorations and furniture, and who might or might not be seconded by a designer; Morel and Seddon assisted by Boileau were more formidable a team than Gillows; the nadir was seen in the likes of Mr. Soho, a credible caricature of the obsequious and nauseatingly inventive upholsterer (see p.347). The third was the furniture pattern book, which proliferated in the same way as the architectural pattern book and which customarily showed furniture unconnected with any setting. Hope's book displayed furniture designs in concordance with the rooms for which they were designed, and Ackermann's *Repository* occasionally displayed furniture in a room, but these were exceptions rather than the rule. Furniture designs shown divorced from any context did not encourage unity of taste (this did not matter so much earlier, when taste was surer and more consistent).

The pattern books show more conveniently than anything else the way in which furniture design evolved, and for that reason may be somewhat misleading; for instance, the distinguished style of George Bullock remained in obscurity until noticed in a book of 1953 by Brian Reade, merely because Bullock did not issue a pattern book (although he was given his due in the pages of Ackermann). There may be others who deserve attention — Vulliamy, to take an example at random. Papworth, an artist of unusual sensitivity and taste, designed a great deal of furniture, mostly now unknown; not unexpectedly, in view of his success in evolving sophisticated architectural combinations of antique and oriental styles, he seems towards the end of the period to have shown an interest in combining antique with Jacobean furniture forms, and it may turn out that some existing anonymous furniture in this vein is his. Certain categories of Regency furniture such as that in the Gothic and, especially, the Chinese styles, are under-represented both in the pattern books and in the *Repository*.

The major pattern books clearly demonstrate changing styles. Sheraton's and Hepplewhite's designs of the 1790s, especially those of the former, freely applied the repertoire of arabesque drawn from antique wall and ceiling decorations (sometimes, no doubt, filtered through Mr. Eckhardt's silks); they use not only the 'arabesques' but such other motifs as velaria, 'Pompeian' maidens and Adam/Angelica Kauffmann-type decorations; all these add charm to the artefacts of the period. Sheraton and Hepplewhite show also the influence of French Romantic Classicism. It is noticeable that Sheraton did not take to the 'Etruscan' idiom in the 1790s, despite the existence, at Carlton House and other great houses, of chairs supplied by Daguerre in an 'Etruscan'/Louis XVI style.

In the new century the Adam/Louis XVI influence receded, to be replaced by the direct influence of the antique, which included a consuming interest in Roman animal heads and paws. Sheraton developed a particularly attractive turned and outsplayed leg, derived from a Roman model, that persisted in bedroom chairs well into Victoria's reign. 'Antique drapery' largely supplanted the earlier festoons. The arabesque and the 'Angelica Kauffmann' Pompeian type decorations fell out of fashion.

The most famous pattern book of the English Regency, Thomas Hope's *Household Furniture and Interior Decoration* of 1807, was conspicuously successful in the way it assimilated antique sources. Despite their variety, and despite his own espousal of the Greek Revival and his interest in Egypt and the exotic, Hope's furniture has a predominantly Roman character; his sources included Roman marble and bronze furniture. The clear-cut ornament, which includes a simple arabesque, not infrequently has an 'Etruscan' air, as, for instance, that on the top and sides of the well known monopodium table[25] eventually to be placed at the Deepdene in a room decorated in the 'Etruscan' style (Pl. LV). In Hope's plates the 'Etruscan' impression is accentuated by the linear method, itself influenced by the drawing technique of Greek vases.

George Smith's *Designs for Household Furniture* of 1808 (the plates were issued from 1804) shows the Hope influence; the book has been unfairly denigrated as the commercialisation of the Hope taste. The designs do not have Hope's unerring distinction, nor do they have the advantage of the beautiful line, but they have vigour and variety and draw on sources, including antique sources, untouched by Hope. Moreover, they include Gothic and Chinese styles.

The long gap that followed the issue of George Smith's 1808 pattern book was filled by the furniture illustrations published from 1809 in Ackermann's *Repository*. These are all second or third hand, and although pretty enough lack finesse, even where they are taken from distinguished sources that already existed in the convenient medium of line. The many pattern books published in the 1820s, increasingly and undiscriminatingly eclectic with a few exceptions (such as Bridgens' distinguished but slight continuation of the tradition of Hope as interpreted by Bullock), exemplify the decline; ill-assimilated and coarsely rendered motifs jostle each other. As far as furniture in the antique style is concerned, Roman influence predominated; the more delicate 'Etruscan' style receded.

The auguries for design had long been recognised by contemporaries as unpropitious; a much increased middle class that sought gentility enlarged the opportunities for going astray. 'There is not a daemon more adverse to good taste than the spirit of novelty'.[26] The rule of taste at the beginning of the period was strong enough to impose some discipline, but the aesthetic theories of Alison and the doctrines of the Picturesque, liberating and creative as they were in many ways, also made for confusion and caprice. The result was that standards of design in furniture suffered the same general decline as other manifestations of visual taste.

Chapter two

# Classical Styles

## Influence of antique sources

The 'archaeological' style may briefly be defined as antique ornament applied to antique forms in an antique manner; the extent to which archaeologically correct forms were allowed to modify or replace more traditional and, it must be said, in some cases more genial forms was a matter of will, and will was driven by fashion. It was not particularly a matter of increased knowledge, for as early as the fifteenth century Mantegna knew enough to give the legs of the bed on which Judith slaughtered Holofernes (Fig. 271) an uncompromisingly archaeological Roman form, more uncompromising and more exact than that of Helen's couch as painted by David in the late 1780s. Mantegna was not alone; the loves of antique ladies gave (amongst others) Giulio Romano and Lambert Sustris the opportunity to depict astonishingly accurate ancient sofas.¹ Raphael's *Virgin with the Fish* in the Prado sits on a stately throne taken from the antique, with arm rests topped by a globe, that is not unlike the state chairs of Napoleonic France and Regency England; his apostles in the Vatican Loggie, a source known to all the cognoscenti and frequently reproduced, sit on sabre-legged benches.² The portrayal of archaeologically exact furniture in paintings was a continuing tradition; Poussin repeatedly pictured grand and convincing antique furniture, which found its way, writ large, on to tapestries; the classical detail of these antique re-creations much resembles that of some of the most splendid pieces of Louis XIV classicising furniture, which themselves were to influence the Regency. Amongst eighteenth-century painters who accustomed the eyes of the public to these ancient forms in antique domestic use were Vien, Greuze, Mengs, Hamilton and West.

From the second half of the seventeenth century onwards, depictions of ancient furniture were reproduced in printed books. The late seventeenth-century publications of Pietro Santi Bartoli were followed in the early eighteenth century by the exhaustive compilations of Montfaucon, which provided easy multiple references to ancient furniture; yet more came from the murals and surviving ancient pieces of furniture excavated from Herculaneum and Pompeii, published from 1757 onwards (the exclusive volumes of the 'Royal edition' of the *Pitture Antiche d'Ercolano* were supplemented in 1804 by a convenient edition produced in Paris by the two sons of Piranesi). Knowledge of such references was general, and there is evidence of their use throughout the eighteenth century; for example, the illustrators of Lord Orrery's translation of Pliny the Younger, printed in 1751, decorated the text with rococo cartouches but showed Pliny himself seated on a chair of accurate Roman form. Regency furniture designers had a plethora of ancient sources at their disposal, and used them.

Regency furniture in the classical style was usually a compound of the forms evolved by designers and makers such as Adam and Jacob with forms and ornament taken more or less directly from the antique (but not necessarily from ancient furniture). It is interesting to notice which ancient furniture forms were domesticated in the nineteenth century and which not. Few were not tried at some time or other; the Roman turned chair leg, often in its slender form and with the foot splayed outwards, persisted throughout the whole period; the Roman type that ended in pointed tip-toe feet was hardly ever used in England, although seemingly the very thing for early Regency parlours. The pointed Roman sofa foot was used, but given the gentle concave curve, also seen on Roman furniture, that robbed it of archaic strangeness. The turned Roman leg served as inspiration for a common type of Regency turned leg, but the varied and exaggerated type of Roman turning copied by Mantegna (often originally in bronze) was rarely used; David used a peculiar 'bobbin' type for his 'Récamier' couch, with

271 *Judith and Holofernes*, by Andrea Mantegna

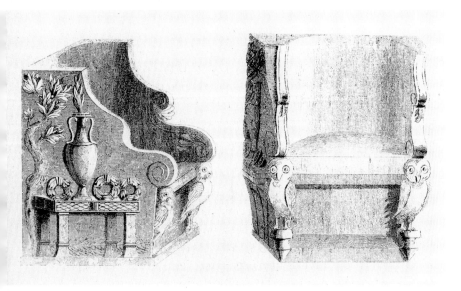

272 'Two ancient chairs', published in *The Antiquities of Athens*, 1794

an authentic pointed foot. The Regency version of Roman turning was often refined to a point where it became more or less assimilated with Regency 'bamboo' (the essential difference is that bamboo is not encircled with rings, but with depressions preceded by a raising of the surface). Compromises were usual; the stately klismos found its reincarnation in the bourgeois Trafalgar chair, for example.

A type of Roman chair that was rarely reproduced in England, save in such adaptations as Thomas Hope's 'Egyptian' chair, was the upright metal or wooden throne with elbow supports and board-like front legs with shaped edges (Fig. 286[a]). The ancient marble throne with concave solid back was seldom used in its original form, save in the grandest settings such as Carlton House (Pl. CXIII), but essentially it is the same form as that which, set on turned or sabre legs, did duty in many a Regency library. The sabre leg itself became ubiquitous; found in both Greek and Roman furniture, it was combined by Regency designers with antique forms with which it had not been associated in antiquity; the most obvious example was the scroll-ended sofa, the 'Grecian couch' set on sabre legs; Roman examples seem usually to have had turned legs. Antique marble benches were adapted for Regency gardens as they had been adapted for gardens for centuries. Amongst the most popular and imitated forms, in part and in the whole, were the famous and beautiful bronze tripods and side tables from Pompeii (Fig. 286[b]).

The lack of continental interest in the Gothic and the exotic (see p.311), meant that furniture designers who looked towards Europe missed the long-evolved and sophisticated tradition enjoyed by the antique taste; the lack accounts for a certain thinness and monotony in Gothic furniture design, and probably for the frequent resort to classical forms as a base for Gothic or exotic detail. It was not until the time of the younger Pugin that Gothic furniture forms were handled with something of the same conviction and accuracy as classical forms.

It is not always possible to be sure of what substance the furniture in antique depictions was made. There is an ancient tradition of producing in other media forms originally made in wood. Sometimes ignorance of the existence of an ancient technique or loss of its method caused difficulties, as with the Regency attempt to reproduce in wood the exaggeratedly outswept leg of the klismos (Fig. 268); difficulties arose because traditionally worked wood cracks at the cross grain; the Regency sabre leg is but a constrained version of the original, which was probably produced by bending with steam.[3] Other features of ancient furniture were easier to imitate, such as the green patination of bronzes, preferred by Hope.[4]

## Holland and the French

The famous 'souper grec' given in 1788 by Mme. Vigée Le Brun (it is no coincidence that she was a painter) was an emanation of the desire

362

to recreate the ancient world that became strong in France in the 1780s; at the supper 'Etruscan' vases were placed on a bare mahogany table and the hostess wore only 'une simple tunique blanche, des fleurs mêlées à ses beaux cheveux. Lorsque les invités entrèrent, ils furent accueillies par le chœur de Gluck "Le Dieu de Paphos et Gnide".'[5] One can understand the enticements of such beautiful masquerades, but possible pitfalls awaited those who admired the archaeological antique in pre-revolutionary France, since it had a politically subversive meaning that it lacked in Italy (see p.97); this may have been why French people of fashion espoused the 'Etruscan' style, more decorative and less 'serious' — that is, until the Revolution. Jacob made chairs for Marie-Antoinette's dairy at Rambouillet in 1787 that were described in a contemporary document as 'of a new pattern in the Etruscan style . . . after the design of . . . Robert' (Hubert Robert, another painter).[6] Surviving chairs from this set are by no means archaeological in the sense that David's or Gavin Hamilton's depicted furniture is archaeological; they apply the 'Etruscan' motifs of elongated diamond shapes, paterae, strings of bay leaves, and an anthemion ornament contained within an oval, in a purely decorative way to classical X frames. Other pieces were made by Jacob for the royal family in an advanced but not archaeologically pedantic taste; for Mme. Elizabeth, he realised designs by Dugourc, Meunier, and Grognard, and for the Prince of Wales' friend, the Duc de Chartres, a design by David for a mahogany bed with *bronzes dorés* in the antique taste.[7]

The 'Etruscan' style was exported to England. 'Etruscan' motifs decorate the 'Louis Seize' forms of chairs supplied by Daguerre to the Prince of Wales and the Duke of Bedford, and an orientalised version of 'Etruscan' and 'Pompeian' ornament was used in the French furniture and ornaments installed in the Chinese Drawing Room at Carlton House (see p.427). And furniture in a Louis XVI style influenced by the antique, by no means uncompromisingly 'archaeological', was bought by aristocratic English clients from Jacob himself. The English liking for mahogany and simplicity may have affected French taste during the 1770s and 1780s, although the lack of figure in some types of mahogany perhaps commended it to those who wished to emulate ancient furniture. English technical mastery may have influenced France; in 1801 Landon mentioned the return to simplicity and praised English workmanship, speaking of French furniture as 'prenant un peu de ce fini d'exécution dont l'Angleterre nous donne des exemples si parfaits et si multipliés'.[8] Some of the French deprecated the English influence; Marigny told Garnier in 1779 that he thought ebony and gilt furniture far more noble than the mahogany furniture ordered by the English,[9] a view soon to be shared by such Englishmen as Beckford and the Prince of Wales.

The English architect who most forwarded French fashions during the 1780s and the early 1790s was Henry Holland, and his patronage by the Prince of Wales at Carlton House opened a new era: 'The age of Regency furniture may be said to have begun when the Prince of Wales appointed Henry Holland to rebuild and refurbish Carlton House . . . in August 1783'.[10] Many Frenchmen were employed on its furnishings and decoration; Gaubert and Weltje (a German) worked for Holland from 1783; Daguerre, Delabrière, Belanger, Dumont le Romain, Pernotin, and perhaps Boileau, who had worked at the Comte d'Artois' 'pavillon' — a name adopted by the Prince — of Bagatelle, came to Carlton House.[11] Bagatelle had shown some of the earliest examples of new fashions, including the tent room and perhaps the 'Etruscan' style itself. In 1786 Daguerre, a leading *marchand-mercier* in France, opened a shop in Piccadilly with Lignereux; after 1789 he was based in London, and eventually took over from Gaubert at Carlton House. The furniture supplied by Holland at this time was much influenced by the 'Louis Seize' style, and did not resemble the more 'archaeological' style that he was to employ after 1795.

The depictions of the Prince's Drawing Room and the Chinese Drawing Room at Carlton House in 1794 gave an idea of the ultra-fashionable furniture of the later 1780s and early 1790s that was associated with Holland's interior decorations (Figs 187, 257). The furniture shown in the 'Drawing Room' is gracefully formal, arranged neatly along the walls but not, one feels, so inexorably that a royal reproof would have descended on the head of a latter-day Mme. de Maintenon for drawing a chair forward.[12] The chairs are much in the Jacob style; the sofas are 'bordered off with three compartments, and covered with figured silk or satin. The ovals may be printed separately, and sewed on. These sofas may have cushions to fill their backs, together with bolsters at each end. In France, where their drawing-rooms are fitted up in the most splendid manner, they use a sett of small and plainer chairs, reserving the others merely as ornaments'.[13]

Obviously the traditions of Louis XIV lived on in France, and 'architectural' chairs retained an importance. This seat furniture was gilded, as were the pier tables ('marble tops and gold frames, or white and gold');[14] the commode, 'painted to suit the furniture' — that is, to accord with the fabrics used for curtains — had 'legs and other parts' in gold to harmonise with the chairs.[15] The tops of commode and pier tables were marble; the commode had a tablet 'in the center, made of an exquisite composition in imitation of statuary marble. These are to be had, of any figure, or on any subject, at Mr. Wedgwood's, near Soho-square'.[16] Wedgwood plaques replaced the Sèvres plaques seen in French furniture of the preceding decades; they were used on French and Russian furniture, amongst others, and it has been remarked above (see p.355) that the plaques themselves not infrequently showed archaeological furniture shapes. The mirrors were surmounted with paintings on glass.

**273** 'Table that was in the Boudoir at Carleton house', design by Henry Holland, c.1790

The features of this and other pieces influenced by Louis XVI furniture, especially the commodes and pier tables with their shaped marble tops, breakfronts, and candelabraform pillars, were to enter the Regency repertoire and to persist throughout the period. Apart from Holland's and the Prince's predilections, it was easy enough for English furniture to assimilate French features; Louis XVI furniture had much in common with the exquisite native neo-classicism of Adam, which itself had 'a delicacy and an elegance seldom surpassed since the Renaissance'.[17] Adam had introduced new forms and combinations, such as the sideboard pedestal flanked by urns, and the classical straight leg taken from antique marble originals, often fluted and tapered to the foot. He had had his French equivalents, such as Neufforge; the neo-classicism of the period crossed national boundaries.

The 'prawn-like' cluster of French designers and craftsmen around Holland prompts the question of how far Holland himself designed the furniture he supplied to the houses in which he worked, especially as some is undoubtedly French. Three considerations are relevant. The first is that whoever the maker or supplier of this furniture, English or French, it could well have been designed by the architect; the second is that as fastidious an architect as Holland probably retained a keen interest in the furniture, especially that which was traditionally 'architectural' — pier tables, mirrors, etc.; the third is that there is no doubt that Holland did design furniture, especially 'architectural' furniture. Designs for pier tables at his own house, Sloane Place, and at Carlton House are attributed to him (Fig. 273); the latter, which has candelabraform front legs, is in something of a 'Weisweiler' taste, and both the candelabraform legs and the arabesque are features that were a little later to appear in Sheraton (Fig. 277).

There is evidence that Holland did not throw off furniture designs lightly, but spent time and trouble, a point relevant when considering the relative responsibility of himself and Tatham for the later Southill designs; he might have needed assistance. A letter of January 1796 from Holland to the Duke of Bedford concerning the furniture at Woburn, where known makers include Ince and Mayhew, Hervé and John Kean, mentioned that 'On the articles of furniture, were anyone to examine the endless number of drawings I have made, and witness the trouble I have had, they would not envy me my charge on that account.'[18]

## Classicism in the 1790s

Thomas Sheraton, in his *Cabinet Maker and Upholsterer's Drawing Book* of 1791–4, presented ideas in current circulation in a coherent and anglicised form; his name is more or less synonymous with the earliest conventional 'Regency' furniture. He observed at the beginning of his book that Hepplewhite's collection of 1788 had, notwithstanding its recent date, contained designs which compared with the 'newest taste' had 'already caught the decline, and perhaps, in a little time, will suddenly die in the disorder'.[19] The remark was not unjustified, being particularly true of some of the chair designs, and as if in reaction the 1794 edition of Hepplewhite's book subdued or omitted rococo themes and emphasised the rectilinear; the new designs included two sheets of typical 'Sheraton' chair backs.[20] In some respects Hepplewhite was as up to date as Sheraton; a 'Library Case' (Fig. 274) shows 'Etruscan' decussations in the astragals, and the rosette is the same motif as that on the advanced cabinet by Holland at Southill (Figs 178, 283; see p.373).

Sheraton's most distinguished inventions emphasised an ultra-refined, small scale domesticity, rather than palatial or country-house grandeur, and this gave the designs longevity; at the very end of the Regency period, unfashionable and utilitarian furniture was still being

**274** Design for a 'Library Case', by George Hepplewhite, 1794

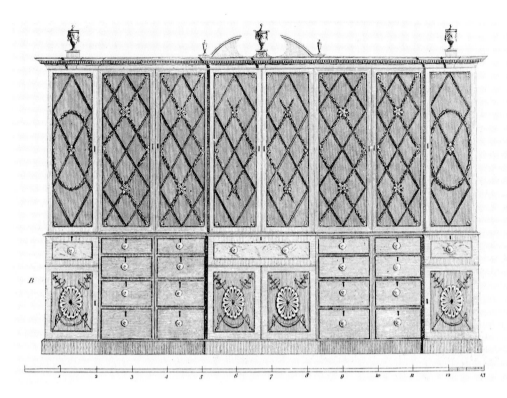

produced in an essentially 'Sheraton' manner. Sheraton's influence was at its height in the 1790s; an attractive style was defined by a man with whose talents it was in perfect harmony.

Many motifs used by Sheraton were inherited from earlier decades; besides the candelabraform pillar mentioned above, which he adapted for bed-posts (an old tradition, they occur in Carpaccio's *St. Ursula* series) and for legs of various kinds, he employed inlays, in coloured and contrasting woods, of delicate and inventive arabesques and garlands inspired by such Roman decorations as those on the ceilings of the 'Domus Aurea'; he used painted decoration in the same idiom, with 'Angelica Kauffmann' figures and groups in the 'Pompeian' taste. He had a liking for wooden rather than marble horizontal surfaces, although the latter were not excluded, and shared the English preference for wooden carved ornament rather than the French for gilt bronze; he was fond of slender rectilinear and turned legs. The designs are noticeably sparing in their use of ornament derived directly from architecture rather than decoration, as are the later furniture designs of Robert Adam.

The colours are usually high and brilliant, with satinwood painted or inlaid; in 1803, Sheraton described the preferred qualities of satinwood in terms that indicate that hot colours were undesirable: 'a highly valuable wood, the best of which is a fine strawcolour cast, and has therefore a cool, light, and pleasing effect in furniture, on which account it has been much in requisition among people of fashion for

above 20 years past'; he added that 'The foxy, or red coloured sattinwood should be avoided'.[21]

Sheraton showed the 'Hepplewhite' shield-shaped back, although he considered it unfashionable. He was more interested in rectilinear chair backs; his group of 'New Designs of Chair-backs' of 1793 (Fig. 275) perfectly expresses Alison's approved aesthetic qualities of 'Fineness and Delicacy'; beside these, most Adam ornament looks robust. Sheraton made it clear that he expected the backs to be simplified in the execution: No. 1, 'intended for painting' may omit the drapery; No. 2 may take away the 'side foliage' and make the bottom of the banister plain. No. 3 may omit the drapery, and if used as a parlour chair, the top rail may be stuffed and covered with red or green leather, or left as mahogany; as a drawing-room chair it should be painted and have the top stuffed. There is some 'goût grec' influence on this last chair; in a much plainer form, chair backs of this shape were to persist throughout the Regency.

There was a vein of common sense in Sheraton, perfectly displayed in the comely and useful 'Lady's Drawing and Writing Table' (Fig. 276). This is the 'Carlton House Table', not originated by Sheraton[22] but popularised in his version: 'These tables are finished neat, either in mahogany or satinwood, with a brass rim around the top part';[23] the rising panel in the centre was made to slide forward. At a slightly later period the table was brought up to date by being given flat supports at either end tied together by a turned pole, and splayed-out sabre legs. In

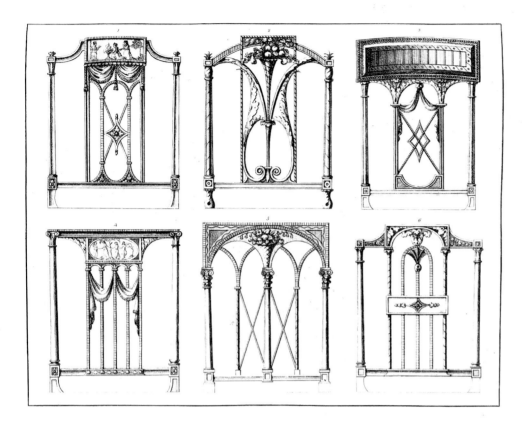

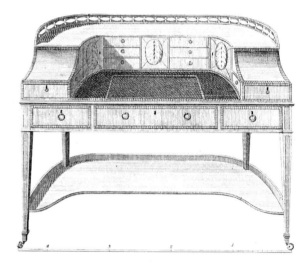

275 'New Designs of Chair-backs', by Thomas Sheraton, 1793

276 Design for 'A Lady's Drawing and Writing Table', by Thomas Sheraton, 1793

277 Design for 'A Cabinet', by Thomas Sheraton, 1793

strong contrast is the dandiacal elegance of a cabinet (Fig. 277) which could also be used for writing purposes; the lopers that drew out by springs to support the cabinet front may be seen resting on the surface. The design was said by Sheraton to be 'new'; it exhibits that peculiar marriage of mechanical ingenuity with decorative frippery that is seen in much Regency furniture meant for female use. Above the fall front is a drawer that locks with the front, and above the drawer an 'ornamented frieze, japanned'; the top is marble edged with brass, practical since the 'flower-pot at the top is supposed to be real, not carved',[24] as presumably were the flowers on the candle branches; those on the stretcher were carved. The profiles of the candle branches are derived from arabesque, as is the design of Sheraton's 'Girandoles' (Fig. 172); placed as the latter are next to an 'Ornament for a Painted Panel', itself drawn from neo-classical arabesque wall decoration, they demonstrate his advice to derive furniture forms from wall decorations. The carving on the legs of the cabinet was to be gilded, as were the bases and capitals of the columns; the legs were to be cross-banded. Such a festive and finical piece as this, glittering with gold and colour and ornamented with flowers, markedly differs in its gaiety and femininity from the solemn or grandiose pieces that were to be the fashion in advanced quarters within ten years; the change could hardly have been greater.

*Above* **CVIII** Design for a sideboard, by Thomas Sheraton, 1804   *Below* **CIX** Design for a sofa, 1806, by Thomas Sheraton

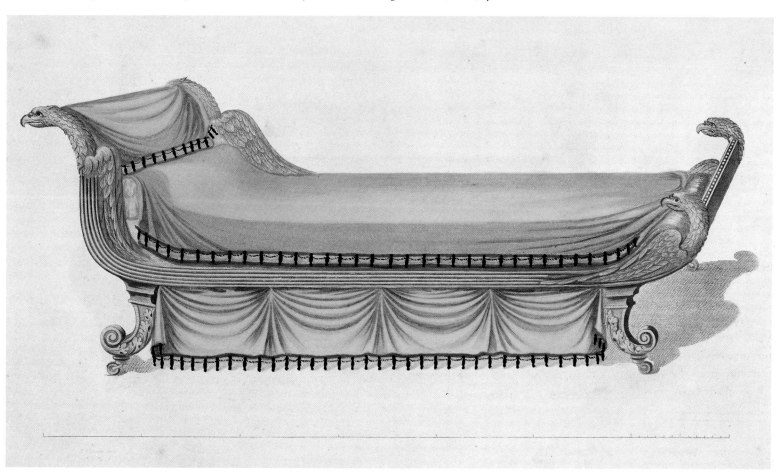

**cx** Design for parlour chairs, by Thomas Sheraton

**cxi** 'Design for a Bed', 1805, by George Smith

## Elementary forms

The French Romantic Classical preoccupation with elementary and disconnected geometric forms, a preoccupation that deeply influenced British architecture during the Regency (see p.97 et seq., p.129 et seq.), has mysterious affinities with a perceptible (although not dominant) strain in the design of English furniture. One says 'mysterious' because the English furniture concerned seems to have more in common in this respect with French architecture than with French furniture (although French furniture does show some interest in simple geometric shapes); in England an early manifestation is seen in the demi-lune commodes of Adam, in which the purity of the semi-cylindrical form was hardly compromised by predominantly flat decoration; this shape continued in fashion into the 1790s, as in 'A Commode' shown by Hepplewhite (Fig. 278), where the demi-lune shape is slightly flattened.

Sheraton published several designs in the 1790s which proved influential as prototypes. The 'Library Table with Secretary Drawer' of 1793 was composed basically of two demi-cylinders and a cube (Fig. 279); as with the Adam commodes, the flat inlaid decoration allows the shapes to predominate. A similar impression is given by 'A SideBoard and Vase Knife Cases';[25] the descent from Adam is clear, but stateliness has been domesticated. Sheraton also showed a sideboard without pedestals, mentioning that 'in spacious dining-rooms, the sideboards are often made without drawers of any sort, having simply a rail a little ornamented, and pedestals with vases at each end, which produce a grand effect'.[26] This last is the Adam sideboard pure, and its constituents were again to become fashionable in the 1820s.

A sideboard of 1804 is startling in its geometric simplicity; it combines a cube and two almost detached cylinders, and has a circular convex mirror set into plain rails; all the inlaid decoration is 'hard edge', and even the brass rails of the cylinders are filled in with triangles (Pl. CVIII). A design of 1804 for a library table shows the same interest in basic forms; the cylinder that holds the candelabrum rests on a segment of a cylinder and a cube, the whole given the fashionable antique trim (Fig. 280).[27] These designs are in an utterly different style from that of the contemporary furniture designed by Sheraton in the 'archaeological' style (and show no trace of the 'lunacy' that has been detected in the latter; perhaps Sheraton was driven mad only by the 'archaeological' style). Other designers found aesthetic pleasure in elementary forms; the 'consular' chairs from Carlton House (Pl. CXIII) have something of it, without, however, the Sheraton 'building-block' element, which soon afterwards went largely out of fashion.

Or rather, it went underground, to resurface with Biedermeier (a style well known to have been influenced by English furniture, and which appeared earlier than has been previously thought) — and eventually to appear again in England with the 'Modernism' of the

**278** Design for a demi-lune commode, by George Hepplewhite, 1794

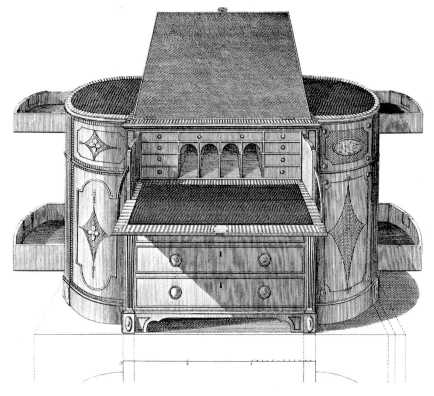

**279** Design for 'A Library Table with Secretary Drawer', by Thomas Sheraton, 1793

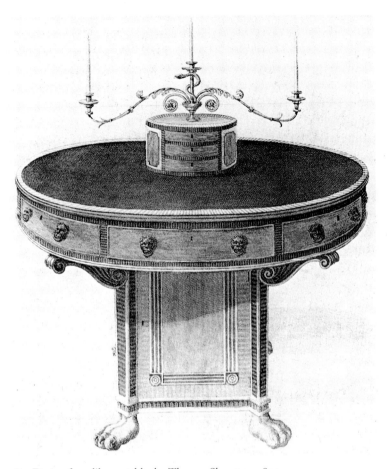

**280** Design for a library table, by Thomas Sheraton, 1804

1930s (itself influenced by Biedermeier furniture through the Wiener Werkstätte). It is possible that a reason for the emergence of the Biedermeier style in the newly liberated states lay in a reaction against the cultural imperialism of the Napoleonic Empire (as the neo-classicism of Nazi Germany and Fascist Italy fell into disgrace after the Second World War). The English had not smarted under Napoleonic defeat, and did not have the same reason for repudiating the French connexion as had the German and Scandinavian states.

There is an indication that an attempt may have been made to interest the English again in geometry. Rudolph Ackermann (see p.391) never lost sight of his German roots, and frequently returned to his native land. He must have noticed what was going on, and a design published in the *Repository* in April 1815 as a 'French Sofa' looks as much German as French. Whatever its nationality, the description emphasises geometry: 'The outline of the seat and back are described by equal radii, and are intersected by small ovals, that combine with them and form a long elipse or oval . . . a portion of this severity is essential to the character of beauty, dignity, and greatness'. Not the usual *Repository* persiflage.

## The Holland transitional style

Furniture in the style of the later 1780s and early 1790s, which customarily used antique motifs as decorative adjuncts in a way unrelated to their antique use, was to be superseded, or rather supplemented, by an 'archaeological' type of furniture based more directly on the furniture shown on Greek vases and Roman murals and sculpture, and extant in marble; such 'archaeological' furniture was being made in France and Italy at the latest by the 1790s, and probably much sooner.[28] The Italians had evinced an interest in advanced neo-classicism earlier than anybody. A gilded wooden klismos chair from the Palazzo Borghese with a back derived from the velarium can be dated to 1782;[29] it is likely that Hope was influenced by Italian 'archaeological' furniture seen during the 1790s in the Borghese Palace in Rome (Fig. 297). An Italian, Bonomi, introduced the klismos chair to England in the 1780s (see p.243); Abildgaard, who had spent time in Italy, introduced it to Denmark; Masreliez went from Rome to Sweden in 1783 and introduced his version of it in about 1790.[30] C. H. Tatham travelled southwards to Naples in 1795, where he must have used his ears and eyes; Sir William Hamilton, living in a locality where antique discoveries were being continually made, some of which strayed into his possession despite strict controls,[31] had had furniture made using details copied from antique furniture.[32]

The advance towards an 'archaeological' style was gradual, and Holland's 'archaeological' furniture is really in something of a transitional style; the furniture for Southill, a commission that began with the house in 1795 (most of the furniture was bought between 1798 and 1802) exhibits the imposition of decorative antique motifs on more or less antique forms rather than the academic re-creation of ancient furniture.

The Southill furniture is of several distinct types. One follows a more or less undiluted mainstream Louis XVI style, as seen in the giltwood chairs supplied for the boudoir, which have fluted and turned front legs; panels, above stuffed backs, were painted with arabesque motifs by Delabrière.[33] These have been attributed to Hervé, and it is possible that Holland had nothing to do with their design, merely acting as a conduit for approved makers. Another style is seen in the large rosewood china cabinet, known to have been in existence by 1800 and to have been made by Marsh;[34] it is in the 'Weisweiler' taste of the Holland design for the Carlton House pier table (Fig. 273; see p.364). There is also a group of interesting and beautiful furniture to which belong the large and small giltwood sofas, a rosewood cabinet and related chiffonier,[35] and a set of elbow chairs.

The sofas have at first glance an air of authentic recreated antiquity. They prove to be an assemblage of elements drawn from diverse sources. The large, upright-ended sofas, for example, have a foot

**281** 'Sedia curule di marmo . . . nel Museo del Cavalier Piranesi . . .', 1779

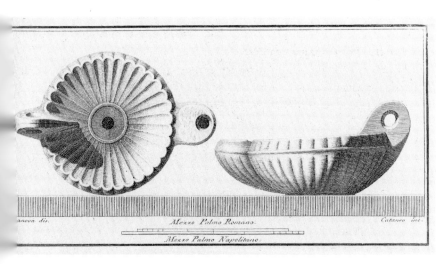

**282** Bowl of a Roman lamp, 1792

**283** A cabinet, designed by Henry Holland for Southill House, Beds., c.1795–1800

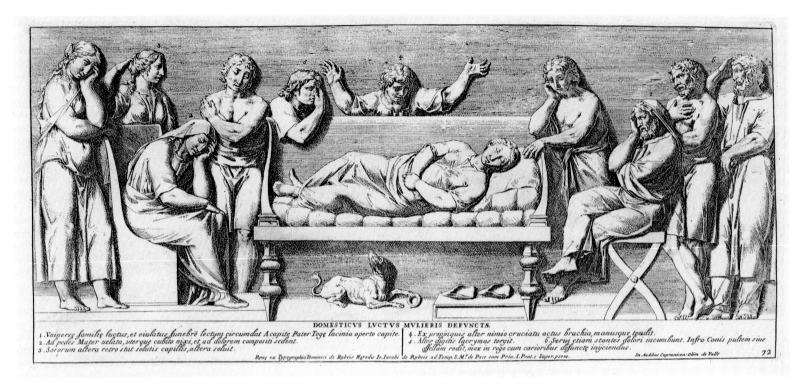

**284** A Roman couch, chair, and X-framed stool, first published by Pietro Santi Bartoli in 1693

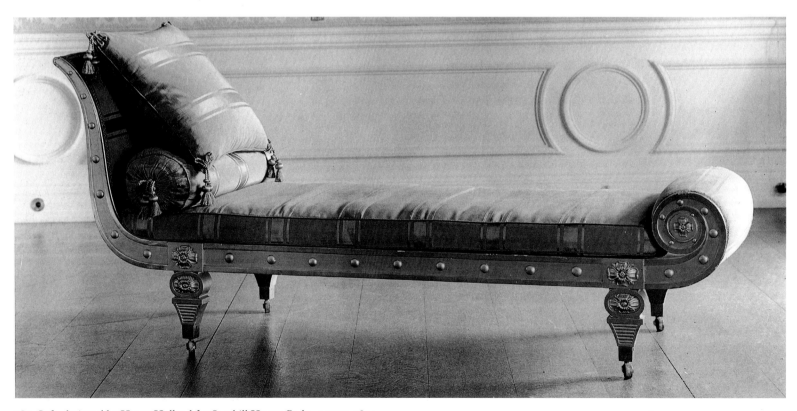

**285** Sofa, designed by Henry Holland for Southill House, Beds., c.1795–1800

inspired by ancient Roman sources that had been employed by Adam (as in the commode for Lady Derby)[36] and by French makers;[37] it is 'eighteenth century' rather than 'archaeological'. The refined 'Récamier' arm of the smaller sofas (Fig. 285) and the ovoid foot of the cabinet and chiffonier (Fig. 283) also come from Roman furniture; an interesting juxtaposition of a similar arm and foot occurs in a lugubrious scene taken from a sarcophagus ('Domesticus luctus mulieris defunctae') engraved by Pietro Santi Bartoli in 1693 (Fig. 284). This sarcophagus had entered the Towneley collection of marbles in 1768 and was displayed in London in Holland's time; Holland himself collected marble fragments.[38] A foot of the same type is seen also in one of two marble chairs illustrated in the third volume of the *Antiquities of Athens*, published in 1794 (Fig. 272); it is certain that Holland would have studied that book closely.

This faceted tapering ovoid foot is apparently peculiar to 'Holland' furniture; neither the foot nor the flat splayed back leg of the chiffonier seem to have been used in contemporary French artefacts, nor did they enter the general repertory of Regency design. The foot of the smaller Southill sofa (Fig. 285), although made up (somewhat clumsily) of elements drawn from the antique (with 'Weisweiler'-type 'ribbing' added), has no antique prototype. (In parenthesis, the support of an occasional table at Southill has similarities with a 'tripus balnearis' shown in the most famous of all ancient paintings, the *Aldobrandini Marriage*; the painting had been continually published, notably by Santi Bartoli and Montfaucon, and had been reproduced on a chimney-piece in 'Athenian' Stuart's Painted Room at Spencer House, where Holland was working from 1785 to 1792.)[39]

One of the most striking motifs seen on the Southill furniture is the vigorous rosette on the front of the cabinet. This is a device that goes back beyond Greece and Rome into remote antiquity;[40] it was revived in the Renaissance and used on Italian and Spanish chests; it appears on English Jacobean furniture. Ancient variants of it were illustrated by Montfaucon[41] and Caylus.[42] It was employed in the late eighteenth century in bisected form for fanlights and other windows. It is illustrated in a form strikingly close to Holland's image in the pages of *Le Lucerne ed i Candelabri d'Ercolano*, published in 1792, where it forms the fluted bowl of a lamp (Fig. 282); another example in the same book,[43] less clear than that reproduced here, has twenty 'petals', exactly the same number as on Holland's cabinet.

The fact that French influence indisputably accounts for some aspects of Holland's furniture style does not necessarily mean that he would have needed a French route to these motifs, or to other motifs employed in these pieces of furniture;[44] all the books were available in England. Nor does the relationship between C. H. Tatham (who joined Holland's team in 1789 — in 1798 Tatham's brother Thomas joined the firm of Elward and Marsh, which did much work for Holland) and Holland necessarily imply that Tatham actually designed any of the furniture associated with Holland. This is of course possible, but one notices that the 'cut and paste' process that created the Southill sofas and cabinet has little in common with what appears to have been Tatham's more pedantic bias, and differs from the closer attention to authentic antiquity that produced the consular chairs and other 'archaeological' pieces at Carlton House, which have also been associated with Tatham.

## The 'archaeological' antique

Holland's amanuensis, C. H. Tatham, lived in Italy from 1794 to 1796. His tastes, as shown in his drawings and architecture, inclined towards the massive and volumetric, with heavy forms arising directly from the floor: his line however was somewhat weak, and can bear no comparison with the romantic power of Piranesi; the forceful rendering of classical acanthus that is such a feature of Regency artefacts, especially those from the later period, must have come from Piranesi rather than Tatham. Tatham appreciated the *matière* of ancient artefacts, and told Holland he thought it 'a pity that other collectors do not so often follow the maxim of the ingenious Cardinal [Borgia, a well-known contemporary collector] . . . you have the several antiquities before you in their pure State such as they were found, unembarrassed by the rude restorations of modern hands . . .'.[45] The concern to present ancient models unaltered extended to his own work: 'I would sooner draw off carefully in bold Chalk any individual figures in your Collection, and have them engraved in the manner of Piranesi's Work, bearing a true Picture of the original . . . giving to the World nothing of my own, but only intrinsic copies of existing models of antiquity'.[46] This is the true 'archaeological' spirit.

He was not backward, in an enthusiastic and friendly correspondence, in urging 'Italian' ideas on Holland: 'I have added two sketches of the famed Candelabra's belonging to the Pope', which 'would be grand Objects to finish the Views of a Suit of Apartments or otherwise, which is often practised with great Success here . . .'. The Italian experience was decisive in propelling Tatham towards a stricter interpretation of antiquity, away from the Louis XVI impress; by 1796 he had designed in Rome a pair of pier tables in advanced neo-classical taste for Lord Bristol.[47]

The result of Tatham's research in Rome was the famous *Etchings of Ornamental Architecture drawn . . . during the years 1794, 1795, and 1796.* Tatham's instinct in thinking this subject more to the hour than the arabesque suggested by Holland (see pp.234–5) was correct; the publication became one of the great Regency source books (it was probably printed in 1800, the date on some of the plates). It was reissued in 1803, 1810, 1826, and 1843; the last two publications united the original *Etchings* with Tatham's 1806 *Etchings Representing Fragments of Grecian and Roman Architectural Ornaments*. Tatham's work must have been of the utmost convenience, and the pieces he illustrated helped to supply Regency furniture with three of its main ingredients. First, the massiveness derived from marble prototypes, as mentioned above; Piranesi and Tatham's enthusiasm for mass and solidity ran diametrically counter to the aesthetic preferences of the immediately preceding period (although Piranesi's arabesque has an attenuated elegance). Speaking in 1806 of silver, Tatham regretted that 'instead of Massiveness, the principal characteristic of good Plate, light insignificant forms have prevailed. . . . Good Chasing may be considered as a branch of Sculpture . . .'.[48] Everything known of him persuades one that he felt furniture also to be a branch of sculpture.

Second, the book pictured the sweeping scrolls and curves that during the Regency supplemented the rectilinear discipline of Adam, Louis XVI and the 1790s Sheraton style. Third, it made generally available the antique zoomorphic ornament that displays on English furniture a primitivistic grimace less often found in France; the force, however, must have come direct from Piranesi, whose beasts and chimeras are extraordinarily expressionistic; on English Regency furniture this became a vivacious and fantastic grotesquerie, often allied with flamboyant richness in materials and finishes.

The barbaric element aroused protest: 'That there is classical authority for all the varieties of masks, and all the combinations of sphinxes, chimeras, hippogriffes, and eagle-winged lions, may be admitted, without admitting their beauty or propriety. . . . It may be

286 'Autels, Trépieds, Candelabres, Lampes, Meubles', published by J. N. L. Durand in 1802

difficult to prove the absurdity of a predilection which is so general; but some of the mixtures in this volume, such as a lion's foot for the root of a flower, a female head fixed on a lion's leg, or by contrast the lion's head dressed in an Egyptian head-dress, are certainly "strange, passing strange".[49] One of the points of Miss Mitford's often quoted description of Rosedale Cottage, a 'cottage orné', is that the furniture had come alive; the 'library Egyptian . . . and swarming with furniture crocodiles and sphinxes. Only think of a crocodile couch and a sphinx sofa' (was Rosedale Cottage modelled on Craven Cottage?)[50] Tatham was attracted towards Egyptian motifs, and the emphasis on strength and volume that he appreciated in certain Roman artefacts was to be found in Egyptian art also.

An instance of the way in which Holland, and ultimately the furniture trade in general, used Tatham's research may be seen in subsequent realisations of the Pope's 'famed Candelabra's' recommended by Tatham to Holland. They were reproduced as Plates 86 and 88 of Tatham's book (they were also reproduced by Durand: see (Fig. 286[c]). Plate 88 was used virtually unaltered as a stove for Carlton House (Fig. 287); the relevant drawing from the Holland sketchbook is dated November 1796. The subject of Plate 86, the 'Barberini Candelabrum', was well known, having been published by Piranesi in 1779;[51] in addition to illustrating it, Tatham sent Holland a replica which arrived in 1796.[52] Two splendid versions in mahogany have come down to modern times; one, now at Kenwood, is unmarked, although Marsh and Tatham have, for obvious reasons, been suggested as the makers;[53] the other, a pair in mahogany with bronze mounts,[54] is inscribed: 'Designed and executed by Vulliamy and Son, London AD 1807' — a repudiation of any involvement by any other designer, including Tatham. Vulliamy is recorded as supplying various stands and plinths to the Prince of Wales in 1807,[55] by which date Holland was dead. The facts counsel caution in making hypotheses.

Thomas Tatham, C. H. Tatham's brother, formed an exclusive partnership in 1803[56] with Marsh (Elward having withdrawn); it worked extensively for the Prince of Wales. At this period Holland was beginning to retire from active work, and C. H. Tatham would have been excellently situated for consultation and for supplying designs for furniture. The lack of direct evidence as to the designer of the later classically inspired Carlton House furniture has been thought hardly material in face of the evidence supplied by its style and its supplier, but the inscription on the Vulliamy torchère mentioned above makes one pause. Whoever designed it, the later Carlton House furniture represents the triumph of the 'archaeological style'; it recreates Roman furniture with overwhelming grandeur and éclat. Everything was gilded; the plain woods or delicately painted surfaces of the late eighteenth century were forgotten. Only boulle or lacquer could hold its own beside the 'high Roman fashion' dominant in the weighty be-

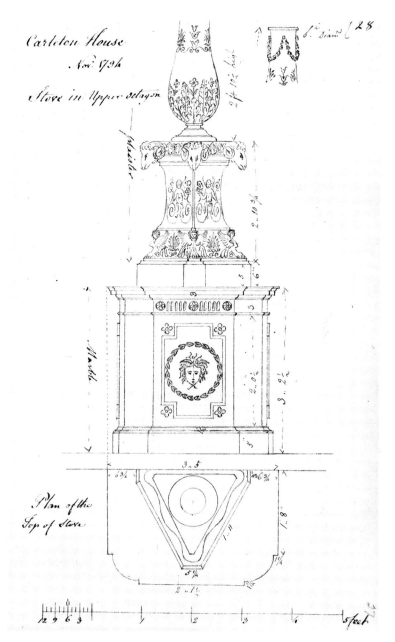

**287** Design for a stove in the Upper Octagon, Carlton House, Nov. 1794

griffined settees of the Blue Velvet Room (Pl. LX)[57] and the magnificent pier tables of the Crimson Drawing Room, themselves supported on vigorous griffins (Pl. LXXI); the last were delivered to Carlton House by Tatham (Thomas), Bailey and Saunders in 1814.[58] The crane candelabrum bases in the latter room, based on an antique original from Hadrian's Villa[59] that had been etched by Piranesi, had been received in July 1813 from Marsh and Tatham[59] and were to reappear at Windsor Castle. The two splendid giltwood chairs from the Throne Room (Pl. CXIII) were derived from ancient seats at San

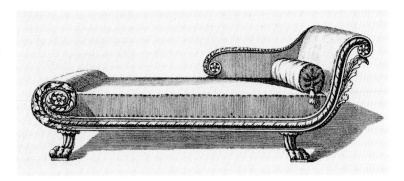

288 Design for 'A Grecian Squab', 1802, by Thomas Sheraton

Gregorio Magno and the Vatican, both illustrated in Tatham's *Etchings*;[60] they were delivered by Marsh and Tatham in 1812.[61]

Sheraton employed the new and more uncompromising 'archaeological' language in designs shown in his *Cabinet Dictionary* of 1803 and *Encyclopaedia* of 1804–08; he, in his one person, encompassed the sharply contrasting styles of the 1790s and the early 1800s. The difference is clearest in the seat furniture. Gone were the spindly elegance and straight lines of the Jacob-like sofas; in their place came the first 'Grecian' squab (couch), of 1802 (Fig. 288), indispensable in most Regency drawing rooms; it is more Roman than Greek with its rolled back arm (Fig. 290) and lion paw feet. Another design for a sofa, of 1806, has eagles at either end in a manner reminiscent of Kent, and the modified sabre leg that was to become common; the sofa is hung with 'antique drapery' in place of the festoons of the 1790s (Pl. CIX).

Sheraton's design of 1803 for a 'Grecian Dining Table' (Fig. 289) was obviously an attempt to reproduce the visual effect of the Roman custom of dining in a recumbent posture, an antique habit which was not revived. The form of the sofas, which have klismos-derived 'sabre' legs and backs, and are covered in a striped material similar to that seen on furniture in ancient wall paintings, resembles that of a hall sofa designed for the Prince of Wales, probably by Henry Holland. They are not unlike extant ancient stone benches that were used in open air theatres, which have the shape of the klismos leg outlined on a solid stone base (used as a model by George Smith in a design for a 'Library Fauteuil' of 1808).[62] The sofas are set in a noticeably spartan (if the epithet be not offensive to the Athenians) dining room, very different from Sheraton's earlier manner; their shape is not far removed from that of the 'Trafalgar' chair (Pl. CXV), of which Sheraton provided the basic form and which, robbed of archaic grace, became the most characteristic and ubiquitous of all Regency chairs.

An example of Sheraton serviceability is provided by his camp chair, 'made to fold up, the back and bottom of which are formed of girth-webbing'.[63] This startlingly simple chair (Fig. 291) was derived from the antique, and displays the tendency towards abstraction that one sees in much ancient art; it appears on Greek vases in a form practically the same as that pictured by Sheraton. It was given every degree of elaboration, and became the ancient and the modern X-framed chair of state. In Sheraton's version it is exactly the same as the X-framed folding chair seen today on every camp site and on every film lot. The Sheraton interpretation of the grander antique X-framed chair appears in two designs of 1803 (Fig. 293); the back of the first shows an antique lyre, which had been usefully illustrated by Montfaucon,[64] its frame realised by a pair of eagles; the second is formed of two formalised cornucopias and is topped by a carrying handle, mobility

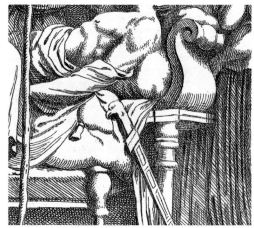

289 Design for a 'Grecian Dining Table', 1803, by Thomas Sheraton

290 Detail of a Roman couch, first published by Pietro Santi Bartoli in 1693

CXII Clock in Egyptian style, now in the Royal Pavilion, Brighton, c.1805

CXIII Council chair made for Carlton House by
Tatham and Co., 1812

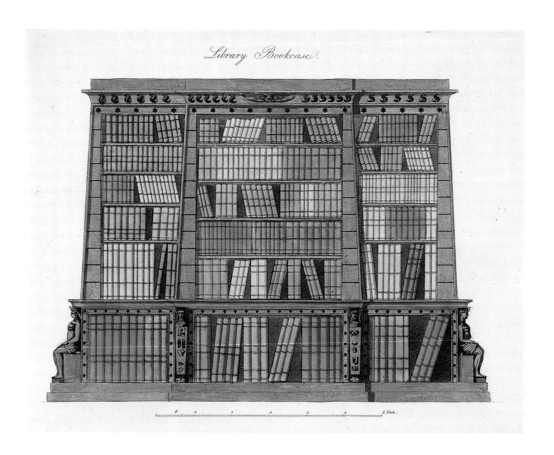

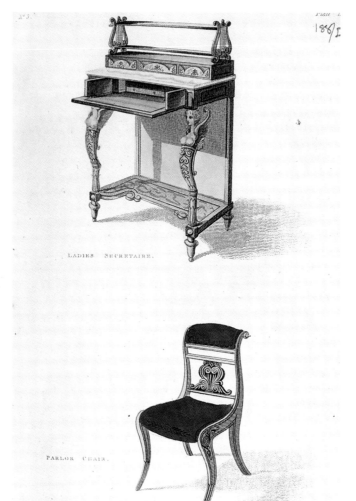

CXIV Design for a 'Library Bookcase',
1805, by George Smith

CXV A 'Ladies Secretaire', and a 'Parlor
Chair', from the *Repository*, 1809

*Opposite* CXVI 'Pocock's Reclining Patent
Chair', from the *Repository*, 1813

CXVII Design for a sofa, sofa-table,
candelabra, and footstool, from the
*Repository*, 1822

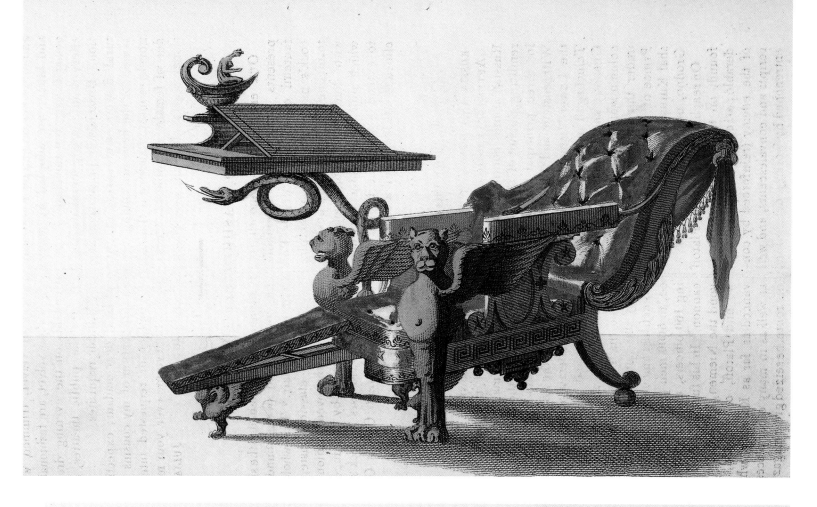

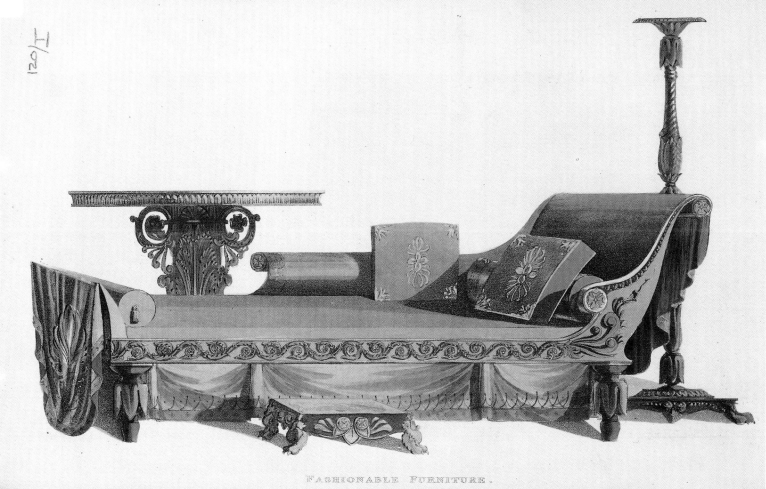

FASHIONABLE FURNITURE.

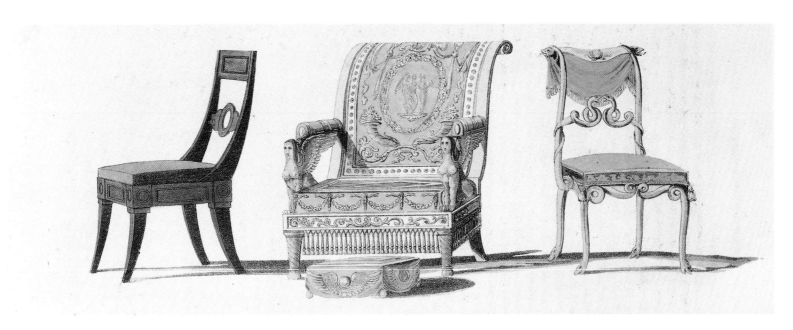

*Above* CXVIII 'Fashionable Chairs', from the *Repository*, 1825 *Below* CXIX 'A Cabinet', from the *Repository*, 1828

recognised in ornament. The chairs anticipate the X-framed chairs of the 1820s.

Sheraton himself attributed his adoption of archaeological antiquity to French influence: he spoke of showing French chairs which 'follow the antique taste and introduce into their arms and legs various heads of animals'.[65] Designers and makers often cited French fashion to gloss their own products. His animal forms are often disconcertingly vivified, whether chimerical or realistic (Fig. 292), giving a disquieting impression of the frigidities of a polite culture being assaulted by barbaric virility.

Another Sheraton motif to which a French origin has been attributed is that of legs turned with rings in relief; the motif, associated with bamboo and chinoiserie, is seen in the work of Weisweiler and Jacob; Holland himself used such turning, and the French influence is unmistakable. However, it has been remarked above that rings formed on bamboo are not raised but depressed, and although rings in relief did become assimilated with chinoiserie their source lay not in Cathay but in classical antiquity — although bamboo itself was also used as a decorative motif by the Romans.[66] The leg was extensively used in early nineteenth-century England, sometimes blended with 'Pompeian' candelabraform shapes and sometimes given the antique pointed foot (in the slender variant, the foot must originally have belonged to metal chairs); the leg was often employed with the foot splayed outwards. Sheraton used it in this last, particularly delicate and beautiful, form (Pl. CX); it survived long into Victorian times, often combined with the balloon back. It should be added that Sheraton published the first English furniture designs in the Egyptian taste; they were merely a matter of applied motifs.

The same mind that conceived the bizarrely animalistic furniture, and the overwrought marine confections that constituted 'Nelson's Chairs', also produced shapes that, sometimes with a little adaptation, became domestic Regency commonplaces. Such were the sofa tables, library tables, dressing tables, sideboards, wash hand stands, work tables, secretaires, bookcases, and other pieces; these often retained Sheraton's earlier elegance, an elegance foreign to the designs of George Smith. The splayed out sabre leg, the brass lion-paw foot, the reeded mouldings, all became part of the workaday Regency language, far removed from the gilded glories of Carlton House. This sort of furniture had no hieratic pretensions; its prototypes were usually wooden or metal, not stone, and the forms it employed had evolved in practical use.

## Thomas Hope

The credit for the inception of the new archaeological style in England was generally given by his contemporaries to Hope. The nature of Hope's achievement was defined by his character; a man of deep feeling, imaginative fancy, and sense of public duty in patronising the arts, who modelled himself on aesthetes and collectors such as Caylus and Albani, he expressed himself in buildings and interiors of striking originality. He believed the art of drawing to be fundamental to the pursuit of excellence in any visual medium, a belief that practical experience confirms; he could become a bore upon the subject (Farington described him in June 1805 as having made too long a speech 'upon the necessity of Artists drawing . . .').[67] He was not alone in thinking drawing important; in 1796 George Cumberland, whose tastes were broad enough for him to consider Blake as having 'extraordinary genius and abilities; the highest, I believe, I shall ever experience',[68] wrote of 'outline' that 'there can be no art without it'. Ultimately, the Regency emphasis on 'outline' may be traced to the

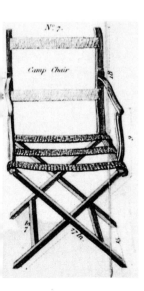

**291** Design for a camp chair, 1803, by Thomas Sheraton
**292** Design for drawing-room chairs, by Thomas Sheraton, 1803

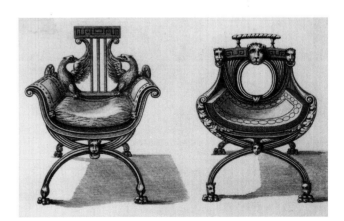

**293** Design for drawing-room chairs, 1804, by Thomas Sheraton

Greek vase, and it was thus that the 'Etruscan' fashion exerted its greatest influence, an influence that transcended the mere employment of 'Etruscan' motifs. Hope's illustrations in his famous *Household Furniture and Interior Decoration* of 1807 avoided the unGreek solecism of 'Outlines thick and thin alternatively, like the flourishes of a penman',[69] for which Cumberland had castigated Flaxman's illustrations to Homer and Aeschylus, and Tischbein's to Hamilton's 'Vases'; *Household Furniture* was not 'finely flourished', but engraved by Aikins and Dawe in a line of uniform thickness. Hope himself made the drawings; surviving sketchbooks show a precise and meticulous hand. Despite their beauty, the engravings falsify the furniture; the disembodied line conveys neither weight nor colour.

Hope's forty days in the wilderness — the wanderings that prepared his career — demonstrate his eclecticism. Four times in Italy, he visited Greece, Sicily, Egypt, Africa, Turkey, Germany, Spain, and Portugal; he numbered the Egyptian, the Grecian, the Etruscan, the Lombardic, the Moorish, the Tartar, the Persian, and the Gothic amongst the styles he had studied (see p.115). Only his self-discipline and taste kept this accumulation of information under control, although he was not an aesthetic puritan. His often quoted 'From an infant . . . I already began dealing in [those] straight lines'[70] has been taken to mean a preference for the ascetically straight over the sensually sinuous line; however, his emphasis appears to have been on precocious ability rather than inherent preference, and whilst the straight line is important in his designs, they do not lack voluptuous curves. Hope's stated aim was to give 'new food to the industry of the poor' and 'new decorum to the expenditure of the rich'; the difficulties that drove him both to design and to draw his own furniture arose from his finding no one person who was 'at once possessed of sufficient intimacy with the stores of literature to suggest ideas' — again the emphasis on associations, an emphasis that displays his faith in high inspiration — and who could draw well enough to execute the designs.[71]

Conception and delineation of his furniture being both Hope's own, three-dimensional execution in England presented further difficulties; 'almost all the least indifferent compositions' had to be based on 'models and casts from Italy'. This last statement appears to relate only to the 'embellishments', the carved and cast ornament; presumably, therefore, the models for these were all Italian. One wonders whether, had there not been a war, Hope would have sent instead to Paris; perhaps not. Paris meant fashion; Italy meant the antique. The ornament was made by Decaix, a 'bronzist', and Bogaert, a carver, both continental craftsmen;[72] Chantrey, whom Hope does not mention in *Household Furniture*, was also employed; he was an assistant to Bogaert.[73]

In discussions of Hope's furniture, its 'archaeological purity' and the scholarly way in which ancient forms were reproduced have been emphasised; Hope himself said that, 'if there was any novelty in my house, it was only in the application of very old forms'.[74] He took the utmost trouble to ensure the accuracy of his antique sources; although he thought Durand useful, the publication lacked both the 'greatest minuteness or the greatest accuracy'.[75] Had he stopped there, his furniture would have been the Regency equivalent of Robsjohn-Gibbing's klismos chair of the 1930s, an accurate facsimile. He did not. His statement continued: 'if the forms of my furniture were more agreeable than the generality . . . it was only owing to my having, not servilely imitated, but endeavoured to make myself master of the spirit of the Antique. . . . Beauty consists not in ornament, it consists in outline — where this is elegant and well understood the simplest object will be pleasing . . .'.[76] Hope well understood his own mental processes; he combined accurately delineated antique motifs in unprecedented and brilliantly original ways, regulated by an unerring taste in 'outline' which he and Cumberland knew comprehended form; drawing is 'the arrangement of the lines which determine form'.[77]

The strength and simplicity of Hope's line, and his judicious selection from other sources, has been demonstrated above (see p.273). His individuality repeatedly shows itself. The difference between his style and that of Percier, for instance, is evident in two related designs for tables, a round table in the case of Percier and Fontaine (Fig. 294) and a rectangular table in the case of Hope (Fig. 295). The exquisite detailed preciosity of the Percier and Fontaine piece, with its light and graceful spring from female sphinx legs, is converted in Hope's hands into a matter of strong, controlled rhythms, virile ornament, and areas of plainness, like the intervals of silence that were appearing in the advanced music of the period; Percier's sphinxes have a slight downwards glance, inherited from the flirtatious rococo, whilst Hope's gaze sternly ahead, as we know that he thought portrait sculpture should gaze. The Hope table was described by its creator as a dressing-table 'in mahogany and gold', with a vase of alabaster upon it; different as it is from that by Percier, it is not a whit inferior.

A reason for the comparative plainness and massiveness of Hope's furniture may be found in his concern for permanence, a concern probably intensified by the romantic *frisson* communicated by those enduring forms in bronze and marble that had survived the collapse of civilisations. He expressed the hope that furniture designed in his manner might 'be preserved in families, from generation to generation, as a valuable portion of the patrimonial estate'; the bronze ornaments, often 'left to exhibit [their] own green patina'[78] — another piece of archaeological romanticism (Henry Holland had placed some of the gilt ornaments on the Southill furniture on green backgrounds, possibly an allusion to bronze?) — were to be reused when their original supports had decayed.

Modern Italian furniture may have provided Hope with ideas (Figs 297, 298). However, the major sources of inspiration were Greece and

**294** 'Table exécutée à Petersbourg pour le Cte. S.', designed by Percier and Fontaine

**295** A dressing-table, by Thomas Hope, 1807

Rome. In speaking of Percier and. Fontaine in his introduction to *Household Furniture*, Hope emphasised what they had themselves stated, that 'study of the antique chef d'oeuvres in Italy' had formed the foundation of their work. The list of sources at the end of Hope's book includes only three that are not textbooks of classical antiquities, whether by Englishmen, Italians, Frenchmen, or Germans, one of the three being an enlightening reference to the vignettes by Percier in Didot's Horace: 'some of which offer exquisite representations of the mode in which the ancient Romans liked to decorate their town and country houses'.[79] The epithet, drawn from the introduction to the Didot volume, 'exquisitissimum', is well deserved; these pictures, which imitate antique gems, are of an entrancing appeal, and represent scenes of ancient life in a way that might well persuade the idealistic observer,

especially one enamoured of Horatian associations, of their easy application to modern life (Fig. 296).[80] They show depictions of furniture in use, and include an idyllic terrace scene with treillage, a flight of steps, and a Reptonian basket overflowing with grapes. They far surpass, in beauty and naturalness, the prints published by Henry Moses of contemporary society ladies and gentlemen using Hope's furniture, which Hope probably instigated in conscious emulation of the Didot vignettes.

The Horace was published in 1799, the year that Hope purchased the house in Duchess Street; dangerous as it is to read too much into a single word, the throb of emotion in Hope's epithet, together with the Moses imitations, leads one to ask how strong an influence those tiny pictures were.

**296** A Roman interior, by Charles Percier, 1799

Hope's synthesising methods in design can be clearly read in the furniture from the Duchess Street 'Egyptian' Room (which he nowhere calls 'Egyptian') (Fig. 264). The remarkable arm chairs, amongst the most forcefully archaic of Hope's inventions, combine elements of the klismos, in the general form of the back and back legs, with a common Greek and Roman type of throne chair illustrated by Caylus[81] and Durand (Fig. 286[a]); it appears in the *Pitture Antiche d'Ercolano*,[82] and it is just possible that Hope saw in the Palazzo Borghese a sofa that used a variant of the throne leg. The winged sphinxes of the chair shown in Durand had been used elsewhere, and Hope substituted the more uncommon touch of 'crouching priests . . . copied from an Egyptian idol in the Vatican'. Other details that gave the chairs Egyptian colour were 'the winged Isis placed in the rail . . . borrowed from an Egyptian mummy-case in the Institute at Bologna; the Canopuses . . . imitated from one in the Capitol; and the other ornaments . . . taken from various monuments at Thebes, Tentyris, etc.'[83] The side tables have turned legs of Roman derivation; the sofa is a synthesis of Roman and Egyptian, embellished, in compliance with Quatremère de Quincy's anathema, not with hieroglyphs, but with little depictions of Anubis and Horus; scorpions decorate the feet, a somewhat uneasy reference so near to the vicinity of the ankle.

As Roman and Greek references were allowed into the 'Egyptian' Room, so were Egyptian references not excluded from other rooms. The Flaxman Room had two candelabra 'composed of a Lotus flower issuing from a bunch of ostrich feathers' (Fig. 299[5]).[84] This flower was a motif of which Hope (with other Regency designers) was fond; he used it as a hanging light in the Ampitheatre at the Deepdene (Fig. 219). The exuberant ostrich-feather base is a more realistic rendering of an Egyptian motif pictured in both Norden's book of 1735[85] and in Quatremère de Quincy's *Architecture Egyptienne* of 1803;[86] Hope listed Norden as a source but not Quatremère, a strange omission given his unmistakable quotation of the latter's opinions.

Another interesting Egyptianising object that stands in the Flaxman Room is 'a clock, carried by a figure of Isis, or the moon, adorned with her crescent' (Pl. CXII).[87] A clock after the same design exists at

Brighton Pavilion; it lacks the crescent, and the head shows no signs of any former attachment; at least three other such clocks are recorded, one of which is signed 'Antoine Ravrio'.[88] The signature does not necessarily mean that Hope did not design the clock, for makers were prepared to make clocks to amateur designs; Tatham, for example, recorded that in 1795 Boschi had executed in Rome a bronze clock 'without any gilding whatever for Lady Spencer after her own design' for £40, and that 'The Workmen having the Moulds could now execute the same for £30'.[89] The maker, left with the moulds, could multiply the images. However, if Hope did design the clock, he deigned to decorate it with meaningless hieroglyphs, contrary to his and Quatremère de Quincy's express prohibition, and contrary to his avoidance of hieroglyphs elsewhere in the house (see pp.191, 343, 345). Moreover, the design itself displays undigested elements from Piranesi (Fig. 300) in a manner foreign to Hope. One can conceive that he bought such a clock, and added the Isis crescent to complete the emblemism of the Flaxman Room, but it is unlikely that he designed it.

Not only did Hope bring together different periods and civilisations in one piece of furniture; genuine ancient and old artefacts were mixed together in carefully assembled ensembles. One of the most idiosyncratic of such creations was his tent room,[90] the 'closet or boudoir' (Fig. 265; see p.270), which contained Egyptian, Hindoo and Chinese objects. There seems to have existed an appetite to swallow

**297** Chimney-piece and chair, from the Italian sketchbook of Thomas Hope

undiluted the products of strange civilisations; the Prince of Wales showed a similar interest in 'ethnic' chinoiserie at the Pavilion of 1802–04 (see p.428).

The most constant inspiration to Hope was the Roman antique. Some objects were virtually unchanged in being converted into modern furniture; such was the 'wine cooler, in the shape of an antique bath or lavacrum' (Fig. 299[4]);[91] its original is illustrated in Durand and elsewhere. Or they were little changed, as are the 'pedestals belonging to a sideboard: imitated from an altar in the villa Borghese' (Fig. 299[6]); this piece was illustrated by Tatham and Durand. The winged paws without heads that terminate the sofas in the 'Third Room containing Greek vases' (Fig. 176) resemble a plate in Flaxman's *Aeschylus*, with the sunken lion head omitted.[92] The superstructures on the library table (Fig. 298[1]) which as Hope says, 'present the shape of ancient Greek house roofs',[93] echo the shape of the cippus on the

chimney-piece of the 'Third Room', one of the sepulchral ambiguities that haunt the archaeological Regency style. The 'stone seats, adorned with sphinxes and Lotus flowers'[94] seen in the Picture Gallery (Fig. 218) — the stone was presumably marble — were derived from an original illustrated by Tatham (Fig. 301), the 'Grand antique Chair executed in parian Marble' that was also drawn upon for the design of the Carlton House consular chairs (Pl. CXIII).

One ancient non-sepulchral form from Herculaneum that Hope employed several times is the beautiful 'athénienne' (Fig. 286[b]). Christened from a painting of 1763 by Vien, *La Vertueuse Athénienne*, it proved infinitely adaptable; it served as a table, a pedestal, a perfume burner, a plant stand, a support for a bowl of goldfish. Hope described one of his versions (Fig. 298[5]) as 'a tripod of bronze: bronze ornaments round the triangular pedestal',[95] one wonders whether the bronze was green, as seems probable. He showed it also as two tripod

**298** Writing table [1 & 2], arm chair [3 & 4] and pedestal [5], by Thomas Hope, 1807

**299** End of a pier table with a carved wooden fringe [1], chair inlaid in metal and ebony [2 & 3], wine cooler [4], candelabrum [5] and sideboard pedestal [6], by Thomas Hope, 1807

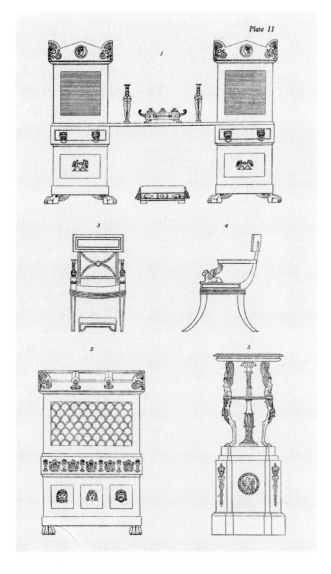

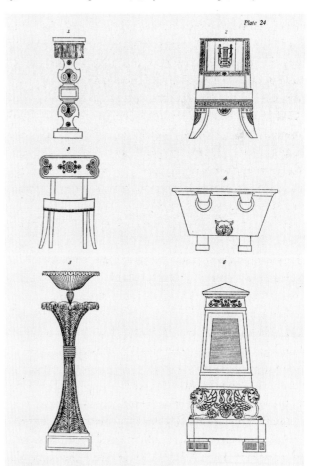

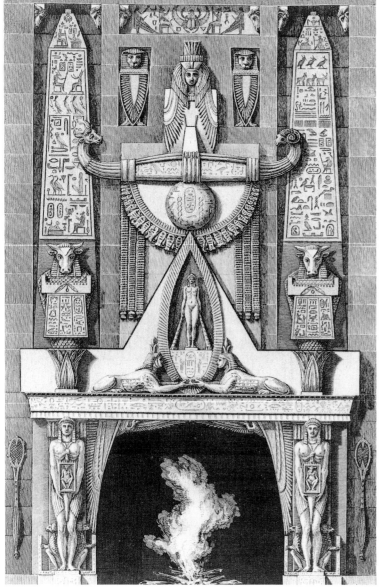

**300** Design for a chimney-piece in the Egyptian style, by G. B. Piranesi, 1769

**301** A 'Grand antique Chair executed in parian Marble from the Collection in the Museum of the Vatican', by C. H. Tatham, 1800

tables of different forms.[96] In one of its original forms the athénienne embodied a kind of ancient gallicism which astonishingly anticipated that early neo-classicism in which lingers the spirit of rococo. Hope rejected this frivolity; he added a heavy base (as did Percier)[97] and substituted a column for the airy spirals of the original, thus producing a static and grave variation.

Given their shared debt to Italy, one questions how far Hope was directly influenced by Percier and Fontaine. He deprecated comparisons between his book and that of 'an artist of my acquaintance, Percier',[98] whom he nevertheless highly praised. There

are points where their designs show similarities; one has been mentioned above. The chair illustrated (Fig. 299[2]) resembles chairs in Percier, if simpler and heavier; certain sofas (Fig. 302[5]) have points of resemblance that indicate Percier rather than a common source. A further example is the 'Chandelier of bronze and gold', which is ornamented, with a poetic allusion to its illumination after nightfall, with 'a crown of stars over a wreath of night-shade' (Fig. 304).[99] The Percier and Fontaine version (Fig. 303) shares the griffins and the symbolism, but with different effect; in place of Hope's disciplined metallic construction is a web-like confection of rock

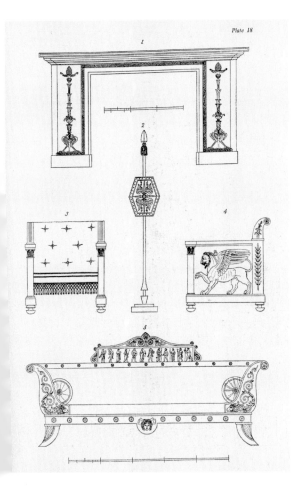

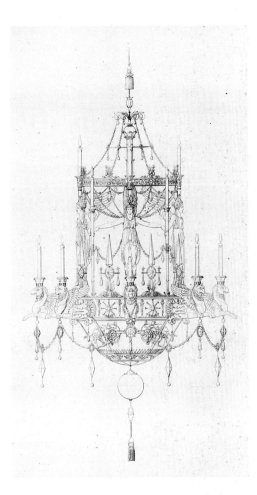

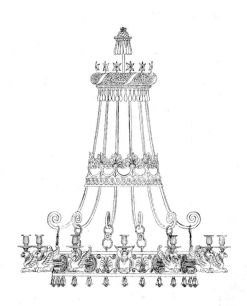

**302** Chimney-piece, chair, pole screen and sofa, by Thomas Hope, 1807

**303** 'Lustre exécutée dans la Maison du C. Ch. . . . à Paris', designed by Percier and Fontaine

**304** Chandelier, by Thomas Hope, 1807

crystal, glass, and gilt-bronze that in its general effect brings to mind certain features of the central gasolier of the Music Room at Brighton Pavilion.

Hope's book, reviled by the Philistines and disliked by voluptuaries, remains incontestably the most distinguished and beautiful of Regency furniture books, and it deeply influenced other designers, including Smith, Bullock, Brown and the Nicholsons. The style it established stands apart from Empire and Restoration styles; massive and severe, but rich and harmonious, even its eccentricities display the force of an original genius. Beside it, Smith is pedestrian and Bullock limited and showy. The influence of Hope's furniture was apparent long before its publication in 1807; he opened his house to the public in 1804, and the cognoscenti flocked in. Samuel Rogers, who designed furniture himself, had apparently seen Hope's designs by January 1803 and was having versions made at that time. Without Hope's contribution, innovation would have rested on Sheraton's version of the *goût grec* and on the Roman style of Carlton House; both were considerable achievements, but, Hope lacking, a vital element would have been missing.

## George Smith

George Smith's *Collection of Designs for Household Furniture* made available many more designs in 'archaeological' mode. Smith has his qualities and made a contribution independent of Hope; differences between their books betoken a difference in attitude. The most telling clue lies in Smith's rejection of the pure line, with its ruthless exposure of deficiencies, its suggestion of idealism and perhaps unattainability, its minimalisation of volume; Smith's furniture casts shadows. He covers the whole range — classical, Gothic, Chinese. His designs are those of a manufacturer; he was by no means as accomplished a designer as Hope, and did not integrate his sources as fully.

There is evidence that he ranged widely in search of ideas. Sphinxes are used on a jardinière design[100] which is reminiscent of that from Mme. Récamier's bedroom (Pl. LVI) published by Krafft and Ransonette. The use Smith made of the *Pitture Antiche d'Ercolano* in devising his 'Decorations' has been mentioned above (see pp.240, 345); from the same source he drew a 'Dejeuné Table' (Fig. 305) virtually unchanged from an antique brazier stand with 'tre pezzi arcuati'

(Fig. 306). This model is found also in Ackermann's *Selection of Ornaments* of 1817–19, and in Agostino Aglio's *Architectural Ornaments* of 1820 (Fig. 308) (the last exhibited much better quality engraving than most pattern books produced in England). Such a picaresque existence is not rare; a good concept has enough vitality to travel. (It was sometimes rejected by the client: a pencilled note in a copy of Smith's 1808 book reads 'Mrs. Holt finds it difficult to suit herself with a pattern: she thinks the pillar of the pattern table too solid and the claw too heavy. She has therefore altered the drawing in pencil at page 76 into more the sort of thing she likes. If possible Mrs Holt intends to call and look at the wood . . .'. Mrs. Holt's pencil drawing is of an irredeemably ordinary table that lacks the fashionable heaviness.)[101]

Smith's plate of 'Drawing Room X Seats' described as 'ornamental and extra seats in elegant Drawing Rooms', which shows three seats together (Fig. 307), came from diverse sources. That on the upper left, with birds' heads as feet, is taken from two slightly differing and famous antique stools from Herculaneum that were published first by Caylus and afterwards by Tatham and Durand (Fig. 286[d]); Tatham informs us that they were covered in modern red cloth, which may indicate that they had been used by the King of Naples.[102] Seats generally similar to Smith's, but with different details, were published side by side in Hope's book,[103] although Smith's upper right design is also substantially the same as one by Percier and Fontaine.[104] Hope provided a few of Smith's designs; the plate of 'Drawing Room chairs in profile'[105] which is dated 1805, well before the publication of Hope's book, shows a chair at the bottom right which is a conflation of two designs shown by Hope; one, an arm chair very like a Jacob design — if it be not an actual Jacob chair[106] — supplied the front leg; the other, a 'large arm-chair' supplied the back and seat.[107] Smith's 'Ladies Dressing Table' (Fig. 309) is probably taken from the same source as Hope's design for a tea-table;[108] both place a sarcophagus shape above a curved pedestal in the manner of the famous red porphyry 'bathing vase' (as Tatham called it) that had been used as the tomb of Pope Clement XII. This 'vase' had been the only smaller antique pictured — in three aspects — by Desgodetz in 1682,[109] and Piranesi portrayed it riding high on the jumbled and broken antique magnificence that litters the most romantic and evocative of his prints.[110] It seems possible that Smith may have looked directly at a picture of the sarcophagus, since unlike Hope he has used the paw feet of the original.

Smith seems to have had a good 'nose' for the topical. For instance, an extraordinary design for a bed of 1805 (Pl. CXI) shows an awareness of the contemporary interest in the primitive (see p.108); without the explanatory text, one would have expected the posts to mimic unworked timber in the sophisticated way that faux bamboo mimicked bamboo; one sees such twiggy conceits in some of the bronze candelabra from Herculaneum.[111] However, for the 'Design in the rustic style . . . suitable to a cottage or country residence . . . the pillars and rails may be selected from rough materials, cleaned and varnished'; the rails are rudimentary temple pediments, each hung with a wreath in a way consonant with Laugierian ideas on the origin of ornament in nature. Another example of Smith's topicality is that at the height of the Egyptian fever, in 1804, he showed alternative designs for a classical sofa with lion or leopard arms, and an Egyptian sofa crawling with hieroglyphs. A strong design for a 'Cheval Dressing Glass', the plate dated 1804 (Fig. 311) is a splendid example of that vigorous Regency style regarded by later generations with horror and disbelief; in solemn weightiness, it combines the Egyptian taste with Tatham-like winged lions at the feet.

Smith was not afraid of employing architectural forms in designing furniture. An intimidating 'Dwarf Library Bookcase' of 1804 (Fig. 310) reproduces at each end virtually unchanged Roman sepulchres, of the type plentifully illustrated by Santi Bartoli and Montfaucon, exactly as they might have appeared along the Appian Way; the application of such literary names as 'Homer' and 'Virgil' to the sepulchres is a naive obfuscation. This is a truly amazing use of the archaeological antique, especially for an age fully alive to the meaning of associations. A 'Stand for Flowers' of 1805 (Fig. 312), which has a stepped construction above a semi-circular aperture, has a strong whiff of ancient Roman columbaria about the arrangement and in the detail of the central urn;

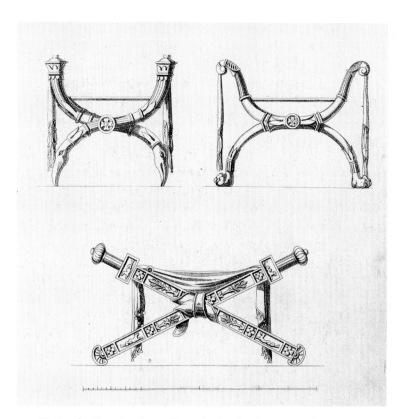

**307** Design for 'Drawing Room X seats', 1807, by George Smith

*Opposite above* **305** Design for a 'Dejeuné Table', 1805, by George Smith

*Opposite below* **306** Roman brazier stands, 1792

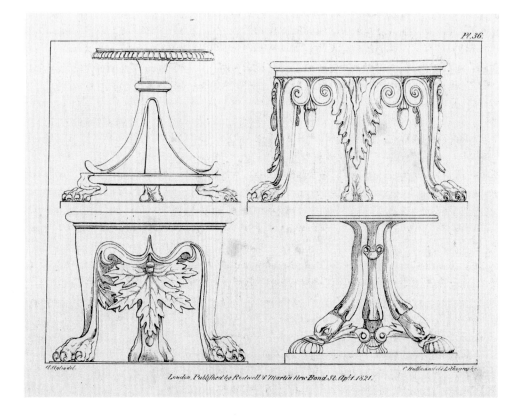

**308** Ancient artefacts, illustrated by Agostino Aglio, 1820

389

**309** Design for a 'Ladies Dressing Table', 1806, by George Smith

**310** Design for a 'Dwarf Library Bookcase', 1804, by George Smith

**311** Design for a 'Cheval Dressing Glass', 1804, by George Smith

**312** Design for a 'Stand for Flowers &c.', 1805, by George Smith

the addition of flowers seals, for the modern observer, the association with the crematorium.

A massive design of 1805 for a Library Bookcase in the Egyptian style (Pl. CXIV), owing nothing to Hope and probably drawn directly from Denon, exemplifies the shift from angularity to solidity, the latter emphasised by the dark mahogany and rosewood that had come into vogue — although many of Smith's designs are still pictured in light-coloured satinwood, pollard oak, or amboyna. His instructions allow much variety: 'Mahogany . . . should be confined to the Parlor and Bedchamber Floors; in furniture for these apartments the less inlay of other woods, the more chaste will be the style. . . . In Drawing Rooms, Boudoirs, Anti Rooms, or other dressed apartments, east and West India Satin-woods, rose-wood, tulip-wood, and the other varieties of woods brought from the East, may be used: with satin and light-coloured woods the decoration may be of ebony or rose-wood: with rosewood let the decorations be ormolu, and the inlay of brass: bronzed metal, though sometimes used with satin-wood, has a cold and poor effect; it suits better on gilt work, and will answer well enough on mahogany'.[112]

Other of Smith's designs betray a variety of influences. One, for a 'Library Fauteuil'[113] shows furniture which though in detail not Piranesian is grouped on a platform in a Piranesi manner, probably inspired directly by Piranesi (Fig. 281). Two 'Library Chairs' have as their front legs realistic Sheraton-like beasts, snarling lions and savage griffins;[114] some Smith beasts look tame, especially the ewe-like rams and stodgy leopards seen on two other library chairs.[115] He has a florid design for the ubiquitous convex mirror,[116] popular throughout the period and decorated in varying degrees of elaboration.

Smith's book of 1808 exemplifies the mainstream, quintessential high Regency style, a fusion of antique and Empire motifs; the designs helped to shape the course of classicism in Regency furniture, which, when all allowance for Gothic, antiquarian and rococo sensibilities has been made, remains by far the most aesthetically successful. Hope and Smith produced, or in the case of Hope probably instigated, publications which took the cause further. Smith in 1812 published *Ornamental designs after the antique*, which showed the robust acanthus, scrolls, and tendrils seen in Piranesi and Tatham. Henry Moses, Hope's amanuensis, published in 1814 *A Collection of Vases, Altars, Paterae, tripods, Candelabra, Sarcophagi etc.* which were meant 'to improve the judgement, and refine the taste of the student',[117] in which words spoke Hope, to whom the volume was dedicated; included were vases from the collections of Soane, Hope, Tatham, the King, the British Museum, Piranesi, the restorer Cavaceppi, and the Musée Napoléon. These publications, together with others such as those of Tatham, Ackermann (the *Ornaments* not the *Repository*), and Aglio (see p.388) and the posthumous republication in 1812 of Sheraton's more advanced

designs in *Household Furniture*, must have helped to give later Regency furniture the liveliness it so often retained at a time when the sinews of design were slackening.

## The 'Repository' and English design

No account of neo-classical furniture design between 1809 and 1825 can afford to neglect the *Repository*, published by Rudolph Ackermann[118] from 1809 to 1828. Ackermann, born in 1764 near Leipzig, had moved to London in the mid-1780s after spending some time in Paris designing carriages, a trade which attracted the highest talents (carriages were 'conspicuous consumption'; the Crace firm began in the same way). His interests were manifold, his perceptions acute. He published the Picturesque, advocated French fashion, and was one of the first business men to install gas.[119] The *Repository* concerned itself with a wide range of subjects, receiving and broadcasting news from all over Europe: Ackermann retained his German contacts, visited Germany, and followed developments in German culture.

Until 1825, when the *Repository* decidedly interested itself for the first time in Gothic furniture (see p.416 et seq.), it consistently emphasised the excellencies of the 'Grecian' style. This term seems at first to have been virtually a synonym for the 'archaeological antique', principally denoting furniture in the 'Etruscan' style; after about 1815 it increasingly comprehended the Roman. The cue for the *Repository*'s classical bias was probably taken from George Smith's intention, proclaimed in the preface to his 1808 book, to promote the cause of classicism. The *Repository* anathematised the Egyptian style in August 1809 as 'barbarous', and thereafter virtually ignored it apart from some decorative detail until May 1822, when an Egyptian-style chimney-piece and overmantel were illustrated. French fashions were closely watched (see pp.393–6); however, the lesson inculcated by Percier and Hope that the furnishings and decoration of a room should be conceived as a whole was only to a certain extent observed; a few plates took in a whole room, as did the 'French Bed Chamber' of May 1815, and window walls were quite often shown with curtains, chimney-pieces, and furniture. On the whole, however, the *Repository*'s tempting individual plates must have encouraged the piecemeal approach.

The 'archaeological' antique is seen in Ackermann's second plate, of March 1809, showing a parlour chair in mahogany inlaid with ebony, with gilt ornaments on the four feet (Pl. CXV); the seat, in red morocco, has 'printed Grecian ornaments in black'. This chair, the klismos domiciled, is the well known 'Trafalgar' chair, in which the profile presents a continuous curve from the toe up the front leg to the back. Sheraton had illustrated chairs of the same type with an almost uninterrupted curve;[120] Hope had shown a 'Side view of a chair'[121] which went even nearer to the true Trafalgar type, in that the scroll on the side of the knee did not interrupt the curve. The sides of the top rail have the little projecting scroll used by Holland. The name 'Trafalgar' seems to have first appeared in print in 1808 in the *London Chair-Makers' and Carvers' Book of Prices*, which implies that the type had by then become generally available.[122]

Shown with this chair is a 'Ladies Secretaire' in rosewood; the female sphinx front legs derive from Herculaneum via the 'athénienne' (see pp.385–6). The text explains that these, and the lyres on the upper part — used with the same emblematic meaning (the lyre of Apollo) on the secretaire as in a library — 'may be carved in wood, and finished in burnished and matt gold, to imitate or-moulu'; this use of carved and gilded wood is as characteristic of English furniture as that of gilt bronze is of French. 'The ornaments on the drawers may be of metal, water gilt', another common practice.

The Regency period produced many pieces of furniture in which precise techniques of cabinet-making and ingeniously simple devices

**313** A Roman chair, first published by Pietro Santi Bartoli in 1693

combined to provide a multiplication of uses in one article. Contrivances of this kind had been produced by French furniture makers since the 1780s; Sheraton had adopted similar devices, and the *Repository* showed not a few, including in October 1811 an example of Merlin's Mechanical Chair, which derived its mechanism from mid-eighteenth century sources.[123] A version of this was used by George IV after he became so unwieldy that he found walking difficult. An advertised advantage was that its wheels would 'propel the chair in any required direction, or with any required velocity, at the pleasure of the operator' — one senses a nascent Mr. Toad.

One of the most bizarre of such constructions, for the sybarite rather than the valetudinarian, was 'Pocock's Reclining Patent Chair' of March 1813 (Pl. CXVI). It was an 'elegant fashionable fauteuil chair: upon Messrs Pocock's patent reclining principle, to incline the back to any position, with double reclining footstools, which slide from under the chair to extend it when the back is reclined to the length of a couch. A reading-desk is attached to the side, and contrived to swing round in front of the chair. The whole is designed with classical taste . . .'.[124] The form of the chair, with its vigorous bronzed leopards, is derived from a model used by Jacob and imitated by Hope[125] and Smith;[126] the frame is decorated with stars and a Greek key pattern, beneath which is a curiously inverted version of the double-scroll motif beloved of Soane, an unfortunate use of a classical motif that hints at the imminent 'Renaissance' revival style. The lively serpent that upholds the reading desk — perhaps emblematic of wisdom, Biblical rather than classical — was probably in bronzed iron (Richard Brown said that serpents, 'to which we have a natural antipathy',[127] should never be used to decorate furniture). The Roman lamp probably held ink in the place of oil. The deep buttoning is an early example of what was to become a fashionable feature; one wonders whether it were sprung — an eighteenth-century use of springs occurs in the exercise chair. The elaborate design is not characteristic of Messrs. Pococke, whose productions were normally plain. Morgan and Sanders also specialised in patented pieces.

Rudolph Ackermann seems consistently to have encouraged students of the fine and applied arts: when his shop opened in 1795 it acted as a cheap library for students. A design of February 1822 for a 'sofa, sofa-table, candelabra, and footstool' (Pl. CXVII) is described as 'the suggestions of an artist unpractised in fabricating such works, and consequently untrammelled by mechanical laws of workmanship and construction'; this suggests a young student whom Ackermann wished to encourage. Although one should not jump to conclusions affecting a period when the language of architecture had a meaning for cabinet makers, the lack of knowledge of cabinet making points to a student of architecture; the curiously flat stem of the table, of which the top is round, appears to have been adapted from the capital of a pilaster. In 1822 the precocious younger Pugin would have been about ten, and his father Augustus had had a long relationship with the *Repository* and with Ackermann.[128] The couch combines forms drawn from Roman furniture (Figs 290, 313), common in the later Regency period, with simple arabesque and 'antique drapery': the candelabrum stem is influenced by 'Pompeian' candelabraform decoration, its base by 'Pompeian' bronze torchères. The text recommends that the 'carved work should be splendidly gilt in matted, sanded, and burnished gold: the furniture, delicate green, of a uniform or mixed colours, and the sub-draperies of a colour in which a red tone should predominate . . .'.

A design for a sofa shown in the 1820s in John Taylor's *Original and Novel Designs for Decorative Household Furniture*, was reproduced in Ackermann's *Repository* in September 1824; a closely related but more accomplished sofa exists at Schloss Charlottenhof.[129] The shape of the arms is abstracted from that of the cornucopia, a motif used by Percier (Pl. CXXXII). A variant has the vigorous Piranesian acanthus decoration so favoured in England in the 1820s.

The neo-classical style continued much in favour with Ackermann during the 1820s. A severe 'klismos' dining-room chair of March 1825 'should be finished in the varnish called French polish', which 'gives considerable brilliance to the wood, preserves its colour, and is benefited by use'; the chair is well within the Percier-Hope tradition. Another, intended for a boudoir, is composed of 'snake-like forms in burnished gold', with seat and drapery in satin;[130] the use of the serpent is probably a free interpretation of a Herculaneum motif (Pl. CXVIII).

## The 'Repository' and French design

If Hope were too independent to be other than marginally influenced by French design, the same could not be said of others. Percier and Fontaine were a main source; another important one was the 'Meubles et Objets de Goût' of Pierre de la Mésangère, wittily called by Mario Praz the 'pinchbeck Percier et Fontaine'. Their engravings (Mésangère's were often not his own designs) were reproduced in the pages of Ackermann's *Repository*, supplemented by Ackermann's *Selection of Ornaments* published in 1817. The Percier designs were invariably simplified and vulgarised in the pages of the *Repository*, whereas the *Selection of Ornaments* conveyed a greater refinement of detail and interpretation; the designs of the 'pinchbeck Percier', crude in their original form, were given neat in the *Repository*.

An 'Imperial Turkey Ottoman, or Circular Sofa', published by Ackermann in January 1811 as made by Morgan and Sanders of brazil wood, is identical, down to the pattern on the cushions, with a 'divan circulaire' published by Pierre de la Mésangère (Fig. 314); the only difference, due to the licence of the colourist, is that light green and yellow in Ackermann replaces pink and blue. Had Morgan and Sanders really made such a straight copy, including the fabrics, or was this an advertising puff? A Mésangère chair reproduced in the next month was unattributed to any English maker, as was a sofa of June 1812.[131] Percier and Fontaine were also plagiarised. A design for a 'Library Table and Chair' (Fig. 315), was published in the *Repository* in May 1812, the year of the reissue of Percier's *Recueil*; the pieces were described as 'two of the most appropriate articles now in use for the nobleman's and gentleman's library'; the table was 'handsomely ornamented with or-moulu brasswork and carved figures; the top covered with green morocco leather, and the chair en suite'. It is mortifying to turn from the English library table, with its faulty proportions and meagre ornament, to its unacknowledged original in the pages of Percier and Fontaine (Fig. 316), which has elaborate decoration applied to well proportioned and simple basic shapes; the transformation of lions into sphinxes in the English version was presumably due to the emblematic

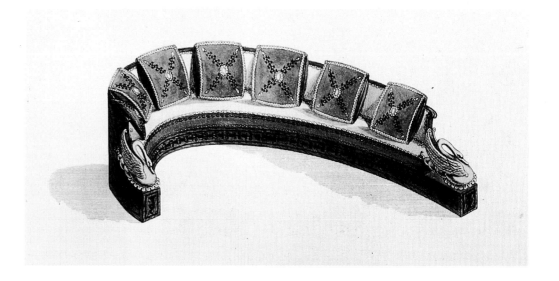

**314** Design for a 'Divan Circulaire', by Pierre de la Mésangère

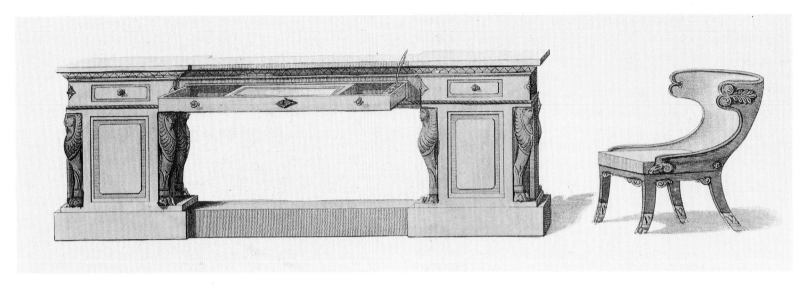

**315** 'A Library Table and Chair', from the *Repository*, 1812

**316** 'Bureau éxécuté à Paris pour Mr. V.', designed by Percier and Fontaine

**317** Design for a bed, published by Ackermann, 1817–19

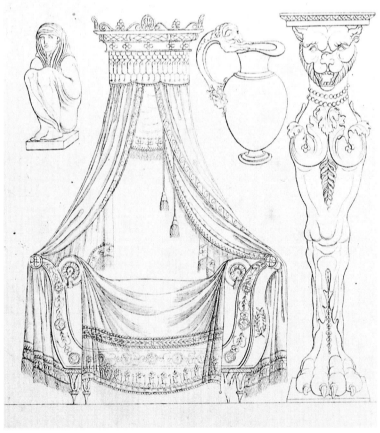

fitness of the Egyptian style for a library. The low swoop of the chair's arms is also reminiscent of Percier and Fontaine. One should add that Percier and Fontaine's furniture designs, like their interior decoration, look more overweighted with decoration in line engraving than in actuality, when unified by colour and tone.

Ackermann's *Selection of Ornaments* reproduced unattributed (Fig. 317) a bed made 'pour Mme M.' by Percier and Fontaine;[132] the excellent quality of this delineation contrasts markedly with its vulgarised representation (source unacknowledged) in the *Repository* of October 1817, where it is given the colours of lilac and buff, similar to those of Mme. Récamier's bedroom. The *Repository* speaks of the design as uniting 'elegant simplicity' with 'so much richness', but despite its preservation of the salient features of the original down even to the position of the tassels, it hopelessly compromises Percier's design; it is not a matter only of the difference between Percier's exquisite line and the muddy approximations of the Ackermann print, hardly disguised by colour; tautness of shape, as in the swell and curve of the arms of the sofa, has been replaced by a flaccid irresolution.

**319** 'Secretaire bookcase', from the *Repository*, 1822

**318** 'Sécrétaire exécute à Paris pour Mr. V.', designed by Percier and Fontaine

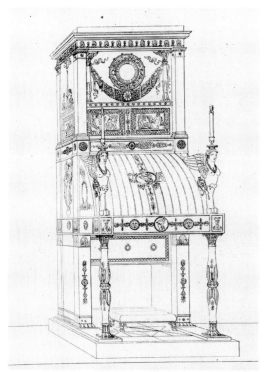

A more open use of Percier occurred in April 1822 when the *Repository* described a secretaire bookcase, of a type recently introduced by Snell of Albemarle Street, as 'after the style so exquisitely perfected by M. Persée, the French architect to Buonaparte. . . . The English style for such furniture is, however, more simply chaste and thence perhaps less liable to be affected by changes in fashion.' A piece of contradictory patriotism followed: 'the English style of furniture has advanced so rapidly into reputation during the last ten years, that the French themselves have now adopted a large portion of its characteristic richness and simplicity'. It is instructive to compare the two (Figs 318, 319). The hieratic sphinxes, medallions on the drawers, and elaborate decoration on the upper part of the cabinet, with its weighty garland beneath a clock — a theme used elsewhere by Percier and Fontaine and adopted by Hope,[133] who used instead of the clock a chaste circle of stars (Fig. 202) — have gone, replaced either by nothing, or by a mean substitute. The effect is of greater diffuseness.

The use of a Percier design by another fashionable British upholsterer is recorded in the *Repository* for March 1825; a chair (Pl. CXVIII) which 'reminds the spectator of the splendid furniture lately executed for his Grace the Duke of Northumberland by Messrs Morell and Hughes' was inspired by a Percier *fauteuil* 'exécutée à Paris pour M. le Ct. de S. en Russie'.[134] The English chair, a simplified and coarsened version of its original, is described as 'very much carved, and should be finished in dead white and gold. The covering is of British satin . . . and embellished with ornamental devices in gold colours on a light blue ground . . .'. The stool, as unlike a Percier design as stool could be, is ornamented with an Egyptian winged disk, no doubt thought congruous with the sphinxes. A 'siège' from the same set had been previously shown in the *Repository* of July 1823, not attributed in any way.

Modern French furniture maintained its influence throughout the period. In 1828, for instance, the *Repository* showed a cabinet (Pl. CXIX) that strongly recalls French Restoration furniture and the style of F.-H.-G. Jacob-Desmalter. This is hardly surprising, since royal taste was powerful, and in January 1825 Jacob-Desmalter had gone to England 'pour se charger de la décoration intérieure de Windsor'.[135] It is a signal of changing tastes that the commentary on the cabinet applauded the usefulness of such pieces not only for jewels and trinkets but for 'exquisitely illuminated missals and other relics of antiquity'.

Plate 28.

*State Bed.*

London, Published Jan.ʸ 1ˢᵗ 1807, by J. Taylor, 59, High Holborn.

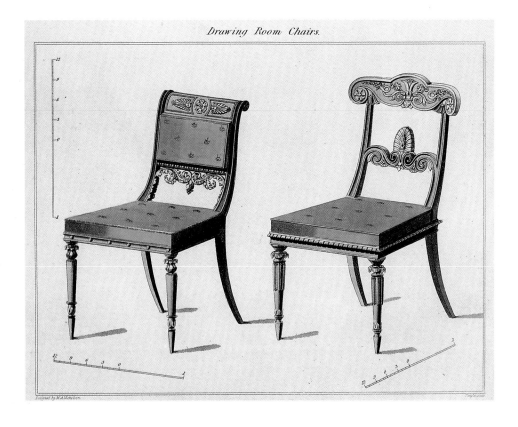

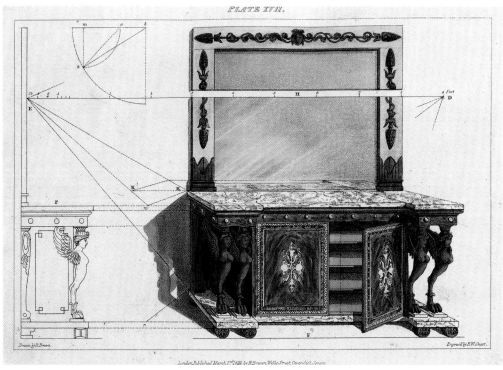

**CXXI** Design for 'Drawing Room Chairs', by P. and M. A. Nicholson, 1826

**CXXII** Cabinet in oak and ebony, brass inlaid, designed by George Bullock, c.1815

**CXXIII** Design for a pier commode and glass, by Richard Brown

*Opposite* **CXXIV** 'Drawing Room Window Curtain', by George Bullock, from the *Repository*, 1816

DRAWING ROOM WINDOW CURTAIN.

CXXV Furniture in Lansdown Tower, Bath, 1844

Chapter three

# Revivalism and Eclecticism

## 'Louis Quatorze' and eclectic furnishing

Before considering the classical successors of Hope and Smith, another creative influence should be mentioned; an influence that originated not in archaeological classicism, nor in the style of the French Empire, but from the activities of the collector and from the wish to emulate the imposing and opulent furniture of the French *ancien régime*, from Louis XIV to the rococo and beyond. The appetite for this style had originated in France itself, which had never forgotten, indeed still has not forgotten, the majestic brilliance of the court of Louis XIV, a memory potent throughout Europe. The furniture designers of the Louis XIV period had invented imposing motifs of which the antique origin was obvious, and that accommodated well with grand Regency interiors; these pieces had thus a double associational value, with antiquity and with Louis XIV. They were prized by the French themselves. Louis XVI, for example, had ordered Jacob to restore twelve boulle cabinets by Oppenord (some of the twelve may be Jacob's faithful copies); the necessary techniques had been continuously practised.[1] Napoleon, who was not interested in recalling the glories of the old dynasty, and did not make a habit of buying antiques — 'Sa Majesté veut faire de neuf et non acheter du vieux'[2] — is nevertheless recorded as having ordered Jacob-Desmalter to make a faithful copy of a Louis XV commode by Joseph Baumhauer in seventeenth-century taste.[3]

After the Revolution the French avant-garde, including Denon and Girodet-Trioson, bought Louis XIV furniture. But it was the rich and voracious English who gained a name for collecting old French furniture, a process made ridiculously easy by the Revolution, which released large quantities of the finest description. The English who showed the most interest were not antiquarians of the Scott or Meyrick type; they were the leaders of society, who set the tone and were slavishly imitated: George IV as prince and king; his intimates Lords Yarmouth, Farnborough and Hertford; Beckford; Elizabeth Duchess of Rutland; and other grandees and connoisseurs. The fashionable taste was sealed by Beau Brummell, the most hypercritical and imitated of dandies, who even in windy exile at Calais 'managed, in spite of his extreme fastidiousness and his poverty, to collect a sufficient quantity of buhl and ormolu to furnish his three rooms in the elegant and costly style of Louis Quartorze . . . He also squandered large sums in bronzes, japanned screens . . . a service of extremely beautiful Sèvres china . . .'.[4]

The glitter and richness of this furniture increasingly appealed to an age that appreciated a dark, vivid sumptuousness; it gave a courtly reflected glory to the new families whose taste was for 'profusion'. Gold was in fashion; gilding was 'His Majesty's taste'; the period extended the use of gilt bronze from the case furniture and ornaments to which the *ancien régime* had largely restricted it to chairs and sofas. Its gleam was omnipresent in avant-garde interiors.[5] As the malicious Samuel Rogers, a friend of Thomas Hope said, obviously of the Deepdene: 'Mr — 's house, the —, is very splendid; it contains a quantity of or-molu. Now, I like to have a kettle in my bed-room, to heat a little water if necessary; but I can't get a kettle at the —, though there is a quantity of or-molu. Lady — says, that when she is at the —, she is obliged to have her clothes unpacked three times a day; for there are no chests-of-drawers, though there is a quantity of or-molu'.[6]

The furniture of Beckford's Dining Room and two Drawing Rooms at Fonthill was much in the taste. The first two rooms contained almost exclusively French, Italian or East Indian ebony, with boulle, lacquer, and *pietra dura*, all of the utmost magnificence; included were two boulle armoires 'designed by Le Brun, from the collection of the Duc d'Aumont', a 'japan commode, formerly belonging to Marie Antoinette', and an 'armoire of buhl and tortoiseshell, made for Lewis XIV'.[7] In the Grand Drawing Room (Fig. 238), French rococo and Empire mingled in the guise of a superb roll-top desk by Riesener from the hôtel d'Orsay (a building rented by Beckford in 1789), a set of water-gilt chairs of about 1800, a circular table 'from Malmaison', and an Aubusson carpet 'of extraordinary costliness', made for St. Cloud in 1814.[8]

The practice of collecting *ancien régime* French furniture had a double effect. It introduced the principle of eclectic furnishing into the grandest interiors, and it provided a repertoire of ornament and techniques that began to be used on contemporary furniture. This process had already begun at one remove, in that Louis XVI furniture had been influenced by the classicism of that of Louis XIV, and had passed this on to English furniture; however, the physical presence of the older furniture was a stronger and more overwhelming influence. It became very necessary, if the grandeur and weight of Louis XIV boulle were to be successfully integrated, that accompanying contemporary furniture should match it.

One way of doing this was to copy it outright, to reproduce old forms faithfully. The French themselves, as mentioned above, had done this occasionally over a long period. The English copied old French furniture extensively during the Regency, the two major London firms associated with boulle being those of Thomas Parker in Air Street and Louis le Gaigneur's 'Buhl manufactory', established in about 1815 in Queen Street. Both reproduced Louis XIV furniture for the Prince Regent. The former supplied a pair of marriage coffers in red tortoiseshell and brass, after a well known model associated with Boulle;[9] the latter two Mazarin desks, supplied in about 1815.[10] Both sets were accurate enough to deceive until well into the twentieth century. The desks were put into the North Drawing Room at Brighton (Pl. XCIX), one of the earliest examples of an eclectic Regency interior, harmonious and judicious; included were the Weisweiler cabinets (original, and faithfully copied by Bailey and Saunders), the Hervé chairs, the candelabra and probably the clock from the Chinese Drawing Room, and a completely modern boulle piano by Mott.

## Bullock and Brown

A more creative use of the characteristics of Louis XIV furniture than the servile copying denounced by many Regency artists and connoisseurs — although Quatremère de Quincy had advocated exact imitation of the antique — was to employ its techniques and forms, bold and grand decoration, massive shapes, and rich brass marquetry, in a manner that was new. The most masterly of those who chose this way was George Bullock, who in his grand classical furniture continued the

Hope tradition, combining with it the techniques of Louis XIV furniture and motifs of his own. Less high-minded and catholic, less inventive and versatile, than Hope — or, as far as the last two qualities are concerned, than Sheraton or Smith — he produced imposing, sometimes grandiose furniture in a forceful style that represents an important aspect of Regency taste.[11]

Richard Brown, who had an as yet undefined working relationship with Bullock, and many of whose designs are completely in the Bullock style,[12] wrote that: 'The late Mr Bullock was the only person who ventured into a new path . . . some of his designs were certainly too massive and ponderous, nevertheless grandeur cannot be obtained without it; such are the standards of his octagon tables. There was great novelty without absurdity, as well as happy relief, in his ornaments; yet many of his articles were considerably overcharged with buhl: sometimes the buhl-work was sunk in brass, and on the other occasions the counterparts was of the same wood as the furniture itself, and the whole surface represented a brazen front. He appears to have been particularly happy in his mouldings, which were of the Grecian taste, sharp, bold, and well relieved. . . . Most of his ornaments were selected from British plants, his woods were of English growth, which were admirably well polished. He has shown that we need not roam to foreign climes for beautiful ornaments, but that we have abundance of plants and flowers equal to the Grecian, which if adopted, would be found as pleasing as the antique.'[13] This passage, with its echoes of Caylus and of Hope — 'the young artist . . . should ascend to those higher, those more copious sources of elegance . . . I mean, in the first place, those of Nature herself . . .'.[14] — reminds one that English cabinet-makers had followed those of France in following Landon's advice to use native woods,[15] a step taken not only because of naval blockades and the shortage of exotic timbers, but because of the imperatives of fashion, as strong as blockades. Bullock extended his interest in native materials to marbles, particularly to the green Mona marble, said in 1816 not only to have 'so considerably increased in reputation and fashion' but to vie in richness of colour with 'the precious marbles of antiquity'.[16]

Bullock's furniture became fashionable, and was generously mentioned in the *Repository*. His influence did not cease with his death: in June 1824 the *Repository* mentioned that his 'character and style' was 'continued with much taste by the chief upholsterers of the day' (a warning against undocumented attributions). Its general effect of a sumptuous boldness was allied with a self-conscious classicism that extended to drapery. A design for an 'English Bed', for instance, given in the *Repository*, has curtains that hang in a resolutely plain manner from tester to floor; the 'abandonment of that profusion of drapery which has long been fashionable, has admitted this more chastened style . . .'.[17] The decorative detail of the curtains is of the 'Etruscan' variety. Bullock treated window curtains in the same fashion; two shown in December 1816 (Fig. 198) and April 1817 have plain 'antique drapery' hanging from the pelmets, instead of elaborate swags; what shows of the walls has 'Etruscan' panelling; the Bullock cabinet in the April 1817 design has on it a massive antique tripod as a lamp. A design of February 1816 (Pl. CXXIV), whilst not quite as austere, shows a strong 'Etruscan' character. The walls have 'Etruscan' panelling; the details of the curtains, including the central arabesque, are 'Etruscan', and to emphasise the point, the Bullock cabinet between the windows is not only full of 'Etruscan' pots, but has a splendidly decorated Greek vase in the place of honour.

The *Repository* called Bullock's furniture 'Grecian'; in May 1816 it used that term to describe his scheme for a library. Much of the repertory of ornament and motifs used in his classical style furniture, especially the case furniture, is 'Etruscan' in origin. From this source come the panels, often with anthemion decoration at the corners, used in commodes and cabinets; they closely resemble the 'Etruscan' compartmentalism of walls (Sheraton's advice comes to mind again); the corners are often stylised into a form resembling that of the antifixae Bullock frequently used as feet (antifixae are seen not only in 'Etruscan' pottery, but on real Etruscan sarcophagi).[18] From the same source came the thyrsus; the anthemion; the large scale simple arabesque; the 'strings' of bay and other leaves; the wreaths with their typical stylised ribbands. It is interesting to notice how the contours of the brass-inlaid anthemion repeat the broad handling of the original vase painting, laid on with a single stroke of the brush; there is no modelling within the contour; the chiselled outline of a sculpted anthemion is different.

Some of these 'Etruscan' features can be seen in a design for a cabinet,[19] realised in several versions in larch wood, ebony, and ebonised wood with brass inlay and gilt-bronze mounts (Pl. CXXII). The development of such cabinets or commodes has been said to be a post-1810 development;[20] certainly none are shown in Hope, but Percier has several and Smith has five, three dated 1804, the other two 1805.[21] Bullock probably looked hard at Smith; one of Smith's 1805 commodes has some similarities with a Bullock commode,[22] and Smith like Bullock favoured 'antique drapery'. The surfaces of Bullock's cabinets are at times virtually flat, relieved only by inlay; the columns are swollen and mannered, not unlike the mouldings in some of Smith's designs.

A design for a candelabrum[23] comes from another source; it is of the familiar Piranesi/Tatham Roman type. The squared-off feet are of a type used by Hope and Percier; they occur as a support for a form of Roman sarcophagus. Other features of the design, especially the palmettes and the human heads on the pedestal in place of the more usual ram or lion, are reminiscent of Percier, as indeed is the general style of the drawing.[24]

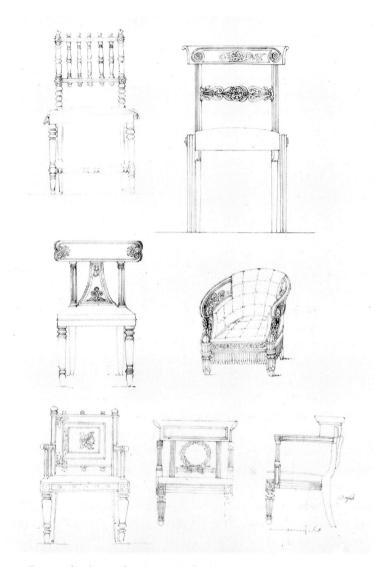

**320** Designs for chairs, after George Bullock, c.1817

Six designs for chairs (Fig. 320) show the variety of antique and other (see p.422) influences affecting Bullock and their absorption into his own style. The chair on the top right, which has sabre legs, was made of oak inlaid with holly;[25] the outward curving upper rail is a French feature that was used by Holland but appears neither in Hope nor Smith. A chair shown as Plate 15 of Percier's *Recueil* has scrolled ornament on the front of the seat, possibly not unrelated to that on the centre rail of Bullock's chair. The chair on the centre left has a top rail related to that in a design by Hope (Fig. 299[3]). The chair on the centre right was illustrated in the *Repository* of September 1817 as a chair 'intended for a Grecian Library'; the legs are a familiar Roman type (Fig. 321). The two chairs shown on the bottom line (one is given in profile view) are typically Bullock in their sturdy late neo-classicism; that on the right was made with slight adaptations (the legs were not

**321** Chairs from 'the repository of Mr. George Bullock', from the *Repository*, 1817

reeded) in at least two versions for Napoleon's house at St. Helena, one in mahogany with ebonised detail, the other in ebonised beech, parcel gilt with brass trimmings.

When, in 1822, Richard Brown's *Rudiments of Drawing Room Cabinet and Upholstery Furniture* appeared, the first comprehensive volume of new furniture designs to follow Smith's 1808 publication, its author expressly recognised a distinct classical tradition. He spoke of its 'new character, bold in the outline, rich and chaste in the ornaments. . . . This style, although in too many instances resembling the Grecian tombs, has evidently risen in a great measure from Mr Hope's mythological work on Household Furniture, Mr Smith's excellent book of Unique Designs [1812 version] and Percier's splendid French work on Interior Decoration.'[26] Brown's other remarks reinforced the idea of inheritance; the cabinet-maker should 'be aided by a store of classic literature, to suggest to him ideas' (this echoes Hope); he should make a 'minute observation' of antique sculpture and ornament; and he should refer to 'books of antiquities, such as Piranesi's, Hamilton's, Tatham's, and Moses''.[27] Hope's idealistic crusade, and Smith's commercialisation of the classical style, had made converts.

Eclecticism, or attitudes to eclecticism, had changed in recent years; the idealistic synthesising of Dance, Soane, and Hope was giving ground to an often indiscriminate jumble. Brown perceived this and distanced himself from it; apartments should be wholly Grecian or Roman, Egyptian or Etruscan, Gothic or Moresque, and not mixed. He showed much interest in the associationalism of Percier and Hope. A library, for example — much reverence was paid throughout the period to the idea of a library, and with reason, since books were essential to neo-classical creativity — a library should be 'furnished in imitation of the antique, and with such busts and prints as relate to science and men of literature and genius', with the use of such emblems as the owl, the laurel, and 'Pegasus, the poet's winged horse'.[28] The emblematic symbolism of designs for a 'Library and Withdrawing Room Chair' (Fig. 322), very Bullock in type, and for a pier commode and glass, with bronzed chimeras (Pl. CXXIII), has been discussed (see p.358). The use of the owl may have been influenced by its presence on a chair illustrated in 1794, in the third volume of the *Antiquities of Athens* (Fig. 272), and in 1814 by Henry Moses in his *Collection of Antique Vases, Altars, Paterae*...[29]

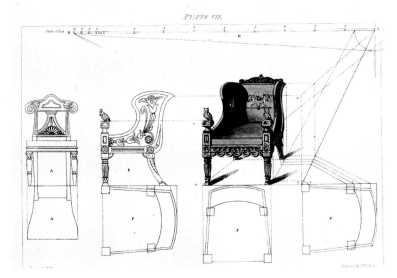

322 Design for a 'Library and Withdrawing Room Chair', by Richard Brown, 1822

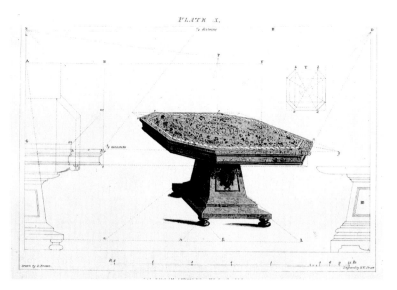

323 Design for a library table, by Richard Brown, 1822

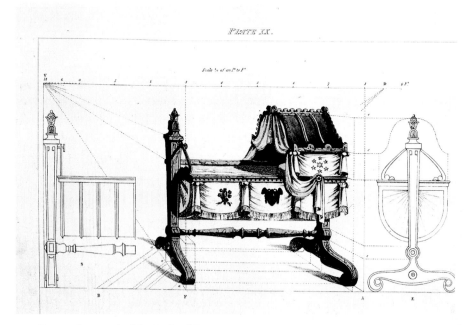

324 Design for a cot-bed, by Richard Brown, 1822

A particularly massive octagon library table (Fig. 323), close to Bullock, is a squared-off derivative of the famous Hope monopodium[30] which had inspired so many versions — including one by Bullock himself in which the curves of the pedestal are replaced by straight lines.[31] The library table exists, with marquetry in place of the masks, which were to have been of Minerva, Mercury, Apollo, and Cadmus;[32] the top was to bear a laurel wreath, as did Hope's monopodium. The mouldings were to be elliptical; Brown remarks that the Greeks always used elliptic curves, the Romans semi-circular, and it is noticeable that in the early nineteenth century many objects that might be expected to have round bases, such as candelabra and lamps, in actuality have elliptical ones. There was some subtlety: 'All the mouldings . . . should be optically studied, that their whole contour may be visible below the eye, as well as when even on the horizon; a circumstance which appears to have been generally overlooked by cabinet-makers up to the present day'.[33] This consideration might well have been overlooked by cabinet-makers, but would be in the forefront of the mind of a sculptor, aware of the distortions required in a figure or moulding intended to be seen from below; it sounds as if it might have been a dictum of Bullock, who had produced some lumpy sculpture, and could help to account for the volumetric emphasis of his mouldings and turnings, seen also in the designs by Brown.

Strong as was Brown's debt to Bullock, some of Brown's designs show the influence of Hope. His 'cot-bed' (Fig. 324), its likeness to Hope emphasised by the use of outline (it looks less classical in the coloured version), is directly related to Hope's 'cradle in mahogany, ornamented in gilt bronze, with emblems of night, of sleep, of dreams, and of hope';[34] the iniquity of oblivion blindly scattereth her poppy on Brown's as well as on Hope's cradle, together with the stars of Night. Hope's 'Spes', a pun on the surname of his own child, is replaced by Brown with 'Nox', an unfortunate substitution were the child of Brown's cradle a girl, in that Night in classical mythology is the daughter of Chaos. Emblemism has its perils.

## The 1820s and after: classicism and revivalism

Domesticated neo-classicism in tasteful equilibrium is well illustrated in Papworth's cosy drawing room of 1814 (Fig. 325). Conceived by an architect who designed much furniture, it lays out for inspection the ideal of fashionable bourgeois comfort. The light of candles and fire falls upon rich draperies and fringes and upon high-waisted women sitting on sabre-legged chairs drawn up to the table; a boy breaks away

in a gesture reminiscent of that of the erotes from the Herculaneum frescoes who draw toy chariots in which are seated other erotes, animals or birds.[35] By the fire stands a screen of Hopean antecedents, its shape derived from an ancient shield; on the chimney-piece are cut-glass candlesticks with the faceted drops that Papworth claimed to have invented. And in the window embrasure stands that most Regency of instruments, with Ossianic associations, the harp. Design is here subjected to the discipline of taste and use; the result has an ideal beauty which was not to last, and by the time Papworth's plate was published in 1823 the signs of change were evident.

The tendencies of the 1820s are present in Taylor's *Original and Novel Designs* of about 1824. A design for a sofa looks back to Hope,[36] but its profile is ominously slack and degraded. Hope's emblematic highmindedness is applied to curtain pelmets (Pl. CXXXI); the mythological opposition of the eagle and the swan is rendered in a way that would domesticate perpetual battle. The acanthus is prominent; in one eccentric design, that for a bed, it flies upwards in a manner that suggests the ostrich plumes used on seventeenth and early eighteenth-century beds. There is much use of vigorous acanthus scrolls in Le Pautre; this increasingly fashionable source may well have reinforced the appeal of acanthus inherited from Piranesi and Tatham.[37] The designs in Taylor live up to the tautologous claims of the title. There are designs for chairs that unmistakably presage the balloon back of the Victorians;[38] others seem to show traces of earlier Georgian influence, including one with a back of a type that used to be called 'Manwaring'.[39] A design for a sofa has chunky 'swans' at either end that recall Kent (Fig. 326). This resemblance to Kent can hardly be accidental: if nothing else indicated an interest, the large number of surviving Regency neo-Kentian console tables supported on eagles would do so. Two such tables in the collection at Brighton Pavilion are made up of eighteenth-century eagle consoles of Kentian type that have been given new Regency bases, mirrored backs, and tops of the fashionable pink porphyry that are (unusually) of solid stone.

The Kentian revival had not been unheralded; signs of an interest in early eighteenth-century styles had appeared early in the nineteenth century. The baroque had been amongst the earliest to be revived; it had appeared in silver by 1804, when Paul Storr began to use the scroll cartouche and scallop shell; he also revived the claw and ball foot. By 1810, rococo motifs were being used in Sheffield plate, and by 1815 Coalport had begun to make rococo vases inspired by Louis XV Sèvres and Chelsea, with applied china flowers after Meissen; hardly surprising, in that all were beginning to be avidly collected. The high rococo designs of Matthias Lock and Thomas Johnson were reprinted, a sure sign of revival.

The Kentian revival was blessed with august associations, owing to the prevailing confusion between Inigo Jones and Kent; the mantle of Jones descended on Kent's furniture, thought by many to be seventeenth century, and therefore appropriate for use with 'Louis Quatorze' schemes (Pls LXXIV, LXXV). It is hardly surprising that there were uncertainties, given past revivals of the same motifs in successive periods. A drawing by Tatham of about 1800 shows an 'Elbow chair from an old Picture of Paul Veronese at Uppark'[40] which has feet that scroll inwards; the detail that has interested Tatham is obviously the broken curve, much used in Louis XIV furniture; one of the somewhat later Southill pieces, a library table, already has legs that are essentially of a 'Louis Quatorze' type.[41] The references of such motifs are multiple.

The Kentian revival is apparent in pieces made for Carlton House; a Kentian settee with lion paw feet and lion arm rests has been said to have been supplied in 1810 by Marsh and Tatham;[42] the central cresting, seen in both Louis XIV and Kent furniture, was used in Carlton House furniture (Pl. LX); this has been regarded as a revival feature, and it may be consciously so, although one of Holland's Southill sofas has a central cresting, as has one of Hope's sofa designs (Fig. 302). There is no doubt that George IV became interested in baroque furniture: in 1818 he bought, through Lord Yarmouth, four bow-front commodes of about 1763 in the style of Langlois, with prominent corner scrolls much in harmony with the aesthetic predilections of the later Regency style. The arm chairs and settees made for the Great and Small Drawing Rooms at Windsor are strongly Kentian in flavour (Pl. LXXIV). Some of the tables are almost equally so, although an admixture of French seventeenth-century influence is visible in the latter.[43] The King bought both English copies of seventeenth-century boulle (see p.402 above) and French interpretations of seventeenth-century styles; an instance of the latter was the acquisition in 1825, through the dealer Robert Fogg from the Watson Taylor sale, of four magnificent 'Louis Quatorze' tables by A. L. Bellangé (who was to live until 1863), with robust legs in steel and gilt bronze that exhibited the typical broken curve.[44] Bullock, incidentally, did not use the broken curve, despite his interest in 'Louis Quatorze'.

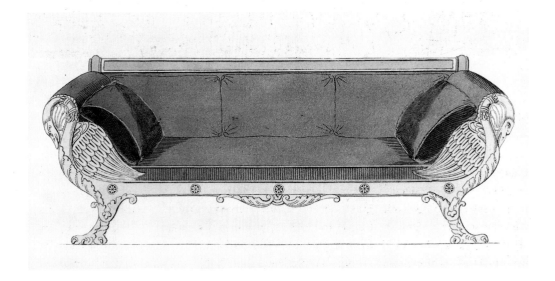

326 Design for a sofa, by J. Taylor, c.1824

Rococo furniture was also revived, especially in the form of chairs. The King had a large set of chairs and sofas made for the Ballroom. Public interest was reflected in the inclusion in pattern-books of 'Louis Quatorze' and rococo. In the later 1820s a few rococo designs appeared amongst late neo-classical examples in Henry Whitaker's *Designs of Cabinet Upholstery Furniture in the Most Modern Style*. One of the many publications of Thomas King, *The Modern Style of Cabinet Work* of 1829 (last reprinted in 1862, a tribute to the proto-Victorian character of the designs), shows how the heavy acanthus of the 1820s was translated into baroque and 'Renaissance revival'. His 'Pier Slabs', so commonly used in the late Regency, have meaningless rosettes on their scrolls (Fig. 327). The text explains that 'in the gilded parts, carving will only be required in the boldest scrolls, or in the massive foliage; while composition ornament may be used for rosettes, enriched mouldings, ornamental borders, and generally in the minute detail'.[45] King also advocated adventitious aids in the manual *Fashionable Window Cornices and Hangings*, which presents 'original designs in which are introduced ornaments of papier mâché, as manufactured by Messrs. Haselden & Co., 24 Golden Square, London'. The designs are almost equally divided between 'Louis Quatorze' and revived rococo, and Gothic; the quality is atrocious, as it is in the same author's *Designs for Carving and Gilding* of 1830, which again advertises 'Louis Quatorze' 'composition ornaments, of the greatest beauty';[46] the plates show rococo candelabra with rococo pier tables.

The eighteenth-century idea that rococo and Gothic were harmonious together survived; the rococo picture frames at Eaton Hall have been mentioned above, and the Saloon contained a sofa and table in revived rococo style; in the Entrance Hall baroque picture frames were juxtaposed with four suits of armour. The boudoir at Bretby (Fig. 242) had revived rococo furniture in a Gothic setting.

Two books of the late 1820s demonstrate contemporary opinion on furniture: the *Decorative Painters' and Glaziers' Guide* of Nathaniel Whittock (1827), and the *Cabinet Maker and Upholsterer's Guide* by George Smith (1826). They write from the standpoints of their respective trades, decorator and cabinet-maker. They concur in thinking French influence highly important: 'It may not be paying an exaggerated encomium to our neighbours the Franks, when we assert the superiority of their inventive faculty in the ornamental parts of design'.[47] Smith, unlike Whittock, discusses designers; in his opinion there 'are no designers now like Hope or Chippendale'.[48] James Wyatt is praised for his influence on 'our domestic movables',[49] an interesting judgment, and two of the King's designers are singled out: Robert Jones, 'who stands at the head of his profession' in ornamental painting[50] and, most of all, 'Mons. Boileau . . . formerly employed in the decoration of Carlton Palace'. The latter was said to have 'an unrivalled taste in decorative painting', a 'light, an airy, and classic style of design

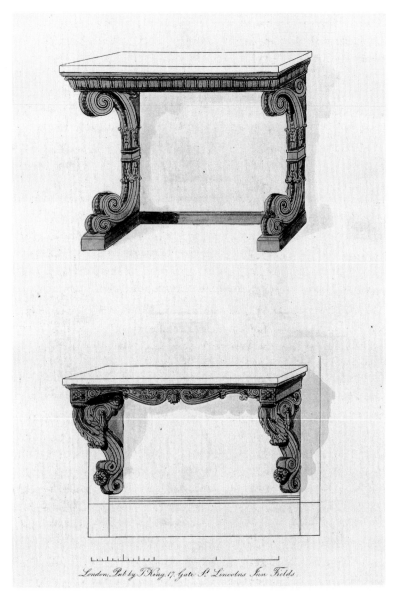

**327** Design for 'Pier Slabs', by Thomas King

for household articles', and he 'has never been surpassed in his designs for ornamental plate and articles for casting in Or molu'.[51] French influence is confirmed by Smith's recommendation of Le Pautre as a source. Advice given almost forty years earlier by Sheraton was repeated by both Smith and Whittock in recommending wallpaper as a source for furniture motifs, the former implicitly,[52] the latter explicitly.[53]

## Exotic and sophisticated techniques

Whittock referred to the fact that 'japanning is now again becoming fashionable'.[54] The imitation of oriental lacquer had never ceased; it had been used in the late eighteenth century by Adam and others, often in juxtaposition with cane (the use of cane is not necessarily an indication of seventeenth-century influence; the French eighteenth century was exceedingly fond of it). Two leaders of fashion, Beckford and the Prince of Wales, were extremely interested in old lacquer, and the strong colours of the early nineteenth century easily accommodated black lacquer. Old lacquer rapidly became popular and costly. Beckford had been early in the field; lacquer had for him an abiding fascination. In August 1797 he wrote to his agent in Paris: 'You are in possession of my sentiments regarding the Bouillon Collection. No pains should be spared to attempt getting hold of it. I am, in fact, still more anxious about the Japans than the pictures.' He thought the former could be bought en bloc, 'for these small trifling toys cannot be very precious in any eyes except such as are affected by the Japan-mania in a violent incurable degree . . .'.[55] In the event, King Edward's Gallery (Fig. 237) contained: 'A very large coffer of japan, once the property of Cardinal Mazarin, and subsequently of the Duc de Bouillon . . . two caskets of gold japan, from the collection of the Duke of Mazarin: with a choice collection of other rare and curious specimens of japan'.[56] There was more lacquer in St. Michael's Gallery.

Modern pieces were made incorporating old lacquer; in 1806–07 the fifth Earl of Jersey bought from John Mclean, for the 'Venetian Drawing Room' at Middleton Park,[57] a 'black Japan Cabinet made to your Japan with lions paws in burnish gild . . . statuary marble top' and an 'enclosed black japan Table, with silk curtains, ormolu ornaments on lions paw feet in burnish gold, made to your marble tops and black Japann'.[58] Attempts were again made to imitate oriental lacquer. Whittock gave recipes from 'an old work on japanning, published in the reign of James the Second', saying that these were the methods that had been employed on the 'old japanned furniture which now obtains such high prices, from the supposition that the art is lost from disuse'.[59] The 'old work' must be that most enchanting of all technical manuals, the frequently reprinted 1688 *Stalker and Parker*, with its humorous style that gently parodies the organ notes of Sir Thomas Browne.

Not only were japanned wooden surfaces used in furniture; Regency commodes occasionally appear that have panels of 'Pontypool' japanned tin. As trays, such japanned wares became highly popular: Whittock mentioned that the 'tortoise shell japan ground', to a receipt by Knuckel, had 'been revived with great success in the Birmingham manufactories', having been used for snuff boxes and dressing boxes, and for the 'tea waiters' which were 'justly esteemed and admired in several parts of Europe'.[60] This combination of japanning and tortoiseshell brings together the characteristics of lacquer and boulle, a minor example of the urge to synthesise. The smooth, hard surface of papier mâché was ideal for japanning, and in 1825 an employee of Jennens and Bettridge introduced the technique, imitated from

Japanese lacquer, of inserting mother o'pearl inlay into japanned papier mâché.[61] The plasticity of papier mâché explains its ready combination with japanning and with the broken curves of revived rococo to produce some of the most popular and characteristic late Regency and early Victorian household utensils and furniture. One of the most favoured subjects for japanning and mother o'pearl inlay was the light and informal chair; Thomas King, for example, shows four bedroom chairs of which the first and second were to be stained, the third and fourth to be japanned.

Whittock went into some detail on the techniques of marbling and graining, commenting that within 'the last ten years a great improvement in the imitation of fancywoods and marbles has brought it into general use', and it is now used in the most 'respectable [meaning rich] houses'.[62] Observation confirms this statement; simulated surfaces can be found in all periods, but they increased in number and in complexity in the later decades of the Regency style; it is significant that this accompanied what in many ways was a revival of the baroque. Amongst the woods for which recipes were given are oak, usually imitated for outside work; 'old wainscot oak', a distinct type, much in demand among the antiquarians; pollard oak; rosewood; and so on. On the eve of a walnut revival, Whittock said that 'walnut tree is not much used as a fancy wood, and therefore no engraved representation is given for it'.[63]

Marbling was excellent, said Whittock, for halls, passages, and the bars of coffee houses (usually 'lined out', not presented as one huge slab); imitations of Siena marble were good for door posts, passages, and furniture painting,[64] although he later condemned the marbling of chairs: 'nothing can be in worse taste'. Where black and gold marble was imitated — probably 'portor' marble, as popular in the Regency period as it was to be in the 1920s and 1930s — it was proper to use gold and silver leaf in the veins. Another illusionistic device was the use of 'gilding, to imitate inlaid brass';[65] this was employed on simulated rosewood chairs, sofas, bookcases, etc. The proper leaf to use was 'pale virgin gold', which assumes a greenish hue like brass when varnished with copal. Whittock mentioned that 'work in imitation of inlaid ebony and ivory is now so fashionable', presumably an allusion to 'pen work'; this was a by-product of antiquarianism, in that it imitated seventeenth-century European or East Indian work, sometimes using Bérainesque arabesque, although all kinds of motifs were employed.

## Late Regency classical eclecticism

The furniture illustrated by Smith in 1826 (some plates dated 1827–8), and by the Nicholsons in their *Practical Cabinet Maker* of 1826 (some plates dated 1827), may stand as a summation of late Regency neo-classical taste. With some clumsiness and disproportion, enough remains of the finer qualities of Regency design to emphasise the soundness of the 'Grecian' tradition. Some unease is apparent; Smith, for example, remarks that recent chair patterns are a mélange of different styles: 'it is not uncommon to find a parlour chair made with turned front feet, the back feet of which will be strictly Grecian, and the yoke for the back partaking of the same style, but supported by Roman columns'.[66] Quite apart from the fact that Smith himself was guilty of a similar solecism, if solecism it were, a rejection of turned front legs associated with back sabre legs would have excluded some of the most beautiful chairs of the Regency. Moreover, turned legs could as easily have Roman affiliations as antiquarian. Loudon repeated the criticism. It is obvious that it was the synthetic method itself, suborned by pedantic historicism, that was coming under attack.

Smith shows two chairs side by side, a French chair and an Indian chair (Fig. 328). The first, in a Louis XIV style that anticipated the puffy curves of Victorian rococo, was to be in rosewood or entirely gilt; the second, an Indian chair, was copied from an ivory chair belonging to Sir George Talbot, and was said to be 'not comfortable'. Both were well in line with royal taste; the Louis XIV style was being installed at Windsor and in 1827 Nash's 'Views of the Royal Pavilion' had shown Indian ivory chairs in the Chippendale style, purchased by the Prince Regent from Queen Charlotte's sale, prominent in the Corridor.

Furniture publicists kept a weather eye on the Court; in 1827, for example, the Nicholsons had published lambrequins; nothing new, they had appeared in 1826 in Ackermann's *Repository* and in the same year in Buckler's *Views of Eaton Hall* (Fig. 241), but they were apposite in that

they were being installed at Windsor (Pl. LXXVI). Smith showed a dressing table: 'The dressing glass is intended as a fixture at the back, after the manner of those in French toilette tables';[67] in April 1828, Ackermann's *Repository* illustrated a toilet table, which by implication is Continental and which is in the sumptuous style of Jacob-Desmalter. The antecedents of both were probably royal, one or several of the toilet tables from Windsor; a design for the south wall of a bedroom[68] at Windsor shows a similar but simpler toilet table, listed by Morel and Seddon as a 'Ladies toilette table of purple wood, with handsome inlaid top, a looking glass at back, with worked muslin drapery over, supported by an ornamented gilt bird and thyrse'.[69] The dressing table with fixed glass was to have innumerable descendants.

Some of these designs look forwards, others backwards. The Nicholsons, for example, have a good circular table, decorated with acanthus and with paw feet, rich and controlled, that is much within the established tradition. It was designed to be gilded and bronzed: the wood looks like pollard oak. They have also, on the other hand, chairs

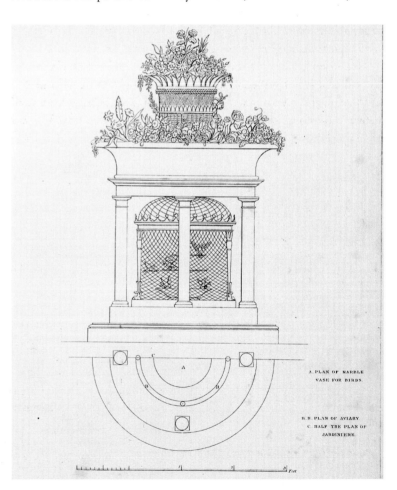

**328** A French and an Indian-style chair, by George Smith, 1826

**329** Design for a 'Jardinière and aviary', by George Smith, 1826

with familiar classical detail applied to forms that were to be in use for the next twenty years or so (Pl. CXXI). One feels that they might well have been content to continue in the Hopean tradition, had not they felt, as did others, compelled to provide novelties: 'to rekindle the dying embers of exhausted pleasure, it becomes necessary to seek out fresh sources of intellectual gratification'.[70]

A design for a sideboard by Smith shows the matured liking for overwhelming mass: 'such a sideboard with its pedestals will require a space of at least 14 feet'.[71] For those bent on displaying wealth, the dining room was a place where plate could be brought out in quantity; the tradition went back centuries, but the mediaeval or Renaissance prince was now replaced by the 'honest British merchant' of *Vanity Fair*; fourteen feet of rosewood or mahogany would take a good deal of vain silver or silver gilt. Weightiness in furniture was not as obligatory as for plate. A design for a jardinière and aviary (Fig. 329), birds and flowers combined, displays the Picturesque in drawing-room captivity. As Smith says: 'In France, this is carried to a very extravagant effect so far as materials and decoration will allow'; he might have added, in the German states also. This example was to be in mahogany and wire; the aviary stands on a marble plinth, 'on which is placed a marble vase containing water for the warbling inhabitants in their wiery castle'.[72]

Smith graded beds in three categories: the four poster, for rooms not less than fifteen feet square; the smaller four poster for cottages and small villas; and the canopy or French bed, suitable for state rooms and alcoves and for nurseries and dressing rooms, an odd but not unreasonable conjunction.[73] He did not forget the cottage orné: a 'Field bed' was suitable for 'the smaller apartment or the principal floor of a mansion' or 'may very well supply the place of a four post bedstead in the principal sleeping apartment of the small villa or cottage orné', a recommendation repeated by Loudon. The Field Bed has 'ornamental cornices supporting the drapery' which may be 'executed in composition and japanned in colours to suit the pattern of the furniture' (the drapery). Speaking of colours in general, Smith describes a restricted palette: 'umbers, siennas, yellow and Roman ochres; vermilion, Venetian red, carmine; madder brown, indigo etc.' are 'all that are likely to be brought into use in colouring either drapery, or cabinet furniture'.[74] Such colours were brilliant but soft.

He gave designs for curtains, such as that for a circular-headed window[75] for a parlour or library; it is less elaborate than that for a drawing room, but none the less the 'valance behind the drapery is supposed to be gathered all over into puckers, such as we see used in the linings of jewel boxes, drawers etc.' which 'when made with silk, produces not only a rich, but beautiful back ground'.[76] This luxurious technique, evocative of the Balzacian demi-monde, was used on the embrasures of the huge French windows in the Music Room at Brighton Pavilion.

An interesting sub-section of English late Regency classically orientated furniture was that designed for Beckford's Lansdown Tower, perhaps by its architect Goodridge (Pls XXX, LXXVII, LXXVIII; see pp.278–81); it was given a plate to itself at the end of English's publication on the building (Pl. CXXV). The impressive pieces, usually of oak, with some use of gilt bronze, recall the weighty

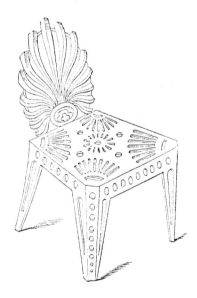

330 An Etruscan lobby chair designed c.1833 by 'Mr. Mallet'

331 Design for a garden seat by James Trubshaw, c.1833, for Lilleshall Hall, Salop.

architectural classicism of the early Italian Renaissance; they bear heavy volutes, consoles, triumphal arches, pilasters, pillars and tablets; there is not a hint of the 'Elizabethan' or 'Jacobean' ornament of the antiquarians. Nor are these pieces slavish copies of earlier furniture; they are unmistakably nineteenth century.

The classical style long survived the Regency, becoming gradually heavier, clumsier, and without grace; it was to be revived, and versions of Percier were to be shown in the Great Exhibition. The Tatham tradition still had vitality, as seen in a Trubshaw design for a garden seat (Fig. 331). Attempts were made to bend classical styles to new materials, as with the extraordinary cast-iron lobby chair designed by 'Mr Mallet' in the 'Etruscan' style, illustrated by Loudon (Fig. 330). The 'Etruscan' label comes from the anthemion back, the decoration on the seat,[77] and the circles on the legs and rails, all to be found on Greek vases. The chair, supposed to be cast in two pieces, would, says Loudon, 'look exceedingly well in the porch of a cottage in the Italian style'.[78] He recommends it should be painted to imitate oak. Perhaps the less said about it the better.

412

Chapter four

# Gothic Styles

## Gothic: impediments and inhibitions

In 1790, Alison had observed that Chinese and Gothic were out of favour, and that the 'Taste which now reigns is that of the ANTIQUE. Everything we now use, is made in imitation of those models which have been lately discovered in Italy'.[1] The lack of critical esteem for the Chinese taste lasted throughout the Regency period and for Gothic furniture until the 1820s; it did not prevent the manufacture of large numbers of Chinese and Gothic style pieces of furniture, but it inhibited any significant movement in design.

After so long a period of classicism, it must have been an effort for the run of the mill cabinet-maker, unversed in the Gothic vocabulary, to think creatively in Gothic terms. The difficulties of working wholly within Gothic concepts may be reflected in a design for Gothic library furniture given in the *Repository* of June 1810 (Pl. CXXIX) (alternatively, the design may show how easily and naturally Regency designers thought in terms of a synthesis). For the backs and back legs of the chairs and the sofa curve back in 'klismos' style, and the Gothic trimmings of the table belie its origin in a type of antique seat illustrated in several versions by Tatham[2] and used for severely classical tables by Hope,[3] Smith[4] and Percier;[5] the designer probably took the basic shape of the table directly from Hope or Smith. One can understand that a designer might find the devising of a Gothic sofa, for which authentic prototypes did not exist, perplexing, but a table should have presented fewer problems. The wood depicted in the Ackermann print is oak 'wainscot' (which meant that it was to be stained dark), but 'may be' mahogany or satin wood, hardly an aid to Gothic authenticity.

This use of antique components in Gothic furniture is at odds with the *Repository*'s purist comment that Gothic furniture should be introduced only where there would then be 'general correspondence' in the appearance of house and furniture. The correspondence was generally observed to the extent that an interest in Gothic furniture was likely to accompany a desire for Gothic decoration; the decided renaissance of the fashion for Gothic furniture in the 1820s was probably a result of certain well reported royal and ducal Gothic decorative schemes (see pp.317, 318, 416). Until then, the taste was probably largely kept alive because of the building, in the wake of the 'succès d'estime et de scandale' of Beckford and Fonthill, of Picturesque country houses in Gothic style (although they frequently had a classical interior), and through the interest taken in the cottage orné, which often showed Gothic partialities.

Until the later 1820s, Gothic furniture detail was habitually modelled on the intricate decorations of Gothic ecclesiastical architecture, exterior and interior; Tudor Gothic was on occasion preferred as being less church-like than earlier Gothic styles. 'Ecclesiastical' Gothic architecture was frequently regarded as somehow more organic in its nature than classical architecture, a concept that led to its being thought of as a growth rather than as a construction (Figs 106, 107). The unsettling effect of this doctrine was compounded by the lack of accepted 'rules' bemoaned by the architects and their clients who wished to revive Gothic architecture; the uncertainties may have inhibited the designers of Gothic furniture, since the art of furniture design was regarded in many quarters as in some ways a minor branch of architecture. Moreover, Laugierian architectural purism may have discouraged the use of a Gothic that was unsteady on its theoretical feet, especially in a period when the classical taste was increasingly and confidently using archaeological furniture forms (often attractively decorated with newly garnered antique motifs). By the 1820s, 'archaeological' attitudes were spreading from classical to Gothic furniture; George Smith in 1826 remarked that it 'has been a great

*Parlor Chairs fronts & profiles.*                    *Plate 38*

**332** Design for 'Parlor Chairs', 1807, by George Smith

mistake' to think that Gothic furniture had been designed after the style of Gothic architecture; 'in those days the furniture for domestic use was massive and heavy, consisting chiefly of bold and highly relieved mouldings, with other members partaking of the round and cable form. Many of the ornaments used about their meubles may be called arabesque, and in some cases they partook very much of the grotesque.'[6]

The caprices of the classical-Gothic synthesis sometimes give Regency Gothic furniture a freakish charm, to which the Puginesque Gothic of the 1820s added a peculiar spiky vitality; these qualities apart, 'ecclesiastical' Gothic seems to have been curiously unflexible for the purposes of designing furniture, and mainstream Regency Gothic tends to lack individuality, designs from different hands often looking much alike. The furniture designs in the classical styles of Sheraton, Holland, Tatham, Hope and Bullock, have a strongly individual character that reflects the personalities of their designers; Gothic had nothing of the

variety, distinction, staying power or proselytising influence of the classical tradition. Regency furniture deprived of Chinese and Gothic would, albeit impoverished, retain considerable merit; Regency chinoiserie and Gothic alone would make but a trifling epilogue to the history of English eighteenth-century furniture.

## Early Regency Gothic

As if to justify Alison's assertion, Sheraton does not mention Gothic in his publications of the 1790s, and its appearance in his *Cabinet Dictionary* is tentative. His *Encyclopaedia* has some flimsy and unconvincing Gothic designs, often with a classical alternative adjacent, as in an 1807 design for two pier tables;[7] neither table contributes anything new, since the Gothic design is undistinguished and the classical is in the Weisweiler/Holland candelabraform manner.

Hope ignored Gothic in his furniture designs; his omission must have been a decisive factor in its comparative neglect in the decade from 1810. Beckford did not, as we have seen, fill Fonthill with Gothic furniture, another influential rejection. George Smith, who included a significant number of Gothic designs in his 1808 book, could call neither on Hope for inspiration nor on Percier and Fontaine, who had expressly repudiated Gothic (see p.311); one can be sure that had the latter produced Gothic designs they would have found their proselytising way into the pages of the *Repository*. None of Smith's Gothic plates are earlier than 1807, including his Drawing Room decoration in the Gothic style; all the other designs for room decorations, in classical styles, are dated 1804. This indicates a late conversion, perhaps as a result of the buzz of interest in the Prince of Wales's Gothic Conservatory and Walsh Porter's Gothic Dining Room at Craven Cottage.

Two interesting designs for 'Parlor Chairs' in Smith's 1808 book (Fig. 332) have features that anticipate his comments of 1828 quoted above. The principal 'Gothic' features are the intersecting arches in the top design, which as late as 1826 Smith saw as the origin of the Gothic style; otherwise, the arches are round. A rudimentary arabesque is used, together with, on the bottom chair, cable moulding; the top chair is decorated with facets, a motif used also by Beckford on his 'Tudor' furniture (Fig. 237). The chairs were to be of 'brown oak, varnished'. The style is Norman rather than anything else; it adds welcome variety to the usual Gothic crockets.

Smith's other Gothic designs are routine. Two sets of 'Hall Chairs' and a 'Hall Sofa' are in accordance with the supposed suitability of Gothic for halls. Smith says of these that 'oak is used with great propriety'; or they may be 'executed in beech-wood and japanned stone-colour, the mouldings, etc. relieved in greys'.[8] Oak was used for practical as well as aesthetic reasons; Gothic dumb waiters 'will admit

*Cylinder Desk and Bookcase.*

*Plate 100*

*London, Published June 1st 1807, by J. Taylor, 59 High Holborn.*

**333** Design for a 'Cylinder Desk and Bookcase', 1807, by George Smith

different intermarriages on the shields') and ornamented with sculpture under canopies. Possibly Smith was looking towards the noble, not to say royal personages who were building Gothic houses in these years.

One of these was the seventh Earl of Bridgewater at Ashridge (see p.180). He, unlike Beckford at Fonthill, chose to have some Gothic furniture, and designs by Wyatville and by Benjamin Dean Wyatt survive; the furniture is competent but unremarkable. More unusual is that from the Gothic Library at Stowe. The library was designed by Soane in academic 'ecclesiastical' Gothic style (see p.316); the furniture is in ebonised mahogany with white bone decoration. It included a pier table (Fig. 334), a chair, and an octagonal table (the octagon was associated with the Gothic style, perhaps because of its use in chapter-houses — Wyatville's table for Ashridge was octagonal). The choice of materials has seventeenth-century associations, and the room contained the standard antiquarian equipment of seventeenth-century ebony East Indian chairs. The new furniture has an air of sombre fantasy; it may have been designed by Soane, but if so, its Gothic is curiously at odds with that of the room.[12]

## 'Repository' and later Regency Gothic

'Ecclesiastical' Gothic designs shown in the early years of the *Repository* included a spiky sequence between February and June 1813 of Gothic conservatory, bedchamber (with an aspiring bed 'formed on the principle of the Gothic crosses of Queen Eleanor' (Pl. XCII)), hall, staircase, and vestibule; there are hints of Fonthill in the hall. In September 1817 three 'Fashionable Chairs' by Bullock appeared, one of which, made for 'a suite of rooms in the Gothic style' is in mainstream 'ecclesiastical' Gothic and carries a shield; it may be an unusually elaborate hall chair (Fig. 321); the design of trefoils in its back is repeated in the apron of an elaborate state chair from Battle Abbey, also attributed to Bullock. A table published in the *Repository* in July 1821 in sturdy Gothic, by J. Taylor of Oakley's, mixes classical and Gothic detail; the detail is picked out in bronzing and the decoration of the piece unites a Gothic arcade at the back, made up of intersecting circles, with bronzed scrolling side pieces in a shape resembling the anthemion. The wood can be oak, or 'mahogany . . . may be used with great propriety, and perhaps the effect of that wood on the whole is richer than that produced by oak'.[13]

The search for an acceptable Gothic idiom continued; in September 1823 Ackermann gave historicist sanction to a Gothic four-poster bed by modelling it on the 'processional canopy of a throne . . . the precursor of the English tester', a not altogether inaccurate assertion; the text concludes that 'recurrence to such sources for designs of furniture in the Gothic style is to be desired'. The counterpane and back panel were in 'Gothic' fabric.[14]

of being made of mahogany, having less open work than some of the Designs in this style; they would look well in wainscot, darkened to imitate old oak . . .'.[9] A 'Cylinder Desk and Bookcase' (Fig. 333), 'though in the Gothic style, may with great propriety be executed in mahogany'; the upper doors should be 'backed with lustring in flutes'. Ogee buttresses, with inconveniently projecting crockets, support the front; the doors of the base are mirrored. Satin wood, 'burnished gold, with parts of bronze, or otherways highly enriched', was proposed for Gothic Drawing Room chairs, the seats to be 'covered with silks, painted satins, painted velvets, superfine cloth, or chintz'.[10]

Architectural 'ecclesiastical' Gothic attains its apotheosis in an almighty design for a State Bed (Pl. CXX); 'there is no kind of work better calculated to produce a grand effect . . . than . . . Gothic'.[11] The bed is enclosed in a chantry-chapel like structure with an open dome formed of ogee arches, liberally bedizened with coats of arms ('the

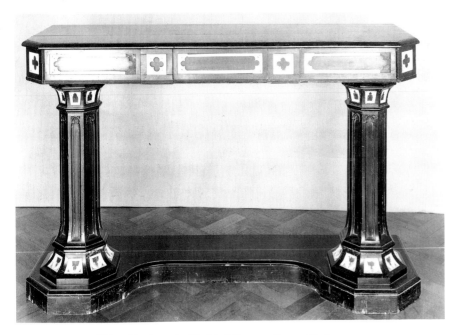

**334** Side table from the Gothic Library at Stowe, Bucks.

The furnishings of Eaton Hall, as recorded in 1826, constituted a large ensemble of Gothic furniture designed in accordance with the house. This was pictured only after two wings had been designed and added from 1823 to 1825 by Benjamin Gummow, Porden's Supervising architect (Porden had died in 1822). The furniture has been attributed to Porden; in giltwood, mahogany, and rosewood, with gilt bronze attachments, it is in the richest Gothic taste. The manner (Fig. 241) isolates gilded Gothic detail on a background of plain wood; the same method is used both on the Dining Room furniture at Windsor[15] and in many of the Gothic plates given in the insistent series of designs, which all seem to be by the Pugins, father and/or son, that appeared in the *Repository* between 1825 and 1827. There are other correspondences between the Eaton Hall and Windsor furniture and the Gothic designs shown in the *Repository*. The form to which the Gothic decoration is applied is usually basically antique; thus the sofa and armchair at Eaton are drawn from Roman models, and an unattributed 'Sofa for a Drawing Room in the Gothic style', shown in the *Repository* in December 1825,[16] has an arm closely similar to that of the Eaton piece.[17] There are other, stray similarities. The double-armed sofa in front of the far window in the Eaton Hall Saloon has scrolled arms and a dipped back rising in the middle, in common with a Gothic sofa published in the *Repository* in November 1826. The mirror in the Drawing Room at Eaton has gilded tracery upon a crimson velvet background; the dining room chairs at Windsor have fabric behind the tracery that decorates their backs. The lambrequins at the Eaton window, paralleled in the apartments at Windsor, are seen also in a

design for a Gothic window published in the *Repository* in February 1826. These coincidences may be due to common sources.[18] However, the long table in the right background of the Eaton Hall Saloon is perhaps significant in this context, in that its unadorned forms seem to have come from a world different from that of the other furniture and might be thought to anticipate the younger Pugin's Gothic, in which construction was to become almost as important as decoration.

From December 1825 the *Repository* published such Gothic pieces as the sofas mentioned, a sideboard, chairs, beds, tables, two pianos, a bookcase, a whist table, a cheval glass, flower stands, candelabra, a

**335** 'Door adjoining Abbot Islip's Chapel, Westminster Abbey', by A. Pugin, 1821

GOTHIC WINDOW CURTAINS.

**CXXVI** 'Gothic Window Curtains', from the *Repository*, 1826

CXXVII A Gothic looking glass, from the *Repository*, 1827

*Opposite above* CXXIX 'Gothic Sopha, Table, Chair & Footstool, for a Library', from the *Repository*, 1810

CXXVIII A 'Gothic table', from the *Repository*, 1826

*Opposite below* CXXX Design for a 'Centre Table' and 'Drawing Room Side Table', by Richard Bridgens, 1838

GOTHIC TABLE.

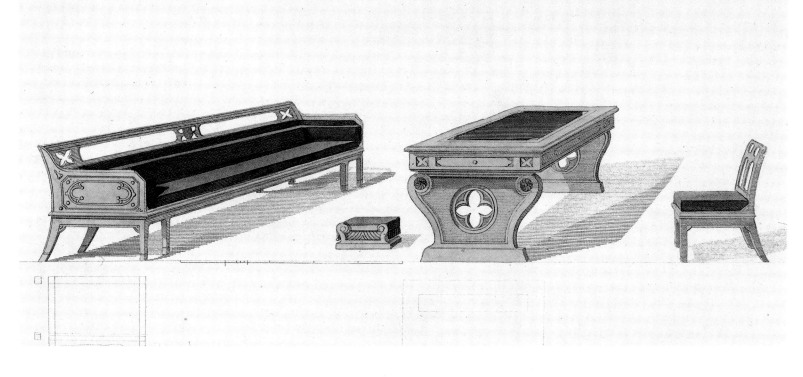

CENTRE TABLE.

DRAWING ROOM SIDE TABLE.

J.Taylor Del

**CXXXI** Design for curtains and pier table, by J. Taylor, c.1824

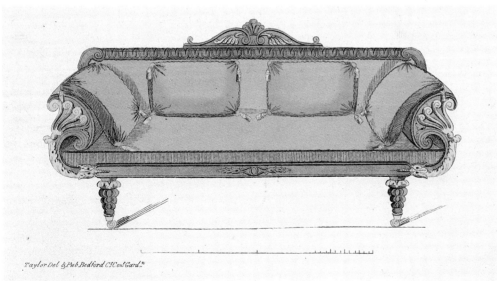

Taylor Del & Pub.Bedford C.H.Cov.t Gard.n

**CXXXII** Design for a sofa, by J. Taylor, c.1824

bureau, and a group consisting of keys, hearth, broom, bell pulls, etc. It showed also the title page of Pugin's *Gothic Furniture*, a sharp assemblage which foreshadows the obsessional intricacies of the Mediaeval Court at the Great Exhibition of 1851. The drawing still exists for a circular 'Gothic Library Table', a form adapted from the classical repertory, which appeared unattributed in the *Repository* in March 1826, and in Pugin's *Gothic Furniture* (Pl. CXXVIII); it has been remarked that the still life on the table is the kind of mediaevalising motif to be expected from the younger Pugin.[19] The Ackermann text draws attention both to the square quatrefoils, which form 'a pleasing variation to the eye from the usual circular quatrefoil', and to the griffins, which 'are taken from that most elegant of Gothic edifices of the latter end of the fifteenth century, the Palais de Justice, at Rouen'; they appear intended to be bronzed, another 'classical' practice.

Two contrasting Gothic beds were illustrated in the *Repository* in April 1826 and February 1827. One is basically a 'French bed' (and has indeed some resemblance to a classical design by Pierre de la Mésangère), with griffins from the tomb of Lord Bourchier in Westminster Abbey, which served as a quarry for antiquarian decorators; the other is a Gothic four poster, with posts that 'resemble the carving on the tomb of Crouchback' in the same building. A romantic design for 'Gothic Window Curtains' (Pl. CXXVI), very much 'Mariana in the moated grange', has a curtain rod that is, as 'of late, continued along the whole length of the room'; the curtains hang simply to the floor without being draped, and a parcel-gilt Gothic commode shows between the windows. The commode has Gothic tracery placed against a green background that matches the curtains; the ogee arch and the tracery above it are of the same type as that above a 'Door adjoining Abbot Islip's Chapel' at Westminster Abbey, illustrated in Augustus Pugin's *Specimens of Gothic Architecture* (Fig. 335). The tracery below the arch has some similarities with that of the 'East Window, Merton College Chapel', from the same publication. And the flowing Gothic tracery of the window seat is like that on the 'parapet of Magdalen Church'. This Gothic furniture is very architectural; a 'Gothic Looking Glass', provided for a dressing room in January 1827, has a frame given strength without weight 'by the introduction of flying buttresses, which, while adding to the strength of the frame, detract nothing from the lightness of its character (Pl. CXXVII); exactly the same could be said of a Gothic cathedral. The wood was to be mahogany or rosewood, and the ornaments wooden or gilt bronze.

**336** 'Gothic Furniture', from the *Repository*, 1819

Debate continued; a 'Gothic Toilette' of August 1827, much in the same style as the other Gothic pieces, was nevertheless said 'to preserve the true domestic Gothic form and details, and to avoid the ecclesiastical style' to which end the 'flat or elliptical arch', was adopted rather than the pointed arch, a general preference already stated by architects. The search for an acceptable Gothic style in furniture had been obliquely referred to a couple of years earlier, in December 1826, when three fanciful Gothic chairs were illustrated, two of which have four sabre legs and one of which has straight front legs with sabre legs at the back: all decidedly mixed in style. The commentator, perhaps to forestall criticism, remarked that the few sixteenth century chairs remaining are 'far from being pure in their details. They are executed in ebony, with ivory occasionally introduced. . . . They are totally unfit for imitation, being clumsy in their design and very heavy'.[20] The reference was obviously to the East Indian seventeenth-century ebony chair, heavy because of the weight of the dense ebony.

One should perhaps notice the hangers on, prominent amongst whom was E. B. Lamb, whose Gothic and Norman furniture designs of the 1830s are repulsive and inept. A clue to Lamb's attitudes is given in his reason for designing a Norman conservatory: 'certainly one of the most awkward things to design in the Norman style; but as I should like such a thing attached to a small villa of this kind, I must make the best I can of it'.[21]

Chapter five

# Antiquarianism

## Eclectic antiquarianism

Before considering the antiquarian alternative to 'ecclesiastical' Gothic, one should notice the interesting furniture placed by Beckford in the Gothic surroundings of Fonthill's King Edward's and St. Michael's galleries (Fig. 237; Pl. LXXXIX).

Prominent in the illustration of King Edward's Gallery, where they stand either side of the alabaster fireplace, are the oak cabinets 'carved in imitation of the style of the Elizabethan age';[1] they are in much the same style as the range of oak tables that stands in the windows, and are curious and distinguished pieces of furniture. Britton was correct in seeing Elizabethan references, especially in the bulbous supports of the upper tier, but the mirror glass gives a 'Regency' air, and the congested and embossed surface decoration is highly original; it may have some relation to decoration encountered on the numerous seventeenth-century East India pieces installed in the house, since to judge from the 'ebony bedstead and furniture [meaning the quilt] part of which belonged to Henry the VII',[2] Beckford shared Walpole's belief that such furniture was Tudor. Something of its ornamental idiom may have strayed to the 'Elizabethan' cabinets. Miscellaneous pieces in King Edward's Gallery included the 'Borghese' *pietra dura* slab, placed upon an oak 'Renaissance' base devised for Beckford, which may be seen in the illustration, and an elaborate South German cabinet of about 1550 attributed to Holbein, both obviously meant to contribute to the 'Tudor' impression.

There was a large quantity of black furniture in both King Edward's and St. Michael's galleries, the use of which put Beckford in the forefront of taste; the East India furniture mentioned above made up a large proportion of this, but seventeenth-century European and modern English pieces, much of it boulle, were also included. In King

Edward's Gallery stood 'two carved ebony tables' and 'two ebony and porcelain coffers';[3] the (obviously modern) torchères were ebonised, as was a set of '6 gallery stools' with twisted legs. At the south end of St. Michael's Gallery (Pl. LXXXIX) were two black, twisted torchères which look as if they may have been English of the Restoration period, perhaps with modern feet; along the Gallery was ranged a grand set of what appear to have been Louis XIV boulle torchères. To these were added 'eleven ebony tables, with slabs of marble, carrying glazed cabinets of buhl and tortoiseshell' (made for Beckford, two of which survive at Charlecote), and East Indian 'chairs and tables of carved ebony'; the chairs were said formerly to have belonged to 'the magnificent and haughty Wolsey, and were part of the splendid furniture of Esher Palace'.[4] The ebony table in the window is probably 'a table of ebony, with torsel feet, which formerly belonged to Cardinal Wolsey'.[5] One feels that Beckford overlooked Wolsey's low birth in the light of his picturesque associations.

Fonthill therefore contained several types of furniture thought generally appropriate for antiquarian schemes apart from 'ecclesiastical' Gothic. These included East India ebony, 'Elizabethan' and Restoration furniture, and boulle; to these, others (not Beckford) added the late seventeenth/early eighteenth-century turned ash provincial chairs that had been taken up by Walpole and others, undeniably quaint whatever their age or provenance. Both the East Indian ebony chairs and the ash chairs rejoice in turning; the latter especially were 'loaded with turnery', as Walpole wrote.[6] The former used the spiral twist; the twist can come near to the cable, which was considered to be a Gothic motif by George Smith. The presence of the spiral twist tends to be taken as evidence of seventeenth-century influence, and often obviously is so; however, its origins in the Salomonic pillar, which was associated with the Temple of Solomon and hence the East, were well known, and when used in conjunction with exotic motifs, as in the Egyptian chairs by the younger Chippendale at Stourhead, the allusion was obviously to the East and not to the seventeenth century. The use of the spiral twist in Roman decoration, and in Roman and mediaeval architecture, was also known. Given the synthesising tendencies of the time, and the fact that Roman leg shapes were imitated in turning, it is often hard to disentangle the sources of the design; the more successful the synthesis, the more difficult the task.

The presence in the turned chair by Bullock (Fig. 320; on the top left of the illustration) of a row of turned knobs along the top rail, and the vestiges of knobs along the sides, suggests a distant relationship with the turned ash chair, although the East India ebony chair is not far away; were the chair ebonised the East India likeness would be strengthened. The seventeenth-century references of these features are intensified by the use of stretchers. An Ackermann illustration of September 1817 of three chairs by Bullock (Fig. 321) shows the range of his style; the first two are mentioned above (see p.403); the third is a chair intended 'for a book room in a mansion built in the seventeenth-century'. This is a design which subsumes seventeenth-century motifs in a convincing creation, new but perfectly adapted to an antiquarian setting. The chair exists, in oak painted and parcel gilt, with gilt brass trimmings;[7] what appears to be a cable pattern in Ackermann becomes a more open twist in the chair, and the chair has no trace of what may in Ackermann be an application of the same red fabric as on the seat (or possibly paint in the same colour as the fabric) to the rails of the back, with only the turned uprights and the centre top of the back exposed.

A typical antiquarian ensemble is seen at Abbotsford, initially provided (see p.327) with furniture by Bullock and Blore. After Bullock's death, Scott acquired an unconnected miscellany of old furniture (Fig. 249). The Library contained a fine and large Gothic desk (in the centre of the room) made by a local joiner, who also put together the 'consulting desk' in the window bay, which with Regency ingenuity revolved, rose, and fell; the uncomfortable monopodia that support the top may have come from London.[8] The two 'Brustolon' Venetian baroque chairs adjacent to the consulting desk were bought from the broker Swaby of Wardour Street; six and two of the set went respectively to two other houses, Belvoir and Newstead. They had been imported by the Abbé Celotti, a dealer who had collaborated with the upholsterer Baldock in acquiring the Fonthill Borghese Table.[9] At the back of the room on the left is a piece in the ebony taste, a fall-front desk almost certainly bought from Baldock.[10] It was described in January 1823 in a letter from Daniel Terry (see p.329) to Scott as 'One of the most solid and superb ebony escritoires I ever saw or think ever was in London it is entirely plain I mean from gilded ornaments Sir but exquisitely carved in panels and mouldings extensive roomy'.[11] It looks as if it were made up from a mid-seventeenth century Flemish chest on

stand: the back was subject to more making up by Terry. Scott had other ebony furniture.

His modern pieces included a brass inlaid dwarf cabinet placed next to the desk; designed by J. S. Moritt of Rokeby, a noted classical scholar, it was made by Bullock from yew from Moritt's Yorkshire estate. Upon it stands a cast taken by Bullock from Shakespeare's memorial bust at Holy Trinity, Stratford; since it has been consistently derided as a work of art, the meaning of the bust was obviously associational. Another Bullock piece, a neo-classical support in yew, mahogany, marble and gilt-bronze, designed to take a silver sepulchral vase containing bones from Athens given to Scott by Byron, stands before the fireplace. One thus saw, in incongruous co-existence in the same room, a group of furniture that included Regency neo-classical, Venetian seventeenth-century baroque, modern Gothic, and made up seventeenth-century ebony. The connecting links are intellectual, or rather associational; the visual harmonies that bound together Beckford's furniture at Fonthill are here tenuous or non-existent.

## 'Elizabethan' or 'Old English'

In March 1813 the *Repository* had shown a most peculiar 'Gothic' design — a 'cottage chair', said to be composed 'after the design which prevailed in the sixteenth century'; it seems to have been actually made, having 'lately been introduced with great advantage as furniture for buildings of the castellated character'; it was recommended for a cottage orné. It is a brutish hybrid, combining outward splayed klismos type legs with a coarsely modelled back composed of cut-out scrolls

337 Design for a 'Window Seat', by Richard Bridgens, 1838

Proof

The Rt. Honble Lady Eleanor Butler and Miss Ponsonby.

"The Ladies of Llangollen."

From a Drawing by LADY LEIGHTON, carefully taken from life.

Drawn on Stone by R.J.LANE A.R.A.

Printed by J. Graf.

J. Ponsonby

Died Decr 8th 1831. Aged 74.

Eleanor Butler

Died June 2nd 1829. Aged 90.

**338** The Ladies of Llangollen in old age at Plas Newydd

and circles in a pattern of undefinable antecedents; as a substitute for Gothic it was hardly satisfactory. It was another result of the search for an alternative to 'ecclesiastical' Gothic furniture, a quest which prompted attempts at Elizabethan and seventeenth-century furniture by Wyatville at Endsleigh and by others. In April 1819 the *Repository* brought forward yet another, hitherto unconsidered, kind of 'Gothic Furniture' (Fig. 336), produced by 'that unsystemised art which is often called Gothic, but which should properly be termed Tedeschi, or old German' which 'prevailed in the mansions of the first rank in Germany in the fifteenth century . . . its fitness and correspondence to some of our own ancient buildings rendered the annexed examples of genuine Tedeschi furniture very desirable'. By 'unsystemised', the *Repository* meant not subject to rules.

The chair, which looks plausibly old,[12] is of a type associated with the name of Francis Cleyn, domiciled in England in the seventeenth century; its form, Italian in origin, became naturalised as that of the hall chair, although the solid scrolled legs were generally placed front and back (rather than at either side) in the English version, a stronger and more logical construction. A set of 'Cleyn' chairs at Holland House was painted white and gold at about this time to go with a newly decorated Jacobean setting — the Audley End 'Jacobean' rooms were also white and gold (see pp.333, 334). The table, small and highly decorated, is more doubtful; it is suspiciously well adapted to Regency requirements, and the thin scrolls at the base seem meagre for its supposed period. One wonders whether Ackermann's draughtsman had used sixteenth or early seventeenth-century designs to concoct or 'help along' a 'Tedeschi' table. The international nature of such early ornament would have made it appropriate for use in any 'Elizabethan' revival, and it is probable that such pattern books were already in use.

The designs of Richard Bridgens, who had been associated with Bullock since at least 1810, incline towards the Elizabethan. It has been suggested that he worked for Bullock and that he 'specialised in the design of furniture and interiors in the Mediaeval and what he [Bridgens] termed the "Old English" styles'.[13] Lacking firm evidence, one cannot tell; in such a many-faceted period as the Regency it seems equally possible that Bullock and Bridgens, like Sheraton and Smith, were prepared to turn their hands to several styles. Bridgens asserted in both the 1825–6 and the 1838 editions of his *Furniture with candelabra* that the contents were 'designed by R. Bridgens', but the syntax of the title page makes it uncertain what exactly his claims were, and some pieces illustrated were acknowledged to be old, such as tables from Penshurst and Christ Church and the famous chair from St. Mary's Hall at Coventry.[14]

Bridgens used old forms and old decoration together, but the result was far from 'authentic'. Modern features occur in his 'Elizabethan' designs; chairs have back sabre legs[15] and he produces such anomalies as

'Elizabethan' chests of drawers[16] (the form did not evolve until the later seventeenth century). His 'Window Seat' (Fig. 337) is entirely hybrid; on the back of a basically Georgian shape is superimposed a mixture of 'Elizabethan' and Restoration motifs, acanthus being employed on the arms. A 'chair and flower stand' is in the Dutch style of about 1700. He took details from architecture, as in work for James Watt of Aston Hall (for whom he made designs after Bullock's death); the overmantel of the Jacobean entrance hall at Aston is utilised as a source for the head of a bed. His designs have vigour (Pl. CXXX). Other designers, such as Papworth, were producing similar concoctions, and Salvin in the 1820s designed striking furniture in the 'Elizabethan' style.

## 'Authenticity'

Whilst the hybrids mentioned above were being designed, exact antiquarianism encouraged the would-be academic copy.[17] Hunt's *Exemplars of Tudor Architecture* of 1830 (see p.184) did not neglect furniture; his judicious text and careful illustrations set a standard that was quickly followed. Loudon illustrated old furniture from Hunt's book, making it clear that he expected it to be copied; he depicted a table in Elizabethan style that looks, in his crude reproduction, authentic; we read however that it was 'designed by Mr Shaw'. Loudon also mentioned that 'Kensett of Mortimer Street' had available 'a correct facsimile of a chair taken from Tintern Abbey', and correct copies of 'two other chairs from Glastonbury; one . . . the abbot's chair, and the other no less remarkable for the simplicity of its construction'.

Along with these 'correct' copies (and some today are perhaps being mistaken for the real thing) were antiquarian essays of the kind seen in Mr. Braikenridge's house (Fig. 250); Loudon said that chests and wardrobes 'might be rendered curious, and highly interesting, though we do not say in correct or architectural taste, by covering them with the Elizabethan, Dutch, Louis XIV, or Francis I, ornaments, which are now to be purchased in abundance', and that such fragments could be obtained from Wilkinson of Oxford Street, and Hanson of John Street, 'from which a judicious compiler of exteriors might clothe skeleton frames . . . at a very trifling expense'.[18] To judge from the survivors, these made up pieces were unified by being glazed with burnt umber (as advised by Whittock for wainscot oak), with deadening effect. Like Regency boulle, they have sometimes proved very deceptive.[19]

They deceived contemporaries; Shaw's *Specimens of Ancient Furniture* of 1836, produced in association with the antiquarians Meyrick and Thomas Lister Parker of Browsholme, has plates dated from 1832: many show real, some doubtful, and some obviously fake old furniture. The 'ebony chair formerly at Strawberry Hill' is included, as are two splendid tables from Hardwick. Shaw's concern for correctness is evident. His mind changed as he wrote; a 'Coach from

Penshurst' said on the plate to be of the 'time of Queen Elizabeth' is given in the text as William III. At times he was too cautious; the famous 'seadog' table from Hardwick, attributed on the plate to Elizabeth or James I, was said in the text to be William III or Queen Anne.

The search for authenticity was by this time far advanced; it is seen not only in various projects for the restoration of old houses, but also in the growing concern for old textiles. Beckford was ahead in (occasionally) using such textiles; by the 1830s the Duke of Devonshire showed in restoring and rehabilitating Hardwick a sensitivity in preserving old fabrics and, most of all, in introducing new, that could be imitated with profit today by those who administer old houses; he realised that it was impossible deliberately to put back the clock and to retain either authenticity or aesthetic consistency. He therefore re-set old needlework into a fabric that deliberately imitated the faded brown of an originally purple cloth; wherever he could, he saved the original. The Green Room had been 'hung with bits of unconnected needlework, and stuffs patched without order, and they were in a state of deplorable decay. I took them down, and, with other fragments now in the hands of my upholsterer at Chatsworth, hope to arrange and save them from decaying still more'.[20] It is remarkable that, living in an age noted for gaudy display, he did not introduce the brash smartness that one sees so often today in similar circumstances: 'All these old beds, once so handsome, are in tatters, and want renovation and repairs, preserving to the utmost their old appearance'.[21] The result was in strong contrast to the zealous innovations at Charlecote and the miscellanies of Abbotsford. The Duke was himself less restrained at Chatsworth, although his aesthetic sensitivity allowed that also to wear well.

# Chinese and Indian

The lack of critical esteem for the Chinese style did not prevent large quantities of furniture in that style being made; it was usually ignored by the pattern books, with charming exceptions (Fig. 339). And a most notable exception was the production by the Prince Regent's designers of brilliantly sophisticated Chinese and Indian style furniture; the quality of this alone justifies one in regarding exotic furniture as a major achievement of the period. The furniture was, of course, intimately linked with the Prince's exotic decorations.

The furniture of the Chinese Drawing Room of the early 1790s seems all to have been either French in origin, or designed and made by French craftsmen in England, or in a French style. It included two sets of chinoiserie pier tables by Weisweiler, one supported by Chinese caryatids (Pl. CVI) and the other (Fig. 256) with a gilt-bronze curtain across its centre. There was a set of giltwood chairs made by Hervé; amongst the ornaments were six candelabra with Chinese maidens and the 'Drummer Boy' clock with its Chinese drummer.[1] The chimney-piece, which has chinoiserie terms, was possibly also French (Holland himself liked chimney-pieces with dandified terms).[2] The style of these objects is a mélange of 'Etruscan', Chinese, and 'Pompeian' motifs. The 'Etruscan' content includes decussated lozenges and hexagons, interlaced arches, and the ambiguous Chinese/'Etruscan' fret and interconnected circles; the Chinese includes upturned roofs (although these occur in the Herculaneum frescoes),[3] the pagoda top of the clock and the elongated caryatids, although the last may have been influenced by the immensely long and fanciful 'due Cariatidi, o Telamoni, che voglian dirsi' (the doubt is understandable) illustrated in the 1779 volume of the *Pitture Antiche d'Ercolano* — the top and base of a table seem almost to be suggested in the print. Other elongated caryatids appear in the arabesques of the ceilings of the Baths of Titus (used by Cipriani as a source for elongated caryatids painted on a ceiling of

old Buckingham House), where one also finds, suggestively, fringed drapery resembling that on the pier tables, and decorated ovals with pointed ends of the type used by Weisweiler.[4] The Hervé chairs, which have serpents around the legs, a reptile used emblematically in many antique sources, are decorated with motifs entirely classical in origin apart from the Chinese figures on the back rails; the figures appear to have been added later. Fabrics used included yellow silk for chairs and ottoman, described as 'brocaded Sattin . . . bordered with Chinese border and welted over with Crimson Ingrain silk'.[5] It will be noticed

**339** Designs for 'Book case doors', 1807, by George Smith

that the Prince of Wales, like Beckford — and even the Duke of Wellington — was not afraid to put yellow next to gilding.

For the earliest chinoiserie decorations at the Pavilion, the 'ethnic' interiors of 1802–04 (see pp.336–8), the Prince imported large quantities of real Chinese furniture and curiosities. It seems probable that some of the flimsier rattan furniture may have been imported flat and made up in England; whether this happened or not, it is certain that genuine Chinese decorative detail in rattan was incorporated into English pieces. Such were the decorative friezes set into the wall cabinets shown in the 1826 Nash view of the Corridor; in 1802 they had lacquer doors (replaced by 1826 with pleated silk), and yellow scagliola tops with ormolu galleries. The simpler 'Chinese export' furniture, as it is usually termed, is seen in the 1826 view of the South Gallery (Pl. CIV). The two tables at the end, which still exist, are made of rattan but have satinwood tops. This kind of furniture, together with the charming and familiar simulated bamboo, was thought as fit for the cottage orné as for the Prince's Marine Pavilion.

The 'ethnic' interiors at Brighton were still in their first youth when George Smith in 1806 produced one of his few designs in the Chinese style — a couple of 'déjeuné tables'. They seem to attempt authenticity, and are as much in the Chambers style as anything else.

The furniture created for the Nash rebuilding of the Pavilion from 1815 onwards is unsurpassed for splendour and magnificence. The view of the Banqueting Room shows the magnificently unbridled rosewood sideboards, their 'larger dragons' added by command of King George IV (Pl. CII). Second thoughts are apparent also in the great Spode gas torchères from the same room, designed by Robert Jones, which have gilt-bronze dragons by Vulliamy that decorate the dark blue columns inspired by the dark blue of Sèvres; the dolphins at the feet are of gilded wood, probably an afterthought. The exotic nature of these torchères, with their green lotus tops, does not entirely disguise their descent from the classical candelabrum, perhaps modified by memories of columns enwreathed with the serpents of Hygeia as depicted in the murals of Herculaneum.

Robert Jones may also have designed the elbow chairs for the Music Room, delivered by Bailey and Saunders in 1817. Originally in lilac and gold, complementary colours of the kind that were thought especially appropriate to the Chinese style, the chair is a brilliant synthesis of classical form (the klismos) and exotic ornament. Jones is known to have designed the sumptuous wall cabinets in ivory and gold for the Saloon, which were delivered too late to be pictured in the Nash book (Pl. CVII). The gilt-bronze 'Indian' arch at the centre and the pillars at the sides are by Vulliamy; the carved and gilded wooden ornament with scrolls and rosettes, more classical than anything else, is supplemented by fragile ornament in bronze gilded to look like wood; the painted decoration is in silver leaf. The most extravagant touch of *luxe* is that all the carved ornament on the front is repeated on its reverse, since the mirror at the back of the cabinet occasionally sends a glancing reflection to the seated spectator.

The Chinese and Indian styles could not be carried further than in the Pavilion; indeed, the building contained the whole gamut of Regency taste, albeit in a unique guise. In total effect, the interiors have more than any other the quality that Loudon characterised as the 'ecstatic', and are marked with the hedonistic refinement that usually characterised the decorating ventures of the King. It is as appropriate a creation as any on which to leave the subject of Regency design; it encapsulates so much of what is best, as well as not a few of the faults, of a remarkable period.

# Epilogue

The author has attempted to chronicle the genesis, progress and dissolution of a style that, amidst all the variety of its aspects, yet has an essential identity that enables us to designate it as 'Regency'. That variety is bewildering, but several characteristics and tendencies stand out beyond the rest.

The core of the style lay in a vocabulary supplied by Greek, Roman and Egyptian antiquity; England had the invaluable support of France and Italy in showing her how to use it, and her achievements in the classical style were of European significance; for the last time in this country the noble images of antiquity were used with unflinching conviction, judgment and panache. The support of Europe was lacking when it came to the use of the varieties of Gothic, and however charming or beautiful the results may at times be, they savour in many cases of provincialism or of pedantic historicism; antiquarianism has both defects in full measure. Only the peculiar virtues of the Picturesque could rescue the situation, and in many cases they do so.

The most creative of tendencies was that towards synthesis, which triumphed in the work of individuals such as Hope and Soane and in the evolution of such entrancing artefacts as the 'picaresque' house and the cottage orné. The most destructive was the increasing power of 'commerce' in intellectual and aesthetic matters; it accompanied the uglifications of the Industrial Revolution, another sinister manifestation. Utilitarianism, which united cultural barbarism with lack of compassion, began its disastrous and successful career. Before his death in 1818 Repton, discerning and sensitive, had already recorded his perception of the commercial and utilitarian threat to the most widely celebrated of the country's beauties, the landscape. By the 1830s destructive tendencies in architecture had become ascendant; at least so thought the most original and inspired of Regency architects — whose work should have been a lamp for his successors — the aged Soane: 'O Architecture! thou Queen of the Fine Arts — my first love — my friend through life and the prop of my declining years, how art thou fallen, fallen, fallen!':[1] when, in 1835, the failure of Soane's 'noble daring' was lamented, it was speculated that he 'soared in a direction directly contrary to the feeling of the day, and failed accordingly . . .'.[2] In 1790, at the beginning of the period, its major political (and aesthetic) theorist Edmund Burke had written that 'To make us love our country, our country ought to be lovely';[3] by 1840 it was already considerably uglier, and well set on the accelerating career it has since followed.

Taken as a whole, the period had been intensely creative, and its achievements — in letters, in architecture and decoration, in town planning, in trade and in war — seem to us, stranded in an almost totally disintegrated culture, with only a 'few late chrysanthemums' in occasional bloom, to have been richly and impressively multifarious.

# Notes

N.B. Standard works quoted are not necessarily the first editions.

INTRODUCTION

1 Musgrave, Clifford: *Regency Furniture* (Faber & Faber, 1970), p.29.
2 Price, Uvedale: *Essays on the Picturesque: Essay on Architecture and Buildings* (J. Mawman, London, 1810), vol. II, p.203.
3 Ibid., p.379.
4 Knight, Richard Payne: *An Analytical Enquiry into the Principles of Taste* (T. Payne & J. White, London, 1806), p.435. Knight echoed d'Hancarville's 'the style of dress did not change from the time of Pericles to that of Harmodius'; the same idea was voiced by Hope.
5 Manwaring, E.W.: *Italian Landscape in Eighteenth Century England* (Oxford University Press, 1925), pp.27–8.
6 See William Mitford: *Principles of Design in Architecture* (London, 1809), p.252. He speaks of ladies 'Ranging the fashionable upholsterer's warehouses, they feel themselves as in a sea of delights, but as in a vessel with a port to seek. Without a compass, they look to Fashion as their polar star, and they give the helm to Fancy.'
7 Peacock, Thomas Love: *Melincourt* (1818; Macmillan, London, 1896), chap. II, p.20.
8 Alison, Archibald: *Essays on the Nature and Principles of Taste* (Edinburgh, 1825), 6th edn., vol. I, pp.37, 89.
9 Although Hope was careful to deny that he was a merchant: 'I, who though of merchants' blood, am not a merchant . . .', *Historical Essay on Architecture* (Murray, 1840), p.XII.
10 The aristocracy that embraced parvenu taste is the same aristocracy that, in the person of the reactionary Duke of Wellington, had objected to soldiers cheering, since it indicated an opinion.

11 Cumberland, George: *Essay of the Utility of Collecting the Best Works of the Ancient Engravers of the Italian School* (W. Nicol, London, 1827), p.vi.
12 Dayes, Edward: *Works of the late Edward Dayes* (T. Maiden, London, 1805), p.203 (from the *Essay on Taste*). Caylus and others had made the same comment, taken from antiquity.
13 Montgomery, J.: *Proceedings of a Public Meeting for . . . a Literary and Philosophical Society in Sheffield, Dec. 12, 1822* (Sheffield, 1822), p.10.
14 Caylus, Comte de: *Recueil d'Antiquités Egyptiennes, Etrusques, Grecques, et Romaines* (Paris, 1761), p.1.
15 D'Hancarville, P.F.: *Antiquités Etrusques, Grecques et Romaines* (Paris, 1785).
16 Laugier, Abbé: *Observations sur l'Architecture* (The Hague and Paris, 1765), p.80. 'Ce n'est que de nos jours que la science de l'Architecture antique a été véritablement approfondie, et qu'on en a établi les règles avec assez de précision pour que l'Artiste puisse travailler sans incertitude et être jugé surement.' In quoting Laugier, the author has corrected the accents.
17 Payne Knight describes a more genial process. Nothing is 'so flexible and ductile as taste in highly polished societies; and consequently no class so small as those who think, feel, and act for themselves in matters belonging to it. Authority begets prejudice — prejudice, fashion — and fashion soon modifies nature to receive all its impressions in their full force': *Edinburgh Review* (1814), p.272.
18 Allison, A.: *Essays*, op. cit., p.64.
19 Fielding, Henry: *Tom Jones* (Odhams, London, 1948), vol. 2, bk. XII, chaps I & X, pp.106, 143. Is the mistake in the Horace quotation deliberate, yet another of the hero's imperfections?
20 Alison, A.: *Essays*, op. cit., p.365.

21 See *Mémoires de l'Institut Royal de France: Classe D'Histoire et de Littérature Ancienne* (Paris, 1818), p.102.
22 See Bindman, D.E.: *John Flaxman R.A.* (Royal Academy, 1979), p.145.
23 Quoted *The Arrogant Connoisseur*, ed. Michael Clarke and Nicholas Penny (Manchester University Press, 1982), p.81.
24 Even as described in John Britton: *The Autobiography of John Britton* (printed for the author, London, 1850), vol. I, p.99.
25 Knight, R.P.: *Analytical Enquiry*, op. cit., p.197.
26 Alison, A.: *Essays*, op. cit., p.65.
27 Peacock, Thomas Love: *Gryll Grange* (Alan Sutton, 1984), chap. XXIV, pp.155–7 (1860, but still a 'Regency' novel).
28 Even the French (D'Arvilly and Baudelaire) recognised Brummell as the archetypal dandy. 'Dandyism appears especially in those periods of transition when democracy has not yet become all-powerful, and when aristocracy is only partially weakened . . . [it] is not . . . an excessive delight in clothes and material elegance. For the perfect dandy, these things are no more than the symbol of the aristocratic superiority of his mind . . . perfection in dress consists of absolute simplicity. . . . Dandyism is, above all, the burning desire to create a personal form of originality within the external limits of social conventions.' Baudelaire: *Selected Writings on Art and Artists*, trans. P.E. Charret (Penguin, 1972), pp.420–1.
29 The relevant passage runs: 'fuggir . . . come un asperissimo e pericoloso scoglio, la affettazione; e, per dir forse una nova parola, usar in ogni cosa una certa sprezzatura, che nasconda l'arte, e dimostri, ciò che si fa e dice, venir fatto senza fatica e quasi senza pensarvi. Da questo credo io che derivi assai la grazia;

perché delle cose rare e ben fatte ognun sa la difficultà, onde in esse la facilità genera grandissima maraviglia.' Baldassare Castiglione: *Il Libro del Cortegiano* (Sansoni, Florence, 1947), p.63. The character of 'James Bond' exemplifies the modern version of *sprezzatura*.

30 Pevsner, Sir Nikolaus: *Studies in Art, Architecture and Design* (Thames & Hudson, 1968), pp.103–04.

31 Alberti, Leon Battista: *Della Architettura di Leon Battista Alberti*, trans. Giacomo Leoni (London, 1739), vol. II, bk. II, p.11.

## Part I: Parks and Gardens

### CHAPTER ONE
### Before 1790: The Antecedents

1 Pope, Alexander: from the 'Prologue designed for Mr. d'Urfey's last play'.

2 Orrery, John, Earl of: *The Letters of Pliny the Younger* (London, 1751), bk. V, Epistle V, pp.380, 385.

3 Walpole, Horace: *Anecdotes of Painting in England . . . the Modern Taste in Gardening . . . with considerable additions by the Rev. James Dallaway* (London, 1827), vol. IV, pp.238, 239.

4 Alberti, Leon Battista: *Della Architettura di Leon Battista Alberti*, trans. Giacomo Leoni (London, 1739), vol. II, bk. X, pp.116, 119.

5 Walpole, H.: *Anecdotes*, op. cit., p.235.

6 Saint-Simon, Duc de: *Mémoires de Saint-Simon*, ed. A. de Boislisle (Paris, 1890), vol. VII, p.192.

7 Walpole, H.: *Anecdotes*, op. cit., p.241.

8 C. Plinius Secundus: *The Historie of the Worlde* (London, 1635), bk. XIX, chap. IV.

9 Walpole, H.: *Anecdotes*, op. cit., pp.268–9.

10 Haskell, Francis, and Penny, Nicholas: *Taste and the Antique* (Yale, 1988), pp.10, 25.

11 Ibid., p.80.

12 Walpole, H.: *Anecdotes*, op. cit., pp.239–40. Walpole was by no means the first to discover nature in Pliny; e.g., Robert Castell had done so in *Villas of the Ancients Illustrated* (The Author, London, 1728). The plan reconstructing Laurentinum (p.16) shows both formal areas and axially planned groves.

13 Orrery, Earl of: *Letters of Pliny*, op. cit., p.385.

14 Ibid., bk. II, Epistle XVII, p.162.

15 Walpole, H.: *Anecdotes*, op. cit., p.240; see Tacitus, bk. XV.

16 Quintus Horatius Flaccus: *The Odes, Epodes, & Cannae Seculare of Horace*, trans. Joseph Davidson (1746), bk. III, Ode XXII.

17 Alberti, L.B.: *Della Architettura*, op. cit., vol. I, bk. VI, p.6.

18 Switzer, Stephen: *Ichonographia Rustica* (London, 1718), vol. III, pp.6, 8.

19 De Jong, Erik: 'Virgilian Paradise: a Dutch Garden near Moscow in the Early 18th Century', *Journal of Garden History*, vol. 1, no. 4, p.323.

20 Nourse, Timothy: *Campania Faelix* (London, 1700), p.322.

21 De Jong, E.: 'Virgilian Paradise . . .', op. cit., p.332.

22 Walpole, H.: *Anecdotes*, op. cit., (Dallaway's addition), p.314.

23 Orrery, Earl of: *Letters of Pliny*, op. cit., bk. VIII, Epistle VIII, p.210.

24 Compare, for instance, with the figures that occur in the 1st century B.C. series depicting the *Odyssey*, from the Esquiline (Vatican, Museo Gregorio Profano). Magnasco, whose figures share similar characteristics, seems to imitate ancient handling of paint and landscape types.

25 Roethlisberger, Marcel: *Claude Lorrain: A Symposium*, ed. Pamela Askew, Studies in the History of Art, vol. 14 (National Gallery of Art, Washington: University Press of New England, 1984), p.63.

26 Ackermann, James: *The Villa* (Thames & Hudson, 1990), p.182.

27 Walpole, H.: *Anecdotes*, op. cit., p.249. He omitted the following line:
    And, to a superstitious eye, the haunt
    Of wood- gods and wood- nymphs.
Milton was not the only English 17th-century poet to anticipate 18th-century gardens. Much of the Capability Brown ideal resides in Marvell:
    The Stiffest Compass could not strike
    A Line more circular and like
    Nor softest Pensel draw a Brow
    So equal as this hill does now . . .
    See what a soft access and wide
    Lyes open to its grassy side . . .
    See then how courteous it ascends,
    And all the way it rises bends . . .
    Upon its crest this Mountain grave
    A Plump of aged trees does wave . . .
Marvell, Andrew: 'Upon the Hill and Grove at Bill-borow'. The editor (Dent, 1968) suggests 'clump' in place of 'Plump', another example of Brown's malign influence? Milton's descriptions were anticipated in 16th-century Italian painting; the landscape added by Titian to Bellini's *Feast of the Gods* (Frick Collection), no doubt meant to represent Mount Parnassus, parallels Milton's descriptions; the tradition revives in Keats and continues in Tennyson's 'Oenone'.

28 Walpole, H.: *Anecdotes*, op. cit., p.249. Significantly, Repton quoted the same passage from Tasso in his *Theory and Practice*, see *The Landscape Gardening and Landscape Architecture of the late Humphry Repton Esq.*, ed. J.C. Loudon (London, 1840), p.162.

29 Rousseau, Jean Jacques: *La Nouvelle Héloise* (1759).

30 Shaftesbury, Earl of: 'I shall no longer resist the Passion growing in me for things of a

natural kind. . . . Even the rude *Rocks*, the mossy *Caverns*, the irregular unwrought *Grotto's* and the broken *Falls* of waters, with all the horrid Graces of the *Wilderness* itself, as representing Nature more, will be the more engaging and appear with a Magnificence beyond the Mockery of Princely Gardens'. Quoted Christopher Hussey: *The Picturesque* (Putnam, 1927), p.56.

31 Wordsworth, William: 'The Prelude'.

32 Burke, Edmund: *Philosophical Enquiry into the Origin of our Ideas of the Sublime & The Beautiful*.

33 Walpole, H.: *Anecdotes*, op. cit., p.314.

34 Ibid., p.279.

35 Gilpin, Rev. William: *Forest Scenery*, ed. Francis Heath (London, 1879), pp.44–50.

36 Repton, Humphry: B.L.Add.Ms. 62112 1058 A., p.101.

37 Beckford, William: *Italy: With Sketches of Spain and Portugal* (London, 1834), vol. 1, pp.184, 300.

38 Walpole, H.: *Anecdotes*, op. cit., Dallaway note p.288.

39 Saint-Simon, Duc de: *Mémoires de Saint-Simon*, op. cit., vol. 28, p.162.

40 Laugier, Abbé: *Essaie sur l'Architecture* (Chez Duchesne, Paris, 1755), pp.236, 240.

41 Rogers, Samuel: *Recollections of the Table-Talk* (Edward Moxon, London, 1856), p.11.

42 Cleland, John: *Memoirs of Maria Brown* (1766, repr. Hamlyn, 1981), p.65.

43 Neale, J.P.: *Views of the Seats of Noblemen and Gentlemen* (W.H. Reid, London, 1818), vol. V, unpaginated.

44 Walpole, H.: *Anecdotes*, p.248.

45 Ibid., p.265.

46 Chambers, Sir William: *A Dissertation on Oriental Gardening* (1772, repr. Gregg, 1972), p.VII. On this page Chambers advocated what became the Regency synthesis: 'neither the artful nor the simple style of Gardening . . . is right: the one being too extravagant a deviation from nature; the other too scrupulous an adherence to her. One manner is absurd; the other insipid and vulgar: a judicious mixture of both would certainly be more perfect than either.'

47 Quoted B. Sprague Allan: *Tides in English Taste: A Background for the Study of Literature* (Harvard University Press, Cambridge, Mass., 1937), vol. 2, p.227.

48 Wordsworth, William: Introduction to 'Lyrical Ballads' (1801 edn.).

49 Walpole, H: *Anecdotes*, op. cit., pp.276, 278.

### CHAPTER TWO
### The 1790s: Associationalism and the Picturesque

1 Repton, Humphry: B.L.Add.Ms. 62112 1058 A., p.214.

2 His influence was not confined to his own times. Christopher Hussey, the historian of the Picturesque, described his theories as 'undeniably true' (*The Picturesque*; Putnam, 1927), p.15.

3 Alison, Archibald: *Essays on the Nature and Principles of Taste* (Edinburgh, 1825), 6th edn., vol. I., p.23.

4 Ibid., p.42.

5 Ibid., p.100.

6 Ibid., pp.43–4.

7 'I pre-attuned my feelings to emotion': Hussey, C.: *The Picturesque*, op. cit., p.127.

8 Manwaring, E.W.: *Italian Landscape in Eighteenth Century England* (Oxford University Press, 1925), p.127.

9 Oxford English Dictionary.

10 Christopher Wren, quoted by James Elmes: *Metropolitan Improvements* (London, 1829), p.32.

11 Alison, A.: *Essays*, op. cit., vol. 2, p.73.

12 Ibid., vol. 1, p.122.

13 Ibid., pp.76, 77.

14 Price, Uvedale: *Essays on the Picturesque* (J. Mawman, London, 1810), vol. 1, p.230.

15 Chambers, Sir William: *A Dissertation on Oriental Gardening* (1772, repr. Gregg, 1972), p.V.

16 Price, U.: *Essays*, op. cit., vol. I, p.246.

17 Ibid.: *Essay on Artificial Water*, vol. II, p.101.

18 Ibid.: *Essay on Artificial Water*, vol. II, p.39.

19 Ibid., vol. I, p.19.

20 Ibid., vol. I, p.125. The reproduction of Claude's *Liber Veritatis* in 1777 by Earlom made his compositions generally accessible. By the time of his death Payne Knight owned 250 Claude drawings.

21 Hogarth had played a part in drawing these qualities to notice.

22 Price, U.: *Essays*, op. cit., vol. I, p.266.

23 Gilpin, Rev. William: *Forest Scenery*, ed. Francis Heath (London, 1879), pp.114–18.

24 Alison, A.: *Essays*, op. cit., vol. I, p.248.

25 Pope, Alexander: 'Imitation of Cowley', line 13.

26 Price, U.: *Essays*, op. cit.: *Essay on Decorations near the House*, vol. II, p.111.

27 Ibid., vol. II, p.156.

28 Ibid., vol. II, p.182.

29 People became excessively nervous in the 1790s. Anna Seward described Knight's poem as 'the Jacobinism of taste' (as a friend of Repton, she was perhaps prejudiced). For Horace Walpole, Knight 'Jacobinically would level the purity of gardens, would as malignantly as Tom Paine or Priestley grill alive Mr. Brown' (quoted *The Arrogant Connoisseur*, ed. Michael Clarke and Nicholas Penny (Manchester University Press, 1982), p.10).

30 Price, U.: *Essays*, op. cit.: *Essay on Decorations near the House*, vol. II, pp.143–4.

31 Ibid., vol. II, p.125.

32 Ibid., vol. II, p.121.

33 Ibid., vol. II, p.112. Charles Percier and Pierre Fontaine commented: 'Les jardins d'Italie présentent le variété et le pittoresque des jardins modernes, sans avoir rien de leur monotone et puérile simplicité': *Choix des Plus Célèbres Maisons . . . de Rome* (Paris, 1809), p.3.

34 Price, U.: *Essays*, op. cit.: *Essay on Artificial Water*, vol. II, p.116.

35 Knight, Richard Payne: 'The Landscape, A Didactic Poem' (London, 1794), p.16.

36 Ibid., p.23.

37 Repton, Humphry: from *Sketches and Hints on Landscape Gardening (1795): The Landscape Gardening and Landscape Architecture of the late Humphry Repton Esq.*, ed. J.C. Loudon (London, 1840), p.99.

38 Knight, R.P.: 'The Landscape', op. cit., p.13.

39 Knight, Richard Payne: *An Analytical Enquiry into the Principles of Taste* (T. Payne & J. White, London, 1806), p.217.

40 Knight, R.P.: *Analytical Enquiry*, op. cit., p.223.

41 Ibid., p.225.

42 Clarke, M., and Penny, N.: *Arrogant Connoisseur*, op. cit., p.42.

43 Price, U.: *Essays*, op. cit.: *Essay on Architecture and Buildings*, vol. II, p.268.

44 Orrery, John, Earl of: *The Letters of Pliny the Younger* (London, 1751), bk. II, Epistle XVII, p.165.

45 Summerson, Sir John: *John Nash* (Allen & Unwin, 1980), p.21.

46 Owen, Felicity, and Brown, David Blayney: *Collector of Genius: A Life of Sir George Beaumont* (Yale University Press, 1988), p.100.

47 Quoted by Pevsner, Sir Nikolaus: *Studies in Art, Architecture & Design* (Thames & Hudson, 1968), p.79.

48 Quoted Dobrée, Bonamy: *Letters of Philip Dormer Stanhope, 4th Earl of Chesterfield* (London and New York, 1932), IV, p.159. Lord Chesterfield, 19 June 1750.

49 Quoted David Watkin: *The English Vision: The Picturesque in Architecture, Landscape and Garden Design* (Murray, 1982), p.91.

50 Reynolds, Sir Joshua; quoted J.C. Loudon: *An Encyclopaedia of Cottage, Farm and Villa Architecture and Furniture . . .* (London, 1857), pp.52–3.

51 Quoted James Elmes: *Metropolitan Improvements* (London, 1829), p.32.

52 This last idea is taken from Montesquieu's *Essay on Taste* (c.1750), a work influential during the Regency; it was from this source that Repton justified his argument for symmetry in flower gardens (Humphry Repton: *Sketches and Hints on Landscape Gardening*, op. cit., p.86). The Morris quotation is taken

from his *Lectures on Architecture*; quoted by Emil Kauffmann: *Architecture in the Age of Reason* (Harvard University Press, 1955), p.23.

53 Kauffmann, E.: *Architecture*, op. cit., p.24.

54 Ibid., p.65.

55 Plaw, John: *Sketches for Country Houses* (Printed W. Stratford for J. Taylor, London, 1800): quoted ibid., p.64.

56 Gandy, Joseph: *Designs for Cottages, Cottage Farms, and other Rural Buildings* (London, 1805), p.IX.

57 Knight, R.P.: *Analytical Enquiry*, op. cit., p.167.

58 Stroud, Dorothy: *Humphry Repton* (Country Life, 1962), p.67.

59 On the title page of the 1818 book of Wyatville designs. Quoted Derek Linstrum: *Sir Jeffry Wyatville* (Clarendon Press, 1972), p.142.

60 Repton, Humphry: *Fragments on the Theory and Practice of Landscape Gardening (1816): The Landscape Gardening and Landscape Architecture of the late Humphry Repton Esq.*, ed. Loudon (London, 1840), p.501.

61 Owen, F., and Brown, D.B.: *Collector of Genius*, op. cit., p.120.

62 Pliny had a 'little garden apartment, which I own is my delight. In truth it is my mistress: I built it; and in it is a particular kind of hot-house, which looks on one side towards the terrace, on the other towards the sea, but on both sides has the advantage of the sun. . . . On the side next the sea, . . . is an elegant little closet: separated only by transparent windows, and a curtain, which can be opened or shut at pleasure, from the room just mentioned.' Orrery's note equates the transparent windows and curtain with modern glass doors: Orrery, Earl of: *Letters of Pliny*, op. cit., bk. II, Epistle XVII, p.167.

## CHAPTER THREE
## Eclecticism

1 Peacock, Thomas Love: *Melincourt* (1818; Macmillan, London, 1896), chap. IV, pp.33–4.

2 See Donald Pilcher: *The Regency Style* (Batsford, 1947), p.21. This short book contains an acute analysis of the period.

3 Trusler, Dr. John: *Practical Husbandry . . . Elements of Modern Gardening* (London, 1790), pp.3, 6, 8.

4 Repton, Humphry: *Sketches and Hints on Landscape Gardening (1795): The Landscape Gardening and Landscape Architecture of the late Humphry Repton Esq.*, ed. J.C. Loudon (London, 1840), p.112: 'I should doubt the taste of any improver, who could despise the congruity, the utility, the order, and the symmetry of the small garden at Trinity College, Oxford, because the clipped hedges

and straight walks would not look well in a picture'.

5 The term 'landscape' first appeared in the late 16th or early 17th century to describe painted scenery; in Milton's 'L'Allegro' the word was used to describe real scenery that appealed in the same way as did a picture; see Nikolaus Pevsner: *Studies in Art, Architecture and Design* (Thames & Hudson, 1968), p.86. Landscape painting was reputed to have been invented by Aeschylus as scenery.

6 Quoted Dorothy Stroud: *Humphry Repton* (Country Life, 1962), pp.28–9.

7 Quoted from the biographical notice written for J.C. Loudon's edn. of *The Landscape Gardening and Landscape Architecture of the late Humphry Repton Esq.*, op. cit., p.6.

8 Repton, Humphry: 'Letter to Uvedale Price Esq', 1794: *The Landscape Gardening and Landscape Architecture of the late Humphry Repton Esq.*, ed. Loudon, op. cit., p.104.

9 From a letter of David Malthus: '. . . I have been often so much disgusted by the affected and technical language of connoisseurship, that I have been sick of pictures for a month, and almost of Nature . . .'. He said that Price and Knight were more like Luther and Calvin than two West Country gentlemen, and would have 'broiled poor Brown'; see D. Stroud: *Humphry Repton*, op. cit., p.91. Knight adjured Repton to take a title more descriptive of his profession than that of landscape architect, 'such as that of walk-maker, shrub-planter, turf cleaner, or rural perfumer' (note to the 2nd edn. of Knight's poem 'The Landscape').

10 Britton, John: *The Auto-biography of John Britton* (London, 1850), vol. I, p.169.

11 Repton, H.: 'A Letter to Uvedale Price Esq': *The Landscape Gardening and Landscape Architecture of the late Humphry Repton Esq.*, ed. Loudon, op. cit., p.104.

12 Ibid., pp.115–16.

13 See J.C. Loudon: *A Treatise on the Improvements proposed for Scone:* Muniments of Earl of Mansfield, National Register of Archives, Edinburgh.

14 Repton, H.: *Sketches and Hints* (1795): *The Landscape Gardening and Landscape Architecture of the late Humphry Repton Esq.*, ed. Loudon, op. cit., p.101.

15 Ibid., p.112.

16 Ibid., p.39.

17 Ibid., p.84.

18 Ibid., p.99.

19 Ibid., p.39.

20 See Marilyn Butler: *Peacock Displayed* (Routledge Kegan Paul, London, 1979). Mrs. Butler says that Peacock's method involves not a parody of individuals but the use of their ideas in the form of Socratic dialogue. The

distinction is fine, and ideas never call for more Madeira.

21 Repton, H.: *Sketches and Hints* (1795), ed. Loudon, op. cit., p.92. One aspect of the Picturesque placed it low in the social hierarchy; e.g. Sydney Smith's remark: 'The Vicar's house is beautiful, the Curate's picturesque'; quoted Christopher Hussey: *The Picturesque* (Putnam, 1927), p.119.

22 B.L. Add. Ms. 62112 1058 A, p.27.

23 Repton, Humphry: *Observations on the Theory and Practice of Landscape Gardening (1803): The Landscape Gardening and Architecture of the late Humphry Repton Esq.*, ed. J.C. Loudon, op. cit., p.238.

24 Ibid., pp.234, 235.

25 'Regularity in that part of a garden which is adjacent to the dwelling-house' and inter-connected small gardens 'so arranged as to inspire all the different emotions that can be raised by gardening' were advocated by Lord Kames: *Elements of Criticism* (1762), a source often quoted by Repton. See G. Carter, P. Goode, K. Laurie: *Humphry Repton Landscape Gardener*, London and Norwich Exhibition (Sainsbury Centre and Victoria & Albert Museum, 1982), p.56.

26 Repton, H.: *Sketches and Hints*, ed. Loudon, op. cit., p.86.

27 Repton, H.: *Observations*, ed. Loudon, op. cit., p.234.

28 Ibid., pp.214–16.

29 One of Percier's illustrations to Didot's Horace, a book that influenced Hope, shows as a re-creation of Roman life an enchanting terrace, with treillage, steps, a Reptonian basket full of grapes, a vase and pot: see *Quinti Horatii Flacci Opera* (Didot, 1799), p.263.

30 Illustrated Charles Percier and Pierre Fontaine: *Choix des Plus Célèbres Maisons de Plaisance de Rome* (Paris, 1809), Pl. 6: 'Vue de la Fontaine et de la Grotte des Potagers de la Villa Albani'.

31 Price, Uvedale: *Essays on the Picturesque: Essay on Decorations near the House* (J. Mawman, London, 1810), vol. 2, p.143. Fashion had not banished trellis from wall decoration; the French or French-inspired arabesque of the 1780s often shows it (e.g. the murals by Valdrès in the Music Room at Stowe, c.1780).

32 Repton, H.: *Observations*, ed. Loudon, op. cit., p.257.

33 Ibid., p.258.

34 Loudon, J.C.: *An Encyclopaedia of Cottage, Farm and Villa Architecture and Furniture* (London, 1857), p.996.

35 Pevsner, Sir Nikolaus: *Studies in Art, Architecture and Design* (Thames & Hudson, 1968), p.152.

36 Repton, H.: *Fragments on the Theory and Practice of Landscape Gardening* (1816, original edn.), p.6.

37 Ibid., p.100.

38 Ibid., p.225.

39 From the Honing Hall Red Book, c.1790; quoted D. Stroud: *Humphry Repton*, op. cit., p.66.

40 Repton, H.: *Sketches and Hints*, ed. Loudon, op. cit., p.95.

41 Ibid., p.64.

42 Ibid., p.104.

43 Repton, H.: *Fragments on the Theory and Practice of Landscape Gardening* (1816, original edn.), p.48.

44 Ibid.

45 Repton, H.: *Fragments* (1816), ed. Loudon, op. cit., p.533.

46 Repton, H.: *Sketches and Hints*, ed. Loudon, op. cit., p.52.

47 B.L. Add. Ms. 62112, 1058 A, p.85.

48 Clifford, Derek: *A History of Garden Design* (Faber & Faber, 1966), pp.164, 165.

49 Ibid., p.184. He lists Curtis's *Botanical Magazine*; Andrews' *Botanists' Repository*; Andrews' monograph on Heaths and Sweet's on *Geraneaceae* as typical.

50 Loudon, J.C.: *The Landscape Gardening*, ed. Loudon, op. cit., p.IX.

51 Loudon, J.C.: *The Gardener's Magazine* (8 Dec. 1832), p.701.

52 Hope, Thomas: *Essay on Gardening*, as transcribed by Mrs. Hofland: *A Descriptive Account of the Mansion and Garden of White-Knights* (London, 1819), p.8.

53 Biver, M.-L.: *Pierre Fontaine* (Librairie Plon, Paris, 1964), p.204: 'De leurs études des palais romains et des villas édifiées dans la campagne, ils rapportent en France l'amour des jeux d'eau, des terrasses fleuries, des escaliers extérieurs, de la polychromie, des plantes grimpantes . . .'.

54 Loudon, J.C.: *Encyclopaedia*, op. cit., p.784.

55 Edgeworth, Maria: *Life and Letters*, ed. Augustus Hare (E. Arnold, London, 1894), vol. 1., p.268, 28 April 1819.

56 Keats, John: 'Hyperion' (c.1818–20).

57 See Alison Kelly: 'Coade Stone in Georgian Gardens', *Garden History*, vol. 16, no. 1 (Spring 1988), pp.111–30.

58 Meason, Gilbert Laing: *The Landscape Architecture of the Great Painters of Italy* (C. Hullmandel, London, 1828), p.61.

59 Percier, Charles, and Fontaine, Pierre: *Recueil des Décorations Intérieures* (P. Didot, Paris, 1812), p.2: 'Le génie de Raphael ne se fait-il pas remarquer dans tous les objets d'ornement qui reçurent son influence?'

60 Loudon, J.C.: *Encyclopaedia*, op. cit., p.771.

61 In 'Review of the Planter's Guide by Sir Henry Steuart', *Quarterly Review*, LXXIV (1828), p.305.

62 Ibid., p.309.

63 B.L. Add. Ms. 62112 1058 A, p.216. A

complete illustrated account of Repton and Nash's garden designs for the Pavilion is given in the author's *The Making of The Royal Pavilion* (Sotheby, 1984).

64 Kelly, Alison: 'Coade Stone', op. cit., p.111.

65 *Windsor and Eton Express*: 7 Aug. 1830.

66 Letter from Princess Augusta to Lord and Lady Arran 13 Sept. 1826: in a collection of extracts in the Royal Library, made by Sir Owen Morshead, from which the *Windsor and Eton Express* references are also drawn.

67 *Windsor and Eton Express*: 6 Sept. 1828.

68 Scott-Elliot, A.H.: 'The Statues by Francavilla in the Royal Collection', *Burlington Magazine* (March 1956), p.78. Statues by Francavilla, like paintings by Bronzino, often have a proto neo-classical look (the Windsor statues were restored in 1856).

69 *Windsor and Eton Express*: 14 Sept. and 13 Oct. 1829.

70 Meason, G.L.: *The Landscape Architecture*, op. cit., p.74.

71 Simo, M.L.: *Loudon and the Landscape* (Yale, 1988), pp.51–2.

72 Price, U.: *Essays*, op. cit., vol. I, p.50; vol. II, *Essay on Architecture and Buildings*, p.329.

73 Austen, Jane: *Sanditon* (Peter Daniels, 1975), p.22. (This passage is part of Jane Austen's original text.)

74 Pilcher, D.: *Regency Style*, op. cit., p.43

75 Britton, John: *Graphical and Literary Illustrations of Fonthill Abbey* (Printed for the author, London, 1823), p.32.

76 Loudon, J.C.: *The Landscape Gardening*, op. cit., p.VI.

77 Of the rustic seats and summer houses: 'I well remember Mr. Papworth stating that they were his designs': Papworth, Wyatt: *J.B. Papworth* (Privately printed, London, 1879), p.381.

78 Many Regency cognoscenti would have recognised a possible antique source in the fragment of a Roman tomb in the Via Asinari, illustrated by Pietro Santi Bartoli in *Gli Antichi Sepolcri*, which might also have served as a source for Bramante's first post-antique revival of associated sculptures and fountains in the Belvedere. See Georgina Masson: *Italian Gardens* (Antique Collectors Club, 1987), p.127.

79 Papworth, J.B.: *Hints on Ornamental Gardening* (London, 1823), p.84.

80 Hofland, Mrs.: *A Descriptive Account*, op. cit., pp.50–99.

81 See J.C. Loudon: *Gardeners' Magazine* (London, 1839), pp.637–72.

82 Repton, H.: *Sketches and Hints*, ed. Loudon, op. cit., p. 80.

83 Pilcher, D.: *Regency Style*, op. cit., p.34.

84 B.L. Add. Ms. 62112 1058 A., p.25.

85 Loudon, Jane: *A Short Account of the Life and Writings of John Claudius Loudon*, repr. by John Gloag in *Mr. Loudon's England* (Oriel Press, 1970), p.189. Loudon had been influenced by Goethe's colour theories, as were Regency decorators (see David Hay: *Laws of Harmonious Colouring Adapted to House Painting*, Edinburgh, 1829; Hay, unlike Loudon, realised that the direct union of opposites was disagreeable, and recommended a third, harmonising colour).

86 Chevalier Charles Sckell, Director General of Gardens in the Kingdom of Bavaria (1833). Quoted Miles Hadfield: *Landscape with Trees* (Country Life, 1967), pp.133–4.

87 Hofland, Mrs.: *A Descriptive Account*, op. cit., p.35.

88 Harding, John: *Hints on the Formation of Gardens and Pleasure Grounds* (1812), unpaginated, pl. 14.

89 Repton, H.: *Observations*, ed. Loudon, op. cit., p.260.

90 Repton, H.: *Fragments*, ed. Loudon, op. cit., p.567.

91 Repton, H.: *Observations*, ed. Loudon, op. cit., p.212.

CHAPTER FOUR
## Garden Buildings and Furnishings

1 Cotton, Charles: *The Wardens of the Rock* (1681); quoted Christopher Hussey: *The Picturesque* (Putnam, 1927), pp.25–6.

2 Browne, Sir Thomas: 'The Garden of Cyrus' from *The Religio Medici amd other Writings* (Dent, 1952), p.169.

3 Kauffmann, Emil: *Architecture in the Age of Reason* (Harvard University Press, 1955), p.104.

4 Watkin, David: *The English Vision: The Picturesque in Architecture, Landscape and Garden Design* (Murray, 1982), p.23.

5 See David Watkin: *Athenian Stuart* (Allen & Unwin, 1982).

6 Loudon, J.C.: *Encyclopaedia of Cottage, Farm & Villa Architecture and Furniture* (London, 1857), pp.996–7.

7 Prospectus issued by James Anderton, Solicitor to the Society forwarding the project: *Proposed Plan for a Grand National Cemetery, 15 March 1830*, V. & A., 1980 93H 138, p.211.

8 Jones, Barbara: *Follies and Grottoes* (Constable, 1974), pp.31–3.

9 Watkin, D.: *The English Vision*, op. cit., p.45.

10 Hazlitt, W., on Claude: quoted E.W. Manwaring: *Italian Landscape in Eighteenth-Century England* (Oxford University Press, 1925), p.43.

11 The proposal in the 1960s by the government historic buildings department to remove the houses built into the West Front of Bury St. Edmunds Abbey showed how far knowledge of, and feeling for, the Picturesque and aesthetic associationalism had faded.

12 Pilcher, Donald: *The Regency Style* (Batsford, 1947), p.3.

13 Knight, Richard Payne: *An Analytical Enquiry into the Principles of Taste* (T. Payne & J. White, London, 1806), p.170.

14 Soane, Sir John: *Lectures on Architecture*, ed. Arthur Bolton (Soane Museum, 1929), Lect. X., p.152.

15 Ibid., p.154.

16 Quoted David Watkin: *The English Vision*, op. cit., p.45.

17 Knapp, J.L.: Ms. 'Sketch of a Tour', unpaginated; Derby Reference Library. Dated by reference to 'dethronement of his Sardinian Majesty'.

18 Pilcher, D.: *Regency Style*, op. cit., p.8.

19 Lugar, Robert: *Architectural Sketches for Cottages, Rural Dwellings . . .* (T. Bensley for J. Taylor, London, 1805), text to pl. VIII.

20 'Eaton Park, Chester', *Garden History Society Journal* (Autumn 1985), pp.130–31.

21 Ibid., p.131.

22 Pückler-Muskau, Prince: *Tour of a German Prince* (London, 1832), vol. III, p.237.

23 Knight, R.P.: *Analytical Enquiry*, op. cit., p.224.

24 Watkin, David: *Thomas Hope and the Neo-classical Idea* (Murray, 1968), p.154.

25 See Bernard Smith: *European Vision and the South Pacific* (Clarendon Press, 1960). p.244.

26 Ibid., p.26; the quotation is from the *Analytical Review* of 1801.

27 Trusler, Dr. John: *Practical Husbandry . . . Elements of Modern Gardening* (London, 1790), p.58.

28 See Sir Nikolaus Pevsner: *Studies in Art, Architecture and Design* (Thames & Hudson, 1968), p.233.

29 Manwaring, E.W.: *Italian Landscape in Eighteenth-Century England* (Oxford University Press, 1925), p.144.

30 Alison, A.: *Essays on the Nature and Principles of Taste* (Edinburgh, 1825), p.322.

31 Chambers, Sir William: *A Dissertation on Oriental Gardening* (1772, repr. Gregg, 1972), p.15.

32 See Patrick Conner: 'The Chinese Garden in Regency England', *Garden History Society Journal* (Spring 1986), pp.42–3.

33 E.g. *Le Pitture Antiche d'Ercolano* (Naples, 1757), vol. I, pl. X, p.49.

34 Conner, Patrick: *Oriental Architecture in the West* (Thames & Hudson, 1979), p.73.

35 Conner, P.: 'The Chinese Garden . . .', op. cit., p.44.

36 Ibid.

37 Robertson, William: *Designs in Architecture for garden chairs, small gates for villas, park*

*entrances, aviarys* . . . (Bulmer & Co., London, 1800), pl. 1.

38 Papworth, J.B.: *Rural Residences* . . . (Ackermann, London, 1818), p.101.

39 Harris, Eileen, and Savage, Nicholas: *British Architectural Books and Writers 1556-1785* (Cambridge University Press, 1990), p.336.

40 Hope's umbrella or parasol was taken from d'Hancarville's *Antiquités Etrusques, Grecques et Romaines* (Paris, 1785), vol. 3, pl. 35.

41 From: *Le Pitture Antiche d'Ercolano* (Naples, 1765), vol. IV, pl. XXII.

42 Papworth, J.B.: *Hints on Ornamental Gardening* (Ackermann, London, 1823), p.101.

43 Ireland's Royal Grounds: Brighton Reference Library grangerised Erridge, vol. 7, f.116.

44 Papworth, J.B.: *Hints*, op. cit., p.53. (The text for the plate illustrated, pl. V, has been misplaced and attached to pl. XIX.)

45 Lever, Jill: *Architects' Designs for Furniture* (Trefoil, London, 1982), p.71.

46 R.I.B.A. Drawings Collection (catalogued as a chimney-piece).

47 Papworth, J.B.: *Hints*, op. cit., p.100.

48 Illustrated John Morley: *Designs and Drawings: The Making of the Royal Pavilion* (Sotheby, 1984), pl. 32.

49 Lugar, Robert: *Architectural Sketches for Cottages*, op. cit., p.3.

50 Robertson, W.: *Designs in Architecture*, op. cit., pl. 15.

51 Masson, Georgina: *Italian Gardens* (Thames & Hudson, 1987), p.20.

52 Richardson, George: *New Designs in Architecture* (printed for the author, London, 1792).

53 Repton, Humphry: *Observations on the Theory and Practice of Landscape Gardening (1803): The Landscape Gardening and Landscape Architecture of the late Humphry Repton Esq.*, ed. J.C. Loudon (London, 1840), p.217.

54 Repton, Humphry: *Fragments on the Theory and Practice of Landscape Gardening (1816): The Landscape Gardening and Landscape Architecture of the late Humphry Repton Esq.*, ed. J.C. Loudon (London, 1840), pp.455-6.

55 Repton, H.: *Observations*, ed. Loudon, op. cit., p.218.

56 There is a contradiction in the representations of the building; J.B. Pipre's interior (W.H. Pyne: *Royal Residences*, London, 1819) shows apparently stone columns. The building gave some trouble: 'The gothic conservatory is covered with glass and without constant attention and continual repair the water cannot be kept out and the profuse enrichments of the ceiling being all of plaster and undefended from wet, but by the glass roof is continually going to decay & falling down . . . as a conservatory the glass roof is not of any use being almost wholly covered with plaster moulding leaving but small perforations for light . . . it is worse than useless . . .'. The buttresses, pinnacles, battlements and mouldings, all in 'Parker's cement', had decayed by 1822. P.R.O. Works 19 11/5; second folder 2.f.45.

57 Repton, H.: *Observations*, ed. Loudon, op. cit., p.217.

58 Papworth, J.B.: *Rural Residences*, op. cit., p.86.

59 Quoted by John Gloag: *Mr. Loudon's England* (Oriel Press, 1970), p.48.

60 Loudon, J.C.: *An Encyclopedia of Cottage, Farm and Villa Architecture and Furniture* (London, 1857), p.980.

61 In 1968, when the author first saw this area in Brighton, it was a Regency paradise. Neglect, injudicious demolition and building, the construction of a car park in place of a wild garden, the destruction of the back of Wilds' house by a department store, have almost destroyed it, although much is retrievable. It is in a 'conservation area'.

62 Pückler-Muskau, Prince: *Tour*, op. cit., vol. III, p.241.

63 This and following quotations are taken from the Rev. Richard Warner: *A tour through the Northern Counties* (Cruttwell, Bath, 1802), pp.173-7.

64 Pückler–Muskau, Prince: *Tour*, op. cit., vol. III, p.247.

65 This and following quotations are taken from J.C. Loudon: *Encyclopaedia*, op. cit., pp.784-9.

66 Stoddard, Sheena: *Mr. Braikenridge's Bristol* (City of Bristol, 1981), pp.38, 39.

CHAPTER FIVE
## Town and Village Planning

1 Quoted Gillian Darley: *Villages of Vision* (Architectural Press, 1975), pp.7, 8.

2 Youngson, J.: *The Making of Classical Edinburgh 1750–1840* (Edinburgh University Press, 1966), p.151.

3 Ibid.

4 From *Critical Observations*, 1771, quoted B. Sprague Allen: *Tides in English Taste: A Background for the Study of Literature* (Harvard University Press, 1937), vol. II, p.222 (now attrib. John Stewart).

5 Alberti, Leon Battista: *Della Architettura*, trans. Giacomo Leoni (London, 1739), bk. IV, p.70.

6 Reynolds, Sir Joshua: Thirteenth Discourse, 11 Dec. 1786.

7 Elsam, Richard: *Hints for improving the condition of the peasantry* (Ackermann, London, 1816), p.24.

8 Price, Uvedale: *Essays on the Picturesque: Essay on Architecture* (J. Mawman, London, 1810), p.346.

9 Elsam, Richard: *Hints on improving*, op. cit., p.21.

10 It was preceded by that of the Prince de Condé at Chantilly (1775), of the Duc d'Orléans at Roncy, and paralleled in 1783 by that of Mme. Elizabeth and the Comtesse de Provence at Montreuil. See Léon Rey: *Le Petit Trianon et le Hameau de Marie Antoinette* (Paris, 1936), p.408. Designed by Mique, the buildings of the Hameau may have been influenced by Hubert Robert. Robert had worked at Ermenonville, designed by Gérardin (who had visited The Leasowes in the 1760s), and at Méréville, designed by Belanger, who had filled a sketch book with famous English gardens.

11 Darley, G.: *Villages of Vision*, op. cit., p.39.

12 Demolished by the Leamington city fathers in about 1960.

13 Gilpin, W.S.: *Picturesque Beauty* (1776); quoted R. Butchart: *Prints and Drawings of Edinburgh* (Edinburgh, 1955), p.25.

14 In James Craig's 1786 'Plan for Improving the city of Edinburgh' quoted J. Youngson: *Making of Classical Edinburgh*, op. cit., p.119.

15 Browne, James: *Picturesque Views of Edinburgh* (Daniel Lizars, 1825), pp.v & vii.

16 Youngson, J.: *Making of Classical Edinburgh*, op. cit., p.95,

17 Ibid., pp.149-52.

18 Ibid., pp.142-3.

19 Shepherd, Thomas: *Modern Athens* (Jones & Co., Finsbury Square, 1829), p.v.

20 Ibid., p.75.

21 Harding, John: *Hints on the Formation of Gardens and Pleasure Grounds* (London, 1812), p.IX.

22 Granville, A.B., M.D., F.R.S.: *Spas of England* (London, 1841), p.223.

23 Warwick County Record Office C.R. 1247/2, 1247/3, 1247/4.

24 One reason for the failure was probably that 'the bulk of the actual development was undertaken by tradesmen and artisans . . . the outstanding feature was the shortness of their horizons and the smallness of their ambitions . . .': C.J. Armison: *The Speculative Development of Leamington Spa* (University of Leicester, 1980), p.140.

25 See John Britton: *Descriptive Sketches of Tunbridge Wells* (London, 1832), p.VII.

26 Miller, Philip: *Decimus Burton*, exhibition catalogue (Eyre & Spottiswoode, 1981), p.22.

27 It had until very recently; they have now disappeared.

## Part II: Exterior Architecture
CHAPTER ONE
## Formative Influences

1 Soane, Sir John: *Lectures on Architecture*, ed. Arthur Bolton (Soane Museum, 1929), Lect. I, p.16. The imaginative use of rules was a commonplace of antiquity, often repeated by moderns. As Clérisseau put it: 'Apprenons

donc des Anciens les règles . . . apprenons aussi à sommettre les règles mêmes au génie': *Antiquités de la France* (Paris, 1778), part I, p. XII. The assertion of many modern architects that ancient motifs become useless for modern purposes would have seemed feeble and ignorant.

2 Ibid., pp.16, 21.

3 Watkin, David: *The Life and Work of C.R. Cockerell R.A.* (Zwemmer, 1974), p.117.

4 Ibid., p.61.

5 *The Farington Diary*, ed. James Grieg (Hutchinson, 1923), vol. II, pp.209, 217.

6 See R. Wittkower: *Architectural Principles in the Age of Humanism* (Norton, U.S.A., 1971); after mentioning Alison and Knight, the author says (p.155): 'Within the terms of a new conception of the world the whole structure of classical aesthetics was systematically broken up, and in this process man's vision underwent a decisive change. Proportion became a matter of individual sensibility and in this respect the architect acquired complete freedom from the bondage of mathematical ratios'.

7 Jameson, Mrs.: *Companion to the most celebrated Private Galleries of Art in London* (London, 1844), p.XXXI.

8 Stuart, James, and Revett, Nicholas: *Antiquities of Athens*, ed. J. Woods (London, 1816), vol. 4, p.XXVII.

9 Chambers, Sir William: *A Treatise on the Decorative Part of Civil Architecture* (1759), ed. Joseph Gwilt (London, 1825), vol. 1, p.231.

10 His theories were anticipated in Cordemoy's *Nouveau Traité de toute l'architecture* of 1708; he refers to Cordemoy in his text.

11 Laugier, Abbé: *Essaie sur L'Architecture* (Chez Duschesne, Paris, 1755), pp.xl–xlii.

12 Laugier, Abbé: *Observations sur l'Architecture* (The Hague and Paris, 1765), p.84.

13 This was not new; it is found in Vitruvius, and Alberti said: 'Nature at first certainly gave us Columns made of Wood, and of a round figure, afterwards by use they came in some places to be cut square . . .', *Della Architettura*, trans. Giacomo Leoni (London, 1739), bk. I, p.14.

14 Laugier, Abbé: *Essaie*, op. cit., p.13.

15 Ibid., pp.23–4.

16 Ibid., p.21.

17 Ibid., p.17.

18 Ibid., pp.29–30.

19 Desgodetz, A.: *Les Edifices Antiques de Rome dessinés et mesurés très exactement* (J.B. Coignard, Paris, 1682), p.66.

20 Alberti, Leon Battista: *Della Architettura*, trans. Giacomo Leoni (London, 1739). vol. II, bk. VI, pp.2, 3, bk. VI, p.20. See also R. Wittkower: *Architectural Principles*, op. cit., pp.33–5.

21 Columns were of course used in a 'Laugierian' way before Laugier: every traveller to Rome saw Bernini's Piazza di San Pietro, and in London some of Hawksmoor's churches curiously anticipate French Romantic Classicism.

22 In the Soane Museum: *Hypnerotomachie . . . de Poliphile* (Paris, 1651), p.17.

23 Laugier, Abbé: *Essaie*, op. cit., p.32.

24 Ibid., p.37.

25 Ibid., p.77.

26 Soane, Sir John: *Lectures*, op. cit., p.6.

27 Milízia, Francesco: *Lives of Celebrated Architects*, trans. Mrs. Edw. Cresy (1826), pp.XXVI, XLix, Iiii.

28 Chambers, Sir William: *A Treatise*, op. cit., vol. II, p.313.

29 Laugier, Abbé: *Essaie*, op. cit., p.56.

30 Laugier, Abbé: *Observations*, op. cit., p.265.

31 Kauffmann, Emil: *Architecture in the Age of Reason* (Harvard University Press, 1955), p.4.

32 Ibid., p.25.

33 Chambers, Sir William: A *Treatise*, op. cit., p.xlv; memoir by Thomas Hardwick.

34 Pevsner, Sir Nikolaus: *Studies in Art, Architecture and Design* (Thames & Hudson, 1968), p.175.

35 Ibid., p.206.

36 Klingender, F. D.: *Art and the Industrial Revolution* (Carrington, 1947), p.65.

37 Colvin, Howard: *Biographical Dictionary of British Architects 1600–1840* (Murray, 1978), p.586.

38 Pevsner, Sir Nikolaus: *Studies*, op. cit., p.175.

39 Chambers, Sir William: *A Treatise*, op. cit., vol. I, p.93.

40 Summerson, Sir John: *Architecture in Britain 1530–1830* (Penguin, 1986), p.482.

41 *Journal of Elizabeth, Lady Holland*, 29 Aug. 1799 (Longmans Green & Co., 1908), vol. II, p.3.

42 Summerson, Sir John: *Architecture in Britain 1530–1830* (Penguin, 1986), p.479.

43 Watkin, D.: *C. R. Cockerell*, op. cit., pp.111–12.

44 R.I.B.A. Drawings Collection.

45 Alberti, much admired by Cockerell, had praised the use of large stones, and gave advice on moving them: see *Della Architettura*, op. cit., vol. II, bk. VI, pp.8–9.

46 Stuart, J., and Revett, N.: *Antiquities of Athens*, ed. W. Reveley (London, 1794), vol. 3, p.IX.

47 Wood, Robert: *Ruins of Baalbec* (London, 1757), pl. XXII.

48 Watkin, D.: *C. R. Cockerell*, op. cit., p.66.

49 Ibid., p.111.

50 Foulston, John: *Public Buildings erected in the West of England* (London, 1838), pl. 80.

51 Dallaway, J.: *Observations on English Architecture* (J. Taylor, London, 1806), p.216.

52 A good description is given in the *Report on Buckingham Palace and Windsor Castle* (Parliamentary Papers P.R.O., vol. 16, pp.272–3). Nash recommended three coats; the first, of tar and chalk, remains elastic; the second was the same, with coarse sand added, to harden it; the third was slates, bedded in whilst boiling hot. This, Nash said, was the most economical covering devised, which he had used for 35 years, and 'at the Pavilion in Brighton, where the work had been done twelve years . . . the water has never penetrated'. He omitted to say that in 1822 the King had been so annoyed by water penetration that Nash dared not appear before him (see John Morley: *Designs and Drawings: The Making of the Royal Pavilion* (Sotheby, 1984, pp.71–2). The culprit may have been Hamlin's mastic; in 1827 the pagoda roofs had to be sheathed in copper, which much altered the effect of the building.

53 Brockman, H. A. N.: *The Caliph of Fonthill* (Werner Laurie, 1956), p.182.

54 Watkin, D.: *C. R. Cockerell*, op. cit., p.68.

55 Pasley, Sir Charles: *Observations on limes, calcareous cements etc.* (London, 1838), pp.12, 181.

56 Hardcastle, Ephraim: *Wine and Walnuts* (Longman, London, 1823), vol. I, p.289.

57 Klingender, F. D.: *Art and the Industrial Revolution*, op. cit., p.108.

58 Ibid.

59 *The Reading Mercury*, 2 April 1826.

60 Meason, Gilbert Laing: *The Landscape Architecture of the Great Painters of Italy* (C. Hullmandel, London, 1828), pp.67–8.

61 Reynolds, Sir Joshua: *The Discourses* (Oxford University Press, 1907), pp.207, 208.

62 Price, Uvedale: *Essays on the Picturesque: Essay on Architecture* (J. Mawman, London, 1810), pp.212, 214.

63 Knight, Richard Payne: *An Analytical Enquiry into the Principles of Taste* (T. Payne & J. White, London, 1806), p.227.

64 Soane, Sir John: *Lectures*, op. cit., Lect. V, p.90.

65 Ibid., Lect. XI, p.175.

66 Price. U.: *Essays*, op. cit., p.221.

67 Knight, R. P.: *Analytical Enquiry*, op. cit., p.160.

68 Ibid., p.225. Presumably Knight would have approved of the Gothic Old St. Paul's with its splendid Corinthian portico added by Inigo Jones.

## CHAPTER TWO
### The Sources of Architectural Vocabulary

1 Invaluable detail as given in John Archer: *The Literature of British Domestic Architecture* (MIT Press, Mass. and London, 1985).

2 Ibid., p.837. The plates are dated up to 1817.

3 Ibid., p.486.

4 Soane, Sir John: *Lectures on Architecture*, ed.

Arthur Bolton (Soane Museum, 1929), Lect. III, p.56.

5 Tatham, C. H. 27 July 1796: Letters and Drawings, V. & A.

6 Milizia, Francesco: *Lives of Celebrated Architects*, trans. Mrs. Edw. Cresy (1826), bk. II.

7 Harris, Eileen, and Savage, Nicholas: *British Architectural Books and Writers, 1556–1785* (Cambridge University Press, 1990), p.352.

8 Archer, J.: *Literature of British Domestic Architecture*, op. cit., p.24.

9 Chambers, Sir William: *A Treatise on the Decorative Part of Civil Architecture*, Joseph Gwilt (1825 edn.), p.XV.

10 Soane, Sir John: *Lectures*, op. cit., Lect. III, p.56.

11 See, for example, the catalogue of the Kissner Collection of books on Rome: Christie's 1990.

12 Kauffmann, Emil: *Architecture in the Age of Reason* (Harvard University Press, 1955), p.210.

13 Hitchcock, Henry-Russell: *Architecture in the Nineteenth and Twentieth Centuries* (Penguin, 1958), pp.21, 432.

14 Dubut, L. A.: *Architecture Civile* (Paris, 1803), unpaginated.

15 Ibid.

16 Smirke, Robert: *Specimens of Continental Architecture* (London, 1806).

17 A book of 26 drawings by Gandy (1825) illustrating various styles (V. & A. Print Room 93 B 18) includes, besides Greek, Roman and Egyptian, the 'Hindoo' and the 'Mahomedan Hindoo' (differentiated); 'Alambra' or 'Arabian'; 'Anglo Norman called Saxon'; 'Wyckham Style' (13th & 14th centuries); 'Burgundian style Rouen'; Turkish and Henry VIII, etc. As the fishing fraternity express it, 'fine mixed feeding'.

18 Repton, Humphry: *Sketches and Hints on Landscape Gardening: The Landscape Gardening and Landscape Architecture of the late Humphry Repton Esq. (1795)* ed. J. C. Loudon (London, 1840), p.53.

19 Soane, Sir John: *Lectures*, op. cit., Lect. XI, p.171.

20 Watkin, David: *The Life and Work of C. R. Cockerell R. A.* (Zwemmer, 1974), p.60.

21 Pergolesi, Michelangelo: *Pergolesi Designs* (M. Dulouchamp, 1801). Pergolesi had worked for Adam.

22 Hussey, Christopher: *The Picturesque* (Putnam, 1927), p.189.

23 But see Leon Battista Alberti: *Della Architettura*, trans. Giacomo Leoni (London, 1739), vol. II, bk. IX, p.79.

24 Adam, Robert: *Ruins of the Palace of the Emperor Diocletian at Spalatro* (Printed for the author, London, 1764), p.9.

25 Soane, Sir John: *Lectures*, op. cit., Lect. VI, p.95.

26 Ibid., Lect. III, pp.52–3.

27 Summerson, Sir John: *Architecture in Britain 1530–1830* (Penguin, 1986), p.452.

28 Laugier, Abbé: *Essaie sur l'Architecture* (Chez Duschesne, Paris, 1755), p.57.

29 *The Farington Diary*, ed. James Grieg (Hutchinson, 1923), vol. II, p.228, 19 April 1804. The French presence became involuntary as well as voluntary: Ackermann's shop, amongst the first to employ emigrés, seldom had less than '50 nobles, priests, and ladies of distinction' at work on fancy goods. By 1809 these had been replaced by natives (Ackermann's *Repository*, vol. I, Jan. 1809, p.54).

30 Repton, Humphry: B. L. Add. Ms. 62112 1058 A, p.194.

31 Colvin, Howard: *Biographical Dictionary of British Architects 1600–1840* (Murray, 1978), p.941.

32 Pilcher, Donald: *The Regency Style* (Batsford, 1947), p.67.

33 Mitchell, Robert: *Plans and Views in Perspective* (Oriental Press, London, 1801), p.1. He included Egyptian with Grecian, Saxon with Gothic, and ignored Chinese and Indian.

CHAPTER THREE
## Classical Styles

1 Laugier, Abbé: *Essaie sur L'Architecture* (Chez Duschesne, Paris, 1755), p.10.

2 Hope, Thomas: *Essay on Architecture* (Murray, 1840), p.24.

3 Richardson, George: *New Designs in Architecture* (Printed for the author, London, 1792), p.2.

4 Watkin, David: *Thomas Hope and the Neoclassical Idea* (Murray, 1968), p.87.

5 Laugier, Abbé: *Observations sur L'Architecture* (The Hague and Paris, 1765), p.67.

6 Illustrated Dorothy Stroud: *The Architecture of Sir John Soane* (Art and Technics, London, 1950), pl. 113.

7 Repton, Humphry: *Observations on the Theory and Practice of Landscape Gardening* (1803), original edn. 5th page after p.148.

8 Illustrated Carter, G., Goode, P., and Laurie, K.: *Humphry Repton Landscape Gardener*, exhibition Sainsbury Centre and Victoria & Albert Museum (Sainsbury Centre, 1982), pp.66, 132.

9 Tatham Sketch Book, R.I.B.A., vol. 2.

10 Cumberland, George: *Thoughts on Outline* (1796), p.3. He thought the *Museo Pio-Clementino* the least accurate publication and the *Pitture Antiche d'Ercolano* the best.

11 Robinson, P. F.: *Designs for Farm Buildings* (James Carpenter, London, 1830), Design X.

12 Meadows, Peter: 'Drawn to Entice', *Country Life* (28 April 1988), p.128.

13 'Défaut c'est lorsqu'au lieu d'isoler les

Colonnes, on les tient engagées dans un mur': Laugier, Abbé: *Essaie*, op. cit., p.13.

14 Richardson, George: *The New Vitruvius Britannicus* (Bulmer & Co., London, 1802), notes to pl. XVI.

15 Pevsner, Sir Nikolaus: *Studies in Art, Architecture and Design* (Thames & Hudson, 1968), p.211.

16 Quoted Damie Stillman: *English Neo-Classical Architecture* (Zwemmer, 1988), p.34.

17 Rosenblum, Robert: *Transformations in late Eighteenth Century Art* (Princeton, 1967), p.123.

18 Hope, Thomas: *Observations on the Plans & Elevations Designed by James Wyatt for Downing College Cambridge in a letter to Thomas Annesley Esq. M.P.* (1804), p.11.

19 Hope, Thomas: *An Historical Essay on Architecture* (Murray, 1840), p.84.

20 'The Deepdene attracts in this respect [by its novelty] exceeding but if the Pompeian style can be so cultivated as to practise well it may supercede the Templar style in which we have so long worked': from Cockerell's diary, quoted John Harris: *Design of the English Country House 1620–1920* (Trefoil, 1985), p.200.

21 Illustration in the Deepdene Volume: Borough of Lambeth Archives.

22 *Il Museo Pio-Clementino* (Rome, 1788), vol. IV, pl. XXIX.

23 Edgeworth, Maria; April 1819 quoted D. Watkin: *Thomas Hope*, op. cit., p.78.

24 See Philippe Duboy: *Lequeu: An Architectural Enigma* (Thames & Hudson, 1986), p.206: 'La Rendez-vous de Bellevue'; p.205: 'Le Pignon de la Pompe à feu'.

25 Loudon, J. C.: *An Encyclopaedia of Cottage, Farm and Villa Architecture and Furniture* (London, 1857), p.783.

26 Such as Schloss Glienicke, and the Gardener's House and Roman Baths at Charlottenhof.

27 The architect Amon Henry Wilds used extensively at Brighton the ammonite capital taken by his father Amon Wilds from Dance. Soane gave the capital high praise in his third Lecture (despite his earlier assertion that it was 'in vain to seek for any addition to' the number of the order, including the invention of 'capitals of a different kind': *Lectures on Architecture*, ed. Arthur Bolton, Soane Museum, 1929, pp.41–3).

28 English, E., and Maddox, W.: *Views of Lansdown Tower Bath* (London, 1844), p.6.

29 Ibid.

30 Meason, Gilbert Laing: *On the Landscape Architecture of the Great Painters of Italy* (C. Hullmandel, London, 1828), p.60.

31 Hunt, T. F.: *Architettura Campestre . . . in the modern or Italian style* (Longman, Rees etc., London, 1827), p.XVIII.

32 Ibid., p.XVII.

33 See L. A. Dubut: *Architecture Civile* (Paris, 1803), pls V, XXXIV, XXIII.

34 Illustrated Tim Mowl and Brian Earnshaw: *Trumpet at a Distant Gate* (Godine, Boston, 1985), p.147.

35 Demolished during the 1970s.

36 Illustrated Dorothy Stroud: *Henry Holland, His Life and Architecture* (Country Life, London, 1966), p. illusts 19–21

37 Stroud, op. cit., p.73.

38 See Damie Stillman: *English Neo-Classical Architecture*, op. cit., p.165.

39 Peyre, M.-J.: *Oeuvres d'Architecture* (1765; Gregg repr. Farnborough, Hants, 1967), p.8.

40 Drawing at Royal Library, Windsor.

41 See R.I.B.A. 35/1 for a disproportioned conjunction of disparate elements.

42 Quoted Clifford Musgrave: *Life in Brighton* (Faber & Faber, 1970), p.125.

43 Watkin, David: *The Life and Work of C. R. Cockerell R. A.* (Zwemmer, 1974), p.81.

44 Archer, John: *The Literature of British Domestic Architecture* (MIT Press, Boston, Mass., 1985), pp.59–67.

45 Middleton, Charles: *Picturesque and architectural views for cottages, farm houses, and country villas* (Edw. Jeffery, London, 1793). Quoted J. Archer: *Literature of Architecture*, op. cit., p.565.

46 Elmes, James: *Metropolitan Improvements* (London, 1829), pp.26, 27.

47 Peacock, Thomas Love: *Melincourt* (1818; Macmillan, London, 1896), chap. XXXIX, p.281.

48 Robinson, John Martin: 'Estate Buildings at Holkham', *Country Life* (21 and 28 Nov. 1974).

49 Robinson, John Martin: *The Wyatts: An Architectural Dynasty* (Oxford University Press, 1979), pp.31, 33.

50 Ibid., p.19.

51 Repton, Humphry: 'Memoirs' B. L. Add. Ms. 62112 1058 A, p.199.

52 See Krafft and Ransonette: *Maisons et Hôtels construits à Paris et dans les Environs de 1771 à 1802* (Paris, 1802), pl. 28.

53 Repton, Humphry: *Designs for the Pavilion at Brighton: The Landscape Gardening and Landscape Architecture of the late Humphry Repton Esq.*, ed. J. C. Loudon (London, 1840), op. cit., p.386.

54 Mordaunt Crook, J.: *The Greek Revival* (Murray, 1972), p.78. Quoting Elmes (1823).

55 Dallaway, James: *Observations on English Architecture* (1806), p.226.

56 Crook, J. M.: *Greek Revival*, op. cit., p.50.

57 Colvin, Howard: *Biographical Dictionary of British Architects 1600–1840* (Murray, 1978), p.941.

58 This solecism is present at the Marine Pavilion, where the Saloon lay behind the colonnade, and where, incidentally, something of the old 'parade' sequence of Saloon, Anti-Chamber and Drawing Room was preserved.

59 Davies, Terence: *John Nash* (David & Charles, 1973).

60 Peyre, M.-J.: *Oeuvres d'Architecture*, op. cit., pl. 2.

61 Repton, Humphry: B. L. Add. Ms. 62112 1058 A, p.38.

62 Stillman, D.: *English Neo-Classical Architecture*, op. cit., p.497.

63 Busby, C. A.: *A Series of Designs for Villas and Country Houses* (Printed for J. Taylor, London, 1808), p.13.

64 Robertson, William: *Designs in Architecture* (W. Bulmer & Co., London & Leipzig, 1800), pl. 15.

65 Quoted J. M. Crook: *Greek Revival*, op. cit., pp.63, 67.

66 Ibid. (quoting Hazlitt), p.67.

67 Ibid. (quoting Arnold's *Library of the Fine Arts*, 1832, p.63).

68 Kauffmann, Emil: *Architecture in the Age of Reason* (Harvard University Press, 1955), p.101.

69 Alberti, Leon Battista: *Della Architettura*, trans. Giacomo Leoni (London, 1739), vol. I, bk. IV, p.74.

70 Wilton-Ely, John: *Piranesi*, Arts Council Catalogue (1978), p.121.

71 Pevsner, Sir Nikolaus: *Studies*, op. cit., p.169.

72 Goethe, J. W.: *Italian Journey*, trans. W. H. Auden and E. Meyer (Penguin, 1970), p.218. For Paestum, see *Paestum and the Doric Revival*, ed. J. R. Serra (Centro Di, 1986), p.102.

73 Forsyth, Joseph: *Remarks on Antiquities, Art and Letters* (London, 1813), pp.339, 341, 343.

74 Colvin, H.: *Biographical Dictionary*, op. cit., p.643.

75 McWilliam, Colin: 'James Playfair's Designs for Ardkinglas': *The Country Seat: Studies in the History of the British Country House*, ed. H. Colvin and J. Harris (Allen Lane, 1970), p.194.

76 Ibid., p.194. Ledoux's scheme is illustrated in Krafft and Ransonette: *Maisons et Hôtels*, op. cit., pl. 72.

77 Colvin, H.: *Biographical Dictionary*, op. cit., p.396.

78 Rosenblum, R.: *Transformations*, op. cit., p.148.

79 Gandy, J. M.: *Designs for Cottages, Cottage Farms, and other Rural Buildings* (Printed for John Harding, London, 1805), pl. XLI.S.

80 Soane, Sir John: *Lectures*, op. cit., Lect. IV, p.70.

81 Ibid., Lect. XI, p.174.

82 Quoted J. M. Robinson: *The Wyatts*, op. cit., p.103.

83 Quoted P. Meadows: 'Drawn to Entice', *Country Life*, op. cit., p.130.

84 B. L. 269 k.6. Although Wood's *Palmyra* (1753) preceded Laugier's *Essaie* (1755).

85 R.I.B.A. Drawings Collection.

86 Thomson, James: *Retreats . . . A Series of Designs . . . for Cottages, Villas, and Ornamental Buildings* (Printed for J. Taylor, London, 1827). Illustrated E. Kauffmann: *Architecture in the Age of Reason*, op. cit., pl. 63.

87 Goodwin, Francis: *Domestic Architecture* (Printed for the author, 1833), vol. I, design 3.

88 Fowler owned the copy of Durand now in the R.I.B.A.

89 Boime, Albert: *Art in an Age of Revolution* (Chicago 1987), p.126.

90 Rosenblum, R.: *Transformations*, op. cit., p.52.

91 Quoted David Irwin: *English Neoclassical Art* (Faber & Faber, 1966), p.60.

92 Hazlitt, William: *Collected Works*, ed. A. R. Waller and A. Glover (Dent, 1903), p.328.

93 Watts, Alaric: *The Cabinet of Modern Art & Literary Souvenirs* (London, 1836), p.219.

94 Hope, T.: *Observations*, op. cit., pp.13–14.

95 Ibid., p.15.

96 Ibid., p.16.

97 Ibid., p.19.

98 Ibid., p.19.

99 Gibbon, Edward: *The Decline and Fall of the Roman Empire* (London, 1818), vol. I, chap. III, p.128.

100 Hope, T.: *Observations*, op. cit., p.20.

101 Ibid., p.35.

102 Ibid., p.27.

103 Ibid., p.33.

104 Ibid., pp.21–2.

105 Crook, J. M.: *The Greek Revival*, op. cit., p.86.

106 Hope, T.: *Observations*, op. cit., p.27.

107 Edgeworth, Maria: *Life and Letters*, ed. Augustus Hare (London, 1894), 1 May 1812, vol. I, p.203.

108 Aikin, Edmund: *An Essay on the Doric Order of Architecture* (London Architectural Society, 1810), pp.10, 12.

109 Watkin, D.: *C. R. Cockerell*, op. cit., p.66.

110 Winckelmann, Abbé: *Reflections on the Painting and Sculpture of the Greeks*, trans. Fuseli (1765), p.30.

111 Aberdeen, Earl of: *An Inquiry into the Principles of Beauty in Grecian Architecture* (Murray, 1822), p.18.

112 Wilkins, William: *Prohisiones Architectonicae* (London, 1837), p.88.

113 A sketch exists showing it fluted: Dorothy Stroud: *George Dance Architect, 1741–1825* (Faber & Faber, 1971), p.201.

114 Quoted J. Mordaunt Crook: 'Grange Park Transformed 1804–09': *The Country Seat*, op. cit., p.221. From the journal of J. L. Mallet, 1823.

115 Hope, T.: *Observations*, op. cit., pp.21–2.

116 Quoted J. M. Crook: 'Grange Park Transformed 1804–09': *The Country Seat*, op. cit., p.223.

117 Youngson, J.: *The Making of Classical Edinburgh 1750–1840* (Edinburgh University Press, 1966), pp.208–11.

118 Kelsall, Charles: *Phantasm of a University* (London, 1814), pp.131, 127–8.

119 Crook, J. M.: 'Grange Park Transformed 1804–09': *The Country Seat*, op. cit., p.223.

120 Watkin, D: *C. R. Cockerell*, op. cit., p.19.

121 Ibid., p.168. Downing uses the Ionic; Laugier had expressed the opinion that the Doric capital was 'le plus simple, et le moins élégant de tous les chapiteaux . . . Rien de moins fastueux, rien même de plus sec et de plus pauvre': *Essaie*, op. cit., p.74.

122 Crook, J. M.: *The Greek Revival*, op. cit., p.130.

123 Loudon, J. C.: *Gardener's Magazine*, 1, (1826), pp.106–07. Loudon indicated that Cockerell was called in to remedy the badly proportioned rooms created by Wilkins.

124 Inwood, H. W.: *The Erechtheion at Athens* (London, 1827), p.154.

125 Watkin, D.: *C. R. Cockerell*, op. cit., p.67.

126 Chambers, Sir William: *A Treatise on the Decorative Part of Civil Architecture*, ed. Joseph Gwilt (1825), p.59.

127 Watts, Alaric: *Cabinet*, op. cit., p.218.

128 Elmes, J.: *Metropolitan Improvements*, op. cit., p.136.

129 Hope, T.: *Observations*, op. cit., p.9.

130 In the Soane Museum copy.

131 Hope, T.: *Historical Essay*, op. cit., p.48.

132 Meason, G. L.: *Landscape Architecture*, op. cit., p.68.

133 Crook, J. M.: *Greek Revival*, op. cit., p.114.

134 Wood, Robert: *Ruins of Baalbek* (London, 1757), op. cit., pl. XXX.

135 Laugier, Abbé: *Observations*, op. cit.; of statues: 'Il est inutile de leur creuser une niche dans l'épaisseur du mur', p.71. *Essaie*, op. cit.; with domes, no roof should appear, 'car il est souverainement ridicule de nous présenter une tour bâtie sur la charpente d'un toit', p.46.

136 Laugier, Abbé: *Essaie*, op. cit. Columns on pedestals looked as if they had been mounted 'sur des échâsses pour suppléer à leur défaut d'élévation', p.24. *Observations*, op. cit. 'N'est-il pas contre nature que des figures se trouvent là où jamais homme ne peut se trouver sans faire craindre pour sa vie?', p.72.

137 Chambers, Sir William: *Treatise*, op. cit., p.374.

138 Elmes, J.: *Metropolitan Improvements*, op. cit., p.130.

139 Soane, Sir John: *Lectures*, op. cit., Lect. II, p.35.

140 'The Odes, Epodes, and Cannae Seculare of Horace': Joseph Davidson (1746), bk. II, Ode XV (Soane Museum copy).

141 He said of the fountain in the Piazza Navona: 'it is impossible not to be pleased with this mighty flight of genius': *Lectures*, op. cit., Lect. IV, p.71.

142 Foulston, John: *The Public Buildings erected in the West of England* (London, 1838), pp.12, 33.

143 Ibid., pp.46–7.

144 Watkin, D.: *C. R. Cockerell*, op. cit., p.19.

145 Elmes, J.: *Metropolitan Improvements*, op. cit., p.25.

146 Price, Uvedale: *Essays on the Picturesque: Essay on Architecture and Buildings* (J. Mawman, London, 1810), p.292.

147 Crook, J. M.: *Greek Revival*, op. cit., p.124.

148 Ackerman, James: *Palladio* (Penguin, 1966), p.92.

149 Summerson, Sir John: *John Nash* (Allen & Unwin, 1980), p.119.

150 Elmes, J.: *Metropolitan Improvements*, op. cit., p.67.

151 *Journal of Lady Holland* (Longmans Green & Co., 1908), vol. II, p.54.

152 Delacroix, Eugène: *Journal*, trans. J. Norton (Phaidon, 1951), p.XIII.

153 Farnborough, Lord: *Short Remarks and Suggestions upon Improvements now carrying on or under consideration* (Hatchards, 1826), p.9.

154 Ibid., p.48.

155 Ibid., pp.16–17.

156 Quoted J. M. Robinson: *The Wyatts*, op. cit., pp.119–20.

157 Quoted Sir John Summerson: *John Nash*, op. cit., p.164.

158 *Remarks on the Improvements now in Progress in St. James's Park Humbly addressed to the Members of Both Houses of Parliament*, c.1827.

159 Parliamentary Papers, P.R.O., vol. 16, pp.306–07.

160 Elmes, J.: *Metropolitan Improvements*, op. cit., p.27.

161 Meason, G. L.: *Landscape Architecture*, op. cit., p.27. It may be relevant that a drawing in the Royal Library attributed to Nash's office, of a mysterious project for a royal palace, has a plethora of pillars (baseless Doric, and Ionic) plus a Corinthian portico (from Carlton House?); the back is Gothic, with Tudor cupolas; R. L. 17182.

162 Lefuel, Hector: *Jacob Desmalter* (Albert Morancé, 1925), p.25.

163 Illustrated Ronald King: *The Quest for Paradise* (Mayflower, 1979), p.35.

164 Chambers, Sir William: *Treatise*, op. cit., p.XXX.

**CHAPTER FOUR**
**Gothic Styles**

1 Mitford, William: *Principles of Design in Architecture* (London, 1809), p.194.

2 Soane, Sir John: *Lectures on Architecture*, ed. Arthur Bolton (Soane Museum, 1929), Lect. V., p.83.

3 Beckford said it would for ever puzzle him how the author of both could be the same man: see Lewis Melville: *Life and Letters of William Beckford* (Heinemann, 1910), p.284. This was a common comment.

4 Alison, Archibald: *Essays on the Nature and Principles of Taste* (Edinburgh, 1825), p.186.

5 Clark, Kenneth: *The Gothic Revival* (Constable, 1928), p.46.

6 Summerson, Sir John: *Architecture in Britain 1530–1830* (Penguin, 1986), p.535.

7 Hope, Thomas: *Historical Essay on Architecture* (Murray, 1840), p.363.

8 Britton, John: 'Essays on the Merits and characteristics of William Shakespere': *Autobiography* (London, 1849), vol. II, Appendix p.23.

9 Pope, Alexander: 'Preface to Shakespeare', 1725.

10 Chambers, Sir William: *A Treatise on the Decorative Part of Civil Architecture*, ed. Joseph Gwilt (Priestley & Weale, London, 1825), p.128.

11 Hall, Sir James: *Essay on the Origin and Principles of Gothic Architecture* (Edinburgh, 1797), pp.5, 16.

12 Ibid., p.12.

13 Ibid., p.4.

14 Walpole, Horace; quoted Kenneth Clark: *Gothic Revival*, op. cit., p.44.

15 Laugier, Abbé: *Observations sur L'Architecture* (Chez Desaint, The Hague and Paris, 1765), p.116.

16 Ibid., p.117. Gaudí's extraordinary constructional devices, as at the Chapel of the Guell Colony, could be entirely justified on Laugierian principles.

17 Ibid., p.130.

18 Ibid., p.137.

19 Ibid., p.239.

20 Ibid., p.115.

21 Sprague Allen, B.: *Tides in English Taste: A Background for the Study of Literature* (Harvard University Press, 1937), vol. II, p.72.

22 Price, Uvedale: *Essays on the Picturesque: Essay on Architecture and Buildings* (J. Mawman, London, 1810), p.264.

23 Repton, Humphry: *Observations on the Theory and Practice of Landscape Gardening (1803): The Landscape Gardening and Landscape Architecture of the late Humphry Repton Esq.*, ed. J. C. Loudon (London, 1840), p.299.

24 Repton, Humphry: *Fragments on the Theory and Practice of Landscape Gardening (1816): The Landscape Gardening and Landscape Architecture of the late Humphry Repton Esq.*, ed. J. C. Loudon (London, 1846), p.425.

25 Macaulay, James: *The Gothic Revival 1745–1845* (Blackie, 1975), p.211.

26 Chambers, Sir William: *Treatise*, op. cit., p.129.

27 Britton, J.: *Auto-biography*, op. cit., vol. II, part II, p.110.

28 Ibid., p.112.

29 Ibid.

30 Mitchell, Robert: *Plans and Views . . . and an Essay to elucidate the Grecian, Roman and Gothic Architecture* (Oriental Press, London, 1801), p.14.

31 Colvin, Howard: *Biographical Dictionary of British Architects 1600–1840* (Murray, 1978), p.234.

32 Ms. 'Arc Arcuto' 1784; unpaginated, Soane Museum.

33 Rickman, Thomas: *Attempt to discriminate the styles of Architecture in England* (Longman etc. & Co., London, 1819), pp.19, 45.

34 Ibid., p.3.

35 Ibid., p.6.

36 Beckford, William: *Recollections of an Excursion to the Monasteries of Alcobaça and Batalha* (1835); see also J. C. Murphy: *Batalha* (1795).

37 Malton, James: *A Collection of Designs for Rural Retreats as Villas Principally in the Gothic and Castle Styles of Architecture* (Carpenter, London, 1803), Design 28.

38 Papworth, J. B.: *Rural Residences* (Ackermann, London, 1818); 'A Gothic Conservatory Designed to be connected with the Mansion'.

39 Malton, James: *Rural Retreats*, op. cit., Design 11, pl. 9.

40 Ibid., p.26.

41 Reproduced Sir John Summerson, David Watkin, and G. Tilman-Mellinghof: *John Soane* (Academy Editions, 1983), p.112.

42 Watkin, David: *The Life and Work of C. R. Cockerell R.A.* (Zwemmer, 1974), p.78.

43 Kelsall, Charles: *A Letter to the Society of the Dilettanti on the Works in Progress at Windsor* (Mela Brittanicus, 1827), p.3.

44 One's thoughts are propelled forward to 1862, when the shrieks of the Queen resounded through the Castle on the death of Prince Albert of Coburg.

45 Ibid., p.21.

46 *Gentlemen's Magazine*, vol. LXX, pt. 1, p.426, quoted James Macaulay: *Gothic Revival*, op. cit., p.175.

47 Alison, A.: *Essays on Taste*, op. cit., p.322.

48 Aspinall, Arthur: *The Correspondence of George Prince of Wales 1770–1812* (Cassell, London, 1963), vol.V; Memo of Sir Robert Wilson, 1804.

49 *The Farington Diary*, ed. James Grieg (Hutchinson, 1923), vol. II, p.150.

50 Peacock, Thomas Love: *Crotchet Castle* (Macmillan, 1927), chap. 1, pp.144–5.

51 Austen, Jane: *Mansfield Park* (1814), chap. IX.

52 Scott, Sir Walter: *Ivanhoe* (1819), chaps XXIII & XXVI.

53 Knight, Richard Payne: *An Analytical Enquiry into the Principles of Taste* (T. Payne & J. White, London, 1806), p.164.

54 Gibbon, Edward: *Decline and Fall of the Roman Empire* (London, 1818), vol. 2, p.181.

55 Macaulay, J.: *Gothic Revival*, op. cit., p.96.

56 Aspinall, A.: *Correspondence of George Prince of Wales*, op. cit., vol. IV; Prince of Wales to Arthur Paget, Belvoir, 7 Jan. 1799.

57 Rowan, Alistair: 'Eastnor Castle', *Country Life* (March 1968), p.606.

58 Royal Library, 1840; 'Designs for Windsor Castle by Jeffry Wyatt Architect'. 'Wyatt' is crossed out in pencil and 'Wyatville' substituted.

59 The Croker Papers, 30 March 1828; ed. Louis Jennings (Murray, 1885), p.414.

60 Ibid.

61 *Illustrations of Windsor Castle by the late Sir Jeffry Wyatville R.A.*, ed. Henry Ashton (John Weale, 1841), vol. II, p.19.

62 See N. Haslam: 'Penrhyn Castle, Gwynedd', *Country Life* (29 Oct. 1987), pp.108–13; (5 Nov.), pp.74–9.

63 Pückler-Muskau, Prince: *Tour of a German Prince* (London, 1832), vol. II, pp.43, 44.

64 Quoted C. Wainwright: *The Romantic Interior* (Yale, 1989), p.244.

65 Ibid., pp.246–7.

66 Malton, James: *Collection of Designs for Rural Retreats*, op. cit., pp.6–7, 31.

67 Robinson, John Martin: *The Wyatts: An Architectural Dynasty* (Oxford University Press, 1979), p.60.

68 This and the following two quotations: Repton, Humphry: *Designs for the Pavillon at Brighton* (J. C. Stadler, London, 1808), p.17.

69 Repton, Humphry: B. L. Add. Ms. 62112 1058 A, p.196.

70 Repton, H.: *Observations on the Theory and Practice of Landscape Gardening (1803): The Landscape Gardening and Landscape Architecture of the late Humphry Repton Esq.*, ed. J. C. Loudon (London, 1840), p.299.

71 Repton, H.: *Fragments on the Theory and Practice of Landscape Gardening (1816); The Landscape Gardening and Landscape Architecture of the late Humphry Repton Esq.*, ed. J. C. Loudon (London, 1840), p.435.

72 Watkin, D.: *C. R. Cockerell*, op. cit., pp.56, 62.

73 See Carter, G., Goode, P., and Laurie, K.: *Humphry Repton Landscape Gardener 1752–1818*, exhibition catalogue (Sainsbury Centre, 1982), p.77.

74 Harcourt, Leslie: *Corsham Court* (A Gothick Dream, 1977), pp.22, 23.

75 Summerson, Sir John: *John Nash*, op. cit., p.38.

76 Rutter, J.: *An Illustrated History and Description of Fonthill Abbey* (C. Knight, London, Shaftesbury, 1823), (outer title page); *Delineations of Fonthill and its Abbey* (Published by the author, London, 1823), (inner title page); London Library copy, p.64.

77 Ibid., p.64.

78 Ibid., p.65.

79 Ibid., p.75.

80 Quoted J. M. Robinson: *The Wyatts*, op. cit., p.60.

81 Rutter, J.: *An Illustrated History*, op. cit., p.109.

82 Ibid., p.110.

83 Illustrated Carter, G., Goode, P., and Laurie, K.: *Humphry Repton*, op. cit., p.57.

84 Pückler-Muskau, Prince: *Tour*, op. cit., vol. III, pp.199–200.

85 Walpole, Horace: *Journals of Visits to Country Seats* (Oxford University Press, 1928), vol. 16, p.30.

86 As Peacock described 'Nightmare Abbey'.

87 Byron, Lord: 'Don Juan', Canto LV.

88 Ibid., Canto LVIII.

89 Jackson-Stops, G.: 'Newstead Abbey . . .', *Country Life* (9 May 1974).

90 See Christopher Hussey: 'Mamhead', *Country Life* (26 May and 2 June 1955).

91 Walker, David: *The Country Seat: Studies in the History of the British Country House*, ed. Howard Colvin and John Harris (Allen Lane, 1970), p.211.

92 Linstrum, Derek: *Sir Jeffry Wyatville* (Clarendon Press, 1972), p.66. The gate now announces a housing estate.

93 See Christopher Hussey: 'Harlaxton Manor Lincs', *Country Life* (11 April 1957), pp.704–07; (18 April) pp.764–7.

94 Seaborne, Malcolm: *The English School* (Routledge, 1971), p.58.

95 The building, in excellent condition, was demolished by Brighton Corporation in 1971 for 'road widening' during the week of a postal strike; a prepared 'spot-listing' was not delivered despite Brighton residents' offers to collect it. Musgrave described in 1970 'a fascinating group of buildings . . . forms as it were a specimen collection of Regency architecture . . . from the black cobble-fronted Brighton vernacular . . . and the adjoining bow-fronted shop with its fine balcony, to the neo-Greek Unitarian Church . . . and the Regency Gothic Central School . . .'. The destruction of Brighton has, since the retirement in 1984 of Mr. Kenneth Fines, a conservation-minded Planning Officer, increased apace.

96 Seaborne, M.: *English School*, op. cit., p.177.

97 Ibid., p.169.

98 Hunt, T. F.: *Exemplars of Tudor Architecture* (Longman etc. & Co., 1830), p.51.

99 Ibid., p.31.

100 Ibid., p.73.

101 Ibid., p.74.

102 Ibid., p.68.

103 See Ralph Hyde: *Panoramia* (Trefoil, 1989), Cat. 99: 'Effect of Fog and Snow seen

through a Ruined Gothic [actually Norman] Colonade'; by Louis Daguerre.

CHAPTER FIVE
Exotic Styles

1 Quoted by G. B. Piranesi: *Di Maniere d'Adornare i Cammini* (Rome, 1769), p.13.
2 *The Inspiration of Egypt*, Brighton Museum Catalogue (1983), ed. P. Conner, p.7.
3 Caylus, Comte de: *Recueil d'Antiquités Egyptiennes, Etrusques, Grecques, et Romaines* (Paris, 1761), vol. II, pl. V.; vol. I, pp.117–18.
4 Parisi, F.: *Descrizione della stanza egizia* (Rome, 1782).
5 *Inspiration*, Brighton Museum Cat., op. cit., p.29.
6 *Edinburgh Review*, vol. I (Jan. 1803), p.330.
7 De Quincy, Quatremère: *De L'Architecture Egyptienne* (Paris, 1803) (Soane copy), pp.207, 208, 209, 221.
8 Ibid.
9 Soane, Sir John: *Lectures on Architecture*, ed. Arthur Bolton (Soane Museum, 1929), Lect. I., p.21.
10 Ibid.
11 Quoted Stanley Mayes: *The Great Belzoni* (Putnam, 1959), p.266.
12 Ackermann's *Repository*, vol. I (1809), p.136.
13 Hope, Thomas: *Historical Essay on Architecture* (Murray, 1840), p.26. Hope's historical judgment was acute; he postulated that Egyptian monuments were only devised to occupy the people 'in moments of leisure', anticipating modern theories of 'hydraulic' civilisations.
14 Busby, C. A.: *A series of designs for villas and country houses* (Printed for J. Taylor, London, 1808), p.11.
15 Randall, James: *A collection of architectural designs* (Printed for J. Taylor, London, 1806), Design IX.
16 Elmes, James: *Metropolitan Improvements* (London, 1829), p.157.
17 Curl, J. S.: *The Egyptian Revival* (Allen & Unwin, 1982), p.124.
18 *Inspiration*, op. cit., p.56.
19 R.I.B.A. Drawings Collection.
20 Foulston, John: *The Public Buildings erected in the West of England* (1838), p.3.
21 *The Mirror*, vol. X (1828), 20 Oct. 1827, p.272.
22 Musgrave, Clifford: *Life in Brighton* (Faber & Faber, 1970), p.228.
23 Klingender, F. D.: *Art and the Industrial Revolution* (Carrington, 1947), p.108.
24 Lamb, Charles: *The Essays of Elia* (Nelson, undated), p.38.
25 Ibid., p.310.
26 See J. S. Curl: *The Egyptian Revival*, op. cit., p.168.
27 Knight, Richard Payne: *An Analytical Enquiry into the Principles of Taste* (T. Payne & J. White, London, 1806), p.216.
28 The religious epic *Bhagavad-gita* and the verse drama *Sakuntala*; Goethe planned to turn the latter into an opera.
29 Maurice, Thomas: *Indian Antiquities or Dissertations etc.* (London, 1806), vol. VI, pp.197, 144.
30 Knight, R. P.: *Analytical Enquiry*, op. cit., p.165. Hodges thought common features of Gothic, Egyptian, Hindu and Moorish buildings derived from a common visual memory of stalactites and caves.
31 Maurice, T.: *Indian Antiquities*, op. cit., vol. I, p.210.
32 Knight, R. P.: *Analytical Enquiry*, op. cit., p.80.
33 Illustrated J. H. Morley: *Designs and Drawings: The Making of the Royal Pavilion* (Sotheby, 1984), p.46.
34 Hope, T.: *Essay on Architecture*, op. cit., p.21.
35 Ibid., p.26.
36 Ibid., p.23.
37 Ibid., p.134.
38 Ibid., p.348.
39 Ibid., p.138.
40 Morley, J. H.: *Designs and Drawings*, op. cit., p.42.
41 *The Farington Diary*, ed. James Grieg (Hutchinson, 1923), vol. III, 20 July 1804. See also Allen Braham: *Architecture of the French Enlightenment* (Thames & Hudson, 1980), p.159.
42 Mitford, William: *Principles of Design in Architecture* (1809), p.193.
43 Jones, Barbara: *Follies and Grottoes* (Constable, 1974), p.64.
44 Conner, Patrick: *Oriental Architecture in the West* (Thames & Hudson, 1979), pp.136, 138.
45 Illustrated J. H. Morley: *Designs and Drawings*, op. cit., pp.74, 75.
46 Reduced by the parsimony and philistinism of national government and local council alike.
47 Marsh, Madeleine: 'Russian Riviera', *Interiors* (Jan. 1989), p.82.
48 Quoted from C. R. Cockerell by Sir John Summerson: *Architecture in Britain 1530–1830* (Penguin, 1986), p.454.
49 Quoted Dorothy Stroud: *George Dance* (Faber & Faber, 1971), p.120.
50 Owen, Felicity, and Brown, David Blaney: *Collector of Genius: A Life of Sir George Beaumont* (Yale University Press, 1988), p.111.
51 Summerson, Sir John, Watkin, David, and G. Tilman-Mellinghof: *John Soane* (Academy Editions, 1983), p.56.
52 Stroud, Dorothy: 'George Dance and Cole Orton House': *The Country Seat, Studies in the History of the British Country House*, ed. Howard Colvin and John Harris (Allen Lane, 1970), pp.217–18.
53 Owen, F., and Brown, D. P.: *Sir George Beaumont*, op. cit., p.132.

CHAPTER SIX
The Regency Synthesis

1 Hope, Thomas: *Historical Essay on Architecture* (Murray, 1840), p.490.
2 Malton, James: *Essay on British Cottage Architecture* (Thomas Malton, 1804), quoted Sir John Summerson: *Architecture in Britain 1530–1830* (Penguin, 1986), p.490.
3 He also recommends that cornices and window frames should be painted stone colour (*Encyclopaedia*; London, 1857), p.270. Venetian blinds could be used with cornice boxes; the latter should be painted stone or cream in the country, green in towns; those on Gothic cottages should imitate oak (ibid. p.262). Shutters were often painted 'green, and other gaudy colours' (p.268). The knobs and nail heads on doors may imitate bronze; this was done by painting them first deep yellow, then green, wiping off the green a little before it was dry (p.267). Loudon thought it proper to insert glass in window canopies to let through the light. Repton advocated that for window frames 'to a gentleman's house the outside of the sashes should be white whether they be of mahogany, of oak, or of deal, because . . . the modern sash-frames are so light, that, unless we see the bars, the houses appear at a distance unfinished, and as having no windows'. In palaces, they should be gilded (*Observations on the Theory and Practice of Landscape Gardening (1803): The Landscape Gardening and Landscape Architecture of the late Humphry Repton Esq.*, ed. J. C. Loudon (London, 1840), p.263.
4 Cottingham, L. N.: *Smith & Founder's Director* (London, 1823).
5 Weale, John: *Designs for ornamental gates, lodges, palisading & iron work of the Royal Parks etc . . . from the executed works of Decimus Burton, Arch., John Nash, Arch., Sydney Smirke, Arch., Sir John Soane, Arch., Robert Stevenson, C. E., Sir John Vanbrugh, Arch., Christopher Wren, Arch.* (John Weale, London, 1841).
6 Roth, Daniel: *Decorative Ironwork* (Daniel Roth, 1976), p.5.
7 Peacock, Thomas Love: *Melincourt* (1818; Macmillan, 1896), chap. XXXII. The new, typically 'Gardenesque' plants listed by the old gentleman may be interpreted as acacias, arbutus, azaleas, aucuba (spotted laurel), and phillyrea. Had Peacock a nurseryman's catalogue in his hands as he wrote the lines?
8 A clue may lie in *A New Book of Cottages and Barns from Nature* by François Vivarès,

published at the early date of 1773. The author has been unable to locate a copy. Vivarès, a French engraver who came to England, stayed and had a brilliant career. See Henry Vivarez: *Pro Domo Mea* (Lille, 1904).

9 Adam sketchbook, Soane 247a.

10 See Léon Rey: *Le Petit Trianon et le Hameau de Marie Antoinette* (Paris, 1936).

11 Smith, J. T. (Keeper of Prints, British Museum): *Remarks on Rural Scenery* (London, 1797), p.7.

12 Price, Uvedale: *Essays on the Picturesque: Essay on Architecture and Buildings* (J. Mawman, London, 1797), pp.367, 368.

13 Ibid., p.358.

14 Ibid., p.341.

15 Smith, J. T.: *Remarks*, op. cit., p.8.

16 Ibid., p.9.

17 Archer, J.: *The Literature of British Domestic Architecture 1715–1842* (MIT Press, Boston, Mass., 1985), p.683.

18 Peacock, T. L.: *Crotchet Castle* (Macmillan, 1927), p.269.

19 R.I.B.A. Album 2.

20 Summerson, Sir John: *John Nash*, op. cit., p.52.

21 Repton, Humphry: *Observations on the Theory and Practice of Landscape Gardening (1803): The Landscape Gardening and Architecture of the late Humphry Repton Esq.*, ed. J. C. Loudon (London, 1840), p.247.

22 Malton, James: *An Essay on British Cottage Architecture* (Hookham & Carpenter, London, 1798), p.5.

23 Malton, J.: *An Essay on British Cottage Architecture* (James Malton, London, 1804), pp.5, 24, 22, 16.

24 Lugar, Robert: *Architectural Sketches for Cottages, Rural Dwellings* (T. Bensley for J. Taylor, London, 1805); quoted by Derek Linstrum: *Sir Jeffry Wyatville* (Clarendon Press, 1972), note 7, p.264.

25 Elsam, Richard: *An essay on rural architecture* (E. Lawrence, London, 1803).

26 Ibid., p.5.

27 Pückler-Muskau, Prince: *Tour of a German Prince* (London, 1832), vol. II, pp.204–05.

28 Summerson, Sir John: *John Nash*, op. cit., p.55.

29 Quoted Sir John Summerson: *John Nash*, op. cit., p.54.

30 Quoted by David Watkin: *The Life and Work of C. R. Cockerell R.A.* (Zwemmer, 1974), p.81.

31 Illustrated R.I.B.A. catalogue.

32 Loudon, J. C.: *Encyclopaedia of Cottage, Farm and Villa Architecture and Furniture* (London, 1857), p.1039.

33 Loudon, J. C.: *Encyclopaedia*, op. cit., p.277.

34 Atkinson, William: *Views of Picturesque Cottages* (T. Gardner, London, 1805), p.19.

35 Bartell, Edmund: *Hints for Picturesque Improvements in Ornamental Cottages* (J.

Taylor, London, 1804), p.10.

36 Loudon, J. C.: *Encyclopaedia*, op. cit., p.262.

37 Ibid., p.263.

38 Ibid., p.261.

39 Ibid., p.266.

40 Linstrum, D.: *Jeffry Wyatville*, op. cit., p.35.

41 Sotheby's, New York, 3 June 1988, Lot 48.

42 Linstrum, D.: *Jeffry Wyatville*, op. cit., p.36.

43 *Guide to the Illustrations and Views of Knowle Cottage, Sidmouth; the elegant Marine Villa Orne of Thos. L. Fish Esq.* (Sidmouth, 1837), pp.1–3.

44 See Sir Owen Morshead: *George IV and Royal Lodge* (Regency Society of Brighton and Hove).

45 Scott, Sir Walter: *The Journal of Sir Walter Scott*, ed. W. E. K. Anderson (Oxford, 1972), p.218.

46 Lieven, Princess: *The Unpublished Diary of Princess Lieven*, ed. Harold Temperley (Cape, 1930), p.119.

47 Quoted D. Linstrum: *Sir Jeffry Wyatville*, op. cit., p.164.

48 Colvin, Howard: *Biographical Dictionary of British Architects 1600–1840* (Murray, 1978), p.809. For Royal Lodge, see *History of the King's Works* (H.M.S.O., 1973), vol. VI, pp.381, 399, 400.

49 Elmes, J.: *Metropolitan Improvements*, op. cit., pp.54–7.

50 Loudon, J. C.: *Encyclopaedia*, op. cit., pp.75–9.

51 Surtees, J.: *Jorrocks Jaunts and Jollities* (1838; Methuen, 1903), pp.47–8.

## Part III: Interior Decoration
### CHAPTER ONE
### Formative Influences

1 Repton, Humphry: *Observations on the Theory and Practice of Landscape Gardening (1803): The Landscape Gardening and Landscape Architecture of the late Humphry Repton, Esq.*, ed. J. C. Loudon (London, 1840), p.283.

2 Repton, Humphry: *Fragments on the Theory and Practice of Landscape Gardening (1816): The Landscape Gardening and Landscape Architecture of the late Humphry Repton, Esq.*, ed. J. C. Loudon (London, 1840), p.457.

3 Joppien, Rudiger: *Philippe James de Loutherbourg* (Kenwood, undated), unpaginated.

4 Ibid.

5 For this and following quotations see Sybil Rosenfeld: *A Short History of Stage Design in Great Britain* (Blackwell, 1973), pp.95–106.

6 Christie, James: *Disquisitions upon the painted Greek vases* (London, 1825), pp.36, 37.

7 Lamb, Charles: *Essays of Elia: The imaginative Faculty* (Nelson, undated), p.309.

8 Wyatville, Sir Jeffry: *Illustrations of Windsor Castle* (J. Weale, 1841), preface.

9 Meason, Gilbert Laing: *On the Landscape Architecture of the Great Painters of Italy* (C. Hullmandel, London, 1828), p.86.

10 Goldicutt, John: *Specimens of ancient decorations from Pompeii* (London, 1825), preface.

11 Gell, Sir William, and Gandy, J. P.: *Pompeiana* (Rodwell & Martin, 1817–19), p.158.

12 Soane reported Vitruvius' complaint that monsters, rather than animals taken from nature, were painted in decorations, and that 'Reeds and Candelabra [were] substituted for columns'; he went on to a more general attack; 'what would he have said on seeing the exterior of a modern Building decorated with the Caducei and other attributes of Mercury, or of an interior enriched with the representations of Winged Figures, and with Lions' Heads in the Cymatium of the Cornice? . . . the outsides of many of our buildings disfigured and disgraced with expensive wooden and oil-cloth Verandas, or Marybone Bird-Cages?' *Lectures on Architecture*, ed. Arthur Bolton (Soane Museum), Lect. VI, p.100.

13 Britton, John: *The Union of Architecture, Sculpture, and Painting* (London, 1827), p.3.

14 Soane, Sir John: *Lectures*, op. cit., Lect. VI, p.98.

15 Ibid.

16 Ibid., Lect. III, p.54.

17 Laugier, Abbé: *Observations sur L'Architecture* (The Hague and Paris, 1765), pp.110–12.

18 Winckelmann, Abbé: *Reflections on the Painting and Sculpture of the Greeks*, trans. Fuseli (1765), p.2.

### CHAPTER TWO
### The Decorated Interior: Classical Styles

1 Adam, Robert: *The Works in Architecture of Robert and James Adam* (The Author, London, 1778), vol. I, p.5. Two hundred years earlier Cellini had taken a different view, expressed equally trenchantly: 'Such arabesques are called grotesques by the ignorant': *The Life of Benvenuto Cellini*, trans. J Addington Symonds (Heron Books, 1968), p.57.

2 Desgodetz, A.: *Les Edifices Antiques de Rome dessinés et mesurés très exactement* (Paris, 1682), pl. 11. This arch frequently appears in 15th-century Italian painting.

3 See Nicole Dacos: *La Découverte de la Domus Aurea et la Formation des Grotesques à la Renaissance* (Warburg Institute, 1969); and Edward Croft-Murray: *Decorative Painting in England* (Country Life, London, 1970), vol. 2, pp.48, 55.

4 Ponce, Nicolas: *Tableaux et Arabesques . . . dans les Thermes de Titus* (Paris, 1838), preface.

5 Tatham Album, Soane Museum: '. . . occupying myself in drawing the front of a beautiful church built by Lombardi called the Madonna delli Miracoli . . .', Venice, 27 July 1796, p.149.

6 Sheraton, Thomas: *Accompaniment to the*

*Cabinet-Maker and Upholsterer's Drawing-Book* (T. Bensley, London, 1794), p.14.

7 There were various sources for dancing maidens, e.g. a famous Roman bas-relief, the 'Nuptiales Chorae', at this time in the Villa Borghese (Fig. 155). See also P. Santi Bartoli: *Picturae Antiquae*, pl. V, and B. de Montfaucon: *L'Antiquité Expliquée*, vol. III, part II, pls CLXXII, CLXXIII.

8 Stillman, Damie: *English Neo-Classical Architecture* (Zwemmer, 1988), p.488.

9 Saunders, George: *A Treatise on Theatres* (Printed for the author, London, 1790), p.39.

10 Tatham, C. H.: 'Letters and Drawings', V. & A., unpaginated.

11 Ibid.

12 Albertolli, Giocondo: *Ornamenti Diversi* (Milan, 1782), e.g. pls VI, XVI.

13 Ibid., pl. XIII.

14 Pergolesi, Michelangelo: *Designs* (M. Dulouchamp, 1801), pl. 33.

15 See J. H. Morley: *Designs and Drawings: The Making of the Royal Pavilion* (Sotheby, 1984), passim, e.g. p.217.

16 Watkin, David: *The Life and Work of C. R. Cockerell R.A.* (Zwemmer, 1974), p.175.

17 Smith, George: *The Cabinet-Maker and Upholsterer's Guide* (London, 1826), p.166.

18 D'Hancarville, P. F.: *Antiquités Etrusques, Grecques et Romaines* (Paris, 1785), vol. I, p.13.

19 Ibid., p.12.

20 Ibid., pp.77, 78.

21 One stimulus for the interest in Greek outline must have been the accuracy with which d'Hancarville reproduced its character. Earlier representations, e.g. by Caylus and Montfaucon, had substituted coarseness for elegance.

22 See Ian Jenkins: 'Adam Buck and Greek Vases', *Burlington Magazine* (June, 1988).

23 Stuart, Lady Louisa: *The Letters of Lady Louisa Stuart*, ed. R. Brimley Johnson (John Lane, 1926), p.110.

24 Quoted C. Willett and P. Cunnington: *Handbook of English Costume in the Nineteenth Century* (Faber & Faber, 1959), p.105. Letter of Emily Eden, 1827.

25 Watson, Sir Francis: *Southill; A Regency House*, ed. Major S. Whitbread (Faber & Faber, 1951), p.40.

26 Adam, Robert: *Works in Architecture*, op. cit., vol. II, pls VII, VIII.

27 See J. H. Morley: *Country Life* (9 May 1991).

28 For Wyatt, see Clifford Musgrave: *Adam and Hepplewhite Furniture* (Faber & Faber, 1966), p.211, pl. 151.

29 Tatham Album, Soane Museum, p.130.

30 Illustrated J. H. Morley: *Country Life* (9 May 1991).

31 Illustrated J. H. Morley: *Designs and Drawings*, op. cit., p.118.

32 'Etruscan' may at times have been used to mean merely 'red and black', e.g. '. . . 1 very neat Etruscan Japand Chinese Lanthorn' (1802), R.A. 25118 (although it is possible that this refers to the ambiguous Etruscan/Chinese type of decoration).

33 Pyne, W. H.: *Royal Residences: Carlton House* (1819), pp.24, 25.

34 Ackermann, Rudolph: *Microcosm of London* (London, 1808), p.108.

35 Whittock, Nathaniel: *The Decorative Painters' and Glaziers' Guide* (1827), p.147, pl. XXXVI.

36 Ibid., p.113.

37 See Peter Thornton: *Authentic Decor* (Weidenfeld & Nicolson, 1984), p.208.

38 *Memoirs of Chateaubriand*, ed. Robert Baldick (Penguin, 1965), p.368.

39 Gell, Sir William, and Gandy, J. P.: *Pompeiana* (Rodwell & Martin, 1817–19), pp.154, 160.

40 Quoted David Watkin: *Thomas Hope and the Neo-Classical Idea* (Murray, 1968), p.69.

41 Joyce, Hetty: 'The Ancient Frescoes from the Villa Negroni', *Art Bulletin* (Providence, Rhode Island; Sept. 1983), p.423.

42 Knight, Richard Payne: *An Analytical Enquiry into the Principles of Taste* (T. Payne & J. White, London, 1806), p.166.

43 Summerson, Sir John: *Heavenly Mansions* (Cresset Press, 1949), p.13.

44 Whittock, N.: *Decorative Painters*, op. cit., p.112.

45 See Desmond Fitzgerald: 'A gallery after the antique', *The Connoisseur*, 181 (1972), pp.2–13. See N. Ponce: *Description des Bains de Titus* (Paris, 1786), pl. 4, 'Murs de la Chambre peinte en fonds noir'. The top two tiers are red, the dado black.

46 *The Age of Neoclassicism:* exhibition catalogue (Arts Council of Great Britain, 1972), p.770.

47 Croft-Murray, E.: *Decorative Painting*, op. cit., vol. 2, p.48.

48 Biver, L.-M.: *Pierre Fontaine* (Librairie Plon, 1964), p.151. See pls 1, 2, and 4 in *Arabesques Antiques des Bains de Livie et de la Ville Adrienne et Les Plafonds de la Villa Madame* by N. Ponce (1789). These designs resemble Percier and Fontaine designs of about 1800; the frescoes in question come from the 'House of Augustus', and Napoleon is recorded as having shown a particular interest in the surviving fragments of the palaces of the Roman Emperors.

49 Some classicising interiors in early Renaissance painting are, allowing for the difference between their volumetric treatment and Percier's line, remarkably like the more palatial Percier and Fontaine style; e.g. see *Sixtus IV in the Vatican Library*, by Melozzo da Forli (Vatican).

50 Joyce, H.: *The Ancient Frescoes*, op. cit., p.438.

51 Soane, Sir John: *Description of the House and Museum on the North Side of Lincoln's Inn Fields* (London, 1830), p.2.

52 Britton, John: *Union of Architecture, Sculpture, and Painting* (Printed for the author, London, 1827), p.19.

53 Percier, Charles and Fontaine, Pierre: *Recueil de Décorations Intérieures* (Paris, 1827 edn.), pl. 61.

54 Pyne, W. H.: *Carlton House*, op. cit., p.25.

55 Soane Museum, vol. 9, no. 10.

56 Some ancient shallow domes with four oculi are recorded.

57 Britton, J.: *Union*, op. cit., p.19.

58 See N. Ponce: *Description*, op. cit., pl. 7, where a tribune with an elaborate vault looks paper thin because of the perspective of the painted floor, which appears to be behind it.

59 Britton, J.: *Union*, op. cit., p.33.

60 Tornezey, M. A.: *Bergeret et Fragonard: Journal inédit d'un voyage en Italie* (Mémoires de la Société des Antiquaires de l'Ouest, Paris, 1895), p.315.

61 Sheraton, Thomas: *The Cabinet-Maker and Upholsterer's Drawing-Book* (T. Bensley, London, 1793; Dover Publications, 1972), p.442.

62 Ibid., p.444.

63 Sheraton, T.: *The Cabinet-Maker and Upholsterer's Drawing-Book* (1793), op. cit., p.443.

64 Ibid., pp.442, 443.

65 *Carlton House*, The Queen's Gallery Catalogue (Balding & Mansell, 1991), p.219.

66 Robinson, J. M.: *Country Life* (25 Oct. 1979), p.1405.

67 Smith, G.: *Cabinet-Maker* (1826), op. cit., pl. CLIII, p.174.

68 Whittock, N.: *Decorative Painters'*, op. cit., p.105.

69 Britton, J.: *Union*, op. cit., p.7.

70 Whittock, N.: *Decorative Painters'*, op. cit. The quotations that follow are taken from pp.105–13.

71 Croft-Murray, E.: *Decorative Painting*, op. cit., vol. 2, p.65.

72 Illustrated in *John Soane*, by Sir John Summerson, David Watkin, and G. Tilman-Mellinghof (Academy Editions, 1983), p.26.

73 Illustrated J. H. Morley: *Designs and Drawings*, op. cit., p.147.

74 Croft-Murray, E.: *Decorative Painting*, op. cit., p.64.

75 *The Architecture of M. Vitruvius Pollio*, trans. W. Newton (James Newton, London, 1791), bk. VII, chap. V, p.163.

76 Mlle. Guimard's dining room illustrated Peter Thornton: *Authentic Decor*, op. cit., p.166.

77 Hyde, Ralph: *Panoramania* (Trefoil, 1989), p.56. There were earlier examples; in the mid-1760s Cipriani (an Italian) painted a landscape panorama around the walls at Standlynch, Wilts, as later at Norbury. The early date of Standlynch, and Cipriani's own background, suggest the classical tradition, e.g. the

continuous garden fresco from the Empress Livia's garden room at Prima Porto (Museo delle Terme, Rome) rather than a Picturesque influence. Gilpin said that Norbury imitated a room painted by Gaspar Poussin in a villa near Rome. Claude had painted four landscapes for the walls of a room in the Palazzo Crescenzi.

78 Aglio, A.: *Sketches . . . of the Interior Temporary Decorations . . . in Wookey-Hall Yorkshire* (Published by the artist, London, 1821). The Ball Room is the only room called 'temporary' in the text, but is this because as well as having temporary decorations it was also a temporary structure?

79 For the general subject see C. Gilbert, J. Lomax and A. Wells-Cole catalogue: *Country House Floors* (Temple Newsam House, Leeds, 1987).

80 Ibid., pp.32–3.

81 Ibid., p.31.

82 Parliamentary Papers, P.R.O., vol. 16, p.96.

83 Quoted C. Gilbert, J. Lomax and A. Wells-Cole: *Country House Floors*, op. cit. (from the *New and Improved Practical Builder*; Peter Nicholson, 1837).

84 Smith, George: *Collection of Designs for Household Furniture* (London, 1808), p.8.

85 E.g. in the tapestry cartoon *The Death of Ananias* (V. & A., Royal loan), an influential source.

86 Soane Museum, Architectural Arabesques, 29.E No. 2.

87 Jones, T. E.: *A Descriptive Account of the Literary Works of John Britton, F.S.A.* (second part of the autobiography; London, 1849), Part II, p.23.

88 Fatma Moussa Mahmoud: *William Beckford of Fonthill*: Geoffrey Bullough: 'Beckford's early travels and his Dream of Delusion' (Kennikar Press, 1972), p.44.

89 Croft-Murray, E.: *Decorative Painting*, op. cit., vol. 2, p.217.

90 Edgeworth, Maria: *Life and Letters*, ed. Augustus Hare (London, 1894), vol. I, p.101.

91 *The Farington Diary*, ed. James Greig (Hutchinson, 1923), vol. II, p.41.

92 *Journal of Elizabeth, Lady Holland* (Longmans, Green & Co., 1908), vol. II, p.150.

93 Biver, M.-L.: *Pierre Fontaine*, op. cit.: 'Le Premier consul ait trouvé que cette pièce ressemblait à une sacristie d'église . . .', p.27.

94 Smith, G.: *Designs for Household Furniture* (1808), op. cit., p.8.

95 Compare the Crimson Drawing Room with the 'State Drawing Room' of 1807 in George Smith's 1808 *Designs for Household Furniture*. Possibly prompted by the activity at Carlton House, the Smith room is in a totally different idiom, thoroughly 'architectural' with Ionic columns and pilasters decorated with arabesque. The Carlton House interiors must

have astounded people who expected something like the Smith room.

96 *Carlton House*, Queen's Gallery Cat., op. cit., p.224.

97 Bellaigue, G. de., and Kirkham, P.: 'George IV and the Furnishing of Windsor Castle', *Furniture History Society Journal* (1972), pp.8, 9.

98 *Windsor and Eton Express*: 26 April 1828.

99 Bellaigue, G. de, and Kirkham, P.: 'George IV', op. cit., p.32.

100 Illustrated Bellaigue, G. de., and Kirkham, P.: 'George IV', op. cit., pl. 32A.

101 *Carlton House*, Queen's Gallery Cat., op. cit., p.74.

102 Percier, C., and Fontaine, P.: *Recueil*, op. cit., pl. 55, p.39.

103 *Carlton House*, Queen's Gallery Cat., op. cit., pp.24, 220.

104 Illustrated Mario Praz: *An Illustrated History of Interior Decoration* (Thames & Hudson, 1964), p.196.

105 Smith, G.: *Cabinet-Maker and Upholsterer's Guide* (1826), op. cit., p.210.

106 Morley, J. H.: *Designs and Drawings*, op. cit., p.189.

107 Illustrated and discussed J. H. Morley: *Designs and Drawings*, op. cit., pp.201–23.

108 Ibid., p.223.

109 Hope, Thomas: *Household Furniture and Interior Decoration* (1807; Tiranti repr., 1978), pp.25–6.

110 From the *Globe*: 2 Sept. 1811; quoted by the *West London Observer*: 9 Sept. 1910, p.5.

111 Tatham Sketch Book, R.I.B.A., vol. 2, 065–6.

112 E.g. the 'Platinum' Room at the Casa del Labrador, Aranjuez: illustrated Percier and Fontaine: *Recueil*, op. cit., pl. 61.

113 Quoted Biver, M.-L.: *Pierre Fontaine*, op. cit., p.49.

114 Hope, T.: *Household Furniture*, op. cit., p.25.

115 Ibid.

116 Percier, C., and Fontaine, P.: *Recueil*, op. cit., pls 30, 55.

117 Elmes, J., quoted Sir John Summerson: *John Nash* (Allen & Unwin, 1980), p.133.

118 Pückler-Muskau, Prince: *Tour of a German Prince* (London, 1832), vol. 4, p.86.

119 Summerson, Sir John: *John Nash*, op. cit., p.133.

120 Pückler-Muskau, Prince: *Tour*, op. cit., vol. 4, p.86.

121 Maddison, John: 'Blickling Hall Norfolk', *Country Life* (March, 1988).

122 Robinson, J. M.: *The Wyatts: An Architectural Dynasty* (Oxford University Press, 1974), p.144.

123 Linstrum, Derek: *Sir Jeffry Wyatville* (Clarendon Press, 1972), p.141.

124 Ibid., p.50.

125 Ibid., p.XXI.

126 Ibid., p.XXI.

127 Colvin, Howard: *Biographical Dictionary of British Architects 1600–1840* (Murray, 1978), pp.654–5.

128 Arrowsmith, H. W.: *The House Decorator and Painter's Guide* (1840), opp. p.52.

129 Frampton, Mary: *Journal*, 13 Sept. 1828, p.337. Notes made by Sir Owen Morshead, Royal Library, Windsor.

130 Watkin, David: *The Life and Work of C. R. Cockerell R.A.* (Zwemmer, 1974), p.81.

131 Ibid., p.31.

132 Bellaigue, G. de, and Kirkham, P.: *George IV*, op. cit., p.23.

133 Ibid.

134 Ibid., p.22.

135 *Carlton House*, Queen's Gallery Cat., op. cit., p.91.

136 Bellaigue, G. de, and Kirkham, P.: *George IV*, op. cit., p.23.

137 Ibid., p.32.

138 Notes made by Sir Owen Morshead; Royal Library, Windsor (Princess Augusta to Ernest, Duke of Cumberland).

139 Rutter, J.: *An Illustrated History and Description of Fonthill Abbey* (Shaftesbury, 1823), p.29.

140 English, E., and Maddox, W.: *Views of Lansdown Tower Bath* (1844), p.7.

141 See Gell, W., and Gandy, J. P.: *Pompeiana*, op. cit., 'House of Pansa', pl. 36.

142 Taken from a printed, undated letter prefacing Lewis Melville: *Life and Letters of William Beckford* (Heinemann, London, 1910); Melville dates this letter to 1823 (p.324). However, the reference to the 'little book-gallery' may refer to Lansdown Tower.

143 Early Renaissance painting had been noticed for some time. In 1775 Romney, who was deeply influenced by antique sculpture, had praised Cimabue, and said that Masaccio's 'strength of character and expression' had been surpassed only by Michelangelo and Raphael. Flaxman was much influenced by early Italian art. The early Renaissance was much discussed and collected after c.1800.

144 Hope has hanging cupboards; compare Beckford's with pl. III of *Household Furniture*, op. cit.

145 A Carpaccio-like study, containing round-headed windows and a table not unlike those at Lansdown Tower in general effect is seen p.151 of the *Hypnerotomachie . . . de Poliphile* (Paris, 1651).

146 Kelsall, Charles: *A Letter to the Society of the Dilettanti on the Works in Progress at Windsor* (Mela Brittanicus, 1827), op. cit., p.55.

147 English, E., and Maddox, W.: *Views of Lansdown*, op. cit., p.6.

148 The millionaire Beckford was economical with scarlet moreen at Fonthill in 1817. Having decided against wallpaper, as too scarlet and difficult to hang, nobody in Salisbury being capable of the job, 'I have

decided to use moreen; eighty yards will be enough, there being no necessity to moreen behind the great cabinet and the two Buhl'. Boyd Alexander: *Life at Fonthill* (Hart-Davis, 1957), p.208.

149 Compare with the chair of 'Jupiter from a Greek vase': Hope, T.: *Costume of the Ancients* (1841), p.115.

150 The similarity of this kind of taste to that of the creators of the German *Wunderkammer* has led to the suggestion that Beckford 'intended that his collection should be modelled on the Wunderkammer he had seen on the Continent'. See M. Snodin and M. Baker: 'Beckford's Silver', *Burlington Magazine* (1980), CXXII, p.744. The present writer can see no evidence of this. Had Beckford really been interested in creating a *Wunderkammer*, the small rooms of Lansdown Tower would have been ideal for the purpose.

151 Repton, Humphry: *Designs for the Pavilion at Brighton* (J. C. Stadler, London, 1808), p.33.

152 Quoted by Peter Thornton: *Authentic Decor*, op. cit., p.149.

153 Meason, Gilbert Laing: *On the Landscape Architecture of the Great Painters of Italy* (C. Hullmandel, London, 1828), vol. 4, p.49.

154 Quoted *Annals of Thomas Banks*, ed. C. F. Bell (Cambridge University Press, 1983), pp.86, 91.

CHAPTER THREE
The Architectural Interior: Classical Styles

1 Pückler-Muskau, Prince: *Tour of a German Prince* (London, 1832), vol. 4, p.49.

2 Illustrated *Country Life* (28 April 1988), p.130.

3 The wonderful ensemble has been dismantled over the last twenty years, a loss of European significance.

4 Quoted David Watkin: *The Life and Work of C. R. Cockerell R.A.* (Zwemmer, 1974), p.71.

5 Hope, Thomas: *Household Furniture and Interior Decoration* (1807; Tiranti repr., London, 1970), p.21.

6 Ibid.

7 Ibid.

8 Ibid., p.33.

9 Redding, Cyrus: *Memoirs of William Beckford of Fonthill* (C. J. Street, London, 1859), vol. II. p.312.

10 Hayden, B. R.: *Life of B. R. Hayden . . . Memoirs* (Longman, 1853), vol. III, p.156. The picture has since suffered a radical cleaning which has removed details seen in early engravings.

11 Britton, J., and Pugin, A.,: *Illustrations of the Public Buildings of London* (J. Taylor, London, 1825), p.220.

12 Richardson, George: *New Designs in Architecture* (Printed for the author, London, 1792), pl. XLII.

13 Illustrated *Country Life*, 28 April 1988, p.131.

14 See E. Aiken: *Essay on the Doric Order of Architecture* (1810), pl. VI: 'Theatre of Marcellus'.

15 Illustrated Dorothy Stroud: *The Architecture of Sir John Soane* (The Studio, London, 1961), pl. 43.

16 *Gryll Grange* (1860), by Thomas Love Peacock. Lord Curryfin may have got the idea from Saunders' *A Treatise on Theatres* (Printed for the author, London, 1790), pp.49–50.

17 Soane, Sir John: *Lectures on Architecture*, ed. Arthur Bolton (Soane Museum, 1929), Lect. II, p.46.

18 Ibid., p.54.

19 Ibid., Lect. VIII, p.127.

20 Illustrated D. Stroud: *Sir John Soane*, op. cit., pl. 120.

21 See the reconstruction in G. A. Guattini: *Monumenti Antichi Inediti* (Rome, 1784), vols 5–6, p.XXXII.

22 Repton, Humphry: *Observations on the Theory and Practice of Landscape Gardening (1803): The Landscape Gardening and Landscape Architecture of the late Humphry Repton Esq.*, ed. J. C. Loudon (London, 1840), p.303.

23 See British Museum clay libation dishes by the potter Sotades, c.460 B.C.: Exh. D.8, 9, 10.

24 Watkin, D.: *C. R. Cockerell*, op. cit., p.172.

25 Now in store awaiting restoration. These are crucial for the total effect.

26 Morley, J. H.: *Designs and Drawings: The Making of the Royal Pavilion* (Sotheby, 1984), p.79.

27 They may have influenced Schinkel; see the cast-iron staircase formerly in Prince Albrecht's Palace, Berlin: illustrated: *K. F. Schinkel*, ed. Michael Snodin (Yale, 1991), p.79.

28 Soane, Sir John: Lectures, op. cit., Lect. IV, p.71,

29 Laugier, Abbé: *Observations sur L'Architecture* (The Hague and Paris, 1765), pp.283–7.

30 See Thomas Hope: *Historical Essay on Architecture* (Murray, 1840), p.461.

31 Papworth, Wyatt: *J. B. Papworth* (London, 1879), pp.107–08.

32 Tatham, C. H.: *Etchings of Ancient Ornamental Architecture . . . drawn in . . . 1744, 1795, and 1796* (London, 1803), p.32.

33 Smith, George: *The Cabinet-Maker and Upholsterer's Guide* (London, 1826), p.164.

34 Papworth, W.: *J. B. Papworth*, op. cit., pp.107–08.

35 Whittock, Nathaniel: *The Decorative Painters' and Glaziers' Guide* (1827), p.192.

36 Linstrum, Derek: *Sir Jeffry Wyatville* (Clarendon Press, 1972), p.176.

37 Smith, G.: *Cabinet-Maker* (1826), op. cit., p.174.

38 Watkin, D.: *C. R. Cockerell*, op. cit., p.52.

39 Soane, Sir John: *Lectures*, op. cit., Lect. XI, p.171.

40 Hope, T.: *Essay on Architecture*, op. cit., p.488.

41 Ibid., p.490.

42 Ibid., pp.491–2.

43 Robinson, John Martin: *The Wyatts: An Architectural Dynasty* (Oxford University Press, 1979), p.60.

44 Croft-Murray, Edward: *Decorative Painting in England* (London, 1970), vol. 2, p.69.

45 Pyne, W. H.: *History of the Royal Residences: Carlton House* (London, 1819), p.58, 'Looking glasses of considerable size, in richly carved and gilt picture frames'.

46 Tatham Papers, V. & A. unpaginated.

47 All illustrated J. H. Morley: *Designs and Drawings*, op. cit.

48 Linstrum, D.: *Sir Jeffry Wyatville*, op. cit., p.193.

49 Alexander, Boyd: *Life at Fonthill* (Hart-Davis, 1957), p.295.

50 Colvin, Howard: *Biographical Dictionary of British Architects 1600–1840* (Murray, 1978), p.153.

51 Quoted J. M. Robinson: *The Wyatts*, op. cit., p.150.

52 Soane, Sir John: *Description of the House and Museum, on the North Side of Lincoln's Inn Fields* (1830), p.50.

53 Hussey, C.: *Country Life* (20 Dec. 1956).

54 Smith, G.: *Cabinet-Maker* (1826), op. cit., p.174.

55 Pückler-Muskau, Prince: *Tour*, op. cit., vol. 4, p.339, 29 April 1828.

56 Quoted from Mrs. Arbuthnot's Journal: John Hardy: 'The Building and Decoration of Apsley House', *Apollo* (Sept. 1973), pp.14, 23, 16.

57 Ibid., p.17.

58 Hardy, John: *Apsley House*, op. cit., p.17.

59 Ibid., p.16.

60 Smith, G.: *Cabinet-Maker* (1826), op. cit., p.173.

61 Ibid., pl. CLII.

62 Ibid., pl. XXXVII.

63 Ibid., p.176.

CHAPTER FOUR
Gothic Styles

1 Stroud, Dorothy: *Humphry Repton* (Country Life, 1962), p.51.

2 *The Farington Diary*, ed. James Grieg (Hutchinson, 1923), vol. II, p.217.

3 Horace Walpole 1774, quoted E. J. Willson: preface to A. Pugin: *Specimens of Gothic Architecture* (1825), 3rd edn., vol. I, p.XIV.

4 Ackermann's *Repository* (March 1809), p.171.

5 Ibid. (March 1811), p.168.

6 Watkin, David: *The Life and Work of C. R. Cockerell R.A.* (Zwemmer, 1974), p.44.

7 Hope, Thomas: *Essay on Historical Architecture* (Murray, 1840), p.458.

8 Quoted by M.-L. Biver: *Pierre Fontaine* (Libraire Plon, 1964), p.207.

9 See Robert Rosenblum: *Transformations in Late Eighteenth Century Art* (Princeton, 1967).

10 Melville, L.: *Life and Letters of William Beckford* (1910), p.105.

11 Britton, John: *The Auto-biography of John Britton* (Printed for the author, London, 1850), vol. I, p.230.

12 Ibid.

13 Fatma Moussa Mahmoud: *William Beckford of Fonthill*, 'Beckford, Vathek and the Orient' (Kennikar Press, 1972), p.70.

14 Boyd Alexander: 'The Decay of Beckford's Genius', in ibid., pp.28–9.

15 Rutter, J.: *An Illustrated History and Description of Fonthill Abbey* (Published by the author, Shaftesbury, 1823), (outer title page); *Delineations of Fonthill and its Abbey* (Published by the author, London, 1823), (inner title page), London Library copy, p.21.

16 Fatma Moussa Mahmoud: *William Beckford*, op. cit., 'Vathek and the Oriental Tale'; note 109.

17 Britton, J.: *The Auto-biography of John Britton*, op. cit., vol. I, p.228.

18 Macaulay, Rose: *They Went to Portugal* (Penguin, 1985), p.141.

19 See Edgar Allan Poe: 'The Assignation, Venice', with its Byronic hero, likened to the Emperor Commodus. Other tales contain other accoutrements (ebony cabinets, rich goblets, etc.) of Beckfordian character (see especially 'Ligeia').

20 Redding, W.: *Memoirs of William Beckford* (London, 1859), p.147.

21 Rutter, J.: *An Illustrated History*, op. cit., p.23.

22 Ibid., p.55.

23 Ibid.

24 Wainwright, C.: *The Romantic Interior* (Yale, 1989), pp.138–9.

25 Rutter, J.: *An Illustrated History*, op. cit., p.54.

26 Ibid., p.53.

27 Beckford's predilection for ebony led to a 1798 plan for Fonthill that sounds like a Poe short story: 'the Revelation Chamber . . . to be 125 feet long and 12 feet wide. It is to be wainscotted with Ebony, and in compartments are to be Historical Pictures by English Artists . . . walls 5 feet thick in which are to be recesses to admit coffins. Beckford's coffin to be placed opposite the door. The room is not to be entered by strangers, to be viewed through wire gratings. The floor is to be Jasper.' Farington, 22 Dec. 1798, from a conversation with Wyatt. Quoted John Wilton-Ely: 'The Genesis and Evolution of Fonthill Abbey', *Architectural History*, 23 (1980), p.44.

28 Ibid., p.35.

29 Wainwright, C.: *Romantic Interior*, op. cit., p.124.

30 Rutter, J.: *An Illustrated History*, op. cit., p.60.

31 Ibid., p.54.

32 Letter 15 Sept. 1817: quoted Boyd Alexander: *Life at Fonthill* (Hart-Davis, 1957), p.221. W. Redding, in his *Memoirs of William Beckford*, op. cit., says that candlesticks best displayed the perspective of the long galleries at night (p.139), a remark probably made by Beckford.

33 Rutter, J.: *An Illustrated History*, op. cit., p.34.

34 Britton, John: *Graphical and Literary Illustrations of Fonthill Abbey* (Printed for the author, London, 1823), p.47.

35 Rutter, J.: *An Illustrated History*, op. cit., p.63.

36 Ibid., p.50.

37 Ibid., p.XXI.

38 Ibid., p.41.

39 Ibid., p.37.

40 Smith, George: *Collection of Designs for Household Furniture* (1808), pl. 150.

41 Repton, Humphry: *Observations on the Theory and Practice of Landscape Gardening (1803): The Landscape Gardening and Landscape Architecture of the late Humphry Repton Esq.*, ed. J. C. Loudon (London, 1840), p.219.

42 Repton, Humphry: *Designs for the Pavillon at Brighton* (J. C. Stadler, London, 1808), p.22.

43 Gibbon, Edward: *Decline and Fall of the Roman Empire* (London, 1818), vol. VI, p.236.

44 Soane, Sir John: *Description of the House and Museum, on the North Side of Lincoln's Inn Fields* (1830), p.6.

45 McCarthy, Michael: *Journal of the Society of Architectural Historians*, vol. XLIV, no. 2 (May 1985), p.136.

46 Ackermann's *Repository* (1811), vol. VI, pp.167–8.

47 *Carlton House*, Queen's Gallery Catalogue (Balding & Mansell, 1991), op. cit., p.225.

48 Royal Archives: Georgian Papers No. 51308–9.

49 Quoted John Cornforth: *The Quest for Comfort* (Barrie & Jenkins, 1978), p.47. The draperies and curtains were initially executed by Gillow, directed by the architect Joseph Kay, Porden's son-in-law (see J. P. Neale: *Views of the Seats of Noblemen*; 1818, vol. I, unpaginated).

50 Quoted by Frances Collard: *Regency Furniture* (Antique Collectors Club, 1985), p.182.

51 *The Farington Diary*, ed. James Grieg (Hutchinson, 1923), 20 July 1804, p.270.

52 Whittock, Nathaniel: *Decorative Painters' and Glaziers' Guide* (1827), p.115.

53 Wedgwood, Alexandra: *A.W.N. Pugin and the Pugin Family* (V. & A., 1985), p.242.

54 Ibid.

55 Royal Library, R.L. 18386.

56 Wedgwood, A.: *A.W.N. Pugin*, op. cit., p.242.

57 Bellaigue, G. de, and Kirkham, P.: 'George IV and the Furnishing of Windsor Castle', *Furniture History Society Journal* (1972), p.15.

58 Ibid., p.20.

59 Sotheby's Catalogue, 9 April 1970, p.15, Lot 160.

60 Britton, J.: *Graphical Illustrations*, op. cit., p.42.

61 *The Mirror of Literature, Amusement and Instruction* (24 Jan. 1824), p.50.

62 For the furnishing of Newstead see: Doris Langley Moore: *Accounts Rendered* (Murray, 1974).

63 Loudon, J.C.: *Encyclopaedia of Cottage, Farm and Villa Architecture and Furniture* (London, 1857), p.1039.

64 Croker, T.C.: *A Walk from London to Fulham* (William Tegg, London, 1860), p.213. Craven Cottage had some affinities with Edward James' wonderfully surrealistic Monkton House in Sussex, in many ways 'Regency Revival'. Its contents were sold by the Trustees of his Foundation after his death, effectively destroying a wonderful creation.

65 Ibid., p.212.

66 Loudon, J.C.: *Encyclopaedia*, op. cit., p.1039

67 Croker, T.C.: *A Walk*, op. cit., pp.217–32.

68 Bartell, Edmund: *Hints for Picturesque Improvements in Ornamented Cottages* (J. Taylor, London, 1804), p.47.

69 Mavror, Elizabeth: *The Ladies of Llangollen* (Michael Joseph, 1971), pp.175–6.

70 Nicholson, S. and G.: *Plas Newydd and Vale Crucis Abbey* (Liverpool, 1824), p.11.

71 *George Bullock Cabinet-Maker* by C. Wainwright, M. Levy, and L. Wood (Murray & Blairman, 1988), p.52.

72 E.g. G.B. Piranesi: *Trofei di Ottaviano Augusto* (Rome, 1753), for splendid classical trophies.

73 *George Bullock*, op. cit., pp.57–61.

74 Parker, T.L.: *Description of Browsholme Hall* (S. Gosnell, London, 1815), p.6.

75 Ollard, Richard: *The Image of the King* (Hodder & Stoughton, 1979), pp.189–90. Quotations from C.S. Lewis, G.M. Trevelyan, et al.

76 Wainwright, C.: *Romantic Interior*, op. cit. p.154.

77 Wainwright, C.: 'Sir Walter Scott and the Furnishing of Abbotsford', *Connoisseur* (Jan. 1977), p.5.

78 Scott, Sir Walter: *The Journal of Sir Walter Scott*, ed. W.E.K. Anderson (Oxford University Press, 1972), March 1828, p.438.

79 Hay, D.R.: *The Laws of the Harmony of Colours adapted to House Painting* (1828), pp.25, 86.

80 Wainwright, C.: *The Romantic Interior*, op. cit., p.167.

81 Ibid.

82 Ibid., p.168.

83 Ibid., pp.199–200.

84 Ibid., pp.188–9.

85 The effect of gaslight was not always happy: 'the sun went down, and suddenly, at the turning of a screw, the room was filled with a gush of splendour worthy of the palace of Aladdin; but, as in the case of Aladdin, the old

lamp would have been better in the upshot. Jewellery sparkled, but cheeks and lips looked cold and wan in this fierce illumination; and the eye was wearied, and the brow ached, if the sitting was at all protracted'; quoted C. Wainwright: *Romantic Interior*, op. cit., p.182.

86 Hay, D.R.: *Laws of Harmony*, op. cit., p.27.

87 All facts, as distinct from comment, in the following account are taken from Sheena Stoddard: *Mr. Braikenridge's Brislington* (Bristol Museum & Art Gallery, 1981).

88 Wainwright, C.: *Romantic Interior*, op. cit., p.247.

89 Quoted ibid., p.255.

90 This and the above quotations are given in C. Wainwright: *Romantic Interior*, op. cit., p.253.

91 Walpole, Horace: *Journals of Visits to Country Seats* (Walpole Society, Oxford University Press, 1928), vol. 16, p.29.

92 See *Audley End House* (1984), P.J. Drury and I.R. Gow, p.30; also Richard Lord Braybroke: *History of Audley End* (London, 1836), p.120.

93 Braybroke, Lord: *Audley End*, op. cit., p.100.

94 Colvin, Howard: *Biographical Dictionary of British Architects 1600–1840* (Murray, 1978), p.392.

95 Braybroke, Lord: *Audley End*, op. cit., p.127.

96 Ibid., p.115.

97 Ibid., p.132.

98 Drury, P.J. and Gow, I.R.: *Audley End House*, op. cit., p.26.

99 Braybroke, Lord: *Audley End*, op. cit., pp.98–9.

100 Illustrated Design No. 9, P.F. Robinson: *Designs for ornamental villas* (J. Carpenter & Son, London, 1827).

101 Ibid., Design No. 9.

102 The Palazzo Lancellotti was pictured in Charles Percier and Pierre Fontaine's *Palais, Maisons et autres édifices modernes dessinées à Rome* (Paris, 1798), pl. 67.

103 Smith, George: *Cabinet-Maker and Upholsterer's Guide* (London, 1826), pl. XCII.

104 Illustrated Charlotte Gere: *Nineteenth-Century Decoration: The Art of the Interior* (Weidenfeld & Nicolson, 1989), p.210.

CHAPTER FIVE
Exotic Styles

1 *Gazette of Fashion* (1822), p.82.

2 Whittock, Nathaniel: *Decorative Painters' and Glaziers' Guide* (1827), p.114.

3 See G. de Bellaigue: 'The Furnishings of the Chinese Drawing Room, Carlton House', *Burlington Magazine*, vol. CIX (Sept. 1967), pp.526, 527.

4 See Sir Williams Chambers: *Designs of Chinese Buildings* (Published for the author, London, 1757), pl. IV.

5 'Fret or Key moulding, has the highest claim to antiquity, existing from the earliest period among the Chinese and Persians, from whence it was carried into Egypt, and from thence into Greece . . .': Smith, George: *The Cabinet-Maker and Upholsterer's Guide* (London, 1826), p.41.

6 Musgrave, Clifford: *Royal Pavilion: Episode in the Romantic* (MacLehose Ltd., 1959), p.34.

7 See J.H. Morley: *Designs and Drawings: The Making of the Royal Pavilion* (Sotheby, 1984), illusts 131, 141, 150.

8 Ibid., p.133.

9 Ibid., p.79.

10 Whittock, N.: *Decorative Painters'*, op. cit., p.114.

11 Ibid., p.115.

12 Quoted by C. Wainwright: *The Romantic Interior* (Yale, 1989), p.183.

13 Whittock, N.: *Decorative Painters'*, op. cit., p.115.

14 A Chinese Ambassador once asked the author what style the Music Room was in. When told 'Chinese' he replied that he thought it looked 'Indian'.

15 See J.H. Morley: *Designs and Drawings*, op. cit., p.213.

16 Ibid., p.204.

17 The quotations are from T. Hope's *Household Furniture and Interior Decoration* (1807; Tiranti repr., 1970), pp.24–5.

18 See, for example, pl. XLIII in Charles Cameron: *Baths of the Romans* (London, 1772); pls 14, 15, 16 in N. Ponce: *Descriptions des Bains de Titus* (Paris, 1786).

19 Illustrated J.H. Morley: *Designs and Drawings*, op. cit., p.84.

20 There must have been conscious emblemism in this. The use of the sunflower is a feature of the Saloon, and the winged solar disk is another sun symbol; Keats, for instance, used the Egyptian solar disk as a symbol of the sun in his classical epic 'Hyperion':
      Two wings this orb,
      Possess'd for glory, two fair argent wings,
      Ever exalted at the God's approach.

21 Ackermann's *Repository* (1809), pp.398–400. Ackermann, Rudolph: *Microcosm of London* (London, 1808), pp.109, 111–12.

22 See J.H. Morley: *Designs and Drawings*, op. cit., p.160

23 Denon, Vivant: *Voyage dans la Basse et la Haute Égypte*, (Paris, 1802), pl. 61: 'Réunion de divers fragmens d'architecture Egyptienne' shows a Doric column without capital or base.

24 See Damie Stillman: *English Neo-Classical Architecture* (Zwemmer, 1988), p.518.

25 Curl, J.S.: *The Egyptian Revival* (Allen & Unwin, London, 1982), p.79, on the Piranesian influence at Cairness.

26 E.g. Piranesi, G.B.: *Diverse Maniere d'adornare i Cammini* (Rome, 1769); see the wall decoration for the Caffè degli Inglesi. The walls of the Egyptian library at White-Knights were 'handsomely painted in distemper, to represent an Egyptian landscape . . .': Hofland, Mrs.: *A Descriptive Account of the Mansion and Garden of White Knights* (1819), p.42.

27 Hope, T.: *Household Furniture*, op. cit., p.27.

28 Ibid., pp.26–7.

29 Piranesi, G.B.: *Diverse Maniere*, op. cit., p.29.

30 Conveniently illustrated, as are all of Smith's 1808 designs, in John Harris: *Regency Furniture Designs 1803–1826* (Tiranti, 1961).

31 For the origin of the designs see *Le Pitture Antiche d'Ercolano* (Naples, 1765), vol. 4, p.337 et seq.

32 B.L. Add. Ms. 62112 1058 A, p.216.

33 Croker, T.C.: *A Walk from London to Fulham* (William Tegg, London, 1860), p.243.

34 *West London Observer*: 9 Sept. 1910, quoting Faulkner *History of Fulham* (London, 1812).

35 Ibid.

36 B.L. 11602, ff. 31. Produced in 1797. He also wrote 'Feudal Times' or 'The Banquet Gallery' (1799) and 'The Traveller', which was set in China, Constantinople, Naples, and England (1806).

37 Whittock, N.: *Decorative Painters'*, op. cit., p.185.

38 *West London Observer*: 1910 (see note 33 above).

39 Illustrated James Elmes: *Metropolitan Improvements* (London, 1829), p.157.

40 Papworth, Wyatt: *J.B. Papworth* (London, 1879), p.9.

41 Ibid., p.68.

42 Ibid., p.61.

43 Wood, Robert: *The Ruins of Palmyra* (London, 1757), pl. XIX.

44 Illustrated John Foulston: *Public Buildings in the West of England* (1838), pl. 90.

45 Pl. CXLVII: George Smith: *Cabinet-Maker* (1826), op. cit., p.168.

46 Whittock, N.: *Decorative Painters'*, op. cit., p.152.

47 *The Edinburgh Review* (1814), pp.288–9.

48 Medwin's *Conversations of Lord Byron*, ed. J. Lovell Jr. (Princeton University Press, 1966), p.48.

49 Hazlitt, William: *Collected Works of William Hazlitt*, ed. Walker and Glover (Dent, 1903), p.348.

50 As at Carlton House. The antique original is illustrated John Wilton-Ely: *Piranesi* (Arts Council, 1987), p.119.

51 Edgeworth, Maria: *The Absentee* (1812; Oxford University Press, 1988), pp.12–13.

CHAPTER SIX
The Cottage

1 Mavror, Elizabeth: *The Ladies of Llangollen* (Michael Joseph, 1971), pp.78, 75.

2 Bartell, Edmund: *Hints for Picturesque Improvements for Ornamental Cottages* (J. Taylor, 1804), p.52.

3 Papworth, J.B.: *Designs for Rural Residences* (Ackermann, London, 1818), p.9 et seq.

4 *Guide to the Illustrations and Views of Knowle Cottage, Sidmouth, the elegant Marine Villa Orne of Thos. L. Fish Esq.* (Sidmouth, 1834), pp.50, 51.

5 Girouard, Mark: *Country Life* (22 Sept. 1966), p.690.

6 On A la Ronde see Barbara Jones: *Follies and Grottoes* (Constable, 1974), p.312; Bea Howe: *Country Life* (3 March 1966); Gillian Walkling: *Traditional Interior Decoration* (Autumn 1986), vol. 1, no. 2.

7 Repton, Humphry: B.L. Add. Ms. 6212 1058 A., p.122.

8 Loudon, J.C.: *Encyclopaedia of Cottage, Farm, and Villa Architecture and Furniture* (London, 1857), p.240.

9 Ibid., pp.271–81.

10 Ibid., pp.344, 346, 325.

11 Cobbett, William: *Rural Rides* (Reeves & Turner, 1885), vol. I, pp.343–7.

**Part IV: Furniture**

CHAPTER ONE

Formative Influences

1 Smith, George: *Cabinet-Maker and Upholsterer's Guide* (London, 1826), p.172.

2 Sheraton, Thomas: *An Accompaniment to the Cabinet-Maker and Upholsterer's Drawing-Book (1794): The Cabinet-Maker and Upholsterer's Drawing-Book* (Dover repr., 1972), p.16.

3 Whittock, Nathaniel: *The Decorative Painter's and Glazier's Guide* (London, 1827), pp.76–7.

4 Alison, Archibald: *Essays on the Nature and Principles of Taste* (Edinburgh, 1825), p.368.

5 Ibid., p.364.

6 Ibid., p.371.

7 Loudon, J. C.: *Encyclopaedia of Cottage, Farm and Villa Architecture and Furniture* (London, 1857), p.1119.

8 *Edinburgh Review* (1807), vol. X. p.478.

9 Scott, Sir Walter: *Quarterly Review* (1828), LXXIV, p.318.

10 Papworth, Wyatt: *J. B. Papworth* (London, 1879), p.37.

11 Morgan, Lady: *The Book of the Boudoir* (1829), p.150.

12 See Simon Redburn: 'J. Maclean and Son', *Furniture History Society Journal*, vol. 14 (1978).

13 Sheraton, Thomas: *Appendix to the Cabinet-Maker's and Upholsterer's Drawing-Book (1793): The Cabinet-Maker and Upholsterer's Drawing Book* (Dover repr., 1972), p.27.

14 Ibid., pp.28–9.

15 Percier, Charles and Fontaine, Pierre: *Recueil des Décorations Intérieures* (Paris, 1827), pp.21, 27.

16 Hope, Thomas: *Household Furniture and Interior Decoration* (1807; Tiranti repr, 1970), p.25.

17 Ibid., p.30.

18 Smith, Rev. Sydney: *Edinburgh Review* (July 1807), p.484.

19 Brown, Richard: *Rudiments of Drawing Room Cabinet and Upholstery Furniture* (London, 1822), pp.31, 44.

20 Stokes, J.: *Complete Cabinet Maker and Upholsterer's Guide* (London, undated), p.39.

21 Ibid., p.40.

22 Watkin, David: *The Life and Work of C. R. Cockerell R.A.* (Zwemmer, 1974), pp.19–20.

23 Irwin, D.: *English Neo-Classical Art* (Faber & Faber, 1966), p.111.

24 Fothergill, Brian: *Sir William Hamilton Envoy Extraordinary* (Faber & Faber, 1969), pp.68, 69.

25 Hope, T.: *Household Furniture*, op. cit., pl. XXXIX.

26 Mitford, William: *Principles of Design in Architecture* (London, 1809), p.251.

CHAPTER TWO

Classical Styles

1 Giulio Romano: *Lovers with Procuress* (Hermitage); Lambert Sustris: *Venus awaiting Mars* (Louvre); illustrated *Lives of the Courtesans* (Rizzoli, New York, 1987), pp.41, 152.

2 Santini: *Architecture et Ornemens de la Loge du Vatican* (Venice, 1783), p.34.

3 Richter, Gisela: *The Furniture of the Greeks, Etruscans, and Romans* (Phaidon, 1966), pp.36, 125.

4 Hope, Thomas: *Household Furniture and Interior Decoration*, (1807; Tiranti repr., 1970), p.29.

5 Quoted Hector Lefuel from *Souvenirs de Mme. Vigée Le Brun* (1865), in *Georges Jacob* (Albert Morancé, 1923), p.114.

6 Honour, Hugh: *Cabinet Makers & Furniture Designers* (Weidenfeld & Nicolson, 1969), p.172.

7 Lefuel, H.: *Georges Jacob*, op. cit., pp.133, 136.

8 Landon, C. P.: *Annales du Musée* (Paris, 1801), p.16.

9 Review by Lindsay Boynton in *Furniture History*, vol. X (1974), p.108.

10 Musgrave, Clifford: *Regency Furniture* (Faber & Faber, 1970), p.29. Still the best general survey of the subject.

11 See Dorothy Stroud: *Henry Holland* (1966), p.74. Miss Stroud thinks the Papworth idea that they were brought over by George Sheringham is unlikely.

12 Watson, F. J. B.: 'Holland and Daguerre', *Apollo* (Oct. 1972), p.282.

13 Sheraton, Thomas: *The Cabinet-Maker and Upholsterer's Drawing-Book* (1791; Dover repr., 1972), p.444.

14 Ibid., p.443.

15 Ibid., p.445.

16 Ibid., pp.444–5.

17 Ward-Jackson, Peter: *English Furniture Designs of the Eighteenth Century* (H.M.S.O., London, 1984), p.23.

18 Stroud, Dorothy: *Henry Holland*, op. cit., p.111.

19 Sheraton, T.: *Drawing-Book*, op. cit., p.10.

20 Hepplewhite, G.: *The Cabinet-Maker and Upholsterer's Guide* (1794, 3rd edn.; Dover repr., 1969), pls 12, 13.

21 Sheraton, Thomas: *The Cabinet Dictionary* (1803), p.314.

22 Shearer has a similar design: pl. 6: *The Cabinet-Maker's London Book of Prices* (1788), and the table was first illustrated in the *Cabinet-Maker's Book of Prices* (1792).

23 Sheraton, T.: *Drawing-Book*, op. cit., p.437.

24 Ibid., p.22.

25 Sheraton, T.: *Appendix . . . to the Drawing-Book*, op. cit., opp. p.42.

26 Sheraton, T.: *Drawing-Book*, op. cit., p.365.

27 Sheraton, T.: *Encyclopaedia*, op. cit., pl. 47.

28 See e.g. the painting *The Marchesa Gentili Roccapaduli*, 1776, which shows a remarkable 'archaeological' Egyptianising pier table and other furniture: Praz, Mario: *An Illustrated History of Interior Decoration* (Thames & Hudson, 1964), p.170.

29 Gonzalez-Palacios, A.: *Il Mobili nei Secoli Italia* (Milan, 1969), vol. 3, p.51, 'Le sedie sono di modello raro, ideate certamente in quegli stessi anni [1782]'.

30 Groth, Hakan: *Neoclassicism in the North* (Thames & Hudson, 1990), pp.72, 73, 220.

31 Goethe, J. W.: *Italian Journey*, trans. W. H. Auden and E. Mayer (Penguin, 1970), p.315.

32 Jaffé, Patricia: *Lady Hamilton* (Shenval, 1972), p.30. Sir William Hamilton was portrayed in the robes of a Knight of the Bath standing beside a table of advanced classical design (National Portrait Gallery).

33 The best account of the Southill furniture is contained in an essay by Sir Francis Watson in *Southill, A Regency House*, ed. Major S. Whitbread (Faber & Faber, 1951). It also has photographs of the major pieces.

34 Stroud, D.: *Henry Holland*, op. cit., p.128.

35 Illustrated Margaret Jourdain: 'Regency Furniture at Southill Park', *Country Life* (7 Dec. 1929), p.844.

36 Adam, Robert: *The Works in Architecture of Robert and James Adam* (London, 1778), pl. VIII.

37 E.g. Cabinet by P. Garnier: Wallace Collection, F.25.

38 Cook, B. F.: *The Towneley Marbles* (British Museum, 1985), p.11.

39 Illustrated M. Jourdain: 'Regency Furniture', op. cit., p.843,

40 See e.g. faience cosmetic vessel Egyptian c.1000 B.C. B.M.EA 71515.

41 Montfaucon, Bernard de: *L'Antiquité Expliquée* (Paris, 1719–24), vol. V, p.81.

42 Caylus, Comte de: *Recueil d'Antiquités Egyptiennes, Etrusques, Grecques et Romaines* (Paris, 1761), vol. V, pl. CVI, p.300.

43 *Le Lucerne ed i Candelabri d'Ercolano* (Naples, 1792), pl. XV, p.93.

44 Sir Francis Watson mentions the 'smaller sofas, single-headed couches and chairs' at Southill which 'derive from antique Roman models. The ébéniste Jacob had used a rather richer version of this pattern . . . for the furniture he had designed for the painter J. L. David's studio as early as 1788. Only the treatment of the feet is heavier in the English version' (Watson, F. J. B.: *Southill*, op. cit., p.29). David is recorded as having furnished his atelier with furniture after the antique, including 'chaises courantes' after 'celles dont la représentation est si fréquente sur les vases dits étrusques' (klismos chairs?); the furniture included 'une chaise curule en bronze, dont les extrémitifs des deux X se terminaient, en haut et en bas, par des têtes et des pieds d'animaux, et . . . un grand siège à dossiers en acajou massif, orné de bronzes dorés et garnis du coussins et de draperies rouges et noires; le tout avait été fidèlement imité de l'antique et exécuté par le plus habil ébéniste de ce temps, Jacob, d'après les dessins de David et de Moreau' (Lefuel, H.: *Georges Jacob*, op. cit., p.142, quoting E.-J. Delécluze: *Louis David* Paris, 1855). This furniture has been taken by Sir Francis and others to be that shown in David's paintings: 'David . . . [designed] models for several pieces of furniture of "archaeological" character, which were realised by Georges Jacob. . . . Unfortunately not one of his pieces is left, and one must be content to study them in some of the master's paintings, like the "Paris and Helen" . . . or the "Death of Socrates"' (A. González-Palacios: *The Age of Louis XVI*, Hamlyn, 1966, p.118): 'Shortly afterwards [after 1785] Georges Jacob received a commission for a suite of furniture in the new style for David's studio and the painter himself provided the designs. Although it no longer survives, we can judge its appearance, for it was used in David's *Amours de Paris et Hélène* painted for the Comte d'Artois two years later.' (Watson, F. J. B.: 'Holland and Daguerre', op. cit., p.286.)

Two studies for the painting by David, one dated 1786, show the form of the sofa evolving. In the second study, which approximates to the finished painting, David modified the arm and substituted a completely different leg; an accurately archaeological leg in the first study was rejected (see *J.-L. David*, Musée du Louvre, Éditions de la Réunion des Musées Nationaux, Paris, 1989, pp.83, 185). Given these alterations, it seems unlikely that David

was working from a sofa, designed by himself or by Jacob, which was before him in actuality. It seems more probable that he used the publications of Roman and Greek furniture that were available to him — one knows that he traced Hamilton's 'Vases' (Boime, Albert: *Art in an Age of Revolution*; Chicago, 1987, p.156) — as they were available to Mengs and later painters. The re-creation of ancient furniture in paintings was common; e.g. Lawrence's *John Philip Kemble as Cato* (1812) shows the actor seated in an extraordinary 'Roman' chair (illustrated *Royal Opera House Retrospective 1732–1982*, Lund Humphries, 1982, Cat. 138).

It is not possible accurately to visualise furniture from a written description, and without harder evidence one cannot assume that the furniture made for David's atelier was that depicted in his paintings; if it were, it would have been 'd'une puissance à la fois majestueuse et brutale' (Lefuel, Hector: *Jacob-Desmalter*, Editions Albert Morancé, 1925, p.32). The piece that seems to have existed — Mme. Récamier's sofa, upon which she reclines in David's portrait of 1800 (a somewhat different version is seen in an 1826 painting of her in retirement at the Abbaye-aux-Bois, illustrated in Mario Praz: *History of Interior Decoration*, op. cit., p.210) — is a suaver version of Roman style; in the context of 1826 it looks tame, but might have seemed 'fidèlement imité de l'antique' in the late 1780s. Perhaps it reflects the style of furniture made for the atelier.

45 Tatham, C. H., V. & A. correspondence; letter to Henry Holland; Naples, 11 Nov. 1795.

46 Ibid., Rome, 4 April 1796.

47 Ibid., 10 July 1795. The design for the pier tables is in the R.I.B.A.

48 Tatham, C. H.: *Designs for Ornamental Plate* (London, 1806), p.1.

49 Review of Tatham's *Ornamental Plate* in the *Eclectic Review*, vol. III, part I (London, 1807), p.364.

50 Mitford, Mary Russell: *Our Village* (Everyman's Library, 1970), p.302.

51 Piranesi, G. B.: *Vasi, Candelabri, Cippi* (Rome, 1778), vol. I, pl. 47.

52 Udy, David: 'The Neoclassicism of Charles Heathcote Tatham', *Connoisseur* (August 1971), p.272.

53 Proudfoot, C. and Watkin, D.: 'The Furniture of C. H. Tatham', *Country Life* (8 June 1972), p.1482.

54 Purchased Trevor Antiques, 1972, for Brighton Pavilion.

55 *Dictionary of English Furniture Makers*, ed. G. Beard and C. Gilbert (W. Maney, Leeds, 1986), p.930.

56 Date given ibid. Other authorities give 1802.

57 *Carlton House*, Queen's Gallery Catalogue (Balding & Mansell, 1992), p.33.

58 Ibid., p.87.

59 The 'Newdigate Candelabrum'; illustrated J. Wilton-Ely: *Piranesi* (Arts Council, 1987), catalogue p.118.

60 Harris, J., Millar, O., and de Bellaigue, G.: *Buckingham Palace* (Nelson, 1968), p.154.

61 Tatham, C. H.: *Etchings . . . of Ancient Ornamental Architecture . . . drawn . . . in . . . 1794, 1795, & 1796* (London, 1803), pls 83, 85.

62 Smith, George: *Collection of Designs for Household Furniture* (London, 1808), pl. 42.

63 Sheraton, T.: *Cabinet Dictionary*, op. cit., p.20.

64 Montfaucon, Bernard de: *L'Antiquité Expliquée*, op. cit., vol. III, 2nd part, pl. CXCI.

65 Quoted Clifford Musgrave: *Regency Furniture*, op. cit., p.41.

66 *Le Lucerne ed i Candelabri d'Ercolano*, vol. I, op. cit., p.320; it shows a simulated bamboo candelabrum in bronze.

67 Watkin, David: *Thomas Hope and the Neoclassical Idea* (Murray, 1968), p.51.

68 Cumberland, George: *Thoughts on Outline* (Robinson, Egerton, London, 1796), p.47.

69 Ibid., pp.8, 16.

70 Hope, Thomas: *Historical Essay on Architecture* (Murray, 1840), p.VI.

71 Hope, T.: *Household Furniture*, op. cit., pp.6, 7.

72 Ibid., p.10.

73 'The ornaments on that mahogany sideboard, and on that stand (in Mr. Roger's dining-room) were carved by [Chantrey]. Chantrey said to me "Do you recollect that, about twenty-five years ago, a journeyman came to your house, from the woodcarver employed by you and Mr. Hope, to talk about these ornaments, and that you gave him a drawing to execute them by?"' The drawing must have been by Hope, who helped Rogers to decorate his house: *Recollections of the Table-Talk of Samuel Rogers* (Edw. Moxon, London, 1856), p.158.

74 From a letter of 1805 to Matthew Boulton. Quoted D. Watkin: *Thomas Hope*, op. cit., p.198.

75 Hope T.: *Household Furniture*, op. cit., p.53.

76 Watkin, D.: *Thomas Hope*, op. cit., p.198.

77 Definition from the Oxford English Dictionary (1984).

78 Hope, T.: *Household Furniture*, op. cit., pp.16, 29.

79 Ibid., p.53.

80 *Quinti Horatii Flacci Opera* (Didot, 1799).

81 Caylus, Comte de: *Recueil d'Antiquités*, op. cit., vol. VI, p.286, pl. LXXXIII.

82 *Le Pitture Antiche d'Ercolano* (Naples, 1765), vol. IV, p.211.

83 Hope, T.: *Household Furniture*, op. cit., p.44

84 Ibid., p.35.

85 Norden, F. L.: *Voyage d'Egypte et de Nubie* (Copenhagen, 1755), pl. CXLIV.

86 Quincy, Q. de: *L'Architecture Egyptienne* (Paris, 1803), pls 1, 9.

87 Hope, T.: *Household Furniture*, op. cit., p.30.

88 Ottomeyer, Hans, and Prischel, Peter: *Vergoldete Bronzen*, vol. 1, fig. 5.3.2.

89 Tatham letters, V. & A., 10 July 1795.

90 Described as 'hung with tent-like drapery' by John Tombs: *The Curiosities of London* (London, 1855), vol. 11, p.489.

91 Hope, T.: *Household Furniture*, op. cit., p.35, and Tatham, C. H.: *Etchings*, op. cit., pl. 72.

92 Flaxman, John: *Compositions from the tragedies of Aeschylus* (London, 1795), pl. 32 (a book listed by Hope as a source).

93 Hope T.: *Household Furniture*, op. cit., p.28.

94 Ibid., p.33.

95 Tatham, C. H.: *Etchings*, op. cit., pl. 85.

96 Ibid., pls 22, 25. For a discussion of this form see M. Praz: *Neoclassicism* (Thames and Hudson, 1959), pp.89–90, and Svend Eriksen and F. J. B. Watson: 'The Athenienne', *Burlington Magazine* (March 1963).

97 Percier, Charles, and Fontaine, Pierre: *Recueil de Décorations Intérieures* (Paris, 1827), op. cit., pl.33.

98 Hope, T.: *Household Furniture*, op. cit., p.14.

99 Ibid., p.38.

100 Smith, G.: *Designs for Household Furniture* (1808), op. cit., pl. 143.

101 Ms. attached to a copy of Smith (1808) in the V. & A. Library.

102 Tatham, C. H.: *Etchings*, op. cit., 'Antique seats executed in Bronze, from the Collection in the Museum at Portici belonging to the King of Naples', p.74.

103 Hope, T.: *Household Furniture*, op. cit., pl. 29, 1 & 2.

104 Percier and Fontaine: *Recueil*, op. cit., pl. 39.5.

105 Smith, G.: *Designs for Household Furniture* (1808), op. cit., pl. 55.

106 Hope, T.: *Household Furniture*, op. cit., pl. 20, 5 & 6.

107 Ibid., pl. 22, 5 & 6. Smith drew his chair from the ingredients of two Hope chairs; Hope assembled the chair in plate 22 from various sources, including the 'Trono di Bacco' (*Museo Pio-Clementino*, edn. Milan, 1818, vol. 7, p.208, pl. XLIV); the end of the arm may be copied from a 'cuillière d'argent' (itself taken from a 'battering-ram') illustrated in Caylus, *Recueil*, op. cit., (vol. V., pl. CIV, p.289). Tatham perhaps served as another source.

108 Ibid., pl. 22.1.

109 Desgodetz, A.: *Les Edifices Antiques de Rome dessinés et mesurés très exactement* (Paris, 1682), p.19.

110 Piranesi, G. B.: *Opere Varie di Architettura, Prospettiva, Grotteschi, Antichita* (Rome, 1750), pl. 5.

111 *Le Lucerne ed i Candelabri*, op. cit., vol. I, p.320.

112 Smith, G.: *Designs for Household Furniture* (1808), op. cit., p.XIV.

113 Ibid., pl. 47

114 Ibid., pl. 45.

115 Ibid., pl. 43.

116 Ibid., pl. 135.

117 Moses, Henry: *A Collection of Antique Vases, Altars, Paterae, Tripods, Candelabra, Sarcophagi etc.* (London, 1814), p.IV.

118 See Agius, P., and Jones, S.: *Ackermann's Regency Furniture and Interiors* (Crowood Press, 1984), a useful compilation with an excellent text.

119 See W. J. Burke: *Rudolph Ackermann* (New York, 1935).

120 Sheraton, T.: *The Cabinet-Maker, Upholsterer, and General Artist's Encyclopaedia* (1805–08), pls 10, 15, 17; reproduced J. Harris: *Regency Furniture Designs 1803–1826* (Tiranti, 1961), pls 13, 10, 12.

121 Hope, T.: *Household Furniture*, op. cit., pl. 40 (6). The scroll back of Hope's chair came, however, from Roman rather than Greek sources.

122 See P. Agius and S. Jones: *Ackermann's Regency Furniture*, op. cit., p.29. A pure type of klismos chair is depicted by d'Hancarville and in Didot's *Horace* (p.385), in which the back leg is bolted on as a separate appendage; the front leg has no bolt and runs in a continuous curve along the seat to the back. The chair is constructed of two pieces, with the construction made apparent, as is true, in a different way, of Hope's chair. A chair with the back leg exactly like the Didot leg is depicted in the *Repository* of January 1810; the front leg, however, is different; it joins the seat at a right angle, and is therefore given an imitation bolt like that on the back leg.

123 See *John Joseph Merlin: The Ingenious Mechanick* (Kenwood, 1985), Cat. B. 19, p.74: Grollier de Servière: *Recueil d'Ouvrager Curieux de Mathématique et de Méchanique* (Paris, 1751).

124 Agius, P., and Jones, S.: *Ackermann's Regency Furniture*, op. cit., p.72.

125 Hope, T.: *Household Furniture*, op. cit., pl. 20.6.

126 Smith, G.: *Designs for Household Furniture* (1808), op. cit., pl. 55.

127 Brown, Richard: *Rudiments of Drawing Room Cabinet and Upholstery Furniture* (London, 1822), p.XII.

128 See Chapter Four, note 17, p.452.

129 The German piece is illustrated by George Himmelheber: *Biedermeier Furniture* (Faber & Faber, 1974), pl. 112.

130 Ackermann's *Repository* (March 1825).

131 Mésangère, P. de la,: *Meubles et Objets de Goût*: Sofa No. 328, Chair No. 311. The Ackermann pieces are reproduced in P. Agius and S. Jones: *Ackermann's Regency Furniture*, op. cit., pp.52, 70.

132 Percier and Fontaine: *Recueil*, op. cit., pl. 19.

133 The motif, common on antique sarcophagi (e.g. see B. de Montfaucon: *L'Antiquité Expliquée*, op. cit., vol. V, part I), is used by Percier, pls 23 (Table de nuit . . . par les frères Jacob), and 38 (Pendule qui doit porter un Buste), and by Hope, pl.14.2. ('Pedestal, belonging to the group of Aurora and Cephalus'.) Hope used stars as employed by Percier in pl. 23, no doubt as appropriate to the dawn theme of the Flaxman Room.

134 Percier and Fontaine: *Recueil*, op. cit., pl. 29.

135 Lefuel, H.: *Jacob-Desmalter*, op. cit., p.16.

CHAPTER THREE
Revivalism and Eclecticism

1 Lefuel, Hector: *Georges Jacob* (Editions Albert Morancé, 1923), p.139.

2 Said of the Reisener jewel cabinet eventually bought by George IV in 1825: Lefuel, Hector: *Jacob-Desmalter* (Editions Albert Morancé, 1925), p.91.

3 Ibid., p.89.

4 Melville, Lewis: *Beau Brummell: His Life and Letters* (Hutchinson, 1924), p.130.

5 Jacob had begun applying it to seat furniture in the 1780s. See Geoffrey de Bellaigue: 'George IV and French Furniture', *Connoisseur* (June 1977), p.119.

6 Rogers, Samuel: *Recollections of the Table-Talk of Samuel Rogers* (Edw. Moxon, 1856), p.243.

7 Rutter, J.: *An Illustrated History and Description of Fonthill Abbey* (Published by the author, Shaftesbury 1823), outer title page: *Delineations of Fonthill and its Abbey* (Published by the author, London, 1823), (inner title page); London Library copy, pp.29, 30.

8 Ibid., p.31.

9 Van Duin, Paul: 'Two Pairs of Boulle Caskets on Stands by Thomas Parker', *Furniture History Society Journal* (1989), pp.214–17.

10 *Dictionary of English Furniture Makers*, ed. G. Beard and C. Gilbert (W. S. Maney & Son, Leeds, 1986), p.536.

11 His sculpture lacks quality.

12 Brown's *Rudiments of Drawing Room Cabinet and Upholstery Furniture* of 1822 was the second edition; the first, of which no copy is known, was probably published in 1819, the year after Bullock's death; see catalogue *George Bullock: Cabinet Maker* (Murray & Blairman, 1988), by C. Wainwright, L. Wood, M. Levy and T. Stevens, p.16.

13 Brown, R.: *Rudiments*, op. cit., p.58.

14 Hope, Thomas: *Household Furniture and Interior Decoration* (1807; Tiranti repr., 1970), p.17.

15 Landon, C. P.: *Annales du Musée* (Paris, 1801), p.16.

16 Ackermann's *Repository* (Oct. 1816), pp.243–4; (Jan. 1816), p.19.
17 Ibid. (Nov. 1816).
18 The *Bullock* catalogue, op. cit., speaks of this foot as possibly having a source in pl.53, no. 4, of Hope's *Household Furniture*, op. cit.; this seems unlikely.
19 Wilkinson Tracings, City Museum Birmingham, p.86.
20 Musgrave, Clifford: *Regency Furniture* (Faber & Faber, 1970), p.100.
21 Smith, George: *Collection of Designs for Household Furniture* (London, 1808), pls 117, 118, 119.
22 Ibid., pl. 117, pp.10, 85.
23 Wilkinson Tracings, City Museum Birmingham, p.117.
24 Percier, Charles, and Fontaine, Pierre: *Recueil de Décorations Intérieures* (Paris, 1827), pl. 59.
25 *Bullock* catalogue, op. cit., no. 27.
26 Brown, R.: *Rudiments*, op. cit., p.X.
27 Ibid.
28 Ibid., p.52.
29 Moses, Henry: *A Collection of Antique Vases, Altars, Paterae, Tripods, Candelabra, Sarcophagi etc.* (1814), p.147.
30 Hope, T.: *Household Furniture*, op. cit., pl. 39.1.2.
31 *Bullock* catalogue, op. cit., p.37.
32 Brown, R.: *Rudiments*, op. cit., p.35.
33 Ibid., pp.42–3.
34 Hope, T.: *Household Furniture*, op. cit., pl. 44, p.42.
35 One sees the gesture in painting long before the 18th century, but the most likely source for the Regency period was Herculaneum, Raphael or Guido Reni. An interesting analysis of the use of classical sources at an early period is to be found in Michael Greenhalgh: *Donatello and his Sources* (Duckworth, 1982).
36 Taylor, J.: *Original and Novel Designs* (undated), pl. 10.
37 The later Regency and early Victorian putto tends to resemble the 17th century rather than the 18th century type (Sheraton gives precise proportions for 'boys or Cupids', drawn from Cipriani); putti in Le Pautre often cavort in acanthus. The frieze designs of Stothard for Buckingham Palace, for instance, owe more to the 17th than to the 18th century.
38 Taylor, J.: *Original and Novel Designs*, op. cit., pl. 16.
39 Ibid., pl. 17.
40 Tatham Sketchbook, R.I.B.A., vol. 2/066–10.
41 Illustrated C. Musgrave: *Regency Furniture*, op. cit., p.74.
42 The documentary evidence for this is now unavailable: see J. Harris, O. Millar, and G. de

Bellaigue: *Buckingham Palace* (Nelson, 1968), p.196.
43 Compare John Vardy: *Some Designs of Mr. Inigo Jones and Mr. William Kent* (London, 1744), pl. 41 with Lots 210 (11) and 210 (111), Sotheby's Catalogue, 9 April 1970.
44 Harris, J., Millar, O., de Bellaigue, G.: *Buckingham Palace*, op. cit., p.175.
45 From the 'Address': T. King: *The Modern Style of Cabinet Work* (London Architectural Library, undated).
46 King, T.: *Designs for Carving and Gilding* (1830), pl. 1.
47 Smith, George: *The Cabinet-Maker and Upholsterer's Guide* (London, 1826), p.104.
48 Ibid., p.193.
49 Ibid., p.V.
50 Ibid., p.104
51 Ibid., p.193.
52 Ibid., p.42, figs 4, 5.
53 Whittock, Nathaniel: *The Decorative Painters' and Glaziers' Guide* (London, 1827), pp.76–7.
54 Ibid., p.90.
55 Wainwright, C.: *The Romantic Interior* (Yale University Press, 1989), p.113.
56 Rutter, J.: *An Illustrated History and Description of Fonthill Abbey* (Published by the author, Shaftesbury, 1823), outer title page: *Delineations of Fonthill and its Abbey* (Published by the author, London, 1823), inner title page, London Library copy, p.35.
57 See Charlotte Gere: *Nineteenth-Century Decoration: The Art of the Interior* (Weidenfeld & Nicolson, 1989), pl.265.
58 Redburn, Simon: 'J. Maclean and Son', *Furniture History Society Journal*, vol. 14 (1978), p.36.
59 Whittock, N.: *Decorative Painters*, op. cit., p.90.
60 Ibid., p.99.
61 Joy, Edward: *English Furniture 1800–1851* (Sotheby Parke Bernet, 1977), p.275.
62 Whittock, N.: *Decorative Painters*, op. cit., p.20.
63 Ibid., p.39.
64 Ibid., p.57.
65 Ibid., p.73.
66 Smith, G.: *Cabinet-Maker* (1826), op. cit., p.187.
67 Ibid., p.97.
68 Illustrated G. de Bellaigue and P. Kirkham: 'George IV and the Furnishing of Windsor Castle', *Furniture History Society Journal* (1972), pl. 24.
69 Ibid., p.33.
70 Nicolson, Peter and Michael Angelo: *The Practical Cabinet-Maker, Upholsterer, and Complete Decorator* (1826), p.VI.
71 Smith, G.: *Cabinet-Maker* (1826), op. cit., p.200.
72 Ibid., p.209.

73 Ibid., p.181.
74 Ibid., p.157.
75 Ibid., pl. XCVI.
76 Ibid.
77 For the seat motifs see d'Hancarville, P. F.: *Antiquités Etrusques, Grecques et Romaines* (Naples, 1766), vol. IV, pl. 121.
78 Loudon, J. C.: *Encyclopaedia of Cottage, Farm and Villa Architecture and Furniture* (London, 1857), p.318.

## CHAPTER FOUR
## Gothic Styles

1 Alison, Archibald: *Essays on the Nature and Principles of Taste* (Edinburgh, 1825), p.195.
2 Tatham, C. H.: *Etchings of Ancient Ornamental Architecture . . . drawn . . . in . . . 1794, 1795, & 1796* (London, 1803), pl. 76.
3 Hope, Thomas: *Household Furniture and Interior Decoration* (1807; Tiranti repr. 1970), pl. 12: 1.6.
4 Smith, George: *Collection of Designs for Household Furniture* (London, 1808), pl. 72.
5 Percier, Charles and Fontaine, Pierre: *Recueil de Décorations Intérieures* (Paris, 1827), pl. 16.
6 Smith, George: *Cabinet-Maker and Upholsterer's Guide* (London, 1826), p.194.
7 Sheraton, T.: *The Cabinet-Maker, Upholsterer, and General Artist's Encyclopaedia* (1805–08), pl. 42; reproduced J. Harris: *Regency Furniture Designs 1803–1826* (Tiranti, 1961), pl. 21.
8 Smith, G.: *Designs for Household Furniture* (1808), op. cit., pls 35, 36.
9 Ibid., p.17, pl. 90.
10 Ibid., pl. 54.
11 Ibid., p.6.
12 See Michael McCarthy: 'Soane's "Saxon" Room at Stowe', *Journal of the Society of Architectural Historians*, vol. XLIV, no. 2 (May 1885), p.142 '. . . I have not seen documentary evidence to warrant a positive identification of the furniture to Soane, though the attribution is probably correct'.
13 Illustrated P. Agius and S. Jones: *Ackermann's Regency Furniture and Interiors* (Crowood Press, 1984), p.137.
14 Illustrated ibid., p.149.
15 Illustrated G. de Bellaigue and P. Kirkham: 'George IV and the Furnishing of Windsor Castle', *Furniture History Society Journal* (1972), pls 7a, 7b.
16 Reproduced P. Agius and S. Jones: *Ackermann's Regency Furniture*, op. cit., p.163.
17 An intriguing sequence is provided in the pages of the *Repository* from the 'Sofa, Sofa-table' etc. of 1822 by 'an artist unpractised in fabricating' (illustrated in this book as Pl. CXVII) to a 'Sofa, Candelabrum, Table, and Footstool' of Feb. 1825 (illustrated p.157 of Agius and Jones) to the Gothic sofa of Dec. 1825 (p.163, Agius and Jones); an ambiguous

classical/Tudor rose, a sort of half-way house to the Gothic, is contained within the circles of the head and foot of the Feb. 1825 sofa; the table of Feb. 1825 exhibits the broken curve and an ambiguously Gothic design around its top. All these designs are closely similar in composition and handling. Could the 'artist unpractised' have been the extremely youthful but very precocious younger Pugin?

18 See J. and J. C. Buckler: *Views of Eaton Hall* (London, 1826). The Grosvenor Estate archives may have the answer.

19 Wedgwood, Alexandra: *A. W. N. Pugin and the Pugin Family* (V. & A., 1985), p.302.

20 Agius, P., and Jones, S.: *Ackermann's Regency Furniture*, op. cit., p.175.

21 Loudon, J. C.: *Architectural Magazine* (19 Nov. 1834), p.340.

## CHAPTER FIVE
## Antiquarianism

1 Britton, John: *Graphical and Literary Illustrations of Fonthill Abbey* (London, 1823), p.45.

2 Ibid., p.48.

3 Rutter, J.: *An Illustrated History and Description of Fonthill Abbey* (Published by the author, Shaftesbury, 1823), outer title page: *Delineations of Fonthill and its Abbey* (Published by the author, London, 1823), inner title page, London Library copy, p.35.

4 Britton, J.: *Graphical . . . Illustrations*, op. cit., p.54.

5 Storer, J.: *Description of Fonthill Abbey* (1812), p.15.

6 Chinnery, V.: *Oak Furniture: The British Tradition* (Antique Collectors Club, 1979),

p.95, illustrations 95–9.

7 Ibid., cat. no. 12, p.75. Bridgens shows what appears to be red paint on the turning: R. Bridgens: *Furniture with Candelabra and Interior Decoration* (Wm. Pickering, London, 1838), p.43.

8 Wainwright, C.: *The Romantic Interior* (Yale, 1989), p.193.

9 Ibid., pp.193–4.

10 Ibid., p.92.

11 Ibid., p.190.

12 See e.g. vol. 1, p.121 Hermann Schmitz: *Das Mobelwerk* (Wasmuth, Berlin, undated).

13 *George Bullock: Cabinet-maker* (Murray & Blairman, 1988), by C. Wainwright, M. Levy, L. Wood, T. Stevens, p.19; see pp.17–20 for a discussion of Bridgens' role and the problems concerning earlier publication of Bridgens' 1838 *Furniture with Candelabra and Interior Decoration designed by R. Bridgens.*

14 Bridgens, R.: *Furniture with Candelabra*, op. cit., pp.37, 55.

15 Ibid., p.31.

16 Ibid., p.49.

17 A splendid set of chairs at Ham House has been put forward as neo-Carolean, exact Regency copies (Peter Thornton and Maurice Tomlin in the *Journal of the Furniture History Society*, 1974). They would be truly remarkable were they Regency, but the author believes on the evidence of their construction that they are 17th century chairs repaired and redecorated in the Regency period. They are discussed in an unpublished catalogue entry in the V. & A. Furniture Department archives and in a copy in the author's possession.

18 Loudon, J. C.: *Encyclopaedia of Cottage, Farm*

*and Villa Architecture and Furniture* (London, 1857), p.1101.

19 The well known buffet with griffins in the V. & A. given by Brigadier Clark is almost certainly a composite fake of this period.

20 6th Duke of Devonshire: *Handbook of Chatsworth* (1845), p.194.

21 Ibid., p.196.

## CHAPTER SIX
## Chinese and Indian

1 Illustrated G. de Bellaigue, J. Harris and O. Millar: *Buckingham Palace* (Nelson, 1968), p.124.

2 In the R.I.B.A. Drawings Collection.

3 Upturned roofs are illustrated e.g.: *Le Pitture Antiche d'Ercolano*, vol. I, p.49 et passim: elongated caryatids, ibid., vol. 5, pl. LXXI. See J. H. Morley: *Country Life* (18 April 1991), pp.118–20.

4 See N. Ponce: *Descriptions des Bains de Titus* (Paris, 1786), pl. 57: *Arabesques Antiques des Bains de Livie et de la Ville Adrienne* (Paris, 1789), pls 5, 7.

5 Bellaigue, G. de: 'The Furnishings of the Chinese Drawing Room, Carlton House', *Burlington Magazine* (Sept. 1967), p.520.

## Epilogue

1 Soane, Sir John: *Description of the House and Museum on the North Side of Lincoln's Inn Fields* (London, 1830), p.50.

2 Cust, Edward: *A Letter to the Right Honourable Sir Robert Peel* (London, 1835).

3 Burke, Edmund: *Reflections on the Revolution in France* (1790), ed. C. C. O'Brien (Penguin, 1968), p.172.

# List of Black and White Illustrations

This list supplements the captions and refers to the source of the illustrations.

**1** A castle in Picturesque scenery by Robert Adam, c.1782 (Soane Museum)

**2** 'Vue Générale de la Villa Pia': from Percier and Fontaine, *Choix des Plus Célèbres Maisons de Plaisance de Rome* (1809) (Soane Museum)

**3** 'A Ground Plan, explained to a lady, who confessed that she did not understand either a plan or map': from Humphry Repton, *Fragments on the Theory & Practice of Landscape Gardening* (1816) (Private collection)

**4** St. Dunstan's Villa, Regent's Park, from the south (1832) (Architectural Association)

**5** Perspective view of a 'House calculated for being decorated with Ivy and Creeper': from J. C. Loudon, *A Treatise on Country Residences* (1806) (Private collection)

**6** A Roman garden, from the *Pitture Antiche d'Ercolano* (1760) (Soane Museum)

**7** 'Fence near the House': from Humphry Repton, *Fragments on the Theory and Practice of Landscape Gardening* (1816) (Private collection)

**8** Beaudesert, Staffs: 'View to the South after Improvement': from Humphry Repton, *Fragments on the Theory and Practice of Landscape Gardening* (1816) (Private collection)

**9** Drumlanrig Castle: design for the garden, 1840, by Sir Charles Barry (R.I.B.A.)

**10** 'Romantic Arches, with Cascades': from William Wrighte, *Grotesque Architecture or Rural Amusement* (1815 edn.) (Victoria and Albert Museum)

**11** 'Modern English Parterre': from John Harding, *Hints on the Formation of Gardens and Pleasure Grounds* (1812) (Soane Museum)

**12** The Ruins at Virginia Water, Windsor, erected 1826–9, by William Delamotte (Royal Library)

**13** 'Cattle Shed & Ruins': from Thomas Elison, *Decorations for Parks and Gardens* (c.1800–10) (British Library)

**14** 'An Ornamental Cottage with Ruins': from Robert Lugar, *Architectural Sketches* (1805) (British Library)

**15** Merlin's Cave, Richmond: designed by William Kent, 1735 (London Borough of Richmond upon Thames)

**16** 'A Seat': from Mrs. Hofland, *Descriptive Account of the Mansion and Garden of White-Knights* (1819) (British Library)

**17** 'Lady seated with her umbrella, footstool, & pyxis, or jewel box from a greek vase': from Thomas Hope, *Costume of the Ancients* (1809) (London Library)

**18** 'Sketch of a hutt . . . at the upper end of garden at Kedleston', by Robert Adam, c.1760–70 (Soane Museum)

**19** 'Larder or dairy': from Thomas Elison, *Decorations for Parks and Gardens* (c.1800–10) (British Library)

**20** 'Apiary for John Allnutt Esqr. Clapham Common, 1813', design by Joseph Gwilt (R.I.B.A.)

**21** 'Danse des Femmes d'Otateiti', by Bartolozzi after G. B. Cipriani (British Museum)

**22** 'The Elevation of a Temple partly in the Chinese Taste': from *New designs for Chinese Temples . . .* by William Halfpenny (1750–2) (Private collection)

**23** The Fishing Temple, Windsor, designed by Sir Jeffry Wyatville, c.1826, by William Delamotte (Royal Library)

**24** 'A Decorative Temple for Park or Grounds in the Chinese Style': by E. Gyfford, from *Designs for small picturesque Cottages and Hunting Boxes* (1807) (Bodleian Library)

**25** 'View of the Temple of Suryah & Fountain of Maha Dao with a distant View of North side of Mansion House', Sezincote House, Gloucs., by John Martin (1817) (British Museum)

**26** 'The General view from the Pavilion': from Humphry Repton, *Designs for the Pavillon at Brighton* (1808) (Brighton Museums)

**27** Garden seats: from W. Robertson, *Designs in architecture, for garden chairs, small gates for villas, park entrances, aviarys, temples, boat Houses, Mausoleums and bridges . . .* (1800) (British Library)

**28** Design for a garden seat: by James Trubshaw, c.1833 (R.I.B.A.)

**29** 'A Pavilion or Summer-House in the Egyptian, or Turkish taste': from Robert Lugar, *Architectural sketches for cottages, rural dwellings, and villas, in the Grecian, Gothic, and fancy styles . . .* (1805) (British Library)

**30** Design for a swimming bath: from W. Robertson, *Designs in Architecture for garden chairs, small gates for villas, park entrances, aviarys, temples, boat houses, mausoleums, and bridges . . .* (1800) (British Library)

**31** 'Design No. 8. The Bath', 1826: from P. F. Robinson, *Designs for Ornamental Villas* (1827) (London Library)

**32** 'Elevation of a Temple with a Greenhouse on each Side': from George Richardson, *New Designs in Architecture* (1792) (Private collection)

**33** 'A Design for an Egyptian Temple proposed to be used as a Greenhouse' for Trentham Hall, Staffs., by C. H. Tatham (1804) (R.I.B.A.)

**34** 'The Interior of the Prince of Wales's Conservatory at Carlton House', designed by Thomas Hopper, 1807 (Royal Library)

**35** 'Design No. 4 Conservatory', 1825: from P. F. Robinson, *Designs for Ornamental Villas* (1827) (London Library)

**36** Lord St. Vincent's greenhouse, 1824: from J. C. Loudon, *The Greenhouse Companion* (1824) (British Library)

**37** 'The Church Way' at Broomwell House,

# Photographic Acknowledgements

GREAT BRITAIN

Architectural Association/Wallace Collection 4
Attingham Park (© National Trust, 1992) L
Birmingham Museums and Art Gallery (by permission of Birmingham Museums and Art Gallery) 320
Bodleian Library (The Bodleian Library, University of Oxford, Vet. A6.c.26, Pls 8 and 20) 24, 54
Brighton Museums (Royal Pavilion, Art Gallery and Museums, Brighton) 26, 66, 128, 139, 147, XVI, XVIII, LXII, LXIII, LXXXVI, CVII, CXII
Brighton Reference Library (East Sussex County Library) 65, 223, 267, II, LII
Bristol City Museums and Art Gallery 37, 250, XXIII
British Library (by permission of the British Library) 13, 14, 16, 19, 27, 29, 30, 36, 137, 138, 140, 155, 156, 164, 181, 193, 197, 220, 221, 225, 281, 282, 296, 300, 306, CXXX
British Museum (by courtesy of the Trustees of the British Museum) 21, 25, 118, 121, 122, 194, 227, 239, 338
Cheshire Museums 76
Christie's (© Christie's) 125, 215, XIV, LXXXVII
*Country Life* 283, 285
William Drummond Gallery LVI
Edinburgh City Library (by courtesy of Edinburgh City Libraries) 41
English Life (English Life Publications Ltd., Derby) LXXXIV
Garrick Club, London 168
Art Gallery and Museum, Glasgow (Glasgow Museums: Art Gallery and Museum, Kelvingrove) XCV
Guildhall Library, Corporation of London 55, 98, 101, 153, 204, 222, 266, XXXVI
Hazlitt, Gooden & Fox Ltd (photograph by courtesy of Hazlitt, Gooden & Fox) LXXXVIII
Mr. Michael Jones 201, 233, 294, 303, 316, 318
Lambeth Archives (London Borough of Lambeth Archives Department) 60, 62, 64, 219, V, VI, LV

London Library 17, 31, 35, 38, 57, 82, 124, 177, 178, 179, 196, 206, 252, 286, 330
The National Gallery (by courtesy of the Trustees, The National Gallery, London) X, XI
National Gallery of Scotland, Edinburgh 249
National Trust (© National Trust, 1991) 254
Private collection 3, 5, 7, 8, 16, 22, 32, 39, 42, 43, 44, 56, 58, 63, 69, 70, 71, 73, 74, 75, 85, 95, 96, 109, 111, 113, 116, 120, 129, 130, 134, 136, 157, 158, 162, 165, 166, 169, 171, 172, 176, 180, 184, 187, 198, 199, 200, 202, 207, 208, 211, 217, 218, 231, 232, 236, 237, 238, 241, 243, 255, 256, 257, 258, 259, 261, 264, 265, 268, 269, 270, 274, 275, 276, 277, 278, 279, 280, 288, 289, 291, 292, 293, 295, 298, 299, 302, 304, 305, 307, 308, 309, 311, 312, 314, 315, 317, 319, 321, 322, 323, 324, 325, 326, 327, 328, 329, 332, 333, 336, 337, 339, IV, VIII, XII, XV, XIX, XX, XXI, XXII, XXIV, XXVIII, XXX, XLII, IL, LI, LX, LXV, LXVIII, LXX, LXXI, LXXII, LXXIII, LXXVII, LXXVIII, LXXXIII, LXXXV, LXXXIX, XC, XCVIII, XCIX, C, CI, CII, CIII, CIV, CVIII, CIX, CX, CXI, CXIV, CXVI, CXVII, CXVIII, CXIX, CXX, CXXI, CXXIII, CXXV, CXXVI, CXXVII, CXXVIII, CXXIX, CXXXI, CXXXII
R.I.B.A. 9, 20, 28, 33, 47, 50, 59, 67, 68, 72, 78, 81, 84, 87, 88, 103, 104, 105, 108, 112, 114, 115, 119, 126, 143, 145, 146, 148, 149, 150, 152, 154, 161, 182, 188, 216, 228, 230, 242, 244, 247, 253, 262, 287, 297, 331, VII, XXXI, XXXII, XXXIII, XXXIV, XLI, XLIII, XLIV, XLVI, LXVI, XCVI
Richmond Library 15
Royal Collection (Royal Collection, St. James's Palace. © 1992, Her Majesty the Queen) LXI, CVI, CXIII
Royal Commission on the Historical Monuments of England 77
Royal Library (Windsor Castle, Royal Library. © 1992, Her Majesty the Queen) 12, 23, 34, 110, 141, 163, 167, 175, 246, 260, LXVII, LXIX, LXIV, LXXIV, LXXV, XCIII
Russell Read XLV

Sir John Soane's Museum (by courtesy of the Trustees of Sir John Soane's Museum, London) 1, 2, 6, 11, 18, 45, 46, 48, 49, 51, 52, 53, 61, 79, 86, 89, 90, 91, 92, 93, 94, 97, 99, 100, 102, 106, 117, 123, 132, 133, 135, 142, 144, 170, 173, 174, 183, 185, 186, 190, 191, 226, 229, 232, 234, 240, 263, 272, 284, 290, 301, 313, XXVI, XXVII, XXXVIII, XXXIX, XLVIII, LVIII, LXXIX, LXXX, LXXXI, LXXXII
Sotheby's (© Sotheby's) LIII, LXXVI, XCIV, CV
Victoria and Albert Museum (by courtesy of the Board of Trustees of the Victoria and Albert Museum, London) 10, 80, 83, 107, 127, 131, 159, 189, 192, 195, 203, 205, 209, 210, 212, 213, 214, 235, 245, 248, 334, III, XIII, XXIX, XXXV, XXXVII, XL, LXV, XCII, CXXIV
Walker Art Gallery, Liverpool CXXII
Miss Marion Waller 251, 335
Warwickshire County Council 40, 151, 160, XXV

AUSTRIA
Graphische Sammlung Albertina, Vienna 271

EIRE
Mrs. Sidney Harpley, Belline, County Kilkenny IX

SWITZERLAND
Geneva Museum (Musée d'art et d'histoire, Ville de Genève) I

UNITED STATES
Cooper-Hewitt Museum (Cooper-Hewitt, National Museum of Design, Smithsonian Institution. Photo: Ken Pelka/courtesy of Art Resource, NY) LIX
The Pierpont Morgan Library (The Pierpont Morgan Library, New York. 1966.9:9) 273
Sayn-Wittgenstein, New York (by courtesy of Sayn-Wittgenstein Fine Art Inc.) XLVII
Yale Center for British Art, Paul Mellon Collection, New Haven, CT XVII, LIV

# Index